DEVON AND CORNWALL RECORD SOCIETY

New Series, Volume 41

Issued to members of the society for the year 1998

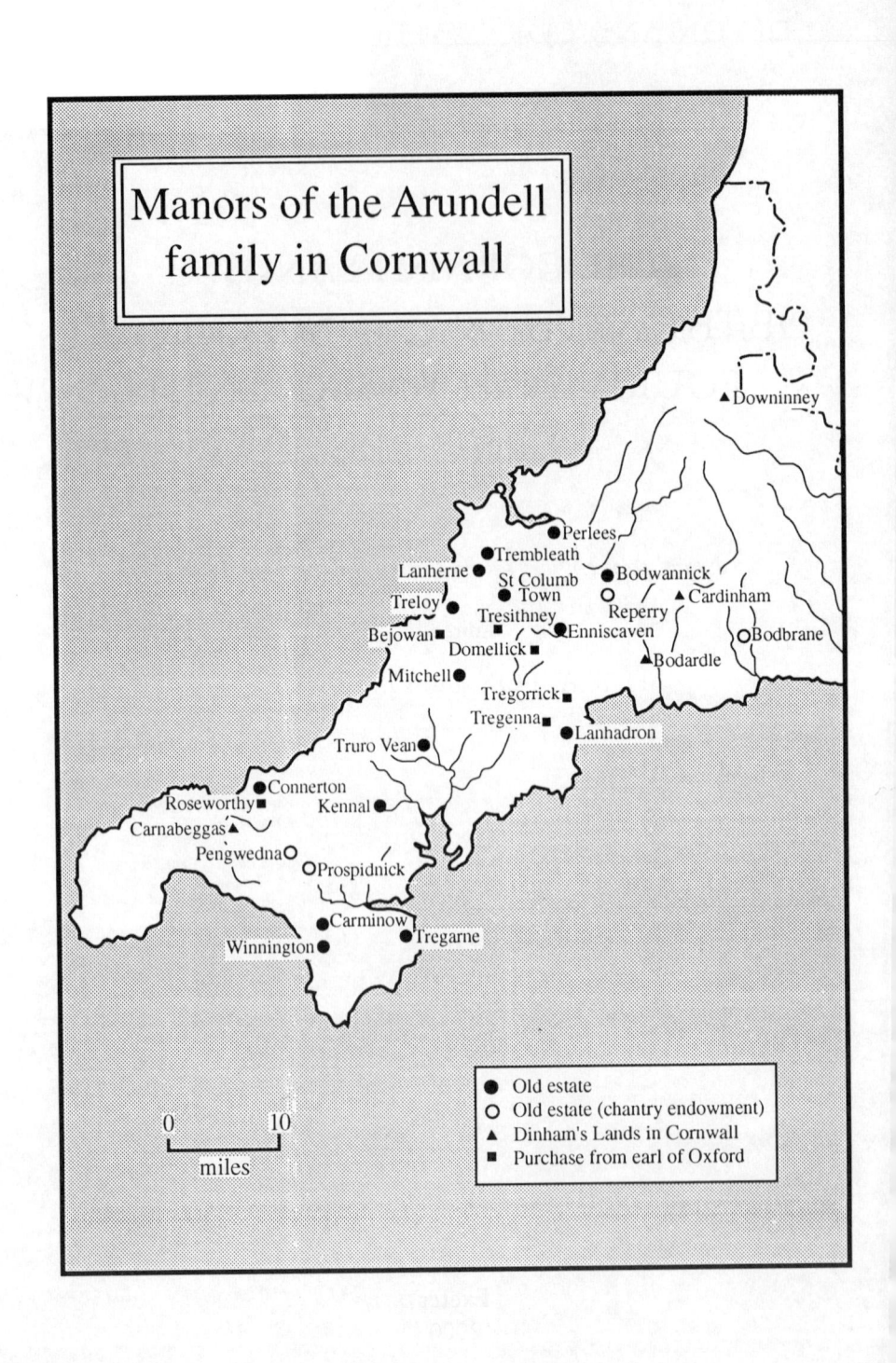

Manors of the Arundell family in Cornwall

▲ Downinney

● Perlees
● Trembleath
Lanherne ●
● St Columb
Treloy ● ● Town
Tresithney ○ Reperry
Bejowan ■ ● Enniscaven
Domellick ■
Mitchell ●
Tregorrick ■
Tregenna ■
Truro Vean ●
● Connerton
Roseworthy ■ Kennal ●
Carnabeggas ▲
Pengwedna ○ ○ Prospidnick
● Carminow
Winnington ● ● Tregarne

● Bodwannick
▲ Cardinham
○ Bodbrane
▲ Bodardle
■ Lanhadron

0   10
miles

● Old estate
○ Old estate (chantry endowment)
▲ Dinham's Lands in Cornwall
■ Purchase from earl of Oxford

DEVON AND CORNWALL RECORD SOCIETY

New Series, Volume 41

THE CORNISH LANDS OF THE ARUNDELLS OF LANHERNE, FOURTEENTH TO SIXTEENTH CENTURIES

Edited by

H. S. A. FOX and O. J. PADEL

Exeter
2000

© Devon and Cornwall Record Society
and H. S. A. Fox and O. J. Padel
2000

*No part of this publication
may be reproduced, stored in a retrieval system,
or transmitted in any form or by any means, electronic,
mechanical, photocopying, recording or otherwise,
without the prior permission of
the copyright holders.*

ISBN 0 901853 41 0

Typeset for the Society by
Colin Bakké Typesetting, Exeter
and printed and bound for the Society by
Short Run Press Ltd, Exeter, Devon

For Margaret Meeres and Isobel Harvey

CONTENTS

Introduction

1. The Arundell family ix
2. The growth of the estate xiii
   The fourteenth century, xv; Luscott inheritance, c.1400, xvi; Soor manors, c.1420, xvii; Lambourne and Lanhadron inheritance, before 1433, xx; other acquisitions, c.1415–30, xxi; gifts to John Arundell's sons, 1420s, xxi; the chantry at St Columb, 1428, xxii; Truro Vean, mid-fifteenth century, xxiv; Chideock inheritance, 1451–80, xxv; creation of Perlees, 1480–99, xxv; Dinham inheritance, 1501, xxvii; earl of Oxford's lands, 1575–76, xxxii; manor of Newland Preeze, 1587, xxxv
3. The documents xxxvii
   Fourteenth-century extents, xxxix; extent of 1451–64, xl; rental of [1480], xlii; extent of 1499, xliv; chantry-endowment manors, xlv; two manors of the earl of Oxford in 1549, xlvi; three manors of the earl of Oxford in 1563, xlvii; survey of Dinham's Lands in 1566, xlviii; extent of 1571, xlviii; three manors of the earl of Oxford in 1575, xlix; rental of c.1586, xlix; later surveys, l
4. The manorial system in Cornwall lii
5. The Cornish landscape in the sixteenth century
   and later lxviii
   Closes and hedges, lxviii; strip-field systems, lxxvii; downs, towns and other features, xciii
6. Conventionary tenements and tenant farmers at the
   close of the Middle Ages ci
   Tenements in decline, ci; resilient tenements, cx; tenants and inheritance, cxiii
7. Overall revenues of the estate cxxi
8. Surnames in the surveys cxxiv
   Patronymic surnames, cxxv; toponymic surnames, cxxvii; other types of surname, cxxix; two-part surnames, cxxxi
9. Editorial conventions cxxxviii

Acknowledgements cxxxix

Appendix: the dating of AR2/1339, [1480] cxli

Bibliography and abbreviations cxlviii

Texts

1. Two fourteenth-century extents
   Lanherne and Trembleath, 1343 1
   Lanhadron, 1385 8
2. Extent of the whole estate, 1451–64 12
3. Rental of the whole estate, [1480] 64
4. Extent of the whole estate, 1499 101
5. Chantry-endowment manors, 15th–16th centuries ... 143
6. Two manors of the earl of Oxford, 1549 156
7. Three manors of the earl of Oxford, 1563 167
8. Survey of Dinham's Lands, 1566 (parts) 173
9. Extent of the whole estate, 1571 (parts) 198
10. Three manors of the earl of Oxford, 1575 207
11. Rental of the whole estate, c.1586 (parts) 235

Indexes

Index of places 241
Index of surnames 253
Index of subjects 276

Maps

Manors of the Arundell family in Cornwall ... ... frontispiece
Tenements of the manor of Connerton cliv
Tenements of the manors of Lanherne and Trembleath ... clv

Family-tree

The Arundells of Lanherne clvi

Introduction

1. THE ARUNDELL FAMILY

The Arundells of Lanherne were one of the foremost families in Cornwall for about 300 years, from the mid-fourteenth century until well into the seventeenth; and their considerable wealth included estates in most parts of the county, as well as elsewhere, notably in Devon and Dorset. We are fortunate that an extensive archive of their estate survives from that period, and has recently come fully into the public domain as a result of its acquisition by Cornwall County Record Office, Truro. The present volume contains rentals and surveys of the Arundells' Cornish lands from the period of their greatest wealth and influence; the documents show the extent of their properties in the county, and thus can serve as a guide to the archive as a whole. Other parts of the archive, such as deeds and leases, manorial court rolls and account rolls, and more miscellaneous documents, are potentially richer than the rentals and surveys in terms of social and economic history; but the user of those documents requires the overall view provided by the surveys in order for their details to be fitted into the larger picture. Part of the purpose of publishing these documents, therefore, is to render the other riches of the archive, yet unpublished, more accessible and comprehensible for the student of local history in medieval Cornwall.

The surname Arundell (or Arundel) is known from various parts of England from the Norman Conquest onwards.[1] The ramifications of the surname have not been fully worked out, and it is unclear whether all bearers of it were ultimately related. The surname may even have more than one derivation, from the Old English place-name Arundel (Sussex) in some cases, and from Old French

---

[1] Yeatman, *House of Arundel*, provides a speculative account of the medieval families.

arondelle 'a swallow' in others.[2] The latter derivation was used in our family's coat-of-arms, and by other bearers of the name, but such allusion of course proves nothing about the actual derivation of the surname. Our family first appears, holding a single manor (Treloy, near Newquay) in the early thirteenth century.[3] The possible relationship of the Cornish Arundells with other, up-country, bearers of the surname is unknown, for lack of records. Nearly a century earlier, in 1130, a Robert Arundell is mentioned in a Cornish context; but he appears in a similar capacity in several other counties, and may belong rather in Dorset.[4] He need have no direct link with the later Cornish family.

The rise of the family in the thirteenth and fourteenth centuries is described in greater detail below ('The growth of the estate'); here a brief summary is needed. After its first appearance in 1216, the family made a series of successful marriages during the thirteenth to the fifteenth centuries; these brought a series of additions to their property. (See the family-tree, p. clvi.) Lanherne itself was one of these additions; but the principal seat of the family moved from Treloy to Trembleath in the parish of St Ervan. Lanherne itself does not seem to have become their principal residence until the later fourteenth, or the early fifteenth, century; the exact date is unclear at present, though it may have been during the 1360s and early 1370s, when there were three John Arundells alive at once, one of Lanherne, one of Treloy, and one of Trembleath.[5]

---

[2] P. H. Reaney and R. M. Wilson, *A Dictionary of English Surnames*, 3rd edition (London, 1991), p. 15; A. Mawer and F. M. Stenton, *The Place-Names of Sussex*, 2 vols, English Place-Name Society, vols 6–7 (Cambridge, 1929–30), I, 136–37; Old French *arondelle* 'swallow', A. Dauzat and others, *Nouveau dictionnaire étymologique et historique [du français]* (Paris, 1971), p. 372, compare Modern French *aronde* 'swallow', p. 46.

[3] *Rot.Litt.Claus.*, I, 247b; *Curia Regis Rolls*, vol. XII, *9 to 10 Henry III*, p. 47.

[4] *Magnum Rotulum Scaccarii vel Magnum Rotulum Pipæ de Anno Tricesimo-Primo Regni Henrici Primi*, edited by Joseph Hunter (London, 1833), pp. 159, etc. Compare Roger Arundel in Somerset and Dorset thirty years later: Pipe Rolls of 1160–61 (6 and 7 Henry II), Pipe Roll Society, vol. 2, p. 59, and vol. 4, p. 47.

[5] See the second inquisition post mortem (1442) of John Arundell who died in 1433–35: PRO, C.139/107, no. 36.

It was during the fourteenth century, too, that a younger branch of the Treloy–Lanherne family arose, the Arundells of Trerice. The exact connection between the two families is not clear, although the documents printed here, and others in the archive, go some way towards elucidating it; it was apparently a younger son of the main family, one Ralph or Randulph, who married Joan, daughter and heiress of Michael de Treres; their son Nicholas thus inherited Trerice and was the progenitor of that line, which from then on functioned effectively as a separate family from that of Lanherne, though retaining tenurial links with the senior branch.[6]

From its height in the fifteenth and sixteenth centuries the family declined in influence (though not at first in wealth), owing to its adherence to the Roman Catholic faith. There was a temporary setback in 1483–84, when Thomas Arundell (the only head of the family for 400 years not to be called John) took part in the duke of Buckingham's rebellion against King Richard III; as a result of the failure of this rebellion Thomas's lands were forfeited to the king, and he died a year later (1485), leaving a son and heir, John, aged only 11.

This John saw the family lands restored under King Henry VII, and lived, apparently quietly, through the changes of King Henry VIII's reign, changes which he must have greatly deplored. He died in 1545, and his eldest son, John, continued the tradition, taking little part in national events; although he must have sympathized with the Prayerbook Rebellion in 1549, he succeeded in remaining uninvolved, even though it was led by a cousin, Humphrey Arundell;[7] this John died in 1557. However, his younger brother, Thomas, led a very different life, mixing in high circles at the court of King Henry VIII. He married Margaret Howard, sister of the king's fifth wife Katherine; and he purchased monastic estates at their dissolution, founding a junior branch of the family at Wardour, in Wiltshire.[8] This branch was to grow in importance,

---

[6] For further details see below, pp. 2, 9, 44, 89, 133, 146 and 157. For this scheme to be right, it is necessary that Odo, son and heir of Michael de Treres, whose wardship and marriage were granted to John Le Soor of Tolverne in 1345 (AR46/8–11), died without heir. Ralph Arundell de Treres was dead by November 1369 (AR1/846 and AR32/1).
[7] Cornwall, *Revolt of the Peasantry*, pp. 120–21 and 232–33.
[8] Twelve important letters of this Thomas Arundell survive from his stays in London: AR25/5–15 and 17.

eclipsing the quieter Cornish branch, until eventually the Cornish male line came to an end when the last Sir John Arundell died in 1701, leaving only a daughter; she was married to one Richard Bellings, who (with her father's approval) took the name of Arundell.

Their son, Richard Bellings Arundell (who died in 1725), in turn had only two daughters, one of whom, Mary Bellings Arundell, neatly perpetuated the family by marrying in 1739 Henry, her seventh cousin once removed, the seventh Lord Arundell of Wardour, and Count of the Holy Roman Empire.[9] (Her sister married but had no children.) In this way the two branches of the family were re-united at Wardour, and the two estates came together. The house at Lanherne was not much used by the family after this, but the Cornish lands continued to be run as a discrete estate. In the late eighteenth century the Cornish lands began to be sold, and most were sold by 1808; shortly afterwards the archive was transferred from Lanherne to Wardour, where it remained until 1991.[10] Lanherne itself was retained by the family, and in 1794 was offered as a home to Carmelite nuns fleeing from the Low Countries; it remains a Carmelite nunnery today. The separate administration of the Cornish estate rendered it easy, when the time came in 1991, for the Lanherne section of the archive to be separated and brought to Cornwall Record Office; the Wardour section is now at Wiltshire Record Office, Trowbridge.

---

[9] For wider details see Webb, *Arundell Family History*; Vivian, *Visitations*, pp. 4 and 7.

[10] For further details see Christine North, 'The Arundell archive', *Journal of the Royal Institution of Cornwall*, [3rd series], 1 (1991–93), 47–57; and Lucy McCann, *Introduction to the Arundell Archive* (Truro, Cornwall County Record Office, 1996).

2. THE GROWTH OF THE ESTATE

From their modest beginnings at Treloy before 1216 the family made a series of good marriages, each of which added to their estate, for over two hundred years; by the mid-fifteenth century the estate was almost at its fullest extent, though the later documents printed here show further additions, some by purchase.[1] The first of these marriages was by Ralph, son of Remfrey Arundell, to Eve, a daughter of Richard de Tremodret or Roche, in around 1250—perhaps slightly earlier, since Remfrey II, Ralph's son, was himself married by 1268.[2] Eve brought with her lands in the hundred of Pyder, notably Trembleath (St Ervan), which became the Arundells' principal residence in the following century; and also some lands further east, in St Minver parish but later attached to the manor of Trembleath. (See below, p. lxv, and the map, p. clv.)

The second marriage came in the next generation, with Remfrey Arundell II, who married the heiress Alice de Lanhern, some time before June 1268. Alice's father John (son of Andrew) de Lanhern was perhaps from a Devonshire family, holding manors of the bishops of Exeter in both counties, though his surname was taken from presumably his preferred residence, in Cornwall. Alice brought with her to the Arundells not only the manor of Lanherne, near to Treloy and Trembleath (and including, at this date, the growing town of St Columb Major: see below, pp. 4–5), but also the Devonshire manors later called Morchard Arundell and Uton Arundell (in the parishes of Morchard Bishop and Crediton), both also held, like Lanherne, of the bishops of Exeter. This was Alice's paternal inheritance; but she brought with her much more than that, for her mother Margery had herself been an heiress, descendant of Richard Pincerna who had received the manor of Connerton, in Penwith, from Robert, son of Robert earl of Gloucester, in about 1155. This was one of the richest manors in west Cornwall, and it

---

[1] This section of the Introduction expands upon remarks made by O. J. Padel, 'The Arundells of Lanherne and their archive', *Cornwall Association of Local Historians, Journal*, 29 (Spring 1995), 8–23.
[2] AR1/64–66; for the marriage of Remfrey II by 1268, see *Cornwall Feet of Fines*, I, no. 216.

was to remain one of the largest in the Arundell estate; it brought with it also the administrative rights of the Hundred of Penwith, the only Cornish hundred to be held in private hands in this way.[3]

It was to be many years before the male line of the Arundells actually came into this rich estate brought to them by Alice de Lanherne; for, having borne Remfrey a son John, she was widowed, and then remarried to a Devonshire man, John de Umfraville. She also had by him a son (who seems to have become a cleric), and by the laws of inheritance her second husband therefore continued to enjoy her estate after her death (between 1302 and 1311), until his own.[4] Since Alice's son, John Arundell I, died before John de Umfraville did, it was her grandson, John Arundell II, who eventually inherited the Lanherne property, at some time between 1311 (when John de Umfraville was still alive) and 1322, when John Arundell II is found described as lord of Connerton—some half-century after Remfrey's marriage with Alice. John II had apparently come of age in June 1318.[5]

In the meantime the family had, through its upward path, taken its place among the gentry of the county. Ralph, who married Eve, was sheriff of Cornwall in 1259–60, and in 1265 he was temporarily placed in charge of Restormel Castle and the barony of Cardinham during Simon de Montfort's rebellion against King Henry III.[6] By 1277 Remfrey II had become lord of the manor and borough of Mitchell, a town on the ancient spine-road through Cornwall, through a purchase made by Ralph his father in about 1270.[7] The

---

[3] Picken, 'Descent of Willington'; Bowles, *Hundred of Penwith*, pp. 19–22, for the grant to Richard Pincerna and its confirmation by King Henry II; and Pool, 'Penheleg manuscript', for the Arundells' later tenure of the Hundred of Penwith.

[4] John son of John de Umfraville a cleric, AR1/82; Alice de Lanherne still alive in 1302, PRO Just.1/117, m.67d. (1302 eyre roll); Alice dead but John de Umfraville her husband still alive in 1311, AR4/415 (lease for term of his life).

[5] John Arundell as lord of Connerton in 1322, AR4/183/1; John due to come of age in June 1318, AR4/347. The bishop of Exeter, who held his wardship, tried unsuccessfully in 1316 to persuade him to marry Joan Kaignes, the bishop's own niece: *Stapeldon*, pp. 33–34.

[6] Ralph as sheriff in 1259–60, AR22/1; his care of Restormel Castle in 1265, AR22/2. The latter deed is reproduced (but misdated and misinterpreted) by Yeatman, *House of Arundel*, plate 34.

purchase presumably represented a deliberate investment in this developing market town; but the town eventually declined, and by the eighteenth century it was among the rottenest of Cornwall's boroughs, and may have been more trouble than it was worth; it was among the first of the Cornish properties to be sold by the Wardour family, in 1775.[8]

Thus in 1300 John Arundell I, the son of Remfrey and Alice and the first of the long line of John Arundells, held the manors of Treloy, Trembleath (with its dependent lands in St Minver) and Mitchell; and he had the expectancy of the reversion of the manors of Lanherne (including St Columb Major), Connerton (together with the Hundred of Penwith) and, in Devon, the manors of Morchard and Uton (later to be called Morchard Arundell and Uton Arundell), after the deaths of his mother Alice and her second husband John de Umfraville. However, as shown above, John Arundell was dead by 1309, so that it was his son who inherited these parts of the estate, after the death of his grandmother's second husband and after himself coming of age in 1318.[9]

The fourteenth century

The Arundell marriages in the fourteenth century have not been studied in detail, and only those which directly concern the acquisition of the estates can be mentioned here. There is even some uncertainty as to how many John Arundells were head of the family during this time. The most important marriage was of a John Arundell, in around 1334, to Elizabeth de Carminow, a daughter of the major west-Cornish family.[10] This is unlikely to be the John

---

[7] Gloucestershire Record Office, D.421/A2/5–6 (deeds, 1270); D.421/A2/8 (deed, 1277); *Placita de Quo Warranto*, p. 109b (Michaelmas term, 1302). The original grant of a weekly market and yearly fair at Mitchell had been made in 1239 by King Henry III, to Walter de Ralegh and Isabel his wife: *Calendar of Charter Rolls*, I, 241. Mitchell is termed a borough in 1305 (Henderson, *Essays*, p. 54) and 1311 (*Anc.Deeds*, IV, A.9373).

[8] AR25/110 and 129 for dealings concerning the borough; AR2/1196 for its sale in 1775.

[9] John Arundell I dead by 1309, AR16/1; John de Umfraville still alive in 1311, AR4/415 (see above).

[10] *Cornwall Feet of Fines*, I, no. 680; 'Beville obituary' (I), p. 21.

who came of age in 1318; more likely to have been his son, though he would be unlikely to have married as early as 1334. Again, there were apparently three John Arundells alive at the same time in the 1360s, distinguished as 'of Lanherne', 'of Treloy', and 'of Trembleath'; all three seem to have died in the 1370s, one of them earlier than his father.

The marriage to Elizabeth Carminow brought the Arundells no immediate gains; but sixty years later, in February 1396, the Carminow heiress Joan died, as a minor aged 10 or 11. Although her family's surname survived down at least to the mid-seventeenth century,[11] this ended the direct line of the family, and the estate was split between the nearest kinsmen, the Arundells of Lanherne and the Trevarthians of Trevarthian (in St Hilary).[12] The partition brought to the Arundells the manors of Carminow, Kennall and Winnington, together with other property, the advowsons of the churches of Whitstone and Philleigh, a small share of Merthen Wood (Constantine; their share was later called Arundell's Wood) and all of Treloweth Wood (St Mewan), later to become an important tinning area. Trevarthian received the manors of Merthen, Trethevas (Landewednack) and Rosuick (St Keverne), most of Merthen Wood, and the advowsons of Ruan Major and Ruan Minor churches. This inheritance is the reason why, in the rental of 1480, the glebe-land of Philleigh and Whitstone parishes, attached to the advowsons of those churches, was listed under Carminow manor (below, p. 85).

Luscott inheritance, c.1400

Later in the fourteenth century, before November 1367, a John Arundell (probably the son of John III and Elizabeth Carminow) married Joan Luscott, a Devonshire heiress. She brought with her the Devonshire estates of Loddiswell, Ideford and Battishorne (Honiton parish), and maybe other lands in that county. After her husband's death she remained in possession of her inheritance, residing at Lanherne and Loddiswell, and granting leases of the

---

[11] CRO Index to Wills, William Carminow of St Teath, esquire.
[12] Inquisition post mortem of Joan Carminow, *Calendar of IPMs*, XVII, 241–42 (nos 615–16); *Anc.Deeds*, IV, A.10409 (and other copies, AR1/192); compare Henderson, *Constantine*, pp. 93–94.

latter.[13] After some years she remarried, to Sir William Lambron (as his second wife also): the earliest evidence yet noted of their marriage is in July 1394, though there are suggestions that it had occurred a little earlier.[14] (Sir William Lambron was also, independently, the father of the next heiress to marry an Arundell, Annora Lambron; this was by his first wife, Joan Lanhadron.) The Devon estates were presumably inherited by John Arundell (who died in 1433–35), her son, after the deaths of Joan and of William Lambron, some time after 1397. The earliest date at which he has been noted holding the five Devon manors (three from the Luscott family and two from the Lanherne one) is September 1407.[15]

Thus in c.1400, after the deaths of Joan his mother and her second husband Sir William Lambron, John Arundell held the Cornish manors of Treloy, Trembleath (including its lands in St Minver), Mitchell, Lanherne (including St Columb Major), Connerton (including the Hundred of Penwith), Carminow, Winnington and Kennall; and the Devonshire manors of Morchard Arundell, Uton Arundell, Battishorne, Ideford and Loddiswell; and perhaps also other properties in Devon.

It is not yet clear what happened to all these Devonshire estates (both the Lanherne and the Luscott inheritances) in later years. They were still in the hands of the family in 1605;[16] but there is little evidence for them in the Lanherne estate after about 1610.

Soor manors, c.1420

With John Arundell who died in 1433–35, the family was at its height. He served King Henry V at sea in 1418–19, when he was in his early fifties; was sheriff of Cornwall four times, and M.P. for the county; and is said to have been known as John Arundell 'the Magnificent', though the fifty-two suits of gold cloth which he was

---

[13] *Brantyngham*, I, 374 (licence for Joan to celebrate in her chapel at Lanherne, 1376); AR20/14 (Joan at Loddiswell, 1391); AR4/2020–25 (leases at Loddiswell granted by Joan, 1376–85).
[14] Married by 1394, AR17/1–2; AR30/5 may suggest it already in 1391. 'Beville obituary' (I), p. 21, misleadingly states that Joan died in 1384.
[15] AR20/16–17, trust leases of the manors.
[16] AR20/51 (final concord, whole estate, November 1605); AR21/28 (draft will of Sir John Arundell, December 1605); compare AR1/546 (sale of part of the manor of Morchard Arundell, 1629).

reputed to have owned at his death do not appear in his will.[17] He was probably the first of the line to make substantial acquisitions of land by purchase, rather than inheritance. In making these he seems to have had two particular aims: providing his younger sons with good estates, and endowing a chantry in St Columb Major (see below).

The family of Soor or Le Sor had held Tolverne, in Philleigh, from as early as the eleventh century.[18] The last of them, Ralph Soor, died between 1409 and 1416;[19] and during the fifteenth century the Arundells acquired three manors formerly Soor's, Tolverne itself, Prospidnick (Sithney) and Bodwannick (Lanivet)—two of them, Tolverne and Prospidnick, within a few years of Ralph Soor's death. However, the mode of acquisition is not clear. It is said that John Arundell I (who died before 1309) had been married to Joan Soor; but no authority has yet been found for that statement.[20] In fact, John Arundell who died in 1433–35 seems to have acquired his interest in Tolverne in 1417–18, along with other manors not formerly Soor's (see below, 'Other acquisitions');[21] so it may be that the eventual acquisition of three Soor manors was due to policy, rather than inheritance. Indeed, in 1371 an entailment of

---

[17] Christopher Allmand, *Henry V* (London, 1992), pp. 224–25 and 228–29, also AR22/5–9; *Lacy*, IV, 20–22, for his will (also AR21/2, a nineteenth-century copy); *Dictionary of National Biography*, s.v. Arundell of Cornwall, for the suits of gold (also AR21/2). The will (dated 18 April 1433) purports to have been proved on 7 June 1433; yet his inquisition post mortem, held in August and October 1435 (13–14 Henry VI) states that he died on Tuesday after Epiphany last, i.e. Tuesday 11 January 1435 (PRO, C.139/72, no. 39); so, too, the inquisition held when his grandson came of age in 1442 (PRO, C.139/107, no. 36). The 'Beville obituary' (I), p. 21, states that he died on 17 January 1433 (i.e. 1434, a Sunday). This discrepancy over the date of his death has yet to be resolved.

[18] *Episcopal Acta, Exeter*, I, 1–2 (no. 1); compare II, 153–54 (no. 170; AR46/1–2), a dispute between Soor and Plympton Priory in c.1188–89.

[19] AR1/225 (Ralph Soor alive in 1409); AR1/346–47 (Thomas Colyn lord of Bodwannick in 1416).

[20] It is asserted by Yeatman, *House of Arundel*, p. 255; and by subsequent authorities, including Vivian, *Visitations*, p. 2. Judging by the reference given by Vivian, this seems to stem from a misapprehension of *Cornwall Feet of Fines*, I, no. 682 (October, 1334).

[21] *Cornwall Feet of Fines*, II, nos 930 and 933.

certain Arundell manors included (in default of Arundell heirs) Ralph Soor of Tolverne and his male heirs; this suggests a marriage-link between the two families, but rather that an Arundell daughter had married a Soor, instead of the other way around.[22] There are also indications of business links between Arundell and Soor in the mid-fourteenth century.[23]

At about the same time as he acquired Tolverne, c.1420, John Arundell also acquired the Soor manor of Prospidnick;[24] it remained a possession of the main line of Arundells, but does not appear very much in the fifteenth-century documentation, because it was made a part of the endowment for the Arundell Chantry in St Columb Major (below). However, a third Soor manor, Bodwannick, appears in the rentals printed here, but does not seem to have come to the Arundells at the same time. After Ralph Soor's death it was in the hands of a kinsman of Arundell, Thomas Colyn de Hellond, who held other properties further west by lease of Arundell; but he seems to have held Bodwannick in his own right.[25] Unlike Tolverne and Prospidnick, Bodwannick is not mentioned among John's lands at his death (1435). It seems to have entered the Arundell estate in 1463–64, just before the date of its earliest rental printed below (February 1464), for it is still absent from the general account of the manors in 1462–63, but present in that of 1463–64.[26] It looks as though it was a deliberate, and later, acquisition.

---

[22] AR20/2; by a similar arrangement in 1404 Ralph Soor left Tolverne, in default of his heirs, to Ralph Arundell (presumably of Trerice), Joan his wife and their heirs, and in default of such heirs to Sir John Arundell (presumably of Lanherne) and his heirs: *Cornwall Feet of Fines*, II, no. 854. It is unclear why the will and testament of Rose, wife of John le Soor de Taluren, appears in the archive (AR46/6–7). John her husband was her executor; and she was apparently daughter of Geoffrey Pridias, and died in April 1342 ('Beville Obituary', II, p. 35).

[23] AR24/3 (1350), AR26/1 (1355) and AR20/2 (1371).

[24] Deed of 1428, recited in his inquisition post mortem (1435), showing John granting the manor of *Pryspynnek Soor* (PRO, C.139/72, no. 39).

[25] As Thomas Colyn's property in 1416–33: AR1/346–53. In 1371 John Colyn of Lelant was married to Rose, kinswoman of Sir John Arundell (AR20/2).

[26] AR2/905, mm. 1–2; compare a dispute with the heirs of Colyn concerning its ownership, in December 1464, AR1/358.

Lambourne and Lanhadron inheritance, before 1433

John Arundell who died in 1433–35 married Annora Lambron, daughter of Sir William Lambron by his first wife, Joan Lanhadron. Joan Lanhadron herself was the heiress of John and Amity Lanhadron. As mentioned above, Sir William Lambron, Annora's father, independently married Joan Luscott, mother of John Arundell, thus marrying his own daughter's mother-in-law; but it is unclear at present which marriage occurred first. John Arundell and Annora must have been married by 1390–1400: John had come of age in about 1387;[27] and his son John Arundell of Bideford was dead by 1424, having himself a son born in 1421. William Lambron and Joan Arundell (née Luscott) were married by 1394.[28] Annora brought with her the inheritances of her father and mother: the manors of Lambourne (Perranzabuloe), Tregarne (St Keverne and St Anthony in Meneage), Nansladron or Lanhadron (St Ewe), Langoran (Goran), Enniscaven (St Dennis) and Penwerris (Budock). John Arundell thus held these manors in his wife's right at his death in 1435. Nansladron (including Langoron), Enniscaven and Tregarne Condurrow remained Arundell manors through to the eighteenth century; the others appear occasionally in accounts during the fifteenth century, but seem to have been lost to the family, or perhaps granted out to junior branches; they do not appear in the rentals printed below. Lambourne itself was certainly granted to a younger son (see below).

Other acquisitions by John Arundell in c.1415–30

In 1417–18 Arundell acquired, along with Soor's manor of Tolverne, the manors of Treveneage and Penberthy (St Hilary), Reperry (Lanivet), and one-third of Pengwedna (Breage).[29] Treveneage and Penberthy, along with Tolverne, were later (in 1426) granted to a younger son, Thomas, and do not appear among the Lanherne lands in this volume; but Pengwedna and Reperry were included in the estate in 1433–34,[30] and remained the property of

---

[27] He was aged 22 in 1387–88, according to the inquisition post mortem of his elder brother Ralph, *Calendar of IPMs*, XVI, no. 507; but aged 28 in 1396, according to that of Joan Carmynowe, *Calendar of IPMs*, XVII, no. 615.

[28] AR17/1–2, dispute between them and John Arundell.

[29] *Cornwall Feet of Fines*, II, nos 930 and 933.

[30] AR2/887, manorial accounts for the estate, 1433–34.

the family through to the eighteenth century. However, they do not appear among the fifteenth-century extents of the main estate printed below, because of being made into part of the chantry-endowment (below).

Similarly the manor of Bodbrane (Duloe) had become Arundell property by about 1430; it appears in the estate account-roll of 1433–34, and in Arundell's inquisition post mortem (1435). Bodbrane had been the property of John Billon of Trethewell in St Eval, a close neighbour of the Arundells at Trembleath or Lanherne (compare the dealings of their predecessors in about 1340: below, pp. 15 and 19). This acquisition was presumably made by purchase, since no marriage connection between the families is known. It occurred after 1398, when John Billon of Trethewell was still lord of Bodbrane; in 1429, John Arundell was able to make a grant including other lands formerly Billon's, so he may have acquired Bodbrane by then too.[31]

Gifts to John Arundell's sons, 1420s

John Arundell's eldest son, John Arundell of Bideford, predeceased his father, being dead by February 1424;[32] he had a son, born in 1421, who was thus the heir to the estate, but due to remain in his minority until 1442. This may be why John Arundell, by now aged about sixty (he was born in 1365–68: see above, n. 27) went to considerable lengths during the 1420s to put his estate into the hands of his other sons, perhaps to ensure that the wardship of his under-age heir should not harm the family estates. However, this action also served to set these other sons up with their own estates, and in one case this created an enduring junior branch of the family: this was Thomas Arundell, whose line remained at Tolverne, in Philleigh, until selling it in 1598 and moving to Truthall, in Sithney.[33] Thomas Arundell received from his father the manors

---

[31] Trelawny deeds of 1398 and 1429, formerly W. M. M. Picken's, now in the RIC, Truro. Compare also *Cornwall Feet of Fines*, II, no. 991, Billon's land of Trethewell, among others, acquired by John Nanfan and others in 1431, also Billon's advowson of St Tudy church; this advowson later belonged to Arundell (Maclean, *Trigg Minor*, III, 314 n. 2).

[32] *Cal.Pat.*, 1442, p. 130; *Inquisitiones Post Mortem* (RC), IV, 216.

[33] Henderson, 'Ecclesiastical antiquities', pp. 409 and 442.

of Treveneage and Penberthy in 1426, Tolverne itself in 1428, and Lanhadron and Lambourne in 1431.[34] Most of these manors disappeared from the Lanherne estate after John's death in 1435, though Lanhadron returned. Thomas's brother Remfrey had received the manors of Treloy and Trink (Lelant) in 1421 (after his marriage to Joan, daughter of Sir John Colshull), Lanherne and St Columb in 1429, other lands in 1430, and Tregarne and Penwerris in 1431. Most of these returned to the Lanherne estate during the fifteenth century, though Remfrey Arundell's widow later married the vigorous John Nanfan, and there was a law-suit in 1456 about her rights of dower.[35]

The chantry at St Columb, 1428

In March 1428 Sir John Arundell founded a chantry (an endowment for the maintenance of priests) at St Columb Major, probably the richest chantry in Cornwall in the Middle Ages. The Lanherne family evidently regarded St Columb Major as their chief ecclesiastical possession: the heads of the family chose to be buried there, rather than in St Mawgan church adjacent to their residence.[36] Even before the chantry was founded, St Columb Major was the most valuable church-living in secular hands in the later Middle Ages.[37] The chantry was endowed with four manors, plus land in St Tudy parish formerly belonging to the Billon family; most of these had been bought by Arundell in the previous ten years, perhaps with the specific aim of creating the chantry. The four manors were Bodbrane, Pengwedna, Prospidnick and Reperry; of these, it is fairly clear that Bodbrane, Pengwedna and Reperry were purchases; and so, probably, was the former Soor manor of Prospidnick.

The endowment was created by settling upon John's son Thomas Arundell five manors, the fifth being Tolverne; later events suggest that Tolverne was intended for Thomas himself and his family,

---

[34] Deeds recited in the inquisition post mortem of John Arundell (1435), PRO C.139/72, no. 39.

[35] AR17/74–77, John Arundel versus Remfrey Arundell (son of Remfrey) and John Nanfan.

[36] Henderson, *St Columb Major*, pp. 45–53; compare John Arundell's will (1433): *Lacy*, IV, 20.

[37] Page, 'Ownership of advowsons', p. 338. As is apparent above, St Columb did not come fully into Arundell ownership until 1310–20.

while the other four were intended as the endowment proper.[38] Those five manors were thus removed from the Lanherne estate; but later in the fifteenth century, John Arundell (Thomas's nephew) claimed that the Tolverne family was failing to maintain his grandfather's chantry, and that the four endowment-manors should revert to the Lanherne line.[39] This happened, but they continued as the endowment for the chantry (which now became the care of the Lanherne family), and so remained outside the family's ordinary estate. That is why they do not appear in the fifteenth-century surveys printed below, nor in the accounts of the whole estate for the period; but they did have their own roll of rentals (below, pp. 143–55). There is evidence that the endowment was not actually sufficient to cover the costs of maintenance, and that the difference was made up by the head of the family.[40]

The chantry served to maintain five priests, who had their own college, adjacent to the church; there is evidence that there was also a school there.[41] Although all the property of chantries fell to the Crown under the Chantry Act of 1545, the family managed to retain the chantry-endowment lands, and even the site of the college, though a law-suit lasting until 1628 was necessary for some of them.[42] From the second half of the sixteenth century the four endowment manors became a normal part of the Lanherne estate. Under Queen Mary the family no doubt hoped to reinstate the chantry, and it actually appears in the manorial accounts for the whole estate in 1558–61, though not thereafter; but that could have been merely a continuation of earlier accounting procedures.[43]

---

[38] For the chantry and its endowment, see Henderson, *St Columb Major*, pp. 38–45. The deed itself is recited in the inquisition post mortem of John Arundell, PRO C.179/32, no. 39, and in its Chancery enrolment, *Cal.Close*, 1430, pp. 35–37. Henderson dated the deed to 1427, but its date is 24 March, 6 Henry VI (1428). See also Snell, *Chantry Certificates*, pp. 16–18.

[39] Henderson, *St Columb Major*, pp. 40–41.

[40] Henderson, *St Columb Major*, p. 42.

[41] Henderson, *St Columb Major*, p. 41.

[42] Henderson, *St Columb Major*, pp. 42–43.

[43] The manors are absent from the estate accounts all through the fifteenth century and down to 1529–30; then manorial accounts for the whole estate are lacking until 1558. The chantry appears as a unit in the accounts for 1558–59 and 1560–61 (AR2/955–956), but from 1561–62 the four manors appear as ordinary ones within the estate (AR2/958).

In addition to this chantry located at St Columb Major church, in 1512–13 the then head of the family, Sir John Arundell who died in 1545, planned to create another chantry, together with an almshouse, at the church of St Mawgan, immediately adjacent to the family residence of Lanherne. He obtained a licence from King Henry VIII, and a foundation-deed was drawn up; but it was never executed.[44] The reason is unknown; it is much too early for Arundell to have prudently anticipated the later events of Henry VIII's reign.

Truro Vean, mid-fifteenth century

Land in *Trurw*, termed a 'manor' (but probably meaning tenements merely) was included by Sir John Arundell (died 1433–35) in a lease of certain of his manors (Connerton, Carminow, Winnington, and Kennall) in 1407, and a tenement there was leased by him in 1426.[45] However, Truro Vean is absent from the manorial accounts of the Arundell estate in 1433–34,[46] and the manor is not mentioned among his properties at his death in 1435, merely 14*s*. rent in the borough of Truro, held of Sir William Bodrugan, knight. The earliest clear evidence for Arundell ownership of Truro Vean, named as such, is in 1445–46; it is not clear when Truro Vean was first termed a manor, but it is so recorded in 1451.[47]

In addition, lands in Carvedras, held of Newham manor (Kenwyn parish) appear in the estate accounts for 1467–68 and 1468–69.[48] These lands were not part of the manor of Truro Vean, and in those years the lands of Carvedras accounted separately from Truro Vean; they do not appear in the rentals printed below. However, a *Carvederas Street* (not the same thing) was part of Truro Vean manor in 1767.[49]

---

[44] AR16/15–16.
[45] AR20/18 (lease, 1407); AR4/2122 (lease, 1426).
[46] AR2/887.
[47] AR2/891 (account of Cornish estate, 1445–46); AR19/10 (pre-nuptial settlement, 1451); it is notable that this is also the date (anomalously early) of its own section within the extent of 1451–64 (below, p. xli and n. and p. 60).
[48] AR2/908, m. 6, and AR2/909, m. 3.
[49] AR2/1189.

Chideock inheritance, 1451–80

In 1451 John Arundell (born in 1421) married, as his second wife, Katherine Chideock; he already had a daughter by his first marriage to Elizabeth daughter of Thomas, Lord Morley.[50] Katherine had also been married before, to William Stafford, and they had a son, Humphrey; so, although Katherine and her sister Margaret (who married Sir William Stourton) were coheirs of their father John Chideock, who died in 1449–50, John Arundell cannot have expected to gain significant property from the marriage. Nor did he need to: at the time, in 1451, he was said to be King Henry VI's wealthiest free tenant in Cornwall, with a yearly income of £2,000.[51] However, Katherine's son Humphrey Stafford, a 'greedy and ambitious man', having been created earl of Devon by King Edward IV in 1469, was killed in Bridgwater, apparently at the hands of a mob, three months later;[52] so the Arundells inherited extensive estates in Dorset and Somerset, including Chideock itself. These do not concern us in the present volume; but Chideock was to remain a part of the Lanherne estate, often administered with the Cornish lands, down to the end.[53]

Creation of Perlees, 1480 × 1499

This manor is something of an enigma. It does not appear in the rentals of c.1460 and 1480; but it does in that of 1499 (below, pp. 140–41); so it must have been acquired or created between 1480 and 1499. Nor is Perlees recorded elsewhere as a manor before the latter date; so it appears to be an eclectic manor, created out of lands recently acquired by the Arundells (see below). Most of the lands, including Perlees itself, were members of the great manor of Pawton, which had belonged to the bishops of Exeter since the ninth century;[54] the lands of Perlees paid high rents mainly to that

---

[50] AR19/8–11, Arundell's pre-nuptial settlement to Katherine, 1451.
[51] *Dictionary of National Biography*, II, 141–43 (Arundell of Cornwall).
[52] Charles Ross, *Edward IV*, 2nd edition (London, 1983), pp. 78 and 132.
[53] A good list of the Chideock lands which came to the Arundells is found in AR2/1229, the accounts of the lands held by Lady Katherine Arundell in her widowhood. See also *Inquisitiones* (RC), IV, 224 (no. 26), for a full list of Chideock lands.
[54] *The Crawford Collection of Early Charters and Documents*, edited by W. S. Napier and W. H. Stevenson (Oxford, 1895), no. VII.

manor or to that of Padstow. No administrative documents of Perlees appear in the Arundell archive earlier than this rental of 1499: the first surviving court roll covers 1500–02, and the earliest surviving estate accounts to include Perlees are those of 1506–07; the preceding set, for 1497–98, does not mention the manor, and the accounts for the intervening years are lacking.[55] This again makes it likely that the manor was created at about the time that it appears in the 1499 rental. The earliest that Perlees is actually referred to as a 'manor' is in 1515;[56] but, as leet courts were held there in 1500–02, it was probably considered one from 1499 onwards.

In the 1499 rental the unit is termed *Penles Treviscan*, with reference to Trevisker in Padstow parish, a conventionary tenement of the manor; two of the manorial courts were held at Trevisker in the earliest extant court roll, in 1500–02.[57] The double name recurs occasionally in the sixteenth century, but the normal name of the manor, from 1500 onwards, was *Penles* or the like.[58] One of the free tenements of the manor, Treniow, is earlier found as a free tenement of Trembleath manor, and in 1499 it seems to have become a free tenement of Perlees instead, while remaining a conventionary tenement of Trembleath (see below, p. 74, n. 9). However, the other free tenements are not previously recorded as Arundell lands. Several of the lands of the manor, including the free tenements of Trenearne and Treniow and the conventionary tenements of Trevisker, Roscullion and Crugmeer, had been held as a group by Joce de Penles and Margaret his wife in 1350; and some of them appear again, still in the hands of the Penles family, in 1410–11.[59] Some of these lands reappear in a grant made by John Scovern to John Arundell, in 1458–59, with one Thomas Lymbery appointed by Arundell to receive seisin; and more in a

---

[55] AR2/418 (court roll, 1500–02); AR2/943 (estate accounts, 1506–07); AR2/942 (estate accounts, 1497–98).
[56] AR20/39, a trust deed of this and two Devonshire manors.
[57] AR2/418; again, at *Trevithcan*, in July 1578, AR4/1595.
[58] *Penlees and Trevyscan* in a manorial account, 1560–61 (AR2/956; but a rough copy of the same account calls the unit *Penlees* simply, AR2/957, fol. 10); *Penles Treviscan* in the 1580s rental, AR2/1343.
[59] *Cornwall Feet of Fines*, I, no. 589, = AR1/376 (1350); and AR1/382–386 (1410–11).

grant made by one John Rosogan to Thomas Lymbery and others in 1465.[60] Thomas Lymbery was later (1478–79) steward of the Arundell lands in Cornwall;[61] and it may well be that he was acting for the family in 1465 in receiving those lands, as in 1459. It thus seems that Perlees manor was created in 1499 out of this group of lands formerly held by the Penles family, plus a few others. It is probably mere coincidence that about 200 years earlier Richard de Mareys had granted to Ralph de Arundell the homage and service of Philip de Penles due for 1½ acres in *Tregiastin*.[62]

Dinham inheritance, 1501

John Arundell (born in 1421) died in 1471 × 1473, and Katherine his wife in 1478 × 1480.[63] In about 1473 their son Thomas Arundell, the only head of the family between 1300 and 1700 not to be christened John, married Katherine Dinham, sister of John Lord Dinham, head of the wealthy and ancient Devonshire family, with extensive lands in Devon, Cornwall and elsewhere as far as Oxfordshire and Buckinghamshire.[64]

The Dinham family had obtained its lands in Cornwall in an unusual manner. In 1268 the heiress Isolda de Cardinan, last of the great Cornish family of Cardinan, sold or gave away much of her estate, presumably in the knowledge that she would die without heirs. Her family had been the greatest feudal barons in Cornwall for approaching 200 years. They had founded the town

---

[60] AR1/389–90 (Scovern to Arundell, 1458–59); AR1/393 (Rosogan to Lymbery, 1465).
[61] AR2/1320 (estate accounts, 1478–79).
[62] AR1/306/1, datable to either c.1260 or the early fourteenth century; *Tregiastin* is probably a poor form for Tregawne, in Withiel, in which the Arundells had an interest in 1334 (*Cornwall Feet of Fines*, I, no. 682, = AR20/1), and in which the Penles family had an interest in 1410 (AR1/384).
[63] John Arundell still alive in 1471, AR23/2; dead in 1473, AR19/18, and *Inquisitiones* (RC), IV, 361 (no. 26). Katherine alive in 1478 (remarried to Sir Roger Leukenore), AR7/10, 12; her will, dated 1479, AR21/6–7; dead in 1480, AR20/30.
[64] The Dinham family is well treated by Pearse Chope, *Book of Hartland*, and Jones, *Family of Dinan*.

of Lostwithiel, built Restormel Castle, and greatly endowed Tywardreath Priory. Isolda settled upon three main beneficiaries for her lands. To Henry Champernowne (*de Campo Arnulphi*) she sold her Cornish manors of Tywardreath and Ludgvan.[65] To Oliver de Dinan she sold her Cornish manors of Bodardle (Lanlivery) and Cardinham, together with the honour of Cardinham, that is the feudal overlordship of the considerable number of manors in Devon and Cornwall which were held of either manor.[66] The third beneficiary was Richard, Earl of Cornwall, to whom she gave others of her properties, and who gave her in return a tenancy for life of his Devonshire manor of Kenton.[67] The reasons for Isolda's choice of beneficiaries are unknown. The resulting ownership of the manor of Cardinham by the Dinham family has understandably caused surmise that there was some connection between the two families; but it is clear that the name of Cardinham existed, independently, long before the Dinhams gained possession of it in 1268. It is possible that there was some kinship between them; but that is unknown at present.[68]

The third Dinham manor in Cornwall, Downinney in Warbstow parish, was bought by Oliver de Dinan shortly afterwards from

---

[65] Oliver, *Monasticon*, p. 43, no. XX (a deed now lost from the Arundell archive). Isolda's seal on this deed is illustrated by Lysons, *Cornwall*, p. lxxix*; and the confirmation by Richard earl of Cornwall survives as AR37/2. This manor of Tywardreath was a secular one, different from that of the Priory.

[66] British Library, Additional MS. 34,792A (Dinham family cartulary, fifteenth century), fols 3r. and 8v.–9r., and AR1/395; see also AR1/842 (Earl Richard's confirmation of the grant). Isolda retained Cardinham and Bodardle for her own lifetime.

[67] PRO, E.36/57 (Earl Edmund's cartulary), fols 33 and 15v.–16.

[68] Lysons, *Cornwall*, p. lxxix, note *e*, notes a similarity between the seals of Cardinan and Dinan, both showing lozenges; he reports a suggestion that the family of Cardinan was perhaps a branch of the Dinans of Brittany, and named their seat *Car-Dinan*, 'Dinan Castle'; as Lysons says, the manor of Cardinham was not originally so named, having gone under the name of Trezance, *Thersent*, in Domesday Book (Picken, 'Trezance, Lahays'). The question is too uncertain to pursue here, but the name Dinan is not found applied to the Cardinan family, and for the time being no kinship is known between the families of Cardinan and Dinan.

John son of William; John was presumably the son of the tenant of Downinney in 1268, William son of Robert.[69]

In addition to the three Dinham manors, the survey of 1566 printed below (pp. 173–97) also includes the 'fees' of Cardinham and *Carbugus*. These were the descendants of the great baronial Honour of Cardinham, composed of the group of twenty-eight manors held in 1086 by Richard fitz Turold, ancestor of the Cardinans (and including the manors of Trezance, later called Cardinham, Tywardreath and Downinney),[70] combined (presumably by marriage) with that group of twenty manors held by Turstin the Sheriff which included the manors of Bodardle (Lanlivery) and Gurlyn (St Erth). Isolda held all this overlordship in 1268. The tenants of these Cornish manors paid their feudal service to the manor of Cardinham, from which the honour took its name, at the 'Great Ditch' outside Bodmin town;[71] but the western manors were instead made dependent upon the small farm of *Carbugus* or Carnabeggas, in St Erth.[72] Hence this insignificant place appears below as having a feudal 'fee' named from it. It was hardly a manor in the true sense (nor is it so termed in the survey of 1566), rather a tenurial convenience; hence, like the Honour of Cardinham, it had no conventionary tenants, only free ones.[73]

The marriage of Thomas Arundell to Katherine Dinham was politically a remarkable one, since the Dinhams were strongly Yorkist, whereas the Arundells were Lancastrian; but this hedging of bets, if such it was, served them well a decade later, when the

---

[69] Dinham Cartulary, fols 13r.–15r. (Oliver's purchase, completed by 1284). The tenants were named in 1268 when Isolda granted the overlordship of the manors in the fee of Cardinham, including Downinney, to Oliver de Dinan (*ibid.*, fols 8v.–9r.).

[70] *Domesday Book: Cornwall*, section 5.3.

[71] See below, pp. 182, etc.; *apud magnum fossatum extra Bodminiam* in 1320 (Dinham Cartulary, fol. 5v.); compare Picken, 'Trezance, Lahays'.

[72] This arrangement is suggested already in 1294 by a document copied into the Dinham Cartulary, fol. 16r.–v.

[73] Carnabeggas is termed a 'manor', held by the co-heirs of Dinham, in 1519 (inquisition post mortem of Richard Vyvyan, PRO C.142/34, no. 39). Leland in c.1540 described it as 'a castel caullid Carnhangibes, as apperith, or maner place now clene down, not far from the bridg': *Itinerary*, I, 192.

Arundell lands were confiscated because of Thomas's participation in Buckingham's rebellion against King Richard III in October 1483. Thomas Arundell cannot have expected his family to inherit much, if any, property from the great Dinham estates in Cornwall, Devon, Somerset and elsewhere, for John Lord Dinham was already married, with two children, and was to remarry after his first wife's death; he also had three brothers and four further sisters in addition to Katherine. Yet all of the men died without living offspring, John Lord Dinham himself being the last in January 1501; so the great Dinham estates were split between the four surviving sisters and their families.[74] These were Sir Edmund Carew, of Mohun's Ottery, aged 36, son and heir of Nicholas, Baron Carew, and of Margery, John Dinham's eldest sister; Elizabeth Lady Fitzwarin, Dinham's second sister, then aged 50 (she later married as her third husband Sir Thomas Brandon); Sir John Arundell, aged 26, son and heir of Thomas Arundell and Katherine, Dinham's third sister; and Joan Lady Zouche, aged 45, Dinham's fourth sister, and wife of John Lord Zouche.[75]

Instead of being split between the four heirs, these lands continued to be run as a single estate, known as 'Dinham's Lands', for some considerable time, with the yearly revenues being divided between the heirs and, eventually, their own descendants or heirs.[76] This was still true in 1566, when a fine survey of the lands was drawn up for Henry Compton, by then one of the four co-heirs of Lord Dinham (see below, pp. xlviii and 173–97). This survey forms the best succinct guide to the Dinham inheritance in Devon and Cornwall, though it does not cover lands further afield. As early as 1506–07 those of Dinham's Lands in Devon and Cornwall were submitting separate accounts from those in Oxfordshire and elsewhere;[77] so the separate survey does not mean that the lands outside Devon and Cornwall had been sold. Indeed, the archive

---

[74] Pearse Chope, 'Manor of Hartland', pp. 434–35, and *Book of Hartland*, pp. 30–37.
[75] See the accounts of 1506–1514 (AR2/1275, 1277, 1279 and 1281); and Pearse Chope, *Book of Hartland*, pp. 36–37.
[76] The account of Dinham's lands in 1590 (AR2/1319) suggests that they were still being so administered at that date.
[77] AR2/1275–76; this arrangement probably goes back to the time of Dinham himself: compare AR2/881 (account of 1489–90).

includes accounts for many of these as late as 1561–62 and 1573–74.[78]

It is thus unclear when, and how, 'Dinham's Lands' ceased operating as a unified group for the four heirs. The last account in the Lanherne archive for the lands as a group is dated 1590.[79] Of the five Cornish units which it contained (three manors and two greater fees), the Arundells later increased their interest in the manor of Cardinham, so that it appears as an Arundell manor in surveys and accounts of the seventeenth and eighteenth centuries, from about from 1597 onwards.[80] They do not seem to have acquired Downinney, and it is not heard of in the later administration of the estate. However, the manor of Bodardle does appear for a while in the manorial accounts of the estate, from 1579–80 to 1611–12; in a slightly later account, of 1620–21, it appears but is deleted. Similarly it appears in two surveys of the estate in this period, a lease-book of 1578 and Codner's Survey of 1618; and Bodardle is also mentioned, along with Cardinham and the other Arundell manors, in two trust deeds of the estate in 1595–97.[81] This suggests that the Arundells acquired some closer interest in the manor for a while, then sold it again in about 1618–20. Unlike the manor of Cardinham, Bodardle does not appear in surveys of the estate after this. (At a later date there are also farming-accounts of Trinity Barton, at Restormel in Lanlivery parish, in 1665–1701;[82] but this does not seem to have been a part of Bodardle manor, since

---

[78] An account of Dinham's Lands in 1561–62 includes Dornford (Wotton parish), Ilbury, Wykham (Banbury parish), Steeple Ashton, Wendlebury, Merton, Horley and Mollington (all in Oxfordshire); and Little Kimble and Cuddington (in Buckinghamshire); and one of 1573–74 includes Souldern, Over Worton, Sesswell's Barton (Steeple Barton parish), Rousham and North Stoke, formerly *Stokebassett alias Stoke Mules* (all in Oxfordshire), and Oving (in Buckinghamshire): AR2/1306 and 1395. Some of the Arundell quarter-shares were sold in a tidy-up of the estates in 1576: AR1/711–17 and 837–38.

[79] AR2/1319.

[80] Manorial accounts, 1596–98 (AR2/1325), 1611–12 (AR2/981) and 1620–21 (AR2/982); then absent until 1659–60 (AR2/1003–04).

[81] AR2/964 (accounts, 1579–80); AR2/982 (accounts, 1611–12); AR2/982 (accounts, 1620–21); AR2/1342 (lease-book, 1578); AR2/1346 (Codner's Survey, 1618); AR20/49–50 (trust deeds, 1595–97).

[82] AR3/410–425.

it is absent in the survey printed below, pp. 194–97. It must represent an independent investment.) As for the two fees, of Cardinham and Carnabeggas, if indeed they were still operating, little more is heard. Since they consisted only of free tenancies, which by now were not worth the cost of their administration, there would have been little incentive to acquire them.[83]

After the break-up of Dinham's Lands the Arundells also retained a close interest in the manor of Hartland, in north Devon; but we are not concerned with that here.

Earl of Oxford's lands, 1575–76

Dinham's Lands were the last major Arundell acquisition by inheritance. However, there were two more acquisitions by purchase before the fortunes of the family began to decline. The greater of these consisted of six manors which Sir John Arundell bought from Edward de Vere, earl of Oxford, in 1575–76;[84] the manors were Bejowan in St Columb Minor, Domellick in St Dennis, Roseworthy in Gwinear, Tregenna in St Ewe, Tregorrick in St Austell and Tresithney in St Columb Major (see below, pp. 156–72 and 207–38). These were all adjacent or close to existing Arundell properties: Bejowan to Treloy, Domellick to Enniscaven, Roseworthy to Connerton, Tregenna and Tregorrick to Lanhadron, and Tresithney to St Columb. At first glance it might seem that this proximity was a factor in selecting the manors, since there were other Cornish manors in the Vere estate which Arundell did not purchase, notably Polsue (St Erme), Penhale and Arrallas (both in St Enoder), Eathorne (Mabe), Rosenithon (St Keverne), Treninick (St Columb Minor) and Predannack Wollas (Mullion).[85] However, some of these other Oxford manors were also close to existing Arundell properties; and the six manors later purchased by Arundell were already treated as a group within the Oxford estate in 1556–57,

---

[83] 'Cardinham fee' is mentioned in the account of 1620–21 (AR2/982).

[84] This is the seventeenth earl, to whom some would give the credit of having written Shakespeare's plays: J. Thomas Looney, *"Shakespeare" Identified in Edward de Vere the Seventeenth Earl of Oxford* (London, 1920).

[85] The Oxford manors in Cornwall in 1449–51 (omitting the six manors later purchased by Arundell) are usefully listed in an account of their whole Cornish estate, AR2/844.

and probably earlier.[86] So it is likely that they were sold as a pre-existing group, albeit one which happened to relate well geographically to the existing Arundell estate. (See the map, frontispiece.)

The documents show Arundell's purchase of the six manors in 1575–76, for just over £3,000.[87] Four years earlier, in June 1571, Edward de Vere had appointed John Arundell chief steward of all his manors in Cornwall and Devon;[88] this may have been some kind of an overture to the negotiations. The three detailed surveys of individual manors, with valuations (see below, pp. xlvii–xlviii and 207–34), dated earlier in 1575, were clearly made as a preliminary to the sale.

The manors were doubtless sold by the earl to support his 'every form of extravagance'.[89] When the sale occurred, four years after he had come of age, he had already 'run up debts of many thousands', and it accords with his practice elsewhere, including the sale of his estate in Essex; indeed, he 'seemed to take delight in selling every acre of his land at ruinously low prices'.[90] Some at least of those Cornish manors not sold to Arundell also appear in other hands by the late sixteenth or very early seventeenth century. At the time of the sale the earl himself was abroad on a fourteen-month holiday in Italy, which cost him over £4,500, much more than he received for the six manors—'the greatest spendthrift tourist of all'.[91]

Some of the six manors bought by Arundell formed a group by inheritance within the Oxford estate. One of them, Tregenna in St Ewe, was actually two manors, in that it had been split, presumably by descent, into the manors of Tregenna Wartha and Tregenna Wollas; they were re-united in the Vere estate, though

---

[86] Estreat rolls for those manors, AR2/734–736 (1556–57, 1557–58 and 1569–70) and court rolls, AR2/737 (1572); earlier account rolls and court rolls covering the Vere manors often seem to group the later Arundell or non-Arundell ones separately; and two trust leases of the family, in 1473 and 1488, cover three and two of the later Arundell manors, again suggesting that they were treated separately from the other Vere manors (AR1/848–849).
[87] AR1/854–862; also AR10/3 (letter of 1574).
[88] AR22/38; Arundell was to receive the sum of £4 yearly for his services.
[89] *Dictionary of National Biography*, s.v. Edward de Vere.
[90] Stone, *Crisis of the Aristocracy*, pp. 264 and 514 (also pp. 295 and 410); *Dictionary of National Biography*, loc. cit.
[91] Stone, *Crisis of the Aristocracy*, p. 701.

occasionally still treated separately. (Note, for instance, the wording 'the manor of Trigennowe Wolas and Trigennowe Wartha' in 1575: below, p. 220.) Four of the six manors (Bejowan, Domellick, Roseworthy and the still undivided Tregenna) had been manors of the Archdeacon or Lercedekne family since at least the mid-thirteenth century.[92] The presumed descent is via Philippa, daughter and coheiress of Warin Lercedekne (died 1400) of Haccombe; she married Hugh Courtenay knight (who died in 1425).[93] Their daughter and coheiress Joan Courtenay married (second) Sir Robert Vere; assuming that this was Robert, who was the younger son of Richard de Vere the eleventh Earl of Oxford (died 1417), and who was also the grandfather of John de Vere the fifteenth earl (who died in 1540), this marriage would presumably explain the presence of certain Lercedekne manors in the estate of the earls of Oxford from about 1500 onwards.[94]

The other two manors and part of another (Tregorrick, Tresithney and Tregenna Wartha) had come to the Veres through Alice, daughter and heiress of Walter Colbroke and Joan Tresithny; she married John de Vere, son of the same Robert Vere (younger son of Richard the eleventh earl), and father of John the fifteenth earl.[95] This latter John (who died in 1540) was thus the first earl to

---

[92] *Cornwall Feet of Fines*, I, no. 453 (Bejowan, Domellick and Roseworthy in 1318); *ibid.*, no. 457 (Tregenna in 1319); *Cal.Pat.*, 1343, p. 181 (Bejowan in 1343); *Black Prince's Register*, II, 28–29 and 32–33 (Roseworthy in 1352); *Brantyngham*, I, 365 (Bejowan in 1375); *Hylle Cartulary*, no. 236 (Domellick in 1401); *Calendar of IPMs*, XIX, no. 217 (Elizabeth widow of Warin Lerchedekene knight; Roseworthy, Bejowan and Domellick, 1407). But the inquisition after the death of Thomas son of Odo Lercedekne, in 1331, mentions only Bejowan of these later Vere manors (*Calendar of IPMs*, VII, no. 345).

[93] Vivian, *Visitations*, p. 107; *Calendar of IPMs*, XIX, no. 217; Maclean, *Trigg Minor*, III, 259.

[94] Vivian, *Visitations*, p. 107; Cokayne, *Complete Peerage*, X, 234–36 and 245–47. However, of those four manors Hugh Courtenay had held only Bejowan and Domellick at his death in 1425 (*Inquisitiones* (RC), IV, 85); Roseworthy and Tregenna are still unaccounted for.

[95] Cokayne, *Complete Peerage*, X, 245–47. A pedigree of 1531 explains the descent of these three manors (AR1/851); see also *Cal.Close*, 1391, p. 269 (John Tregorrek and others, lands in Tregorrek and Tresithny), and AR1/844 (feoffment in trust to Joan, formerly wife of Walter Colbroke, 1488, with remainder to Alice, lately wife of John Veer).

inherit all six manors which were later to be sold to Arundell.[96] Most of the other Oxford manors (Eathorne, Penhale, Polsue, Predannack Wollas and Rosenithon) had come to the family by a much earlier marriage, of Richard, eleventh earl (c.1385–1417; father of Robert the grandfather of John the fifteenth earl); he had married (second) Alice, sister and coheiress of Richard Sergeaux; the Sergeaux family had in turn inherited some of them from the Seneschal family in the earlier fourteenth century.[97] This is the reason why the six manors bought by Arundell may have constituted a sub-group within the Oxford estate, composed of two fairly recent inheritances. All six manors were in areas with considerable potential for tinning, and this may have been a further motive for the investment. They were demonstrating this potential, and also the value of their woods for serving the tinning industry, very soon after their purchase.[98]

Manor of Newland Preeze, 1587

This manor does not appear in the documents printed below, as it was purchased too late to be included in any sixteenth-century survey. It was created in the thirteenth century by the lords of Cardinham, being carved out of the lands of Cardinham itself for the Peverell family;[99] it remained in that family and their successors until Henry earl of Huntingdon sold it in 1564 to Roger Copping, whose family had been yeoman tenants of the manor for at least

---

[96] Apparently none of the manors was in the Oxford estate in 1449–51 (AR2/844); the manors of Roseworthy, Bejowan and Tregenna [Wollas] were within it by 1473 (AR1/848), and Domellick by 1488–89 (AR2/846). Tregenna [Wartha], and by implication Tresithney and Tregorrick, were still in Colbroke's hands in 1468 (AR1/440); the earliest clear evidence in the Lanherne archive for all three in the Oxford estate is 1527–28 (AR2/856).

[97] Henderson, *Mabe*, p. 29; Henderson, 'St Keverne', p. 74; Cokayne, *Complete Peerage*, X, 234–36; *Inquisitiones* (RC), III, 260 (Richard Sergeaux knight, 1399–1400, manors including Eathorne, Rosenithon, Predannack, Penhale and Polsue). Note the grant of Oxford manors, including these five, during the minority of John the thirteenth earl: *Cal.Pat.*, 1463, p. 287.

[98] Freeth, 'Ministers accounts'.

[99] AR1/462 (deed of 1307–08, citing an earlier charter, now lost).

100 years.[100] Copping appears in 1566, holding Newland Preeze as a free tenement of the manor of Cardinham (below, p. 177). Twenty-three years later, in 1587, John Copping of St Neot sold his share of the manor to Sir John Arundell; but the Copping family still remained as tenants of the manor in 1717.[101] The tenements of the manor in 1659 were (free) Newland, Bilgars, Old Cardinham, and Preeze (all in Cardinham), Treswigger, *Haycroft* (lost), Pengelly, Penrose, and Scribble (Blisland), Bradford and East Rose (St Breward); (conventionary) Newland, Haygrove, Combe Park and Blowing House (Cardinham) and Poldew (Blisland).[102] Within Cardinham parish, the tenements of Newland Preeze manor were intermingled with those of Cardinham manor itself.

---

[100] AR1/466–469 (sale, 1564); AR1/464 (William Copping as tenant, 1464).
[101] AR1/472–477 (sale, 1587); RIC rental of 1717.
[102] RIC MS.; the spellings have been modernised. The tenements are substantially the same in Copping's deed of 1564 (AR1/468).

3. THE DOCUMENTS

The documents printed below vary greatly in nature and purpose, covering as they do a span of almost 250 years. The distinction between types of survey, particularly between a 'rental' and an 'extent', was not rigidly observed, and no doubt varied over the ages. Discussion on the subject has tended to concentrate on the thirteenth century, earlier than the earliest document printed here (1343). Lennard established that an 'extent' originally must include valuations, a definition endorsed by Lomas and Harvey;[1] yet, of the documents printed here, only some of the sixteenth-century ones contain true valuations, and they do not call themselves 'extents'. Lomas also suggested that, in its true sense, 'the extent had become superfluous by the fifteenth century' and was largely replaced by the rental; the list of documents which he considered from around the country ends in 1409.[2] Harvey has confirmed that, by the fifteenth century, the rental had become very similar to, and indeed had largely replaced, the extent; 'the distinctions between the different sorts of medieval survey are not always clear-cut in practice.'[3] This suggests that even those of our documents which do actually call themselves 'extents' may have had more the purpose of a rental, and perhaps the term 'extent' was used out of habit. We have tried to observe the usage of the documents themselves, but have not attempted precision nor, necessarily, consistency; 'survey' is used as a general term covering all such documents. Even a 'rental' may vary between a formal list of rents due (such as that of 1480, below) and an informal list of rents collected or to be collected; the documents covering the chantry-endowment manors (below, pp. 143–55) are closer to the latter category.

The three fifteenth-century surveys of the whole manor are spaced almost exactly at twenty-year intervals, being dated 1451–64 (mainly 1459–60), 1480 (by deduction: see below) and 1499.

---

[1] Lennard, 'What is a manorial extent?'; Lomas, 'Development of the manorial extent'; Harvey, *Manorial Records*, pp. 20–22.
[2] Lomas, 'Development of the manorial extent', pp. 270–73.
[3] Harvey, *Manorial Records*, pp. 22–23; see also Harvey, *Cuxham Records*, pp. 72–78.

Whether this was due to policy or to chance is not clear; but the turnover of conventionary tenants at this period (see below) was such that a rental would have been very dated after twenty years. It is possible that the 1451–64 extent was the first such covering the estate as a whole (as opposed to ones covering individual manors, such as the fourteenth-century documents printed here), and so was perhaps regarded as having a particular authority, especially in relation to free tenements and their descents. The extent of 1499 was in places considerably updated at a later date or dates (particularly in the town of St Columb), and gives the impression of being a document which continued in use for some time; so it is possible that the gap following it (the next survey extant covering the whole estate being that of 1571) represents a real one in terms of the management of the estate.[4] If these two surmises are correct (that the extent of 1451–64 was the first such for the estate as a whole, and that the gap following 1499 was a real one), then the surviving documents provide an interesting record of what was needed in the way of administrative documents in the fifteenth and sixteenth centuries; but it is possible that documents have been lost. At all events, the existence of three such surveys, at roughly equal intervals in the second half of the fifteenth century, adds to their interest, in making it possible to study aspects of the manorial system which could not be treated from a single survey.

It must be emphasized that even the 'whole-estate' surveys do not quite give a complete picture of the Arundell lands in Cornwall. At times there are glimpses of other properties which do not appear in the documents printed below, presumably because they did not form part of any Arundell manor. The inquisition post mortem of John Arundell (died 1433–35) mentions various properties which do not appear in this book, such as smallholdings at Tremorkin (St Neot) and St Tudy (part of the chantry-endowment), and land in Killiow, Bolotho and Nansilgans (all in Kea).[5] A 'manor' of Trefrink and Penpol (named from Trink, in Lelant, and Penpol, in Phillack) appears in the estate accounts, and in deeds of the estate, in the fifteenth century; it had already been held by the family in

---

[4] A rental of St Columb town (only) exists from 1537: AR2/189.
[5] PRO, C.139/72, no. 39.

1391, and was still apparently part of the estate in 1477;[6] yet it does not appear in the rental of 1451–64, except insofar as Trink was held as free tenements of Connerton manor (below, pp. 44 and 47). We have already seen how the Arundell lands in Truro included lands in Carvedras, not part of Truro Vean manor; a reeve's account for them appears in the estate accounts between 1459 and 1475, so that we might expect to see those lands in the extent of 1451–64.[7] Similarly land in Trewinnion (in St Enoder) appears in the accounts in 1467–69 and 1474–75, paying high rent to the manor of Degembris (in Newlyn East);[8] and lands in Sticker and Treloweth, both in St Mewan and part of the former Carminow estate, appear in 1476–77.[9] None of these appears in the fifteenth-century surveys. Finally, the last section of the 1480 rental (below, pp. 99–100) is of a kind not represented in the other surveys, and seems to cover some lands not mentioned otherwise. Although most tenements were indeed placed under some manor or other, if only for administrative convenience, what appears printed below is surveys of the manors held, not necessarily surveys of all property.

Fourteenth-century extents, AR2/1336 and AR2/376

The extent of Lanherne and Trembleath in 1343 (AR2/1336) is the earliest manorial survey in the archive. This is late by up-country standards; but the preservation of earlier manorial documents from Cornwall has not been good. The document consists of a single piece of parchment, written on both sides. It purports to cover *duas partes* 'two parts' of the 'manor' (singular) of Lanherne and Trembleath; since Lanherne was still considered to include the town of St Columb at this date, this survey actually deals (in part) with three of the fifteenth-century manors. The phrase *duas partes* could mean either 'the two parts', if the manor was regarded as falling into two subdivisions (i.e. Lanherne and Trembleath), or 'two-thirds'. Joan, presumably mother of John Arundell II, had been dowered with a two-thirds share of the 'vill' of Trembleath in 1323,

---

[6] AR2/885 (receipts from Arundell manors, 1387–88); AR20/29 (deed of whole estate, 1477).
[7] AR2/904–906, 908–910, and 912.
[8] AR2/908–909 and 912.
[9] AR2/915; for the Carminow inheritance, AR1/192 and *Anc.Deeds*, IV, A.10409, and see above, pp. xv–xvi.

and she was still alive, and living at Trembleath, in 1339.[10] It is therefore possible that this survey of two-thirds of Lanherne and Trembleath represents a survey of her dower-shares, made while she was still living. This would explain why a good number of the tenements mentioned in 1459–60, both free and conventionary, do not appear in 1343. In addition some of the tenements listed in 1343 do not appear later, notably several in St Minver (Gunvenna, Trelawder, Weens and either Treglyn or Treglynes). The reason for this is unclear.

The extent of Lanhadron in 1385 (AR2/376) was drawn up before the manor became Arundell property; Annora's marriage to John Arundell (who died in 1433–35), which brought this manor and others to the Arundell family, must have occurred by about 1395, but it is unlikely to have been as early as 1385 (see above). When the extent was drawn up the manor must still have been in the hands of Annora's parents, William Lambron and his first wife Joan (née Lanhadron), if she was still alive. One-third of the manor had previously been held in dower by Amity, wife of John Lanhadron (and Joan's mother);[11] it was possibly on the occasion of the manor being re-united that this extent was drawn up. This document, like that of 1343, consists of a single membrane, written on both sides; on the reverse are added ten entries from the proceedings of a manorial court of Lanhadron, dated 1 February 1402. The entries all relate to the receipt of conventionary land by tenants; they are not printed below. There is other evidence in the document that it was updated, including the amalgamation of tenements (see below, p. 11 and notes).

Extent of 1451–64, AR2/1337

This is a splendid parchment roll, over 32 feet long, in excellent condition except for some decay at the head. As already mentioned,

---

[10] AR3/29, John Arundell's appointment of attorneys to deliver seisin to Joan, 1323 (there is no mention of Lanherne or St Columb). AR27/1, licence to Lady Joan Arundell to celebrate mass in her chapel at Trembleath, 1339. For two similar divisions in dower see below (Amity Lanhadron).

[11] *Cornwall Feet of Fines*, I, no. 673 (= AR1/262); for a similar arrangement in Devon in c.1400 see AR17/72.

it provides the earliest survey of the Arundell estate as a whole. It is therefore of great value in its list of tenants and their tenements. However, like the later surveys of 1480 and 1499, this roll omits the four manors which formed the chantry-endowment. For them we are dependent upon another roll specially devoted to them (below, pp. 143–55).

There is considerable variation within this roll in the years in which the surveys were made (one manor in 1451, one in 1456, seven in 1459–60, four in 1463 and one in 1464; two sections are undated). This is puzzling: the roll seems thus to be a composite one, though copied in a single hand (except for a few minor alterations). There is no geographical grouping of the manors surveyed in different years; so this cannot have been a matter of practical convenience in administration. Presumably the roll was actually written in about 1464, the date of the latest survey included (that of Bodwannick); but Bodwannick is followed by three manors which were actually surveyed earlier. The date of the Bodwannick survey is immediately after that manor became part of the estate in 1463–64 (see above, 'Soor manors'). It may be that the survey was completed in 1463, without Bodwannick, and the addition of a new manor to the estate caused this fresh copy to be made a year later. The last two manors in the roll, Enniscaven and Truro Vean, are also those with anomalously early dates (1456 and 1451). These seem to be 'tidying-up' sections, not freshly surveyed in 1459–63 but entered here for completeness. The variation in dating may possibly relate to some tenurial arrangement within the family, but that remains unclear at present.[12]

Two of the surveys are undated: the town of St Columb (p. 35) and the second section covering Trembleath (p. 54). In the first case this may be because St Columb was still (as in 1343) considered to be part of Lanherne manor which it follows, so that no additional date was necessary. In the second case the tenements listed duplicate those of 1459, but some of the tenants are different: it seems

---

[12] 1451 was also the year in which John Arundell married Katherine, daughter of Sir John Chideock; the Arundell manors of Carminow, Trembleath, Connerton, Tregarne, Kennall, Lanherne, St Columb, Mitchell and Truro Vean were settled upon her; also their manors of Penwerris, Lambourne and Rinsey (not in the extent of 1451–64), further manors in Devonshire, and Ravensbury in Surrey (AR19/8–11).

likely that the survey is of a slightly later date (perhaps 1463–64, as its place within the roll would suggest).

The extent of the manor and borough of Mitchell is missing from the roll. An endorsement on the roll informs us, 'Methsole cut off from the within and sent to Lord Arundell to London: Feby 1771.' This was shortly before the manor of Mitchell was sold by the Wardour family in 1775 to the Scawens of Carshalton (Surrey). Several early deeds concerning the manor went with the extent, presumably at the same time. By a happy chance, these now survive in Gloucester Record Office, so the relevant item is here printed as part of its parent document.[13] It cannot be assigned to its right place, however. The single membrane has sewing-holes at both ends, so it must have come from somewhere in the middle of the roll; but it is unknown where. The only guess that can be hazarded is that Mitchell could have been adjacent to one of the other three sections dated 1463, Connerton, Lanhadron and Rescassa. The survey is not quite complete: it gives only one conventionary tenement for the manor, instead of the later three (below, pp. 63 and 95), and it also lacks a total of rents from the conventionary tenants, and an overall total for the manor. However, the missing part must have been so small that it cannot have amounted to a whole membrane. Most probably the missing part formed the top of the following membrane, and was cut off and sent to London along with the surviving whole membrane; that membrane from which it was cut would then have had new sewing-holes made, and will now be unrecognizable in the main roll. It is most unlikely that the fragment still survives, since it would be very small, would have no heading and would be meaningless on its own.

Rental of [1480], AR2/1339

This document is a great paper roll, over 23 feet long; it is decayed at its head and foot, and the losses at the head (see p. 65) include

---

[13] Gloucestershire Record Office, collection D.421/A2 (the extent is no. 25); see below, p. 61 and n. For the sale in 1775, see AR2/1196 (audit book for that year). A note in the Gloucestershire catalogue points out that Tryphena, the heiress of the Scawens, had married in 1759 the second Earl Bathurst, of Cirencester (1714–94); the records might have passed to the Bathurst family's Lydney branch, of which Lord Bledisloe, the present owner of the documents, is a member.

the only occasion on which a full date, including the year, was given. The date of the roll can, however, be established with some confidence as 1480. (See the Appendix for detailed discussion.) Some of the names of tenements in the left-hand margin have also been lost, in whole or part; but in many cases these can be identified with certainty by comparison with personal names, place-names and tenurial details in the surveys of 1451–63 and 1499 (e.g. pp. 65–66, 78 and 83–84).

It is uncertain whether this roll would have described itself as an 'extent' or a 'rental'. When it is mentioned in the account-rolls (see the Appendix) it is always a 'rental'; but so is that of 1499, which actually calls itself an 'extent' instead. However, two facts make this survey slightly different in kind from those of 1451–63 and 1499. One is that it contains certain details not found in the other documents, notably one section dealing with miscellaneous rents and with receipts from the demesne lands (below, pp. 99–100), and under Carminow manor the rents from the glebe-lands of Philleigh and Whitstone parishes (p. 85), which are absent in 1459 and 1499;[14] the other is that in five cases (Treloy, Truro Vean, Kennall, Tregarne and Carminow, pp. 69, 77, 78, 80 and 85) it gives chief or outgoing rents, as well as revenues. These factors suggest that this is a document of a slightly different kind from the other two; so it is here termed a 'rental', in accordance with its description in the contemporary rolls.

The other problem concerning AR2/1339 is the absence of the manor of Lanhadron, present in the extents of 1451–64 and 1499. It could be surmised that it was originally the first manor on the roll, and has been lost without trace; but the condition of the roll does not otherwise suggest such severe damage, and there are hints suggesting that Lanhadron was deliberately omitted. In the account for 1478–79 of the general receivers of the Arundell estate in Devon and Cornwall, the remark appears that the revenues paid to Thomas Arundell, the head of the estate, included 'the revenues of Lanhaddroun and the revenues of the lands falling to him through

---

[14] These glebe-lands, attached to the advowsons of those churches, were listed here because they were part of the Carminow inheritance (above, p. xvi), not because they were members of Carminow manor in any tenurial sense.

the death of Katherine Arundell'.[15] This suggests that Lanhadron had not been part of the main estate lately, for whatever reason. Furthermore, Lanhadron is occasionally absent from the manorial accounts of the whole estate. It is so in 1467–69,[16] but present again from 1469–70 onwards.[17] Although its omission from the rental of 1480 cannot be directly due to whatever reason was operating twelve years earlier, it may be that some arrangement in tenure or accounting was liable to cause it to be treated separately from the rest of the estate. It could have been leased or mortgaged, perhaps to pay debts of John Arundell (died 1471–73) or his son Thomas (died 1485).[18] Perhaps further work on the archive will throw light on the matter.

Extent of 1499, AR2/1340

This is a more straightforward document than the rental of 1480. It has the form of a book, instead of a roll; it is clearly legible except for some fading, especially on the first few pages. In contents it covers the same manors as the surveys of 1451–64 and 1480 (including Lanhadron), but with the addition of the manor of Perlees and Trevisker, probably newly created from recent purchases (see above). This survey continued to be used for nearly thirty years, and perhaps longer (the next surviving rental for the whole estate does not occur until 1571);[19] consequently it contains additions and updatings, not always legible; these occur particularly in the town of St Columb and the manors of Lanherne and Treloy. Further evidence for its later use comes from the manorial accounts, where

---

[15] AR2/1320; this is Katherine (Chideock), Thomas Arundell's mother, who died in c.1478–79, not Katherine (Dinham), his wife. The lands settled upon Katherine (Chideock) in 1451 did not include Lanhadron: AR19/8–11.

[16] AR2/908–909.

[17] AR2/910; the name is missing but the manor is identifiable. Note the receipt by Thomas Arundell and Katherine his wife of the 'manors' of Lanhadron and St Goran in 1474 (AR19/22), implying that they had been leased or mortgaged.

[18] For these debts, see for instance AR20/29 (lease to pay off debts, 1477; not including Lanhadron), AR2/921 (no. 12), AR2/927, AR2/1235 and AR2/1237 (general receiver's accounts for the estate, 1480–81, 1488–89 and 1489–90).

[19] AR2/1341, a 'renewal' of the extent of 1451–64 (see above).

it is cited in a similar fashion to the 1480 rental. It is notable that, although the document itself claims to be an 'extent' (see under St Columb and Treloy, pp. 102 and 110), the account rolls always refer to it as a 'rental' instead. The rolls contain greater detail than the book itself about the days on which the manors were surveyed; they may have been referring to another copy which has not survived (perhaps a working-copy, as opposed to this fair copy), or to other documents which recorded the dates of the surveys. The following are the references to the document noted in the account rolls:

>Connerton, 'rental renewed 8 January 1499';
>Perlees, 'rental renewed 11 January 1499';
>Lanhadron, 'rental renewed 11 January 1499';
>Mitchell, 'rental renewed 11 January 1499';
>Treloy, 'rental renewed 12 January 1499';
>Lanherne, 'rental renewed 12 January 1499';
>Trembleath, 'rental renewed 12 January 1499';
>Bodwennack, 'rental renewed 12 January 1499';
>Enniscaven, 'rental renewed 12 January 1499';
>Truro Vean, 'rental renewed 12 January 1499';
>Kennall, 'rental renewed 12 January 1499';
>Winnington, 'rental renewed 12 January 1499';
>Carminow, 'rental renewed 12 January 1499'.[20]

This can hardly represent a physical circuit of the manors, as in 1480 (see the Appendix); presumably the survey was renewed at a central point (probably Lanherne or St Columb), using information brought in from the manors.

Chantry-endowment manors, AR2/1338

All the fifteenth-century surveys omit the four manors (Bodbrane, Pengwedna, Prospidnick and Reperry) set aside as the endowment for the chantry at St Columb. However, these are covered in a roll dealing specifically with those manors; parts of it are printed here. This roll consists of a variety of paper and parchment leaves, of dates varying from 1461–62 to 1559, plus several undated ones. They mostly have the informal character of working documents, rather than fair copies. There are extracts from court rolls (of

---

[20] All from the manorial account roll of 1528–29 (AR2/952), except for Perlees, which is from that of 1508–09 (AR2/945).

Bodbrane 1461–62, and of Pengwedna and Prospidnick, 1546–49), particularly of entries concerning tenancies. Anomalously, there is one rental of the manor of Carminow, appearing on the dorse of a rental of Reperry (both undated); this may be significant, in suggesting that the administration of the chantry-endowment manors was sometimes performed by the same men as that of the main estate, even though their accounting was completely separate. The four manors are consistently absent from the manorial accounts for the estate in the fifteenth century.

Several of the leaves duplicate one another; thus a rental of Pengwedna, 1468–69, appears on both rot. 4d. and rot. 18r., and one of Bodbrane in 1515 on both rot. 6r. and rot. 13. In some cases of duplication, one or other copy gives slightly more information; variants have been noted in the footnotes where they are significant. Since the material for these manors is so much smaller in quantity than that for the main estate, texts of two different dates have been printed for each manor (except for Bodbrane, for which only one text is available), in an attempt to remedy the deficiency. For the same reason, the entries for these four manors in the rental of 1571 (below) have also been printed (pp. 198–206), in an attempt to provide coverage, albeit later, approaching that of the main estate.

Two manors of the earl of Oxford in 1549, AR2/1333

This informal rental of Roseworthy and Bejowan manors, consisting of paper leaves sewn together at the top, was made under the ownership of the sixteenth earl, the father of Edward de Vere who sold the six manors to Arundell twenty-six years later. It is carelessly written, probably by an up-country administrator who was unfamiliar with the Cornish names, for it contains some basic errors in spelling (such as *Bossevargham*, *Warthaye* and *Spernam*, p. 158, and *Tallkarnye*, p. 161), and other carelessnesses among the names (see for instance pp. 162n. and 164n.); but also a few good spellings showing the contemporary pronunciation, such as were not often used by local administrators more familiar with the traditional spellings.[21] The totals of rents seem slightly confused in places. The

---

[21] A striking instance is *Roose Vydney* (p. 157), showing one of the earliest known examples of the sixteenth-century west-Cornish sound-change *-nn-* > *-dn-*.

text is printed here as being the earliest survey covering any of the Oxford manors in Cornwall.

The rental must have come into the Arundell archive at the time of the purchase of the six manors, along with various court rolls and other documents concerned with the administration of the manors. The reason why it covers only two of the six manors is unknown. There may of course have been other rentals, which have not survived, for the other manors. At the end the rental contains notes concerning five of the six manors, omitting Domellick; this provides further evidence that the manors were being treated as a group within the Oxford estate (compare below).

Three manors of the earl of Oxford in 1563, PRO, SP12/31, no. 30

This document too was made while the manors were still in Oxford ownership, in this case while the heir to the sixteenth earl (died 1562) was a minor (Edward de Vere, born 1550). The estate was thus in the Crown's hands, and this partial survey seems to owe its creation, and its preservation in the State Papers, to that fact.[22] It includes all six Oxford manors bought by Arundell twelve years later; unfortunately it omits the free tenants, so for these we are dependent upon other surveys: the earlier one of 1549 in the case of Bejowan and Roseworthy; and the later surveys of 1575 (below) for those of Tregorrick and Tresithney; but for the free tenements of Domellick and Tregorrick we have to wait until the first Arundell survey after the purchase of the manors, namely that of c.1586 (below), when both free and conventionary tenants were given for these small manors.

Only three manors from the survey are printed here (Domellick, Roseworthy and Tregorrick); the other three are omitted (Bejowan, Tregenna and Tresithney), because the much fuller surveys of 1575 are available.[23] What is remarkable is that this 1563 survey covers only those Oxford manors sold to Arundell twelve years later: it omits the other Cornish manors in the Oxford estate. Like other evidence mentioned above (pp. xxxii–xxxiii), this suggests that the

---

[22] *Handbook of British Chronology*, edited by E. B. Fryde and others, 3rd edn (London, 1986), p. 477.

[23] All six manors are printed by Stoate, *Cornwall Manorial Rentals*, pp. 126–32; our readings differ slightly in a few places.

six manors were somehow considered as a separate group within the Oxford estate. Even so, the other Oxford manors in Cornwall, such as Polsue, Eathorne and Rosenithon, should also have needed to be surveyed in 1563 when the estate was in wardship, and it is not clear why these six manors alone were covered.

Survey of Dinham's Lands in 1566, DRO, Z17/3/19

This fine book was produced for Henry Compton, one of the four joint owners of Dinham's Lands in 1566. It covers the seventeen Devonshire manors of the Dinham estate, plus that of Corton Denham in Somerset; two small groups of tenements not classified as manors (Langford Lester, in Ugborough parish, and Newton Poppleford); and five Cornish units, the three manors of Bodardle, Cardinham and Downinney, the fee of Cardinham and also that of *Carbugus* or Carnabeggas, in St Erth. This book was bought from a second-hand bookseller in Barnstaple in 1885, was acquired by Richard Pearse Chope, the historian of Hartland, and was bequeathed by him to Devon Record Office in 1938.[24]

This is the earliest of the detailed sixteenth-century surveys, giving much more information than earlier documents. In particular, for the conventionary tenements it gives details of leases, and the names and sizes of fields. By this period there are detailed accounts of how such surveys were drawn up; study of these illuminates our understanding of the texts.[25]

Extent of 1571, AR2/1341

This paper book covers the fifteen manors of the 1499 extent, plus the four chantry-endowment manors, which were by now fully integrated into the main estate. There was also to be a twentieth section, covering the Hundred of Penwith; but it was left blank. The Dinham manors of Cardinham and Bodardle (let alone the other Cornish components of Dinham's Lands) do not appear. From this survey, only the four chantry-endowment manors are printed here, in order to supplement the less adequate documentation which they possess in the earlier period. This survey calls itself a 'renewal' of an extent dated 12 May 1460 (38 Henry VI), which

---

[24] Pearse Chope, 'Manor of Hartland', p. 435, and 'Lord Dynham's lands', though the latter is unreliable on the Cornish manors.
[25] Kerridge, *Surveys of Pembroke Manors*, pp. x–xiii.

is clearly our extent of 1451–64, using for the whole the date of the survey of Lanherne, which is the first manor copied into the book (though not the first on the earlier roll). However, that of 1451–64 does not contain the four manors printed here, and they must have been obtained from some other source; this survey was not simply a renewal of the earlier one.

AR2/1341 was itself updated by numerous insertions and deletions. Hands different from the one which wrote the main text have added new names of tenants, especially among the free tenants. Some of the names printed below in this survey therefore may refer to dates later than 1571, though probably not much later.

Three manors of the earl of Oxford in 1575, AR2/464, 477 and 482

These three separate surveys of Bejowan, Tregenna and Tresithney were evidently made with a view to the impending sale. They were clearly made at the same time as one another, and by the same surveyors, not only from their internal information, but from the similar format and handwriting of all three. They give lists of the tenants and their rents, and consistently provide information about leases; in addition they contain sections giving 'value if improved'. These sections relate to the potential value of the manor when sold; they contain further information concerning details such as field-names, land-use and roofing-materials of buildings. It is possible that equally-detailed surveys were made of the other three Oxford manors (Domellick, Roseworthy and Tregorrick) before their sale; but unfortunately these have not survived, if they were made.

Rental of c.1586, AR2/1343

When this survey was made the Arundell estate was at almost its fullest extent. It is undated, but internal evidence indicates a date in or close to 1586. It covers the nineteen manors of the 1571 survey (the fifteen of 1499 plus the four chantry-endowment manors), plus the six Oxford manors bought in 1575. The manor of Newland Preeze was not included, presumably because this survey was made before its purchase in 1587; nor are the Dinham manors of Cardinham and Bodardle, later in Arundell hands.

There are several clues as to the date of this document. In the manor of Treloy, under the free tenement of Trencreek (St Columb

Minor), a reference to 'the account for 1581' appears, showing that this rental is later than that year. The description of Roseworthy manor mentions several dates. The entry for the tenement of *Strete, Penpons* and *Roseangrowes* mentions a relief paid by Alexander Penhelege, gentleman, in 26 Elizabeth, 1584, 'as appears in the account for that year';[26] the entry for *Ponseferrys* cites the account for 1578; and the entry for *Penhale Wartha* mentions both a relief paid in 1585 and also homage paid for the tenement on 6 November in that year. The rental is therefore assumed to be later than that, but earlier than October 1587, when the purchase of Newland Preeze was completed;[27] it could have been made a little later if for some reason the recently-purchased manor was omitted. In all manors this rental contains many blanks among the free tenants; as elsewhere, these tenants were by now not worth the trouble of following up their transmission by inheritance, and they were therefore often either cited in terms of tenants from an earlier document (or the unspecified 'heirs' of those tenants), or left completely blank. The only two manors printed below from this document are Domellick and Tregorrick, for which no complete earlier survey is available, since that of 1563, including these manors, omits the free tenements altogether. However, it is also quoted fairly often in the footnotes to earlier surveys, since it contains useful detail updating the information of earlier surveys, and sometimes (though not consistently) it gives the parishes in which tenements were located.

Later surveys, seventeenth and eighteenth centuries

The Lanherne archive contains various later surveys, not printed here; they are often useful for elucidating or expanding upon details of the earlier documents. One particularly worth mentioning is 'Codner's Survey' of 1618, which also contains an essay on the different types of relief in Cornish tenures, and how they differ from those elsewhere in England, on fees Gloucester and fees Mortain, and on the Cornish acre.[28]

---

[26] His father, also Alexander Penheleg, had died by 1582: Pool, 'Penheleg manuscript', p. 165 n. 18.

[27] AR1/476 (final concord, Michaelmas term, 1587).

[28] AR2/1346; also cited occasionally below are rentals for the whole estate in 1739, 1756 and 1760 (AR2/1356, 1360–61), and a useful book of leases for the western manors made in 1740 (AR2/1358).

Two other surveys are frequently cited in the footnotes of the text. The first is a fine survey of the estate made in April 1659 ('the eleaventh yeare of the Raigne of our Soveraigne Lord Kinge Charles the Second'). It covers the twenty-five manors of the survey of c.1586 (the nineteen manors of the old estate, plus the six Oxford manors), but with the omission of the towns of St Columb and Mitchell; it also includes Newland Preeze, but for some reason not Cardinham (nor Bodardle, apparently in Arundell hands for a while before being sold in about 1618–20).[29] This survey provides all the feudal information of earlier documents, and occasionally gives the parishes in which tenements were located, thus providing a useful link between the medieval surveys and the modern map. It appears to have escaped from Wardour during the last century; it was given in 1919 to Charles Henderson by Sir Langdon Bonython, of Adelaide (Australia), and later bequeathed by Henderson to the Royal Institution of Cornwall, Truro.[30]

The last survey to be regularly cited is, strictly, not a rental, but a registration of Arundell's estates as a recusant. This dates from 1717, the time of Richard Bellings Arundell; it lists all the lands in great detail, including rents, and therefore serves the same function for our purposes as the rental of 1659. It contains all twenty-seven manors of the full Arundell estate (the nineteen of the old estate, the six Oxford manors, and Newland Preeze and Cardinham; not Bodardle), and also lists the tin-bounds.[31] This survey too is therefore very useful for checking or explaining details in the earlier documents, and is often cited (as '1717 survey') in the notes to the texts printed below.

---

[29] Compare Cardinham, absent from the estate accounts until 1659, but present after that date (AR2/1003–04); see also above, p. xxxi.

[30] RIC, Henderson MSS, Arundell Rental 1659. The free tenements ('high-rents') of Connerton manor were printed from this document by Bowles, *Hundred of Penwith*, pp. 35–44; since the other documents printed by him do not seem to have returned to the archive, this may have been the occasion of its escape.

[31] The complete document is RIC, MS Brooks 35; there is another copy in the archive itself, AR28/24, omitting the free tenants.

4. THE MANORIAL SYSTEM IN CORNWALL

Probably few users of this volume, other than some professional historians, will have a clear understanding of the workings of the manorial system, as manifested in the medieval documents; we cannot claim that ourselves. But it is incumbent upon the editors of a volume such as this to attempt to explain what is actually meant by the entries printed below. The discussion which follows is not intended for professionals with a thorough knowledge of the medieval land-holding system in Cornwall. Because of the paucity of clear statements about some aspects of that system, there may be some errors or misrepresentations in what follows: anyone who detects them is encouraged to publish a better account.

First, the manor. Primarily this was an economic and administrative entity: 'a single administrative unit of a landed estate, whether or not it contained a residence of the holder'.[1] One of the largest manors in Cornwall, from before 1086 down to the eighteenth century, was Connerton, in Penwith; it is uncertain whether it has ever possessed a residence for its owner, though there are hints in the thirteenth century. One of the salient features of a manor was its entitlement to hold manorial courts; but Harvey has emphasized that this was a consequent feature of the manor, rather than originally a defining one.[2] A manor was not necessarily a discrete area of land: it often embraced outlying areas, and the land of two or more manors could thus be intertwined (see below). Moreover, a particular farm or hamlet might owe allegiance to more than one manor, either through being subdivided into separate holdings, or at different levels of the land-holding pyramid: examples of both appear in the following pages. But at a time when hardly anyone could be said to own land, and most were occupying rented land higher or lower on the scale of sub-tenants, the manorial system was the method of organizing land-tenure.

The most important feature of a manor from the present point of view was thus that it possessed **tenements**, units of land which

---

[1] Harvey, *Manorial Records*, p. 1.
[2] Harvey, *Manorial Records*, p. 2.

were held of it (i.e. owed allegiance to it). The holders of these were the **tenants** of the manor. Virtually everyone in the Middle Ages would have been a tenant of one or more manors; and they would have been acutely conscious of the allegiance that they owed, and the duties which this allegiance entailed. As will be seen below, the tenements were divided into two fundamental types, **free** and **conventionary** tenements. The differences between the two basic types were far-reaching.[3]

The **free tenants** were obviously those of higher status; they were in theory free to quit their tenancies if they wished, unlike the conventionary tenants. Even more importantly, their tenancies were normally inherited by right, and could not be taken away by the lord; and their rents were normally fixed. In the pages which follow will be seen striking examples of rents of free tenements which remained the same for many years. In the 1385 rental of Lanhadron manor, the free tenement of Pill (in Lanlivery) paid yearly 1 *lb*. cummin (p. 8, below); in 1499 this was given as '1 *lb*. of cummin, value 4*d*.' (p. 117), and in the survey of 1717, over 330 years after the earlier rental, this tenement still owed 4*d*. yearly. Similarly in the manor of Trembleath, the rents paid in 1717 for the two free tenements of Carlumb and Blakes Keiro, both in St Minver, were respectively 1*d*. and 3*s*. 4*d*., as they had been almost 260 years earlier, in 1459 (below, p. 24). This is not to say that rents of free tenements were immutable; the rents could change over the years, whether or not they were supposed to. But they changed much more slowly than those of conventionary tenements—so much so that the rents paid by free tenements can often be a useful clue to identifying those tenements in documents many years later.

The free tenant had other duties as well as his rent. Like all tenants, he had to **pay suit of court** (attend) at the manorial courts, to acknowledge his allegiance. If he was fortunate this would only be required twice yearly, at the major (leet) courts; others had to pay suit at the ordinary courts, held (in theory) every three weeks

---

[3] A more thorough discussion of the different types of tenure on the Duchy manors is given by Hatcher, *Duchy of Cornwall*, chapter 3, 'The obligations and legal status of tenants' (pp. 52–79); and Hull, *Caption of Seisin*, 'The tenants of the "antiqua maneria"' (pp. xxvi–xliii); and, for a wider context, Dyer, *Standards of Living*, pp. 10–13, and J. L. Bolton, *The Medieval English Economy 1150–1500* (London, 1980), pp. 17–31 (esp. pp. 28–29) and 236–45.

('common suit of court'). In either case, a sum of money could be paid instead of attendance; this was a **fine for suit of court** (i.e. instead of it). No doubt this was standard practice higher up the social scale; in the rentals of Roseworthy and Bejowan manors in 1549 (below, pp. 156–66) the official drawing up the rental so took it for granted that the free tenants would pay the fines instead of attending, that he included the fines as if they were a standard part of the rent. Practices such as this, particularly when silently assumed, may sometimes account for changes over the years in the rents of free tenements.

There are two types of free tenancy in the Cornish rentals, tenancy **in socage** and tenancy **by knight's service** (military service). The former was the lower in status. For our purposes it can be thought of as the basic form of free tenure, with most or all of any services which it once entailed long since commuted to a money payment: it was 'the great residuary tenure',[4] in that a free tenant held in socage if he did not hold by some other specified form of free tenure. Apart from the theoretical obligation of military service (which might not have applied at all for a socage tenancy, or if it did would not have been at the knightly level), the chief difference between socage and knight's service was the doubtful privilege of one who held by the latter, that if he died while his heir was still a minor, the heir became a ward of the landlord, who then enjoyed the revenues of the estate until the heir came of age. This lucrative right could be farmed out by the landlord, and substantial sums were paid for the benefit. Free tenants were of very varying status. At one end of the scale, they might be lords of manors in their own right, including members of the nobility, perhaps of higher social standing than the landlord: see, for instance, the marquess of Dorset as a free tenant on Connerton manor in 1480 (below, p. 88, etc.). Such tenants might never have visited their various landholdings. At the other end, there would be yeoman farmers, resident upon their single properties.

The entries in the rentals for free tenants say how much land they held in the tenement, in terms of (usually) 'Cornish acres' or their subdivision, the ferling (quarter-acre). Needless to say, this was a fiscal acre, not a measured one.[5] It would be futile to attempt

---

[4] Finberg, *Tavistock Abbey*, p. 73, citing F. Pollock and F. W. Maitland, *History of English Law*, 2 vols (Cambridge, 1911), I, 294.

[5] The difference is clearly drawn by Harvey, *Manorial Records*, p. 16.

to identify these acreages on the ground, because the point of the fiscal 'acre' was not the measurement of the land but how much tax a holder should pay on a particular occasion, reckoned at a given amount per 'acre'. The acreage was thus a nominal assessment of the land-holding, similar to the ratable value of a house today. According to Carew, writing in 1602, the Cornish acre was one-quarter of a knight's fee.[6] Two systems of tax-assessment for land were in use in Cornwall in the Middle Ages, the 'fee Mortain' and the 'fee Gloucester'. A knight's fee Mortain was reckoned as only five-eighths the size of a fee Gloucester, and therefore, in a taxation (or 'aid') imposed at a given rate, it paid only five-eighths as much per fiscal acre.[7] The origins of this distinction lay in the vast estates, in Cornwall and elsewhere, held by Robert Count of Mortain, half-brother of William the Conqueror, in the late eleventh century, and by Robert earl of Gloucester in the mid-twelfth. In theory it was those lands which had been held ultimately of the Mortain estate (including the lands of the earldom of Cornwall or held of it) which would be assessed by the one method, and those held ultimately of the Gloucester estate by the other.[8]

When a free tenant died and was succeeded by his heir, that heir had to pay **homage** (or homage and fealty) and **relief** on taking over the tenancy. Homage was the acknowledgement of the landlord's overlordship. Relief was a money payment, at a fixed amount, for being allowed to take over the tenement.

Finally, the free tenant had to pay the yearly rent for his land; this might be as high as a few shillings, or as low as nothing. It might be a payment in kind, such as a pair of spurs, 1 *lb*. of cummin, or a single rose. No doubt these payments in kind were very often commuted to cash instead, and a cash equivalent is usually given.

---

[6] Carew, *Survey of Cornwall* (1602 edn), p. 36r.
[7] *Inquisitions and Assessments relating to Feudal Aids*, 6 vols (London, 1899–1920), I, 385. Carew reckoned the ratio as two-thirds instead (*Survey of Cornwall*, 1602 edn, p. 38v.); this was presumably a late approximation.
[8] Picken, 'Descent of Willington' and 'Feudality of Pendrim', and references given there; the essay on land-tenure in Codner's Survey (above, p. l) also discusses the differing assessments; and, more generally, Frank Stenton, *The First Century of English Feudalism*, 2nd edn (Oxford, 1961), chapter 5, 'Knights' fees and the knight's service' (pp. 152–91) (p. 164 on the small fees Mortain).

As mentioned earlier, free tenancies normally passed by inheritance. If there was a surviving male relative, he inherited alone; if not, then the female relatives inherited jointly. In England at this period, and at this level of society, the custom was primogeniture for males, but failing that partible inheritance for females.[9] This meant that free tenements often became subdivided. For instance, a free tenement at Trelavour, in the manor of Enniscaven, held by Oliver Tregassowe in 1456 (p. 59), was held in 1480 by 'the heir(s) of Oliver Tregassowe' (p. 96). By 1499 the holders were given as four different men (p. 139); although the survey did not say so, these men probably held by right of their wives, who would have been daughters or other female relations of Oliver Tregassowe. Again, a free tenement at Tregonning and elsewhere in the manor of Kennall, held by John Trethaek in 1460 (p. 19), was held by John Stanlowe and John Baker, 'by right of their wives', in 1480 (pp. 77–78); these wives were presumably the heirs of John Trethaek, though again that was not stated.

The result of this process was that the holders of free tenements could become hard to trace; frequently among the free tenements in following pages the words 'The heir(s) of ...' appear, instead of the actual name of a tenant. This does not necessarily mean that the heir could not be traced: it may be that the scribe could easily have discovered the name (it may even have been the direct son and heir); but he found it easier, while updating an older document, to repeat the name he found there, with the let-out phrase 'the heir(s) of', or to leave a blank to be filled in later when the true heirs could be established. But in the later period, when the rents remained at the same low level and tenancies had often passed through a female line, perhaps with subdivision, the value of chasing up a free rent of a few pence was not worth the time spent on it. It is no wonder that many later rentals (though not those in the Arundell archive) do not bother with free tenements, and list only the conventionaries; the rental of the earl of Oxford's manors, 1563, provides an example of such an omission (below, pp. 167–72).

Conventionary tenements would have been seen, by the time of our documents, as the real 'meat' of the manor, in that it was these which provided a useful income for the lord, and over which he exercised close control. Two other names for this group of

---

[9] e.g. Dyer, *Standards of Living*, pp. 39 and 44.

tenements also appear in the records. 'Customary' was a wider term for the non-free tenements, since they were held 'by custom of the manor'. For our purposes conventionary and customary tenements amount to the same thing in the documents printed below; the conventionary tenements in Cornwall probably represent a particular type of customary tenement, though the term was virtually universal in the county. The two are sometimes distinguished from one another, for instance at Carminow manor in the 1659 rental, where conventionary and customary tenements are listed separately; the difference is not clear (but see below). The last name in this category of tenancies is 'copyhold' (for tenements held 'by copy of court roll'); this was a later development, of the fifteenth and particularly the sixteenth centuries. The tenants cited below as holding 'by copy' in the sixteenth century held by this tenure.[10]

The differences between the conventionary tenements and the free tenements were extensive. The rents of conventionary tenements could be increased when the tenant changed, and the results appear in the rentals printed below, where the manorial income from conventionary tenements is always well above that from free tenements. This is true even in the manor of Connerton, with its astonishingly long list of free tenants and a comparatively short list of conventionaries (pp. 39–48).[11] A conventionary tenant had more in the way of duties; since these were normally the same for all conventionary tenants on a particular manor, they did not need to be listed each time, but could be covered by a standard phrase, such as 'service as usual in the manor', or the like. (See, for instance, p. 10 below, where the first tenant's services were specified in 1385, and the subsequent ones refer back to that entry.) The days' work was often commuted into a money payment (again, this sometimes seems to be assumed, for example in the listing of 'work silver' at Bodbrane in 1468–69: below, p. 151.) The conventionary tenant had to pay an **entry-fine** on taking over his tenement, comparable with the relief paid by a free tenant; like the free tenant, he must attend the manorial court, paying **common suit** at the regular sessions,

---

[10] For instance, in 1549 (pp. 159 and 164); in 1563 (pp. 168 and 171); and in 1566 (pp. 174–76, etc.).

[11] The sole exceptions are the towns of St Columb and Mitchell, where the townsmen were free, so the free rents outweigh the others (e.g. p. 95); but there the development of 'tenants for term of years' gave the landlord greater control (e.g. p. 70).

held in theory every three weeks; and he must grind his corn at the lord's mill, paying to do so, of course. When he died, a 'best beast' was taken as **heriot**; or, if he wished to leave before his tenancy had run its time, a **farleu** was charged. He also had to act in turn as reeve of the manor, whose duties were, among other things, to collect the dues and report on them to the lord. Most importantly, he had to pay a substantial and economic rent for his tenement, usually at the four quarter-days still used today (Christmas, mid-Lent or Easter, Midsummer and Michaelmas, though many variations occur), plus often one or more capons at Michaelmas or Christmas (for instance in Bodwannick manor in 1464, pp. 56–58).

Conventionary tenements were originally so called because the leases for them were granted by agreement (*conventio*) every seven years, when tenants would bid to hold the properties.[12] This system was still operating on the Duchy manors in the fifteenth century, but it is unclear whether it did so on private estates such as that of the Arundells; however, the term continued in use. Confusingly, conventionary tenements could originally be either 'free' or 'unfree', at least on the Duchy manors;[13] the classification would have been determined by the status of the tenant, rather than that of the tenement. Of course, the holder of a 'free conventionary' still had far more by way of burdens and duties than one holding a true free tenement. Unlike the Duchy rolls, the Arundell surveys make no distinction between free and unfree conventionaries. But later still, in the seventeenth century, a contrast appears between customary and conventionary tenements: this is seen, for example, in Codner's survey of the Arundell estate in 1618,[14] and again on Carminow manor in the 1659 rental. Codner distinguished conventionary tenants, holding by lease, from customary tenants, holding by copy of court roll. It is possible that this in some way perpetuated an earlier distinction between free and unfree conventionaries; but, if so, then such a distinction would need to have been present, though invisible, in the fifteenth-century surveys. It may be rather that the seventeenth-century distinction was a new one which had arisen with copyhold tenure.

---

[12] Hatcher, 'Non-manorialism', pp. 2–7.
[13] Hatcher, 'Non-manorialism', pp. 3 and 7, and *Duchy of Cornwall*, pp. 53, 58 and 63–64.
[14] AR2/1346.

A few other categories of tenants remain to be mentioned. Tenants of the demesne land appear on Lanherne and Trembleath in the earliest rental, 1343 (p. 4, at St Columb) and in the fifteenth century on several manors, Carminow, Connerton, Lanherne and Trembleath; but it is notable that only on Connerton and Carminow was a rent being received in all three fifteenth-century rentals. On Lanherne and Trembleath the demesne was 'in hand' (i.e. in the lord's hands, presumably being farmed as demesne) in 1460 and 1499.[15] In the earliest rental of Lanherne and Trembleath (but not in any later ones), there are also two other categories of tenants apart from the conventionaries, 'cottars' (*coterelli*) and bondmen or villeins (*nativi*). By the fifteenth century these two categories had disappeared, as they also had on the Duchy manors.[16]

It would seem that it might be very much in a lord's financial interest to alter some free tenements to conventionary ones, provided that he did not thereby jeopardize his ability to supply the military service due from his land. One possible attempt at this appears in the pages below. In Winnington manor in 1460 there is an unusual entry concerning Sowanna (Gunwalloe), which, though a free tenement, had come by inheritance to a *nativus* or bondman. It was to be granted as conventionary land instead; but in fact it continued to be listed as a free tenement (below, p. 18 and n.). If this was actually an attempt to convert a free tenement to a conventionary one (and that is not certain), it did not succeed. By and large, although tenements might come and go on a manor, usually for reasons which are far from clear, the status of a particular tenement within the manor seems normally to have been very stable.

It is hoped that the above will to some extent serve to explain individual entries in the surveys. However, there is another aspect of the manorial structure which cannot be ignored: the geographical spread of tenements of any given manor. A single place may appear as a free tenement of one manor and as a conventionary tenement

---

[15] Carminow, pp. 16, 85 and 127; Connerton, pp. 46, 90–91 and 134; Lanherne, pp. 35, 99–100 and 110; Lanhadron, p. 53. At Trembleath the demesne seems to have been situated at Trembleath, Tregwinyo and Trenayles in c.1460 (p. 55), and at Trembleath in 1480 (pp. 75–76, not called demesne) and 1499 (p. 107).

[16] Hatcher, *Duchy of Cornwall*, p. 62, and 'Non-manorialism', pp. 9–10: the difference between conventionaries and villeins on the Duchy manors was last recognised in 1406.

of another; and the tenements of a single manor can extend over several different parishes, intermingled with the tenements of other manors. To take an extreme example, the final free tenement listed in the manor of Connerton, in the westernmost part of Cornwall, was itself another manor, that of Welcombe in Devon, 65 miles away. This was true already in 1463, and it was still so in 1659, nearly 200 years later, even though the yearly rent was merely 'one clove gillyflower'. In 1717 the manor of Welcombe was omitted altogether as a tenement of Connerton. Geographically it provides an extreme instance, but of a pattern which was widespread throughout Cornwall. (See the map, p. cliv.)

Structures such as this need some explanation. That offered here is one deriving from the complex tenurial histories of properties, histories often lost except for their later effects seen in these documents. The way in which the system worked was as follows. Land being the primary asset of value in the central and late Middle Ages, it was often 'given', for example to relations or retainers. This 'gift' could not be absolute, for nobody held land in absolute freehold: all land was held, directly or through an intermediate lord, of the king. So what was 'given' was a tenancy. In exchange for this tenancy the recipient had to acknowledge the donor as his landlord, by paying the rent asked and recognizing the allegiance of the land in the manner already described. If the landlord was being particularly generous, for instance in giving land to one of his younger sons in order to set him up with an estate, the rent might be nominal, such as 'a red rose, if asked'; but some recognition of the allegiance was considered essential. Of course, the 'gift' may actually have been a purchase: the recipient may have paid, with money or otherwise, for the grant; but it would still be termed a 'gift' in the deed commemorating it.

That was how the system operated from the donor's viewpoint. We must now examine it from that of the recipient. If he was otherwise unpropertied, then of course he simply became a tenant of the donor's manor, like many of the people appearing in the following pages. However, if the recipient was a significant landholder, then he had to fit the new property into the structure of his own estate, since he would probably not be intending to live there himself, but to sub-let it in turn. He did this generally by deeming it a tenement of one of his own manors. Thus a piece of land may appear, in the rentals printed below, as a tenement of one of the Arundell manors; but that need not be the full story, for our manor may also have owed rent for it to some other, non-Arundell, manor from which it had previously been a 'gift'. This 'superior' rent, paid by one manor to another for one of its own tenements, is termed a **high rent** (*altus redditus*) or **chief rent** (*capitalis redditus*) or, in some later documents, a **rent resolute** (i.e. a rent paid out by the manor).[17] These high rents are often not mentioned in the surveys—though sometimes they may be, especially at a later date (see, for instance, pp. 11, 16, 69, 160 and 166; and excellent lists in the surveys of Oxford manors in 1575, pp. 214, 223–24, and 231). For this reason it must be emphasized that the surveys often tell only a part of the story, albeit a major part. For the rents paid *by* a manor for some of its properties, we must turn to the manorial account rolls, in which the Arundell archive is also rich. (The other source where these tenures are regularly seen is the inquisitions post mortem, where the tenure of each property, after they have been listed, is given: 'held of X's manor of B', and the type of tenure stated, if known.)

It will be seen that the system of rents and high rents incorporates a vast amount of history, in terms of previous gifts, which is now lost and which will, in many cases, never be recovered. These tenures encapsulate whole networks of human relationships in the twelfth and thirteenth centuries (possibly even earlier in some cases), networks of which all record, except for the tenures commemorating them, has often been subsequently lost.

Of course, the recipient of the property need not necessarily retain it simply as part of his estate: he might himself grant it out to another, who would in turn incorporate it into *his* estate, paying a rent to our recipient, who in turn paid high rent for it to the original donor. Not only may many of the free tenements listed here have paid a high rent to some other estate, but irrespective of that, they may also have constituted manors in their own right in the estate of the holder—thus having their own tenements and tenants, with which the compiler of the Arundell surveys was not concerned. A good example is the manor of Newland Preeze, held of the manor of Cardinham as a free tenement (below, p. 177), but consituting a manor in its own right, later purchased by the Arundells (see above, p. xxxv).

---

[17] The term 'high rent' was also used, confusingly, to mean 'rents of free tenants', for instance by Bowles in listing the free tenements of Connerton manor from the 1659 rental (*Hundred of Penwith*, p. 35).

A simple example may first be cited. In about 1250 one Stephen son of Roger de *Gliuion* (Gluvian, in St Columb Major and Mawgan in Pyder) gave to Ralph de Arundell land in *Kalestoc Ruald* (Little Callestick, in Perranzabuloe), together with 'the men belonging to the land', who are then listed: Roger de Limoges and Richard de Kalestoc, tenants in *Kalestoc Ruald*, and Odo de Red and the heir of Reginald de Red, tenants in *Red* (the hamlet of Rees, in Perranzabuloe).[18] Apart from Ralph's 'homage and service', the only rent asked was a pair of white gloves each Easter. We do not know why Stephen made this gift to Ralph Arundell, though further work on the records may discover some relationship, whether of kinship or otherwise, providing a hint. Ralph deemed these lands to be tenements of his manor of Treloy some miles away, this being the only manor which he held in his own right at the time, although his marriage to Eve de Tremodret had brought him the lands at Trembleath which were later to be so important to the Arundells. Thus we find, in 1460, one Thomas Trevaignoun holding (among other lands) Little Callestick and Rees of Arundell's manor of Treloy (below, p. 28). What the rental does not tell us, though the account rolls do, is that Arundell's manor of Treloy at this period paid yearly a high rent for Rees of 1*d*., instead of the pair of gloves, to the manor of Gluvian.[19] The reason for this situation was the grant of Stephen to Ralph, two centuries earlier.

This system can also explain the fact, mentioned earlier, that Welcombe manor near Hartland, in Devon, was held as a free tenement of Connerton manor in Penwith. A grant survives, undated but evidently made in about 1240, whereby Richard son of John gave his land of *Walcomb'* to John de La Herne, in marriage with Richard's daughter Margery.[20] The rent was the surprisingly high sum of 60*s.* yearly (an unresolved problem). Richard son of John

---

[18] AR1/4; the date comes from the people involved and the witnesses to the deed.
[19] AR2/46 (reeve's account for Treloy, 1421–22); AR2/894, m. 3 (reeve's account for Treloy, 1447–48); AR2/919, p. 7 (reeve's account for Treloy, 1479–80). Callestick is not mentioned, an unexplained anomaly. 1*d*. was a standard rate for a pair of white gloves: compare below, pp. 22 and 42; also AR1/73 and, in Dorset, AR1/1075; but ½*d*. instead in AR1/74–75.
[20] AR1/103; there is a poor reproduction in Yeatman, *House of Arundel*, plate 29.

was the grandson of Richard Pincerna, to whom the manor of Connerton had been granted by Robert, son of Earl Robert of Gloucester, in about 1155.[21] We do not know how Richard came to possess this land at Welcombe, in addition to the manor of Connerton: probably by grant of a superior lord, or by inheritance from an ancestor who had in turn received it by grant. John de La Herne consequently held Welcombe of Richard son of John; since Richard's chief property in the region was the manor of Connerton, John held it of that manor, meaning that he paid his rent for Welcombe to the receiver for Connerton, and performed any other services, such as suit of court, there too. John, who already resided at Lanherne (as his surname indicates), would have let Welcombe to a sub-tenant, probably at once; he need never have visited the place. Our records suggest that when he did so, he himself demanded only the token rent of 'one clove gillyflower'. This sub-tenant would have held it of John de La Herne, and was not concerned with John's own rent for it, paid to his father-in-law. In due course, perhaps immediately, the sub-tenant or his heir came to deem Welcombe itself a 'manor', holding its own courts, and with its dependent farms and hamlets as tenements of Welcombe.

However, since John de La Herne had married Richard's heiress, eventually he (through his wife Margery), or his own heir (in this case Alice de Lanherne, who eventually married Remfrey Arundell) inherited the parent-manor, Connerton, of which he himself held Welcombe. Presumably, at this point, he would have stopped paying the 60s. yearly rent for it, now owed to himself. The sub-tenant, who had held Welcombe of John (who in turn held it of Connerton), would now hold it directly of John's manor of Connerton; hence the situation recorded in the surveys down to 1659, whereby the manor of Welcombe was held of that manor, and paid token rent to it. In this case we are fortunate in possessing the charter (or one of them) which gave rise to the later arrangement; but in many more cases the deeds have been lost, and only the later tenure remains as a hint of what had happened.

The next example is one which, in contrast, lacks any explanatory documentation. The manor of Treloy had one conventionary tenement called Trethowell, which can be shown by later rentals, by sixteenth-century leases and by the persons involved in it to be

---

[21] Picken, 'Descent of Willington'.

Trethowell in Kea parish, fifteen miles due south of Treloy, not the nearer places called Trethewell within the Arundell heartlands of St Columb Major and St Eval.[22] Although not as far removed from its manorial centre as Welcombe was from Connerton, this conventionary tenement was distant, even by Cornish standards. In this instance no deeds have survived to tell us how the property entered the Arundell estate; nor is anything known about its earlier history. All that is known is that the manor of Treloy paid for it a high rent to the manor of Landegea, at Old Kea churchtown a mile from Trethowell.[23] Again, this high rent appears only in the account rolls, not in the rentals. The earliest date at which the property is found in Arundell hands is 1374, which may indeed be the date of its acquisition.[24] It is unknown why it was made a tenement of Treloy manor: if it had come into Arundell hands very early, say at about the same time as Callestick and Rees (mid-thirteenth century), then the reason would again be that Treloy was the only available manor for it to be attached to; but if the fine of 1374 represents its arrival into the estate, as seems likely, then the reason may have been the comparatively arbitrary one, that the John Arundell who acquired the property was (at the time) not yet in possession of the full estate, but had already been set up at Treloy. If so, that would have been the natural manor for him to attach the property to, and the attachment then continued after he (or his heir) came into the full estate. We may also wonder, though the question cannot be answered, why it was made a conventionary and not a free tenement. Clearly it was to the landlord's advantage to do so, in that an economic rent could be charged. If it was not until 1374 that the property came into the estate, it may be that this provides an explanation: by and large, the free tenements seem to have become more stable at an earlier date, and it may be that by the late fourteenth century, the conventionaries were the natural, as well as the profitable, category for new acquisitions. Or it may have depended upon the status of the tenants holding the property at the time that

---

[22] Below, p. 31 and n.; confusingly, the Arundell manor of Trembleath paid a yearly rent to the manor of Trethewell (St Eval) for the leat of Millingworth mill: e.g. AR2/915 (bailiff's account, 1476–77).

[23] '1d. to lord of *Landege* for chief rent of *Trethowall*' 1479–80 (AR2/919, p. 7); 'to lord of *Landegee* for chief rent of *Trethowell*' 1491–92 (AR2/931, m. 2), manorial account rolls.

[24] *Cornwall Feet of Fines*, I, no. 695.

the acquisition was made, and therefore upon its previous history within its parent manor of Landegea.

The same type of explanation also tells us why the manor of Trembleath had a cluster of free and conventionary tenements seven miles away in the parish of St Minver, across the Camel estuary and in a different hundred (Trigg instead of Pyder): Trevanger, Keiro, either Treglyn or Treglynes, Gunvenna and Tredrizzick (below, pp. 2–3 and 6; 24–25; and subsequent surveys; see map, p. clv). Both Trembleath and Tredrizzick came to the family through Ralph's marriage with Eve de Tremodret in the mid-thirteenth century; and the deeds survive whereby the properties were given (and later confirmed, in 1259) by Eve's father, Richard de Tremodret or de Rupe.[25] Interestingly, when the lands were given, Tredrizzick was called a 'manor', and Trembleath was said to be held 'as one acre of the fee of *Tredreysuc*, because it is one acre of land of that fee'. A decade or so later Robert de la Roche, son and heir of Richard de Tremodret, probably at the time when he inherited his estate from his father, acknowledged the fealty of Ralph de Arundell for 'one knight's fee in *Tredreyseck* and *Trembleyd*'.[26] Yet, by the time manorial records become available a century later, the situation had been reversed: Trembleath had become a manor, and Tredrizzick was a conventionary tenement of it (p. 6). Whatever the reason, the linkage of the two properties was due to the fact that they had come to the family from the same source; and then it was natural, when other properties in the same area came into the family slightly later from a different source, to place them together; for instance, Treglyn in St Minver came to the Arundells in around 1260, in a gift quite separate from that of Tredrizzick; yet it too appears as a free tenement of Lanherne and Trembleath manor in 1343 (p. 2).[27]

That was the basic system. However, over the years changes occurred to make it more complex. Manors changed hands over the centuries, particularly by inheritance but also by other means. If a lord's manor paid high rent to another manor for a particular tenement, and the same lord later acquired rights over the second manor, he would owe the high rent to himself. A straightforward

---

[25] AR1/62–65.
[26] AR1/72.
[27] Gift by Roger de Trewelwart (Trevelver in St Minver) to Ralph de Arundel of one acre in *Tinglun* (probably Treglyn in St Minver), c.1260, AR1/22.

example of this is seen in the tenements of Treloy manor which paid high rent to the manor of Bejowan, in the same parish of St Columb Minor.[28] The originating cause of these high rents is not known, though it was presumably similar to those cases already examined. Then in 1575 Sir John Arundell purchased the manor of Bejowan from the earl of Oxford, and therefore owed these high rents, paid by the manor of Treloy, to himself as lord of Bejowan. We cannot know whether these small payments were actually made each year. Accuracy of accounting in the various manors would seem to require that they were; but it would take considerable research in the records, by one thoroughly conversant with manorial accounting, to establish the point, if it were possible at all.

Another simple example can be cited. Nanterrow, in Gwithian, was a free tenement of Connerton manor (pp. 43, 88 and 132; see map, p. cliv). What the survey does not tell us is that Connerton paid a high rent for Nanterrow to the manor of Roseworthy; it is recorded, for instance, in the beadle's account for the manor in 1448–49.[29] Nanterrow must have been granted by the lord of Roseworthy to the lord of Connerton at some time in the past. It is predictable, therefore, that among the free tenants of Roseworthy manor, when they are first recorded in 1549 (still under the earl of Oxford's ownership) Nanterrow appears, held by Sir John Arundell of Lanherne, knight. The Arundells held it of Roseworthy manor, but in absorbing it into their own estate had deemed it a tenement of Connerton manor. Again, we cannot know whether they continued to pay the yearly '2s. 6d or a pair of gilt spurs' after Arundell acquired Roseworthy manor in 1575.

In a less direct example, Picken has remarked how in the fourteenth century Edward de Courtenay, the eleventh earl of Devon, inherited the honour of Plympton castle from his father; he also held, as mesne or intermediate lord, the manor of Pendrim near Looe of the Ferrers family, having inherited it from his mother. His overlords at Pendrim, the Ferrers, in turn held Pendrim of the earl's

---

[28] In 1421–22 the manor of Treloy paid high rent to the manor of Bejowan for its free tenements of Keskeys and Tolcarne Merock, and its conventionary tenements of Kestle and Treviglas (below, pp. 29–31): AR2/46.

[29] AR2/896; at this date it was the only rent paid out by the manor of Connerton.

own honour of Plympton Castle—'a circular kind of service', as Picken has said.[30]

No doubt this system seems crazily complex and illogical to the modern reader who first encounters it; however, it had evolved logically over the years, and in reality was no more complex, and no less logical, than the Common Agricultural Policy today.

---

[30] Picken, 'Feudality of Pendrim'.

5. THE CORNISH LANDSCAPE IN THE SIXTEENTH CENTURY AND LATER

Manorial surveys which list all of the fields of all customary holdings on a manor—such as some of those printed below—bring the landscape alive before our eyes.[1] Some of the features to look out for are discussed in this section (which is based upon sixteenth- and early seventeenth-century surveys both in the Arundell collection and in other archives) in the hope that readers will search for more examples of this relatively common class of document and use them as fully as they deserve to be used in the service of landscape history.

Closes and hedges

Manorial surveys are valuable repositories of information about closes (i.e. enclosed fields), their names, their sizes and (occasionally) their situation. Take, as just one example, Robert Davy's holding at Lower Trezance (now Teason, Cardinham), surveyed in 1566.[2]

Orchard and garden	—
Close Above Towne	2½ acres
Hollywill Parke	2½ acres
Middel Parke	3 acres
lez Bye	3 acres
Clieff Parke	1½ acres
close under garden	2 acres
Downe Close	2 acres

The order in which the closes are given is interesting because it suggests that the surveyor walked through this enclosed farm listing and estimating the sizes of the fields as he went, and we can almost imagine ourselves walking with him. We begin in the orchard and garden which adjoined the farmhouse, proceed into *Close Above*

---

[1] Free tenements, as opposed to customary ones, were not surveyed in detail, so information about their fields does not survive in these documents.
[2] Below, p. 178.

Towne (i.e. the field lying directly above the 'town' or farmstead), then through other closes or 'parks' including *Middel Parke*, about half way through the perambulation, and we end up in what was almost certainly the field furthest from the farmstead, *Downe Close* next to (probably taken out of) the rough pasture or downland, perhaps near the spot named on modern maps as Fore Down. Small hints among the names of fields in other sixteenth-century surveys suggest that they too were listed in the order in which the surveyor encountered them on the ground in a perambulation which began at the farmstead and ended at the farm's outer boundary. Thus on the manor of Tresithney (St Columb Major), surveyed in 1575, the last closes listed for four of the tenements are *Parke Anythen (park + an + eithin*: 'gorse close'), *Utter* (i.e. 'outer') *Feilde*, a close 'at the lane end' and a close 'taken ... from the common'.[3] In each case the nature of the land or the described location indicates a field at some distance from the farmstead.

The surveyor's perambulation of Robert Davy's holding at Lower Trezance cannot have taken long, for it was a small farm of just over 16 acres and its closes were all very small individually. In this last respect it was by no means unusual because enclosed Cornish landscapes in the sixteenth century tended to be minutely compartmentalized into closes which were tiny compared, say, with the ten-acre fields recommended to farmers in some parts of England where land was enclosed by act of parliament in the eighteenth and nineteenth centuries.[4] From some of the surveys printed in this volume the following figures for average size of closes may be calculated.[5]

Manor of Downinney, 1566	3.8 acres
Manor of Cardinham, 1566	2.3 acres
Manor of Bodardle, 1566	2.0 acres
Manor of Tregenna, 1575	3.1 acres

---

[3] Below, pp. 232–4.
[4] Hoskins, *Making of the English Landscape*, p. 145.
[5] The figures exclude large portions of newly enclosed waste. They also exclude demesne closes, which tended to be larger, matching the large acreage of some demesnes. See, for example, the two closes of 16 acres each on the demesne of Tresithney: below, p. 233. At Bodardle the surveyor estimated the size of closes on some tenements but gave acreages more precisely on others; only the more precise ones have been used here.

The variation between manors is interesting and is what might be expected from careful observation of the Cornish landscape today. For example, many of the holdings on the manor of Bodardle (with the smallest closes of all) had been laboriously created from the stone-strewn slopes south of Helman Tor; small size here in part reflects the sheer difficulty surrounding the creation of these fields, many of which still today contain boulders too massive to be removed.

On manors such as Bodardle where the circumstances of land reclamation led to the creation of closes very small in size, they nevertheless tended to persist over time; there is little evidence for enlargement, suggesting that farmers in fact had a preference for agricultural landscapes which were minutely fragmented into small enclosed compartments. And that preference was sometimes expressed when a farmer decided to create two or more closes where there had been only one before. At Tresithney (St Columb Major) a close of six acres was described in the survey of 1575 as 'now in two parts divided'; it was 'moory or meadow ground', so perhaps its division with a new hedge was the beginnings of a small scheme of improvement. At Porth Veor (St Columb Minor), according to the same survey, one farmer was engaged in the creation of even smaller closes, for what was already one 'little close of pasture' containing one acre was now 'in two parts divided'; the two new closes so made were 'near unto the tenement' (i.e. farmhouse) so we probably have here an example of the creation of new very small paddocks for the close supervision of livestock, or the making of gardens or orchards.[6] There are no references in the surveys printed here to the opposite process, removal of hedges in order to enlarge fields. It is the same in manorial surveys from other estates: these contain few references to the enlargement of closes and many references to division: for example, surveyors noted that a six-acre field on the manor of Hornacott (North Tamerton) in 1614 had been 'in three parts divided' and that a seven-acre field at Trewartha (Veryan) in the 1690s was 'now divided into four parts'.[7]

A preference among farmers for small closes made much sense in the context of sixteenth-century Cornish farming practice. To begin with, the crop rotations of the county tended to favour farms divided into many small compartments. Richard Carew, whose farming experience was gained during the decades in which some

---

[6] Below, pp. 233 and 216.
[7] PRO, SC12/30/27; CRO, AD/51.

of our surveys were made, described in 1602 how Cornish farmers were accustomed to take crops of wheat and oats from a close for a year or two and were 'then driven to give it at least seven or eight years leyre' (i.e. 'ley' or pasture forming part of a rotation which involved both arable crops and grass); a later Cornish source (1675) specifies six or seven years as the length of the period during which closes remained as ley pasture between each cropping.[8] Such practice was by no means confined to south-western England, but the South-West was its stronghold and as late as the nineteenth century agricultural writers remarked on how different it was from the short three-year rotations with bare, ploughed fallows (rather than ley grass), found in many other parts of England.[9] Where, as in Cornwall, rotations took, say, eight years to complete (two years under crops followed by six years of ley pasture), the ideal number of compartments into which a farm might be divided was eight. If we imagine a 30-acre farm the average size of the compartments would therefore be between three and four acres and they were, of necessity, enclosed because they served as pastures for livestock during the long years between each cropping; on a smaller farm where the same rotation was practised the closes would be correspondingly smaller. These are over-simplistic calculations but they nevertheless go some way towards explaining the small size of closes in regions where ley farming was practised.

Farms laid out in numerous small closes were also ideal for intensive livestock farming, as the Devonian John Hooker noted in c.1600 when he explained that livestock in his native county were moved from one field to another so that 'by their often changes they feed still as it were upon a new springing grass';[10] in other words, the grass of all the closes on a farm was kept fresh and untrampled with the exception of that occupied by livestock at any one time (the same end as is secured today by moving an electric fence within a large field). Management of this kind was obviously very suitable for dairy cattle and also for young animals which needed the most close supervision; hence the small closes called Lamb Close or Lamb Park on some of the tenements whose surveys

---

[8] Carew, *Survey of Cornwall* (ed. Halliday), p. 102; Anon., 'Improvement of Cornwall', p. 295.

[9] 'There is hardly any branch of husbandry in Cornwall so incompletely performed as [bare fallowing]': Worgan, *General View*, p. 54.

[10] Blake, 'Hooker's Synopsis Chorographical', p. 344.

are printed in this volume. Its benefits were recognized too in a sixteenth-century report which stated that the wool of Cornish sheep had once been 'hairy and coarse' on account of badly managed grazing in 'wild country' (that is, on moors and downs); the report then goes on to say that fleeces were now much improved (a trend noted also by Carew), the implication being that some sheep at least had been removed from the moors and more carefully managed on enclosed farmland.[11]

Careful management of livestock in small closes may be contrasted with systems which allowed them to roam on open spaces without much supervision. If large enough and not over-stocked, the rough pastures of moors and downs were ideal for use as extensive grazings for certain types of livestock, for example immature store cattle with some years yet to live before their final fattening; this must have been recognized at an early date and was what lay behind a statement by the bailiff of the episcopal manor of Cargoll (Newlyn) in 1408 when he complained that some types of demesne animal which 'should common on the waste' were occupying superior pasture which should have been put to better use.[12] If extensive grazing was applied to farmland there was a tendency for the hedges to be allowed to decay, for the small fields which they surrounded were no longer necessary. Thus a survey of a tenement at Medland (Temple) described the farm as 'for many years ... kept as feeding so that the names of the fields are forgotten', while a surveyor at Stuffle (St Neot), another 'feeding farm' also on the flanks of Bodmin Moor, wrote of the holding as 'all pasture ground, the inner hedges down, the fields without names'.[13] In the surveys printed below there are perhaps hints of this kind of development on the manor of Cardinham where Eleanor Mold occupied holdings in Benorth, where she lived, and also a moorside holding at Higher Cardeast where there was no inhabited house, only a sheephouse associated with a number of closes which were large by Cornish standards. Higher up on the same manor, now deserted and reclaimed by the waste of Cardinham Moor, though some field boundaries still survive, was one of the tenements called

---

[11] *Tudor Economic Documents*, eds Tawney and Power, I, 194–5; Carew, *Survey of Cornwall* (ed. Halliday), p. 106.
[12] DRO, W1258M/E/24.
[13] Lanhydrock Atlas (at Lanhydrock House); for Stuffle see also Austin et al., 'Tin and agriculture', pp. 34 and 233.

Colvannick; this may have become a 'feeding farm' before being finally deserted, but its decline almost certainly took place after the date of the survey printed here, which mentions inhabited houses and typical small closes at all of the farms bearing the name of Colvannick.[14]

Small closes were well adapted to the arable farming practices of Cornwall in the sixteenth century and also to the intensive side of pastoral farming. The smaller the closes on a farm, then the greater was the total length of the hedges and banks or walls which surrounded them, and these boundaries themselves were thought to be an asset: in Hooker, again, we read that Devonshire farmland was 'all the more profitable' for being 'divided and severed with mighty great hedges and ditches'.[15] From the middle of the nineteenth century onwards, when removal of hedges began to be advocated, the very acreage occupied by hedgebanks came to be regarded as a waste of valuable land. Such an attitude would have seemed strange in the sixteenth century, so when a surveyor of an Arundell property found that the farm measured 47 acres 'from out bound to out bound', but only 40 acres if the closes were measured individually, he rightly concluded that the balance was 'taken up ... with the hedges', without passing any adverse comment on this situation.[16] Sixteenth-century written surveys rarely include details of the acreage occupied by hedges, but some later maps do and this probably reveals that they were regarded as assets.[17] Clearly they

---

[14] Below, p. 185; see pp. 178–9 and 183–5 for all the tenements at Colvannick; for the deserted site just south of Colvannick Tor see Johnson and Rose, *Bodmin Moor*, pp. 83–4.
[15] Blake, 'Hooker's Synopsis Chorographical', p. 344.
[16] AR2/1347, seventeenth-century survey book.
[17] In PRO, SC12 33/25, is a rare example of a seventeenth-century survey (of a tenement in Cardinham parish) which appears to measure the acreage occupied by the hedges. For maps from the end of the eighteenth century which give the acreage occupied by the hedges see CRO, RH/1344 (property in St Erth and St Hilary) and AD/216/4 (Medlyn in Wendron). Both were surveyed by Alexander Law. A few tithe apportionments give the acreage occupied by hedges, e.g. those of Ludgvan and Rame (CRO), Cornwood and Beaford (DRO). Writing in 1811, Worgan considered that 'so many are the advantages to the occupier from these fences [i.e. hedges] that ... the landlord is well justified in taking the measurement of his fences with his fields': *General View*, pp. 48–9.

provided excellent shelter for livestock and crops alike. In addition, and especially where the closes of farms were intermixed, as they often were in Cornwall, a hedge (of earth or stone) provided a stout and virtually indisputable property boundary: a surveyor at Holwood (Quethiock) had this attribute in mind when he observed that 'every man's land is severally [i.e. separately] known and hedged and enclosed'.[18] So far we have found no contemporary statement from Cornwall revealing attitudes towards the hedge as a legal property boundary which is as clear as one from the Devonshire manor of Kenton in 1599: there it was said before the manor court that removal of hedges was 'contrary to our custom' because it would result in future disputes over boundaries. But when we read in a survey of Caradon Prior (Linkinhorne) about special 'viewers of the decays of edifices and fences', and of frequent presentments before manorial courts of those tenants who did allow their hedges to become delapidated, we are witnessing a perception among lords and tenants alike of their value in providing, among other things, strong and indisputable boundaries.[19]

Hedges were all the more valuable if they supported trees, as was specifically recognized by a surveyor of West Antony manor in the early seventeenth century who noted that the manor's hedges made up for a lack of woodland; the same point was made by a surveyor at Uphay (Axminster), Devon, who noted that although there were 'no woods ... other than the hedgerows', tenants were nevertheless assured of 'sufficient fuel and timber ... for their necessary expense'.[20] In view of the great value of trees to landlord and tenant alike, and of the abundance of hedges in Cornwall, it is surprising that timber in hedges is not more frequently mentioned in manorial surveys. The occasional survey from the South West lists trees with great precision and a few estate maps show individual trees.[21]

---

[18] CRO, ME/1591.
[19] DRO, 1508M/Lon./manor/Kenton/2; Welch, 'Survey of Duchy manors', p. 34; CRO, WM/168 (manorial courts of Bray and Trenode in Morval) and CRO, ME/1630, court book of Rame.
[20] Welch, 'Survey of Duchy manors', p. 291; DRO, 123M/E/31.
[21] Thus a survey of Axminster drawn up in 1574 enumerates 8,394 trees: DRO, 123M/E/72. An example of an estate map showing the position of trees in detail is CRO, EN/1367, containing a map of properties in St Gluvias. Many estate maps use a stylized tree symbol for hedges.

But usually we are left guessing as to whether sporadic mention of hedgerow trees (or no mention) indicates few trees in the landscape or failure on the part of the surveyor to record them. Surveys which make no mention of hedgerow trees are the most common, a good example being that made of Dinham's Lands printed below. An example of a survey which gives only sporadic references to them is one made in 1601–2 covering some of the manors annexed to the Duchy of Cornwall. Trees are mentioned in far fewer than one-tenth of the entries, for example 'in the hedges ashes and elms to the value of 10s.', relating to a messuage and meadow in St Austell town.[22] Another good example is the survey (1575), printed below, of the manors of Bejowan, Tregenna and Tresithney. It is the most detailed of surveys, measuring land down to the nearest perch, but for only four holdings are details of hedgerow trees given: at Kestle (St Columb Minor) where there were some small elms next to the farmhouses, twelve elms on a holding at Withiel churchtown, fourteen elms and four ashes in a close in St Austell town, and seven elms near the farmstead at Tresawsen (Perranzabuloe).[23] This highly specific counting of trees on a very small proportion of the holdings listed in this survey would suggest that we should take lack of mention of trees on the other holdings at face value: the first two of the manors are near the windswept western coast of mid-Cornwall, where many hedges are treeless today. Finally, some surveys contain explicit statements about lack of hedgerow timber: 'such scarcity that it will scant suffice ... to repair the customary tenements' on the manor of Landulph; some tenants with 'no timber ... to repair ... decays' on the manor of Caradon Prior (Linkinhorne and North Hill). Reference in the survey of 1566, printed below, to 'a certain wood ... limited for the reparations of the tenants in Cardinham and Bodardle' suggests that on those manors, too, hedgerow timber may have been insufficient.[24] In some senses it is difficult to reconcile the evidence of surveys with the evidence of leases, for the latter frequently reserve all timber,

---

[22] PRO, E315/414, a highly detailed survey containing, as well as field names, minute details about the tenants' houses and gardens (including a bee garden in one case).
[23] Below, pp. 219, 225–6 and 232.
[24] BL, Harl. MS. 71; Welch, 'Survey of Duchy manors', p. 34; below, p. 187.

or named species of trees, to the landlord; it is difficult to decide whether such reservation clauses refer to actual trees or potential trees.[25]

A general impression, and it is no more than that, is that enclosed landscapes in sixteenth-century Cornwall were not much adorned with trees. We must not forget, of course, that there would have been variations over the face of the county and changes over time. When John Norden wrote that 'the greatest want that the county has is wood and timber', he added that scarcity was most greatly felt in the four western hundreds which were 'almost bereft of this benefit'.[26] His observation is confirmed by a sixteenth-century surveyor at Leigh Durrant (Pillaton) in eastern Cornwall: he found the tenants there to be 'more civil than in the west part of Cornwall and better disposed to plant and set and furnish their habitations with orchards'.[27] Generally more windswept than the east, more populous and with tinning more widespread, the western parts of the county had long, of necessity, resorted to gorse (furze) and peat for domestic fuel and smelting. A change may have occurred in the seventeenth century, perhaps as a result of changing attitudes towards timber provision. For example, in the third decade of the seventeenth century, some leases granted for tenements on the estate of the Duchy of Cornwall stipulated that a number of new trees should be planted every year. By the end of the seventeenth century Cornish glebe terriers show that the county's incumbents were enthusiastic planters of trees, both for their economic value and 'for the defence of the dwelling house from the north-west winds' (at windswept Tintagel).[28] By then new attitudes towards planting, partly stimulated perhaps by the publication of John

---

[25] For a sample of Cornish leases mentioning timber trees, see Padel, 'Queries from Cornish documents', pp. 141–2; abstracts of Arundell leases with references to trees occur in AR2/1346.

[26] Norden, *Cornwall*, p.18; half a century earlier, Leland frequently commented upon the lack of trees in Cornwall: *Itinerary*, I, for example pp. 173, 175 (*bis*) and 178.

[27] BL, Harl. MS. 71.

[28] *Parliamentary Survey*, ed. Pounds, I, *passim* (e.g. pp. 2, 6 and 9); *Calendar of Cornish Glebe Terriers*, ed. Potts, p. 159. See also Potts's index, giving references to many species of trees (some 'new planted') and to nurseries.

Evelyn's *Sylva* (1664) and by royal and private example, may have begun to affect the Cornish scene.[29]

Readers of the sixteenth-century surveys with field-names printed below, and of other similar Cornish manorial surveys, will soon realize that the word most commonly used for an enclosed field was 'park', either in Cornish (e.g. *Park Anythen, park + an + eithin*: 'furzy enclosure') or the English (e.g. *Furze Park*); the latter is also very frequent in Devon, a county where enclosed landscapes were in many senses similar to those of Cornwall. It can be also found as a common noun so that, for example, the rental of 1480, printed below, refers to a *parcus* (Latin rendering of the vernacular) in Helston town.[30] A brief etymological collection from the late sixteenth century states that 'Cornish men term them [closes] by ... parks', while a seventeenth-century farmer from Ashburton, coaxed into explaining local terminology before an exchequer commission concerned with enclosure from the waste, decided to satisfy the lawyers doubly by stating that 'in the vulgar speech of the Devonshire people', a close 'is called a park and that which is not enclosed is not usually called by the name of a park'.[31]

Strip-field systems

Here and there the sixteenth-century surveys printed in this volume give a picture of a type of field landscape which was quite distinct from the enclosures and hedges described above: a landscape in which arable land was divided up into many small, unenclosed strips. For example, to the east of the hamlet of Trebelzue (St Columb Minor), on land now occupied by one of the runways of St Mawgan airfield, a survey of 1575 describes one expanse of arable land belonging to the hamlet, amounting to at least 68 acres in all, minutely divided into at least 114 strips.[32] In the surveys printed

---

[29] Albion, *Forests and Sea Power*, pp. 130–2; Thomas, *Natural World*, pp. 198–9.
[30] Below, p. 83; compare '4 parks [*parci*] lying together', p. 176.
[31] BL, Cott. Faust. V.15, fol. 133v.; PRO, E134 3 Jas I/East.2.
[32] Below, pp. 215–16 and 218. There may have been more acres and strips here, because there was a free tenement at Trebelzue for which we have no precise details. It is listed in 1549 and in *c*.1586, but, oddly, not in 1575: below, p. 164, and AR2/1343.

here the following terminology points clearly to field landscapes of this kind: 'intermingled parcels', 'sundry parcels' or 'diverse parcels' within named fields; land in 'common fields'; and the term 'stitchmeal' (literally 'in separate pieces') which is also enshrined in Carew's *Survey of Cornwall* where he wrote of farmers who 'rubbed forth their estate in the poorest plight', their land lying 'all in common, or only divided by stitch-meal'.[33]

It should come as no surprise to find some evidence of strip-field systems in the surveys printed here, for as long ago as the 1920s Henderson was collecting materials for a paper entitled 'Evidence for the open field system in Cornwall' (unfortunately never published). A little later on Rowse devoted several pages of his *Tudor Cornwall* to the subject.[34] Indeed, the evidence which he used came partly from surveys (some printed below, pp. 167–72) of some of the earl of Oxford's Cornish manors; these surveys were made while the under-age earl was a ward of the Crown, and they remained among the State Papers (see above, pp. xlvii–xlviii). Henderson and Rowse made important contributions by showing that there had once been some strip-field cultivation in Cornwall whereas previous opinion had thought that there had been little or none: a county where 'the arable lands ... were very largely enclosed' and which was 'without ... common field at the end of the sixteenth century'.[35]

Rowse thought that cultivation in strips in Tudor Cornwall was rare, 'exceptional' and 'on its way to extinction', a view in which he was influenced by two topographical writers.[36] The first was Richard Carew of Antony, in the far east of Cornwall, who seemed to distance himself from what he thought of as the primitive 'mingle-mangle' system which characterized estates 'in the poorest plight'—he said that it had existed 'in times not past the remembrance of some yet living', implying that it was exceptional at the time of the writing of his *Survey of Cornwall* (begun perhaps in the late 1580s, revised between 1598 and 1602) but was still remembered by the very old.[37] Carew constantly stressed the agricultural

---

[33] Carew, *Survey of Cornwall* (ed. Halliday), p. 138.
[34] Henderson collection at RIC; Rowse, *Tudor Cornwall*, pp. 33–6.
[35] Gray, *English Field Systems*, p. 266; Gonner, *Common Land*, map D.
[36] Rowse, *Tudor Cornwall*, pp. 35–6.
[37] Carew, *Survey of Cornwall* (ed. Halliday), p. 138; for the date, pp. 47–8 of Halliday's Introduction.

THE CORNISH LANDSCAPE   lxxix

and commercial advances of his own times and it was perhaps because of this pride in his county's progress that he played down the extent of surviving strip-field systems. Rowse cites a survey of part of the estate of the Duchy of Cornwall made early in the seventeenth century in which the unnamed surveyor writes, of the manor of Leigh Durrant (Pillaton), that 'some part ... lieth in common fields which is hardly found in any manor of his Highness else in Cornwall'.[38] The survey can now be shown to have been the work of John Norden.[39] It is not a survey of the ancient manors of the Duchy but of the 'annexed manors' which had been tacked onto the old estate following the attainder in 1538 of Henry Courtenay, marquess of Exeter, and the dissolution of St Stephen's Priory, Launceston, and St Andrew's, Tywardreath. Because of the history of their ownership, almost all of these annexed manors lay in the eastern parts of Cornwall: out of 28, no less than 21 were situated east of St Austell Bay and 19 east of the River Looe. This is significant, because all of the evidence shows that in the sixteenth century strip-field systems were to be found far more frequently in the west of Cornwall than in the east. Norden's statement is not a general one about Cornwall at large (as sometimes claimed), nor a statement about the Duchy estate as a whole; rather, it is relevant (like the words of Carew, an easterner) to the farming landscape of eastern Cornwall early in the seventeenth century. There had once been strip-field systems associated with hamlets in the eastern half of the county, but by Carew's and Norden's day most of them had become enclosed, partly as a result of the needs of pastoral

---

[38] Rowse, *Tudor Cornwall*, p. 35.
[39] Rowse cites PRO, LR2/207, a composite volume containing several surveys, one of which (undated and not bearing the name of the surveyor) is a virtually complete survey of all of the annexed Cornish manors of the Duchy of Cornwall. It is not a full survey with field names but takes the form of an abbreviation, lists of tenants (omitting free tenants) and the total acreage, rent, nature of tenure and value of each tenement; notes on some of the tenants (e.g. 'a perverse fellow' and 'toleration emboldens to do ill'—of a tenant who dug slate without licence); and 'Observations' touching on tenures, liberties, distance from market towns, etc. Another copy of this abbreviation has been printed by Welch, 'Survey of Duchy manors'. The full survey, from which these abbreviations were made, is Duchy of Cornwall Archives, E.m.5., 'Surveys in Cornwall'; it bears the name of John Norden.

farming.[40] Medieval references to strip-field systems in eastern Cornwall occur at Trevia (Lanteglos by Camelford) in 1356–7 and at Trevollard (Lanreath) in 1446.[41] There were late survivals of hamlet strip-field systems in the east at Blarrick (Antony) in 1578 and at Pendrift (Blisland) in 1611–12.[42]

Carew and Norden therefore led Rowse to conclude that in the Tudor age strip-field systems were largely things of the past. That conclusion must now be qualified: while it is true to say that closes covered the greatest part of the Cornish cultivated landscape in the sixteenth century, especially in eastern parts of the county, strip-field cultivation would have been a fairly familiar sight to any traveller willing to seek out isolated hamlets, especially in the west. Several explanations may be put forward to account tentatively for this westerly distribution. First, there is little doubt that the eastern parts were the more pastoral, and indeed a survey of Tinten (St Tudy), made around the middle of the sixteenth century, explicitly states that enclosure of the 'late ... common fields' there was carried out so that the land could be 'converted into pasture and employed to feeding and grassing of cattle';[43] clearly closes held in severalty, rather than intermixed open strips, were needed for that activity. Surveys which include details of land-use show that the number of acres of pasture outnumbered (often greatly) those of arable on properties in eastern Cornwall, while the reverse was true in the west; and we must not forget Carew's remark about farmers in the north-east of the county who fed yearly 'great droves of cattle' sent there temporarily by graziers from Somerset and Devon. A little later, a seventeenth-century writer described 'little tillage more than for necessary use' in parts of eastern Cornwall.[44] Second, in western Cornwall arable farming was encouraged by a greater density of population than in the east, by demands for bread

---

[40] Below (Tinten, mid-sixteenth century), and Fox, 'Chronology of enclosure'.

[41] Below, p. lxxxix (Trevia), and CRO, R/2068 (Trevollard), an exchange of strips in 1446, probably a prelude to enclosure. See also Johnson and Rose, *Bodmin Moor*, pp. 106–14.

[42] CRO, ME/1591 (Blarrick, 1578); below, p. lxxxiv (Pendrift, 1611–12).

[43] BL, Harl. MS. 71.

[44] Pounds, 'Lanhydrock Atlas', pp. 24–5 (a statistical analysis of land use at the end of the seventeenth century); Carew, *Survey of Cornwall* (ed. Halliday), p. 107; BL, Add. MS. 33,420, fol. 126, a description of East Hundred by 'Edward Kneebone of Westcot, gent.'

THE CORNISH LANDSCAPE   lxxxi

from a numerous population engaged in non-farming occupations (such as tinning and fishing) and by ready access to sea-sand which was still thought of as indispensable to cultivation; arable farming was possible where the land lay all in strips, but intensive pastoral farming was not. Third, the later survival of strip-field systems in the west may be another sign of a remoteness also expressed, for example, in later survival of the Cornish language there.

Taking simply the evidence of those of the sixteenth-century surveys printed in this volume which describe the tenants' fields in detail, there is no sign of surviving strip-field cultivation on the manor of Cardinham on the southern flanks of Bodmin Moor, nor on the manor of Bodardle, many of whose farms lay on the steep slopes of the granite hills west of Lostwithiel, nor on the manor of Downinney in the north-east, close to the county boundary with Devon. But as soon as one turns to the more westerly manors the evidence becomes abundant. On the manor of Bejowan, with tenements largely in the parishes of St Columb Major and Minor just inland from Newquay, there is evidence for arable strips at the hamlet of Trebelzue, already mentioned ('pieces ... in a common field', land 'in diverse parcels divided'), at Bedrugga ('intermingled parcels'), at Tolcarne Merock ('intermingled parcels'), at Kestle ('diverse parcels') and at Porth Veor (arable lands 'in diverse parcels' and in 'sundry small parcels' within named fields). A few miles directly east of Bejowan is the manorial centre of Tresithney (St Columb Major); on this manor at least one of the hamlets, Bosoughan, had some land lying in intermixed strips.[45] If we add to these examples the documentary evidence for strip-field systems from other (non-Arundell) manors in the vicinity—for example, the hamlets of Tregurrian, Trevarrian (both St Mawgan in Pyder), Tredinnick (St Issey) and Towan (St Merryn)[46]—as well as the evidence of modern maps from the tithe maps to the Ordnance Survey's 'Explorers', which clearly show former open strips fossilized by hedgebanks—for example, at Engollan (St Eval),

---

[45] Trebelzue, pp. 215–16 and 218; Bedrugga, pp. 214–15; Tolcarne Merock, pp. 217–18; Kestle, pp. 218–19; Porth Veor, pp. 216–17; Bosoughan, p. 232. The land in 'stitchmeal' at Porth Veor and at Bosoughan (Tresithney manor) appears in the Oxford survey of 1563 (PRO, SP12/31, no. 30).

[46] PRO, E315/388; below, p. 140; Lanhydrock Atlas (at Lanhydrock House).

Penrose (St Ervan) and Trencreek (St Columb Minor)[47]—then it becomes clear that at one time a good proportion of the land lying inland from the coast between Padstow and Newquay would once have been cultivated in strip-field systems. A sixteenth-century traveller between these two places would have seen some hedgebanks, for many farms had closes as well as strips, as the surveys make clear, while strips often lay within quite small enclosed fields; but he would have come away with a strong, if not prevailing, sense of cultivation in strips to produce the 'fruitful grain' which John Leland noted as he passed through this country in the early sixteenth century.[48]

There is much evidence for strip cultivation in the western half of the county in surveys of other, non-Arundell manors. One of the fields subdivided into strips at Trebelzue, mentioned above, was described by its surveyors as next to 'the way leading towards Tregoryan' and had they walked down the lane to reach the hamlet of Tregurrian they would have found an extensive strip-field system which has left some traces on the map still today. This was surveyed in 1606 as part of the manor of Carnanton (St Mawgan in Pyder) then in the hands of the Crown, the surveyors in entry after entry enumerating acres *in communibus campis* [in common fields] ... in stychemeal'; the lands of the adjacent hamlet of Trevarrian were described in exactly the same way in the same survey.[49] Then again, a survey of the Trevanion estate, made in the reign of Henry VIII, adopts a classification of land which formally acknowledges that many farms had both closes and unenclosed strips: the surveyor divides the acreage of each farm into three categories, *in claus'* (enclosed), *vasta* (waste) and 'in stitches' (i.e. in strips, the word being the first element in 'stitchmeal', mentioned above). The survey reveals holdings with a good proportion of their land in stitches on the manors of Boswellick (St Allen), Penhale (St Enoder), Tolgarrick (St Stephen in Brannel) and Trewellard (St Just in Penwith): all are in the western parts of Cornwall.[50] Final examples of strip-field cultivation may be taken from the

---

[47] For a good example of fossilized strips see the map of Tregurrian and Trevarrian in Flatrès, *Géographie rurale*, fig. 40, based on the tithe map of St Mawgan in Pyder.
[48] Leland, *Itinerary*, I, 317.
[49] PRO, E135/388; see also above, n. 47.
[50] BL, Add. Roll 32,958.

Lanhydrock Atlas, a mapped survey of the Robartes estate made in the late 1690s by Joel Gascoyne. The survey contains many maps showing land subdivided into strips, among the best examples being one of Predannack Wollas (Mullion) on the western side of the Lizard peninsula, which reveals that almost all of the land of the hamlet, outlying rough pasture and furze excepted, was, or had recently been, divided into unenclosed strips; a map of Garrah, just to the north of Predannack, with a very extensive area of strips; and one of Bollowall (St Just in Penwith), near the western cliffs, as far west as one can go, where almost the whole of the cultivated territory of the hamlet was subdivided into minute strips, called 'stitches' by the surveyor.[51] All of these examples, and many others, show that the county of Cornwall can no longer be described as 'very largely enclosed' in the sixteenth century, a conclusion which is bound to affect calculations which historians may make in the future about the pace of enclosure in England generally.[52] No detailed research has been carried out on enclosure of these remaining strip-field systems, although it has been suggested that this took place in the seventeenth century.[53] Certainly by the eighteenth and nineteenth centuries few hamlets retained complete strip-field systems surrounding the settlement, although the periodic cultivation of downs (outfield cultivation) still involved division of the rough pastures into strips by those farmers who had rights on them (see below, pp. xcv–xcvi).

The early development of strip-field systems in Cornwall is, as Rowse rightly said, 'a mute process of which we have no evidence'.[54] Sixteenth-century surveys, as well as earlier rentals, do however shed a little light upon the rationale (if not the ultimate origins) of the strips associated with the Cornish hamlet. The surveys printed here, and others, allow us to calculate the average size of strips at some places, and a sample of such calculations is given here. In the surveys of 1575 printed below there are strips of an average size of one rood (quarter-acre) at Bedrugga (*Bodrogowe Fielde* and *Higher*

---

[51] Lanhydrock Atlas (at Lanhydrock House).
[52] In his brave attempt to calculate, century by century, the pace of enclosure in England, Wordie (following Gonner: above, n. 35) begins with a Cornwall which was assumed to be wholly enclosed by 1600: 'English enclosure', p. 489.
[53] Whetter, *Cornwall in the Seventeenth Century*, p. 22.
[54] Rowse, *Tudor Cornwall*, p. 36.

Feild), average two roods (half-acre) at Tolcarne Merock (*Penclyes*) and average four roods (one acre) at Tresawsen (*Greate Feilde*) (below, pp. 214, 217 and 232). In other documents there were strips averaging two and three roods at Pendrift in Blisland (*Undertown* and *Willand*) in 1611–12, and averaging one rood at Bollowall in St Just in Penwith (all fields) in c.1696.[55]

What is remarkable about these figures is the minute size of the strips in most cases. The number of parcels into which a piece of land was divided was normally far in excess of the number of tenants who could ever have had an interest in it, so that, for example, a field at the hamlet of Trebelzue called West Field, of just over eight acres, was divided among three tenants into twenty-one strips.[56] This fact must be significant and provides a lead into a greater understanding of strip-field systems in Cornwall. One explanation which has been put forward to explain fragmentation of land into strips in some other parts of England is that each tenant occupied many small parcels intermixed with those of his neighbours so that it was impossible for anybody to withdraw from the system by enclosing his portions, because they were too small.[57] This explanation is reasonable enough but needs another, underlying, motive to account for the strong desire among participants to retain their strip-field system and not to allow any individual to withdraw from it through enclosure; to retain a system in which all participants were shareholders.

It is worth exploring the concept of shareholders in relation to the Cornish hamlet and its strips, for it may take us a little further in our understanding of the settlement type and its field system. The theme may be introduced with some figures showing the rents paid by tenants at the hamlet of Porth Veor on the manor of Bejowan (St Columb Minor), according to the rental of 1549 printed below; the hamlet was surrounded by a complex strip-field system.[58]

---

[55] Duchy of Cornwall archives, E.m.5, 'Surveys in Cornwall' (Pendrift); Lanhydrock Atlas (Bollowall).
[56] Below, pp. 215–16 and 218. These figures are for the non-free tenants. There was also a free tenement here: above, n. 32.
[57] Dahlman, *Open Field System*, pp. 124–5.
[58] Below, p. 165, for the rental; pp. 216–17 for arable land 'in diverse parcels' at Porth Veor; p. 212 for the ghost of the four tenements of 1549.

Tenant	Rent	Shares (of 7s.1d.)
James Roberd	28s. 4d.	4
Joan Olde	14s. 2d.	2
Robert Rychard	7s. 1d.	1
Joan Opye	7s. 1d.	1
Totals	56s. 8d.	8

The lord of the manor expected the hamlet to bring in 56s. 8d. in 1549; the total rent was still the same in 1575; it remained at 56s. 8d. in c.1586, by which time the manor had passed to the Arundells, and, indeed, was still the same in the early seventeenth century.[59] This total rent is a good round figure: it was common in the Middle Ages (when the rent was no doubt set) to reckon in marks (two-thirds of £1, that is 13s. 4d.) or in fractions of a mark, and 56s. 8d. comes out as four marks and one-quarter of a mark. Far odder, at first glance, are the rents paid by the tenants in 1549. The sum of 7s. 1d. paid by both Rychard and Opye looks awkward: why not plain 7s.? The answer soon becomes clear from a close inspection of the individual sums which shows that the total rent payable to the lord had been split into eight shares, 7s. 1d. being one-eighth of 56s. 8d. Conceivably there could formerly have been eight tenants at Porth Veor, each paying an equal share, though this cannot be proved because there are no rentals for this manor earlier than 1549. Alternatively, a group of tenants with unequal capacities for investing in the land had at some point in time split the rent into eight shares, each one then electing to pay for a certain number according to his or her wealth. Now James Roberd, the largest shareholder, would have been justifiably aggrieved if he did not have access to a good deal more land than, say, Joan Opye (a smallholder) and, from the relationship between their respective rents, he would be expected to claim four times as much if share-holding in rents was matched by shareholding in land.

In order to demonstrate the last point and to explore the age of the system of shareholding we need rentals or surveys which give both rents and precise acreages. The medieval Arundell rentals printed in this volume do not satisfy both criteria, so it is necessary to take a short sideways step into some manors on the estate of the Duchy of Cornwall which has medieval documents slightly

---

[59] Below, pp. 216–17; AR2/1343 (survey, c.1586) and AR2/1346 (survey, 1618).

fuller in content. Examples of rents and acreages in 1337 from two Duchy hamlets—Trewen in Lanteglos by Camelford (manor of Helstone in Trigg) and Trecaine in Creed (manor of Tybesta)—are given here.[60]

Trewen

Tenant	Rent	Acreage	Shares (of 9½ acres and 3s. 4d.)
Andrew Trewenna	6s. 8d.	19	2
Roger Sage	6s. 8d.	19	2
John de Trewenna	6s. 8d.	19	2
Warin Vda	3s. 4d.	9½	1
John de Trewenna	3s. 4d.	9½	1
Totals	26s. 8d.	76	8

Trecaine

Tenant	Rent	Acreage	Shares (of 8½ acres and 2s. 8d.)
Gervase Popa	7s.[61]	25½	3
William Gynnon	8s.	25½	3
Richard Snou	5s. 4d.	17	2
Richard Snou	2s. 8d.	8½	1
Totals	23s.	76½	9

The rent columns here show the same features which we have already seen at Porth Veor, a total rent divided into shares of which some tenants have one, some more than one. The columns for acreage are highly instructive, for they show that the number of acres occupied by each tenant was directly and precisely in proportion to the number of shares held and, therefore, to rent paid: thus a tenement with one share at Trecaine held 8½ acres and paid 2s. 8d. while a tenement with two shares held 17 acres and paid 5s. 4d. These are groups of tenants among whom there is an established custom of stakes or shares in the cultivated territory of the hamlet.

Satisfied that we can use rents as surrogates for acreages we can return to the Arundell estate and turn to consider how the share system coped with changes over time in numbers of tenants: no hamlet is static and we might, in general, expect to find growth in numbers of tenants in the thirteenth century and the early fourteenth, contraction after 1348 and through into the fifteenth

---

[60] *Caption of Seisin*, ed. Hull, pp. 21 and 58–9.
[61] The logic of the multiples indicates that this sum should have been 8s; the figure of 7s. may be an error for 8s. or a rent reduction.

century, with perhaps some growth again in numbers of tenants in the sixteenth century. As an example we take the hamlet of Tregona (St Eval) in the manor of Trembleath.[62]

1459

Tenant	Rent	Shares (each of 3s. 4d.)
John Carbura	13s. 4d.	4
John Treghar	13s. 4d.	4
John Scovarn	16s. 8d.	5
Ralph Carpenter	23s. 4d.	7
John Carbura	13s. 4d.	4
Totals	80s.	24

1480

Tenant	Rent	Shares (each of 22s. 6½d.)
Thomas Richard	22s. 7d.	1
Thomas Dunston	22s. 6½d.	1
John Pascawe	22s. 6½d.	1
Totals	67s. 8d.	3

1499

Tenant	Rent	Shares (each of 26s. 8d.)
William Laurens	26s. 8d.	1
John Laurens	26s. 8d.	1
John Heyly	26s. 8d.	1
Totals	80s.	3

c.1586

Tenant	Rent	Shares (each of 13s. 4d.)
Fridisweda Renold	13s. 4d.	1
Elizabeth William	13s. 4d.	1
Wilmot Jeffry	26s. 8d.	2
Robert Doungye	26s. 8d.	2
Totals	80s.	6

These figures need little commentary. The total rent required from the hamlet of Tregona by the Arundell family was usually 80s., though with a reduction of one mark in 1480, at a time when other rent reductions were being made in Trembleath manor.[63] In 1459 there were 24 shares, the five tenants holding varying numbers; in 1480 and 1499 there were three tenants with three equal shares; in c.1586 there were four tenants with varying shares. Here we see a

---

[62] Below, pp. 26, 75 and 107; figures for c.1586 from AR2/1343.
[63] See below, pp. ci–ciii.

share system capable of accommodating changing permutations of numbers of tenants and, within the tenant body, variations in wealth and in capacity to invest in land. The total rent payable was like a common pool to which tenants contributed differing amounts (and amounts which varied over time) according to their number and the capacity of each to pay.

Two general points may be made about the system of variable shares described above. First, the shares were clearly *divisions* of a total. To take just one example: the precise mathematical relationship between the sizes of holdings at Tregona in 1459—with some tenants occupying four twenty-fourths of the land, another occupying seven twenty-fourths, and so on—could not possibly have arisen through spontaneous growth of each of those holdings over time. The outcome could only have been achieved through *division* of the total cultivated land of the hamlet into 24 shares which were then taken by the tenants, some receiving more, some less. This point may be illustrated with a simple example from the manor of Tybesta (Creed) on the Duchy estate. There, at the hamlet of Trewinnow Vean in 1356–7, three tenants each held ten and one-third acres; again, a precise equality which is unlikely to have arisen through the spontaneous evolution of those three holdings. And sure enough a few decades earlier, in 1337, we find only one holding at Trewinnow, a single farm of 31 acres. At some time between 1337 and 1356–7 it was divided into three equal shares of ten and one-third acres each.[64]

A second point is an extension of the first: precise division of the land into shares would have been greatly facilitated if the land were fragmented into small strips. This point can be developed best if we first take the very simple example of Trewinnow Vean. The single farm of 1337 presumably consisted of closes held in severalty. It is highly unlikely that the sizes of these closes allowed them to be allocated to the three new tenants there, following the tripartite division, in such a way as to give each a precisely equal share, down to the nearest third of an acre; so some degree of parcellation of the land into strips may have accompanied the division. We can return to Tregona (St Eval) for a more complex example. If the land of the hamlet of Tregona comprised closes of varying sizes it is highly unlikely that they could have been

---

[64] PRO, E306 2/1; *Caption of Seisin*, ed. Hull, p. 58.

allocated, undivided, among the five tenants of 1459 so that each received acreages precisely in proportion to his (or her) shares in the total rent for the hamlet (or vice versa). It is even more unlikely that closes could have been the basis of the differing allocations of land represented by the revised shareholding arrangements apparent in the rentals of 1480, 1499 and c.1586. If, on the other hand, the land of Tregona comprised numerous small strips, all of these differing allocations could have been made with ease on each occasion with an exactly fair distribution of acres among the tenants in proportion to their share of the rent. If split up into small strips, the arable territory of a hamlet could be used as a common pool from which tenants took shares of differing acreages in proportion to the shares which they contributed to the financial pool which was the total rent for the hamlet.

The explanation given above has a good deal of further support in the evidence. A reference of 1405–6 from the Duchy archive, relating to Trecaine in Creed (Tybesta manor), states that three holdings there, probably vacant as a result of run-down farming after the Black Death, were to be 'equally divided' (*equaliter dividend'*) between the hamlet's surviving tenants.[65] Another reference from the Duchy archive, from 1356–7 and relating to the hamlet of Trevia in Lanteglos by Camelford (manor of Helstone in Trigg), explains that the burden of 22*d.* rent, unpaid by one of the tenants probably because of poverty, had been taken over and shared out as an obligation among the other inhabitants of the hamlet. They also shared out among themselves an amount of land which was the equivalent of a rent of 22*d.*, 'because', the scribe wrote, as if to record expected practice, 'each ferling of land should be divided between all [tenants] so that the whole arable land of this vill is let among the tenants'.[66] These two references are important because they allow us to witness what was probably a well-established custom of land sharing among the tenants of a hamlet. An excellent, because highly explicit, illustration of the share system comes from the fields of Zennor churchtown as they are described in the parish's glebe terriers. In 1616 the glebe was reckoned to be

---

[65] PRO, E306 2/7. Some land in this hamlet had been in a poor state in the later fourteenth century: PRO, E306 2/2. A share system operated here, holdings being of 8½ acres (one share), 17 acres (two shares) or 25½ acres (three shares).

[66] PRO, E306 2/1; and again in 1371, Duchy of Cornwall Archives, no. 475.

'one-fifth part of the whole churchtown', that is to have a one-fifth share in its land, the four other shares belonging to other farms there. The small closes around Zennor, with their huge virtually irremovable stone walls, are unlikely to have fallen into five groups, each group with precisely the same acreage. The solution, therefore, to the task of dividing the land precisely into five was to split the closes into strips, most of less than one acre; from this pool of strips each of the shareholders took one-fifth. That this had been done is quite clear from a series of glebe terriers which describe the minute strips ('stitches') of the glebe (usually bounded by those of other tenants in the churchtown), and which state that the land 'lieth in stich meal'.[67] Finally, the identical terminology of two fourteenth-century charters relating to Trevellion (Luxulyan) and Little Lantyan (Lostwithiel) is highly instructive. Holdings at both places were described as *sullonatim inter vicinos* ('divided into strips [selions] among neighbours').[68] This striking, and highly unusual, terminology seems to stress the involvement of neighbours in the organized sharing-out of their land. It implies that the territory of these hamlets was thought of as common to their inhabitants; therefore there was no need to define the location of the strips precisely, it being sufficient to state that they formed part of a field system in which allocation of shares was the responsibility of neighbours.

The slight vagueness of the phrase 'divided into strips among neighbours' (with no more precise details of the location of strips) is interesting because it has a counterpart in Cornish documents from the sixteenth and seventeenth centuries. In these one sometimes comes across a holding whose lands are described as, for example, 'within the vill and fields of Trevelsue' (Trebelzue in St Columb Minor).[69] This terminology is not entirely unknown in documents from other south-western counties, but occurs far more frequently in Cornish collections than in any others. It is a little vague and seems to suggest that the holding could not be disentangled from other lands in the same hamlet. Could this have been so because the holding was intricately intermixed with other

---

[67] Rolfe, 'Cornish parsons', p. 28 (quoting CRO, ARD/TER/145, glebe terrier of 1616); *Calendar of Cornish Glebe Terriers*, ed. Potts, pp. 176–7.
[68] RIC, Henderson Calendar 19, p. 314; CRO, CN/788.
[69] Below, p. 213.

shareholdings in the same hamlet? As far as Trebelzue is concerned, that was certainly the case: its highly sub-divided strip-field system has already been mentioned several times in this Introduction. Another example from the Arundell estate comes from Tregona (St Eval) whose share-holding system has already been described above: a lease of 1584 describes 30 acres there as 'in the fields and hamlet and waste of Tregona'.[70] From beyond the Arundell estate an Elizabethan survey refers to a holding 'in the vill and fields of Penpoll' (Phillack), while a map of the 1690s shows the existence of strips there.[71] This terminology hints strongly at a concept of holdings which were thought to have a share in the whole territory of the hamlet in which they were situated.

Further support for the idea of the Cornish hamlet as a body of shareholders comes from evidence relating not to the arable land, but to other resources. At the very core of a hamlet's territory was its 'town place' or 'town floor', the small open space onto which the farmsteads faced. This was usually common to the community: a lease of 1684 relating to a holding in the hamlet of Trevanson (St Breock) allowed the tenant 'liberty to keep pigs and geese on the town place or town floor' and 'common pasture on the town floor' belonged to holdings in the hamlets of Tregurrian and Trevarrian (St Mawgan in Pyder), surveyed in 1606. The survey of holdings at Trebelzue, rather unusually, measures the town place and shows that each tenant theoretically had a precisely similar acreage down to the nearest perch, which was probably the tenants' way of expressing the notion of equal shares in its capacity to support the grazing of young livestock and poultry.[72] On the outskirts of a hamlet's territory lay its common pasture (in some cases separated from the arable by a boundary feature whose maintenance may have been regarded as a common responsibility among the tenants, for in one of the surveys printed below it is called the 'town wall');[73] and rights to common pasture, too, were shared among holdings. Thus on the manor of Eastway (Morwenstow), according to Norden's survey, the stint of sheep on the common pasture

---

[70] AR2/1346.
[71] DRO, W1258M/E/29 (survey of Penpoll, Phillack); Lanhydrock Atlas (c.1696; at Lanhydrock House).
[72] RIC, Henderson Calendar 2, p. 122 (lease, 1684); PRO, E315/388 (survey, 1606); below, pp. 215–16 and 218 (Trebelzue).
[73] Below, p. 177; also p. 175 for land 'above the wall'.

was in units of five, tenants having allowances of 5, 10, 20 or 30 sheep according to the sizes of their holdings; common of pasture upon Bin Down (Morval), was 'according to the proportion' (i.e. to holding size); on the manor of Landrayne (North Hill), a sixteenth-century surveyor noted that 'tenants ... have common ... [for] as much of all kinds of cattle as their several in-grounds will bear in winter'; Zennor glebe, with a one-fifth share in the arable which has already been described above, also had 'one-fifth part throughout the commons on the down and cliff for pasture and fuel'.[74] All of these cases show a system of shares in the use of common pasture, these being proportionable to shares in the arable. Where other common facilities or institutions existed—such as a shared corn-drying kiln, a communally held fulling mill, or a chapel or guild attached to a hamlet—we may suppose that the costs of their upkeep were shared out in a similar way. From Devon one documented example has been found of a by-law enacted at the lowly level of the hamlet, but this is a rare survival; no doubt the many disputes which must have arisen at this level, about strip boundaries, common pasture, crop rotations and so on, were normally settled by oral resolution.[75]

Through their strip-field systems, attested as far back as the fourteenth century, we therefore begin tentatively to understand something of the workings, and the working life, of the Cornish hamlet.[76] The rules and rhythms of these settlements were determined not by lords but by small groups of farming families con-

---

[74] Duchy of Cornwall Archives, E.m.5., 'Surveys in Cornwall'; see also Welch, 'Survey of Duchy manors', p. 4, where the stint at Eastway is described as 'a set proportion of sheep among themselves [the tenants]'; also CRO, WM/32 (Bin Down), and *Calendar of Cornish Glebe Terriers*, ed. Potts, p. 177.

[75] For a shared corn-drying barn at Brown Willy hamlet see P. Herring in Johnson and Rose, *Bodmin Moor*, p. 93; AR2/887, an account roll of 1433–4, for a fulling mill, on Trembleath manor, leased in common by tenants; Mattingly, 'Medieval parish guilds', p. 313, for an example of a guild serving a hamlet community; DRO, 902M/M33, by-law (*ordinatio*) made by the inhabitants of the hamlet of Bugford (manor and parish of Stoke Fleming) about common pasture. Normally, by-laws were enacted at the level of the manor, not of the hamlet.

[76] An even earlier reference (1248) to a selion, at Lemail (Egloshayle), appears in AR1/57.

forming by custom to established practices. Lords set the burden of total rent to be paid by tenants in a hamlet, often a 'round sum'. Tenants then shared out that burden according to their differing capacities to pay. Shares in rent paid were matched by shares in arable land and other resources. Because the number of tenants living in a hamlet changed over time, as did relative numbers of richer and not so well off farmers, the land needed to be re-allocated from time to time and this could be done most precisely if the arable were sub-divided into small strips. Strip-field systems in Cornwall were not, as Rowse thought, 'radiated by the foreign influence of the towns';[77] they were intrinsic to the hamlet, a settlement type of ancient origins, and as such they were thoroughly local in character.

Downs, towns and other features

It is to be expected that surveys from the sixteenth and seventeenth centuries can tell us a great deal about downs (unenclosed pastures) and their uses, for they were then a more prominent feature of the Cornish scene than they are today; all commentators on Cornish agriculture, from the sixteenth century to the nineteenth, have noted the disappearance of downs at the expense of enclosure and, indeed, that process is evident in the surveys printed in this volume.[78] Management of downs as common pastures varied according

---

[77] Rowse, *Tudor Cornwall*, p. 35. By 'foreign' Rowse meant English, believing that a majority of the population of the county's early boroughs was English not Cornish. Rowse was thinking of the areas of cultivated strips associated with many Cornish boroughs (Henderson, *Essays*, p. 67); these probably originated through sub-division of town commons among burgesses, and they therefore have little direct relevance to the strip-field systems of rural hamlets.

[78] Rowse, *Tudor Cornwall*, pp. 36–7; Whetter, *Cornwall in the Seventeenth Century*, pp. 54–5; Rowe, *Cornwall in the Industrial Revolution*, pp. 224–6. For recent enclosure of downland in the surveys printed below see, for example, pp. 174 ('Treglissedowne newly enclosed'), 175 ('down newly enclosed'), 232 ('close of pasture newly taken out of the common of Tresawsyn'), and 234 ('close of pasture taken out of the common'). There are many cases in the surveys of closes called, for example, 'Neweground', 'Newe Downe Close' or 'Down Park' (e.g. pp. 179, 233 and 184): these names also signify relatively recent enclosure.

to the local custom of the manor. We learn that on the 'great waste of moor and heath' belonging to the Cardinham manor, drifting (i.e. rounding up animals, partly in order to seek out those of outsiders) was the responsibility of the free tenants; while Goss Moor was inter-commoned not only by tenants of Domellick manor (St Dennis) but also by those of other adjacent lordships.[79] On Roseworthy manor (Gwinear), downs (one described as '40 acres of very good pasture ground') were common pasture 'without stint', but at some other places, as we have seen, the pasture of downs was restricted, tenants enjoying pasture for so many animals according to their shares.[80]

Of all the products yielded by the downs, other than grazing, tin was the most valuable. On some of the moors of Bodardle manor the tenants themselves managed the collection of the lord's toll tin, electing one of their number to carry it away in sacks. Here the lord's toll was at a rate of one-sixteenth of the product, whereas on Goss Moor, belonging partly to the manor of Domellick, the rate was one-thirteenth; clearly, as was also the case with multure (the lord's toll of grain ground at mills), the rate was fixed by local customs agreed by lord and tenant. Tin, of course, was to be found beneath cultivated land as well as on downs and wastes, as is clear from a reference to 'all the broken ground for the tin works' on a tenement belonging to the manor of Bejowan (St Columb Major).[81]

Finally, it was typical of Cornwall, and indeed of the whole of the South-West, for there to be no firm dividing line between the use of downs for grazing and their use as temporary arable 'outfields' ploughed and cropped for a year or so and then allowed to revert to rough grazing.[82] None of the surveys printed in this volume refers to this practice unequivocally although 'arable land

---

[79] Below, pp. 187 and 171.
[80] Below, p. 170; for stints see above, pp. xci–xcii.
[81] Below, pp. 197, 171 and 213. The medieval manorial accounts for Cardinham also contain references to toll tin: AR2/446 (reeves' accounts, 1435–55).
[82] William Marshall thought that the 'cultivation of commonable lands is ... peculiar to this extremity of the island' [i.e. Cornwall, Somerset and Devon]: *Rural Economy*, II, 226. He was correct about the prevalence of the practice in the South-West, though incorrect in thinking that it was restricted to that province; see also Fox, 'Outfield cultivation'.

upon the Down', belonging to some of the tenants of Downinney (Warbstow), may have been of this type; the surveyor here describes permanent enclosures in a different way.[83] Other surveys are more explicit. At Climsland Prior (Stoke Climsland) in 1649 a surveyor noted that the tenants were accustomed to 'enclose part of the ... down and sow it for one year and then throw it open again'; on Bin Down (Morval) tenants had rights of tillage 'according to the proportion'. Tenants at Millook (Poundstock) were allowed to pass over the common pasture of the hamlet only when it was 'out of tillage'; here a stint of two bullocks out of a total of sixty (when the down was uncultivated) was equated by the surveyor as the equivalent of one-twentieth of the area when it was cultivated.[84] Surveys rarely add much more detail to enable us to bring this practice of outfield cultivation to life. For that we have to rely on other documents (sometimes quite late ones, for this traditional practice persisted into the nineteenth century). Seventeenth-century equity cases from Devon have led to the survival of transcripts of the voices of tenant farmers as they described parts of a common in the parish of Ashburton which were 'sometimes enclosed with frith and sometimes lay open', or parts of a common in Sidbury parish which were 'tilled ... about 100 years ago ... and the show and sign of ridges of tillage do yet plainly appear'.[85] Much later, there is detailed nineteenth-century correspondence relating to Treligga commons (St Teath) and Tregurrian commons (St Mawgan in Pyder) which describes breaking them up for tillage and their complex division into a large number of strips divided by low ridges of turf.[86] Strip-field cultivation in Cornwall therefore continued into the nineteenth century on periodically-cultivated outfields and, from the reference relating to Millook (above), it is

---

[83] Permanent enclosures are described as 'a close called a down newly enclosed' and 'moor in severalty': below, pp. 175–6.
[84] *Parliamentary Survey*, ed. Pounds, I, 34; CRO, WM/32; Lanhydrock Atlas (at Lanhydrock House).
[85] PRO, E134 2 Jas.I/Hil.15 and 5 Jas.I/Mich.1.
[86] 'We are now breaking it up for tillage' (June, 1856); 'I had no idea that there were so many pieces of land' (October, 1870); '... stitches, the boundaries of which are most distinctly indicated by the ridges of furze or turf, ... tilled with corn ... usually about once in twenty-five or thirty years' (1833): CRO, F/271–2 and W/2.

clear that tenants had shares in the outfield, when tilled, which were in proportion to the number of animals they could graze when it was not tilled; this was the last breath of the old share-holding system which applied at earlier dates to the arable land immediately surrounding the hamlet, as we have already seen.

Useful references to towns in estate surveys occur in two contexts. Firstly, surveyors sometimes give thumbnail descriptions of the towns nearest to the rural manor which is being surveyed. The purpose of this practice was, undoubtedly, to give some indication of how profitable farming on the manor might be, for profitability depended in part on ease of access to markets close at hand: tenements on the manor of Leigh Durrant (Pillaton) were said by a sixteenth-century surveyor to be very profitable because 'there is such ... sale of all kinds of victuals to the town of Plymouth'.[87] John Norden included a question about market towns in his 'Articles of survey' (a set of questions to be addressed) for his survey of the annexed manors of the Duchy of Cornwall, made in 1611–12. This regularly includes brief notes on towns: for example, Landulph manor was 'distant from Saltash but one mile by boat and three miles by land'; Stratton market was still active enough to be recommended as an outlet for tenants on the manors of Eastway (Morwenstow) and Boyton.[88] The survey of 1563, printed in part in this volume, describes Helston, Penzance and St Ives as 'towns of ... note for market or other repair or traffic' while Tregony was 'a market town of much access' and St Columb Major a 'little market town'.[89]

Surveys also give good details about the towns which belonged to the estate which was being surveyed. The Arundell estate contained some scattered urban properties[90] and also included the whole of two towns, the 'little market town' of St Columb Major and the borough of Mitchell (St Enoder). In the sixteenth and early

---

[87] BL, Harl. MS. 71.
[88] Duchy of Cornwall Archives, E.m.5, 'Surveys in Cornwall'; Welch, 'Survey of Duchy manors', pp. 278, 5 and 7.
[89] Below, p. 168; PRO, SP12/31, no. 30; Carew, *Survey of Cornwall* (ed. Halliday), p. 220, describes St Columb Major as 'a mean town'.
[90] For example, property in Bodmin which was part of the manor of Reperry, and property in Helston which belonged to the manor of Prospidnick: below, pp. 200–1 and 205.

seventeenth centuries neither came into that category of decayed urban places about which some commentators on the Cornish scene were so scathing: 'a poor village ... peopled with twelve dwellings and thirteen cuckolds' (Carew on the borough of Crafthole in Sheviock); 'the meanest and and poorest that can bear the name of a town' (Norden on Boscastle in Forrabury).[91]

Of the two towns belonging to the Arundell family, St Columb Major was the larger. Codner's survey of the early seventeenth century lists about 50 dwellings here, which might indicate a population of around 250 or so, a large concentration of people by the Cornish standards of the day.[92] It also shows a town in which there was constant replenishment and change in the building stock: one dwelling was described as 'once four houses'; there were 'newly built' houses as well as a 'decayed tenement'. The dimensions of some houses are given, commonly 12ft or 13ft wide, with lengths varying from 18ft to 20ft (three cases) to 38ft (one case). The smaller dimensions clearly indicate the narrow street frontage while the longer ones represent the extension of the house backwards into its long garden plot. Most of the buildings mentioned in the survey are described simply as 'houses' or 'tenements', but a little more detail is added about a few. Clearly different from the rest of the urban property was the 'great house called Tremaynes House', a one-time residence of that family.[93] A church house, a sexton's house and several shops (either workshops or retail shops) are also listed. Mention of two fulling mills (of which only one was working in the early seventeenth century), either within or close to the town, of an inn bearing the 'sign of the wolf' (from the Arundells' fourteenth-century arms, alluding to their residence at

---

[91] Carew, *Survey of Cornwall* (ed. Halliday), p. 177; Norden, *Cornwall*, p. 54.

[92] AR2/1346. The figure of 250 is arrived at by multiplying the number of dwellings by a rough approximation for household size taken from *Household and Family in Past Times*, edited by P. Laslett and R. Wall (Cambridge, 1972), pp. 138, 192 and 195; it takes no account of sub-letting of parts of tenements.

[93] The family is recorded in the town during the late fifteenth century (below, pp. 38, 72 and 103); it was still in the parish in 1569 (*Muster Roll*, ed. Douch, p. 33); but Codner does not name the family, so they had presumably gone from the town by 1618.

Trembleath)[94] and of a place 'where the fish market is kept' help us to envisage a lively urban scene and to imagine some of the occupations of the town. Accumulation of many properties in the hands of single individuals and many references to sub-leasing in the survey both point to an active market in urban property.

Mitchell was the smaller of the two Arundell towns. Its origins as a borough probably date from some time after 1239 when the lord of the manor of Degembris obtained a royal charter for a yearly fair here on the feast of St Francis and a weekly market. The borough was purchased by Sir Ralph Arundell towards the end of the thirteenth century.[95] Codner's early seventeenth-century survey which is so comparatively rich in references to the urban scene at St Columb Major is rather disappointing as far as Mitchell is concerned. At that time the borough contained 23 tenements held 'in free burgage' and the survey, like that of St Columb, contains abundant evidence of the accumulation of properties by individual speculators, who then sub-let them. The most interesting detail concerns the fair of St Francis: a close called *Fareparke* was leased out with the proviso that the Arundell family could enter it each year to erect 'standings' and 'other things necessary for the fair'; the medieval chapel of St Francis was apparently still intact and was used at the time of the fair; the profits were at farm (leased) for 26s. 8d.[96]

The sixteenth-century surveys printed below are relatively uninformative about farm buildings in the landscape. The survey of Dinham's Lands made in 1566 acknowledges that some tenements

---

[94] The place-name Trembleath means 'the farm of the wolf' (Old Cornish *bleit* 'wolf'), and a wolf was depicted on some Arundell seals in the fourteenth and fifteenth centuries, indicating an appreciation of the Cornish language at the highest level of west-Cornish society in the late fourteenth and early fifteenth centuries: illustrated in Lysons, *Cornwall*, p. lxxix*, nos 4–5 (from AR4/2122, dated 1426, and AR20/3, dated 1371; also the seal on AR20/7, again dated 1371).

[95] See above, pp. xiv–xv; Henderson, *Essays*, p. 54; Beresford, *New Towns*, pp. 408–9. Mitchell was a borough by 1311 (*Anc.Deeds*, IV, A.9373).

[96] Henderson's study of the medieval court rolls of the borough of Mitchell (*Essays*, pp. 54–60) gives much additional information. He states that the chapel 'became derelict at the Reformation' and was 'a mere heap of stones in 1745'; and that the profits of the fair were around 30s. in the early sixteenth century (*ibid.*, pp. 56–7).

contained, as well as the farmhouse, 'other buildings necessary for husbandry' but gives no more detail; the survey made in 1575 before the sale of the earl of Oxford's manors to the Arundell family describes the roofing material of each house (slate or thatch), but adds no more information about vernacular architecture. Other surveys (though a minority) give fuller descriptions of houses, for example 'one hall, a chamber adjoining to the higher end of the same hall, a little room severed within the same hall, a chamber over the said hall, a little chamber ..., a sheep house and a little chamber at the end of the same, a dry house, a barn, a little room adjoining, two piggs' houses and a little house in the lane'—an excellent picture of a farmhouse and its associated buildings on the manor of Carminow, taken from Codner's survey of the Arundell lands in the early seventeenth century.[97] It is not clear why more manorial surveys do not contain such detail, because the rent for a tenement and, especially, the fine (or entry money) depended in part on the quality of the accommodation and farm buildings. The answer may possibly be that surveyors, who were always unpopular with the tenants (the latter fearing that what a surveyor recorded would result in rent increases), realized that too much intrusion into the very dwellings of farmers would be to over-step the mark.[98]

Manorial surveys, including those printed below, provide excellent detail about management of woods; their study would in part make good our lack of knowledge of the history of woodland in post-medieval Cornwall.[99] Lack of space precludes detailed

---

[97] AR2/1346; this survey is largely based upon leases which do sometimes contain details of farmhouses. Surveys not entirely based upon leases more rarely have such descriptions. Three examples are PRO, E315/414 (survey, 1601–2, of manors annexed to the Duchy of Cornwall); DRO, 1508M/estate/valuations/4 (survey of the manor of Kenton, Devon, 1598); and Kerridge, *Surveys of Pembroke Manors*, throughout.

[98] For the unpopularity of surveyors see Norden, *Surveiors Dialogue*, I, 4.

[99] The surveys printed below mention, for example, woods reserved to lords for their great timber, the time elapsed since the last cutting being specified precisely by the surveyor (p. 187); wood-pasture leased to tenants with the proviso that no grazing should take place until six years had elapsed since felling, to allow regeneration (p. 181); woodland which was used for grazing and coppicing (p. 227), normally compartmentalized to allow for both of these activities; and woodland in which tenants had rights of housebote, that is permission to take timber for repairs to their houses (p. 187).

examination of all of the other features of the Cornish scene which come alive to the reader of these surveys—for example, quarries dotting the landscape,[100] and several types of buildings associated with the tin industry and with fishing.[101] These are all illuminated by manorial surveys, a class of document which, perhaps more than any other, transports the historian back into the landscapes of their time.

---

[100] For the field-name *Quarry Park* or the like see below, pp. 183 and 200. Exceptionally, in a seventeenth-century survey of Tintagel, 21 coastal slate-quarries are listed: *Parliamentary Survey*, ed. Pounds, II, 183–4. For a medieval quarry on the manor of Winnington see below, p. 129. But the survey of Truro Vean manor in 1499 does not mention the quarry which was there four years later (below, p. 121 n. 26).

[101] For blowing-mills see pp. 116, 123, 150, 168 and 205. Codner's survey of 1618 (AR2/1346) gives good detail about a stamping-mill at Nance (Lelant; Connerton manor), with its 'dressing places' and 'leats to carry the water to the mill'; the same survey (Carminow manor) mentions 'a house called a capstan house', implying the paraphernalia for fishing. *Capson Howse* (Gunwalloe; Carminow manor) was leased in 1582 and 1612 (AR4/820–1).

6. CONVENTIONARY TENEMENTS AND TENANT FARMERS AT THE CLOSE OF THE MIDDLE AGES

Tenements in decline

The medieval rentals printed here contain less information about the landscape than the sixteenth-century surveys do. But the fact that these rentals survive in a series, a new one being drawn up every 20 years or so, makes them exceptionally useful for studies of tenements and families of tenant farmers during the latter half of the fifteenth century. Here we offer some introductory comments on how such topics might be approached, based upon an analysis of rentals of a few of the manors. It is hoped that these comments will stimulate others to use the material printed below in order to undertake more detailed analyses for the other manors, and to add data from court rolls and account rolls in the Arundell archive, for these also contain much information on tenements and tenants. In what follows all conclusions are based upon examination of conventionary tenements only. Free tenements, which were very numerous on some manors, deserve their own study.

Among the conventionary lands the most frequently mentioned unit of occupancy in the medieval rentals is the tenement or holding. Some of the post-medieval surveys describe it in more detail: a farmhouse 'in which the tenant lives', enclosed fields and arable strips in any combination, with, perhaps, rights of grazing upon commons. Such detail is lacking in the medieval rentals but these do, at least, allow a count to be made of changing numbers of tenements on each manor over the last 50 years or so of the Middle Ages. This is done, in the figures below, for the manors of Trembleath (St Ervan) and Treloy (St Columb Minor), about three miles north and two miles south, respectively, of Lanherne, and a little way inland from the north Cornish coast; the figures also show changes in rents paid.

	Trembleath		
	1459	1480	1499
Occupancies	17	13	14
Conventionary rents	£13 19s. 3d.	£12 2s. 6d.	£14 7s. 2d.

Treloy

	1460	1480	1499
Occupancies	18	13	12
Conventionary rents	£13 1s. 10½d.	£12 15s. 4d.	£12 6s. 8d.

The first point to make about these figures is a cautionary one. They are intended to provide an overall index of how well, or otherwise, the body of tenant farmers was doing on these two manors during the second half of the fifteenth century. For comparisons between the rental years to be valid, it is essential that like is compared with like; therefore, if a tenement is for some reason absent from one rental, it must be excluded from all of the figures. A case in point is the tenement at Trethias (St Merryn) on the manor of Trembleath. It is missing from the conventionary tenants in the rental of 1459, but is present in 1480 and 1499 when it paid a rent of 8s.[1] If included in the table it might give the impression that occupancies and rents were decreasing less than was actually the case.[2] The figures should not be employed to show how much, in rents, the Arundell family was receiving from these two manors; for that, the sub-totals and totals in the rentals printed below may be used (see pp. cxxi–cxxiii). Rather, they indicate changes in the tenants' capacity to pay rent, and in demand for land, fewer occupancies probably reflecting reduced demand.

Having made this cautionary point, we may discuss the figures in more detail by using the example of Trembleath manor between 1459 and 1480. Rents declined by 36s. 9d.: this sum was made up of quite large reductions at Penrose (reduction of 8s. 9d.) and Tregona (12s. 4d.) and a smaller one at Chapel (1s. 4d.); further, the mill which paid 16s. in 1459 was described in 1480 as

---

[1] There was a free tenement at Trethias in 1459 (below, p 24). The first appearance of a conventionary tenement there, in 1480, is clearly a new addition to the rental, because it has been placed at the end, after the mill (below, p. 75). The free tenant at Trethias is also given in 1480 and 1499 (below, pp. 73 and 105), which argues against any replacement of free by conventionary tenure here.

[2] Other examples of tenements excluded from the figures are one presumably at Treniow (Trembleath manor), occurring only in the 1499 rental; another at Trekenning (Treloy manor) which was lost to the manor through an exchange; and Trembleath demesne.

unoccupied and contributing no rent.³ The fall in rents is thus made up of reductions of varying amounts and one nil rent because of a vacancy. Occupancies fell by four, from seventeen to thirteen, a drop which is accounted for as follows: the vacancy of the mill, a decline of occupancies from five to three at the hamlet of Tregona and a decline from three to two at Engollan. The last may serve as a detailed example. In 1459 there were three tenements there, occupied by William Vycar, William Carbura and Robert Endure; in 1480 the first of these tenements remained, now held by Martin Wolcock, but the other two had been engrossed (added together), and were now held by Ivo Symon. Reductions of the rents of individual tenements lay behind the declining cash figures above; engrossing of tenements was largely responsible for decline in the number of occupancies.⁴

It must not be forgotten that the years covered by the figures take in only the tail-end of a long period of depression in the English countryside with its roots in the early fourteenth century, so that if earlier rentals had survived for these two manors it is almost certain that they would show an even greater degree of decline.⁵ Several underlying causes lay behind depression in the countryside during the late fourteenth century and much of the fifteenth. There was a severe fall in population as a result of the Black Death of 1348, of subsequent outbreaks of plague and of aspects of mortality and fertility much discussed by historical demographers; as a result there was a reduced and sluggish demand for the produce of the land affecting both arable and pastoral farming, but especially the former, and an unwillingness among farmers to make long-term investments.⁶ Such difficulties did not affect all parts of every county with equal severity (as we shall see later), though few regions altogether escaped.

Figures for the manors of Trembleath and Treloy show that some tenant farmers were in difficulty, especially in the 20 years between 1459–60 and 1480. The rentals upon which they are based, and also manorial account rolls, reveal temporarily vacant holdings,

---

³ The four reductions given here total 38s. 5d.; one rent on the manor was increased by 1s. 8d., making a net reduction of 36s. 9d.
⁴ On Trembleath manor there was an apparent increase between 1480 and 1499, the result of reoccupation of the mill.
⁵ For Cornwall see Hatcher, *Duchy of Cornwall*, pp. 81–4 and 102–21.
⁶ The most recent general discussion is Bolton, 'World upside down'.

amalgamations (resulting in declining numbers of occupancies), reductions in rents and a rapid turnover of tenements among farming families, a sure sign (among other things) of reluctance to invest in land for the long term. On both manors there was one holding which seems to have been in especial difficulties, for precise reasons which the rentals do not tell us: perhaps the land had become especially 'feeble' or 'moorish' (terms used by Duchy officials for similar cases). One, Trebby (St Columb Major), was already empty in 1460, for the compiler of the rental failed to name its occupier; by 1480 there was still no occupier, but the Arundell family had persuaded the whole body of tenants on the manor to pay its rent of 10s. collectively. They may have divided it up among themselves or, more probably, used its fields as common pasture; they may have delapidated it further (as common tenants with little personal interest in it) for by 1499 it is described as 'waste', with the nostalgic words 'used to pay 10s.'[7] The other holding in especial difficulties was at Trenayles (St Ervan). By 1459 it had already reached the degrading stage of being let in common to all the tenants of the manor. Even this arrangement did not work, for the tenants were failing to pay its rent in 1459 and by 1480 it had been absorbed into an adjacent tenement whose tenant paid very little for it.[8] As well as these two farm holdings, the mills of both manors were in difficulties, that of Trembleath being vacant and 'decayed' in 1480, as we have seen, and that of Treloy being rented for only 13s. 4d. in 1480, compared with 20s. in the earlier rental.[9] A decayed mill provides an index of how badly a manor's tenant farmers were faring at arable farming: farmers in difficulties brought less grain to be ground at the manorial mill, payments made to the miller were reduced accordingly and he was unable to pay his full rent to the landlord and unable to maintain the mill.

Rent reductions show that tenants were (or thought they were, or claimed to be) making smaller profits and they therefore reflect depression in farming. Whereas, in the thirteenth century, tenants and would-be tenants were numerous and land scarce, by the fifteenth century the relationship was reversed, with tenants relatively scarce and land relatively abundant; under such circumstances they were able to bargain with landlords and to negotiate lower

---

[7] Below, pp. 31, 69 and 113.
[8] Below, pp. 27 and 75.
[9] Below, pp. 75, 69 and 31.

rents. The results of bargaining are to be read in many Arundell manorial account rolls from the fifteenth century in the section of the account called rent 'defects' (failures). Only two examples need be given here: from an account roll of Treloy manor for 1421–2 where it is recorded that Peter Sherp's holding should render 14s. 3d., 'whereas', laments the reeve, 'it is let to him for 11s. this year'; and from the manor of Carminow (Mawgan in Meneage) in 1476–7 where Richard Jankyn had bargained for a rent reduction from 23s. 6d. to 20s.[10] The results of such bargaining for rent, as they affected particular holdings, may also be seen in the rentals printed in this volume.

Rent reductions reflect tenant farmers in difficulties. But there were also improvements in their position during the fifteenth century, one being the lord's willingness to subsidize repair of his tenants' buildings. A tenant's reluctance to repair buildings shows under-capitalized farming and an unwillingness to invest in the property. A landlord's acceptance of the costs of repair shows a desire to retain or attract tenants and is an especial feature of English agricultural history during years of depression.[11] Thus in 1421–2 the Arundells employed craftsmen to repair the house of John Prynke on Treloy manor, saving him 25s. 4d. on items such as the great timbers and the thatching; in 1489–90 they paid out large sums to the tenants of Trembleath so that they could set about repairing their houses.[12]

A second improvement in the position of tenants during the fifteenth century was in the size of farms. With fewer people competing for land than there were in the early fourteenth century before the Black Death, opportunities existed for the enterprising tenant to enlarge his farmland through engrossing of holdings. Many examples may be drawn from the rentals printed below. Thus from Treloy manor we can see how, in 1460, two tenants each held 'half the vill' of Trethowell (Kea) and how, by 1480, the two holdings there had been engrossed into one, then held by Walter John

---

[10] AR2/46 (reeve's account, Treloy, 1421–2) and AR2/914 (manorial accounts, 1476–7).

[11] Dyer, 'English peasant buildings', pp. 22–3; Fox, 'Occupation of the land', pp. 170–2 for the South-West; Clay, 'Landlords and estate management', p. 226.

[12] AR2/46 (reeve's account, Treloy, 1421–2) and AR2/928, m. 10 (reeve's account, Trembleath, 1489–90).

Jagowe; the one holding persisted into the sixteenth and seventeenth centuries when it was described as 'the whole vill' of Trethowell.[13] On the same manor, at the hamlet of Treloy itself, there were four tenants in 1460, one with a three-sixths share of the whole vill and three each with shares of one-sixth; 20 years later there were only two tenants there, each with half the vill.[14] By careful linkage of holdings recorded in these late medieval rentals to rentals and surveys of the sixteenth and seventeenth centuries it is possible to estimate what gains by enterprising tenants meant in terms of acreage: for example, the two holdings of 20 acres at Trethowell gave way to one of 40 acres between 1460 and 1480; at Treloy in 1460 some of the holdings had been of about 15 acres in size whereas the two which had emerged by 1480 were each of 44 acres.[15] These are only two examples but the figures suggest that on many Arundell manors gains in the size of holdings may have been similar to those on some manors of the estate of the Duchy of Cornwall: a doubling in the average size of holding from 21 to 40 acres on the manor of Tybesta (Creed) between 1337 and 1497 and a rise in average size from 17 to 26 acres on the manor of Helstone in Trigg (Lanteglos by Camelford) over the same period.[16]

A traveller through the Cornish landscape of the late fifteenth century would have seen, on some manors, holdings in various stages of decay as well as farms which were managing to survive. There would have been holdings which were still tenanted but on which under-capitalization showed itself in decaying farmhouses and farm buildings, such as those cases—mentioned above—in which the Arundell family eventually subsidized the tenant by helping with the costs of repair. There would have been farms forsaken by their previous occupier (either through death or forfeiture) which the Arundell family then managed to let out to a syndicate of tenants; we have seen this happening for a time at Trebby and at Trenayles, and there are other examples elsewhere in Cornwall,

---

[13] Below, pp. 31 and 69; AR2/1343 (survey, c.1586) and AR2/1346 (survey, 1618).
[14] Below, pp. 30 and 68.
[15] Based on acreages given in AR2/1343 and AR2/1346.
[16] Fox, 'Tenant farming', p. 724; see also Hatcher, *Duchy of Cornwall*, pp. 226–8.

and also in Devon.[17] Management by a syndicate of tenants, who probably used the farm as a common pasture, was hardly conducive to investment and repair, so this was a dangerous stage in the history of a tenement. If that solution failed, and if no taker presented himself, the farm would fall 'into the lord's hands through lack of tenants' as the account rolls put it. This did not mean complete abandonment of the land: for example, in 1421–2 the reeve of Treloy reported in his financial account that there were several holdings on the manor lying 'waste' without regular tenants but he was able to make a little profit from them by partially selling the 'herbage', that is, by letting them field by field to any tenants who wished to take out a short lease, probably for a matter of months, of some pasture on the cheap.[18]

Many tenements which went through these vicissitudes during the fourteenth and fifteenth centuries did in fact survive as recognizable units into the sixteenth and seventeenth centuries. Others became lost as two or more tenements were amalgamated; in some cases they came to be permanently reckoned as one and are described as *sub una tenura* in the rentals (literally 'under one holding', meaning, from the point of view of the lord who had the documents drawn up, that the rents and other burdens had been amalgamated into one).[19] A tenant with two or more holdings would probably allow one farmhouse to decay and on some estates this was specifically sanctioned by the lord so as not to burden engrossing tenants with the upkeep of too many buildings.[20] Very often engrossing of this kind was internal to the hamlet— in other words, one tenement at a particular hamlet was added to another[21]—and this had important repercussions for settlement patterns. Accompanying the rise in the size of holdings as engrossing took place was a reduction in the number of occupancies. To return to examples already given: at Treloy itself the hamlet decreased in size from having four occupancies in 1460 to having just two in 1480 and at Trethowell two were reduced to one between the same dates. Multiplied many times over, developments such as these wrought significant changes in the pattern of settlement:

---

[17] Fox, 'Occupation of the land', p. 170.
[18] AR2/46 (reeve's account, Treloy, 1421–2).
[19] Below, e.g. pp. 20 and 48; see also p. 10.
[20] Fox, 'Occupation of the land', p. 171.
[21] Hatcher, *Duchy of Cornwall*, pp. 230–1.

some hamlets declined in size and many others were replaced by a single farm. These processes were going on throughout the South-West during the later Middle Ages and are important because they affected the appearance of the landscape in all subsequent centuries down to the present day: there were still two farmsteads at Treloy in the sixteenth and seventeenth centuries and still a single farmstead at Trethowell.[22] They are important, too, because some places became even more isolated, especially where (as so often happened) a single farmstead replaced what had once been a small community of farmers.

Changes taking place in the fourteenth and fifteenth centuries could also lead to loss of settlement from the landscape, in other words to desertion. Basically this could happen in two different ways. The first was when farmsteads were abandoned and the land belonging to them reverted to rough pasture. This is what seeems to have occurred at Trenayles, already mentioned above, in the manor of Trembleath. The place was once an independent farm, as the *Tre-* element in the name suggests. From the middle of the fifteenth century onwards its land was used in a variety of ways but in all cases there is a suggestion of its run-down quality. In 1499 it was rented by John Keiser (perhaps a son of Richard Keiser who farmed nearby Tregwinyo at this time); the rent was a meagre 3s. 4d., which suggests that the farmhouse had already decayed and that the land was unkempt. At some time in the sixteenth century the Arundell family took it in hand, perhaps as rough grazing. At other times the land of Trenayles was used in common; this was the case in 1459 and in the tithe apportionment of the middle of the nineteenth century two very large fields called *Trenyles*, with no associated farmstead, are described as 'common'.[23] Another example of reversion to waste comes from the settlement called Goosehill (in Advent parish), high on Bodmin Moor on the Duchy manor of Helstone in Trigg, which had three messuages in 1337 but in 1498 was recorded as unoccupied pasture.[24]

---

[22] Fox, 'Occupation of the land', pp. 164–7; AR2/1343 and AR2/1346.
[23] Below, pp. 27, 75 and 107; AR2/1343, 'Used to be leased into the lord's hands to his own use'; CRO, St Ervan tithe apportionment. The fields called *Trenyles* are exposed and windswept. Like others on the slopes of Bear's Downs, they have been divided up with remarkably straight hedges, almost certainly an indication of relatively recent enclosure.
[24] *Caption of Seisin*, ed. Hull, pp. 16 and 18; PRO, E306 2/16; Christie and Rose, 'Davidstow Moor', pp. 179–80.

Desertion also occurred where the fields of one place became permanently attached to, and farmed from, another nearby but distinct settlement.[25] The beginnings of the demise of the now lost place called *Nanskerres* (Sithney) may possibly be recorded in a court roll entry of 1521–2 where Thomas Nantrysak was said to have 'encroached certain land at ... Nanskyrwys and brought it into his own land of Nantrysak'.[26] This was an unsanctioned case of the addition of part of one farm to another. More usually attachment involved the sanctioned leasing by one tenant of two or more holdings from the lord. Thus on the manor of Cardinham in 1566, Robert Davy held one tenement at Lower Trezance (now Teason) with 'the house in which he lives' and also a tenement at Benorth on which, the surveyor noted explicitly, there was no dwelling house; Eleanor Mold lived in a farmhouse on her tenement at Benorth while at Higher Cardeast she held another tenement on which, significantly, there was only a sheephouse, possibly the former farmhouse there converted to use for animals.[27] The joining of tenements in this way would of course lead to desertion of settlement only if all farmhouses at a particular spot became uninhabited.

The rentals and surveys printed below, from the fourteenth, fifteenth and sixteenth centuries, contain many references to places which were inhabited when the documents were drawn up but which are now 'lost', that is not named on maps of the nineteenth century and later. The Cornish landscape is not able to boast true deserted villages of the type found in the Midlands of England but it is littered with the remains of abandoned and shrunken farms and hamlets. This point may be illustrated from two directions: from the evidence of the landscape itself as revealed, for example, in the 'rapid identification survey' recently carried out for Stratton Hundred by the Cornwall Archaeological Unit or in the useful parochial checklists published in *Cornish Archaeology*;[28] and from

---

[25] Fox, 'Peasant farmers', pp. 50–1.
[26] Below, p. 147, n. 14; this could refer either to rough pasture or to land already in cultivation.
[27] Below, pp. 178, 184 and 185.
[28] See *Medieval Settlement Research Group Annual Report*, 8 (1993), 45, for a summary, by P. Herring, of the 'rapid identification survey', in which 21 previously unrecorded deserted hamlets were found and 87 shrunken hamlets.

documents such as these rentals and surveys which name places that are no longer inhabited. All of the 'lost' places mentioned in the transcripts which follow need to be investigated in detail by local researchers with the help of other documents in the Arundell collection, perhaps especially the magnificent series of leases. When this has been done we shall probably learn that the process of desertion of farms and settlement sites was a long-drawn-out one extending well into the nineteenth and twentieth centuries.

Resilient tenements

In the previous section we have discussed rents and numbers of tenements on two Arundell manors where the trend was a downward one during the last half of the fifteenth century. It is probably true to say that such a trend was experienced on a majority of English manors during this period, but it was not, however, the experience of them all. On the Arundell estate it is possible to find places which appear to have had economies far more resilient than those of Trembleath and Treloy discussed above. Two manors have been chosen in order to examine that theme, Connerton (Gwithian) in the far west, with tenements on either side of the Hayle estuary, and Bodwannick (Lanivet), with some of its holdings within three miles of the large (by medieval Cornish standards) town of Bodmin and with lands lying between the two medieval stannary districts of Fowymore (Bodmin Moor) and Blackmore. Summary statistics for these two manors, derived in the same way as those for Trembleath and Treloy, are given below.[29]

	Connerton		
	1463	1480	1499
Occupancies	29	29	27
Conventionary rents	£21 1s. 8d.	£20 10s. 0d.	£20 9s. 0d.

	Bodwannick		
	1464	1480	1499
Occupancies	23	23	23
Conventionary rents	£17 14s. 4d.	£17 16s. 4d.	£18 0s. 1d.

---

[29] For an explanation of how the figures were arrived at see earlier in this section (Trembleath and Treloy, pp. ci–cii). The figures exclude tenements which cannot be traced in all three rentals, for example a tenement at Penfentin in Gwithian which occurs only in the 1499 rental for Connerton manor.

On both manors rents held up in a most satisfactory way during the last half of the fifteeenth century. The largest downturn was on Connerton manor between 1463 and 1480, but it was only of 11*s*. 8*d*., the result of reductions of 1*s*. or 2*s*. in the rent of a small number of tenements. Connerton's figure for 1499 is rather deceptive. It is just slightly lower than that for 1480, but the small drop conceals small rent increases for a good number of tenements and one large decrease for the tenement at Vow (St Ives parish) where, for some reason, rent was reduced from 28*s*. to 20*s*. On Bodwannick manor rents in fact show a small upward trend between 1464 and 1499. The second of the three rentals, for 1480, reveals that one tenement was subject to an increase in rent since 1464; the third rental, for 1499, shows modest increases for five tenements. There were no rent reductions on this manor during the last half of the fifteenth century.

We should seek reasons for the contrasting fortunes of Trembleath and Treloy on the one hand, and Connerton and Bodwannick on the other, in contrasts in the profitability of farming. Hatcher was the first to point out that whereas farmers on some manors belonging to the Duchy of Cornwall fared relatively well during the fifteenth century and were able to withstand increases in rent, others were more depressed; he perceptively linked the differences to local contrasts in demand for agricultural produce. He argued that where the size of local populations was swollen by the presence of tinners, cloth workers and other consumers of produce from farms—in regions with what he called 'diversified' economies—then farmers prospered accordingly and landlords were able to increase rents;[30] converse conditions, with relatively limited local markets for farm produce, led to greater difficulties for farmers and, in places, reductions in their rents. Hatcher's arguments may be extended to the Arundell estate, although his tentative conclusion that western Cornwall was relatively depressed during the fifteenth century, and the east relatively prosperous, should perhaps be abandoned; the local economic geography of the county in the Middle Ages was highly complex, so that a simple bipartite division of that kind is unlikely to have existed.

For the manors of Bodwannick and Connerton there are plenty of indications of that economic diversity which was often associ-

---

[30] Hatcher, 'A diversified economy', pp. 224–6.

ated with relatively buoyant farm rents during the later Middle Ages. The rental of 1499 records a blowing-mill on the manor of Bodwannick, and a generation later the parish of Lanivet (in which the manor was situated) recorded over 70 reputed tinners as passing muster there.[31] In Cornwall and in Devon the two industries of tinning and cloth-making were often found together, perhaps because spinning and weaving were occupations practised by tinners' wives or seasonally by the tinners themselves when tin working was impossible or unattractive.[32] And, sure enough, the rental of 1464 records a fulling mill on Bodwannick manor, occupied by John Touker for a yearly payment of 12s. 8d.; Andrew Touker was occupier in the rental of 1499, by which time the payment had been increased to 13s.[33] There is no means of estimating the number of people who were wholly or partly engaged in the probably linked occupations of tinning and cloth-working in the vicinity of the manor, nor of estimating the demand which they exerted for foodstuffs; both may have been considerable, with a correspondingly great effect on the profitability of agriculture and on rents for agricultural land. Nearness to the town of Bodmin must have further enhanced the profitability of farming at Bodwannick. Before the Black Death the town was almost certainly the largest in Cornwall; it was probably smaller in the late fifteenth century, though still the 'chiefest' town in the county, with a plentiful market in the sixteenth century.[34] The population of Bodmin, and buyers coming to its market, cannot have failed to exert demands on the farming population of a manor as close to it as Bodwannick was.

Connerton manor was also well situated in respect to markets. The conventionary tenements of the manor lay in six parishes altogether (Gwithian, Phillack, Gwinear, Crowan, Lelant and St Ives) in all of which lived tinners according to the muster roll of c.1535; indeed, some of the names in the rental of 1499 printed below may be linked to those in the muster roll: thus John Frawen who occupied a tenement at Penpoll (Phillack) is probably the same person (or from the same family) as the John Frawen of the muster

---

[31] Below, p. 116; *Cornwall Military Survey*, ed. Stoate, pp. 177–8.
[32] Fox, 'Medieval rural industry'; a good example of a manor with both industries was Cardinham in the fifteenth century: AR2/446–50.
[33] Below, pp. 58 and 116.
[34] Below, p. 171; Norden, *Cornwall*, p. 50.

roll.[35] The Arundell archive itself contains references to tinning within Connerton: for example, the account roll of the reeve there for 1467–8 records that 7s. 7d. was received from toll of tin 'in diverse moors within the manor this year'.[36] Besides demands for foodstuffs from tinners, the town of St Ives, with a population largely involved in fishing and trading, must have exerted some extra demand; it contained a minimum of 280 people in 1377, by no means in the lowest class of small Cornish towns at that time.[37]

By contrast, the manors of Trembleath and Treloy, where rents were declining during the last half of the fifteenth century, lay in an industrial and urban backwater. They lay outside any of the stannary districts: the cores of the nearest, the stannaries of Tywarnhaile and Blackmore, were 16 and 10 miles away respectively. The whole of the north Cornish coastlands, from Newquay northwards to the county boundary, were something of an economic backwater in the later Middle Ages, with few industries and few towns of any note; and, consequently, the relatively depressed nature of its agricultural base resulted in reduction of lay subsidy payments (in the reassessment of 1446) of over 30 per cent in the case of most parishes and of over 50 per cent in the case of some.[38]

Tenants and inheritance

The inheritance of tenements is another topic which may easily be studied with the help of late medieval rentals and surveys printed in this volume. To what degree were the farms listed in these rentals 'family farms'? How normal was it for a farm to descend from father to son, or was non-hereditary descent dominant? Dr Ros Faith began her pioneering study of these matters with the following passage.

> The idea that land 'ought to descend in the blood of the men who held it of old' is of course common in many peasant societies. One would guess that it was common, although tacitly so, in most English

---

[35] *Cornwall Military Survey*, ed. Stoate, pp. 140–3 and 148–9; *ibid.*, p. 142, and below, p. 135, for John Frawen.
[36] AR2/908, m. 1.
[37] Maclean, 'Poll tax', p. 39; the poll tax figure has been inflated by the very low multiplier of 1.5 in order to take into account unrecorded people.
[38] Pounds, 'Taxation', p. 166.

rural districts at least until the time of the enclosure movement. But there does seem to have been a period in English history—roughly that of the fourteenth and fifteenth centuries—when in many rural communities this fundamental idea was in practice abandoned.[39]

Using the evidence of land transactions in court rolls (from manors in Berkshire and other counties) she discovered that those involving the family were at a very low ebb in the fifteenth century: 13 per cent on one manor, for example, 17 per cent on another. Since she wrote many historians have found the same thing in other parts of England during the fifteenth century: for example in Durham, in Devon, in Huntingdonshire and in the West Midlands.[40] Two basic factors are held responsible for this development. First, given the high mortality in the period many tenants must have died without any son (or son of age) to succeed to the holding. Second, the existence of many vacant tenements encouraged a young man to take up a holding other than the patrimony, instead of waiting until his father died in order to succeed to the family's land. The bond between family and land was therefore broken to be replaced by a new mobility which saw tenements being taken by one family after another, and tenants migrating between tenements. The spiral of non-family succession was an upward one, for each time, say, that a young man took on a non-family holding he set off a succession of similar inheritances: on his father's farm which may then have passed out of the family, and on the farm of the man (unless he was landless) who eventually did move into his father's farm. The vacant holdings created a potential market which an estate agent today would describe as having 'no chains'.

The fifteenth-century rentals printed here, spaced as they are at convenient intervals of about 20 years, offer the enticing possibility of a shorthand method of investigating these topics for the Arundell estate, a method which relies simply on tracing tenements and their occupants between rentals, thus avoiding time-consuming study of land transactions recorded in court rolls. The ease with which a tenement may be traced from one rental to another greatly assists this kind of investigation (tenements are

---

[39] Faith, 'Peasant families', pp. 86–7.
[40] Lomas, 'South-east Durham', pp. 295–301; Fox, 'Tenant farming', pp. 726–9; DeWindt, *Land and People*, pp. 133–5; Dyer, *Lords and Peasants*, pp. 301–5, and 'Size of peasant holdings', pp. 283–6.

classified in the rentals according to the place in which they were situated; distinguishing between two or more tenements at the same place is usually, but not always, rendered possible by differences in rents paid). There are, however, problems. First, if, say, a tenement is held by a John Jago at one date and by a Philip Opy twenty years later, we can say that it has changed hands at least once, though we do not know whether or not there was one, or more than one, intervening tenant. Second, and common to all similar investigations by whatever method, there is the problem of equating name with family.[41] It is unlikely that Philip Opy was the son of John Jago, but he may have been, for example, a nephew. There has been much discussion of this issue, which cannot be completely resolved; all that can be said is that in the situation which we shall find on the Arundell estate—one of remarkably few transfers to sons on conventionary tenements—it would be highly surprising if a reluctance of sons to take over the patrimony existed alongside, say, an attraction by nephews to the holdings of their uncles. Finally there is the problem of the fluidity of bynames: only when they cease to be fluid and become hereditary surnames can an analysis of tenements and families be entirely watertight. Surnames had apparently become very largely hereditary in Devon by the fifteenth century but this does not mean that all surnames in the adjoining county had become entirely fixed by then, for Cornish personal names have their own peculiarities.[42] Study of lay subsidy rolls and other documents indicates that as late as the sixteenth century some Cornish families, when they migrated to a new place, changed their surnames to the name of that place (see also below, p. cxxvii–cxxviii). Users of this volume may wish, by exploiting the indices, to search for examples of this process. One which emerges from study of the families of Treloy manor concerns the occupants of a tenement at Trethowell (Kea), Walter John Jagowe according to the rental of 1480 and John Trethowall in the 1499 rental. These were certainly two different people, for they have different forenames. It seems that a John X (whose name we shall never know unless a chance survival of a record in a court roll tells us) came to Trethowell between 1480 and 1499 and, subsequent to that move, he came to

---

[41] Dyer, 'Families and land', pp. 307–11.
[42] Postles and McKinley, *Surnames of Devon*, pp. 91–2 and 105–6; Padel, 'Cornish surnames in 1327'; compare below, pp. cxxiv–cxxviii.

be called 'Trethowell'. There is probably no firm answer to the question of how common changes of surname were during the period covered by the fifteenth-century rentals printed here, but they were probably not prevalent enough to affect greatly any conclusion about farms and farming families which are drawn from them.

If we turn initially to Trembleath and Treloy, the two manors discussed first in an earlier section of this Introduction, we find hereditary succession on conventionary tenements at such a low ebb as to be virtually non-existent. Out of approximately 30 conventionary tenements, the same family name is found on only two between 1459–60 and 1480: at Treloy itself John Bynny appears in the first rental and John Benny in the second, the latter being either the same person as the former, or (probably) a son; at Crigmurrick (St Merryn) a Robert Coulyng held a tenement at both dates. It was more or less the same between 1480 and 1499: at only three holdings was there continuity of surname, almost certainly indicating hereditary descent, one of these holdings being at Crigmurrick which continued to be held by a Robert Coulyng (possibly the same man as in 1480 or possibly a son with the same forename).[43] The holding at Crigmurrick was therefore the only one out of about thirty which the same family held throughout the last forty years of the fifteenth century. Very interesting is the contrast provided by Connerton and Bodwannick, the other two manors described above in the section on resilient tenements. Combined, the two manors contained about 55 holdings, of which eighteen apparently remained in the same family between 1463–4 and 1480, and sixteen between 1480 and 1499.[44]

Discussion must focus upon two issues, first the very real contrast which existed between the manors and, second, the possible presence of any circumstances peculiarly Cornish to account for the rather low figures for hereditary tenure even at Connerton and Bodwannick, and the very low figures at Trembleath and

---

[43] This may be a special case of the longevity of a family at a particular tenement: Robert Coulyng had inherited it from his mother, and the family was still there in 1543: AR3/32 and AR4/67.

[44] In the manor of Tregarne, the conventionary tenement of Boden Vean remained in the same family over three generations between 1447 and 1499 (below, pp. cxxvi, 23, 80 and 124).

Treloy (matched by others, also very low, from other estates in the county).[45] The contrast between the two sets of manors is very much what is to be expected given their contrasting economies. The sluggish economies of Trembleath and Treloy may have encouraged sons to emigrate, abandoning their fathers' holdings, to look for more attractive opportunities elsewhere; perhaps their places were eventually taken by unrelated incomers (possibly younger sons from other manors, or former tinners), who were first-time farmers, attracted by the depressed farm rents on these manors. Turnover of this kind on holding after holding for generation after generation resulted in the almost complete replacement of names and families on these two manors between 1459–60 and 1499. On the manors of Connerton and Bodwannick, with their relatively buoyant economies, the attitude of sons to their fathers' farms was somewhat different. A significant number remained on their home manor, probably because they saw a fair future there. This meant that in 1499 there were several families which had been on the manor and on the same farms at least since the early 1460s: for example, at the hamlet of Bodwannick itself, two holdings were held by two members of the Broude family in 1464, and by 1499 three of the four holdings there were occupied by that family; the corn mill was held by members of the Briand family throughout the late fifteenth century, and indeed later.[46]

Were there other reasons for the generally weak state of hereditary succession on all of the manors discussed above? Three will be discussed here. First, as has been suggested for other mining regions, the many opportunities which existed in Cornwall at large for sons to accumulate a little capital in tin mining (and related occupations such as turf cutting) no doubt encouraged young men to leave their farms, to save over several years, then to take on farm holdings which were more attractive than their fathers', or which became vacant before their fathers'.[47] Migration to find permanent or seasonal work in the stannaries was a possibility for all Cornishmen. Secondly, a distinctive feature of the land market

---

[45] Fox, 'Tenant farming', p. 727, for the estate of the Duchy of Cornwall; see also Hatcher, *Duchy of Cornwall*, pp. 220–1, for rapid turnover of tenants, although individual tenancies did often exceed 7 years.
[46] Below, p. 57n.
[47] Blanchard, 'Industrial employment', pp. 259–60.

on some Cornish estates seems to have specifically encouraged non-hereditary succession to holdings: this was the 'assession' system developed most fully on the lands of the Duchy of Cornwall, but also present on some other estates. Under this system, all conventionary tenants simultaneously surrendered their holdings at an 'assession' held every seven years, each to be bargained for anew and awarded to the highest bidder, with no concession at all for hereditary descent of tenements. The system was deliberately introduced so that the Duchy could maximize income, at frequent intervals, from tenements which were held by a 'convention' (agreement) between lord and tenant; a sitting tenant could be ousted, at each assession, by 'him as would give most' (in rent and fine) and it was only the occasional, lucky, tenant who was able to remain unchallenged 'because no other man came'. The presence of a manor on which this system was practised must have stimulated the land market of the whole district, encouraging immigration into it at frequent intervals when assessions were held and creating a further flurry of vacancies, or potential vacancies, on the manors from which those immigrants came; even if the system had been restricted to the Duchy estate, it is likely to have caused a good deal of stirring in the Cornish land market generally, for the Duchy manors were well dispersed throughout the county.[48]

Finally, we must consider prevalence of service in husbandry as possibly another reason for low incidence of hereditary tenure. In those parts of the county where service in husbandry dominated—that is, where it was usual for a farm's labour force to be made up of young, living-in servants on yearly contracts drawn from outside the family—this encouraged mobility among young men (so that there was an increased possibility that they might eventually take up farms beyond the horizons of the manors of their birth) and also encouraged the thrift and regular savings which were necessary in order to enter a tenancy. Where, on the other hand, there prevailed the other principal type of rural labour in the Middle Ages—the cottage labourer who hired himself out by the day or week to a variety of masters—a lesser degree of mobility and lesser likelihood of thrift produced a situation in which it was less common for young men to migrate and to be able to take up a

---

[48] For the assession system see Hatcher, *Duchy of Cornwall*, pp. 74–6; Fox, 'Tenant farming', p. 728 and n.

tenement of their own. The subject of farm labour in Cornwall is very much an under-researched one, both for the Middle Ages and for later periods. We do know, however, that in the nineteenth century living-in service in husbandry prevailed and was more deeply rooted there, and in Devon, than in any other county in southern England.[49] This late survival may hint at roots which stretched far back in time. For the Middle Ages, all that we have for the South-West is a study of farm workers in Devon which shows that service in husbandry was very common in those parts of the county which touched upon Cornwall.[50] One small hint from Cornish sources is the absence of large numbers of landless cottage holdings in later medieval rentals and other sources. Only a very small number are recorded in the medieval rentals and post-medieval rentals and surveys of the Arundell estate. On the manors of Lanherne and Trembleath seven cottars are named in the rental of 1343 but these had dwindled in number by the later fifteenth century, 'cottars' never again appearing as a sub-heading in the rentals printed below;[51] it is the same on the Duchy estate where cottars, and cottages, are very rare indeed according to the survey made in 1337.[52] These Cornish documents will appear very strange to readers familiar with rentals and surveys from some other parts of England where cottage holdings were more numerous. An insignificant amount of cottage labour is a sure sign that tenants with sons too young to work on the farm, or those whose sons had left home, or those with farms too large to be worked with family labour, must have looked to servants in husbandry in order to make good the deficit. And, as we have said, service in husbandry is usually associated with high degrees of mobility among young people and the opportunity for savings which might eventually lead to occupancy of a farm away from their home manor.

Whatever the reasons for the high degree of transfers of farms outside the family revealed by the rentals printed below, there can be no doubt that these documents describe a late medieval countryside in which there was relatively little continuity of occupancy

---

[49] Kussmaul, *Servants in Husbandry*, pp. 20 and 131.
[50] Fox, 'Servants, cottagers and tied cottages', pp. 4–9.
[51] Below, pp. 4–5; pp. 33, 66 and 109 for the decline of cottages on the Lanherne manor.
[52] *Caption of Seisin*, ed. Hull.

between one generation and the next and a good deal of mobility as people moved from one manor to another. The idea of unchanging medieval rural societies, full of family continuities with a distant past, should perhaps be abandoned. It is hoped that the rentals printed below, together with the index of names, will enable users of the volume to follow up this suggestion in more detail.

7. OVERALL REVENUES OF THE ESTATE

The existence of three surveys at twenty-year intervals in the second half of the fifteenth century invites analysis of the income provided by their estate for the wealthiest family in late-medieval Cornwall. It must again be stressed that the surveys do not provide the whole story: we have already seen that there were some minor Cornish lands which do not appear in these surveys; even in the manors listed here there were other revenues (shown in the manorial accounts) in addition to the rents, such as profits from the manorial courts and toll of tin; there were probably direct interests in the tinning industry too;[1] and there were also the lands in Devon, Dorset and elsewhere.

Therefore the actual income of the family will have been very different from the estate revenues shown here. Indeed, if John Arundell's alleged yearly income of £2,000 in 1451 is correct, then the rents of the Cornish manors surveyed in 1451–64 provided little more than a tenth of his income;[2] and these amounts are gross income and do not generally include outgoing payments. £200 yearly would have been an average income for a knight in the earlier fifteenth century;[3] so we should expect that of the Arundells to have been considerably higher, if only to have given rise to the legends about this John Arundell and his grandfather, 'the Magnificent'.

What follows is only a preliminary analysis, since too many of the total sums are uncertain. Moreover, these surveys record only what the lords expected to collect in rents; the sums actually received varied from year to year according to the capacity of individual tenants to pay. The table shows that the overall revenues expected were stable, showing a slight rise from 1460 to 1499; only

---

[1] Direct involvement by the Arundells in the tinning industry is seen, for instance, in 1342 (AR1/113) and 1503–05 (AR26/2); the lord's tin-works at *Polgoyth* (St Ewe) and elsewhere are mentioned in 1495 (AR2/348 m. 3).
[2] See above, p. xxv.
[3] Dyer, *Standards of Living*, pp. 27–48 (especially p. 31).

Treloy fell significantly in that period. Within that general picture, however, there were minor differences. Most manors were extremely stable throughout the forty years: Bodwannick (rise of nearly £2), Connerton, Enniscaven, Kennall, Lanhadron (judging by the two figures only), Tregarne and Winnington are notable; probably Mitchell as well, if the full figure for 1463 were available. Those manors which showed a significant rise in our documents were either towns (St Columb and Truro Vean), or those where demesne farming was abandoned (Carminow and Trembleath). In the case of Carminow and Trembleath the rents arising from the demesne lands, about £5 at Carminow in 1499 (p. 127; compare pp. 16 and 85), and £7–8 at Trembleath in both 1480 and 1499 (pp. 75–76 and 107), account for the rises in the expected revenue. The figures at Lanherne are difficult to interpret, because of differences in reckoning between the three surveys; the demesne land seems to have been in hand in 1460 and 1499 (pp. 35 and 110). Apart from this factor all three manors were probably stable throughout the period. At Connerton, too, demesne farming had already been abandoned before the earliest survey in 1463 (p. 46).

There may have been a particular reason (not apparent) for the rise at St Columb; it is anyway striking how much more profitable the town of St Columb was than the town of Mitchell, despite the geographical advantage of the latter. From the lords' point of view, the fact of being located in a tinning area does not seem to have boosted the overall revenues expected in rent on a manor, though it may have affected the rents of individual tenements (see above, p. cxi): the obvious tinning manors were Bodwannick, Connerton, Enniscaven and Lanhadron, and their overall revenues as a group display no difference from the non-tinning manors. Of course, tinning may have affected other revenues of a manor (not visible in these surveys); but it had no obvious effect on the overall rents.

It is hoped that these remarks, cursory though they are, will be of some use as a preliminary analysis of the revenues shown in the surveys.

OVERALL REVENUES   cxxiii

Total revenues from the Arundell manors in the three fifteenth-century surveys.

Manor	1451–63	1480[4]	1499
Bodwannick	£18 10s. 0d.(?)	£19 11s. 6d.	£20 8s. 2d.
Carminow	£15 10s. 10d.	£15 8s. 4d.	£21 15s. 4d.
St Columb	£26 4s. 8d.	£32 18s. 10d.(?)	£38 4s. 8½d.
Connerton	£39 17s. 8d.	£39 12s. 7¼d.	£39 15s. 11d.
Enniscaven	£3 1s. 3d.	£3 1s. 7d.	£3 2s. 3½d.
Kennall	£6 4s. 5½d.	£6 2s. 3½d.	£6 7s. 7½d.
Lanhadron	£18 4s. 7½d.[5]	—	£19 11s. 4½d.
Lanherne	£16 19s. 5d.[6]	£11 18s. 5d.[7]	£24 18s. 11d.
Mitchell	£3 11s. 11½d.[8]	£4 1s. 3½d.	£4 4s. 9½d.
Tregarne	£11 6s. 8½d.	£11 5s. 2½d.	£11 6s. 9½d.
Treloy	£16 12s. 9d.	£14 6s. 6½d.	£14 19s. 6¼d.
Trembleath	£12 10s. 1d.	£20 12s. 6½d.	£24 13s. 4d.
Truro Vean	£0 9s. 0d.[9]	£5 6s. 5d.	£6 19s. 2d.
Winnington	£7 6s. 4½d.(?)	£7 6s. 3½d.	£7 6s. 3½d.
Total	£203 3s. 1½d.(?)[10]	£195 3s. 9¾d.(?)[11]	£243 14s. 5½d.[12]

---

[4] Outgoing payments, given for several manors in this rental, have been ignored, since they do not usually appear in the other two surveys.
[5] Including Rescassa.
[6] Or £23 12s. 9d. including the demesne land, 'in hand'.
[7] Not including demesne land (at end of roll); but even without that, the actual total should be anyway about £5 higher (see p. 66 n.).
[8] Two conventionary tenements, totalling about 9s., are missing.
[9] Not including conventionary tenements, worth about £5.
[10] Plus about £5 9s. for conventionary tenements at Mitchell and Truro Vean.
[11] Plus about £18–19 for Lanhadron if included.
[12] Omitting Perlees (£10 18s. 1d.).

8. SURNAMES IN THE SURVEYS

Space does not allow a full examination of the personal names found in the surveys; but a few salient points should be mentioned here, particularly for those perhaps unfamiliar with Cornish nomenclature at this period. The surnames demonstrate characteristics which have already been noted as typical of late-medieval Cornish naming, and also two features which have not been remarked upon before. The features which have been observed elsewhere are two forms of fluidity in surnames, first the use of the father's christian name as a surname (e.g. Ralph John, son of John Thomas, in *c.*1510–20, p. 148n.), and second the fresh adoption of place-names as surnames (e.g. Pascoe Kerne, p. 199, also called Pascoe Kerne of Tresylian, p. 229, and Pascoe Tresylyan, p. 209, all in 1571–75).[1] Further instances of both of these characteristics will be examined below. Of the two further distinctive features which have not been noticed before, the first is the lack of descriptive ('nickname') surnames, and the comparative lack of occupational ones. The vast majority of surnames in this volume, probably well over 90 per cent, are either local ones (derived either from a place-name, or from a description of a person's residence) or familial (derived from a father's or ancestor's christian name). The second feature is the frequency of three-part names, of various kinds: names such as John Tomme Harry and John Petit Predannek abound, causing obvious problems of indexing.

All of these four aspects deserve examination. One or two questions of definition must first be dealt with. 'Surname' is used here in the sense of 'the distinguishing name (or names) following the christian name' (some scholars prefer the term 'byname'); when such a surname persists over three or more generations in one family it becomes an 'inherited surname'. Much effort has been expended on the question, 'When did surnames become hereditary?' Postles and McKinley have provided a welcome recent discussion

---

[1] Padel, 'Cornish surnames in 1327', and 'From place-name to surname in Cornwall'.

for the adjacent county of Devon.[2] Basically the answer is that it depends partly upon the social level: many Norman lords already brought inherited surnames with them when they arrived in 1066, but at the lower levels of society it was not until the fourteenth century that hereditary surnames became widespread in much of England. However, in Cornwall, as we shall see, it was common even in the sixteenth century for surnames to be fluid, and this at more than one level of society.

Patronymic surnames

First, the use of a father's christian name as a surname. Examination of the index will show examples of this. Jeffrey Browne and his son James held a tenement at Riviere (Phillack) in 1549; and the same tenement was held by James Jeffrey 'son of Jeffrey Browne' in 1563 (below, pp. 159 and 169). In 1509 John Thomas held a tenement at Pengwedna (Breage); a slightly later rental (after 1516) gives the holders as John Thomas, his wife Mabel, and their children Thomas John, William John, Ralph John and Alice John (p. 148 and n.). Further east, though still in the western half of Cornwall, we find John Roberd, and his sons Henry John and Richard John, holding a tenement at Trebelzue (St Columb Minor) in 1549. All of these examples provide ample evidence that surnames were not fully hereditary, and that people might take a surname from the father's christian name, as late as the middle of the sixteenth century in western Cornwall.

Taken on their own, the examples portray a situation very similar to that found in Wales at the same period, and very different from that of most of England.[3] However, there are also plenty of counter-examples, even within the category of patronymic surnames, contrasting with the examples just cited. 'Thomasine John daughter of James John' occurs on the same manor as James Jeffrey son of Jeffrey Browne, again in 1563 (p. 169); and in 1549 there were Alan John and his son Thomas John (p. 159). Although they are not easy to show, examples such as these were probably

---

[2] McKinley, 'Evolution of hereditary surnames in Devon', in Postles, *Surnames of Devon*, pp. 81–107.
[3] Morgan, 'Rise of hereditary Welsh surnames'.

common in the fifteenth century too, even in the far west of the county.

At the intermediate stage, a family connection is demonstrable between William Tomperowe, otherwise William Toma Berowe, holding land at Boden Vean (St Anthony in Meneage) in 1460 and 1480 (pp. 23 and 80), and John Will Perow, holding the same tenement in 1499 (p. 124); that William was John's father is shown by John's appearance ten years earlier, as reeve of the manor, under the name John William Tomma Perow.[4] His grandfather was presumably the Thomas Perowe who died in 1447, also holding land at Boden Vean.[5] We thus have Thomas Perowe (died 1447), his son William Tomperow (living 1460 and 1480), and his son John Will Perow, or John William Tomma Perow (living 1489–99). The name under which John was referred to in 1499, John Will Perow, used his father's christian name as his own middle name, followed by the inherited surname Perow or Berowe; his name in 1489, John William Tomma Perow, used both the father's and then the grandfather's christian names as middle names, again followed by the inherited surname. This case belongs in the category of three-part names, to be discussed later; but it is significant here as showing christian names being used as meaningful patronymics, combined with an inherited surname as well.

At the present level of knowledge it is impossible to ascertain how the pattern was determined in a given case: we cannot predict whether a John, son of Alan Thomas, would have been called John Thomas or John Alan. All we can do is note the currency of the two patterns. Prys Morgan has pointed out that in Wales a similar fluidity of surnames was firmly established at the same period and later (sixteenth and seventeenth centuries). This fluidity gradually gave way to inherited surnames, but it happened at a period when the stock of christian names was an extremely limited one, resulting in the proverbially limited range of Welsh surnames today.[6] It looks as though the situation with regard to patronymics in Cornwall was similar in the fifteenth and sixteenth centuries to that

---

[4] Reeve's acount for Tregarne manor, 1388–89, AR2/926, m. 3.
[5] Court roll of Tregarne manor, 8 May 1447 (AR2/380, m. 2); William Toma Perowe was mentioned as the tenant at Boden Vean nine months later, on 19 February 1448 (*ibid.*, m. 3).
[6] Morgan, 'Rise of hereditary Welsh surnames'.

in Wales, though with much more of the inherited usage as well, as in most of England. (However, an equivalent of the Welsh patronymic connective *ap* or *map* is never found in Cornwall.)[7]

Toponymic surnames

The second type of fluidity, already known, is the adoption of fresh toponymic surnames by persons changing residence in our period. Examples are again plentiful in the surveys; one has been noted above, in the context of the high turnover of tenancies (Walter John Jagowe in 1480 replaced by John Trethowall in 1499 at Trethowell, in Kea: pp. cxv–cxvi, 69 and 113). In many cases below, a conventionary tenant bears the name of his tenement as a surname, such as (in 1499) Henry Pennans at Pennance Vean (Gwithian) and William Nans at Nance (Lelant) (pp. 135–36), Ralph Cleise at Clies (Mawgan in Meneage), Richard Trispreson at Tresprison (Mullion), and James Tolle at Toll (Gunwalloe) (pp. 126 and 128–29). The historical evidence concerning the general shortness of tenures at this period, discussed above, suggests that it was often these men themselves, rather than their fathers, who had received those surnames, and perhaps after comparatively brief residence at the places.

Once again, counter-examples can readily be produced. Richard Beauripper, holding land at Chyvarloe (Gunwalloe) in 1480, probably took his surname from Berepper, in the same parish; yet the tenement at Berepper was held by Laurence James in 1480 (p. 84). John Bossosowe, holding land at Penfentin (Gwithian) in 1499 (p. 134), was probably named from the farm of Bejawsa or Bejosah, in the neighbouring parish of Camborne and in a different manor. Frequent as these counter-examples are, however, the numbers of people bearing the names of their tenements as surnames, in a society where great mobility can be demonstrated, is too great to be explicable other than by the fresh adoption of place-name surnames at our period.

---

[7] There is a single instance in the south-west, the curiously English-sounding *Ælfric map Happes*, witness to a manumission in Exeter in c.1090: *The Leofric Missal*, edited by F. E. Warren (Oxford, 1883), p. 1a; for the date, N. E. Ker, *Catalogue of Manuscripts Containing Anglo-Saxon* (Oxford, 1957), pp. 378–79, and D. A. E. Pelteret, *Slavery in Early Mediaeval England* (Woodbridge, 1995), p. 141. Thanks are due to Dr David Thornton for his kindness in pointing out this individual.

This fluidity has already been noted, on other evidence, in the fourteenth century;[8] the evidence here is that it was still the case in the fifteenth century, and in mid-Cornwall. We have already seen that Pascoe Kerne (p. 199), also called Pascoe Kerne of Tresylian (p. 229), is also found as Pascoe Tresylyan (p. 209), all in 1571–75; the likelihood is that Kerne was his inherited surname, but in residing at Tresillian (Newlyn East), he had adopted the name of his residence as an alternative surname, which was sometimes used on its own. Pascoe was by no means low down the social scale. His son John rose from calling himself 'merchant' in 1573 to 'gentleman' in 1579; he was still calling himself John Kerne alias Tresylian at the later date.[9] John Cheverton alias Boessywen, holding a free tenement at Bejowan (St Columb Minor), is another obvious example of the same phenomenon (p. 164).

Once again one cannot, at the moment, account for such fluidity, nor predict the circumstances under which it occurred; but a fondness for having as a surname the name of one's residence is apparent.[10] Normally, of course, people's surnames were bestowed by others; but here we seem to see attempts by people to influence their own surnames. This fondness may have been especially strong among the rising yeoman class. From other material, Henderson has shown how a Thomas family, which moved in 1585 to Carnsew in Mabe parish, adopted the surname Carnsew, first as an alias, later (1641) as their sole surname, retained even though they had by then moved to the neighbouring parish of Budock; and that the family which owned Carveth, in the same parish, adopted the surname Carveth during the sixteenth century.[11] The great Cornish family of Trelawny provides a tempting example of a different kind. The family surname came from the modest farm of Trelawny, in Altarnun parish; but in the late sixteenth century they acquired the manor of Trelawne (in Pelynt). It is interesting to wonder whether the similarity of the place-name to their existing surname formed part of the motivation for the acquisition.[12]

---

[8] Padel, 'Cornish surnames in 1327'.
[9] AR14/6–7, leases to him of the toll of tin in certain duchy manors.
[10] Already suggested by Padel, 'Place-name to surname in Cornwall'.
[11] Henderson, *Mabe*, pp. 32–33; for the Carnsew family in Budock in 1641 and 1660–64 see *Cornwall Protestation Returns*, ed. Stoate, p. 4, and *Cornwall Hearth and Poll Taxes*, ed. Stoate, pp. 130 and 186.
[12] Padel, 'Place-name to surname in Cornwall'.

Other types of surname

The third distinctive feature shown by the material is the comparative lack of descriptive ('nickname') and occupational surnames. All over the western world, surnames can be broadly classified into four types: local (from place-names or descriptions of residence), familial (patronymics and the like), occupational, and descriptive ('nicknames').[13] Even though the classification cannot be rigidly applied, it serves well for an initial examination. In our material the overall figures, all very approximate, for the different types are (out of a total of approximately 795 different surnames): local 362, familial 149, descriptive 89, and occupational 60.[14] However, these figures are highly misleading, for a glance at the Index of Personal Names will show that many surnames have only a single bearer, or very few, while many others have a large number. The occupational and descriptive ('nickname') surnames tend to have very few bearers, and so have many of the numerous local ones; while most of the familial surnames, such as John, Thomas or William and their derivatives, have large numbers. If a count could be made of individuals, rather than names, the preponderance of local and familial surnames over occupational and descriptive ones would be far greater.

This imbalance is especially disappointing, since occupational and descriptive surnames are those where Cornish-language surnames have the opportunity to appear. The Arundell estate in the fifteenth century was almost all situated west of Bodmin, and it included several manors in the far west, so Cornish would have been widely spoken in most of their manors at that period; yet the number of Cornish-language surnames (apart from place-names) appearing in the following pages is limited. It is gratifying to see that all three men surnamed *Melender* or *Melynder* 'miller' actually occupied mills (pp. 21, 23 and 84), emphasizing again that surnames at this date meant what they said, and were not inherited meaninglessly; and it is striking that there are three instances of this name, but only

---

[13] Reaney and Wilson, *Dictionary of English Surnames*, pp. xiv–xlv.
[14] These figures include all names from both the fifteenth- and the sixteenth-century material printed below. About 135 surnames cannot be counted, because their origin is either multiple, such as *Hogge* (either a pet-form of *Roger*, so familial, or *hog* 'pig', so a nickname), or obscure.

one of *Miller*. The low proportion of occupational surnames applied throughout west Cornwall, not only within the Cornish-speaking community. Other notable occupational surnames in Cornish include *Gweader* 'weaver' (equivalent to Latin *Textor* and English *Webbe* 'weaver'); *Trehar* 'taylor' (equivalent to Latin *Cissor* and English *Tailor*, etc.; once again the Cornish is rather commoner than the English);[15] and the various forms of *gof* 'smith', *Goff*, *Gooff*, *Goef* and *Engooff* (equivalent to Latin *Faber* and English *Smyth*; probably also *Ingowe* and *Angowgh*, since these are unlikely to be Cornish *cogh* 'red'). *Marrek* (p. 55) is likely to be a translation of *Knyght* (p. 37), though there is probably no connection between the two individuals named; but it is unclear in what sense this could count as an occupational name.

These examples show that Cornish-language surnames could enter into the record: Cornish names were not being translated into Latin or English, nor ignored. Indeed, their greater frequency over their English equivalents is itself telling, albeit on a very small scale; it emphasizes the west-Cornish nature of the Arundell estate. Cornish would have been the dominant language (though evidently not the only one) on most of the Arundell manors in the fifteenth century, with the exceptions of Bodbrane, probably Bodwannick and Perlees, and maybe Truro Vean. Among the English-language occupational surnames it is again striking to find the only three instances of *Touker* referring to the occupants of the fulling-mill on Bodwannick manor (pp. 58, 98 and 116); and perhaps significant that, on this manor close to Bodmin town, the name is in English: the Cornish equivalent *Troghyer does not occur in these surveys.[16] Other occupational surnames occurring only in English include *Carter*, *Sadler*, *Skynner* and *Tanner*; as one might expect, these occur mainly in the towns in the fifteenth century, serving to strengthen the long-held impression that, in western Cornwall,

---

[15] The equivalence between the two is nicely shown by comparing John Androwe *Treghar*, the second conventionary tenant at Tregona (Trembleath manor) in 1459 (p. 26), with Thomas Androwe *Taylour*, the second tenant at Tregona in the undated section of the same survey (p. 54).

[16] It occurs, in the forms *Trockear*, *Trokyer*, and the like, in Penwith and Kerrier hundreds in the Subsidy of 1524: *Cornwall Subsidies*, ed. Stoate, pp. 2, 39, etc.

towns such as Mitchell and St Columb were more English-speaking than the surrounding countryside.

Descriptive or 'nickname' surnames are similarly scarce. Among the few which do appear are the charming John *Pengwyn* 'whitehead' (p. 104), the well-attested *Scovarn* or *Scovern* 'ear' ('big-eared'?), *Byan* or *Vyan* 'little', *Hire* or *Enhere* 'tall', and the surprisingly rare *Seys* 'Englishman' (p. 10 only); *Du* 'black' does not appear at all. One interesting name is that of Simon *Kentrevek* 'the neighbour' (pp. 15, 19 and 84); its significance is unclear. The scarcity of this descriptive type reflects the similar situation seen in Cornwall, much earlier, in the Lay Subsidy of 1327; while descriptive surnames are somewhat commoner there (five examples of *Seys*, and several of *Du*), the overall pattern is much the same, with a great dearth of surnames from this category and the occupational one.[17] The dearth is equally true among the English-language surnames in our documents; about the only example of the picturesque phrasal type, common in most of England, is *Sherdewyne* 'shear-the-wind' ('swift'), found distinctively in St Columb Major from 1456 to 1499.[18] This imbalance of the different types of surname must reflect an actual state of affairs in western Cornwall in the late Middle Ages: the overwhelming majority of people bore surnames consisting of either patronyms or place-names.

Two-part surnames

The final type of name to be examined is the characteristic three-part names, consisting of a christian name plus two-part surname. Although these form a distinctive category among the surnames appearing below, they actually belong to several different kinds when analysed. We have already examined the example of William Tomperowe and his son, John Will Perow; in their case the two-part surname consists of a patronymic plus an inherited surname (probably also a patronymic in origin; perhaps a derivative of Peter). However, in other cases, such as John Petit Predannek, it was the

---

[17] Padel, 'Cornish surnames in 1327'.
[18] In 1456, AR2/902, m. 7 (account roll); 1458, AR1/177 (deed); for the surname, Reaney and Wilson, *Dictionary of English Surnames*, p. 405. A thirteenth-century example in Somerset appears in another deed, AR1/718.

middle part which was an inherited surname, while the final part was a place-name. Clearly there are various types of these names, which need to be distinguished from one another.

The commonest type of two-part surname, by some margin, is that where both parts are derived from christian names; examples such as John Toma Davy, Roger Jakluky, Randolph Hicke Edward (*Hick* being a derivative of *Richard*), Richard Tom Rawlyn (*Rawlyn* being from *Ralph*), and numerous others can be found in the Index.[19] In such cases the natural assumption is that the two parts of the surname give the father's and grandfather's christian names (John Toma Davy = John, son of Thomas, son of David, and so on); however, the example of John Will Perow, whose grandfather turns out to have been called Thomas Perowe, cautions us against assuming this too readily. Nevertheless, it is very likely that, in many instances, names of this type do give us the father's and grandfather's christian names, necessary in a society where the stock of christian names was very limited, and where many people were distinguished only by patronymics: men such as John Toma Davy and John Tomme Harry shared both their own and their father's christian names, so they could be distinguished from one another by their grandfathers' christian names. Only detailed work in the court rolls, where available, might be capable of proving this in any given case.

What is particularly interesting about these names is that their appearance is restricted in chronology, geography and the type of document where they occur. They are absent from the Lay Subsidy of 1327; rather than indicating that such names were not in use at that date, that absence may be due to the comparatively formal nature of the source. In deeds and leases they occur, but not very frequently. One example is John Jakherry, named in a lease of lands in Trembleath manor in 1480 (compare him on p. 76, below); but it is notable that one his companions in the lease, named there as John Norton, appears in the rental as John Harry Norton, with a middle patronymic (p. 76).[20] This may indicate the different levels of formality of the lease (a document with legal import and status) and the rental (a private administrative document within the manor). Oto John Symon and Nicholas John Symon, brothers,

---

[19] It is notable that in such names the middle one, in particular, and often the final one as well, are normally pet-forms.
[20] AR4/185 (Trembleath, 1480).

appear in a lease of various lands in Truro Vean of 1498, reciting an earlier lease to their father John Symon in 1481. (These two brothers must be the same as Oto Norton and Nicholas Symon holding the same lands a year later, in 1499: below, pp. 120–1).[21] It may be that this type of two-part surname, which has a colloquial feel, was not generally felt suitable for use in more formal documents of this kind; it is also possible that the type was particularly current lower down the social scale, though it certainly was not restricted to that range. (The Symon brothers, judging from their holdings in Truro Vean, were quite significant tenants within the manor.)

The surnames composed of two christian names occur with reasonable frequency in the sixteenth-century subsidies, in contrast with that of 1327. The contrast may be due to the later subsidies reaching farther down the social scale than that of 1327; but an alternative or additional explanation could be that the increase in literacy by the 1520s caused a decrease of formality in the later documents. However, in these later subsidies this type of surname is present only in the western half of the county: instances appear in all four western hundreds, but they are virtually, if not entirely, absent from the eastern ones. For example, in Penwith, we find John Thomas William (Ludgvan, 1524) and William Jack Stephyn (St Hilary, 1524);[22] in Kerrier, John William Richard (Penryn, 1524) and Werin John Stephin (Constantine, 1543);[23] in Powder, John Jak Pascowe (St Just in Roseland, 1525) and Oto Tom Harry (Truro, 1543);[24] in Pyder, Ralph John Davy (Cubert, 1543) and Tebat Jac William (St Columb Major, 1543).[25] The corresponding absence of this type from the five eastern hundreds in the same sources is striking.

This geographical range is borne out by the court rolls. These surnames are very well represented in all the Arundell court rolls of the fifteenth century, but the manors are all in the western half of the county.[26] By contrast, they appear to be absent from the

---

[21] AR4/1043 (Truro Vean, 1498).
[22] *Cornwall Subsidies*, ed. Stoate, pp. 16–17.
[23] *Cornwall Subsidies*, ed. Stoate, pp. 24 and 28.
[24] *Cornwall Subsidies*, ed. Stoate, pp. 55 and 57.
[25] *Cornwall Subsidies*, ed. Stoate, pp. 76 and 82.
[26] Unfortunately the court rolls of the only east-Cornish Arundell manor, Bodbrane, do not commence until 1519–20 (AR2/320).

court rolls of the manor of Cardinham, in east Cornwall, and of the borough of Fowey, technically in west Cornwall but at the easternmost border and, as a town and port, probably more anglicized than other areas of west Cornwall.[27] Although such names may yet be found in east Cornwall, it seems quite possible that this type of three-part name, specifically where the middle name is the father's christian name, and especially where both parts of the surname are derived from christian names, is distinctive of areas where the Cornish language was still spoken at our period. If further work proves this to be so, the presence or absence of the type may turn out to be a useful indication of the strength of Cornish-speaking in a given area in the fifteenth and sixteenth centuries.

Two four-part names remain to be considered. The exceptional case of Richard Jankyn Wylkyn de Seynt Irven, a tenant at Trembleath (St Ervan) in c.1463–64 (p. 54), remains unexplained. He is clearly the man known earlier (1459) as Richard Jankyn Wilkyn (p. 26), and probably the one known later as Richard Seynterven or Synt Ervyn in 1480 and 1499 (pp. 76 and 107). As Richard Jankyn Wylkyn he fits into the pattern examined above, but he seems also to have had a local surname (hereditary?) of his parish of residence; hence his simpler name in 1480 and 1499. The decision how to refer to him was presumably that of the individual scribe. Moreover, either the family surname was a well-established one, or St Ervan parish was particularly prone to spawning toponymic surnames, for men with the same surname occur on the manor at other dates: Thomas Harry Seynt Erven in 1446 (not obviously related to Richard Jankyn Wylkyn), and John Seynyrvan in 1537; also (probably the same as the last) John Synt Irvan, living in the parish of St Ervan in 1543.[28] The other instance does not occur in the surveys, but John Will Perow (in 1499, p. 124) was called John William Tomma Perow in 1489 (see above, p. cxxvi), having his grandfather's as well as his father's christian name before (seemingly) an inherited surname. Even these fine four-part names (incorporating three-part surnames) cannot compete with an

---

[27] Court rolls of Fowey, 1416–1540, ART2/1; court rolls of Cardinham, AR2/447, m. 4 (1476–77), AR2/449, m. 4 (1482–83), and AR2/450, mm. 8–9 (1496–97); but it has not been possible to do exhaustive searches of these rolls.

[28] AR2/50, m. 1 (court roll of Trembleath, 1446); AR2/81 (court roll, 1537); *Cornwall Subsidies*, ed. Stoate, p. 83 (St Ervan parish, 1543).

individual in north-east Wales in the fourteenth century, who was referred to in a court roll as Gwilym ab Einion Vaghan Tasker de Harwold, making him the proud possessor of one of each type of surname, with a patronymic (*ab Einion*), an epithet (*Vaghan* 'little'), an occupational surname (*Tasker* 'one who performs piece-work') and a local name (*de Harwold*, from Harrold in Bedfordshire).[29]

The second-commonest type of two-part surname is that where the final part was a place-name. Here the final part served various functions. In some cases it clearly served as a distinuishing marker between people with the same surname: the most obvious example is the various John Arundells (de Lanherne, de Treres, de Talvern, etc.). These place-names may have been felt to be additional surnames, virtually hereditary, denoting the branch of the family to which a person belonged. However, this is less evidently true in some other cases, such as John Petit Predannek (pp. 28, 111; his family had been established at Predannack Wartha for over 200 years),[30] Thomas Keligrew de Arwennak (p. 123), and Richard Botreaux de Coisvogherth (p. 87; presumably of Coswarth, in Colan, where the Botreaux family had held land since at least 1327). In these cases the third part seems rather to have been used simply as an honorary suffix to indicate the family's residence, or to show that the person mentioned was of the family's chief line— just the kind of usage which perhaps gave rise to the feeling that it was proper to reside at the place indicated by one's surname.

However, this explanation will not work for cases such as John Henry Carthu (p. 165), Thomas Henry Trevethek (p. 136), John Jak Wone (p. 80), for the men in question do not seem to have been resident at the places denoted. In these cases the two-part surname seems to consist of a hereditary toponymic surname, supplemented

---

[29] Court roll of Dyffryn Clwyd lordship, court of Llannerch commote, 30 April 1360 (PRO, SC2/218/8, m. 21d.). For *Tasker*, see Reaney and Wilson, *Dictionary of English Surnames*, p. 440; for *Harwold* = Harrold, see A. Mawer and F. M. Stenton, *The Place-Names of Bedfordshire and Huntingdonshire*, English Place-Name Society, 2 (1926), p. 32; and for the link between Dyffryn Clwyd and Bedfordshire, see Padel, 'Locational surnames in fourteenth-century Denbighshire', pp. 290 and 297. Thanks are due to Dr Andrew Barrell for his kindness in drawing this individual to our attention.

[30] e.g. in 1289, *Cornwall Feet of Fines*, I, no. 330.

by a transient patronymic one ('John, son of Henry, Carthu', and the like). The situation is somewhat similar in the case of John Dauy Mena, holding a free tenement at Mennawartha (manor of Enniscaven) in 1499 (p. 137), for he actually held the place from which his surname came. He seems likely to be the same man as John Mena, holding the same tenement in 1456 and 1480; so here again the middle section is presumably the father's christian name, serving as an optional patronymic; John's 'real' surname was derived from his residence. So where the third part is a place-name, in some cases (such as John Petit Predannek and John Arundell Trerys) the second element can be seen as the 'real' surname, and the third a distinguishing or honorific addition; while in others the third is the 'real' surname, and the middle one an optional patronymic.

The great majority of two-part surnames contain either a patronymic or a place-name as the final element. However, both other categories are represented in this position, albeit in very small numbers. There are four instances of occupational names: John Androwe *Treghar* and Thomas Androwe *Taylour* have already been noted (pp. 26 and 54). The two men were probably related (either brothers or father and son); and they are very likely to have plied the trade indicated by their second surname. David *Cryer Melender* (manor of Tregarne, p. 23) had two occupational surnames. It is very unlikely that he actually practiced both occupations, though not impossible (*crier* could mean 'announcer in court', for instance); but more likely linguistically that the first was an inherited surname, while the second was certainly his occupation.[31] John Perowe *Sergeaunt* (p. 47, Connerton manor, 1463) seems to be different again; here the third part may be occupational (either 'servant' or 'summoner to the court'), or descriptive ('free tenant holding by petty serjeanty')—if the latter, then here it was necessarily hereditary, since he was a conventionary tenant.[32]

Finally there is one, and only one, case of the descriptive *Vyan* 'little' added as a third element: John Wolcok Vyan (p. 38); this would seem such a natural way to distinguish (say) a father and son of the same name, that it is surprising it is not commoner. Even this man was referred to simply as John Wolcock twenty years

---

[31] Reaney and Wilson, *Dictionary of English Surnames*, pp. 116–17, *s.v.* Crier, Cryer.
[32] Note another John Perowe in the same manor and parish (p. 47), or the same man held two tenements.

later, in 1480 (p. 71).[33] Overall, therefore, the relative numbers of the four categories of surname in final position within two-part surnames closely reflect the relative numbers of those categories in surnames generally within the material, with patronymics much the commonest, place-names well represented, and occupational and descriptive names very much rarer.

The interest of the three-part names, particularly those where the surname is composed of two christian names or their derivatives, emerges from a study of manorial surveys and court rolls. Although the type is present in the sixteenth-century subsidies, its importance and distribution have not been observed before. The absence of the type from the Lay Subsidy of 1327 has also hindered the appreciation of its significance. It is likely that, as with other studies of medieval surnames, the sources used have a major effect upon the data obtained. This is partly because of the ways in which the different records were drawn up. Manorial sources, especially court rolls but also surveys such as are printed here, seem to be the richest in the variety of usage that they show, partly because they are the most likely to show the local usage within the community, and partly because they make it possible to observe individuals and their families over periods of time. Subsidies, on the other hand, although they offer consistent coverage over large areas, in a manner which manorial records cannot provide, do not offer the same close reflection and depth of local usage.[34]

---

[33] In the case of John Cleys Mottry and Martin Hicke Gelda (pp. 14 and 90), the third elements are obscure.

[34] Compare Padel, 'Locational surnames in fourteenth-century Denbighshire', p. 283.

9. EDITORIAL CONVENTIONS

The documents printed here are all written in Latin, except for the surveys of the earl of Oxford's manors in 1563 (pp. 167–72) and parts of the surveys of 1566 and 1575 (pp. 173–97 and 208–34). They have been summarized rather than translated, since the repetitive and formulaic contents do not merit printing in full. However, phrases of doubtful reading or meaning, or ones of historical interest, have been printed in full, in italics within round brackets. Names of places, and surnames of people, have been printed as they appear in the manuscript (though with some obvious abbreviations expanded); christian names have been translated into their modern equivalents, but with the manuscript reading given (again in italics within round brackets) in cases of doubt. Similarly in headings of sections within a given survey, everything printed in the text appears in the manuscript, unless it is within square brackets; thus, on p. 13, the heading **Carmynowe** is as in the manuscript. Likewise sub-headings, printed for distinctness' sake in italics within the text, are translations of manuscript headings, unless they appear within square brackets.

Words which are absent from the manuscript for some reason (usually decay or scribal omission), but which can be supplied with confidence, are printed within square brackets, in roman type as being part of the text. All editorial comment also appears within square brackets, but in italics. This includes identifications of place-name forms, with their parishes. It is hoped that this will serve adequately to distinguish, within the text itself, editorial comment and modern spellings from the all-important manuscript readings.

In the footnotes, introduction and indexes, place-name forms cited from manuscripts are cited in italics; but personal names receive the same treatment as in the text, namely modernization of the christian names and retention of the spelling of surnames. Thus on p. 1, note 3, the names of John Dauney and John de Arundel (in roman type), and also the place-names printed in italics, are as taken from the printed Calendar of Inquisitions Post Mortem.

For indexing policies see the introductions to the indexes; for abbreviations and references see pp. cxlviii–cliv, below.

ACKNOWLEDGEMENTS

Our first thanks go to the keepers of the documents printed here, for the opportunities to consult them and permission to print them. Chiefly this means Christine North, Cornwall County Archivist, and Cornwall County Council, which now owns the Lanherne archive in the care of Cornwall Record Office. The archive was purchased by the County Council with the help of a major grant from the National Heritage Memorial Fund. To Christine North's kindness we owe our use, not only of all the documents printed here except for those on pp. 61–63 and 167–97, but also of many others cited from the archive. Crown copyright material in the Public Record Office (SP12/31, no. 30) is reproduced by permission of the Controller of Her Majesty's Stationery Office (pp. 167–72). Parts of the Dinham Survey are reproduced by kind permission of John Draisey and Devon Record Office (pp. 173–97); and the rental of Mitchell in 1463 by kind permission of Lord Bledisloe, through David Smith and Gloucestershire Record Office (pp. 61–63); David Smith also gave helpful assistance over consulting this manuscript. Angela Broome of the Royal Institution of Cornwall helpfully made the Arundell surveys of 1659 and 1717 available for our use.

One of us was privileged to work on the Arundell archive while it was still at Wardour, and is happy to thank Lord Talbot for his accommodation and hospitality. The other was fortunate to have occasion to catalogue part of the Lanherne archive for Cornwall Record Office, with the help of a grant from the Leverhulme Trust to the Cornwall Heritage Trust, and our thanks are gladly given to those charitable bodies. A generous gift by the late Dr A. L. Rowse to the Devon and Cornwall Record Society has made it possible to publish a volume which otherwise would have overstretched the Society's yearly resources. We also give our thanks to people who have discussed aspects of the work with us, notably Dr Brian Golding, Dr Isobel Harvey, Peter Herring, Dr Mari Jones, Professor Richard Hoyle, Dr Joanna Mattingly, Professor Nicholas Orme, Dr David Postles, and David Thomas of Cornwall Record Office. Kenneth Smith, who designed and drew the maps, and Dr Michael Thompson, both Honorary Visiting Fellows at the Department of English Local History, University of Leicester, helped in many

cxxxix

practical and other ways; John Heathcote Ball and Dr Phillip Lindley, both of Leicester, identified the artist of the watercolour used on the cover. Margaret Bunt typed parts of the text preparatory to typesetting; Colin Bakké typeset the Introduction and indexes and parts of the text, and Mrs Pauline Whitmore provided much practical help. Margery Rowe generously and efficiently saved us from difficulty by seeing the volume through the press.

Our greatest practical debt is to Dr Alan James, who diligently and painstakingly compiled the indexes of place-names and personal names. A glance at these will show how much thoughtful work has gone into them; since a volume such as this is used largely through its indexes, all readers will share our gratitude to him.

Although both editors are happy to take joint responsibility for all of the Introduction, it may be helpful for them to admit that H.F. is chiefly responsible for sections 5 and 6, on the Cornish landscape and on tenements and tenants, while O.J.P. is chiefly responsible for sections 1–4 and 8, on the family and the growth of the estate, the documents, the manorial system in Cornwall, and the surnames.

APPENDIX:
THE DATING OF AR2/1339 [1480]

The entry for the first manor in this roll was dated by day, month and year (presumably regnal). Entries for subsequent manors are dated, first as 'the same day', later by successive days (6–13) in September, 'of the same year'. Thus the year was given only once in the roll, and that is now lost through decay. An approximate date is provided by the watermark, which is similar to one in another document dated to 1469.[1] Internal evidence agrees with this approximate date. Within the roll a few charters are cited, of which the latest is dated 1453–54 (32 Henry VI: p. 72).

Some clues about dating can naturally be obtained from the tenants mentioned within the roll, when they are also known from other sources. Dating from tenants is not infallible, particularly from the free tenants (who are the easier ones to trace), since free tenancies, passing normally by inheritance, were not always updated assiduously or speedily, so that their names can be some years out of date in a roll such as this. However, when the roll does recognize a known and dated change, a *terminus post quem* is provided. One such case is that of a free tenement at Trink, in Connerton manor: in 1463 this was held by an unnamed 'heir of William Trefrynk'; in AR2/1339 by 'Stephen Calmady, sometime William Trefyng' (sic), and in 1499 again by Stephen Calmady (below, pp. 44, 89 and 133). In 1476–77 relief was paid in the manor upon the death of John Calmady, evidently Stephen's predecessor;[2] so our roll, showing awareness that Stephen had succeeded John Calmady, must be dated later than 1476.

Conventionary tenants can provide the same kind of clue. In the manor of Tregarne, one John Chynale took a tenement at Tregevis

---

[1] [Henry Thomas] Scott and Samuel Davey, *A Guide to Collectors of Historical Documents, Literary Manuscripts and Autograph Letters, etc.* (London, 1891), Appendix of watermarks, [6th plate], upper illustration. Our thanks to David Thomas, Cornwall Record Office, for pointing this out.
[2] Account for the manor of Connerton, 1476–77, AR2/915.

in 1476 for a term of seven years.[3] He is seen holding that tenement in AR2/1339 (below, p. 80), but in the extents of 1460 and 1499 he is not named there, nor elsewhere. In theory, his term in 1476 could have been a renewal, and it may have been extended after it ended in 1483, so his tenancy cannot provide a precise range of dates; but a date within a few years of 1476 is at least suggested. In the same manor, the tenant of the mill in AR2/1339 was one John Phelipp (below, p. 80). He is also recorded at the mill in 1479,[4] but in 1476 one John Cornhogh had taken a lease of the mill, for term of fourteen years.[5] Either John Cornhogh and John Phelipp were different men, in which case Cornhogh must have failed to complete his term and have been replaced by Phelipp between 1476 and 1499, or John Cornhogh's name had been changed to John Phelipp after his arrival at the mill in 1476. In either case he provides a *terminus post quem* for AR2/1339 of 1476–79. He was still the tenant of the mill in 1499 (below, p. 125), so his tenancy cannot help at the later end. Similarly in the manor of Lanherne, Isabel Trewarvena held a cottage at Lanvean in AR2/1339 (below, p. 66); she is absent in both 1460 and 1499, but is mentioned in 1490–91 as holding a tenement there.[6] This provides a *terminus ante quem* of 1491–99.

A group of three Arundell leases of some lands in Trembleath manor, dated 23 September 1480, shows tenants who all appear in AR2/1339. The first was made to Thomas Tremayle, Nicholas Janyn, John Iwyn and John Tregarthyn, and grants them jointly a close called *Le Parke Enys* and one-quarter of the land in Trenayles; the second is to Martin Wolcok, Thomas Dungy, John Jakherry and John Norton, and grants them jointly a close called *Le West Clo[se]*, plus another quarter of Trenayles; the last is to William Badcok alone, and grants him the whole of Tregwinyo, plus half of Trenayles. These grants are closely reflected in AR2/1339: William Baddecok there holds the 'whole vill' of Tregwinyo and Trenayles,

---

[3] Court roll of Tregarne manor, between April and September 1476 (AR2/380, m. 11).

[4] Court roll of Tregarne manor, April 1479 (AR2/380, m. 12); he was presented for illegally leasing his buildings and hedges (*domos et sepes*) and for abuse and misuse of the lord's timber, and was fined 40s.

[5] Court roll of Tregarne manor, between April and September 1476 (AR2/380, m. 11).

[6] Account of Lanherne manor, 1490–91, AR2/172.

APPENDIX   cxliii

and the eight men who received the two closes appear successively under Trembleath itself (below, pp. 75–6). The correspondence of tenants indicates a closeness of date. AR2/1339 ought therefore to be dated later than these leases, but it will be seen below that its date is in fact likely to be about three weeks earlier than them. Assuming that the date, deduced on other grounds, is correct, either the leases renewed existing tenancies, or the new tenants were prematurely entered, or this copy of the rental, perhaps written a few weeks after the actual survey was made, silently incorporated the new tenancies.

The final section of AR2/1339, much decayed, is of a kind not found in the other surveys (pp. 99–100). The section seems to cover demesne lands (including those of Lanherne and Carminow) and other miscellaneous incomes. Although obscure through decay, the parts dealing with Lanherne have much detail in common with the manorial accounts of 1478–79 and 1490–91, both of which also have sections dealing specifically with the demesne lands.[7] The tenant of *Cowclose* in AR2/1339, Thomas Clerke (below, p. 99), also appears in the main entry for Lanherne manor, holding a conventionary tenement at Trevelgue and the rabbit-island (p. 65); he is again named as holding the rabbit-warren in the account of 1476–77.[8] Another tenant in this section, Thomas Tregoys, was the general receiver for the Arundell estate during the years 1477–92, and was the bailiff of Lanherne in 1478–79, and of the demesne land there in 1479–80.[9]

Two further pieces of this kind of evidence can be given. Within the roll, two entries in the town of St Columb appear to have been added after it was written (below, p. 73), namely a bakehouse now rented by Luke Carter, and the rent for a holding of Mark Knygh'

---

[7] AR2/916, m. 2 (manorial accounts; 1478–79); AR2/172 (reeve's account for Lanherne and bailiff's account for *Lanherne Parke*, the demesne land; 1490–91).

[8] Reeve's account of Lanherne, 1476–77 (AR2/914, m. 2); but AR2/1339 also names John Ricard as holding the farm of rabbits at Lanherne (below, p. 99).

[9] Account of Ideford (Devon) for 1477–78, AR2/490 (Thomas Tregose, lord's receiver); manorial accounts for 1491–92, AR2/490, fol. 12 (Thomas Tregoys, receiver; but not in AR2/935, 1492–93); manorial accounts for 1478–79, AR2/916, m. 2 (Thomas Tregoys, bailiff at Lanherne); the same for 1479–80, AR2/919, p. 5 (Thomas Tregoys, bailiff of the demesne land).

being remitted or granted (*remiss*') to Holy Trinity chapel. These tenancies both receive particular mention in the manorial account of 1479–80, where the bakehouse is described as 'in the lord's hands' this year, and a payment is made, 'of the lord's charity', to the keeper of Holy Trinity chapel from the rent of a chamber lately held by Mark Knight.[10] Evidently these slightly-later additions to AR2/1339 reflect the situation specifically mentioned in the account for 1480.

Finally, it is notable that the four reeves mentioned in the manorial accounts of 1479–80 all appear as tenants in their respective manors in AR2/1339: Walter Tresawell, Trembleath (at Manuels, p. 75), Oliver Darre, Bodwennack (at Laninval, p. 98), Thomas Crugowe, St Columb (pp. 72–73; also in 1499, p. 103) and Richard Beauripper, Carminow (at Chyvarloe, p. 84).[11] With the exception of Crugowe, these men do not appear in the extents of 1451–64 or 1499. This fit of reeves in 1479–80 with tenants named in AR2/1339 is better than that of the reeves named in the surviving accounts of any other year. In 1476–77 three out of five reeves named in the accounts appear as tenants on their manors in AR2/1339;[12] in 1478–79 two out of two reeves in the (partial) accounts;[13] in 1482–83 five out of nine reeves;[14] in 1484–85 four out of five (one

---

[10] AR2/919, p. 4.
[11] AR2/919; there is also a reeve named at Lanhadron, but that manor is absent from AR2/1339 (see above). For the other manors in this account the bailiffs reported instead; none of them appears in AR2/1339 (except for Thomas Tregoys, bailiff of the demesne land: see above), but the office of bailiff was not a tenant's duty like that of reeve.
[12] AR2/914: John Broyder in the manor of Carminow (compare p. 84), Thomas Hykke in Enniscaven (compare p. 96), and Reginald Cary in Mitchell (compare p. 94: the 'heir of Reginald Cary' must himself have been called Reginald Cary, as shown by his appearance in 1499, p. 98). Reeves of this year lacking in AR2/1339 were Thomas John Matthy (Lanherne and Treloy) and John Tremenhyre (Tregarne).
[13] AR2/916: Peter Tolle in Winnington (compare p. 82) and Thomas Michell in Enniscaven (compare p. 96).
[14] AR2/923: John Jamys in Carminow (compare p. 84), Ralph Roys in Winnington (compare p. 82), Laurence Erlond in Treloy (compare p. 69), Richard Oppy in Bodwannick (compare p. 98) and Thomas Michell (again) in Enniscaven (compare p. 96); the reeves not found in AR2/1339 are John Penmeneth in Kennall, Andrew Hicke in Lanherne and Mabena Wolcok in Trembleath.

of these appearing again in 1499, as does the fifth, not in AR2/ 1339);[15] and in 1488–89 three or four out of eleven reeves named in the accounts (while four others of them appear instead in the 1499 extent).[16] The general impression from this evidence is of 1478–80 as the period when the reeves fit best with the tenants named in AR2/1339, and that by 1489 the manorial reeves named in the accounts agree as well, or better, with tenants found in the extent of 1499, rather than with those found in AR2/1339.

There is probably more evidence of this sort to be obtained from a detailed study of particular manors; but what has been given is sufficient to give a general impression of a date around 1476–90, or more closely about 1478–85. This date is confirmed by another kind of evidence. The dates of the various surveys in the roll portray a tight geographical circuit, making a logical progression around the county, as follows (compare the map, frontispiece):

> first day, the adjacent manors of Lanherne, Treloy, St Columb and Trembleath (below, pp. 65–73); date unknown, the day being lost along with the year, but from what follows it will be apparent that this session took place a day or two before the next survey, therefore 4 or 5 September;
> 6 September, Truro Vean and Kennall (below, pp. 76–77);
> 7 September, Tregarne (p. 79);
> 9 September, Winnington and Carminow (pp. 81–82);
> 10 September, Connerton (p. 85);
> 11 September, Mitchell and Enniscaven (pp. 93–95);
> 13 September, Bodwannick (p. 96).

---

[15] AR2/924: Thomas Jobe in Treloy (compare p. 69), John Harry in Carminow (compare p. 84; again in 1499, p. 126), John Trenowth esq. in Mitchell (compare p. 93) and Adam John in Kennall (compare p. 78); the fifth reeve was James Tolle in Winnington, present in 1499 at the tenement occupied by Peter Tolle in AR2/1339 (pp. 82 and 129).

[16] AR2/926: Ralph Rose in Winnington (compare p. 82), William Richard in Enniscaven (compare p. 96); at Bodwannick the reeve was John Luky through his attorney Richard Oppy (compare p. 98); all four of these were still present in 1499 (pp. 129, 140 and 115–16). Reeves in 1488–89 absent in AR2/1339 but present in 1499 were Thomas Tomm in Carminow (compare p. 126), John William Tomma Perowe in Tregarne (compare p. 126, John Will Perow; and see above, p. cxxvi), John Hykke in Kennall (compare p. 123), and Thomas Hellond in Mitchell (compare p. 138). Reeves absent from both surveys are Thomas Treloy in Treloy, John Gwyndreth in Lanherne, and Thomas Hayly in Trembleath.

In the manorial accounts, the reeves or other officers making the account sometimes referred to a particular rental, and when it was made, as authority for the rents collected. The dates of the individual surveys given above correspond exactly with ones given in various years in the manorial accounts, referring to a rental renewed in 1480, and used between 1480 and 1493. In the accounts the formula used each time was 'set rents (*redditus assisi*) according to a rental newly made ...'. These mentions in the yearly accounts are as follows.

>1479–80:
>Trembleath, 'a rental newly made 4 September 1480 (20 Edward IV)'.
>St Columb, 'a rental newly made 4 September 1480'.
>Tregarne, 'a rental newly made 7 September 1480'.
>Connerton, 'a rental newly made 10 September 1480'.
>Truro Vean, 'a rental newly made 6 September 1480'.
>Treloy, ' a rental newly made 4 September 1480'.
>Carminow, 'a rental newly made 9 September 1480'.[17]
>1484–85:
>Mitchell, 'a rental newly made 11 September 1480 (20 Edward IV)'.
>Kennall, 'a rental newly made 6 September 1480'.[18]
>1489–90:
>Bodwannick, 'a rental newly made 13 December [*sic*] 1480 (20 Edward IV)'.[19]
>1492–93:
>Trembleath, 'a roll renewed in 1480 (20 Edward IV)'.[20]

From this it is clear, both that the rental made in 1480 continued to be used for at least thirteen years, and that the days correspond exactly to those of AR2/1339, except for the month at Bodwennack, which in any case is anomalous, and probably erroneous. It might be argued that this was a natural geographical circuit, which could have been followed in other years too; to this it can be replied that the succession of dates portrayed in the 1499 extent is quite

---

[17] All from reeves' accounts, 1479–80, AR2/919; the rental which they mention was thus only a few weeks old when these accounts were drawn up at Michaelmas.

[18] Reeves' accounts, 1484–85, AR2/924, p. 5.

[19] Reeves' accounts, 1489–90, AR2/928, m. 8; the other entries show that 'December' here is a slip for 'September', irrespective of whether the rental named is AR2/1339.

[20] Reeves' accounts, 1492–93, AR2/933.

different (see above, p. xlv), and that the correspondence of days and manors is too exact for that explanation to be convincing. If the identity of AR2/1339 and the rental made in 1480 is accepted, then the account rolls establish the day on which the first four manors were surveyed as 4, not 5, September.

However, there is one anomaly which argues against equating AR2/1339 with the rental renewed in 1480. The description of Connerton is specifically stated to have been made on 'Monday 10 September', the only occasion when a week-day as well as a date was given. But in 1480 10 September was not a Monday but a Sunday. We cannot plead that the scribe wrote '10' in error for '11', for the date is confirmed by the account-roll of the same year. We can only suppose that the scribe of the rental, for some reason, wrote 'Monday' incorrectly instead of 'Sunday' in that entry.[21] One conceivable reason might have been to observe a convention of not acknowledging in writing the fact of working on a Sunday.

It therefore seems that AR2/1339 can be ascribed with confidence to the year 1480, being the rental of that year mentioned in various accounts. This accords well with the date-range provided by the evidence of the tenants. New rentals were not made very often. That of 1499 continued to be cited in the accounts, in a similar manner to that of 1480 already seen, as late as 1527–28 (see above). No other references in the accounts to renewals of rentals, at dates other than 1480 and 1499, have been noted. Moreover, the dating of AR2/1339 to 1480 produces two twenty-year intervals between the three fifteenth-century documents printed here; it seems very unlikely that an additional, lost rental could reasonably be posited, as would be necessary if AR2/1339 were not the recorded document of 1480. The ascription of AR2/1339 to 1480 is therefore here accepted as established.

---

[21] In the following years around our period, 10 September did fall on a Monday: 1470, 1481, 1487, 1492, 1498. But 1470 is too early, for reasons given above; 1481 is very improbable given that another rental had been compiled only a year earlier; and 1498 is equally improbable since another was compiled a year later. This leaves 1487 and 1492 as possible dates; the reason for preferring 1480, despite its discrepant week-day, is the evidence of the circuit, combined with Ockham's razor; and the fact that the rental of 1480 was still being cited in 1493.

BIBLIOGRAPHY AND ABBREVIATIONS

Albion, R. G., *Forests and Sea Power* (Cambridge, Mass., 1926).
Anc.Deeds: *Catalogue of Ancient Deeds in the Public Record Office*, 6 vols (London, 1890–1915).
Anon., 'The improvement of Cornwall by sea sand', *Philosophical Transactions of the Royal Society of London*, 10 (1675), 293–6.
AR: document in the archive of Arundell of Lanherne, CRO.
Austin, D., G. A. M. Gerrard and T. A. P. Greeves, 'Tin and agriculture in the Middle Ages and beyond: landscape archaeology in St Neot parish, Cornwall', *Cornish Archaeology*, 28 (1989), 5–251.
'Beville Obituary': (I) C. Henderson, 'The Beville Obituary', *Devon and Cornwall Notes and Queries*, 16 (1931–31), 17–26; (II) W. M. M. Picken, 'The Beville Obituary II', *ibid.*, 36 (1987–91), 354–62, and 37 (1992–96), 35–41.
Beresford, M., *New Towns of the Middle Ages. Town Plantation in England, Wales and Gascony* (London, 1967).
BL: (manuscript in) British Library, London.
Black Prince's Register: *Register of Edward the Black Prince*, 4 vols (London, 1930–33).
Blake, W. J., 'Hooker's Synopsis Chorographical of Devonshire', *Transactions of the Devonshire Association*, 47 (1915), 334–48.
Blanchard, I., 'Industrial employment and the rural land market 1380–1520', in *Land, Kinship and Lifecycle*, edited by R. M. Smith (Cambridge, 1984), pp. 227–75.
Bolton, J., '"The world upside down": plague as an agent of economic and social change', in *The Black Death in England*, edited by M. Ormrod and P. Lindley (Stamford, 1996), pp. 17–78.
Bowles, Charles, *A Short Account of the Hundred of Penwith, in the County of Cornwall* (Shaftesbury, 1805).
Brantyngham: *The Register of Thomas de Brantyngham, Bishop of Exeter (A.D. 1370–1394)*, edited by F. C. Hingeston-Randolph, 2 vols (London and Exeter, 1901–06).
Cal.Close: *Calendar of Close Rolls*.
A Calendar of Cornish Glebe Terriers 1673–1735, edited by Richard Potts, Devon and Cornwall Record Society, n.s., 19 (1974).
Calendar of IPMs: *Calendar of Inquisitions Post Mortem* (see also *Inquisitiones*).
Cal.Pat.: *Calendar of Patent Rolls*.
Caption of Seisin: see Hull.
Carew, Richard, *The Survey of Cornwall* (London, 1602).

BIBLIOGRAPHY AND ABBREVIATIONS   cxlix

Carew, Richard, *The Survey of Cornwall*, edited by F. E. Halliday (London, 1953).
Christie, P., and P. Rose, 'Davidstow Moor, Cornwall: the medieval and later sites', *Cornish Archaeology*, 26 (1987), 163–95.
Clay, C., 'Landlords and estate management in England', in *The Agrarian History of England and Wales*, V, *1640–1750*, edited by Joan Thirsk, part ii (Cambridge, 1985), pp. 119–251.
Complete Peerage: G. E. Cokayne, *The Complete Peerage*, edited by V. Gibbs and others, 13 vols (London, 1910–59).
Cornwall Feet of Fines, edited by J. Hambley Rowe, 2 vols, Devon and Cornwall Record Society (Exeter, 1914–50).
Cornwall Military Survey, see Stoate.
Cornwall, Julian, *The Revolt of the Peasantry 1549* (London, 1977).
CRO: (document in) Cornwall Record Office, Truro.
Dahlman, C. J., *The Open Field System and Beyond. A Property Rights Analysis of an Economic Institution* (Cambridge, 1980).
DeWindt, E. B., *Land and People in Holywell-cum-Needingworth. Structures of Tenure and Patterns of Social Organisation in an East Midlands Village 1252–1457* (Toronto, 1971).
Domesday Book (general editor John Morris), vol. 10, *Cornwall*, edited by C. and F. Thorn (Chichester, 1979).
Douch, *Muster Roll*: *The Cornwall Muster Roll for 1569*, edited by H. L. Douch (Almondsbury, 1984).
DRO: (document in) Devon Record Office, Exeter.
Dyer, C., *Lords and Peasants in a Changing Society. The Estates of the Bishopric of Worcester, 680–1540* (Cambridge, 1980).
Dyer, C., *Standards of Living in the Later Middle Ages. Social Change in England c.1200–1520* (Cambridge, 1989).
Dyer, C., 'Changes in the link between families and land in the West Midlands in the fourteenth and fifteenth centuries', in *Land, Kinship and Lifecycle*, edited by R. M. Smith (Cambridge, 1984), pp. 305–11.
Dyer, C., 'Changes in the size of peasant holdings in some West Midland villages 1400–1540', in *Land, Kinship and Lifecycle*, edited by R. M. Smith (Cambridge, 1984), pp. 277–94.
Dyer, C., 'English peasant buildings in the later Middle Ages', *Medieval Archaeology*, 30 (1986), 19–45.
Episcopal Acta, Exeter: *English Episcopal Acta*, vols XI–XII, *Exeter 1046–1184* and *Exeter 1186–1257*, edited by Frank Barlow (Oxford, 1996).
Faith, R. J., 'Peasant families and inheritance customs in medieval England', *Agricultural History Review*, 14 (1966), 77–95.
Finberg, H. P. R., *Tavistock Abbey*, 2nd edition (Newton Abbot, 1969).
Flatrès, P., *Géographie rurale de quatre contrées celtiques. Irelande, Galles, Cornwall et Man* (Rennes, 1957).

Fox, H. S. A., 'Medieval rural industry', in *An Historical Atlas of South-West England*, edited by R. J. P. Kain and W. L. D. Ravenhill (Exeter, forthcoming), pp. 346–53.

Fox, H. S. A., 'The chronology of enclosure and economic develoment in medieval Devon', *Economic History Review*, 2nd series, 28 (1975), 181–202.

Fox, H. S. A., 'Peasant farmers, patterns of settlement and *pays*: transformations in the landscapes of Devon and Cornwall during the later middle ages', in *Landscape and Townscape in the South West*, edited by R. Higham (Exeter, 1989), pp. 41–73.

Fox, H. S. A., 'Outfield cultivation in Devon and Cornwall: a reinterpretation', in *Husbandry and Marketing in the South-West 1500–1800*, edited by M. Havinden (Exeter, 1975), pp. 19–38.

Fox, H. S. A., 'Servants, cottagers and tied cottages during the later middle ages: towards a regional dimension', *Rural History*, 6 (1995), 1–30.

Fox, H. S. A., 'Occupation of the land: Devon and Cornwall', in *The Agrarian History of England and Wales*, III, *1348–1500*, edited by E. Miller (Cambridge, 1991), pp. 152–74.

Fox, H. S. A., 'Tenant farming and tenant farmers: Devon and Cornwall', in *The Agrarian History of England and Wales*, III, *1348–1500*, edited by E. Miller (Cambridge, 1991), pp. 722–43.

Freeth, G., 'On some extracts from the ministers accounts, relating to the Arundell estates in Cornwall', *Journal of the Royal Institution of Cornwall*, 5 (1874–78), 285–93.

Gonner, E. C. K., *Common Land and Inclosure* (London, 1912).

Gray, H. L., *English Field Systems* (Cambridge, Mass., 1915).

Harvey, *Cuxham Records*: P. D. A. Harvey, *Manorial Records of Cuxham, Oxfordshire, circa 1200–1359* (London, 1976).

Harvey, P. D. A., *Manorial Records* (London, 1984).

Hatcher, John, *Rural Economy and Society in the Duchy of Cornwall 1300–1500* (Cambridge, 1970).

Hatcher, J., 'Non-manorialism in medieval Cornwall', *Agricultural History Review*, 18 (1970), 1–16.

Hatcher, 'A diversified economy: later medieval Cornwall', *Economic History Review*, 2nd series, 22 (1969), 208–27.

Henderson, 'Beville obituary': see 'Beville'.

Henderson, Charles, *A History of the Parish of Constantine in Cornwall*, edited by G. H. Doble (Truro, 1937).

Henderson, Charles, 'The ecclesiastical antiquities of the four western hundreds of Cornwall', *Journal of the Royal Institution of Cornwall*, n.s. 2 (1953–56), iii–iv, and 3 (1957–60), ii and iv (page numbering consecutive throughout).

Henderson, Charles, *Essays in Cornish History*, edited by A. L. Rowse and M. I. Henderson (Oxford, 1935).

Henderson, Charles, *Mabe Church and Parish, Cornwall* (Long Compton, c.1930).

BIBLIOGRAPHY AND ABBREVIATIONS cli

Henderson, Charles, *St Columb Major Church and Parish* (Long Compton, 1930).
Henderson, Charles, 'The topography of the parish of St Keverne', *Annual Reports of the Royal Cornwall Polytechnic Society*, n.s. 7 (1931–33), 49–75 and 185–92, and 8 (1934–36), 14–25.
Hoskins, W. G., *The Making of the English Landscape* (London, 1955).
Hull, P. L. (ed.), *The Caption of Seisin of the Duchy of Cornwall (1337)*, Devon and Cornwall Record Society, n.s., 17 (1971).
The Hylle Cartulary, edited by R. W. Dunning, Somerset Record Society, 68 (1968).
Inquisitiones (RC): *Calendarium Inquisitionum Post Mortem sive Escaetorum*, Record Commission, 4 vols (London, 1806–28) (see also *Calendar of Inquisitions Post Mortem*).
Johnson, N., and P. Rose, *Bodmin Moor. An Archaeological Survey*, I, *The Human Lanscape to c.1800* (Truro, 1994).
Jones, Michael, *The Family of Dinan in England in the Middle Ages* (Dinan, 1987).
Kerridge, E. (ed.), *Surveys of the Manors of Philip, First Earl of Pembroke and Montgomery 1631–2*, Wiltshire Archaeological and Natural History Society, Records Branch, 9 (1953).
Kussmaul, A., *Servants in Husbandry in Early Modern England* (Cambridge, 1981).
Lacy: *The Register of Edmund Lacy, Bishop of Exeter, 1420–1455*, edited by G. R. Dunstan, 5 vols, Devon and Cornwall Record Society (in conjunction with the Canterbury and York Society), n.s., vols 7, 10, 13, 16, 18 (1961–72).
Leland, *Itinerary*: *The Itinerary of John Leland in or about the Years 1535–1543*, edited by Lucy Toulmin Smith, 5 vols (London, 1906–10).
Lennard, Reginald, 'What is a manorial extent?', *English Historical Review*, 44 (1929), 256–63.
Lomas, T., 'The development of the manorial extent', *Journal of the Society of Archivists*, 6 (1978–81), 260–73.
Lomas, T., 'South-east Durham: late fourteenth and fifteenth centuries', in *The Peasant Land Market in Medieval England*, edited by P. D. A. Harvey (Oxford, 1984), pp. 253–327.
Lysons, *Cornwall*: Daniel Lysons, *Magna Britannia*, vol. III, *Cornwall* (London, 1814).
Mackie, J. D., *The Early Tudors 1485–1558* (Oxford, 1952).
Maclean, J. 'Poll tax account for the county of Cornwall, 51st Edward III, A.D. 1377', *Journal of the Royal Institution of Cornwall*, 4 (1871–73), 27–41.
Maclean, Sir John, *The Parochial and Family History of the Deanery of Trigg Minor*, 3 vols (London and Bodmin, 1873–79).
Marshall, W., *The Rural Economy of the West of England*, 2 vols (London, 1796).

Mattingly, J., 'The medieval parish guilds of Cornwall', *Journal of the Royal Institution of Cornwall*, n.s., 10 (1986–90), 290–329.
Morgan, Prys, 'The rise of Welsh hereditary surnames', *Nomina*, 10 (1986), 121–35.
Muster Roll, see Douch.
Neilson, N., *Customary Rents*, Oxford Studies in Social and Legal History, 2 (Oxford, 1910).
Norden, J., *Speculi Britanniae Pars. A Topographical and Historical Description of Cornwall* (London, 1728; cited from new edition, Newcastle, 1966).
Norden, J., *The Surveiors Dialogue*, 4th edn (London, 1738).
O.E.D.: The Oxford English Dictionary.
Oliver, George, *Monasticon Dioecesis Exoniensis* (Exeter, 1846).
Padel, O. J., *Cornish Place-Name Elements*, English Place-Name Society, 56/57 (1985).
Padel, O. J., 'Cornish surnames in 1327', *Nomina*, 9 (1985), 81–87.
Padel, O. J., 'From Cornish place-name to surname in Cornwall', *Journal of the Cornwall Family History Society*, 35 (March 1985), 19–20.
Padel, O. J., 'Locational surnames in fourteenth-century Denbighshire', in *Names, Places and People. An Onomastic Miscellany in Memory of John McNeal Dodgson*, edited by A. R. Rumble and A. D. Mills (Stamford, 1997), pp. 279–300.
Padel, O. J., 'Queries from Cornish documents', *Devon and Cornwall Notes and Queries*, 36 (1987–91), 140–7.
Page, Mark, 'The ownership of advowsons in thirteenth-century Cornwall', *Devon and Cornwall Notes and Queries*, 37 (1992–96), 336–41.
The Parliamentary Survey of the Duchy of Cornwall, edited by N. J. G. Pounds, 2 vols, Devon and Cornwall Record Society, n.s., 25 and 27 (1982–84).
Pearse Chope, R., *The Book of Hartland* (Torquay, 1940).
Pearse Chope, R., 'The early history of the manor of Hartland', *Transactions of the Devonshire Association*, 34 (1902), 418–54.
Pearse Chope, R., 'The Lord Dynham's lands', *Transactions of the Devonshire Association*, 43 (1911), 269–92.
Picken, W. M. M., 'The descent of the Devonshire family of Willington from Robert, earl of Gloucester', in W. M. M. Picken, *A Medieval Cornish Miscellany* (Chichester, forthcoming).
Picken, W. M. M., 'The feudality of Pendrim manor', in W. M. M. Picken, *A Medieval Cornish Miscellany* (Chichester, forthcoming).
Picken, W. M. M., 'Trezance, Lahays and the Manor of Cardinham', *Devon and Cornwall Notes and Queries*, 26 (1954–55), 203–08.
Placita de Quo Warranto temporibus Edw. I. II. & III., Record Commission (London, 1818).
Pool, P. A. S., 'The Penheleg manuscript', *Journal of the Royal Institution of Cornwall*, n.s., 3 (1957–60), 163–228.

BIBLIOGRAPHY AND ABBREVIATIONS   cliii

Postles, David, with Richard McKinley, *The Surnames of Devon*, English Surnames Series, 6 (Oxford, 1995).
PRO: (document at) The Public Record Office, London.
Pounds, N. J. G., 'Taxation and wealth in late medieval Cornwall', *Journal of the Royal Instititon of Cornwall*, n.s., 6 (1969-72), 154-67.
Pounds, N. J. G., 'Lanhydrock Atlas', *Antiquity*, 19 (1945), 20-6.
RIC: (document at) The Royal Institution of Cornwall, Truro.
Rolfe, J. S., 'Cornish parsons and parsonages of the XVII century', *126th Annual Report of the Royal Cornwall Polytechnic Society* (1959), 21-50.
Rot.Litt.Claus.: *Rotuli Litterarum Clausarum*, edited by T. D. Hardy, 2 vols, Record Commission (London, 1833-44).
Rowe, J., *Cornwall in the Age of the Industrial Revolution* (Liverpool, 1953).
Rowse, A. L., *Tudor Cornwall* (London, 1941).
Snell, L. S., *The Chantry Certificates for Cornwall* (Exeter, 1953).
Stapeldon: *The Register of Walter de Stapeldon, Bishop of Exeter, (A.D. 1307-1326)*, edited by F. C. Hingeston-Randolph (Exeter, 1892).
Stoate, T. L. (ed.), *Cornwall Manorial Rentals and Surveys* (Bristol, 1988).
Stoate, T. L. (ed.), *Cornwall Hearth and Poll Taxes 1660-1664* (Almondsbury, 1981).
Stoate, T. L. (ed.), *Cornwall Protestation Returns* (Almondsbury, 1974).
Stoate, T. L. (ed.), *Cornwall Subsidies in the Reign of Henry VIII* (Almondsbury, 1985).
Stoate, T. L. (ed.), *The Cornwall Military Survey 1522, with the Loan Books and a Tinners Muster Roll c.1535* (Almondsbury, 1987).
Thomas, K., *Man and the Natural World. Attitudes in England 1500-1800* (London, 1983).
Tudor Economic Documents, edited by R. H. Tawney and E. Power, 3 vols (London, 1924).
Vivian, J. L. (ed.), *The Visitations of the County of Cornwall, comprising the Heralds' Visitations of 1530, 1573, and 1620* (Exeter, 1887).
Webb, Edward Dorian (ed.), *Notes by the 12th Lord Arundell of Wardour on the Family History* (London, 1916).
Welch, C. E., 'A survey of some Duchy manors', *Devon and Cornwall Notes and Queries*, 29 (1962-64), 161-4, 196-200, 214-17, 241-3, 276-9 and 290-3; and 30 (1965-7), 4-7, 33-6, 67-70 and 102-5.
Whetter, James, *Cornwall in the Seventeenth Century* (Padstow, 1974).
Wordie, J. R., 'The chronology of English enclosure, 1500-1914', *Economic History Review*, 2nd series, 36 (1983), 483-505.
Worgan, G. B., *A General View of the Agriculture of the County of Cornwall* (London, 1811).
Yeatman, J. P., *The Early Genealogical History of the House of Arundel, being an Account of the Origin of the Families of Montgomery, Albini, Fitzalan, and Howard, from the Time of the Conquest of Normandy by Rollo the Great* (London, 1883).

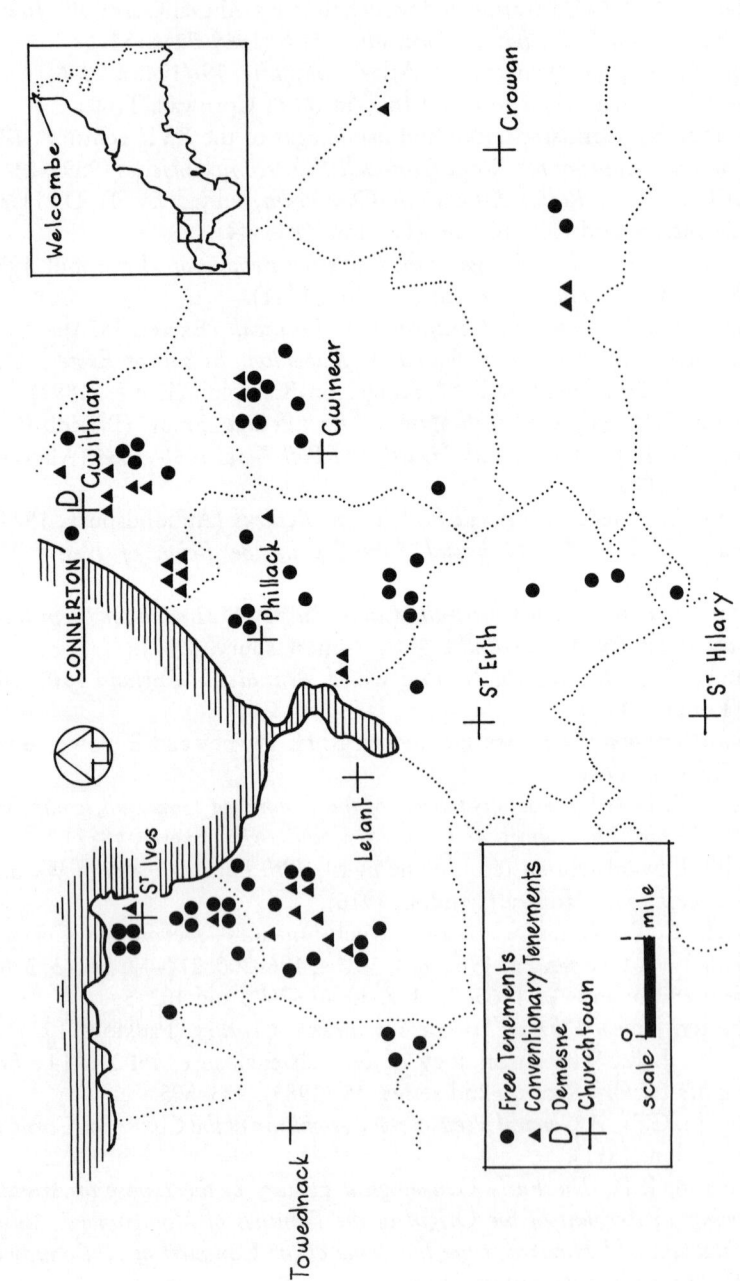

Tenement of the manor of Connerton in 1463 (excluding unlocated tenements)

MAPS

Tenements of the manors of Lanherne and Trembleath in 1459-60 (excluding unlocated tenements)

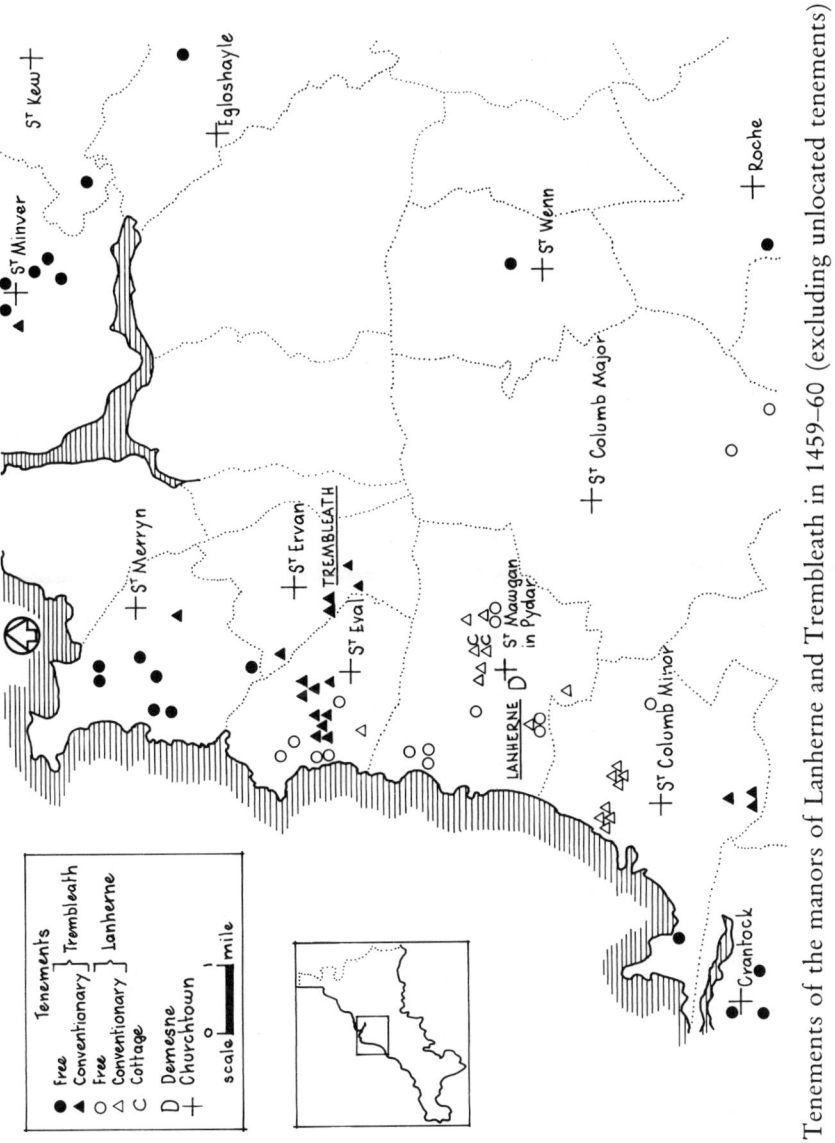

THE ARUNDELLS OF LANHERNE
Outline of the medieval family

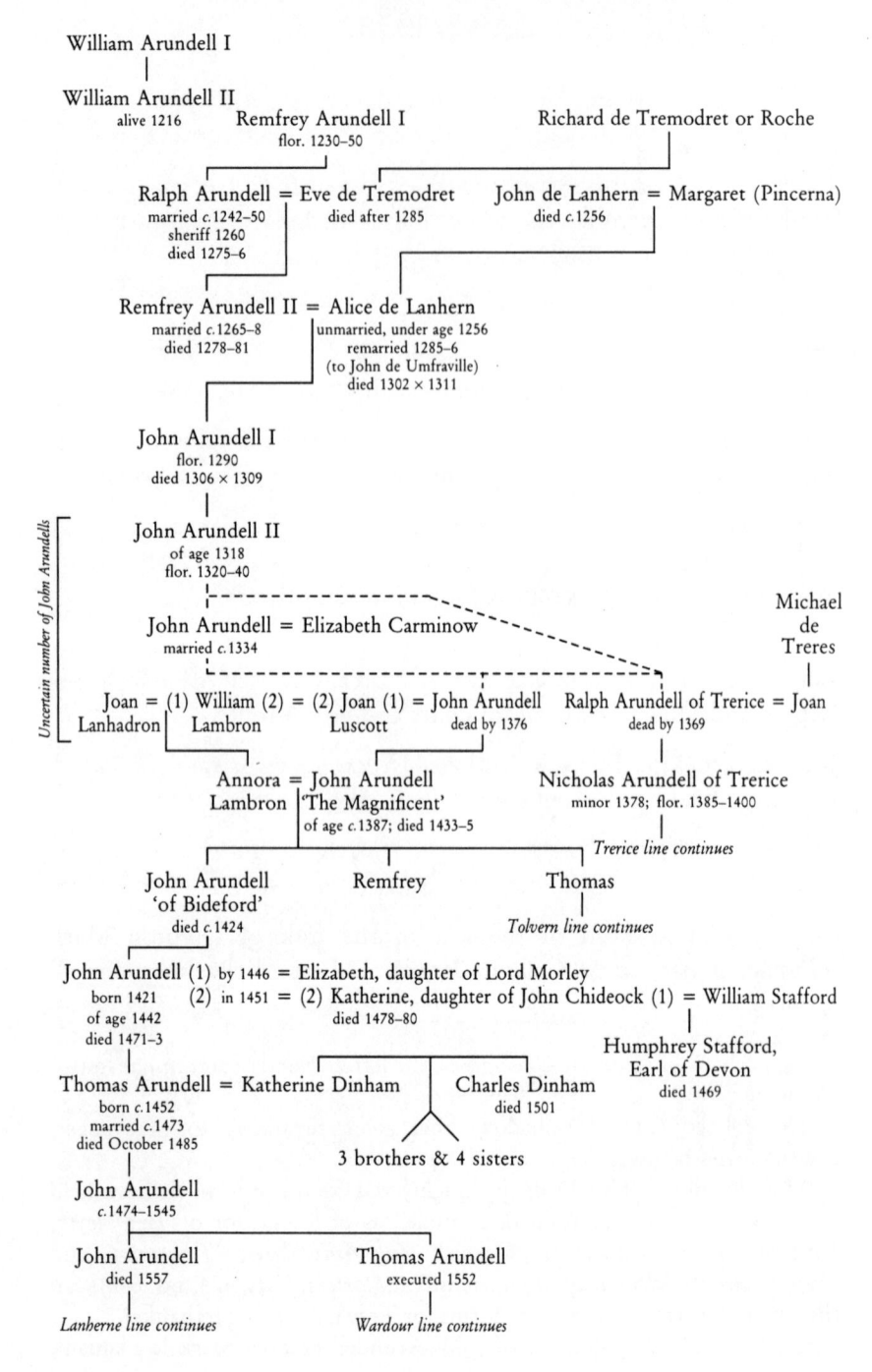

William Arundell I
|
William Arundell II
alive 1216   Remfrey Arundell I   Richard de Tremodret or Roche
                    flor. 1230–50

Ralph Arundell = Eve de Tremodret   John de Lanhern = Margaret (Pincerna)
married c.1242–50   died after 1285   died c.1256
sheriff 1260
died 1275–6

Remfrey Arundell II = Alice de Lanhern
married c.1265–8   unmarried, under age 1256
died 1278–81   remarried 1285–6
                     (to John de Umfraville)
                     died 1302 × 1311

John Arundell I
flor. 1290
died 1306 × 1309

John Arundell II
of age 1318
flor. 1320–40
                                                                        Michael
John Arundell = Elizabeth Carminow   de
married c.1334   Treres

Joan = (1) William (2) = (2) Joan (1) = John Arundell   Ralph Arundell of Trerice = Joan
Lanhadron   Lambron   Luscott   dead by 1376   dead by 1369

Uncertain number of John Arundells

Annora = John Arundell   Nicholas Arundell of Trerice
Lambron 'The Magnificent'   minor 1378; flor. 1385–1400
         of age c.1387; died 1433–5
                                                    Trerice line continues

John Arundell   Remfrey   Thomas
'of Bideford' |
died c.1424   Tolvern line continues

John Arundell (1) by 1446 = Elizabeth, daughter of Lord Morley
born 1421   (2) in 1451 = (2) Katherine, daughter of John Chideock (1) = William Stafford
of age 1442   died 1478–80
died 1471–3
                                                           Humphrey Stafford,
Thomas Arundell = Katherine Dinham   Charles Dinham   Earl of Devon
born c.1452   died 1501   died 1469
married c.1473
died October 1485
                                  3 brothers & 4 sisters
John Arundell
c.1474–1545

John Arundell   Thomas Arundell
died 1557   executed 1552
| |
Lanherne line continues *Wardour line continues*

LANHERNE & TREMBLEATH, 1343
(AR2/1336)

Manor of Lanhern and Trembleyth
[*Lanherne, in St Mawgan in Pyder, and Trembleath, in St Ervan*]

Extent of two-thirds (*duas partes*) of the manor [*sic, singular*] of Lanhern and Trembleyth, made Thursday before St Dunstan, 17 Edward III [15 May 1343].

Free tenants

John Lercedekne, 1 acre in Gauerghen[1] [*Gaverigan, in St Columb Major*]; 12*d.* at Michaelmas, common suit of court.

John de Tynten, 1 acre and 3 ferlings in Hengolon [*Engollan, in St Eval*]; 3*s.* 11*d.* at Sts Philip and James and All Saints, suit of court.

John Dawene, 2 acres in Ammalgres ['1 acre in Treuengar', *deleted*][2] and 1 acre in Trethauek [*Middle Amble, in St Kew, and Trethauke, in St Minver*],[3] by knight's service; common suit of court.

John de Penfos [*Penvose, in St Mawgan in Pyder*], 1 acre there, by knight's service; 4*s.* at St Andrew's, Easter, Nativity of St John the Baptist and Michaelmas, suit of court and suit of mill.

John Lercedekne, 1 acre in Ruthefos [*Ruthvoes, in St Columb Major*], by knight's service; suit of court.

John de Treueglos, ½ acre in Arlyn [*Harlyn, in St Merryn*]; homage and fealty.

Mark Flamank, head of the leat of the mill of Glyuion Mark [*Gluvian Marth, in St Columb Major*]; 12*d.* at Michaelmas, for all service.[4]

---

[1] *Sic*, perhaps in error for *Gauergwen*; the letters *h* and *w* are similar in this hand.
[2] The deleted entry foreshadows that given separately for Trevanger, eleven entries below.
[3] After his death John Dauney, knight, was found in 1346 to have held (among other lands) of John de Arundel, as of his manor of *Trembleyth*, 3 messuages and 3 acres Cornish in *Ammalgres, Treuruson* and *Trewartharon* (*Calendar of Inquisitions Post Mortem*, VIII, 474, no. 648); can the two latter names be corrupt forms for Trevanger and Trethauke?
[4] In October 1323 John son of John Arundell granted Mark le Flamank

[*St Columb town, in St Columb Major*]:
John de Nanscuuel, 3 plots (*placeas*) in the vill of Sancta Columba Maior; 3s. at Michaelmas; 2 suits of court, at 1 May and Michaelmas, in the vill of Sancta Columba and not elsewhere.

Odo de Nanscuuel, 1 plot there; 12*d.* at Michaelmas, 2 suits of court as above.

John de Rosworugan, 1 plot there; 12*d.* at the same date, suit as above.

John de Reswalstus, 1 plot there; 12*d.* at the same date, 2 suits of court as above.

Ralph Petycru, 3 plots there; 3s. at the same date, 2 suits of court as above.

John Soor de Sancto Austel, 1 house (*domus*) with a garden there; 6*d.* at the same date, 2 suits of court as above.

John Dawene,[5] 1 acre in Treuengar [*Trevanger, in St Minver*], by knight's service; 8½*d.* and 2 parts of a farthing (*ferling*'), at St Petrock's [4 June].

John Walesbrew, 3 acres in Cayrou [*Blakes Keiro, otherwise Keiro Veor, in St Minver*],[6] by knight's service; 2s. 2*d.* at the same date, suit of court.

Ralph Darundel, 1 acre in Kynyafos [*Carnewas, in St Eval*], for term of life; 2s. at Michaelmas.[7]

John Virly,[8] 1 acre in Tynglun [*either Treglyn or Treglynes, in St Minver*];[9] 5s. at two dates, and 20*d.* to lord of Bliston [*Blisland*].

---

permission to build a leat for his mill in *Gliuyon Mark*' upon Arundell's land of Lanherne; the yearly rent of 12*d.* was to be paid at Michaelmas and Sts Philip and James (AR3/145).

[5] The name appears as *Dalbene*, the letters *lb* and *w* being similar.

[6] The fuller name given in Whalesborough's entry in the extent of 1459, below (p. 24), provides the identification.

[7] This is presumably the Ralph or Randulph who married Joan, daughter and heiress of Michael de Trerys; their son Nicholas was ancestor of the Trerice branch of the family: Henderson,'The Beville obituary' (I), p. 25, and below, p. 9 n. 26.

[8] cf. the lost place-name *Virly* in 1334, evidently in St Minver parish: *Cornwall Feet of Fines*, I, no. 682 (= AR20/1).

[9] It has not yet proved possible to distinguish conclusively between the early spellings of Treglyn and Treglynes, so it is not certain to which of these places *Tynglun* refers, though Treglyn is more likely.

Joan who was wife of Bartholomew de Berkle, ½ of Goyen Vinov [*Gunvenna, in St Minver*];[10] 2s. 2d.

Total [*of free tenants*], 31s. 5½d. and 2 parts of a farthing (*ferling*).

Conventionary tenants

John Denesel, Treyudres [*Trevedras, in St Mawgan in Pyder*];[11] 20s. at the four main dates.

Reginald Ceny, ½ acre in Penfos [*Penvose, in St Mawgan in Pyder*]; 6s. 8d. at St Andrew's, Easter, Nativity of St John the Baptist and Michaelmas, suit of court.

Treuelghy [*Trevelgue, in St Columb Minor*]:
Vincent *de eadem*, 1 acre and 1 ferling in Treuelghy;[12] 22s. 10½d., suit of court.
1 ferling there which is waste used to pay 5s. 8½d. [*added later*].
John Huwet', 3 ferlings in Treuelghy; 17s. 1d., suit of court.
Maud Gonfold,[13] 1 ferling; 5s. 8½d., suit of court.
Roger de Treuelghy, 3 ferlings; 17s. 1d., suit of court.

Hengolon [*Engollan, in St Eval*]:
John Pafford, ½ acre in Hengolon; 7s., suit of court.
John de Hengolon,[14] ½ acre there; 7s., suit of court.

J. Billoun:[15]

William Wyghen, 1 ferling there [*i.e. in Engollan?*]; 3s. 6d., suit of court.
John Roche, land of Tregonben [*Tregonning, in St Mawgan in Pyder*],[16] for term of years; worth 20s. yearly.

---

[10] *Tynglun* and *Goenfynou* appear together as part of the dower-lands of Eve, the widow of Ralph Arundell, in 1276 (AR19/1). In 1322-23 Bartholomew Berkele had been a witness to a group of deeds forming an internal Arundell transaction, concerning lands including Trelawder and Gunvenna (AR1/84 and AR4/183/1-2).
[11] The spelling is erroneous, probably an error for *Treuudrys*.
[12] Four years after the date of this rental, in July 1347, Sir John Arundell mortgaged his conventionary tenements at Trevelgue for 60 marks, while retaining the tenants' suit of court and mill; the four conventionary tenants are named as Vincent de Treuelgy, John Andreu, John Huwet, and Roger *de eadem* (AR1/114-115).
[13] '*iacens*', added later over her name (i.e. land lying in the lord's hands?).
[14] 'William Trip' [?], added over this name.
[15] See below (p. 5 n. 19).

Hilary Doly, 1 messuage and 1 piece (*pecia*) of land in Enysuaugan ['*Enysmaugan*' *(lost)*, in St Mawgan in Pyder]; 2s. 6d.

Penros [*Penrose, in St Ervan*]:
Stephen de Trenewit, 2 parts of ½ acre of land of Penros; 8s., of which 12d. to the lord of Pouton.[17]

Dounrew [*unidentified*]:
Elias Dounrew, 1 parcel of land in Dounrew; 7s., suit of court.
Alice who was wife of Simon Treluri, 1 parcel of land there; 4s., suit of court.
John Gerues, 1 parcel of land in Dounrew; 4s., suit of court.
John (*Ioh'e*) *de eadem*, 2 parts of 1½ acres; 16d., suit of court.

Total [*of conventionary tenants*], £7 19s. 5½d.

Demesne land of Sancta Columba [*St Columb Major*]:
Thomas Basset, 1 messuage and ¼ of the demesne and the mill; 33s. 4d. at the said dates, suit of court.
Peter Pencors, 1 messuage and ¼ of the demesne and the mill; 33s. 4d., suit of court.
Nicholas Huchoun, 1 messuage and one-eighth of the demesne and the mill; 16s. 8d., suit of court.
Richard Carmynov, 1 messuage and one-eighth of the demesne and the mill; 16s. 8d., suit of court.
Ralph Folfrank, Roberta who was wife of Creheer [?], and John Paler, 1 messuage and ¼ of the demesne and the mill; 33s. 4d., suit of court.

Cottars (*coterelli*):

John Paler, 1 cot-land (*coterell'*); 18d., suit of court.
Maud Crak, 1 smallholding (*bordell'*); 2s., suit of court.

[16] This must be the conventionary tenement of Lanherne manor called *Tregonben* in 1376, 1391 and 1429 (AR4/2130; AR20/14 and /19), *Tregenwen* in 1457 (AR20/20), and *Tregonwen* in 1457–60 (AR20/22–23 and /26; all intra- familial deeds); *Tregonvan* in 1460 and 1499 (AR2/1337 and /1340; below, pp. 34 and 109); *Tregonnen* 1477 (AR2/914, m. 2) and *Tregonnian* 1491 (AR2/172; manorial accounts); *Tregonvan* 1532 (AR2/157; court roll); its parish is shown by John Tregonben, taxpayer in St Mawgan in Pyder, 1327 Lay Subsidy. (In most instances the *n* could of course be read as *u*.) In 1659 and 1717 the corresponding tenement is called *Tregonnan*, specified in 1717 as being in St Mawgan in Pyder.
[17] The bishop of Exeter's manor of Pawton, in St Breock.

MANOR OF LANHERNE AND TREMBLEATH 5

Stephen Badyn, 1 messuage with garden; 4s., suit of court.
Joan Henr', 1 messuage; 4s., suit of court.
Ralph Folfrank, 1 messuage with garden; 4s., suit of court.
William Summonur, 1 messuage with garden; 4s., suit of court.
Joan Treghures, 1 cot-land (*cotell*'); 18*d*., suit of court.

Total [*of demesne land and cottars*], £7 14s. 4*d*.

Bondmen (*nativi*):

Treuelghy [*Trevelgue, in St Columb Minor*]:
Joce de Treuelghy, 1 acre; 22s. 6*d*., suit of court.
Benedict Stouka [*or* Stonka], 3 ferlings; 17s. 1*d*., suit of court.

Tregheustek [*Tregustick, in St Columb Minor*]:[18]
Roger Leta, 1 acre; 22s. 6*d*., suit of court.
John Stouka [*or* Stonka], 1 acre; 22s. 6*d*., suit of court.
William *de eadem*, ½ acre; 11s. 5*d*., suit of court.

J. Billoun:[19]

Thomas Budda, 1 acre 3 ferlings in Tregona [*Tregona, in St Eval*]; 31s. 4*d*., suit of court.
Mark Budda, 1 acre in Hengolon [*Engollan, in St Eval*]; 14s.

---

[18] The Arundells had interests in both Tregustick in Withiel and Tregustick in St Columb Minor; but it was the one in St Columb Minor which was a conventionary tenement of Lanherne manor. See, for instance, leases dated 1558–1611 (AR4/473–477), and a presentment in a court of Lanherne of 1455 that tenants at Trevelgue had blocked the sanding-way of Tregustick (AR2/133, m. 1; Trevelgue lies between Tregustick in St Columb Minor and the sea).

[19] On 18 May 1339 John Arundell had mortgaged 2 messuages with 1 acre and 3 ferlings of land in *Tregona*, and 1 messuage with 1 acre of land in *Hengolon*, to John Byllun de Trethywol (Trethewell, in St Eval parish). Arundell was to pay 20 marks of silver to Byllun by 3 October 1339 (AR1/85). The heading 'J. Billoun' in the rental probably relates to this mortgage, the rent from the properties being payable to Byllun. But the situation is complicated by the fact that three months later, on 4 August 1339, Arundell mortgaged the same properties to Roger and John Caylewy, again for 20 silver marks, to be repaid by 1 May 1340 (AR1/86–87). This was done with Byllun's knowledge, for he was the first witness to the deeds of the new mortgage. However, the evidence of this heading in the rental suggests that the first mortgage, to Byllun, was still in force in 1343. Note the same heading for some properties among the conventionaries (p. 3).

Chevage:
William Piterel, John Pig', John Hardi, Marina de Lanuighan, William Quarter', Thomas Pernel, Joan Pernel, 1*d*. each; total 7*d*.

Mills:
The mill of Lanhern used to pay 40*s*. for the lord's part (*pro parte domini*).
Molend' Goeth[20] used to pay 40*d*.

Total [*of mills*], 43*s*. 4*d*.

Tredreysec [*Tredrizzick, in St Minver*]:
Henry Walter, 3 ferlings there; 17*s*., suit of court.
Richard Paul, 3 ferlings there; 17*s*., suit of court.
Geoffrey *de eadem*, 1½ ferlings there; 4*s*., suit of court.
John Wennon', 1½ ferlings there; 4*s*., suit of court.

Trelawader [*Trelawder, in St Minver*]:[21]
Roger *de eadem*, ½ acre there; 7*s*., suit of court.
John Walter, ½ acre there; 7*s*., suit of court.

Woyn [*Weens, in either St Minver or St Kew*]:[22]
Richard atte Hendr', vill of Woyn; 22*s*., suit of court.

Total [*for Tredrizzick, Trelawder and Weens?*], 108*s*. [*sic; read* 78*s*.?]

Lanuighan [*Lanvean, in St Mawgan in Pyder*]:
Odo Textor, ½ acre in Lanuighan; 9*s*., suit of court.

---

[20] Unidentified, but evidently a former **Melingoth* 'old mill', partly translated into Latin; it was presumably an older mill replaced by the Lanherne mill already mentioned.
[21] Not found in later surveys, but the Roche family (from whom the Arundells obtained their other lands in St Minver parish) had an 8-year interest in the place in 1234 (AR1/50); and it appears among Arundell lands named in a group of leases within the family in 1322–23, which also mention several of the tenants given here (AR1/84 and AR4/183/1–2).
[22] Weens in St Minver parish is close to Treglyn and Gunvenna (see above, in the free tenements, pp. 2–3), but is not otherwise recorded as Arundell property; Weens in St Kew parish, adjacent to Hendra, appears in a final concord dated 1328, effected between William de Tremur with Joan his wife and Joan, widow of John Arundell of *Trembleith* (*Cornwall Feet of Fines*, I, no. 500, = AR1/821), but concerning non-Arundell properties. The identification is therefore uncertain between the two places, and no later mentions in the Arundell archive occur to assist a decision.

MANOR OF LANHERNE AND TREMBLEATH

Thomas Ton, 3 ferlings there; 13s. 6d., suit of court.
Robert *de eadem*, 3 ferlings there; 13s. 6d.
Peter *de eadem*, 1 ferling there; 4s. 6d.
John Ionnian, 1 house and 1 acre English; 2s. 6d.

Total [for Lanvean], 43s.

[*Total for the manor, including free tenants, conventionary tenants, demesne land, cottars, bondmen, Billoun's lands, chevage, mills and other named lands*, £32 11s. 6d. and 2 parts of a farthing.]

LANHADRON, 1385 (AR2/376)

Nansladron [*Nansladron or Lanhadron, in St Ewe*]
Extent of the manor of Nansladron, made by oath of William Stork' and Ralph Roscorlan, Thursday after St Mathias, 8 Richard II [2 March 1385].

[*Free tenants*]

Welle [*unidentified, in Lanlivery*]:[23]
John Stonart, 1 acre Cornish, by knight's service; 2 suits of court at the 2 leet courts.

Peel [*Pill, in Lanlivery*]:
Thomas Courtes, 1 acre Cornish, by knight's service; 1 *lb.* cummin at Michaelmas, with 2 suits of court.

Pengilly and Karloes [*Pengelly, in St Ewe, and Carloose, in Creed*]:
The heirs of Silvester Tregenfren,[24] 2½ acres Cornish, by knight's service; 15*d.* at Michaelmas, with [*blank*] suit of court . . .[25]

Bossulyon [*Bossillian, in Creed*]:
The heirs of Ralph Maenheyr, ½ acre Cornish in socage; 12*d.* at Michaelmas and 2 suits of court at the 2 leet courts.

Bonhordon [*Benhurden, in Goran*]:
Thomas Treuelwyth, ½ acre Cornish, by knight's service; 3*d.* at Michaelmas, 2 suits of court at the leet courts, at Seyngoran, not elsewhere.

Roscorlan [*Rescorla, in St Ewe*]:
The heirs of Richard Botthet, 1 acre Cornish, by knight's service; 12*d.* at Easter and 12*d.* at Michaelmas, common suit of court. [*Entry deleted*, 'because below, namely with Stephen Dodda'].

---

[23] This free tenement appears as *Wille* again in 1463, and as *Will Parke* in 1499 (below, pp. 49 and 117); in 1659 it is 'Wille in the same parish' [of Lanlivery], held by Walter Kendall; but it does not appear thereafter.

[24] On 12 October 1285 John son of Silvester de Tregenwran (who took his surname from Tregarthen, in Ludgvan) acknowledged to Serlo de Lanlaron, the then holder of Lanhadron, his duty to pay suit of court to Serlo every three weeks at *Lanlaron* for tenements which he held of Serlo in *Karlud* and *Pengelli* (AR1/249).

[25] A further word, after *sect' cur'*, is not legible.

Seyncryda [*Creed churchtown*]:
The heirs of Michael Treres,[26] 1 acre Cornish at Sancta Cryda, by knight's service; ['6*d*. and a pair of white gloves at Michaelmas, without suit of court', *deleted*] and scutage when it arises, for all service.

Trewaruene [*Trewarmenna, in Creed*]:
Reginald Tretherf, 1 acre Cornish, in socage; 15*d*. at Easter and Michaelmas [for all service, *deleted*] and a pair of gloves.

Tregerthyk and Nansgronek [*Tregerrick and 'Nansfrinick alias Nanruan' (lost, near Tregerrick); both in Goran*]:
The heirs of William Boddrugan, [3, *deleted*] acres Cornish [4, by charter, *added later*], and 1 ferling Cornish in Nansgronek, by knight's service; a pair of iron spurs or 12*d*. at Michaelmas; 2 suits of court, at the courts after the Exaltation of the Cross and Michaelmas.

Crukconerwoles [*(Lower) Cotna, in Goran*]:
The same heirs, 1 ferling Cornish, by knight's service, and 1 corn mill; 6*d*. at Michaelmas, for all service.

Hountyndon [*Hunting Down; also 'Bloughan' (lost) and Castle, otherwise Little Lantyan; all in Lanlivery*]:
The same heirs, in Hountyndon, Bloflond and Castel, ½ fee, by knight's service.

Stephen Dodda, 1 acre Cornish in Roscorlan [*Rescorla, in St Ewe*]; 12*d*. at Sts Philip and James and Michaelmas, and 2 suits of court.

Total [*of free tenants*], 6*s*. 9*d*., plus 1 pair of iron spurs, 1 pair of gloves, and 1 *lb*. cummin.

Conventionary tenants

Roscorlan [*Rescorla, in St Ewe*]:
Ralph Roscorlan, 1 parcel there, which he formerly held at will; 12*s*.

---

[26] In 1345 the wardship and marriage of Odo son of Michael de Treres, then under age, was sold by William de Campo Arnulphi to John le Soor de Taluren, in Philleigh (AR46/9-11). This Odo must have died without issue, for Joan, daughter and heir of Michael de Trerys, married Randulph Arundell, lord of *Kenhawis* and of *Karenver* and *Wotfold* (Carnewas, in St Eval, and Crenver and Oatfield, in Crowan); their son was Nicholas Arundell of *Trerys*, ancestor of the Trerice branch of the family: see Henderson, 'The Beville obituary' (I), p. 25, and above, p. 2 and n.

and 4 days' work ploughing, harrowing, reaping and carrying the lord's corn; suit of court and mill.

Thomas Crukdur, 1 parcel, at the lord's will; 12s. and service as above [*entry deleted*].

Henry Rescorlan, 1 parcel, at the lord's will; 9s. and service as above.

Richard Watkyn, 1 parcel, for the same term (*ad terminum predictum*); 5s. and 3 days' work reaping, harrowing and carrying the lord's corn; suit of court and mill.

William Braggour, 1 parcel, for the same term (*ad terminum predictum*); 10s. and all services as [above].

Lanhewy [*Lanuah, in St Ewe*]:
Thomas Couk' [?], 1 parcel, for the same term; 7s. 6d. and 3 days' work as above; suit of court and mill.

Thomas Mayow, 1 parcel, for the same term; 7s. 6d. with all services, as above.

John Mester, 1 parcel; 2s. and suit of court.

Seyngoran [*Goran churchtown*]:
Sir John Vicar', 1 parcel, for the same term; 17s.

Richard Vicar, 1 parcel; 17s. and 2 days' work reaping and carrying corn, and suit of court.

['John Martyn', *deleted*] Richard Viker, 1 parcel, at the lord's will; 8s. 6d. and service as above.

Matthew Bothet [?], 1 parcel, for the same term; 8s. 6d. and 2 suits of court and days' work, but not to be reeve or tithingman.

Crukconer Wartha [*Cotna, in Goran*]:
William Stork, 1 parcel, for the same term; 12s. and service as above.

Thomas Wyn, 1 parcel, for the same term; 6s. 8d. and service as above.

John Seys, 1 parcel, for the same term; 7s. and service as above.

Penhal [*Penhale, in Goran*]:
Andrew Mangyer, 1 parcel, for the same term; [14s., *deleted*] 27s. 4d. and all service, as above ['and it is held as a single holding', *added in same hand as* '27s. 4d.'].

John Andrev [*blank*].[27]

Meneyt3gwyens [*Menagwins, in Goran*]:
Alice Meneythgwyns ['John Nicol', *written above*], 1 parcel, for the

---

[27] Evidently John Andrev's holding had been incorporated in that of Andrew Mangyer.

same term; 8s. 6d., and all service, as above.

Waste land (*terra vasta*): 1 parcel formerly of Luke Vincent used to pay 18d.; 1 parcel formerly of John Ponsnewyth used to pay 2s.; 1 parcel formerly of *Pasket* [sic] used to pay 18d.[28]

Bossu [*Bosue, in St Ewe*]:
Nicholas Cissor, 8s. [*deleted?*] 12s. 6d.
Thomas Jedwart, for [?], 6s. 8d.
[Nicholas Auny, *deleted*] Roger Penhalov, 8s. 4d.
[Simon Bossu, 5s., Thomas Slaffe, 4s., *deleted*] Thomas Welle, 12s. 6d.

Penhal [*Penhale, in Goran*]:
Andrew Mangeyr, 13s. 4d. [*deleted, because given above*]

Lanworan [*Goran churchtown*]:
John Hagge, 22s.
Richard Godzhis, 11s. and 3 capons.

Sub-total [68s., *deleted*] 76s. and 3 capons.
Total [*new?*] *of conventionary tenants*, £13 6s. 2d.

Mill:
[Thomas Welle, *deleted*] Richard Wraan, 26s. 8d.

Total [*original? of conventionary tenants?*], £9 0s. 14d.

Total [*original? of free and conventionary tenants*], £9 9s. 5d., plus 1 pair of iron spurs, 1 pair of gloves, and 1 *lb*. cummin.[29]

From which total the lord pays to the chief lords:
to the lord of Tewyn, for the leat of Nansladron mill, 18d.;[30]
to the lord of Debesta, for Pengilly, 18d.;
to the same, fine [*blank; for suit of court*], 13d.[31]

---

[28] All these four entries are deleted, and replaced by one at the end of the whole rental: 'John Nicol pays, for the whole vill of Mene3gwens, 12s. 2d.'.
[29] The various totals do not make sense; but, because of the updatings to the rents, it is not readily possible to disentangle them.
[30] *Tewyn* is the Duchy manor of Tewington, in St Austell parish; in 1379-80 the manor of Lanhadron paid 12d. 'to the lord prince for the leat of Nansladron mill' (AR2/837, m. 1); and in 1386-87 it paid 18d. 'to the lord of Tewyn for the leat of Nansladron mill' (AR2/838, m. 1).
[31] *Debesta* is the Duchy manor of Tybesta, in Creed parish; the account of Lanhadron in 1408-09 (9-10 Henry IV) supplies the missing detail of the payment: 'fine for suit of court for Trewaruene, 13d.' (AR2/837, m. 2).

EXTENT, WHOLE ESTATE, 1451-64

(AR2/1337 + Gloucestershire Record Office, D.421/A2/25)

Contents

Manor of Carminow, 1459	13
Manor of Winnington, 1460	17
Manor of Kennall, 1460	19
Manor of Tregarne, 1460	21
Manor of Trembleath (1), 1459	24
Manor of Treloy, 1460	27
Manor of Lanherne, 1460	32
Town of St Columb	35
Manor of Connerton, 1463	39
Manor of Lanhadron, 1463	49
Rescassa, 1463	53
Manor of Trembleath (2)	54
Manor of Bodwannick, 1464	55
Manor of Enniscaven, 1456	58
Manor of Truro Vean, 1451	60

Manor and borough of Mitchell, 1463 ... 61

EXTENT OF 1451-64

Carmynowe
[*Carminow, in Mawgan in Meneage*]

Extent made Monday before St Thomas the Apostle, 39 Henry VI [17 December 1459], by William Payoun, William Treghar and Simon Kentrevek.

Free tenants

Redalan, Huthnans, Karioghall, Treneer, Ruddour and Tilligowe [*Redallan, Huthnance, Crawle, Trenear, Ruthdower, and Treliggo, all in Breage*]:
The heir of Warin Lercedekne, Redalan, Huthnans, Karioghall, Ruddor, Treneer and Tilligowe, as ½ knight's fee; by homage, fealty and scutage, for all service.

Treueglos, Treuemder, Tregenryth [*Treveglos, Tremeader, Tregerthen* [?] *and 'Carlibby' (lost), all in Zennor*]:[1]
The heir of Richard Sergeaux knight, 1 acre Cornish in Treueglos, 3 acres Cornish in Treuemeder, 1 acre in Tregenryth, and 1 ferling in Carleb, by knight's service; by homage and fealty.

Tregedyll [*Tregiddle, in Cury*]:
John Petyt Predannek, 1 acre Cornish, in socage, by homage and fealty, with suit of court every three weeks; yearly rent, at [All Saints?] and Sts Philip and James, Apostles, 12*d*.

Gurlyn and Treuelyhan [*Gurlyn and Trelean, both in St Erth*]:
The heir of Ralph Soer holds 2 parts of Gurlyn and ½ of Trevelyhan, which were sometime given in free marriage with one Margery daughter of Carmynov.

Grous [*Angrouse, in Mullion*]:
The heir of Reginald Godrevy, 3 acres at Grous, by homage and fealty, with suit of court every 3 weeks; yearly rent, at the four principal dates in the manor, 5*s*.

Rosmodro [*Rosemorder, in Manaccan*]:
Ralph Reskymer, ½ [acre] Cornish in Rosmodro, by homage and fealty; yearly rent, at the four chief dates, for all service, 20*s*.

---

[1] Later surveys (1659, 1717) specify the parish as Zennor.

Polgrun [*Polgrean, in Cury*]:
James Nanfan, 1 [acre] Cornish at Polgr...en, in socage, by homage and fealty, with suit of court every 3 weeks; yearly rent, at the four principal dates, 20s.

Helstonburgh [*Helston town*]:
The heir of Pascoe Cotha, . . . plots (*placeas*) . . . and . . .; yearly rent, at the four principal dates, 6s.

[*Total of free tenants, £1 12s.*]

Conventionary tenants

Lammargh [*Lamarth, in Mawgan in Meneage*]:
Thomas Wille, 1 acre Cornish, that is the whole vill, at the lord's [will]; yearly rent, at the four chief dates usual in the manor, namely St Andrew, mid-Lent, St James the Apostle and Michaelmas, with all other services as all conventionary tenants do, a better beast (*melius averium*) when it arises [as heriot], suit of mill, and other customs as the custom anciently is; 11s.

Bronywyk Wartha, Bronywyk Wolles [*Higher and Lower Burnuick, in Mawgan in Meneage*]:
William Ive, ½ acre and ½ ferling in Bronywyk Wartha, and 1½ ferlings in Bronywyk Woles, at the lord's will; yearly rent, at the same dates, with services as other conventionary tenants do, 23s. 6d.

Hendre, Chynythyn, Killyancreth [*Hendra and 'Chynythen' (lost), in Cury, and Killianker, in Mawgan in Meneage*]:
John Hicke, in Hendre ½ acre Cornish and in Chynythyn ½ ferling, at the lord's will; yearly rent, at the same dates, with all other services as other conventionary tenants do, 17s.
John Jakke Robyn, in Hendre 3 ferlings and in Kyllyancreth 1 acre, at the lord's will; yearly rent, at the same dates, with all other services as other conventionary tenants do, 17s.

Cleys, Olynsy [*'Clies Olingey' (lost), part of Clies, in Mawgan in Meneage*]:
John Cleys Mottry, in Cleys and in Olensy 3 ferlings, at the lord's will; yearly rent, at the same dates, with all other services as above, 16s.

Chywarloo contains 4 acres Cornish [*Chyvarloe, in Gunwalloe; also 'Treworlyn' (lost), presumably in Gunwalloe*]:[2]

[2] Compare the place called *Trewurlyn*, mentioned in a court roll of the

Richard Sweyn, in Chiwarloo, 1 holding, at the lord's will; yearly rent, with service as above, 10s.

Walter Polpenruth, 1 holding there, at the lord's will; yearly rent, with service as above, 10s. 8d.

Richard Cleys, 1 holding there, at the lord's will; yearly rent, with service as above, 6s. 8d.

James Hopkyn, 1 holding there, at the lord's will; yearly rent, with service as above, 10s.

John Cleys, 1 holding there, at the lord's will; yearly rent, with service as above, 12s.

Geoffrey Porthbyan, 1 holding there, at the lord's will; yearly rent, with service as above, 10s.

Benedict (*Ben'*) Renaudyn, 1 holding there called Treworlyn, at the lord's will; yearly rent, with service as above, 10s.

Nanspyan [*Nampean, in Gunwalloe*]:
Richard *de eadem*, ½ acre, at the lord's will; yearly rent, with service as above, 15s.

Gome [*'Goome' (lost), near Anhay, in Gunwalloe*]:
John Robyn, 1 ferling, at the lord's will; yearly rent, with service as above, 5s.

Hendredodda [*Burgess, in Gunwalloe; also 'Chynythen' (lost), in Cury*]:[3]
Simon Kentrevek, ½ acre there, and in Chyneythyn ½ ferling; yearly rent, with service as above, 16s.

Chynals [*Chinalls, in Gunwalloe*]:
Walter Treleek, 3 ferlings, at the lord's will; yearly rent, with service as above, 13s. 4d.

Beauripper [*Berepper, in Gunwalloe*]:
Simon Kentrevek, 1 ferling, at the lord's will; yearly rent, with service as above, 9s.

Hee [*Anhay, in Gunwalloe*]:
William Treghar, 3 ferlings, at the lord's will; yearly rent, with service as above, 25s. 8d.

William Payoun, 3 ferlings, at the lord's will; yearly rent, with

manor in 1488–90: AR2/219, m. 2.
[3] In a seventeenth-century book of leases and letters appears a lease, dated December 1680, for a tenement (singular) called 'Hendradoda alias Burges and Rossehender', parcel of the manors of Carminow and Winnington (AR8/21, fol. [3r]).

service as above, 21s.

Morreb Loo, Polscovornogowe, Cleys Men ['*Morebloe*' *(lost), in Gunwalloe;* '*Polscovornogow*' *and* '*Clies Men*', *unidentified*]:
At Polscovornogowe there are 2 acres, at Cleys Meen 1 acre, and at Morreb Loo 4 acres [*no tenant or rent given*].

Mills:
Thomas Raffull, 1 mill with land annexed to it, *viz.* the lower mill; yearly rent, with service as other conventionary tenants do, 20s.
The higher mill is now vacant and remains in the lord's hands; it is ruinous and decayed; it used to pay [*blank*].[4]

Total of conventionary tenants and mills, [*blank*; £13 18s. 10d.]

Total of free and conventionary tenants and mills,
[*blank*; £15 10s. 10d.]

Demesne land of Carmenowe

Peter Gerveys, the farmer there, pays for the farm of the demesne land of Carmynov, together with the land of Bronnov [*Burnow, in Cury*], at the same dates, maintaining all the houses with thatching-straw (*cum stram' tect'*) and all the hedges, and at the end of the term he is to surrender and hand them over in as good a state as he received them, [*blank*].

Payment of rent (*acquietanc' redd'*)

To the lord bishop of Exeter, for Carmenov, 6s. at the feasts of All Saints and Sts Philip and James, Apostles, and suit of court;[5]
to John Pedit, for Crous,[6] at the same feasts, 5s.;
to the lord of Lucyes,[7] for Rosmordro, 20d.

* * *

---

[4] Compare perhaps the 'new mill' of Carminow, the building of which appears in the reeve's account in 1491–92 (AR2/931, fol. 3).
[5] In the account rolls the payment to the bishop of Exeter was made for the conventionary tenement of Lamarth only, e.g. in 1433–34 and 1469–70 (AR2/887, m. 5, and AR2/910, p. 2).
[6] The free tenement of Angrouse (see above) was held of Petit's manor of Predannack (Wartha), in Mullion, as seen in the account rolls, e.g. in 1433–34 and 1454–55 (AR2/887, m. 5, and AR2/900, m. 7).
[7] The manor of Rosuick or *Lucyes*, in St Keverne.

Wynyantoun
[Winnington, in Gunwalloe]

Extent made Tuesday before St Hilary, 38 Henry VI [8 January 1460].

Free tenants

Tregowres, Hengeyther and Cornhough [*Tregowris, Nangither and Carno, all in St Keverne*]:
Ralph Reskymer, 2 acres Cornish, in socage; yearly rent, at St Andrew the Apostle, mid-Lent, St James and Michaelmas, with common suit of court every 3 weeks, 10s. 2d.

Trerys, Trenans Bian and Treseys [*Trerise, in Ruan Major; Trenance Vean, in Mullion; and Trezise, in St Martin in Meneage*]:
The heir of Richard Sergeaux, 1 acre Cornish in Trerys, by homage and fealty for all service.
The same heir, ½ acre Cornish in Trenans Bian, in socage; yearly rent, at the same feasts, with suit of court, 2s. 5½d.
The same heir, ½ acre Cornish in Treseys, in socage; yearly rent, with suit of court, as above, 2s.

Bossym and Pentyr [*Bochym and Pentire, both in Cury*]:
The heir of William le Brit, 1 acre Cornish, by knight's service; suit of court every 3 weeks, for all service; [*blank*].

Trevenwoen alias Trnowne [*sic*][8] [*Trenoon, in Ruan Major*]:
The heir of William Erysy, ½ acre Cornish in Trenowoen, in socage; yearly rent, at the same feasts, 6s. 8d.

Hendre [*Hendra, in Ruan Major*]:
Thomas Massely, 3 ferlings, in socage; yearly rent, with suit of court, as above, 3s. 8¼d.
The heir of Henry de Hendre, 1 ferling, in socage; yearly rent, with suit of court, as above, 14¾d.

Trespryson [*Tresprison, in Mullion*]:
The heir of Henry Tresprysoun, ½ acre Cornish, in socage; yearly rent, with suit of court, as above, 2s. 5½d.

Erysy [*Erisey, in Grade*]:
Henry Bodrugan, ½ acre Cornish, in Erysy; yearly rent, with suit of court, as above, 20d.

---

[8] *alias Trnowne* added later, in a different hand.

Tregadreth Mur, Tregadreth Bihan, Treris, Nansplough [*Tregaddra, in Mawgan in Meneage, and Trease and Nanplough, both in Cury*]:
The heir of Thomas de Tregadreth, 2 acres and 1 ferling in Tregadreth Mur, Tregadreth Bian, Trerys and Nansplough; yearly rent, at the same feasts, with suit of court, as above, 20*d*.

Seyntsewana [*Sowanna, in Gunwalloe*]:
½ acre Cornish, which used to pay yearly 4*s*. 11*d*., is in the lord's hand, because it descended by hereditary right to Matthew de Seynt Sewana, a bondman (*nativus*) of the lord, as elsewhere stated (*ut alias pres'*); now it is granted as conventionary land (*traditur convencionar'*), as below.[9]

Total [*of free tenants, blank;* 37*s*. 4½*d*. (?)]

Conventionary tenants

Toll [*Toll, in Gunwalloe*]:
John Nensy, 3 ferlings; yearly rent, at St Andrew the Apostle, mid-Lent, St James and Michaelmas, with suit of court and of Carmynowe mill, and other services as other conventionary tenants of the manor do, 20*s*.

Gonensy Cok [*'Goninsey Cock' (lost), close to Chepye, in Gunwalloe*]:
Matthew Hicke, in Gonensy, 1 acre Cornish; yearly rent, with suit of court and service as above, 10*s*.

Gonensy Pye [*Chepye, in Gunwalloe*]:[10]
John Nicholl, 3 ferlings; yearly rent, at the same feasts, as above, 12*s*. [?]

---

[9] Is this entry at all defensive? The promised mention does not appear. The tenement is absent from the 1480 rental, and appears between the free and conventionary tenements (but with no rent given) in 1499 (p. 128). It remained as a free tenement of the manor (with the rent unchanged) in the sixteenth-century surveys (and in 1571 also as a conventionary tenement, deleted: AR2/1341), and is absent altogether from those of 1659 and 1717.
[10] In a lease of 1783 the single tenement of 'Goninsey Cock and Goninsey Pye otherwise Chepy' appears (AR4/998); although the name Chepye is itself ancient (first recorded in 1492, and named from the le Py family, recorded in the parish in the 1327 Lay Subsidy), evidently Goninsey Pye (as well as Goninsey Cock) became merged with it at some time before the late eighteenth century; compare also *Trenowith iuxta Gonensy* in a deed of 1457 listing tenements of Winnington manor (AR20/23); Trenoweth is adjacent to Chepye in Gunwalloe parish.

Trenewith [*Trenoweth, in Gunwalloe*]:
John Robyn, 1 acre Cornish; yearly rent, at the same feasts, as above, 17s.

Roos [*'Rosehendra' (lost), in Cury*]:[11]
Simon Kentrevek, 1 ferling; yearly rent, at the same feasts, with suit of court, as above, 4s.

Nynsy [*Hingey, in Gunwalloe*]:[12]
John Pascov, 1 acre Cornish; yearly rent, at the same feasts, with suit of court, as above, 16s.

Wynyanton [*Winnington, in Gunwalloe*]:
James Tabard, 1 acre Cornish; yearly rent, at the same feasts, 12s.
Thomas Oby, 1½ acres Cornish; yearly rent, at the same feasts, 20s.

Total [*of conventionary tenants, blank;* 109s.]

There are also various casual profits, *viz.* of marriage, scutage, aids, escheats, heriots, wreck of sea, and strays, from the Hundred of Kirriar.[13]

Total *of free and conventionary tenants,* [*blank;* £7 6s. 4½d. (?)]

* * *

Kenell
[*Kennall, in Stithians*]

Extent made Wednesday before St Hilary, 38 Henry VI [9 January 1460].

[*Free tenants*]

Tregonan, Penmena, Treskewys and Trembruth [*Tregonning, Penmenor, Treskewes, and Trembroath, all in Stithians*]:
John Trethaek, 2 acres Cornish, in socage; yearly rent, at mid-Lent

---

[11] See above, under *Hendredodda* alias Burgess (p.15).
[12] A lease of the lands of manor in 1783 calls this tenement '*Hengey* otherwise *Nensey*' (AR4/1001).
[13] Roger de Carminow had in 1302 proved that he had the right to waif and stray in the Hundred of Kerrier, as an appurtenance of his manors of Winnington, Merthen (in Constantine) and Tamerton (*Placita de Quo Warranto*, p. 109b); at the division of the Carminow estates in 1396 it came to Arundell along with the manors of Carminow, Kennall and Winnington (*Catalogue of Ancient Deeds*, IV, A.10409, = AR1/192/1-2).

and Michaelmas, with 1 suit of court, at the next court after Michaelmas, and relief when it arises, 4s.

Ressegh [*Roseath, in Stithians*]:
John Ressegh, ½ acre Cornish, by knight's service; 2 suits of court, at May-day and Michaelmas, and he is to have housebote and 2 days' worth of turbary in Kennall moor (*duas dietas blestar' in mora de Kenell*); yearly rent, at the same dates, with relief when it arises, 3s.

Enys [*Ennis, in Stithians*]:
The heir of Henry de Enys, 3 parts of an acre Cornish, in knight's service; suit of court every 3 weeks; yearly rent, at the same dates, with relief when it arises, 14¾d.
The heir of John Auny, 1 ferling, by knight's service; suit of court as the heir of Henry de Enys; yearly rent, with relief when it arises, 14¾d.

Tregonan [*Tregonning, in Stithians*]:
The heir of William de Trencryk, ½ acre Cornish, in socage; 3-weekly suit of court; yearly rent, at the same dates, with relief when it arises, 2s.

Hendre [*Hendra, in Stithians*]:
Thomas Durant, ½ acre Cornish, by knight's service; 2 suits of court at the 2 leet courts; yearly rent, at the same dates, with relief when it arises, 3s.

Total [*of free tenants*], 14s. 5½d.

Conventionary tenants

Kenell [*Kennall, in Stithians*]:
Walter Cissor, 2 holdings as one, with 1 heriot (*duas tenuras sub una tenura et una herieto* [*sic*]); suit of court and mill, to be reeve when chosen, and all other services as other conventionary tenants do; yearly rent, at 4 dates, *viz.* St Andrew the Apostle, mid-Lent, St James the Apostle and Michaelmas, 18s.
William Tomma, 1 holding; suit of court and mill, and all other service, as above; yearly rent, 13s. 4d.
Richard Wilcok, 1 holding; suit of court and mill, and all other service as above; yearly rent, 13s. 4d.
Andrew Envelyn, 1 holding; suit of court and mill, and all other service, as above; yearly rent, 8s. 6d.

Treberueth [*Trebarveth, in Stithians*]:
John Noiel, 2 holdings; the same service, with suit of court, as above; yearly rent, at the same feasts, 16s. 6d.[14]

Tremenhir [*Tremenheere, in Stithians*]:
Peter Tremenhyr, 1 holding; the same service, as above; yearly rent, at the same feasts, 10s.

Trembroyth [*Trembroath, in Stithians*]:
William Hopkyn, 1 holding; the same service, as above; yearly rent, at the same feasts, 8s. 6d.
John Pascov, 1 holding; the same service, as above; yearly rent, at the same feasts, 8s. 6d.

Kenell mill [*in Stithians*]:[15]
Ralph Melender, the lord's mill; yearly rent, at the same feasts, 13s. 4d.

Total [*of conventionary tenants*], 110s.

Total of free and conventionary tenants, [*blank;* £6 4s. 5½d.]

* * *

Tregarn
[*Tregarne, in St Keverne*]

Extent made 8 January, 38 Henry VI [1460], by John Renawdyn, John Parson, William Tregarn and others.

[*Free tenants*]

Trelanvian [*Trelanvean, in St Keverne*]:
Ralph Reskymer, ½ acre Cornish [*tenure not given*]; yearly rent, at St Andrew the Apostle, mid-Lent, St James the Apostle and Michaelmas, with 2 suits of court at the 2 leet courts, and relief when it arises, 7s.

Comgwynnan [*Polgwidnan, in St Keverne*]:
The heir of Henry Chynals, [*blank*]; yearly rent, without suit of court, ½d.

---

[14] John Noiell was reeve of the manor in 1467–68: account roll (AR2/908, m. 2).
[15] Detailed accounts of recent repairs to this mill appear in the reeves' accounts for 1446–47 and 1447–48 (AR2/892 and 894, m. 2).

Tregarn [*Tregarne, in St Keverne*]:
Henry Boden, [*blank*]; yearly rent, with suit of court every 3 weeks, and relief when it arises, 12*d*.

Moungleth [*Mongleath, in Budock*]:
Simon Kyllygrewe, [*blank*]; yearly rent, with suit of court every 3 weeks, and relief when it arises, 2*s*.

Nansdreysek [*Nancetrisack, in Sithney*]:
The heir of John Arundell, knight,[16] [*blank*]; yearly rent, as above, 6*d*.

Penwerres [*Penwerris, in Budock*]:
The same heir, the whole vill; yearly rent, 1 pair of white gloves or 1*d*.

Gylly [*Gilly, in Mawgan in Meneage*]:
John Pedyt, [*blank*]; yearly rent, with 2 suits of court, 1*d*.

Baghowe [*Bahow, in St Keverne*]:
Richard Baghowe, [*blank*]; yearly rent, 7*s*.

Total of free tenants, [*blank*; 17s. 8½d.*]

Conventionary tenants

Tregarn [*Tregarne, in St Keverne*]:
John Polgwest, 1 holding; yearly rent, at St Andrew the Apostle, mid-Lent, St James the Apostle and Michaelmas, with suit of court and mill, and other services according to the custom of the manor, 20*s*.
Walter Mata, 1 holding; yearly rent, with other service and suit of court as above, 12*s*. 2*d*.
William Menughter, 1 holding; yearly rent, with other service and suit of court as above, 13*s*. 8*d*.

Helwyn [*Halwyn, in St Keverne*]:
Thomas Pascov, 1 holding; yearly rent, at the same dates, with suit of court as above, 12*s*.
Nicholas Helwyn, 1 holding; yearly rent, at the same dates, with suit of court as above, 12*s*.

---

[16] From the 1499 rental (below, p. 123) it is apparent that this was Arundell of Tolverne (in Philleigh), not of Lanherne. Nancetrisack was also held as a conventionary tenement of Prospidnick manor (pp. 147, 150), paying 6*d*. high rent to Tregarne manor (account, 1433–4, AR2/887, m. 2).

Tregevys [*Tregevas, in St Martin in Meneage*]:
John Renawdyn, ½ of the vill; yearly rent, at the same dates, 16s.
Richard Renawdyn, the other ½ of the vill; yearly rent, with suit of court as above, 16s.

Hendrevyk [*Landrivick, in Manaccan*]:
Robert Hendrevyk, the whole vill; yearly rent, at the same dates, with suit of court as above, 15s.

Condorowe [*Condurrow, in St Anthony in Meneage*]:
Peter Soer, 1 holding; yearly rent, at the same dates, with suit of court and other service as above, 10s. 4d.
John Hopkyn, 1 holding; yearly rent, at the same dates, with suit of court and other service as above, 10s. 4d.
John Parson, 1 holding; yearly rent, at the same dates, with suit of court and other service as above, 10s. 4d.
Geoffrey de Condorowe, 1 holding; yearly rent, at the same dates, with suit of court and other service as above, 10s. 4d.

Penpoll [*Penpoll, in St Anthony in Meneage*]:[17]
John Soer, 1 holding; yearly rent, at the same dates, with suit of court and other service as above, 9s.

Boden Vian [*Boden Vean, in St Anthony in Meneage*]:
William Tomperowe, 1 holding; yearly rent, at the same dates, with suit of court and other service as above, 20s.

The mill [*Tregarne Mill, in St Keverne*]:
David Cryer Melender, the mill of Tregarn, repairing and maintaining it at his own costs; yearly rent, 22s.

[*Total of conventionary tenants*, £10 9s. 2d.]

[*Total of free and conventionary tenants*, £11 6s. 8½d.]

* * *

---

[17] By the time of the rental of c.1586 Penpoll, in St Anthony in Meneage, had been altered to a free tenement of this manor (AR2/1343).

Trembleyth
[*Trembleath, in St Ervan*][18]

Extent made 20 October, 38 Henry VI [1459], by William Vycar, John Carbura, William Carbura, John Heyly and others.

Free tenants

Lamayll,[19] Arlyn, Trevayhov, Trethias, Treyarnan, Trevur, Tewyn [*Lemail (in Egloshayle), Harlyn, Trevio,*[20] *Trethias, Treyarnon, Treveor and Towan (all in St Merryn)*]:
Thomas Rescarrek, William Pencors and Hugh Boscawen, co-heirs of Laurence Arundell, in Trevayhov 1 acre Cornish, in Trethias ½ acre, in Treyarnan ½ acre, in Tewyn ½ acre, in Trevur ½ acre, and in Arlyn ½ acre,[21] by knight's service; yearly rent 1 pair of gilt spurs or 3s. 4d, at the 4 dates usual in the manor, with suit of court every 3 weeks: 3s. 4d.

Kerowe Lom [*Carlumb, in St Minver*]:
Thomas Rescarrek, 2 acres Cornish, by knight's service; yearly rent, with suit of court as above, 1d.

Kerowe Mur [*Blakes Keiro, otherwise Keiro Veor, in St Minver*]:
Thomas Whalisbrewe, 2 acres Cornish, by knight's service; yearly rent, with suit of court as above, 3s. 4d.

Ammall, Trevanger, Seynt Mynfre, and Trethavek [*(Middle) Amble (in St Kew),*[22] *Trevanger, St Minver and Trethauke (all in St Minver)*]:
Thomas Mohoun, in Ammall 1 acre Cornish, in Trevanger 1 acre, in Seynt Mynfre 1 acre and in Trethavek ½ acre, by knight's service; yearly rent, with 3-weekly suit of court as above, 12½d.

Arlyn [*Harlyn, in St Merryn*]:[23]
John Coulyng, by right of Katherine his wife, ½ acre Cornish, by knight's service; yearly rent, with 3-weekly suit of court, [*blank*].

---

[18] The conventionary tenements of this manor are duplicated in a later section: below, pp. 54–55.
[19] Lemail, though specified in the marginal heading, is omitted in the text.
[20] Identification provided by later surveys; compare *Tregahu* in c.1240 and *Tregayhu* in 1259 (deeds, AR1/51 and AR1/66).
[21] 'and now Cowelyng holds' (*et modo Cowelyng habet*), added above *Arlyn*; see the separate entry, below, for the same information.
[22] For the identification see the rental of 1343 (above, p. 1).
[23] See also under *Lamayll*, etc., above.

Restelek [*Retallick, in Roche*]:[24]
The heir of John Hopkyn, 1 acre Cornish, by knight's service, with suit of court at the 2 leet courts; yearly rent, at the same dates, 6*d*.

Trevelwith [*Trevella, in Crantock*]:
John Trevelwith, 1 acre Cornish; yearly rent, at the same 4 dates, without suit of court, 4*s*.

Langorowe [*Langurra, at Crantock churchtown*]:
John Quynell, ½ acre Cornish in socage, with common suit of court; yearly rent, 6*d*.

Tewyn [*Towan, in St Columb Minor*]:[25]
Remfrey Arundell, ½ acre Cornish in socage; yearly rent, without suit of court, 3*d*.

Trefewha [*Trevowah, in Crantock*]:
Robert Trefewha, ½ acre Cornish in socage; yearly rent, with common suit of court, 13½*d*.

Skywys [*(Great) Skewes, in St Wenn*]:[26]
The heir of John Arundell, knight, 2 acres Cornish in socage; no rent, but suit of court every 3 weeks.

Total [*of free tenants*], 14*s*. 2*d*.

Conventionary tenants

Trethreysek [*Tredrizzick, in St Minver*]:
Thomas Blake, 1 holding; yearly rent at Christmas, Easter, Nativity of St John the Baptist and Michaelmas, plus a day's work at harvest, and other services according to the custom of the manor, 13*s*. 4*d*.

Penros [*Penrose, in St Ervan*]:
John Penros, Richard Jaktomma [*blank left for further names*], 1 holding; yearly rent at the same feasts, and to be reeve when chosen, and all other services according to the custom of the manor, 14*s*.

---

[24] The identification is provided by later surveys, and by an acknowledgement by Arundell of receipt of homage from George Fursedon in 1579 for Fursedon's tenement of *Restellecke*, endorsed *c*.1600 as being in Trembleath manor and Roche parish (AR3/36).
[25] This free tenement is called *Tewyn in St Colomb Loer* in the rental of *c*.1586 (AR2/1343).
[26] A court roll of the manor in 1527–28 provides the identification: *Skewys Veor*, held by Thomas Tretherff of this manor (AR2/952, m. 2).

Tregona [*Tregona, in St Eval*]:
John Carbura, 1 holding, services as above; yearly rent at the same feasts, 13s. 4d.
John Androwe Treghar, 1 holding, services as above; yearly rent at the same feasts, 13s. 4d.
John Scovarn, 1 holding, by the same service, as above; yearly rent, at the same feasts, 16s. 8d.
Ralph Carpentar', 1 holding, by the same service; yearly rent, at the same feasts, 23s. 4d.
John Carbura junior, 1 holding, service as above; yearly rent, at the same feasts, 13s. 4d.

Hengolan [*Engollan, in St Eval*]:
William Vycar, 1 holding, service as above; yearly rent, at the same feasts, 16s. 3d.
William Carbura, 1 holding, service as above; yearly rent, at the same feasts, 13s. 4d.
Robert Endure, 1 holding, service as above; yearly rent, at the same feasts, 13s. 4d.

Helwen [*Halwyn, in St Eval, at Engollan*]:[27]
Richard Mechell, the whole vill, service as above; yearly rent, at the same feasts, 13s.

Trembleyth [*Trembleath, in St Ervan*]:
John Laury, 1 holding, service as above; yearly rent, at the same feasts, 15s. 3½d.
John Heyly, 1 holding, service as above; yearly rent, at the same feasts, 13s. 4d.

Crukmorrek [*Crigmurrick, in St Merryn*]:
Robert Coulyng, ½ acre Cornish at the lord's will; yearly rent, at the same dates, 10s.

Trembleyth [*Trembleath, in St Ervan*]:
Richard Jankyn Wilkyn, a parcel of land on the east side, called Trembleyth close (*claus' de Trembleyth*) beside Ton Engrous and the land of Trewynnek; suit of court twice yearly; yearly rent, for term

---

[27] For the identification, see leases of *Helwyn*, with *Hengollan*, as a conventionary tenement of this manor in 1540–59 (AR4/75–77); also a lease, 1684, of the 'towne and villadge of Hengollan and Helwyn', in St Eval (AR4/80). Halwyn survived as two fields at Engollan in 1841. The same pair formed a free tenement of Lanherne manor: see below, p. 32.

of years by the lord's charter, 6s. 8d.[28]

Trevyngonyov [*Tregwinyo, otherwise Trevengenow, in St Ervan*]:
William Tom Androwe, the whole vill, service as above; yearly rent, at the same feasts, 10s.
He also holds a close called Parke Trembleyth; yearly rent, at the same feasts, 33s. 4d.

Treveneyles [*Trenayles, near Tregwinyo, in St Ervan*]:
The tenants of Trembleyth hold Treveneyles in common among themselves; yearly rent, at the same feasts, [*blank*].

Menuwels [*Manuels, in St Columb Minor*]:
Eurinus Jakrobyn, 1 holding, service as above; yearly rent, at the same feasts, 20s.
Richard Donowe, 1 holding, service as above; yearly rent, at the same feasts, 20s.

Chapell [*Chapel, in St Columb Minor*]:
[*blank*] Gouernour, 1 holding, service as above; yearly rent, at the same feasts, 6s. 8d.

Melynnew[t] [*Millingworth, in St Ervan*]:
John Scovarn junior, the lord's mill of Melynnewith; yearly rent, at the same feasts, 16s.; to repair the mill at his own expense, except that the lord shall provide mill-stones and timber when needed.

Total of conventionary tenants, 'without Trembleyth, Treuenayll and Trevyngonyowe',[29] £11 15s. 11d.

[*Total of free and conventionary tenants*, £12 10s. 1d. (?).]

* * *

Treloy
[*Treloy, in St Columb Minor*]

Extent made Friday before the Nativity of St John the Baptist, 38 Henry VI [20 June 1460], by John Mathy, John Benny and others.

Free tenants

Polgrun [*Polgreen, in Newlyn East*]:
The heir of Mark Mighelstowe, 3 acres Cornish, by knight's service;

---

[28] Trewinnick, in St Ervan (not Arundell land); *Ton Engrous* is unknown.
[29] These tenements seem actually to be included here; for their omission, as demesne land of the manor, see the later entry (below, p. 55).

suit of court every 3 weeks; yearly rent, at the 4 dates usual in the manor, 5s.

Gargus [*Gargas, in Cuby*]:
Thomas Trevaignoun, [*blank*] Cornish, by knight's service; yearly rent, with common suit of court, 12d.

Bosuelek [*Boswellick, in St Allen*]:
The same Thomas, [*blank*] Cornish, by knight's service; yearly rent, with suit of court as above, 6d.

Reys [*Rees, in Perranzabuloe*]:
The same Thomas, ½ acre Cornish in Reys, by knight's service; yearly rent, with suit of court as above, 1d.

Kelestek [*Callestock-ruall, otherwise Little Callestick, in Perranzabuloe; also Bryanick, at St Agnes churchtown*]:
The same Thomas, [*blank*] Cornish in Kelestek Ruald and Breanek, [*tenure blank*]; yearly rent, 2s.

Trencruk [*Trencreek, in St Columb Minor*]:
John Pedyt Predannek, 1 acre Cornish, in socage; yearly rent, with suit of court as above, 12d.
The heir of Henry Trencruk, 1 acre Cornish, in socage; yearly rent, with suit of court as above, 2s. 8d.

Wiket [*Wicket, in Newlyn East*]:
John Copleston, ½ acre Cornish, in socage, by right of his wife, daughter and heiress of John Hanly; suit of court every 3 weeks; yearly rent, 10d.

Trelegh [*Traleath, in Newlyn East*]:
The same John, ½ acre in Trelegh, in socage, by his wife's right as above; yearly rent, with suit of court as above, 10d.

Trelast [*Trelaske, in Cubert*]:
The heir of Richard Gluvyon, 4 acres Cornish, in socage; yearly rent, with common suit of court, 20d.

Pentyr Vian [*Pentirevean, otherwise East Pentire, in Crantock*]:
Francis Jannowe, 1 acre Cornish, in socage; yearly rent, with common suit of court, 2s.

Trefewa [*Trevowah, in Crantock*]:
The heir of Maud Trefewa, 1 acre Cornish and ½ ferling, in socage; yearly rent, with common suit of court, 2s. 6½d.

James Nanfan, 1 ferling, in socage; yearly rent, at the same dates, with common suit of court, 4*d*.

Helwyn [*Halwyn, in Crantock*]:
Thomas Wyndesore, 1 parcel of land; yearly rent, at the same dates, with common suit of court, 6*d*.

Tresavian [*Tresean, in Cubert*]:
John Trevele, ½ acre Cornish, in socage; yearly rent, with common suit of court, 12*d*.

Hendre Paull [*Hendra Paul, in St Columb Minor*]:
John Trethias, ½ acre Cornish, by knight's service; yearly rent, with common suit of court, 3*s*.

Trevargh [*Trevarth, in Gwennap*]:[30]
Henry Bodrugan, [*blank*] Cornish; yearly rent, without suit of court, 5*s*.

Talkarn Morepp [*Tolcarne Merock, in St Mawgan in Pyder*]:
Paul Benny, 1 acre Cornish, in socage; yearly rent, with suit of court and mill, 17*s*.

Hendre Moistell ['*Hendra Mussell', in St Columb Minor*]:[31]
Peter Seyntaubyn, John Bray Treworlas, Richard Carvegh and John Boys, 1 acre Cornish in Hendre Moystell, by right of their wives, co-heiresses of William de Tremur, by knight's service; yearly rent, with suit of court twice, 13¾*d*.

Trenynnek [*Treninick, in St Columb Minor*]:
Robert [*sic; read* John?] le Veer, earl of Oxford, 6 acres Cornish in Trenynnek, by knight's service; yearly rent, with common suit of court, 1 *lb*. pepper.

Caskeys [*(Higher) Keskeys, in St Columb Minor*]:
Richard Rosougan, ½ acre Cornish, by right of Joan his wife, daughter of Thomas Bosveysek; yearly rent, with suit of court twice, 13*d*.

---

[30] Documents in CRO ME/189-197 deal with Bodrugan's tenure of Trevarth in Gwennap; the earliest is a quitclaim dated 1291 by Thomas lord of Pensignance (in Gwennap) to Sir Henry de Bodrugan of the land of Trevarth. In 1421-22 and 1479-80 the manor of Treloy paid a rent to the lord of Inkpen for this tenement (AR2/46 and AR2/919).

[31] It is not certain whether *Hendra Mussell* was at Hendra near Manuels or Hendra near Treloy, both in St Columb Minor.

Penrynburgh [*Penryn town, in St Gluvias*]:
John Body de Penrynburgh [*blank*].

Total of free tenants, 50s. 2¾d.

Conventionary tenants

Treloy and Niewetoun [*Treloy and 'Newton' (lost), in St Columb Minor*]:
John Hicke Mathy, 2 acres Cornish in Treloy, at the lord's will; suit of court and mill, a day's work at harvest, to be reeve and tithingman when chosen, and all other services as other conventionary tenants do, and a best beast as heriot; yearly rent, 36s. 8d.

John Perys, ½ acre and one-third of ½ acre Cornish in Treloy, at the lord's will; services as above; yearly rent, payable at the 4 dates usual in the manor, 12s. 2¾d.

John Tyek, ½ acre and one-third of ½ acre Cornish in Treloy, at the lord's will; services as above; yearly rent, at the same 4 dates, 12s. 2¾d.

John Benny, ½ acre and one-third of ½ acre Cornish in Treloy, at the lord's will; services as above; yearly rent, at the usual dates, 12s. 2¾d.

Pentyr [*(West) Pentire, in Crantock*]:
Francis Pentyr, ½ acre Cornish, service as above; yearly rent, 9s.

Bodrugowe [*Bedrugga, in St Columb Minor*]:
Thomas Groby, ½ acre Cornish, service as above; yearly rent, at the same dates, 6s.

Talkarn [*Tolcarne, in St Mawgan in Pyder*]:[32]
Laurence Benny, ½ acre Cornish, service as above; yearly rent, at the same dates, 11s.

Tripkunyn [*Trekenning, in St Columb Major*]:
John Skauerel, ½ acre Cornish, as above; yearly rent, at the same dates, 15s.

Kestell [*Kestle, in St Columb Minor*]:
Thomas Penros, [*blank*] Cornish, as above; yearly rent, at the same dates, 17s.

---

[32] Seemingly Tolcarne Merock, in St Mawgan in Pyder, the same as the free tenement: so in c.1586, '*Talcarnmerack* in St Mawgan' (AR2/1343).

Treveglos [*Treviglas, in St Columb Minor*]:
John Symon, ½ acre Cornish, as above; yearly rent, at the same dates, 12s.
John Huwet, 1 ferling, as above; yearly rent, at the same dates, 7s. 8d.
John Ady, 1 ferling, as above; yearly rent, at the same dates, 6s. 8d.
John Perowe, weaver (*textor*), 1 house and 1 selion containing 1 acre English; services as above; yearly rent, at the same dates, 4s. 6d.

Trewothowall [*Trethowell, in Kea*]:[33]
John de Trewothowall, ½ of the vill, as above; yearly rent, 13s. 4d.
Francis of the same (*de eadem*), the other ½ of the vill, as above; yearly rent, 13s. 4d.

Myngan [*'Mingham' (lost), in St Columb Major*]:
Richard Olyuer, the whole vill, by the lord's charter, for term of years; yearly rent, as above, 18s.

Trepedannen [*Trebudannon, in St Columb Major*]:
John Tomma, 1 ferling; service as above; yearly rent, at the same dates, 10s.

Penpoll [*Penpoll, in Crantock*]:
Ralph Volanty, the whole vill; service as above; yearly rent, at the same feasts, 40s.

Trehibeowe [*Trebby, in St Columb Minor*]:
[*blank*]; service as above; yearly rent at the same feasts, 10s.

Penrynburgh [*Penryn town, in St Gluvias*]:
John Body, by the lord's charter, for term of years; yearly rent, at the same feasts, without suit of court, 10s.

Strete Newham [*'Strete Newham', otherwise 'Newhamstret' (lost), in Truro (in Kenwyn)*]:
1 garden there; yearly rent, 8d.

Melenvran [*mill at Mellanvrane, in St Columb Minor*]:
Henry Huwet, 1 holding with 1 selion and a parcel of moor below the mill, bounded by the corn-mill; yearly rent, 20s.

[*Total of conventionary tenants, £14 7s. 6¼d.*]

[*Total of free and conventionary tenants, £16 12s. 9d.*]

* * *

---

[33] See AR4/42–45, leases dated 1588–1619 of Trethowell, specified as being in Kea parish and Treloy manor, to the Husband family of Kea.

Lanhern
[*Lanherne, in St Mawgan in Pyder*]

Extent made 12 May, 38 Henry VI [1460].

Free tenants

Ruthfos and Gauergan [*Ruthvoes and Gaverigan, in St Columb Major*]:
The heir of Warin Lercedekne knight, 3 acres Cornish in socage; yearly rent, at the 4 dates usual in the manor, with suit of court every 3 weeks and relief when it arises, 12*d*.

Nanstornan [*Nantornan, in St Columb Minor*]:
Thomas Nanswhidan, 1 acre Cornish, by knight's service; yearly rent, with suit of court as above, 2*s*. 2*d*.

Penfos [*Penvose, in St Mawgan in Pyder*]:
The same Thomas, 1 acre Cornish, by knight's service; yearly rent, with common suit of court, 12*d*.

Polgrun [*Polgreen, in St Mawgan in Pyder*]:
Roger Polgrun, 1 acre Cornish, by knight's service; yearly rent, with common suit of court, 2*s*. 3*d*.

Bodruthyn [*Bedruthan, in St Eval*]:
John Nanfan, 1 acre Cornish, by knight's service; yearly rent, with common suit of court, 1 *lb*. cummin.

Trenans [*Trenance, in St Mawgan in Pyder*]:
James Flamank, 2 acres Cornish, by knight's service; yearly rent, with common suit of court, 16*d*.

Penfos [*Penvose, in St Mawgan in Pyder*]:
Stephen Mark and John Felipp, coheirs, 1 acre Cornish, by knight's service; yearly rent, with common suit of court, 4*s*.

Helwyn and Hengolan [*Halwyn and Engollan, in St Eval*]:[34]
The heir of John Tynten, 3 [?] acres Cornish,[35] by knight's service; yearly rent, with suit of court as above, 3*s*. 11*d*.

Porth [*Mawgan Porth, in St Mawgan in Pyder*]:
John Porth, 1 acre Cornish in socage; yearly rent, without suit of court, 15*d*.

---

[34] See above, p. 26 (conventionary tenement of Trembleath manor).
[35] The figure '3' has been altered, possibly to '6'.

John Coulyng and Ralph Porth, 1 acre Cornish in socage; yearly rent, without suit of court, 15*d*.

Elwans, Bodruthyn, Pentyr [*Efflins, Bedruthan and Pentire, in St Eval*]:
Oto Colyn, [*blank*] acres Cornish in socage; yearly rent, without suit of court, 1 red rose.

Trewaruena [*Trevenna, in St Mawgan in Pyder*]:
The heir of Thomas Knapp, 3 ferlings, by knight's service; yearly rent, with common suit of court, 4*s*. 6*d*.
John Martyn Barry, by right of his wife, 3 ferlings, by knight's service; yearly rent, with common suit of court, 4*s*. 6*d*.

Total of free tenants, 27s. 2d.

Conventionary tenants

Treuudrys [*Trevedras, in St Mawgan in Pyder*]:
John Faber ['the smith'], the whole vill; yearly rent, payable at the 4 usual dates, with common suit of court and other services as the other conventionary tenants do according to the custom of the manor, 20*s*.

Trewaruena [*Trevenna, in St Mawgan in Pyder*]:
George Queynte, 1 holding; yearly rent, with other services as above, 9*s*.

Lanvyan [*Lanvean, in St Mawgan in Pyder*]:
Thomas Goef, 1 cottage (*unum cotag'*) and 1 acre English; yearly rent, 20*d*.
John Salt, 1 cottage; yearly rent, as above, 12*d*. [*altered?*].
John Scovarn, 1 holding; yearly rent, as above, 9*s*.
John Fenten, 2 holdings; yearly rent, as above, 18*s*.

[*blank in margin*]:[36]
John Gweader, 1 holding; yearly rent, as above, 9*s*.
John Scovarn, 1 holding; yearly rent, as above, 9*s*.

Penpons Lanhern [*Penpont, in St Mawgan in Pyder*]:
Thomas Snele, 1 holding; yearly rent, as above, 5*s*.

---

[36] These two entries may refer to the lost *Newham*, named in the 1499 extent (below, p. 109), but not named here; however, in the rental of *c*.1586 that land was held with Penpont, as a free tenement of Lanherne: '*Penpons* and a meadow called *Newham*' (AR2/1343).

Wyndessore [*Windsor, in St Mawgan in Pyder*]:
The same Thomas, the whole vill of Wyndesore; yearly rent, as above, 13s. 4d.

Enysmaugan [*'Enysmaugan' (lost), in St Mawgan in Pyder*]:
Juliana Trous; yearly rent, 2s.

Tregonvan [*Tregonning, in St Mawgan in Pyder*]:
John Joopp, by the same service, as above; yearly rent, 16s.

Tregoustek [*Tregustick, in St Columb Minor*]:
Thomas Janyn, lord's bondman, 1 holding, by the same service; yearly rent, 20s.
John Janyn, lord's bondman, 1 holding, by the same service; yearly rent, 20s.
Richard Mayowe, 1 holding; yearly rent, as above, 10s.
Salmon' Richard', 1 holding; yearly rent, as above, 10s.

Trevelgy [*Trevelgue, in St Columb Minor*]:
John Huet, 1 holding; yearly rent, as above, 11s. 8d.
John Tyek, 1 holding, as above; yearly rent, 11s. 8d.
Thomas Willyam, 1 holding lately held by Thomas Perowe; yearly rent, 11s. 8d.
John Erlond, 1 holding; yearly rent, as above, 11s. 8d.

Penfos [*Penvose, in St Mawgan in Pyder*]:
Stephen Mark, 1 holding, as above; yearly rent, 8s. 4d.

Kenewes [*Carnewas, in St Eval*]:
John Laury and John Budy, the whole vill, by the same service; yearly rent, 19s.

Carnantoun meadow (*pratum de Carnantoun*) [*meadow named from Carnanton, in St Mawgan in Pyder*]:[37]
Remains in the lord's hands; it was accustomed to pay yearly 3s. 4d.

Hellenpark [*'Halyn Parke' (lost), in St Mawgan in Pyder*]:[38]
Remains in the lord's hands; it was accustomed to pay yearly 7d.

---

[37] Carnanton, near to Lanherne, was not an Arundell manor; but this meadow named from it occurs in Lanherne manor already in 1390-91: account roll (AR2/886, m. 5).
[38] 'Halling Parke' in the rental of c.1586 (AR2/1343); 'Halyn Parke' in the surveys of 1659 and 1717.

Lanhern Doune:
Remains in the lord's hands; it was accustomed to pay yearly 8s.

Mill of Lanherne:
John Scovarn, at the lord's will; yearly rent, 53s. 4d.

[*Total of conventionary tenants*, £15 12s. 3d.]

Demesne land of Lanhern:
It was accustomed to pay yearly, in addition to things received and reserved in the lord's hands (*ultra except' et reservat' in manibus domini*) £6 13s. 4d.

Total of free, conventionary and bond tenants, [blank; £23 12s. 9d.; but £16 19s. 5d. without the demesne land, in hand.]

* * *

Vill of Sancta Columba
[*St Columb town, in St Columb Major; no date given*]

Free tenants

Ralph Tripkunyn, those holdings which were held by Luke Pluven; yearly rent, at the 4 dates usual in the manor, with suit of court at the two leet courts and other services and customs as the other free tenants do, 6d.

The same Ralph, 1 close; yearly rent, at the 4 dates, over and above 3s. 4d. reserved in the lord's hands for various holdings there to be newly built (*ultra 3s. 4d. reservat' in manibus domini pro divers' ten' ibidem de novo edificand'*), 5s.

John Clemov, 1 holding newly built, for term of years; yearly rent, with 2 suits of court at the 2 leet courts, plus relief when it arises and other services as the other free tenants do, 4s.

Odo Moyll, 1 holding, for term of years, lately held by John Clemov, to be newly built (*de novo edificand'*); rent, as above, 11d.

The same Odo, 1 holding, lately held by John Felghour, with a parcel of land annexed to it; yearly rent, with the same service, as above, 2s.

The same Odo, a parcel of land opposite that holding, for term of years; yearly rent, with the same service, 4s.

John Michell, 1 holding; yearly rent, with 2 suits of court and other services as the other free tenants do, 2s. 8d.

The same John, 1 holding, now inhabited by William Michell, next to a holding lately held by John Russell; yearly rent, with the same service, as above, 2s. 8d.

The same John, 2 holdings opposite the cross; yearly rent, with other services, as above, 8s.

The same John, 5 gardens; yearly rent, with other services as above, 4s. 6d.

The same John, 1 close called Parkenfenten; yearly rent, with other services, as above, 2s.

The same John, 2 holdings; yearly rent, with other services, as above, 10d.

The same John, 1 close beside the cross in the lane (*iuxta crucem in venella*); yearly rent, with other services, as above, 20s.

The same John, 1 close with another holding annexed to it, leading to the town well (*ducens ad fontem eiusdem ville*), sometime held by John Russell; yearly rent, with the same service, as above, 21s. 8d.

The heir of Michael Udy, 1 holding; yearly rent, with suit of court, as above, 20d.

John Shirdewyn, a parcel of a tenement of the same heir of Michael Udy (*parcell' ten' dict' her' Mich' Udy*); [yearly] rent, 8d.

Richard Goff, [1 holding], for term of years; yearly rent, with other services, as above, 3s. 4d.

Odo Vyuyan, [1 holding], for term of years; yearly rent, with other services, as above, 12d.

The heir of Robert Olyuer, 2 holdings, for term of years; yearly rent, with other services, as above, 2s. 8d.

Remfrey Arundell knight, 1 holding lately held by the heir(s) of Trewynhelek; yearly rent, with other services, as above, 9d.

Ralph Tripkunyn, 1 holding, lately held by Andrew (*Andrie*) Treghar, for term of years; yearly rent, with the same service, as above, 4s.

Mark (*Marchus*) Tomas, 1 holding, for term of years; yearly rent, with other services, as above, 4s.

Richard Paule, 1 holding, lately held by John Doll, for term of years; yearly rent, with services as above, 4s.

1 tenement, lately held by Mark Knyght, remains in the lord's hands; granted to Robert Udy, clerk, to hold at the lord's will; it was accustomed to pay yearly 8s.

Thomas Enys, 3 holdings; yearly rent, with other services, as above, 2s. 1d.

Nicholas Tresithny, John Nanscuvell and John Erysy, 3 holdings; yearly rent, with other services, 3s.

Maud Trenowth and David Tregarrek, 1 holding; yearly rent, with other services, as above, 12d.

The same Maud and David, 1 holding newly assigned (*de novo assesso*); yearly rent, 6d.

John Trevga, 1 holding lately held by William Facy, for term of years; yearly rent, with other services, 4s.

Thomas Tresithny, 1 holding; yearly rent, with other services, as above, 4s.

The same Thomas, 1 holding, with a close annexed to it; yearly rent, with other services, 12s.

The same Thomas, 1 holding; yearly rent, with other services, as above, 12d.

Thomas Tresithny and Nicholas Tresithny, 1 holding lately held by John Russell, for term of years; yearly rent, with other services, as above, 20d.

Nicholas Tresithny, 1 close sometime held by John Byan; yearly rent, with other services, as above, 7s.

The same Nicholas, a smithy (*fabricale*); yearly rent, with other services, as above, 12d.

Richard Resougan, 4 holdings; yearly rent, with other services, as above, 12d.

The heir of Michael Crabba, 1 holding, for term of years; yearly rent, with other services, as above, 2s. 6d.

Paul Benny, 1 holding sometime held by John Russell; yearly rent, with other services, as above, 6s. 8d.

The heir of John Russell, 1 holding sometime held by Ralph Basset; yearly rent, with other services, as above, 5s.

John Carn, 1 holding, for term of years; yearly rent, with other services, as above, 3s. 4d.

Michael Tom Symon, 1 holding, for term of years; yearly rent, with other services, as above, 3s. 4d.

The heir of John Wolcok Vyan, 1 holding, for term of years; yearly rent, with other services, as above, 3s. 5d.

Oliver Paull, 1 holding, for term of years, sometime held by John Renavdyn; yearly rent, with other services, 9s.

The heir of John Renavdyn, 1 holding, for term of years; yearly rent, with other services, as above, 3s. 4d.

Paul Benny, 1 holding, for term of years; yearly rent, with other services, as above, 9d.

Michael Gregor, 1 holding, for term of years; yearly rent, with other services, as above, 2s.

Stephen Mouna, 1 holding, for term of years; yearly rent, with other services, as above, 4s.

Thomas Facy, 1 holding; yearly rent, with other services, as above, 1d.

John Tremeen, [1 holding] newly assigned to him (*de novo sibi assess'*), opposite the cross, sometime held by John Russell, for term of years; yearly rent, with other services, as above, 18d.

Luke Kerter, a bakehouse (*domus pistrine*); yearly rent, 8s.

[*Sub-total of free tenants*], £9 19s.

The Great Close (*Magnum clausum*):

Richard Tomeov, a parcel of land within the great close, services as above; yearly rent, 15s.
John Michell, a parcel of land, services as above; yearly rent, 15s.
John Shirdewyn and Richard Shirdewyn jointly, a parcel of land, for the same services; yearly rent, 15s.
John Felipp and Walter Noell between them, a parcel of land, services as above; yearly rent, 15s.

William Michell and Richard Vyuyan between them, a parcel of land, services as above; yearly rent, 15s.

John Shirdewyn, 1 parcel of land newly let for a building-plot (*de novo assess' pro placea terre edificand'*), services as above; yearly rent, 4s. 4d.

John Strangman, 1 parcel of land newly let for a building-plot, services as above; yearly rent, 2s. 10d.

John Felipp, 1 parcel of land newly let for a building-plot, services as above; yearly rent, 4s. 4d.

Nicholas Treluddrov, 1 parcel of land newly let for a building-plot, services as above; yearly rent, 3s. 4d.

Walter Noiell, 1 parcel of land newly let for a building-plot, services as above; yearly rent, 6s. 8d.

The close beside the mill of Sancta Columba, with a parcel of moor annexed to it, is worth yearly 23s. 4d.

[*Sub-total of the Great Close*], 119s. 10d.

The mill used to pay yearly £10.

The fair and market used to pay yearly 6d.

Richard Tresafnowe, 1 parcel of land for building (*de novo edificand'*); yearly rent, with services as above, 2s.[39]

Ralph Janyn, 1 parcel of land to be newly built (*de novo edificand'*); yearly rent, with services as above, 20d.

Robert Urban, 1 holding, for term of years; yearly rent, 20d.

[*Total for whole town, £26 4s. 8d.*]

* * *

Conartoun
[*Connerton, in Gwithian*]

Extent made Thursday before St Margaret, 3 Edward IV [14 July 1463].

Free tenants

Trencrome, Nansavallen [*Trencrom and 'Nansavallan' (lost), both in Lelant*]:[40]

William lord of Botreaux, 1 acre Cornish, in socage; yearly rent, at

---
[39] 'Tresafnowe nil', added later, in margin.
[40] *Nansavallan* is located in Lelant parish in the surveys of 1659 and 1717.

the 4 chief dates, with common suit of court every 3 weeks, 4s.
The same William, the water (*aqua*) of Lananta;[41] yearly rent, at Easter, 6d.; also for offering and aid (*offr' et auxilium*), at Michaelmas, 3d.[42]

Boswithgy and Boscudyn [*Bosworgey and Boscudden, in St Erth*]:
The same William, for 1 acre Cornish, with the tithing of Conertun (*cum decenna de Conertun*), [*blank*].[43]

Talscoys [*Taskus, in Gwinear*]:
The heir of Michael Petit, ½ acre Cornish, in socage; yearly rent, at the 4 chief dates, with suit of court as above, 15d.

Bosuerghes [*unidentified*]:[44]
The heir of William Manyer, 5 acres English, in socage; common suit of court, [*blank*]

Amalibri, Nanscludry, Chienglasen [*Amalebra, Nancledra and Chylason, all in Towednack*]:
The heir of Nigel de Loryng, 2 acres Cornish, in socage; yearly rent, at the same dates, with common suit of court as above, 8s.

Polkenhorn [*Polkinghorne, in Gwinear*]:
The same heir, ½ acre Cornish; yearly rent, at Michaelmas, 12d.

---

[41] In the account roll of the manor for 1468–69 this is called the 'water running from *Boyskerrys* to *Lananta*' (AR2/909, m. 1d), presumably the stream rising south-west of Boskerris (SW 519376), flowing south-west then east into the southern branch of the Hayle estuary, below Lelant church.

[42] This phrase appears several times among the free tenements of Connerton manor, worded differently in each of the fifteenth-century surveys; *offr'* is elucidated by an entry in the 1499 extent (p. 130, below), where it is written in full as *offretorium ad festum Sancti Michaelis*. In the 1480 rental the phrase was consistently written as *offr' auxilii*, as if 'offering *of* aid'; but 'offering *and* aid', as here, is perhaps correct. By the time of the 1659 and 1717 surveys the phrase was given as 'aid' alone; compare Hatcher, *Duchy of Cornwall*, p. 69, for *auxilium* on the Duchy manors. The due may be connected with the attachment of the Hundred of Penwith to the manor; the manor of Winnington claimed (among other casual profits) aids from the Hundred of Kerrier (above, p. 19).

[43] In the rental of c.1586 (AR2/1343) it is stated that the holder of this tenement 'will be tithingman when it arises' (*et erit decenn' infra manerium predictum quando acciderit*).

[44] The acreage, 5 again in the 1480 rental (p. 85), is altered to 25 English acres in 1499 (p. 130) and c.1586; thereafter the tenement disappears.

Trenauwyn Wartha [*Trenowin, in Gwinear*]:
The same heir, 1 ferling; yearly rent, at Michaelmas, with common suit of court as above, 1 *lb.* of cummin [4*d.*, *added later*]

Eglos Heill [*Egloshayle, at Phillack churchtown*]:
The heir of William Tregos, ½ acre Cornish at Eglos Hel, in socage; yearly rent, at Michaelmas, with common suit of court, 6s. 9*d.*

Trethengy [*Trethingy, in Phillack*]:
The same heir, 1 acre Cornish, in socage; yearly rent, at the same feast, 1*d.*; and for offering and aid at the same feast, 3*d.*

Conerwartha [*Connorwartha, at Gwithian churchtown*]:
Odo Resgerens, by right of Alice his wife, ½ acre Cornish; yearly rent, at the same feast, with suit of court as above, 12*d.*

Ponsreles [*'Ponsfrellas' (lost), in Gwithian*]:[45]
The same Odo, ½ acre Cornish; yearly rent, at the same feast, with common suit of court, 1*d.*

Graften [*'Grafton' (lost), in Gwithian*]:
The same Odo, 1 ferling; yearly rent, at the 4 chief dates, with common suit of court, 2s.

Treuasek and Fentenlegh [*Trevassack and Ventonleague, in Phillack*]:
John Penros, 2 acres Cornish, by knight's service as is seen by an indenture held by the lord; yearly rent, at the same dates, with common suit of court, as above, 3s.

Arde [*Ayr, in St Ives parish*]:
John Hell Porthia, one-third of an acre Cornish, in socage; yearly rent, at the same 4 dates, with common suit of court, as above, 2s.

Hendre [*Hendra, in St Ives parish*]:
The heir of William Fitz Waultere, 1 acre Cornish, by knight's service; yearly rent, at Easter, with suit of court once at Michaelmas, 1 pair of gilt spurs or 6*d.*

Trenawyn [*Trenowin, in Gwinear*]:
The heir of Robert Cras, 1 acre Cornish, in socage; yearly rent, at Michaelmas, with 2 suits of court at the leet courts, 12*d.*

Hellenwoen [*Hellynoon, in Lelant*]:
The heir of Richard Eyr, 1 croft; yearly rent, at the 4 chief dates,

---

[45] *Ponfrelis* in the rental of c.1586 (AR2/1343); *Ponsfrelles alias Ponsvorhelles* (held with *Conner Wartha*) in that of 1659.

with 2 suits of court, as above, 2s.

Carewyn [*Carwyn, in Phillack*]:
Thomas Godolghan, 1 acre Cornish, in socage; yearly rent, at Michaelmas, with common suit of court, as above, 2s.

Boskeures Woles [*Boskerris Woollas, in Lelant*]:
The heir of John Treburgheur [?], ½ acre Cornish in Boskeureswoles, by knight's service; yearly rent, at the 4 chief dates, with common suit of court, as above, 6s. 8d.

Tregeuyn [*probably Treven, in St Erth*]:[46]
The heir of Richard Eyr, 2 acres Cornish; yearly rent, at the 4 chief dates, with 2 suits of court at the 2 leet courts, 5s.

Carneny, Carbons, Chiengwael, Eglosheill, Trewelisyk Heyll [*Carninney, Carbis and Chyangweal, in Lelant; Egloshayle, in Phillack; and Trelissick, in St Erth*]:
The heir of Nigel de Loryng, 1 acre Cornish in Carneny [and] Carbons, 1 ferling in Chiengwael, ½ acre Cornish in Eglosheyll and ½ acre Cornish in Trewelisyk Heyll, all in socage; yearly rent, at Michaelmas, with common suit of court, as above, 7s. 7d.; also offering and aid at the same feast, 3d.

Trethegember [*Tregembo, in St Hilary*]:
William Gourlyn, 1 acre Cornish, in socage; yearly rent, at the 4 dates, with common suit of court, as above, 12d.

Gournogov and Westva [*'Carnogowe' (lost) and Westway, in Lelant*]:
The heir of Philip Trembras, 1 acre Cornish in Gournogov and Westua, by knight's service; yearly rent, at Michaelmas, 1 pair of gloves, value 1d., with common suit of court, as above: 1d.

Arde [*Ayr, in St Ives parish*]:
The heir of John Colyn de Lananta,[47] one-third of an acre Cornish, by knight's service; yearly rent, at the 4 dates, with common suit of court, as above, 16d.

---

[46] This tenement appears as *Tregevyn* in the 1480 rental, as *Trenywyn* (or *Tregywyn*) in the 1499 rental (below, pp. 87 and 131), and as *Tregennen* in the rental of c.1586 (AR2/1343); in that of 1659 it is *Trevyen alias Tregynwin*, located in St Erth parish.

[47] With this and the next entry compare the earlier receipt of homage, in 1448, by John Arundell from Oto Colyn de Hellond (son of John Colyn de Hellond) (Helland parish), for land in *Trevalscoys, Hendre* and *Arthya*, held of Arundell's manor of Connerton (AR3/80).

Trevalscoys [*Trevaskis, in Gwinear*]:
The same heir, one-third of an acre Cornish, by knight's service; yearly rent, at the same dates, with common suit of court, as above, 12*d*.

Trewronnan [*Trevarnon, in Gwithian*]:
The heir of Reginald Renward, 2 acres Cornish in Trewronnon, in socage; yearly rent, at Michaelmas, without suit of court, 6*d*.

Trenowith [*Trenoweth, in Gwinear*]:
The heir of William Manyer, 2 parts of 1 acre Cornish in Trenewth iuxta Trevalscoys, in socage; yearly rent, at the same dates, with common suit of court, 2*s*.; also for offering and aid, at Michaelmas, 2*d*.

Trewoen, Legha [*Trewoone and Leah, both in Phillack*]:
The heir of John Corloys, 1 ferling in the vill of Trewoen and Legha, in socage; yearly rent, at 3 dates, *viz.* St Andrew the Apostle, mid-Lent and St James the Apostle, with common suit of court, 15*d*.; also for offering and aid, at Michaelmas, 1½*d*.

Trewoen, Legha [*Trewoone and Leah, both in Phillack*]:
The heir of Olimpias (*Olimpi'*) Boys, 1 ferling, in socage; yearly rent, at 3 dates, *viz.* St Andrew the Apostle, mid-Lent and St James the Apostle, with common suit of court, 15*d*.

Eglosheyll [*Egloshayle, at Phillack churchtown*]:
The heir of the same Olimpias (*dicte Olimp'*), 1 ferling in Egglosheyll, in socage; yearly rent, at Michaelmas, with 2 suits of court at the 2 leet courts, 13¼*d*.; also for offering and aid at the same feast [Michaelmas], 1½*d*.

Nansderov [*Nanterrow, in Gwithian*]:
The heir of Thomas Burwik, 2 acres Cornish, by knight's service; yearly rent, at the 4 dates usual in the manor, with common suit of court, 10*s*.; also for offering, at Michaelmas, 4*d*.

Pennans [*Pennance, in Gwithian*]:
The heir of Alan Manyer, ½ ferling, in socage; yearly rent, at Michaelmas, with common suit of court, ¼ *lb*. pepper; also for aid, at the same feast, 1*d*.
The same heir, ½ ferling, in socage; yearly rent, at Michaelmas, with common suit of court, ¼ *lb*. pepper; also for aid, at same feast, 1*d*.
The heir of Joan Pennans, ½ ferling, in socage; yearly rent, at the

same feast, with common suit of court, ¼ *lb*. pepper; but now pays nothing, because in the lord's hands through escheat, and charged in the conventionary rents (*in redd' conv'*);[48] also for aid, at the same feast, 1*d*.; but now pays nothing, because in the lord's hands through escheat, as above.

The heir of John Goef, ½ ferling, in socage; yearly rent, at the same feast, with common suit of court, ¼ *lb*. pepper; but now pays nothing, because in the lord's hands through escheat, as above; also for aid, at the same feast of Michaelmas, 1*d*.; but now pays nothing, because in the lord's hands through escheat, as above.

Treffrynk, Ard' [*Trink, in Lelant, and Ayr, in St Ives parish*]:
The heir of John Aly Carnarthur, in Trefrynk 1 acre Cornish and in Ard' one-third of an acre Cornish, in socage; yearly rent, at the 4 chief dates, with common suit of court, 4*s*. 8*d*.; also for offering and aid, at the same feast of Michaelmas, 3*d*.

Trefrynke [*Trink, in Lelant*]:
The heir of William Trefrynk, ½ acre Cornish, in socage; yearly rent, at the 4 chief dates, with common suit of court, 2*s*. 6*d*.

Ard' [*Ayr, in St Ives parish*]:
The heir of John Hell Porthia, one-sixth of an acre Cornish, in socage; yearly rent, at the same dates, with common suit of court, 12*d*.

Helles byan [*Hellesvean, in St Ives parish*]:
The same heir, ½ ferling in Hellesbyghan, in socage; yearly rent, at the same dates, with common suit of court, 16*d*.

Carenuer, Wotfold [*Crenver and Oatfield, both in Crowan*]:
The heir of Nicholas Trerys, [*blank*];[49] yearly rent, for all service, 1 grain of wheat.

---

[48] This comment, here and in the following entry, was added later.
[49] This is of course Nicholas Arundell Trerys, an early member of the Trerice line. The original grant of these properties had been made on 5th March 1358, by Sir John Arundel, lord of Connerton, to Ralph Arundel de Trerys (AR1/104); this must have been close to the beginning of that line. Nicholas, son of Ralph Arundell Treres, was a minor in 1378 (AR41/6), and was alive, as Nicholas Arundell de Trereys, in 1400 (AR4/180). Compare notes on pp. 2 and 9, above, and Henderson, 'The Beville obituary' (I), p. 25.

MANOR OF CONNERTON 45

Treuleghian [*Treloyan, in St Ives parish*]:
The heir of John Oen, in Treleghan, ½ acre Cornish; yearly rent, at the 4 dates, with common suit of court, 3s.

Boskeures Wartha [*Boskerris Wartha, in Lelant*]:
The heir of Nicholas Tremayn, ½ acre Cornish, by knight's service; yearly rent, at the same dates, with common suit of court, 2s.; also for offering and aid, at Michaelmas, 3d.

Treulyghion [*Treloyan, in St Ives parish*]:
The heir of John Wilkyn Veel, 1 ferling, in socage; yearly rent, at the 4 chief dates, with common suit of court, 4s.
The heir of John Hire, 1 ferling, in socage; yearly rent, at the 4 chief dates, with common suit of court, 2s.

Tregene [*Tregenna, in St Ives parish*]:
The heir of Henry Willy, 1 ferling; yearly rent, at the same dates, with common suit of court, 2s.
The heir of Richard Riche, ½ acre Cornish, by knight's service; yearly rent, at the same dates, with common suit of court, 20d.; also for offering and aid, at Michaelmas, 3d.;
The heir of Alan Tregene, 1 ferling; yearly rent, at the same dates, with common suit of court, 2s; also for offering and aid, at Michaelmas, 3d.

Goyswyn [*Lanyon, formerly 'Coswinwolward', in Gwinear*]:[50]
John Lanyeyn, the heir of John Hicka, in Goswyn, 2 acres Cornish, in socage; yearly rent, with common suit of court, 6s. at the 3 dates stated, and 20d. at Michaelmas (= 7s. 8d.); also for offering and aid, at Michaelmas, 3d.

A sanding-way (*via sabul'*) [*at Pulsack, in Phillack*]:
The heir of Nicholas Polulsek, for a way leading from Polulsek to the sand, 6d.

Treualscus [*Trevaskis, in Gwinear*]:
The heir of John Hamely, in Trevalscoys 1 ferling; yearly rent, 12d.
The heir of John Totam, 1 ferling; yearly rent, 12d.

Welcomb iuxta Hertlond [*Welcombe (parish), in Devon*]:
The heir of Robert Corun [?], the manor of Welcomb iuxta

---

[50] Relief for the death of John Lanyeyn, holding 2 acres at *Coyswynwulward*, was paid in 1476–77 (account roll, AR2/915); in the rental of 1659 *Cosewin Wolver* was held by Tobias Lanyon, gentleman.

Hertelond, by service etc., because he showed a charter to John Cork, sometime steward of Sir John Arundell, knight, at Launceston; however, it is not certified here whether by knight's service or in socage, therefore to be distrained to show, etc.; rent 1 clove gillyflower.

Total of free tenants, 114s. 10½d. and ½ lb. pepper.[51]

[*Conventionary tenants*]

Demesne land of Conartoun [*Connerton, in Gwithian*]:
Various tenants hold the whole of the demesne land; yearly rent, at the 4 chief dates, with common suit of court, as follows:
John Rawe, 1 holding; yearly rent, 19s. 6d.
Humphrey (*Umfrus*') Hichopkyn, 1 holding; yearly rent, 19s. 6d.
Richard Carnky, 1 holding; yearly rent, 16s. 8½d.
Margaret Jamys, 1 holding; yearly rent, 11s.
Ralph Merceur (*M'ce*'), 1 holding; yearly rent, 25s.
Simon Purlad, 1 holding; yearly rent, 25s.
William Louda, 1 holding; yearly rent, 11s.
James Laurens, 1 holding; yearly rent, 8s. 4d.
Stephen Rawe, 1 holding; yearly rent, 11s. 1d.
Richard Geffre, 1 holding; yearly rent, 19s. 4d.
Simon Jakenhell, 1 holding; yearly rent, 33s. 4d.

Engarrek [*Angarrack, in Phillack*]:
Henry Caran, 1 holding; yearly rent, 18s.

Nansgracyes [*Negosias, otherwise Nantasier, in Gwithian*]:
Richard Jakenhell, 1 holding; yearly rent, 23s.

Talseghan [*Tolzethan, in Gwithian*]:
Martin Daune, 1 holding; yearly rent, 26s. 8d.
The same Martin, 1 parcel of moor called Hallas; yearly rent, 8d.

Pennans Vueer, Hall envelyn, Gargasen [*Pennance (Veor), 'Halenvelan' and 'Gargason' (both lost), all in Gwithian*]:[52]
James Hicke, the whole vill; yearly rent, 38s. 8d.

---

[51] A different total, of £4 18s. 2½d., seems to be implied by the totals given at the end of the manor.
[52] Compare land held in *Hall Envelyn* and *Cargassen*, in 1454–55 (account roll, AR2/900, m. 5); also the tenement of *Pennans Veer, Hallenvellan, Gargasen* in the rental of c.1586 (AR2/1343).

Pennans Vian [*Pennance Vean, in Gwithian*]:
John Perowe, 1 holding; yearly rent, 13s. 4d.

Engewe [*Angew, in Gwithian*]:
John Jagowe, 1 holding; yearly rent, 14s.
John Tomma, 1 holding; yearly rent, 14s.

Uppetoun [*Upton, in Gwithian*]:
John Hopkyn, 1 holding; yearly rent, 18s.
John Perowe Sergeaunt, 1 holding (together with 3s. 4d. for a parcel of land at Esterloo) [*added later*]; yearly rent, 12s. 4d.[53]
John Kellyan, 1 holding; yearly rent, 18s.
John Heruy, 1 holding; yearly rent, 9s.
Thomas Hicke, 1 holding; yearly rent, 18s.

Esterloo [*'Easter Low' (lost in the sand), in Gwithian*]:[54]
Jankyn Jakraulyn, 1 holding; yearly rent, 12s.
Richard Esterloo, 1 holding; yearly rent, 12s.

Penpoll iuxta Lananta [*Penpoll, in Phillack*]:
Thomas Penpoll, 1 holding; yearly rent, 24s.
John Jake Felipp, 1 holding; yearly rent, 24s.

Trevalscoys [*Trevaskis, in Gwinear*]:
John Priour, 1 holding; yearly rent, 10s.
Richard Nicholl, 1 holding; yearly rent, 10s.

Dryme [*Drym, in Crowan*]:
Francis Ive, 1 holding; yearly rent, 20s.
John Daune, 1 holding; yearly rent, 20s.

Treffrynke, Nans [*Trink and Nance, in Lelant*]:
Roger Trevaignon, 1 holding; yearly rent, 15s.
William Nans, 1 holding; yearly rent, 13s.

Vynwyn [*Venwyn, in Lelant*]:
William Vynwyn, 1 holding; yearly rent, 18s. 8d.

---

[53] It is unclear whether the rent of 3s. 4d. (which is not entered separately in the rents column) is included in the total of 12s. 4d., or additional to it.

[54] Compare a lease recited in an eighteenth-century survey: 'Easter Low. Peter Curnow, by lease dated 16 June 1675 holdeth all those lands and tenements called *Easter-low* with appurtenances, being a common, the most part thereof is covered with sand, all lying in the parish of Gwithian, for 99 years' (AR2/1358, fol. 34v., no. 29).

Gorfos [*Vorvas, in Lelant*]:
Joan Gorfos, 1 holding; yearly rent, 10s.

Boskerrys [*Boskerris, in Lelant*]:
Nicholas Jakgillowe, 1 holding; yearly rent, 13s. 4d.
Stephen Gregor, 1 holding; yearly rent, 10s.

Treloighion [*Treloyan, in St Ives parish*]:
John Laury, 1 holding; yearly rent, 10s.

Fowyer [*Vow, in St Ives parish*]:
Thomas Foggeur, 1 holding; yearly rent, 28s.

Polleowe [*Poleo, in Crowan*]:
John Polkynhorn, 1 holding; yearly rent, 6s.[55]

Enwythen [*Withen, in Lelant*]:[56]
Richard Renawdon, 1 parcel of land; yearly rent, 8s.

Total of conventionary tenants [including demesne], £34 19s. 5½d.

Total of free and conventionary tenants, £39 17s. 8d.

[*A schedule of rough notes concerning tenements in the manor is attached to the membrane at this point; it reads as follows.*]

Wethan, Porthrepter [*Withen and 'Barrepta' (lost), near Carbis, in Lelant*]:
['Peter John Alan', *deleted*] Henry Rawe; yearly rent, 8s.
Henry Trevysithek, 1 holding; yearly rent, 8d.
Philip Merceur; yearly rent, 4d.
William Vynwyn; yearly rent, 2d.
John Fyttok; yearly rent, 2d.
James Hicke, at Pennansvur [*Pennance, in Gwithian*], 3 holdings as 1 holding (*tres tenuras sub una tenura*); he used to pay 36s.; also for 20 acres in Conerdon, and 1 parcel of moor in Hale..., 6s. 8d.
... water (*aqua*) of [*blank*], 8d.
Total 42s. 8d.; and reeve has received only 38s., therefore to be inquired concerning 4s. more, according to his charter (*per cartam*

---

[55] The text has 'vj.s. ij.s.', but the 'ij.s.' appears to be an error. In 1410 John Arundell leased the whole vill of *Pollyov* to John Polkenhorn and Margaret his wife, for term of their lives, rent 6s. yearly (AR4/318); and Nicholas Polkynhorn was entered as paying the same rent in the rentals of 1480 and 1499 (below, pp. 92 and 136).

[56] This whole entry is added later; it is unclear whether it was included in the total or not.

suam), if he is shown to be excused (*si probatur excusari*).

The water of Lananta pays yearly 12*d*.[57]
Moor of Nansterov [*Nanterrow, in Gwithian*], Humphrey Syluester holds there; he pays 8*d*.[58]
Memorandum to view an extent of the lord of Botreaux with William Rosmoddres, *viz.* for Boswithgy and Boscudyn [*Bosworgey and Boscudden, in St Erth*], *viz.* how large a part of 1 knight's fee.[59]
Fowyer [*Vow, in St Ives parish*], granted to Oto Trevnw^t and his heirs of body; yearly rent, after a certain term, 20*s*.; and a charter was made for Conerton to John Michall, and written by John Tomas, 4 Edward IV [1464–65]. To be inquired of the lord concerning the charter.

* * *

Lanhaddroun
[*Nansladron or Lanhadron, in St Ewe*]

Extent made Wednesday before St Thomas the Martyr, 3 Edward IV [28 December 1463].

[*Free tenants*]

Pille [*Pill, in Lanlivery*]:
Robert Courteys, [1] acre Cornish, [by knight's service];[60] 2 suits of court; rent, 1 *lb*. cummin.

Wille [*lost, in Lanlivery*]:[61]
The heir of Robert Kayll, [1] acre Cornish, [by knight's service]; 2 suits of court; yearly rent, 6*d*.

Pengelly [*Pengelly, in St Ewe*]:[62]
The heir of Margery Ilcomb, *viz.* Henry Bodrugan, esquire, [2] acres Cornish, [by knight's service]; suit of court every 3 weeks; yearly rent, 12*d*.

---

[57] The words *curr' ad* are written above 'water of Lananta'; see p. 40, n. 41.
[58] Different from Nanterrow itself (p. 43): compare pp. 88–89 and 93.
[59] Actually 1 acre Cornish (¼ knight's fee): see p. 40, above.
[60] The acreages and service in this and the next three entries are left blank in the manuscript, and have been supplied from the 1499 rental (p. 117).
[61] For the identification see the 1385 rental (above, p. 8, n. 23).
[62] This tenement paid a fine for suit of court to the manor of Tybesta (1385 rental, above, p. 11); it is identified in 1717 as being in St Ewe parish.

Carloys [*Carloose, in Creed*]:
The heir of Nicholas Prouest, [½] acre Cornish, [by knight's service]; 2 suits of court; yearly rent, 2s.

Tregirthik [*Tregerrick, in Goran*]:
Henry Bodrugan, esquire, 1 acre Cornish, in socage; 2 suits of court; rent, 1 pair of spurs, value 12d.

Nansgrenek ['*Nansfrinick alias Nanruan' (lost), in Goran*]:[63]
The same Henry, 1 acre Cornish, [*service blank*]; 2 suits of court; rent [*blank*].

Crukconerwoles [*(Lower) Cotna, in Goran*]:
The same Henry, for the leat (*bed'*) of the mill of Crukkoner Woles, 6d.

Seynt Crida [*Creed churchtown*]:
The heir of Thomas Carmynov, [1, *deleted*] acre(s) Cornish, by knight's service; 2 suits of court, at the leet courts; yearly rent, 12½d.

Bossulyan [*Bossillian, in Creed*]:
The heir of Walter Menhyr, *viz.* John Trevilian, esquire, [½] acre Cornish, [in socage];[64] 2 suits of court, at the leet courts; yearly rent, 12½d.

Trewaruena [*Trewarmenna, in Creed*]:
The heir of Reginald Tretherf, [1?] acre Cornish, [in socage]; 2 suits of court, at the leet courts; yearly rent, 17½d.

Roscorlan [*Rescorla, in St Ewe*]:
The heir of Dodda,[65] [*blank*] acre(s) Cornish; 2 suits of court; but 2 parts of the rent are seized into the lord's hand, through escheat; the reversion of the third part of the rent is in dower with the wife lately of the heir of Dodda when it arises [?] (*cum uxore nuper hered' Dodda qu' accider'*), whence in the lord's hands 16d., and 8d. for dower when it arises: 8d. [*underlined for deletion*]. (Nil, because the

---

[63] The place-name (in the margin) has been altered or added later, though not the entry itself; the modern form is provided by the survey of 1717.

[64] The acreage and service in this entry and the next are again blank, and have been supplied from the 1499 rental (below, pp. 117–18); the acreage at Trewarmenna is given as '2' in 1499, but as '1' in 1385 (above, p. 9), and as this manuscript gives *acram* (singular), it is presumed that '1' acre was intended.

[65] 'nil', added above the phrase.

MANOR OF LANHADRON 51

whole tenement is in the lord's hands, and is charged among the conventionary rents, in the hands of Nicholas Cousyn.) [*Sentence added later.*]

Total of free tenants, [*blank;* 8s. 6½d. (?)][66]

Conventionary tenants

Roscorlan [*Rescorla, in St Ewe*]:
John Iveron, 1 holding; suit of court every 3 weeks, and all other services and customs as the conventionary tenants do; yearly rent, at the 4 chief dates in the manor, 10s. 8d.
William Miller, 1 holding; service as above; yearly rent, 10s. 8d.
John Iveron,[67] 1 holding; service as above; yearly rent, 10s. 4d.
John Jagowe, 1 holding; service as above; yearly rent, 18s.

Bossu [*Bosue, in St Ewe*]:
Robert Felipp, 1 holding; service as above; yearly rent, 22s.
Edward Randowe, 1 holding; service as above; yearly rent, 12s. 6d.
Joan Ude, 1 holding; service as above; yearly rent, 12s.

Lanywy [*Lanuah, in St Ewe*]:
1 holding lately in the hands of John Janyn, now waste; it used to pay 7s. 6d.
1 holding lately in the hands of Janyn Bakeur, now waste; it used to pay 7s. 6d.
1 cottage lately in the hands of Isolda Gatty, now waste; it used to pay 2s.

Laworan [*at Goran churchtown*]:
John Goly, 1 holding; service as above; yearly rent, 17s.
Randolph (*Randocus*) Hicke Edward, 1 holding; service as above; yearly rent, 9s. 4d.
John Quyke, 1 holding; service as above; yearly rent, 20s.
William Toma Dauy, 1 holding; service as above; yearly rent, 8s. 8d.

Crukconer [*Cotna, in Goran*]:
Nicholas Hicke, 1 holding; service as above; yearly rent, 10s.
The same Nicholas, the whole vill [*sic*]; service as above; yearly rent, 16s.

---

[66] Note the absence, from this list of free tenements, of Hunting Down, *Bloughan* and Castle (all in Lanlivery), present as a tenement in the rentals of 1385 and 1499 (pp. 9 and 117).
[67] Name added later, over an erasure.

Laworan [*at Goran churchtown*]:
Joan Nawen, 1 holding; service as above; yearly rent, 10s. 4d.

Penhall [*Penhale, in Goran*]:
John Toma Dauy, 1 holding; service as above; yearly rent, 10s.;
1 holding now waste, lately in the hands of the same John Dauy; it used to pay 10s.

Menagwyns [*Menagwins, in Goran*]:
Richard Jake Hicke, 1 holding; service as above; yearly rent, 5s. 4d.

Laworan [*at Goran churchtown*]:
The same Richard, 1 holding, sometime held by Richard Abbas; yearly rent, 4s. 3d.

Bonhurdon [*Benhurden, in Goran*]:
John Jaket, the whole vill, by the lord's charter; service as above; yearly rent, 26s. 8d.

Corn-mill [*Lanhadron mill*]:
Emma (*Emmota*) wife of John Tyrell,[68] the lord's mill of Lanhaddron; 2 suits of court; yearly rent, 46s. 8d.

Penbruglith [*Pengrugla, in St Ewe*]:
The land there used to pay 6s. yearly, but half of it is now granted by the lord to Oliver Wise, esquire, in exchange for the same amount of land at Pentewyn [*Pentewan, in Mevagissey*], enclosed in the lord's park of Lanhaddroun, as seen in the lord's account roll; 3s.

Hallendaves [*lost, presumably in St Ewe*]:[69]
Remains in the lord's hands, because it is enclosed within the park of Lanhaddroun; it used to pay [*blank*].

Laworan [*Goran churchtown*]:
Nicholas Cornuall, 1 workshop, by the cross (*shoppa iuxta crucem*);

---

[68] John Tyrell, when himself the miller, had been presented in the manorial court on 22 April 1445, for failing to be present in the mill to receive the tenants' grain, and for taking the lord's timber and using it for mills outside the manor at St Austell and St Columb (AR2/339, m. 6); on 29 September 1445 he bound himself to John Arundell esquire in £20 for keeping the mill well (AR3/348). Thirteen years later, on 25 April 1458, he was again presented in the manorial court, this time for using the corn-mill to grind black tin, hence burdening the tenants excessively in the provision of millstones (AR2/341, m. 2).

[69] *Halendevas*, rental of c.1586 (AR2/1343).

yearly rent, 2s.

Total of conventionary tenants, [blank; £15 12s. 5d. (?)]

The demesne land of Lanhaddroun remains in the lord's hands; it is worth yearly [*blank*].

[Total of free and conventionary tenants and demesne land, blank; £16 1s. 1½d. (?)]

* * *

Rescasa
[*Rescassa, in Goran*][70]

Extent made Wednesday before St Thomas the Martyr, 3 Edward IV [28 December 1463].

Free tenants

Rescasa [*Rescassa, in Goran*]:
Thomas Rescasa, [*blank*] acre(s) Cornish; suit of court there; yearly rent, 18d.

Conventionary tenants

Rescasa [*Rescassa, in Goran*]:
Richard Hoer, 1 holding; suit of court of Lanhaddron manor; yearly rent, 8s.
John Wolcok, 1 holding; service as above; yearly rent, 20s.
Thomas Geffre, 1 holding; service as above; yearly rent, 8s.
William Tregengy, 1 holding; service as above; yearly rent, 6s.

Total of free and conventionary tenants, 43s. 6d.

* * *

---

[70] Rescassa was not a manor, being a free tenement of the Duchy manor of Tybesta (*Caption of Seisin*, ed. Hull, p. 57); but Ralph Tripkunyn had in 1459 surrendered his interest in it to John Arundell, in exchange for tenements at Trebudannon and Trekenning (AR1/48 and 268-269); it had not yet been assimilated into an Arundell manor, hence its separate description here, and it still formed a separate accounting unit in 1466-67 (AR2/906); by 1499 it had been fully absorbed into Lanhadron manor (p. 118), the closest Arundell property to which it naturally became attached. In the rental of *c*.1586 (AR2/1343) the manor of Lanhadron paid a chief rent to the lordship of Tybesta for *Rescasa*. Tripkunyn had acquired his interest in Rescassa in 1441 (*Cornwall Feet of Fines*, II, no. 1051). Note the absence of Rescassa from the 1385 extent (pp. 8-11); see also below, p. 113 and n. 11.

Trembleyth

[*Trembleath, in St Ervan; no date given*][71]

Conventionary tenants

Trethreysek [*Tredrizzick, in St Minver*]:
John Spernall, 1 holding; yearly rent, 13s. 4d.

Penros [*Penrose, in St Ervan*]:
Reginald Coysvghford, 1 holding; yearly rent, (with suit of court) [*added later*], 14s.

Tregona [*Tregona, in St Eval*]:
John Carbura, 1 holding; yearly rent, with suit of court every 3 weeks, 13s. 4d.
Thomas Androwe Taylour, 1 holding; yearly rent, with suit of court as above, 16s. 8d.
Ralph Carbura, 1 holding; yearly rent, with suit of court as above, 20s.
William Vyan, 1 holding; yearly rent, with suit of court as above, 16s. 8d.
Robert Dure, 1 holding; yearly rent, with suit of court as above, 13s. 4d.

Hengolan [*Engollan, in St Eval*]:
Ivo (*Ivonus*) Symon, 1 holding; yearly rent, with suit of court as above, 26s. 8d.
Martin Wolcok, 1 holding; yearly rent, with suit of court as above, 16s. 3d.

Helwyn [*Halwyn, in St Eval, at Engollan*]:
William Helwyn, 1 holding; yearly rent, with suit of court as above, 13s.

Trembleyth [*Trembleath, in St Ervan*]:
Richard Jankyn Wylkyn de Seynt Irven, a certain parcel (*certam parcell'*) on the east side of the new close of Trembleyth, and land of Trewynnek on the east side of that parcel, and Ton Angrous on the

---

[71] This section seems to duplicate the main entry for the conventionary tenants of the manor (pp. 25–27, above); the tenements are listed in the same order (with the omission of Trembleath, Tregwinyo and Trenayles, here mentioned as demesne land, at the end); the rents are usually the same, and the tenants sometimes so. This series may be slightly later, since the tenants given here have less in common with those of 1459 (above) than with those of 1480 (below, p. 75).

north side of it; yearly rent, with 2 suits of court, 6s. 8d.

Crukmorek [*Crigmurrick, in St Merryn*]:
Robert Coulyng, at the lord's will, ½ acre Cornish by gift of John Raulyn de Penros, in exchange for ½ acre Cornish in Penros of the lord's land, delivered to John Raulyn in exchange for this land in the vill of Crukmorek; yearly rent, with suit of court as above, 10s.[72]

Menuwels [*Manuels, in St Columb Minor*]:
John Noell, 1 holding, with suit of court twice yearly; yearly rent, 20s.
John Smyth; yearly rent, with suit of court twice yearly, 20s.

Chapell [*Chapel, in St Columb Minor*]:
Martin Marrek, 1 holding; yearly rent, with suit of court twice yearly, 5s. 4d.

Melyn Newith [*Millingworth, in St Ervan*]:
The mill is now unoccupied; it used to pay yearly 18s.

Total of conventionary tenants, [*blank*; £12 3s. 3d. (?)]

Demesne land

Trembleyth, Trevyngonyowe, Trevynneylys [*Trembleath, Tregwinyo (otherwise Trevengenow) and Trenayles, all in St Ervan*]:[73]
Remain in the lord's hands; they used to pay yearly [*blank*].

* * *

Boswenek
[*Bodwannick, in Lanivet*]

Extent made St Peter's Chair, 3 Edward IV [22 February 1464].

Free tenants

Resevelyn [*Rosevallon, in Bodmin parish*]:
William Pencors, Thomas Reskarrek and the heir of Boscawen, co-heirs, the whole vill; yearly rent, with 2 suits of court, 20d.

Boskeyr [*Boskear, in Bodmin parish*]:
Edmund Beket, by right of his wife, sometime [held by] Thomas

---

[72] The deeds effecting the exchange are dated 1466 (AR1/89–90); Arundell and Cowlyng had a dispute about this exchange in c.1486 (AR3/32).
[73] These tenements are here correctly excluded, unlike in the previous entries for the manor (above, p. 27).

Lanhergy (*de iure uxoris sue, quondam Thome Lanhergy*); yearly rent, with common suit of court, 12*d.*

Treffry [*Treffry, in Lanhydrock*]:
John Felpp, [*blank*]; yearly rent, with 2 suits of court, 4*s.* 6*d.*

Boskedek [*Bokiddick, in Lanivet*]:
Thomas Rescassa, [*blank*]; yearly rent, with common suit of court, 5*d.*

Trefry [*Treffry, in Lanhydrock*]:
John Perys, [*blank*]; yearly rent, with 2 suits of court, 18*d.*

Boskedek [*Bokiddick, in Lanivet*]:
Thomas Lacy, [*blank*]; yearly rent, with 2 suits of court, 20*d.*

Seynt Laurens [*St Lawrence, in Bodmin parish*]:[74]
William Hoigge, 1 holding; yearly rent, with 2 suits of court, 6*d.*

Trefry [*Treffry, in Lanhydrock*]:
Thomas Trefrye, [*blank*]; yearly rent, with 2 suits of court, 3*s.*
Thomas Lanhergy, [*blank*]; yearly rent, with 2 suits of court, 12*d.*[75]

Total of free tenants, [*blank*; 15*s.* 3*d.*][76]

Conventionary tenants

Boswenek [*Bodwannick, in Lanivet*]:
John Robyn, 1 holding; yearly rent, with suit of court every 3 weeks, 32*s.* and 3 capons.
Thomas Brode, 1 holding; yearly rent, with suit of court as above, 12*s.* 6*d.* and 3 capons.
William Brande, 1 holding; yearly rent, with suit of court as above, 12*s.* 6*d.* and 3 capons.
John Symon, 1 holding; yearly rent, with suit of court as above, 32*s.* and 7 capons.

Atleye [*Atley, in Lanivet*]:
John Laye, 1 holding; yearly rent, with suit of court as above, 21*s.* and 6 capons.

---

[74] This free tenement at St Lawrence is actually to be identified with *Frogham* (near to St Lawrence, but in Lanivet parish): compare the rentals of 1480 and 1499 (below, pp. 97 and 114).
[75] Whole entry added later.
[76] A small running-total gives '14*s.* 3*d.*', failing to include the last entry.

Tremayll [*Tremayle, in Lanivet*]:
Richard Brenton; yearly rent, with suit of court as above, 16s.
Odo Raulyn; yearly rent, with suit of court as above, 14s. and 4 capons.

Lanytte [*Lanet, in Lanivet*]:
Henry Laughe;[77] yearly rent, with suit of court as above, 18s. 8d.

Seyntlaurens [*St Lawrence, in Bodmin parish*]:
John Walter; yearly rent, with suit of court twice, 5s.

Lanytte [*Lanet, in Lanivet*]:
Nicholas Martyn; yearly rent, with suit of court, 13s. 4d. and 2 capons.

Lanynwell [*Laninval, in Lanivet*]:
Oura Oppy; yearly rent, with suit of court, 10s. 6d. and 1 capon.
John Hoskyn; yearly rent, with suit of court, 12s. and 3 capons.
Thomas Tresougan; yearly rent, with suit of court, 19s. 6d. and 3 capons.

Boskedek [*Bokiddick, in Lanivet*]:
Thomas Hankyn [or Haukyn]; yearly rent, with suit of court, 8s. and 2 capons.

Wodely le Ouera [*Higher Woodley, in Lanivet*]:
John Hurde; yearly rent, with suit of court, 13s. 4d. and 2 capons.
John Willyam; yearly rent, with suit of court, 14s. and 2 capons.

Wodely le Nethera [*Lower Woodley, in Lanivet*]:
John Brode; yearly rent, with suit of court as above, 9s. and 2 capons.
John Vdy; yearly rent, with suit of court as above, 10s. and 2 capons.
Richard Betty; yearly rent, with suit of court as above, 12s. and 2 capons.

Corn-mill:
Reginald Briand; yearly rent, with suit of court as above, 24s. and 2 capons.[78]

---

[77] Joan, relict of Henry Lawe, was regranted a lease of the same tenement in November 1467, for the same yearly rent: AR1/362.
[78] The corn-mill was still held by the Bryand family in 1541 and 1558, when leases of it were regranted to members of the family (AR4/1498-99); no longer so in 1578, though the family was still in the area (AR4/1500).

Fulling-mill:
John Toukeur; yearly rent, with suit of court as above, 12s. 8d. and 2 capons.

Atte Fourde [*Forda, in Lanivet*]:
William Brenton; yearly rent, with suit of court as above, 16s. and 2 capons.

Newetoun [*Newton, in Lanivet*]:
Thomas Betty; yearly rent, with suit of court as above, 8s. and 2 capons.

Wodely Nethera [*Lower Woodley, in Lanivet*]:
William Richov; yearly rent, with suit of court as above, 14s. and 2 capons.

[*St Lawrence, in Bodmin parish*]:[79]
Henry Laughe, 1 holding together with his holding, as a single holding, at Seynt Laurens on the western side of the king's highway, through Richard Tomyov (*per Ricardum Tomyov*); rent [*blank*]; it used to pay yearly 14s.: nil.

Seynt Laurens [*St Lawrence, in Bodmin parish*]:
Nicholas Joopp, 1 holding formerly held by Henry Laughe; yearly rent, with suit of court, 10s.

Total of free and conventionary tenants, [*blank*; £18 10s. (?)], *plus 57 capons.*

* * *

Enyscavyn
[*Enniscaven, in St Dennis*]

Extent made Thursday before Michaelmas, 35 Henry VI [23 September 1456].

Free tenants

Enyscavyn [*Enniscaven, in St Dennis*]:
Nicholas Carmynowe, [*blank*]; yearly rent, with common suit of court, 4s. 6d.
Richard Gauergan, by right of his wife, [*blank*]; yearly rent, with common suit of court, 13½d.

---

[79] Marginal comment, 'Vacant here, because let to Nicholas Jopp'; the entry is superseded by the following one, which has been added later.

Mena [*Menawollas, in St Dennis*]:[80]
John Cornuwayll[81] and Nicholas Pascowe, co-heirs by right of their wives, ½ acre Cornish; yearly rent, with common suit of court, 5¾d., 1 pair of white gloves, and 1½d. for tin-fine (*pro fine stanni*).

Trelowargh [*Trelavour, in St Dennis*]:
John Grigor, [*blank*]; yearly rent, with 2 suits of court, 5¾d.

Menawartha [*Mennawartha, in St Dennis*]:
John Mena, [*blank*]; yearly rent, with common suit of court, 8½d.

Trelowargh [*Trelavour, in St Dennis*]:
Oliver Tregassowe, [*blank*]; yearly rent, with 2 suits of court, 3s.

Total of free tenants, 10s. 4½d. [sic; 10s. 5d.?]

Conventionary tenants

Nenys [*Ennis, in St Dennis*]:[82]
William Dagoun, 1 holding; yearly rent, with suit of court, 3s. 4d.

Trelowargh [*Trelavour, in St Dennis*]:
John Olyuer, 2 holdings; yearly rent, 14s. 6d.
The wife of John Hopkyn, 1 holding; yearly rent, 3s.
Richard Betty, 1 holding; yearly rent, 10s.

Enyscavyn [*Enniscaven, in St Dennis*]:
John Basset, 1 holding; yearly rent, 10s.
Richard Wilcok, 1 holding; yearly rent, 10s.

Total of conventionary tenants, 50s. 10d.

Total of free and conventionary tenants, [blank; £3 1s. 3d.]

* * *

---

[80] This tenement appears as *Mena Wolas* in the rental of c.1586 (AR2/1343), paying yearly 7¾d. and 1 pair of white gloves, plus 1½d. as tin-fine.

[81] In 1446 John Cornewayll paid homage and fealty to John Arundell for lands held of him by knight's service in the vill of *Grynwyth*, manor not stated (AR3/337). The place is unidentified (it can hardly be Greenwith, in Perranarworthal parish, the only place known with a name resembling the form); nor is a John Cornwall otherwise known as a tenant of Arundell at this time; so it is tempting to suggest that *Grynwyth* was in some way an alternative name of this free tenement of Menawollas. A John Cornuell de Roche, occurring in 1444, may also be the same person (ART6/1).

[82] Name here originally *Enys*, with *N*- added later; in the rental of c.1586 it appears as *Ennysveer* (AR2/1343).

Truruvyan

[Truro Vean, in St Clement]

Extent made Thursday before All Saints, 30 Henry VI [28 October 1451].

[Free tenants]

Robert Coulyng, 1 close called Runeboughetoun;[83] yearly rent, with 2 suits of court, 2s. 6d.

The heir of Spernan, 1 close there; yearly rent, with 2 suits of court, as above, 4s. 6d.

Robert Cuthbert and Richard Carvegh, 1 close there sometime held by Richard Trefry; yearly rent, with 2 suits of court, 2s.

The heir of Thomas Wylle, *[blank]* there.

William Trevenour, *[blank]* there.

Laurence Trewounwall, *[blank]* there.

Total of free tenants, [blank; 9s.][84]

* * *

---

[83] This tenement appears as *Runeboughton alias Gwele Connyam* in the renewal of this rental in 1571 (AR2/1341), and in the rental of *c*.1586 (AR2/1343); but in the manorial accounts *Gwealcunnion* and *Runbovetown* (or *Rumbovetown*) were separate tenements, e.g. in 1692–93 (AR2/1048 and 1052). For *Gwealcunnion* see below, p. 120, n. 20.

[84] No conventionary tenants are given, whereas the rentals of 1480 and 1499 have good lists (below, pp. 77 and 120–21); it is likely that a membrane listing these has been lost from the roll (perhaps at the time that the membrane containing Mitchell was cut off: see below, p. 61).

Methsholl
[Mitchell, in St Enoder][85]

Extent made Thursday before the Nativity of St John the Baptist, 3 Edward IV [23 June 1463].

[*Free tenants*]

John Trenowth, esquire, 2 plots formerly held by William Scatera, and 1 plot formerly held by Walter Wynkele; yearly rent, with suit of court every 3 weeks, 3s. 11½d.

The same John, 1 plot which Thomas Treiagu had by gift of William Berban; yearly rent, with suit of court as above, 3s. 6d.

The same John, 1 plot with a moorland (*landa*) called Goenenbayly, both of which the same Thomas had by gift of Joce Faber ['the smith']; yearly rent, with suit of court as above, 2s. 6d.

The same John, 1 plot which he had by gift of John Skyt; yearly rent, with suit of court as above, 12d.

The same John, 1 plot which he had by gift of the same John Skyt; yearly rent, with suit of court as above, 7d.

The same John, 1 plot formerly held by the same Thomas Treiagu by gift of Thomas Burges; yearly rent, with suit of court as above, 9d.

The same John, 2 plots formerly held by John Hogen; yearly rent, with suit of court as above, 15d.

The same John, 2 plots formerly held by Richard Higon; yearly rent, with suit of court as above, 18d.

The same John, the moorland (*landa*) of Goenmargh [*Goamarth (field), in St Enoder*]; suit of court as above; yearly rent, at three dates, *viz.* the Invention of the Holy Cross, the Nativity of St John

---

[85] An eighteenth-century endorsement on the roll states, 'Methsole cut off from the within & sent to Lord Arundell to London: Feby 1771.' The manor was sold in 1775 (AR2/1196). The membrane is still detached, now Gloucestershire Record Office, D.421/A2/25, where it is kept company by several important thirteenth-century deeds concerning the manor; they and the present membrane evidently left the archive as part of the sale. However, the description of the manor is incomplete (see the end), and it is likely that there was another part, now lost. It is unclear whereabouts in the roll the whole section would have been placed.

the Baptist and St Francis, 6s.

The heir of Henry Conyn, 1 house called Chienpoll; yearly rent, with 2 suits of court, ½d.

The same heir, 3 plots and ¼ of the moorland (*landa*) of Goenbayly; yearly rent, with suit of court every 3 weeks, 8s. 8d.

The same heir, 1 plot formerly held by Maydov; yearly rent, with suit of court as above, 9d.

The heir of John de Sancto Albino, 1 plot which he had by gift of Stephen Heuos, and 1 acre English which he purchased (*perquisivit*) from William Gillot; yearly rent, with suit of court as above, 15d.

The heir of Reginald Tretherf, 1 acre in the moorland (*landa*) called Kaergrugyer; yearly rent, without suit of court, 5d.

The same heir, 1 parcel of land formerly held by Simon Fal in Gunenmargh [*Goamarth (field), in St Enoder*]; yearly rent, with suit of court as above, 18d.

The same heir, 1 plot formerly held by his father, 1 plot opposite, 3 acres in the moorland (*landa*) beside Fosbras, ½ plot, all formerly held by *Gunneta*, 8 acres in the moorland (*landa*) beside Kaergrugyer, and 1 acre English between the ways leading to St Michael's Mount (*mons Sancti Michaelis*) and Truru; yearly rent, with suit of court as above, 2s. 7d.

The same heir, 1 plot formerly held by Simon Fal, 4 acres English in the ground (*terra*) called Sikerlych, and ½ acre English formerly held by Henry Longes; yearly rent, with suit of court as above, 2s. 2d.

The heir of John Fowy, 4 plots; yearly rent, with suit of court as above, 2s. 9½d.

The same heir, 2 acres English next to land lately held by Simon Fal; yearly rent, with suit of court as above, 6d.

The heir of Joan daughter of John Fowy, 1 plot formerly held by Robert Roncyn; yearly rent, with suit of court as above, 8d.

The heir of Michael Treuarʒan and William Treuelgyn, 1 plot with its portion in Gunenbally, formerly held by John Marke; rent, without suit of court, paid through the heir of Reginald Tretherf, 8s. 2d.

John Treuysa, 1 plot and 2 acres English in Gunenmargh; yearly rent, with 2 suits of court, 9d.

The heir of William Fynda, 3 plots with their portion in Gunenbally, *viz.* ¼ part of it; suit of court as above; yearly rent, in addition to 21d. rent which the lord has released to him in exchange for 1 messuage and 1 acre in the town of Medesholl held by the said Joan (*quos predicta Johanna habuit*) 18d. (formerly 3s. 3d.).

The heir of Alice Skynner, 1 plot formerly held by Stephen Heuos [*or* Henos]; yearly rent, with suit of court as above, 6d.

The heir of John Fowy, the acre of St Francis (*acram Sancti Francisci*); yearly rent 4d. to the lord, and 6d. to St Francis: 4d.

The heir of Reginald Cary, 1 plot formerly held by William Bonda; yearly rent, with suit of court as above, 4d.

The heir of Richard de Nansdelyowe, ½ acre Cornish; yearly rent at Michaelmas, with suit of court as above, 4s.[86]

Total of free tenants, [*blank;* £2 17s. 11½d.]

Conventionary tenants

John Perkyn, 1 holding formerly in the hands of Martin Gros; yearly rent, 14s.[87]

---

[86] This free tenement was evidently at Nantillio (in St Enoder), though that is only implied in the text; compare the rentals of 1480 and 1499 (below, pp. 94 and 138).
[87] The extent of the manor breaks off here, presumably through the loss of a further membrane; but the 1480 rental lists only three conventionary tenants, and that of 1499 just two, holding evidently the same three tenements (see below, pp. 95 and 139); so at most only two tenements, and the total sums for the conventionary tenants and for the whole manor, are missing here.

RENTAL, WHOLE ESTATE, [1480]
(AR2/1339)

Contents

Manor of [Lanherne]	65
Manor of Treloy	67
Town of St Columb with Trenhillocks ...	70
Manor of Trembleath	73
Manor of Truro Vean	76
Manor of Kennall	77
Manor of Tregarne	79
Manor of Winnington	81
Manor of Carminow	82
Manor of Connerton	85
Manor and borough of Mitchell	93
Manor of Enniscaven	95
Manor of Bodwannick	96
Miscellaneous lands	99

RENTAL OF [1480]

[*Lanherne, in St Mawgan in Pyder*][1]
[Rental renewed 4 September 1480.]

[*Free tenants*]

[*About six free tenements missing, including Ruthvoes and Gaverigan (St Columb Major), Nantornan (St Columb Minor), Penvose, Polgreen, Trenance (St Mawgan in Pyder), and Bedruthan (St Eval)*]

[*Probably Engollan, with or without Halwyn, in St Eval*]:
... Cornish, by knight's service ...

[*Mawgan Porth, in St Mawgan in Pyder*]:
... Cornish, in socage; suit as above; ...
... [The heirs] of Ralph Porth, 1 acre Cornish, in socage; no suit of court; ... [rent payable at] the chief dates ...

[*Efflins, Bedruthan and Pentire, in St Eval*]:
... 2 acres Cornish in Elwans, Bodrut... [and Pen]tir ..., in socage ...

Total [27s. 2d. *deleted*], 1 *lb*. cummin (4d.), 1 red rose.
Total [*of free tenants*], 27s. 6d.

Conventionary tenants

Trevelgy [*Trevelgue, in St Columb Minor*]:
John Bloyowe, 1 holding there; yearly rent, at 4 dates, 44s.
Thomas Clerke, mowable meadow with the rabbit-island (*pratum falcabile cum insula cuniculorum*); yearly rent, at 4 dates, [26s. 8d. *deleted*] 28s. 4d.
...danyn [?], 1 holding there; yearly rent, at 4 dates, 25s.
...yowe, 1 holding; yearly rent, at 4 dates, 8s. 4d.
... [1] holding; yearly rent, at 4 dates, 16s. 8d.
... 4 dates, 8s. 4d.
... 1 holding; yearly rent, at 4 dates, 20s.

...s [= *Carnewas, in St Eval*]:
John Laury, ½ the vill there; yearly rent, at 4 dates, 9s. 6d.

---

[1] The beginning of this paper roll is much damaged, with loss of material, including the date; see the Introduction, pp. xlii–xliv and cxli–cxlvii.

the other half remains in hand; pays through the bailiff (*per ballivum*) at the same dates, 9s. 6d.

... [*Tregonning, in St Mawgan in Pyder*]:
William Faven, 1 holding; yearly rent, at 4 dates, 20s.

...rvenac [= *Trevenna, in St Mawgan in Pyder*]:
George Dunstan, 1 holding there; yearly rent, at 4 dates, 9s.

Lanvyan [*Lanvean, in St Mawgan in Pyder*]:
John Fynten, 1 holding there; 18s.
John Jak, 1 holding there; 18s.
[John, *deleted*] Ralph Came, 1 acre Cornish; 9s.
Isabel Trewarvena, 1 cottage and 1 acre English; this year [20d. *deleted*] 2s., and following year 2s.
1 cottage in hand, waste and decayed; formerly 12d.

Penpons [*Penpont, in St Mawgan in Pyder*]:
Thomas Snelle, 1 holding with a garden; [7s. *deleted, twice*] 5s.

Wyndesore [*Windsor, in St Mawgan in Pyder*]:
John Fynten, John Jaktomme, and John Jakke, the whole vill; 16s.
Thomas Snelle, 1 small meadow; 2s.
William Trose, 1 holding with a garden there; 2s.

Mill: John Nanscuvell; 33s. 4d.

Lanheron doune: the tenants and outsiders (*tenentes et extranei*) pay there, at the same dates, 8s.

Meadow (*pratum*) of Carnanton [*named from Carnanton, in St Mawgan in Pyder*]: Reginald Crabbe; 3s. 4d.

Hellenparke [*'Halyn parke' (lost), in St Mawgan in Pyder*]:
Rector of Lanheroun church [*St Mawgan in Pyder*], 1 parcel; 7d.

  Total [*of conventionary tenants, etc.*], £10 10s. 11d. [7d. *deleted*][2]

 [*Total of free and conventionary tenants*, £11 18s. 5d. *or* £17 4s. 5d.]

Demesne of Lanheroun:
[*blank*] ... at the end of the roll (*in fine libri*).[3]

* * *

---

[2] The true total of the conventionary rents seems to be £15 6s. 11d., and there is no obvious reason for the discrepancy; compare the totals of £15 12s. 3d. in 1460 (above, p. 35), but over £23 in 1499 (below, p. 110).

[3] See pp. 99–100, below.

Treloye
[Treloy, in St Columb Minor]

Rental renewed the same day and year [4 September 1480].

Free tenants

Wiket and Treleghe [*Wicket and Traleath, in Newlyn East*]:
Ralph Copleston, 1 acre Cornish, by knight's service; 3-weekly suit; yearly rent, at the 4 usual dates, 20*d*.

Polgrun [*Polgreen, in Newlyn East*]:
The heirs of Myghelstowe, 3 acres Cornish, by knight's service; suit as above; at 4 dates, 5*s*.

Trelast [*Trelaske, in Cubert*]:
Oliver Wyse, 4 acres Cornish, in socage; suit as above; at the same dates, 20*d*.

Tresavian [*Tresean, in Cubert*]:
The heir(s) of Trevele, ½ acre Cornish, in socage; suit as above; at the same dates, 12*d*.

Trefewha [*Trevowah, in Crantock*]:
The heir(s) of Trewurga, 1 acre and ½ ferling Cornish, in socage; suit as above; at 4 usual dates, 2*s*. 6½*d*.
The heirs of Nanffan, 1 ferling Cornish, in socage; suit as above; at the same dates, 4*d*.

Helwyn [*Halwyn, in Crantock*]:
The heirs of Wyndesore, 1 parcel of land, by knight's service; suit as above; at the 4 usual dates, 6*d*.

Pentyre Eyther [?] [*Pentirevean, otherwise East Pentire, in Crantock*]:
John Tremayn, ½ acre Cornish, in socage; suit as above; at the same dates, 2*s*.

Trencruke [*Trencreek, in St Columb Minor*]:
Thomas Kylligrewe junior, 1 acre Cornish, in socage; suit as above; at the 4 usual dates, 12*d*.
The heir(s) of Ralph Trencruk, 1 acre Cornish, in socage; suit as above; at the 4 usual dates, 2*s*. 8*d*.

Hendrewarde Paule [*Hendra Paul, in St Columb Minor*]:
John Tretheas, ½ acre Cornish, by knight's service; suit as above; at the same dates, 3*s*.
John Tyek, ½ acre Cornish, by knight's service; suit as above; at the

same dates, 3s. [*margin*: Memo, 2s. 5d. de Warde [?] *terre eiusdem &c. et dat'* 15d. (14d. *deleted*).][4]

Hendre Mustell [*'Hendra Mussell' (lost), in St Columb Minor*]:
The heir(s) of Tremure now Thomas Seyntabyn, 1 acre Cornish, by knight's service; suit as above; at 4 dates, 13¾d.

Bosvelek, Reys [*Boswellick, in St Allen, and Rees, in Perranzabuloe*]:
John Trevaynon esq., 1 acre Cornish, by knight's service; suit as above; at the 4 usual dates, 6d.
The same John, ½ acre Cornish, by knight's service; suit as above; at the same dates, 1d.

Gargous, Kelestek [*Gargas, in Cuby, and Callestock-ruall, otherwise Little Callestick, in Perranzabuloe; also Bryanick, at St Agnes churchtown*]:
The same John, 2 acres Cornish there, by knight's service; suit as above; at the same dates, 12d.
Thomas Trevaignoun, in Kelestek Ruold and Breanek, 1 acre Cornish; at the same dates, 2s.
Respited until (*resp' quousque*) [*in margin*].

Trencruk, Trenynnek [*Trencreek and Treninick, both in St Columb Minor*]:
The heirs of Sergeaux, 6 acres Cornish there, by knight's service; suit as above; the same heirs, 6 acres Cornish there, by knight's service; suit as above; [jointly]1 *lb*. pepper.

Carskeys [*(Higher) Keskeys, in St Columb Minor*]:
John Rossogan, ½ acre Cornish, by knight's service; 2 suits; at the same dates, 13d.

Total [of free tenants], 30s. 2¼d. and 1 *lb*. pepper.[5]

Conventionary tenants

Treloy [*Treloy, in St Columb Minor*]:
Thomas John, 1 holding and 2 acres Cornish, at will; suit of court and mill, and to be reeve when it arises; at 4 usual dates, 36s. 8d., and for a day's work at harvest (*pro diet' autumpni*), 2d.
John Bynny, 2 acres Cornish, at will; suit as above; at the same dates, 36s. 8¼d., and for a day's work, 2d.

---

[4] The meaning of this marginale is not clear.
[5] This total does not include the cryptic amounts mentioned in the margin under Hendra Paul.

Trethowell [*Trethowell, in Kea*]:
Walter John Jagowe, 1 acre Cornish, at will; suit as above; at the same dates, 26s. 8d.

Myngan [*'Mingham' (lost), in St Columb Major*]:
Oto Moyle, the whole vill, by charter; suit of court; at 2 dates, 18s.

Kystall [*Kestle, in St Columb Minor*]:
Laurence Erlond, one-third acre Cornish, at will; at 4 dates, 17s.

Penpoll [*Penpoll, in Crantock*]:
John Stephen, the whole vill, at will; at 4 usual dates, 30s.

Pentyre Eyther' [*Pentirevean, otherwise East Pentire, in Crantock*]:
John Hopkyn, ½ acre Cornish, at will; at 4 dates, 6s.

Melyn Vraan [*Mellanvrane, in St Columb Minor*]:
Thomas Jobbe, 1 holding with a selion (*cum sullone*) of land and the mill, at will; at 4 dates, 13s. 4d.

Trevegglos [*Treviglas, in St Columb Minor*]:
Oto Goff, one-third acre Cornish, at will; at 4 dates, 24s.
Robert Melyonek chaplain, 1 acre Cornish; at 4 dates, 2s. 4d.

Bodrugowe [*Bedrugga, in St Columb Minor*]:
John Hykke, ½ acre Cornish, at will; at 4 dates, 6s. 8d.

Talcarn Morrep [*Tolcarne Merock, in St Mawgan in Pyder*]:
Robert Denys, one-third of the vill; at 4 dates, 28s.

Trebeowe [*Trebby, in St Columb Minor*]:
The lord's tenants; at the same dates, 10s.

Strete Neuham [*'Strete Newham', otherwise 'Newhamstret' (lost), in Truro (in Kenwyn parish)*]:
Richard Skeberyowe, 1 garden; at the same dates, 8d.

Total [*of conventionary tenants*], £12 16s. 4¼d.

Total [*of free and conventionary tenants*], £14 6s. 6½d.;[6] from which deduct 36s. 4d. [*for outgoing payments*]; remains clear yearly £13 9s. 10½d.

* * *

---

[6] An incorrect total, £15 6s. 2½d., is first given (deleted); and the nett total is derived from this figure. The true nett total is £12 10s. 2½d.

Seynt Columb' and Trewynhelek
[*St Columb town and Trenhillocks, in St Columb Major*]

Rental renewed the same day and year [4 September 1480].

Free tenants and tenants for term of years

Ralph Trypkunyn holds freely those holdings which were lately of Luke Pluven; 2 suits of court, and other services as other tenants have been accustomed to do, except for (*ultra*) 3s. 8d. for 1 close there, reserved for the lord (*reservat' domino*) for various tenements in the same newly to be built; rent at 4 dates, 5s. 6d.

John Clemowe, 1 holding newly built, for term of years; 2 suits of court, and 12d. for relief; rent at 4 dates and other services, 4s.

Oto Moyle, 2 holdings (2s. 11d.) with 2 parcels of land (4s.), by charter, for term of years; suit and other services as above; rent at 4 dates, 6s. 11d.

John Michell, 7 holdings, 5 gardens, 2 closes (15s., in the Great Close) and certain parcels of land, by charter; suit and services as other tenants; rent at 4 dates, 77s.

Heirs of Michael Vdy, 1 holding, by charter; rent at 4 dates, 20d.

John Serdewyne, 1 parcel (8d.), holding of the said heir of Vdy, 1 close of land (26s. 8d.) at Trewenhelek [*Trenhillocks, in St Columb Major*], 1 close (7s. 6d.) at Seyntcolumb and 1 holding (4s. 4d.) at Seyntcolumb, by charter; suit and services as other tenants; rent at 4 dates, 39s. 2d.

Richard Goff, 1 holding, by charter; suit and services as other tenants; rent at 4 dates, 3s. 4d.

Odo Viuyan, 1 holding, by charter; suit and services as other tenants; rent at 4 dates, 12d.

The heir(s) of Robert Olyuer, 2 holdings, by charter dated Sunday before Easter 1 Hen V [16 April 1413]; suit and services as other tenants; rent at 4 dates, 2s. 8d.

[*marginal addition, concerning 8d. increment.*]

The heirs of Remfrey Arundell, 1 holding lately of the heir(s) of Trewenhelek [*Trenhillocks*]; the same suit and services; rent at the same dates, 9d.

Mark Thomas, 1 holding for term of years, by charter; the same suit

ST COLUMB TOWN

and services; rent, 4s.

Thomas Budy and heir(s) of John Jamys, 1 holding, by charter; rent etc. as above, 2s. 6d.

Richard Paule, 1 holding (4s.) lately of John Dolle, for term of years from 3 Hen VI [1424-25], 1 parcel (9d.) and 1 close (20s.) at Trewenhelek [*Trenhillocks*]; rent, etc., as above, 24s. 9d.

Remfrey Eneys, 3 holdings by charter; rent, etc., as above, 2s. 1d.

Nicholas Tresythny and John Heresy, 1 close (7s. 11d.) and 1 smithy (*fabrica*) (12d.), by charter; rent, etc., as above, 8s. 11d. [*the 11d. added later; margin*: 11d. increment];
the same Nicholas and John Heresy, 2 holdings; suit and services as other tenants; rent, 2s.

Thomas Tresythny, 1 holding (4s.), 1 holding with a close (12s.), 1 holding (12d.) and 1 holding (20d.), by charter; suit, etc., as above; 18s. 8d.

John Nanscuvell, 1 holding there; suit, etc., as above; 12d.

David Tregarrek, 2 holdings there; suit, etc., as above; 18d.

John Trevga, 1 holding; suit, etc., as above; 8s. [4s. *deleted; margin:*] increment 4s. [2s., *deleted*].

John Rossogan, 4 holdings; suit, etc., as above; 12d.

The heirs of Michael Crabbe, 1 holding there by charter; suit, etc., as above; 2s. 7d.

The heirs of John Russell, 1 holding (5s.) and 1 holding (6s. 8d.) now of Richard Paul; suit and services as other tenants; 11s. 8d.

Vivian Carun' [?], 1 holding (3s. 4d.) and 1 close (36s. 8d.) at Trewenhelek [*Trenhillocks*]; suit, etc., as above; 40s.

Michael Tomme Symon, 1 holding; suit, etc., as above; 3s. 4d.

The heir(s) of John Wolcock, 1 holding there; suit, etc., as above, 3s. 5d.

Michael Stevyn, 1 holding there; suit, etc., as above; 9s.

Richard Harry, 1 holding there; suit, etc., as above; 3s. 4d.

Michael Gregory, 1 holding there; suit, etc., as above; 2s.

Stephen Movna, 1 holding (2s. 8d.) and 32 feet of land (16d.), by charter, 1 close (3s. 9d.) in the Great Close, and 1 close (6s. 8d) [query whether he has or not, because he has not a charter; 10d. increment, *added later*]; 14s. 5d.

Thomas Crugowe, 1 holding, by charter, 38′ × 12′; suit, etc., as above; 1d.

John Tremayne, 1 holding, by charter dated 32 Hen. VI [1453–54]; suit, etc., as above; 19d.

Richard Tomyowe, 1 parcel of land (10s.) in the Great Close and 1 close (23s.) at Trewenhelek [*Trenhillocks*]; suit, etc., as above; 33s.

John Watta, 1 holding (6s. 8d.) and 1 close (4s. 4d.) in the Great Close; suit, etc., as above; 11s.

Richard Serdewyne, 2 closes there (in the Great Close), by charter; suit, etc., as above; 7s. 6d.

John Trosse, 1 close (in the Great Close); suit, etc., as above; 6s. 11d.

William Michell, 1 close (in the Great Close; 7s. 6d.) and 1 holding (2s. 4d.); suit, etc., as above; 9s. 10d.

John Harry, 1 holding (2s. 10d.) and 2 closes (12s. 8d.; at Trewenhelek [*Trenhillocks*]); suit, etc., as above; 15s. 6d.

Michael Peryn, 1 holding (4s. 4d.) and 1 close (5s.; in the Great Close); suit, etc., as above; 9s. 4d.

Nicholas Treloddrowe, 1 parcel of land (3s. 4d.) and 1 holding (9s.) with a close of land (at Trewenhelek [*Trenhillocks*]); suit, etc., as above; 12s. 4d.

Richard Treysathnov, 1 parcel of land; suit, etc., as above; 2s.

Richard Janyn, 1 holding, by charter; suit, etc., as above; 20d.

Robert Sutter, 1 holding, by charter; suit, etc., as above; 20d.

John Jenkyn alias Pascowe, 1 close (at Trewenhelek [*Trenhillocks*]); suit, etc., as above; 13s. 4d. [*margin*: Memo of 8d. [?] increment of John Laury the following year, in addition to 4s. 4d. previously charged.]

Thomas Trehar, a parcel of the vill of Trewynhelek [*Trenhillocks*]; 16s.

Thomas Crugowe, 3 mills and 2 closes there; £10 6s. 8d.

[*added later:*]

Luke Carter, a bakehouse (*domus pristrine*) [*sic*]; 8s.

Mark Knygh', 1 holding; 8s. ['leased [?] to Holy Trinity Chapel (*remess'* [?] *capelle Sancte Trinitatis*), 8s.', *interlinear*].

Total, £32 19s.
Total, £32 3s. ...
Total, £32 18s. 10d., ... thus proved 10s. ...[7]

* * *

Trembloyth [*sic*]
[*Trembleath, in St Ervan*]

Rental renewed the same day and year [4 September 1480].

Free tenants

...mayle, Arlyn, [T]revayhov, [T]rethias, Treyarnan, [T]revur, Tewyn [*Lemail (in Egloshayle), Harlyn, Trevio, Trethias, Treyarnon, Treveor and Towan (all in St Merryn)*]:[8]
Thomas Raskerrak, William Pencors and Hugh Boscaffyn, co-heirs of Laurence Arundell, in Trevayhov 1 acre Cornish, in Treythias ½ acre Cornish, in Treyarnan ½ acre Cornish, in Tewyn ½ acre Cornish, in Trevur ½ acre Cornish, and in Arlyn ½ acre Cornish, by knight's service; 3-weekly suit of court; 1 pair of gilt spurs or 3s. 4d. at the 4 usual dates.

Kerow Lome [*Carlumb, in St Minver*]:
Thomas Raskerrak, 2 acres Cornish by knight's service; suit as above; at Michaelmas 1d.

Kerowe Mur [*Blakes Keiro, otherwise Keiro Veor, in St Minver*]:
Thomas Whalesburgh, 2 acres Cornish by knight's service; suit as above; 3s. 4d.

Ammell, Trevanger, Seyntmynfre and [T]reythavek [*(Middle) Amble, in St Kew; Trevanger, St Minver and Trethauke, all in St Minver*]:
Thomas Movne, in Ammell 1 acre Cornish, in Trevanger 1 acre

---

[7] It is not clear how to reconcile these various totals, with each other or with the rents given.
[8] Compare the rental of 1459, again with Lemail appearing in the heading, but not in the text (above, p. 24).

Cornish, in Seyntmynfre ½ acre Cornish, in Trethavek 1 acre Cornish, by knight's service; 3-weekly suit of court; 3s. 4d.

Arlyn [*Harlyn, in St Merryn*]:
John Coulyng, by right of Katherine his wife, ½ acre Cornish, by knight's service; suit of court [*only*].

Restelek [*Retallick, in Roche*]:
The heirs of William Hopkyn, 1 acre Cornish, by knight's service; suit at the 2 leet courts; 6d.

Trevelwith [*Trevella, in Crantock*]:
John Trevelwith, 1 acre Cornish by knight's service; 3-weekly suit of court; 4s.

Langorowe [*Langurra, at Crantock churchtown*]:
John Quynell, ½ acre Cornish in socage; 3-weekly suit of court; 6d.

Tewyn [*Towan, in St Columb Minor*]:
Heir(s) of Remfrey Arundell, ½ acre Cornish in socage, without suit; 3d.

Trefewha [*Trevowah, in Crantock*]:
Robert Trefewha, ½ acre Cornish in socage; 3-weekly suit; 13½d.

Skywys [*(Great) Skewes, in St Wenn*]:
Heir(s) of John Arundell knight, 2 acres Cornish in socage; 3-weekly suit of court. [Query rent [?], *added.*]

Treneyowe [*Treniow, in Padstow, presumably*]:[9]
Thomas Ruffos, 1 acre Cornish by knight's service; 4s.

Total [*of free tenants, blank;* 19s. 5½d.]

---

[9] This free tenement is lacking in the earlier extents, and also in that of 1499; but it reappears thereafter, in the rentals of c.1586 and 1659 ('held by heirs of Ruffos now [*blank*]': compare the tenant here). In 1499 Treniow appears, oddly, as a *conventionary* tenement of Trembleath (the first to be listed, and paying the same rent as here: below, p. 106). Treniow was also a free tenement of Perlees manor, from its first appearance in 1499 (p. 140). In the account rolls of Trembleath manor, Treniow appears as a member in 1468-93, paying high rent to the lord of Padstow (accounts, AR2/908, m. 3; AR2/910, fol. 4; AR2/915 and AR2/933); and again in 1470 (court roll, AR2/64, m. 2); and in Perlees manor in 1509 (account roll, AR2/945, fol. 9), paying high rent to Padstow borough.

Conventionary tenants

Trethrisek [*Tredrizzick, in St Minver*]:
Vicar of Sancta Menfreda [*St Minver*], 1 acre Cornish; 13s. 4d. Query concerning 2d. for days' work at harvest (*Q'r de 2d. de diet' autumni*).

Penros [*Penrose, in St Ervan*]:
Reginald Coysvogherth, 1 holding at will; 5s. 3d.

Tregona [*Tregona, in St Eval*]:
Thomas Richard, 1 holding; 22s. 7d.
Thomas Dunston, 1 holding; 22s. 6½d.
John Pascawe, 1 holding; 22s. 6½d.

Hengolan [*Engollan, in St Eval*]:
Martin Wolcok, 1 holding; 16s. 3d.
Ivo Symon, 2 holdings; 26s. 8d.

Helwen [*Halwyn, in St Eval, at Engollan*]:
James Iwyn, 1 holding; 13s.[10]

Crukmorek [*Crigmurrick, in St Merryn*]:
Robert Coulyng, ½ acre Cornish; 10s.

Trevyngonyowe, Trevenellys [*Tregwinyo (otherwise Trevengenow) and Trenayles, near Tregwinyo, both in St Ervan*]:
William Baddecok, the whole vill [*singular*]; 45s.

Menewels [*Manuels, in St Columb Minor*]:
Walter Tresawell, 1 holding; 20s.
John Roberd, 1 holding; 20s.

Chapell [*Chapel, in St Columb Minor*]:
Martin Robyn, 1 holding; 5s. 4d.

Melynnewith [*Millingworth, in St Ervan*]:
The mill there; in hand, decayed (*decas'*).

Trethias [*Trethias, in St Merryn*]:
Henry Bailly, 1 acre Cornish; 8s.

Sub-total of conventionary tenants, £12 10s. 6d.

Trembloyth [*Trembleath, in St Ervan*]:
John Tregarthyn, 1 close; 13s. 6½d. [4d. deleted].

---

[10] The name *Trembloyth* appears, deleted, after this entry.

John Yewan, 1 close; 13s. 6½d. [4d. *deleted*]
Nicholas Jenyn, 1 close; 13s. 6½d. [4d. *deleted*]
Thomas Tremayle, 1 close; 13s. 6½d. [4d. *deleted*]
Thomas Dunge, 1 close; 13s. 6½d. [4d. *deleted*]
John Jakharry, 1 close; 13s. 6½d. [4d. *deleted*]
John Harry Norton, 1 close; 13s. 6½d. [4d. *deleted*]
Martin Wolcok, 1 close; 13s. 6½d. [4d. *deleted*]
John Trewynean, 1 close; 6s. 8d.
Richard Seynterven, 1 close; 6s. 8d.
Richard Jaktomme and Henry Richard, 1 close; 6s. 8d.
John Stephen, 1 close; 6s. 8d.
Richard Seynterven, 1 close, by charter; 6s. 8d.

Total [*of Trembleath tenants*], £7 20d.
[*Total of all conventionary tenants*, £19 12s. 2d.]

Total [*of free and all conventionary tenants*], £20 12s. 6½d.[11]

* * *

Treruvian
[*Truro Vean, in St Clement*]

Rental renewed 6 September, the same year [1480].

[*Free tenants*]

Robert Coulyng, 1 close called Runeboughton, freely; 2 suits of court; at 4 dates, 2s. 6d.

Henry Cutbert and Richard Carvegh, 1 close sometime of Richard Trefry; 2 suits of court; at 4 dates, 2s.

William Trevenour, 1 close, freely; 2 suits of court; 6d.

The heir(s) of Laurence Trewonwall, 1 close in Gwelequonyam, freely; 2 suits of court; 3d.

The heir(s) of Thomas Wille, 1 close in Gwelequonyam, freely; 2 suits of court; 8d.

Robert Janyn chaplain, 1 holding, for term of years; 2s.
[*margin*: remains in hand; *interlinear*: to be granted (*tradatur*) to John Norton, for term of years; [*margin*: increment [?] 12d. Leased (*dimiss'*) to John Norton.]

---

[11] This seems to imply a total of 20s. 4½d. for the free tenants, rather than the 19s. 5½d. given earlier.

The heir(s) of David Spernan, 1 close, freely; 2 suits of court; 4s. 6d. [*margin*: query 8s.]

Total [*of free tenants*], 12s. 5d.

Conventionary tenants

John Nortoun, in various places, with (*cum*) 6s. 8d. increment of rent there [*sic*]; at 4 dates, 74s. 2d.
[*interlinear*: Ralph Treberveth and Walter Kern *reper'* [?] all the lands and holdings which John Norton lately held there, for term of 20 years, for yearly rent, £4 0s. 10d.]

Thomas Laugher,[12] 2 closes (in Gwelequonyam), at will; 8s. 2d.

Henry Stoute, 1 close, at will; 2s.

William Veyse, 1 close in Carvoddros [*Carvedras, in Kenwyn*], at will; 6s. 8d.

William Langher, 1 garden in Carvoddros, at will; 2s.

Joan Crabbe, 1 parcel, at will; 12d.

Walter Curlean, ½ messuage with ½ garden, at will; 10d.

1 close, rent 10s., in hands of the prior of the brothers of Truru;[13] query how (*quere quomodo*), [*blank*].

Total [*of conventionary tenants*], £4 14s. [?]

Total [*of free and conventionary tenants*], 106s. 5d.;
from which is deducted for chief rent, 5s. 8d.;
remains 100s. 9d.

* * *

Kenell
[*Kennall, in Stithians*]

Rental renewed 6 September, the same year [1480].

[*Free tenants*]

Tregonan, Penmena [*Tregonning and Penmenor; also Treskewes and Trembroath; all in Stithians*]:
John Stanlowe and John Baker, by right of their wives, 2 acres

---
[12] The name could alternatively be read as *Langher*.
[13] The Dominican friary; see Henderson, 'Ecclesiastical antiquities', pp. 257–62 (p. 258).

Cornish in Tregonan, Penmena, Trescuwys and Trembroyth, in socage; at 2 dates (mid-Lent and Michaelmas), 4s.

Ressegh [*Roseath, in Stithians*]:
Joan Ressegh, ½ acre Cornish, by knight's service; 2 suits of court; at the same dates, 3s.

Enys [*Ennis, in Stithians*]:
The heir(s) of Ralph Enys, ½ acre Cornish, by knight's service; 3-weekly suit of court; 14¾d.
Martin Robert, 1 ferling, by knight's service; suit as above; 14¾d.

Tregonan [*Tregonning, in Stithians*]:
The heir(s) of William Trencrik [*sic*], ½ acre Cornish, in socage; suit as above; 2s.

Hendr' [*Hendra, in Stithians*]:
John Durant, ½ acre Cornish in Hendr', by knight's service; 2 suits of court; 3s.

Total [of free tenants], 14s. 5½d. [sic]

Conventionary tenants

...l [*Kennall, in Stithians*]:
John Nole, 1 holding, by copy; at 4 dates, 26s. 8d.
Adam John, 1 holding, at will; at 4 dates, 13s. 4d.
Walter Hopkyn, 1 holding in Kenell, at will; 13s. 4d.

Trebuet [*for 'Treberuet'; Trebarveth, in Stithians*]:
Richard Treberuet, 1 holding, at will; at 4 dates, 16s. 6d.

Tremenhere [*Tremenheere, in Stithians*]:
John Sewragh, 1 holding, at will; 10s.

Trembroyth [*Trembroath, in Stithians*]:
John Pascowe, 1 holding, at will; 8s. 6d.
Pentecost (*Pentacost*) Jak Pascowe, 1 holding, at will; 8s. 6d.

Mill of Kenell:
Edward Thomas, the mill; 11s.

Total [of conventionary tenants], 107s. 10d.

Total [of free and conventionary tenants], £6 2s. 3½d.;
from which is to be deducted for chief rent, 20s.;
remains 102s. 3½d.

* * *

Tregaryn
[*Tregarne, in St Keverne*]

Rental renewed 7 September, the same year [1480].

Free tenants

Trelanvyan [*Trelanvean, in St Keverne*]:
John Reskymour, ½ acre Cornish, by knight's service; 2 suits of court; at 4 dates, 7s.

Comguyneon [*Polgwidnan, in St Keverne*]:
The heir(s) of Chynals, ½ acre Cornish, by knight's service; no suit of court; at Michaelmas only, ½d.

Tregaryn [*Tregarne, in St Keverne*]:
Thomas Boden, ½ acre Cornish, by knight's service; 3-weekly suit of court; 12d.

Monglyth [*Mongleath, in Budock*]:
The heir(s) of Killygrewe, 1 acre Cornish, by knight's service; suit as above; 2s.

Nansdrisek [*Nancetrisack, in Sithney*]:
The heirs of John Arundell,[14] ½ acre Cornish, by knight's service; 6d.

Penweres [*Penwerris, in Budock*]:
Richard Kendell, the whole vill, in socage; at Michaelmas, 1 pair of gloves or 1d.

[G]illy [*Gilly, in Mawgan in Meneage*]:
John Petit, ½ acre Cornish, in socage; 2 suits of court; at Michaelmas only, 1d.

Baghowe [*Bahow, in St Keverne*]:
Richard Baghowe, 1 acre Cornish, in socage; no suit; 7s.

Total [of free tenants], 17s. 8½d.

Conventionary tenants

Tregaryn [*Tregarne, in St Keverne*]:
Thomas Golla, 1 holding, at will; suit of court and mill; at St Andrew, mid-Lent, St James and Michaelmas, 20s.
Joan Janyn and Nicholas Roberd, 1 holding; 12s. 2d.

---
[14] John Arundell of Tolverne, in Philleigh parish (compare p. 22, n. 16).

Richard Tomaluky, 1 holding; 13s. 8d.

Helwyn [*Halwyn, in St Keverne*]:
John Jak Wone, 1 holding; 16s.
John William, 1 holding; 8s.

The mill:
John Phelipp, the mill; to repair it in everything except timber; 22s.

Bodenvian [*Boden Vean, in St Anthony in Meneage*]:
William Toma Berowe, 1 holding; 20s.

Hendrevik [*Landrivick, in Manaccan*]:
John Tomma, the whole vill; 13s. 4d.

Penpoll [*Penpoll, in St Anthony in Meneage*]:
John Sadeler, 1 holding; 9s.

Condorowe [*Condurrow, in St Anthony in Meneage*]:
Henry Hopkyn, 1 holding; 10s. 4d.
John Peryn, 1 holding; 10s. 4d.
John Geffrey, 1 holding, at will; 10s. 4d.
John Perowe, 1 holding, at will; 10s. 4d.

Tregevis [*Tregevas, in St Martin in Meneage*]:
Richard Renoudon, 1 holding; 21s.
John Chynale, 1 holding; 11s. 8d.
[*margin*: query concerning 4d. more]

Total [*of conventionary tenants*], £10 [?] 7s. 6d. [2d. deleted]

Total [*of free and conventionary tenants*], £11 5s. 2½d.
[4s. 10½d. deleted; 14d. deleted];
from which is to be deducted for chief rent 11s. 5½d.;
remains £10 13s. 5d.[15]

* * *

---

[15] The nett total is deduced from the original total of £11 4s. 10½d., not from the revised one of £11 5s. 2½d.; but in any case the total for conventionary tenants does not seem to agree with the rents cited.

Wynnyanton
[*Winnington, in Gunwalloe*]

Rental renewed 9 September, the same year [1480].

Free tenants

Trerys, Trenans Vian and Tresoy [*sic*] [*Trerise in Ruan Major, Trenance Vean in Mullion, and Trezise in St Martin in Meneage*]:
The heir of Richard Sergeaux knight, 1 acre Cornish in Trerys; homage and fealty, for all service;
the same heir, ½ acre Cornish in Trenans Vyan, in socage; 3-weekly suit of court; at St Andrew, mid-Lent, St James and Michaelmas, 3s. 5½d.;
the same heir, ½ acre Cornish in Treseys, in socage; suit etc.; 2s.

Tregowris, Hengeyther, Cornhough [*Tregowris, Nangither and Carno, all in St Keverne*]:
John Reskymour [*interlinear*: 11s. query], 2 acres Cornish, in socage; 3-weekly suit of court; 10s. 2d.

Bossym, Pentir [*Bochym and Pentire, both in Cury*]:
Richard Wydeslade, 1 acre Cornish, by knight's service; suit as above; 4s. 11d.

Hendr' [*Hendra, in Ruan Major*]:
Richard Bonythorn [*sic*], 3 ferlings, by knight's service; suit as above; 3s. 8¼d.
The heirs of Henry Hendr', 1 ferling, in socage; suit as above; 14¾d.

Trenowen [*Trenoon, in Ruan Major*]:
Thomas Erysy, 1 acre Cornish, by knight's service; no suit; 6s. 8d.

Tresprison [*Tresprison, in Mullion*]:
Richard Tresprison, ½ acre Cornish, in socage; suit as above; 2s. 6d.

Erysy [*Erisey, in Grade*]:
Henry Bodrugan, ½ acre Cornish, by knight's service; suit as above; 20d.

Tregaddrith Mur, Tregaddrith Vyan, Trerys, Nansplough [*Tregaddra, in Mawgan in Meneage, and Trease and Nanplough, both in Cury*]:
Thomas Chamond, 2 acres 1 ferling Cornish, by knight's service; 3-weekly suit of court; 20d.

Total [*of free tenants*], 37s. 11½d. [33s. 0½d., *deleted*]

Conventionary tenants

Trenowith [*Trenoweth, in Gunwalloe*]:
John Bossustowe, 1 holding, at will; suits of court and mill of Carmynowe; 17s.

Nansy [*Hingey, in Gunwalloe*]:
Ralph Rois, 1 holding, at will; suit as above; 16s.

Gun͞sy͞py, Chypy [*Chepye, in Gunwalloe*]:[16]
John Nicoll, 1 holding, at will; 20s.

Roos ['*Rosehendra' (lost), in Cury*]:
John Broider, 1 parcel, at will; 2s.

Tolle [*Toll, in Gunwalloe*]:
Peter Tolle, 3 ferlings, at will; 20s.

Curte [*Court, in Gunwalloe*]:[17]
John London [*or* Loudon], 1 holding, at will; 12s.

Wynnyanton [*Winnington, in Gunwalloe*]:
Isabel Raffull, 1 holding, at will; 10s.
Robert Oby, 1 holding, at will; 10s.
John Gerueys, 1 house, but tenure is unknown; 16d.

Total [*of conventionary tenants*], 108s. 4d. [£6 3s. *deleted*]

Total [*of free and conventionary tenants*], £7 6s. 3½d. [16½d. *deleted*]

* * *

Carmynowe
[*Carminow, in Mawgan in Meneage*]

Rental renewed the same day and year [9 September 1480].

Free tenants

Redalan, Huthnans, Karioghall, Trener, Roddour and Tilligow [*Redallan, Huthnance, Crawle, Trenear, Ruthdower and Treliggo, all in Breage*]:
The heir(s) of Warin Archedeken, in Redalan, Huthnans,

---

[16] The first name is for *Goninsypy*, close to Chepye and merged with it by 1499 (below, p. 129): see above, in the 1460 extent (p. 18).

[17] This may be the same tenement as *Chicastell* in 1499 (below, p. 129), which is the later *Choy Castle* (lost), adjacent to Gunwalloe church and so to the modern farm of Court.

Karyoghall, Roddour and Tilligowe, ½ knight's fee; homage, fealty and scutage, for all service.

[T]reueglos, ...omder [*sic*], Tregenrith [*Treveglos, Tremeader and Tregerthen* [?]; *also 'Carlibby' (lost), all in Zennor*]:
The heir(s) of Richard Sergeaux knight, 1 acre Cornish in Treueglos, 3 acres in Treuemeder, 1 acre in Tregenrith, and 1 ferling in Carleb, by knight's service; homage and fealty.

Tregedell [*Tregiddle, in Cury*]:
John Petyt Perdannek [*sic*], 1 acre Cornish in Tregedell, in socage, by homage and fealty; 3-weekly suit of court; at All Saints and St James, 12*d*.

Gurlyn and Trevelyham [*Gurlyn and Trelean, both in St Erth*]:
The heirs of Ralph Soer, 2 parts of the vill of Gurlyn and ½ the vill of Trelevylyham [*sic*], by knight's service; sometime given with one Margery, daughter of Carmynowe.

Grous [*Angrouse, in Mullion*]:
William Gurlyn, 3 acres at Grous, lately of the heir(s) of Reginald Godrevy, by homage, fealty and 3-weekly suit of court; at the 4 usual feasts, 5*s*.

...modr' [*Rosemorder, in Manaccan*]:
Ralph Reskymmour, ½ acre Cornish in Rosmodr', by homage and fealty; at the 4 usual feasts, for all service, 20*d*.

Polgrun [*Polgrean, in Cury*]:
James Nanffan, 1 acre Cornish in Polgrun, in socage; homage, fealty and 3-weekly suit of court; 20*s*.

Helstonburgh [*Helston town*]:
William Jak Dauy, 2½ plots and 1 field (*parcus*) in Helstonburgh, in socage; 6*s*.

Total [*of free tenants*], 33*s*. 8*d*.

Conventionary tenants

..amargh [*Lamarth, in Mawgan in Meneage*]:
Ralph Lamargh, the whole vill of Lamargh, by charter; suit of court and mill; [3*s*. 11*d*. *deleted*] 11*s*.

[Br]onnywyk Warth', [B]ronnyw..k Wolas [*Higher and Lower Burnuick, in Mawgan in Meneage*]:
Richard Jenkyn, ½ acre and ½ ferling in Bronnyweke Warth', and

1½ ferlings in Bronnywyke Wolas, by charter; 20s.

[He]ndre, [C]hinithin [*Hendra and 'Chynythen' (lost), in Cury*]:[18]
John Hikke, ½ acre in Hendr' and ½ ferling in Chynythyn, at will; 17s.

[H]endre, [K]illiancreth [*Hendra, in Cury, and Killianker, in Mawgan in Meneage*]:
John Jamys, 3 ferlings in Hendre and 1 acre in Bylyancreth [*sic*], at will; 17s.

Cleys Olinsie [*'Clies Olingey' (lost), part of Clies, in Mawgan in Meneage*]:
Henry Cleys, in Cleys and Clensy [*sic*], 3 ferlings, at will; 16s.

...e [*Anhay, in Gunwalloe*]:
Ralph Hee, 3 ferlings, at will; 19s.
Richard Nanspian, 1 holding, at will; 30s. 8d.

... Dodde [*'Hendradodda' (= Burgess), in Gunwalloe; also 'Chynythen' (lost), in Cury*]:
John Broidier, ½ ferling in Chynythyn and ½ acre in Hendre Dodde; 16s.

...ls [*Chinalls, in Gunwalloe*]:
Walter Trelek, 3 ferlings, at will; 13s. 4d.

...pper [*Berepper, in Gunwalloe*]:
Laurence Jamys, 1 ferling, at will; 9s.

...arlo [*Chyvarloe, in Gunwalloe*]:
John Burges, 2 holdings in Chiwarloo; 20s. [*margin*: query, 21s. 8d.]
Richard Beauripper, 1 holding, at will; 12s.
John London [*or* Loudon], 1 holding, at will; 10s.
Simon Kentrevek, 1 holding, at will; 10s.
John Jamys, 1 holding, at will; 6s. 8d.
John Gregory, 1 holding, at will; 10s.

. . . [*Nampean, in Gunwalloe*]:
John Harry, ½ acre Cornish, at will; 14s.

[*The mill*]:
Thomas Melynder, the corn-mill there, at will; 20s.

---

[18] The marginal names in this entry and the two following have all been rewritten at a rather later date (except for *Cleys* in the next entry but one), so may not be reliable fifteenth-century forms.

MANOR OF CARMINOW   85

[*Glebe-land of other parishes (see above, pp. xvi and xliii)*]:
The rector of Seynt Fyle [*parish of Philleigh*] yearly, for his glebe, 12*d*.
The rector of Whitston [*parish of Whitstone*] yearly, for his glebe, 2*s*.

Total [*of conventionary tenants, etc.*], £13 14*s*. 8*d*.

[*Demesne*]:
... demesne there
... bailiff through agistment ... sheaf (*garbam*).
Thus because it is unknown [still, *deleted*] at present [?].

Total [*of free and conventionary tenants*], £15 8*s*. 4*d*.;
from which is deducted for chief rents, 12*s*. 1*d*.;
remains £14 16*s*. 3*d*.

* * *

[Co]nertoun
[*Connerton, in Gwithian*]

Rental renewed Monday 10 September, the same year [1480].[19]

[*Free tenants*]

[*Trencrom and 'Nansavallan' (lost), both in Lelant*]:
The heirs of William Botreaux, 1 acre Cornish in Trencrom and Nansavallan, in socage; 3-weekly suit of court; 4*s*. Also at Michaelmas, for offering of aid (*pro offr' auxilii*), 3*d*.;[20]
the same heirs, the water of Lenanta [*stream at Lelant*]; at Easter, 6*d*.

[*Bosworgey and Boscudden, both in St Erth*]:
The same heir [*sic*], 1 acre Cornish in Boswythgy and Boscudyn, by service of ¼ knight's fee; no suit or rent.

[*Taskus, in Gwinear*]:
John Petyt, heir of Michael Petyt, ½ acre Cornish in Talscoys, in socage; 3-weekly suit of court; 15*d*.

[*'Bosverghes', unidentified*]:
The heirs of [Carsulsek, *deleted*] Carsullek, sometime of William Manyer, 5 acres English in Bosverghes, in socage; 3-weekly suit of court; but rent to be inquired, because it is still unknown; 13*d*.

---

[19] 'Monday' seems to be an error for 'Sunday': see the Introduction.
[20] This phrase is consistently written *pro offr' auxilii* in this rental, as if 'for offering *of* aid'; but it may be that 'offering *and* aid', as in 1463 and 1499, was intended.

[*Trenoweth, in Gwinear*]:
The same heir of Carsullek, ½ acre Cornish in Trenowith, sometime of William Manyer, in socage; 3-weekly suit of court; at 4 dates, 2s. Also for offering of aid, at Easter, 3d.

[*Amalebra, Nancledra and Chylason, all in Towednack*]:
John Broughton [sic], sometime of Nigel Loryng, 2 acres Cornish in Amalibry, Nanscludry and Chyclasen [sic], in socage; 3-weekly suit of court; 8s.

[*Polkinghorne, in Gwinear*]:
The same John Boughton [sic], sometime of Nigel Loryng, ½ acre Cornish in Polkynhorn, by knight's service; at Michaelmas, 12d.

[*Trenowin, in Gwinear*]:
James Tregaryn, lately of Nigel Loryng, 1 ferling Cornish in Trenawyn Wartha; 3-weekly suit of court; at Michaelmas, 1 *lb.* cummin [or] 4d.

[*Egloshayle, at Phillack churchtown*]:
John Arundell Talvern, sometime of William Tregoys, ½ acre Cornish in Egloshayle, in socage; 3-weekly suit of court; at Michaelmas, 6s. 9d.

[*Trethingy, in Phillack*]:
The same John, sometime of the same William, 1 acre Cornish in Trethengy, in socage; 3-weekly suit of court; at Michaelmas, 1d. Also for offering of aid, at the same feast, 3d.

[*Connorwartha, at Gwithian churchtown*]:
The heir(s) of Laurence Sheryston, sometime of Odo Resgerens by right of Alice his wife, ½ acre Cornish in Conerwartha, in socage; 3-weekly suit of court; at Michaelmas, 12d.

[*'Ponsfrellas' (lost), in Gwithian*]:
The same heir, sometime of the same Odo, ½ acre Cornish in Ponfreles, in socage; 3-weekly suit of court; at Michaelmas, 1d.

[*'Grafton' (lost), in Gwithian*]:
The same heir, sometime of the same Odo, 1 ferling in Graften, by knight's service; 3-weekly suit of court; at 4 dates, 2s.

[*Trevassack and Ventonleague, both in Phillack*]:
The heir(s) of Remfrey Arundell knight, sometime of John Penros, 2 acres Cornish in Trevasek and Fentenlege, by knight's service;

3-weekly suit of court; rent at 4 dates, by indenture remaining with the lord, 3s.

[*Ayr, in St Ives parish*]:
Robert Nanscothen, sometime of John Helle de Porthia, one-third of an acre Cornish in Ardy [sic], in socage; 2s.

[*Hendra, in St Ives parish*]:
The heir(s) of Odo Colyn, sometime of William Fitzwater, 1 acre Cornish in Hendre, by knight's service; suit of court at Michaelmas [*only*]; at Easter, 1 pair of gilt spurs or 6d.

[*Ayr, in St Ives parish*]:
The same heir, sometime of John Colyn de Lenanta, one-third of an acre Cornish in Ardy, by knight's service; 3-weekly suit; 16d.

[*Trevaskis, in Gwinear*]:
The same heir, sometime of the same John Colyn, one-third of an acre Cornish in Trevalscoys, by knight's service; 3-weekly suit; 12d.

[*Trenowin, in Gwinear*]:
William Moune, sometime of Thomas Cras, 1 acre Cornish in Trenawyn, in socage; 2 suits, at the leet courts; at Michaelmas, 12d.

[*Hellynoon, in Lelant*]:
The same William, sometime of Richard Eyer, 1 croft in Hellenwone, in socage; 2 suits; at 4 dates, 2s.

[*probably Treven, in St Erth*]:
The same William, sometime of the same Richard Eyer, 2 acres Cornish in Tregevyn, in socage; 2 suits of court; 5s.

[*'Carnogowe' (lost) and Westway, both in Lelant*]:
The same William, sometime of Philip Trembras, 1 acre Cornish in Gurvosowe and Westva, by knight's service; 3-weekly suit of court; at Michaelmas, 1 pair of gloves, value 1d.

[*Carwyn, in Phillack*]:
John Gotholhan, sometime of Thomas Gotholhan, 1 acre Cornish in Carewyn, in socage; 3-weekly suit; at Michaelmas only, 2s.

[*Boskerris Woollas, in Lelant*]:
Richard Botreaux de Coisvogherth [*Coswarth alias Cotford, in Colan*], sometime of John Trevogherth, 1 acre Cornish in Boskirris Wolas, by knight's service; 3-weekly suit of court; at 4 dates, 6s. 8d.

[*Carninney, Carbis and Chyangweal, in Lelant; Egloshayle, in Phillack; and Trelissick, in St Erth*]:
Marquess of Dorset, by right of Cecily his wife, daughter of the lord of Haryngton, sometime of Nigel Loryng, 1 acre Cornish in Carnyny Carbons, 1 ferling in Chyengweke [*sic*], ½ acre Cornish in Egloshayle, and ½ acre Cornish in Trewylysik Hayle, in socage; 3-weekly suit of court; at Michaelmas, 7s. 7d. Also for offering of aid, at the same feast, 3d.

[*Tregembo, in St Hilary*]:
William Rosmoddros, sometime of William Gurlyn, 1 acre Cornish in Trethegember, in socage; 3-weekly suit of court; 12d. Also for offering of aid, at Michaelmas, 3d.

[*Trevarnon, in Gwithian*]:
William Clemowe, sometime of Reginald Raynward, 1 acre Cornish in Trewronnan, in socage; no suit; at Michaelmas, 3d.
Thomas Trevnwyth, by right of Isabel his wife, sometime of said Reginald Reynward [*sic*], 1 acre Cornish in Trewronnan, in socage; no suit; at Michaelmas, 3d.

[*Trewoone and Leah, both in Phillack*]:
James Tomlyn, sometime of John Corlys, 1 ferling in Trewoyn and Legha, in socage; 3-weekly suit of court; at 3 dates (St Andrew, mid-Lent and St James), 15d.

[*Egloshayle, at Phillack churchtown*]:
John Boys, sometime of Walter Reskere, 1 ferling Cornish in Egloshayle, in socage; 2 suits, at the 2 leet courts; at Michaelmas only, 13½d. Also for offering of aid, 1½d.

[*Trewoone and Leah, both in Phillack*]:
The same John, sometime of Olimpus (*Olimpi*) Boys, 1 ferling in Trewoyn and Legha, in socage; 3-weekly suit of court; at 3 dates (St Andrew, mid-Lent and St James), 15d.

[*Egloshayle, at Phillack churchtown*]:
The same John, sometime of the same Olimpus (*dicti Olimpi*), 1 ferling in Egloshayle, in socage; 2 suits, at the leet courts; at Michaelmas, 13¼d. Also for offering of aid, at the same feast, 1½d.

[*Nanterrow, in Gwithian*]:
Walter Kyllywyn, John Talcoys [*sic*], and Thomas Penwern, coheirs, sometime of Thomas Burwyk by right of Isabel his wife, 2 acres

Cornish in Nansterov, by knight's service; 3-weekly suit of court; at 4 dates, 10s. Also for offering, at Michaelmas, 4d.

[*Pennance, in Gwithian*]:
Walter Bolenowe, by right of Joan his wife, sometime of Alan Manyer, ½ (*dimietat'*) ferling in Pennans, in socage; 3-weekly suit of court; at Michaelmas, ¼ *lb.* pepper. Also for offering of aid, at Michaelmas, 1½d.;
the same Walter, by right of Joan his wife, sometime of the same Alan, ½ ferling in Pennans, in socage; 3-weekly suit of court; at the same feast, ¼ *lb.* pepper. Also for offering of aid, at Michaelmas, 1½d.

[*Trink, in Lelant; also Ayr, in St Ives parish*]:
Walter Carnarthur, sometime of John Aly Carnarthur, 1 acre Cornish in Trefrynk, in socage, and one-third of an acre Cornish in Ardy [*sic*], in socage; 3-weekly suit of court; at 4 dates, 4s. 8d. Also for offering of aid, 3d.
Stephen Calmady, sometime of William Trefyng,[21] ½ acre Cornish there [*i.e.* at *Trink*]; 3-weekly suit of court; at 4 dates, 2s. 6d.

[*Crenver, Oatfield and Nancegollan, all in Crowan*]:
The heirs of John Trerys, sometime of Nicholas Trerys,[22] in Carenver, Wotfold and Nansengolon, in socage; for all services, 1 grain of wheat.

[*Treloyan, in St Ives parish*]:
John Enhere and John Treloyghen, coheirs, 1 ferling in Treloyghen, in socage; 3-weekly suit of court; at 4 dates, 3s. [?]

[*Boskerris Wartha, in Lelant*]:
Thomas Tremayn, sometime of Nicholas Tremayn, ½ acre Cornish in Boskyures Wartha, by knight's service; 3-weekly suit of court; 2s. Also for offering of aid, at Michaelmas, 3d.

[*Tregenna, in St Ives parish*]:
Peter Plymmayn and Robert Ruys by right of his wife, sometime of Henry Wylly, 1 ferling in Tregene, in socage; 3-weekly suit; 2s.
Peter Tregena, sometime of Richard Reche, ½ acre Cornish in

---

[21] *Trefyng* seems to be an error for *Trefrynk* (i.e. Trink).
[22] These are of course John and Nicholas Arundell of Trerice: see note to the 1463 rental (p. 44), and compare the 1499 rental (p. 133). Nancegollan, close to Oatfield and Crenver, is never elsewhere mentioned as part of this tenement, and may be named merely for locating the properties.

Tregena, by knight's service; 3-weekly suit of court; 20*d*. Also for offering of aid, at Michaelmas, 3*d*.
Joan, lately wife of Stephen Boys, and Margaret Glyn, daughters of Alan Tregena, 1 ferling in Tregena, in socage; 3-weekly suit; 2*s*. Also for offering of aid, at Michaelmas, 3*d*.

[*Lanyon, formerly 'Coswinwolward', in Gwinear*]:
John Lanyeen, sometime of John Hicke, 2 acres Cornish in Coyswyn, in socage; 3-weekly suit of court; 7*s*. 8*d*. Also for offering of aid, at Michaelmas, 3*d*.

[*Stream from Trevarnon, in Gwithian, through Pulsack, in Phillack*]:
John Polsulsek, now Nanspian, owes yearly for having the water running from the spring of Trevrunon through the lord's land called Praas Gulcer to Pulsulsek, 6*d*.

[*Treloyan, in St Ives parish*]:
Marion (*Mariona*) Polpeer, 1 ferling in Treloyghan, in socage; 3-weekly suit of court; 18*d*.
Martin Hicke Gelda, 1 ferling in Treloyghan, in socage; 3-weekly suit of court; 5*s*. 6*d*.

[*Trevaskis, in Gwinear*]:
Alan Trevalscoys, lately heir of John Hamely, ½ acre Cornish in Trevalscoys; 3-weekly suit of court; 2*s*.

[*Welcombe (parish), near Hartland, Devon*]:
The heirs of Robert Corun, the manor of Welcomb by Hertelond, by service etc., because he showed a charter to John Corke, sometime steward of John Arundell knight, at Launceston; however, it is not certified here how he holds, by knight's service or in socage; to be distrained to show, etc.; 1 clove gillyflower.

[*A sanding-way at Pulsack, in Phillack*]:
The heirs of Nicholas Polsulsek, the way from Polsulsek to the sand; 6*d*.

Total [*of free tenants*], 115*s*. 3¾*d*.

Conventionary tenants

Conertoun, demesne land [*Connerton, at Gwithian churchtown*]:

Thomas Kelean, 1 holding, at will; 33*s*. 4*d*.
Richard Carnky, 1 holding, at will; 19*s*. 8*d*.
Hervey Rawe, 1 holding, at will; 11*s*. 1*d*.

Michael Loude, 1 holding, at will; 8s. 4d.
John Stephen, 1 holding, at will; 11s.
Richard Hoskyn, 1 holding, at will; 26s.
Stephen Kelean, 1 holding, at will; 11s.
Ralph Mercer, 1 holding, at will; 26s.
A holding lately of Richard Pennans pays through the bailiff, by the third sheaf, this year (*per ballivum per tertiam garbam hoc anno*), 19s. 6d.
John Rawe, 1 holding, at will; 19s. 6d.
James Laurence, 1 holding, at will; 16s. 8½d.

Sub-total [of demesne land, blank; £10 2s. 1½d.]

Garrek [*Angarrack, in Phillack*]:
Simon Prelot, 1 holding, at will; 16s.

Nanscaseas [*Negosias, otherwise Nantasier, in Gwithian*]:
Richard Hopkyn, the whole vill, at will; 23s.

Talseghan ['*Halenvelan' (lost), at Tolzethan, in Gwithian*]:
Richard Giffra, the meadow there called Haleanvelyn, at will; 26s. 8d.

Pennans Mur [*Pennance (Veor), in Gwithian*]:[23]
Nicholas Janyn, 1 holding, at will; 19s. 4d.
Michael Robert, 1 holding, at will; 19s. 4d.

Pennans Vian [*Pennance Vean, in Gwithian*]:
Walter Bolenowe, 1 holding, at will; 13s. 4d.

Gewe [*Angew, in Gwithian*]:
John Jagowe, 1 holding, at will; [14s. 6d. *deleted*] 16s.
John Tomma, 1 holding, at will; [13s. 6d. *deleted*] 14s.

Uppeton, Uppetoun [*Upton, in Gwithian*]:
John Hopkyn, 1 holding, at will; 16s.
John Clerke, 1 holding, at will; 8s.
Walter Jamys, 1 holding, at will; 16s.
William Jak Hervy, 1 holding, at will; 8s.
A holding formerly of Michael Jenkyn, in hand, pays through the bailiff, by the third sheaf (*per ballivum per tertiam garbam*), 16s.

---

[23] After *Pennans Mur* the letters *Cu* appear, presumably an error, though the lost tenement of *Gargason*, which appears with Pennance in 1463 (p. 46) and after it in 1499 (p. 135), may possibly have been intended.

Est'loo ['*Easter Low' (lost in the sand), in Gwithian*]:
John Cok, 1 holding, at will; 12s.
Richard Herry, 1 holding, at will; 12s.

Poleov [*Poleo, in Crowan*]:
Nicholas Polkynhorn, 1 holding, at will; 6s.

Trevalscoys [*Trevaskis, in Gwinear*]:
John Tomma, 1 holding, at will; 10s.
Oto Salman, 1 holding, at will; 10s.

Drym [*Drym, in Crowan*]:
Roger Fraunceys, 1 holding, at will; 20s.
John Priour, 1 holding, at will; 20s.

Penpoll [*Penpoll, in Phillack*]:
John Gondry, 1 holding, at will; 24s.
Thomas Geffrey, 1 holding, at will; 24s.

Vynwyn [*Venwyn, in Lelant*]:
William Vynwyn, 1 holding, at will; 18s. 8d.

Nans [*Nance, in Lelant*]:
William Nans, 1 holding, at will; 11s.

Trefrynk [*Trink, in Lelant*]:
John Gunere [*sic; for* Gundre?],[24] 1 holding, at will; 13s. 4d.

Gurfos Arundell [*Vorvas, in Lelant*]:
Richard Hopkyn, 1 holding, at will; 10s.

Wethen [*Withen, in Lelant*]:
Richard Trewanyan, 1 holding, at will; 8s.

Treloghan [*Treloyan, in St Ives parish*]:
Michael Niclys, 1 holding, at will; 10s.

Fowyer [*Vow, in St Ives parish*]:
James Nicholl, [1 holding, at will, *deleted*] the whole vill, by charter; 28s. [20s., *deleted*]

Boskyrrys Wolas [*Boskerris Woollas, in Lelant*]:
John Jenyn, 1 holding, at will; 13s. 4d.
Stephen Gregory, 1 holding, at will; 10s.

---

[24] Compare John Gondry, three entries earlier.

Porthrypp' ['*Barrepta*' (lost), near Carbis, in Lelant]:[25]
Warin Tomlyn, 1 parcel; 4*d*.
William Vynwyn, 1 parcel; 2*d*.
Henry Trevisithik, 1 parcel, 8*d*.
Henry Tomme Gregory, 1 parcel; 4*d*.

[*moor at Nanterrow, in Gwithian*]:
Ralph Mercer, for the moor of Nansterowe, 8*d*.

Water of Lananta [*stream at Lelant*]:
Pays yearly at the same dates, 12*d*.

[*Total of conventionary tenants only*, £23 15*s*. 2*d*.]

Total [*of demesne and conventionary tenants*], £33 17*s*. ... [3½*d*.]

Total [*of free, demesne and conventionary tenants*], £39 12*s*. ... [7¼*d*.]

* * *

Methsholl
[*Mitchell, in St Enoder*]

Rental renewed 11 September, the same year [1480].

Free tenants

John Trenowyth, 2 plots (3*s*. 11½*d*.) lately of William Scatera; 1 plot lately of Walter Wynkele; 1 plot (3*s*. 6*d*.) sometime of William Berban, afterwards of Thomas Treiagu; 1 plot (2*s*. 6*d*.) with the moorland (*landa*) called Goenenbayly, lately of the same Thomas Treiagu; 1 plot (12*d*.) lately of John Skyt; 1 plot (7*d*.) lately of the same John Skyt; 1 plot (9*d*.) lately of Thomas Burgeys, afterwards of Thomas Treyagu; 2 plots (15*d*.) lately of John Hogen; 2 plots (18*d*.) lately of Richard Hogen; and the moorland (*landa*) (6*s*.) of Goenmargh [*Goamarth (field), in St Enoder*]; 3-weekly suit of court; at 3 dates (Invention of the Cross, Nativity of St John the Baptist, and St Francis), 21*s*. 0½*d*.

The heirs of Henry Conyn, 1 house (*domus*) (½*d*.) called Chienpoll (2 suits of court); 3 plots (8*s*. 8*d*.) and ¼ of the moorland (*landa*) of Goenbayly; 1 plot (9*d*.) lately of Maydov; 3-weekly suit of court; at the same dates, 9*s*. ... [5½*d*.]

John Tretherf, 1 acre (5*d*.) in the moorland (*landa*) called Kaergrugyer; 1 parcel (18*d*.) lately of Simon Falle in Gunenmargh

---

[25] Name renewed or added later.

[*Goamarth, in St Enoder*]; 1 parcel (2s. 7d.) which his father previously held, and 1 plot opposite; 3 acres in the moorland (*landa*) beside Fosbras and ½ plot, which (*quas*) Gunneta previously held; 8 acres in the moorland (*landa*) beside Kaergrugyer; 1 acre English between the ways to the Mount of St Michael and Truru; 1 plot (2s.) which Simon Falle previously held; 4 acres English in the land called Sikerlych; ½ acre English which Henry Longes previously held; 1 plot (15d.) [which] the heirs of Sanctus Albinus had by gift of Agnes Skyt; 1 acre English which the same heirs had by gift of Stephen Heuos; and 1 acre which he bought (*perquisivit*) from William Gillot; 3-weekly suit of court; at the same 3 dates, [*amount lost;* 7s. 9d.?]

John Tresithny, 4 plots (2s. 9½d.), lately of the heir of John Fowy; 2 acres English (6d.), lately of Simon Falle, afterwards of the same heir; and 1 plot (8d.), lately of Joan daughter of John Fowy; 3-weekly suit of court; at the same 3 dates, 3s. 11½d.

The heirs of Laurence Sheriston, 1 plot with its portion in Gunenbayly, lately of the heir(s) of Michael Treuarʒan and William Treuelgyn, which Robert Roncyn previously held; no suit; by hand of Reginald Tretherf, at the same 3 dates, 8s. 2d.

Henry Trevisa, 1 plot and 2 acres English in Gunenmargh [*Goamarth (field), in St Enoder*]; 2 suits of court; at same 3 dates, 9d.

The heir(s) of Alice Skynner, 1 plot, previously of Stephen Heuos; suit as above; as above, 6d.

The heirs of John Fowy, the acre of St Francis; to St Francis 6d., and to the lord 4d.

The heir(s) of Reginald Cary, 1 plot which William Bonda previously held; suit as above; as above, 4d.

The heir(s) of Richard Nansdyllyowe, ½ acre Cornish at Nansdyllyowe [*Nantillio, in St Enoder*]; suit as above; at Michaelmas, 4s.

Ralph Fynda, 3 plots with their portion in Gunenbally, *viz.* ¼ part there, lately of William Fynda; suit as above; rent, at the same dates, apart from (*ultra*) 21d. rent which the lord has released to him, given in exchange for 1 messuage and 1 acre in the vill of Medesholl (formerly 3s. 3d.), 18d.

Martin Raulyn, the acre An Poule (*acram an Poule*); 4*d*.

Total [*of free tenants*], 58*s*. 3...*d*.[26]

Conventionary tenants[27]

Methesholl
Martin Raulyn, 1 holding, at will; 14*s*.

Nansdyllyow [*Nantillio, in St Enoder*]:
Richard Nansdillyowe, 1 holding, at will; 5*s*.

Cruk Bras [*unidentified*]:
The reeve of Methesholl, Cruk Bras; 4*s*.

Total [*of conventionary tenants*], 23*s*.

Total [*of free and conventionary tenants*], £4 0*s*. 15½*d*.

* * *

[En]yscavyn
[*Enniscaven, in St Dennis*]

Rental renewed 13 September, the same year [1480].

Free tenants

Enyscavyn [*Enniscaven, in St Dennis*]:
Nicholas Roche, ½ acre Cornish, by knight's service; 3-weekly suit of court; at the Purification of the Blessed Virgin Mary and Michaelmas, 4*s*. 6*d*.
William Gauergan, ¼ of ½ acre Cornish, by knight's service; suit as above; at the same feasts, 13½*d*.

Mena [*Menawollas, in St Dennis*]:
John Cornewall and Nicholas Pascowe, coheirs by right of their wives, ½ acre Cornish, by knight's service; 3-weekly suit of court; at the same feasts, 7¾*d*. [and] 1 pair of white gloves.
Also for tin-fine, 1½*d*.

---

[26] The grand total for the manor implies a total here of 58*s*. 3½*d*., though the rents given seem to total 58*s*. 1½*d*. instead.

[27] This is the earliest complete list of the conventionary tenants of Mitchell, the rental of 1463 being partly deficient here (see above, p. 63). In the 1499 rental (below, p. 139) and that of *c*.1586 (AR2/1343) the third tenement is called *Gonhughell*, instead of *Cruk Bras*, but it was presumably the same place.

[Tre]lovargh [*Trelavour, in St Dennis*]:
John Gregory, ¼ acre Cornish, by knight's service; 2 suits of court; at the same feasts, 5¾d.

...wartha [*Mennawartha, in St Dennis*]:
John Mena, ¼ acre Cornish, by knight's service; common suit of court; at the same feasts, 8½d.

...vargh [*Trelavour, in St Dennis*]:
The heir(s) of Oliver Tregassowe, ¼ acre Cornish, by knight's service; 2 suits of court; at the same feasts, 3s.

Total [of free tenants], 10s. 7d., 1 pair of gloves.

Conventionary tenants

..nys [*Ennis, in St Dennis*]:
William Dagon, 1 holding, at will; at 4 dates, 3s. 4d.

Trelovargh [*Trelavour, in St Dennis*]:
William Richard, 2 holdings, at will; 17s. 6d.
John Hauke, 1 holding, at will; 10s.

...vyn [*Enniscaven, in St Dennis*]:
Thomas Michell, 1 holding, at will; 10s.
Thomas Hicke, 1 holding, at will; 10s.

Total [of conventionary tenants], 50s. 10d.

Total [of free and conventionary tenants], 61s. 7d. [*sic*], and 1 pair of gloves.

* * *

Bodewenek
[*Bodwannick, in Lanivet*]

Rental renewed 13 September, the same year [1480].

[*Free*] tenants

...lyn [*Rosevallon, in Bodmin parish*]:
Richard Flamak, the whole vill, in socage; 2 suits of court; at Michaelmas, 20d.

...yr [*Boskear, in Bodmin parish*]:
John Bere, ½ acre Cornish, by knight's service; 3-weekly suit of court; at the same feast, 12d.

Treffry [*Treffry, in Lanhydrock*]:
John Phelip, ½ acre Cornish, by knight's service; 3-weekly suit of court; at the same feast, 4s. 6d.

Boskedek [*Bokiddick, in Lanivet*]:
Thomas Rescassa, 1 ferling Cornish, by knight's service; 3-weekly suit of court; at the same feast, 5d.

Treffry [*Treffry, in Lanhydrock*]:
Heirs of John Perys, 1 ferling Cornish, by knight's service; 2 suits of court; at the same feast, 18d.

Boskedek [*Bokiddick, in Lanivet*]:
The heirs of Alice Lacy, 3 ferlings Cornish, by knight's service; 2 suits of court; at the same feast, 20d.

Frogham [*'Frogham' (lost) in Lanivet*][28]:
Thomas Hogge, 1 tenement (*tenementum*), by knight's service; 2 suits of court; at the same feast, 6d.

Treffry [*Treffry, in Lanhydrock*]:
John Treffry, ½ acre Cornish, by knight's service; 2 suits of court; at the same feast, 3s.

[*Tremayle, in Lanivet, and a down named from it*]:
Thomas Lanhergy, 2 acres within Tremayledoune and Tremayle, by knight's service; 2 suits of court; at the same feast [query whence (*quere inde*), *added later*], 12d.

Total [*of free tenants*], 15s. 3d.

Conventionary tenants

Bodwennek [*Bodwannick, in Lanivet*]:
John Brode senior, 1 holding, at will; common suit of court; 32s., [plus] 4 capons.
John Hicke, 1 holding, at will; 12s. 6d., plus 3 capons.
William Broude, 1 holding, at will; 12s. 6d., plus 3 capons.
Thomasia Broude, 1 holding, by charter; 32s. 4d., plus 7 capons.

...y [*Atley, in Lanivet*]:
John Ley, the whole vill, at will; 21s., plus 6 capons.

---

[28] *Frogham in St Lawrence* in the rental of c.1586 (AR2/1343); *Tregam alias Frogham* (in Lanivet parish), tenants the feoffees of the parish, 1717 survey. The lost *Frogham* in Lanivet was evidently very close to St Lawrence in Bodmin parish; compare the entry in the 1499 rental (below, p. 114).

...mayle [*Tremayle, in Lanivet*]:
Richard Oppy, ½ of the vill, at will; 16s.
Thomasia Raulyn, other ½ of the vill, at will; 14s., plus 4 capons.

Lanytta [*Lanet, in Lanivet*]:
John Tregassowe, ½ of the vill, by charter; 18s. 8d.
William German, other ½ of the vill, at will; 13s. 4d., plus 2 capons.

...yle [*Tremayle, in Lanivet*]:
John Harry, 2 closes, by charter; 7s. 6d.

... [*Laninval, in Lanivet*]:
... Oppy, one-third of the vill, at will; 10s. 6d., plus 1 capon.
[Oliver] Darre, one-third of the vill, at will; 12s., plus 3 capons.[29]
... Tresogan, one-third of the vill, at will; 19s. 6d. ... [*lost*]

... [*Bokiddick, in Lanivet*]:
...y [= Luky?], the whole demesne land (*terra domini*), at will; ... [8s.? *see note at end*.]

... [*Higher Woodley, in Lanivet*]:
... Hurde, ½ of the vill, at will; 13s. 4d., ...
John William, other ½ of the vill; 14s., ...

..odeley ...hera [*Lower Woodley, in Lanivet*]:
John Oppy, 1 holding, at will; 9s., ...
John Vdy, 1 holding, at will; 10s., plus 2 capons.
Richard Betty, 1 holding, at will; 14s., plus 2 capons.
Richard Luky, 1 holding, at will; 14s., plus 2 capons.

The mills:
Reginald Bryand, the corn-mill; 24s., plus 2 [?] [capons].
John Touker, the tucking-mill; 12s. 8d., ...

...teforde [*Forda, in Lanivet*]:
John Germayne, 1 holding, at will; 16s., plus 2 capons.

Neutoun [*Newton, in Lanivet*]:
Thomas Betty, the whole vill, at will; 8s., plus 2 capons.

Seyntlaurens [*St Lawrence, in Bodmin parish*]:
Thomas Rogger, 1 holding, at will; 10s. 6d.

---

[29] The christian name is lost, but can be supplied with confidence from the manorial account of 1479–80, where Oliver Darre is named as the reeve of the manor that year: AR2/919, p. 3; see also the Introduction (Appendix).

The spring [*fons*] of Lanynwell [*water-course running from Laninval to Stephen Gelly, both in Lanivet*]:³⁰
John Tomme Harry, the water running from Lanynwell to Stymgelly; at the same dates, 3*d*.

Richard Flamak, the weir (*gurges*) of the mill of Gere [*Tregear, in Bodmin parish*]; at 4 dates, 8*d*.

Total [*of conventionary tenants*], £18 ... [16*s*. 3*d*.?]³¹

Total [*of free and conventionary tenants*], £19 11*s*. 6*d*.

* * *

[*Miscellaneous incomes, including farm of demesne lands*]

...en ...ovton
The hamlet (*hameletta*) there is worth yearly, in total, 13*s*.

...
The hamlet there is worth yearly, in total, [*lost*].

. . . [*Demesne tenants of Lanherne Park?*]:³²
Thomas Clerke, 1 close called Cowclose; yearly, 10*s*.
John Ricard, 1 close called Oldeparke; this year, 16*s*.
Humphrey Denshill, the great meadow; this year, 20*s*.
Thomas Tregoys, the small meadow; this year, 5*s*.
The meadow 'abouetheberne' and the meadow 'abouetheforge' remain in hand, and are mown to the lord's use.
The wood in Oldeparke remains in hand and pays, through Thomas Treys, [*amount, if any, lost*].

. . . [*rabbit-island in Lanherne manor?*]
John Ricard holds the farm of rabbits (*firma cuniculorum*) there, and pays this year, [*lost*].

---

³⁰ Compare the 1499 rental (below, p. 116); in that of c.1586 this is again described as 'Fount of Lannyvell . . . water running from Lannivell towards Stingelly' (AR2/1343).
³¹ The visible conventionary rents add up to a total of £18 8*s*. 3*d*., while a total of £18 16*s*. 3*d*. is needed to make the overall sum given for the manor. This suggests that the lost rent for the tenement of Bokiddick was 8*s*., assuming that all the figures are correct.
³² The accounts for Lanherne in 1478–79 and 1490–91 are closely related to some of what can be made out here (AR2/916, m. 2, and AR2/172).

...m'
Is worth yearly clear (*de claro*), [*lost*].

... barton lands (*terre bertone*):
Thomas Southwode holds the great meadow; yearly, [*lost*].
The same, the small meadow; yearly, [*lost*].
The same, the garden (*gardinum*) there; this year, [*lost*].

... [*Hundred of Penwith?*]:
The hundred there is worth by estimation yearly, [*lost*].

...yn [*Penryn town?*]:
A holding [?] (*ten'*) there is worth yearly, [*lost*].

...ynowe ... [*Carminow demesne?*]:
Is worth yearly by estimation, and pays, through agistment (*per agistamentum*), [*lost*].

———————————

RENTAL, WHOLE ESTATE, 1499 (AR2/1340)

Contents

Town of St Columb with Trenhillocks	102
Manor of Trembleath	105
Manor of Lanherne	108
Manor of Treloy	110
Manor of Bodwannick	114
Manor of Lanhadron	117
Manor of Truro Vean	120
Manor of Kennall	122
Manor of Tregarne	123
Manor of Carminow	125
Manor of Winnington	127
Manor of Connerton	130
Manor and borough of Mitchell	137
Manor of Enniscaven	139
Perlees and Trevisker	140

EXTENT OF 1499

Seyntcolumbe and Trewynhelek
[*St Columb town and Trenhillocks, in St Columb Major*]

Extent made 21 January 14 Henry [VII, 1499], by John Michell and Thomas Crugowe, free tenants (*liberi*), Richard Paul and Richard Herry, plot-holders (*placionar'*), and Richard Tomenty and Reginald Caiser, conventionary tenants.

Free tenants

Edmund Arundell, knight, 1 tenement; 10*d*.

Peter Bevyll esquire, 1 tenement and 1 close called Park Tresithney, for himself and his heirs; 12*s.*;
the same, 2 tenements, as above; 12*s*.

The heir(s) of Nicholas Tresithny, 2 tenements and 1 close; 10*s*.

John Resogan, 1 tenement; 1*d.*, 2 suits of court.

Thomas Nenys, 3 tenements; 2*s*. 1*d*.

James Tripkunyn, 1 [?] tenement; 6*d.*;
the same, 1 close in exchange; used to pay 5*s*.

Thomas Crugow, 3 . . . of John Russell; 11*s*. 8*d.*;
the same, 1 piece (*pec'*) of land; 1*d*.

John Nanskevell, 1 tenement; 12*d*.

Heir(s) of Erysy, 1 tenement; 12*d*.

Thomas Tomyow, 3 [?] closes; 23*s*.[1]

John Boscawen and John Treg...rrek, 2 tenements with certain [?] gardens (*certis* [?] *gardinis*) annexed; 15*d*. [?]

John Michell, 1 close called Park Engrowse; 20*s*. [?];
the same John, 1 tenement where he now lives, with 2 gardens (*ortis*) annexed and 1 piece . . . 6 virgates . . . called . . ., beside a plot of John Clymov, . . . ; 3*s*. 4*d*. [?];
the same, land along the road to the well (*terra per viam ad fontem*), and 1 close by the town well (*fons*), called Parke Enfenten, for

---

[1] Marginal note to this entry and the following one: 'Note a charter made by John Arundell knight'.

himself and his heirs; 12s.

The same John, 1 tenement with 1 close lately of John Russell; 21s. 6d. [?]

The same, 1 tenement lately Michael Jagowe's, . . . charter; 3s. 0½d.

[*Tenants for*] *term of years*

The same John, 2 plots, one 20′ × 24′, the other 24′ × 24′. . . , term 28 years, by charter; 3s. 4d.

Richard Hawell, 1 plot, term 80 years; 15d.

Thomas Budy, 1 plot, term [*blank*]; 15d.

Richard Herry, 1 plot, term 55 years; 3s. 4d.

Michael Cokyn, 1 plot, 40′ × 90′, term 57 years, by charter; 3s. 4d.; the same, 1 plot, 8...′ × 24′, term 43 years; 3s. 5d.; the same, 1 close, term 60 years; 9s.

Mark Thomas, 1 tenement, with 1 garden (*ortus*) annexed, term 26 years; 4d.

Ralph Restalek, 1 plot, 48′ × 24′, term 44 years; 2s.

Nicholas Bawdyn, 1 plot, term 80 years; 4s.

Reginald Crabbe [now John Adam cap[ellanus] [?], *added later*], 1 plot, 60′ × 24′, term 11 years; 2s. 8d.

John Sherdewyne, 1 plot, 52′ × 50′ [?], term 56 years; 4s. 4d.; the same, 1 piece of land, 16′ long, term 36 years; 8d.; the same, 3 closes, term 65 years; 26s. 8d.; the same, . . . close(s), term 66 [?] years; 7s. 6d.

Thomas Stevyn [Richard Tyek, *added later*], 1 plot, . . . annexed, term [*blank*]; 9s.

Richard Michell chaplain (*cap'*), 1 plot, term 66 years; 2s. 4d. The same, 1 close, term 66 years; 7s. 6d.

Vivian (*Vevyanus*) Carne, 1 plot, term 35 years; 3s. 4d.; the same, 2 closes, term 67 years; 36s. 8d.; the same, 1 plot lately Michael Tom Symon, term 35 years; 3s. 4d.

John Tregois, 1 plot, term 83 years; 8s.

Alice Tremayn, [1 plot, 38′ × 12′, term 53 years, *added later*]; 19d.

John Harry, 1 plot, 34′ × 90′, term 56 years; 2s. 10d.

The same, 2 closes, term 66 years; 12s. 8d.

John Peryn, 1 plot, 52′ × 90′, term 67 years; 4s. 4d.
The same, 1 close, term 71 years; 5s.
The same, 1 close, term 60 years; 5s.

William Watt, 1 plot, 52′ × 90′, term 56 years; 6s. 8d.
The same, 1 close, term [blank]; 4s. 4d.

Richard Couswarn, 2 plots, 120′ × 90′, and 1 close lately of John Crosse, at the lord's will, term 80 years; 17s.
The same, . . . close(s), term 66 years; 3s 9d.

John Pengwyn, 1 plot, 80′ × 24′, term 80 years; 3s. 4d.
The same, 1 lane (*venella*); 3d.
The same, 1 piece of land for his rushes (*pro russibus suis*); 4d.

Ralph Jenyn, 1 plot, 48′ × 24′, term 77 years; 2s.

John Mowna, 1 plot, 24′ × 24′, term 80 years; 2s. 4d.
The same, 1 plot, 64′ long, term 44 years; 2s. 8d.

Richard Moile, 1 plot, term 52 years; 2s. 11d.
The same, 1 plot, 52′ × 90′, term 56 years; 4s.

John Clemow, 1 plot, 112′ × 24′, term 28 years; 4s. 8d.

Richard Sherard, 1 plot and 1 close, term 65 years; 16s.

Odo Gooff, 1 plot, term 52 years; 3s. 4d.

John Peen, 1 plot, 42′ [?] × 24′, term 70 years; 20d.

Richard Paule, 1 plot, 18′ × 18′, term 37 years; 9d. [?]
The same, 1 plot, term 26 years; 4s.
The same, 1 close in Trewynhelek, term 67 years; 20s.

John Pascow, 1 close, term 65 years; 13s. 4d.[2]
The same, 1 close at the lord's will; 7s. 6d.

John Barbour, 1 close at [will]; 7s.
The same John, 1 lane; 3d.

Remfrey Sherdewyne, 2 closes, term 66 years; 7s. 6d.

John Duront, 1 close, term [blank]; 7s.

John Laurens, 1 close, term 60 years; 5s.

---

[2] An obscure set of numbers is added over 'close', and '99' over '65'.

John Treluddrow [Reginald Treher, *over*], 1 close, term 60 years; 5s.

Odo Fevian, 1 plot, 40′ × 30′, term 50 years; 12d.

Odo Trewolvas, 1 plot, term 43 years; 20d.

Thomas Nicoll, 1 plot, 48′ × 24′, term 80 years; 4s.

Reginald Keiser, 1 close called Parke Envelyn, term [*blank*]; 20s.

Ralph Retalek, 1 lane, at lord's will; 6d.

1 chamber (*camera*) called Knyght is Chamber; used to pay 8s.

Likewise for . . . called . . .; used to pay 8s.

Likewise Reginald Keiser holds 3 mills; £13

> *Total of free tenants and tenants for term of years, £38 4s. 8½d.*

* * *

Trembleith
[Trembleath, in St Ervan]

Free tenants

Restelek [*Retallick, in Roche*]:
The heir(s) of William Hopkyn, 1 acre Cornish, by knight's service; 2 suits of court; rent at 4 dates, 7d.

Langorow [*Langurra, at Crantock churchtown*]:
The heir(s) of Richard Quyell, ½ acre Cornish; common suit of court; now in hand because he died without heir; 7d.

Treffewa [*Trevowah, in Crantock*]:
Gregory Trefewa, ½ acre Cornish, in socage; common suit of court; 13½d.

Lamayle, Arlyn, Trevayow, Trethias, Treyarnan, Trever, Tewyn [*Lemail (in Egloshayle), Harlyn, Trevio, Trethias, Treyarnon, Treveor and Towan (all in St Merryn)*]:
John Restarrok,[3] the heir of William Pencors and Richard Boskawen Roos, co-heirs of Laurence Arundell, in Trevayow 1 acre Cornish, in Trethias ½ acre, in Treyarn..n ½ acre, in Tewyn ½ acre, in Trever ½ acre and in Arlyn ½ acre Cornish, by knight's service; 1 pair of gilt spurs or 40d., payable at 4 dates, with 3-weekly suit of court.

---

[3] Poor spelling for *Rescarrok*: see Maclean, *Trigg Minor*, I, 437.

Kerowlom [*Carlumb, in St Minver*]:
The same John, 2 acres Cornish, by knight's service; common suit of court; 1*d*.

Kerow Meur [*Blakes Keiro, otherwise Keiro Veor, in St Minver*]:
John Trevylyan esquire, 2 acres Cornish, by knight's service; common suit of court; 40*d*.

Ammall, Trevang', Seyntmenver, Trethawek [*(Middle) Amble (in St Kew), Trevanger, St Minver and Trethauke (all in St Minver)*]:
Thomas Moune, in Am...l 1 acre Cornish, in Trevang' 1 acre, in Seynt Mynver ½ acre, in Trethawek 1 acre Cornish, by knight's service; common suit of court; 12½*d*.

Arlyn [*Harlyn, in St Merryn*]:
John Coulyng, ½ acre Cornish, by knight's service; 3-weekly suit of court; nil.

Trevelwith [*Trevella, in Crantock*]:
John Trevelwith, 1 acre Cornish, by knight's service; without suit of court; 4*s*.

Tewyn [*Towan, in St Columb Minor*]:
Edmund Arundell, ½ acre Cornish, by knight's service; common suit of court; 3*d*.

Skewys [*(Great) Skewes, in St Wenn*]:
John Tretherff, 2 acres Cornish, in socage; common suit of court; nil.

Total of free tenants, 14*s*. 4*d*.

Conventionary tenants

Trenoyow [*Treniow, in Padstow, presumably*]:[4]
Elizabeth Trepkunyn, 1 ferling; 4*s*.

Trethias [*Trethias, in St Merryn*]:
John Trethias, ½ acre Cornish; 8*s*.

Tredreysek [*Tredrizzick, in St Minver*]:
William Fisher, 1 holding; 13*s*. 4*d*. and 1 day's work at harvest or 2*d*.

---

[4] This seems to be a one-off entry: Treniow in Padstow is otherwise found (in 1480, c.1586 and 1659: see note to the 1480 rental, above, p. 74) as a *free* tenement of Trembleath manor (with larger acreage, but the same rent as here); and as a free tenement of Perlees manor from that manor's first appearance in 1499 (below, p. 140).

Penros [*Penrose, in St Ervan*]:
Henry Ric', ½ acre, leased to him for term of his life and of Nicola his wife and William his son; 7s.

Tregona [*Tregona, in St Eval*]:
William Laurens, 1 holding; 26s. 8d.
John Laurens, 1 holding: 26s. 8d.
John Heyly, 1 holding; 26s. 8d.

Hengolan [*Engollan, in St Eval*]:
Thomas Donston, 1 holding; 33s. 4d.
Sampson Kerter, 1 holding; 10s.

Helwyn [*Halwyn, in St Eval, at Engollan*]:
John Foy [?], 1 holding; 13s. 4d.

Crukmorok [*Crigmurrick, in St Merryn*]:
Robert Coulyng, 1 holding; 10s.

Dolga Trembleith [*unidentified*]:
Richard Synt Ervyn, a parcel of land, for term of 50 years; 6s. 8d.

Trevyngonyow [*Tregwinyo, otherwise Trevengenow, in St Ervan*]:
Richard Keiser, the whole vill; 50s.

Melynnow[t] [*Millingworth, in St Ervan*]:
The same Richard, the mill; [16s., *deleted*] 20s.

Trewheneylys [*Trenayles, near Tregwinyo, in St Ervan*]:
John Keiser; 3s. 4d.

Menuels [*Manuels, in St Columb Minor*]:
John Tresawell, 1 acre; 20s.
Richard Cok, 1 holding; 20s.

Chapell [*Chapel, in St Columb Minor*]:
Richard Coke, 1 holding; 6s. 8d.

Demesne land of Trembleith:
Remains in hand; used to pay £8 13s. 4d.

> Total [*of conventionary tenants and demesne*], £23 19s. 0d.[5]
>
> Total *of free and conventionary tenants*, £24 13s. 4d.

* * *

---

[5] The total omits the 2d. for a day's work, mentioned under Tredrizzick.

Lanhern

[*Lanherne, in St Mawgan in Pyder*]

Free tenants

Ruthfos and Gau'gan [*Ruthvoes and Gaverigan, in St Columb Major*]:
The heir(s) of Larcedeken knight [and now Veur, *added later*], 3 acres Cornish, in socage; common suit of court; 12*d*.

Nanstornan [*Nantornan, in St Columb Minor*]:
John Nanswhiden, 1 acre Cornish, by knight's service; common suit; 2*s*. 2*d*.

Penffoos [*Penvose, in St Mawgan in Pyder*]:
The same John, 1 acre Cornish, by knight's service; common suit of court; 12*d*.

Polgreen [*Polgreen, in St Mawgan in Pyder*]:
Thomas Polgren, 1 acre Cornish, by knight's service; common suit of court; 2*s*. 3*d*.

Bodruthyn [*Bedruthan, in St Eval*]:
Richard Nanfan, 1 acre Cornish, by knight's service; common suit of court; 1 *lb*. cummin or 4*d*.

Trenans [*Trenance, in St Mawgan in Pyder*]:
Richard Flamak, 2 acres Cornish, by knight's service; common suit of court; 16*d*.

Penfoos [*Penvose, in St Mawgan in Pyder*]:
John Budy, by right of his wife, and John Phelip, . . . Cornish, by knight's service; common suit of court; 4*s*.

Hengolen [*Engollan, in St Eval*]:
John Tentyn, 3 acres Cornish, by knight's service; . . . ; 3*s*. 11*d*.

Porth [*Mawgan Porth, in St Mawgan in Pyder*]:
John Couswarn, 1 acre Cornish, in socage; no suit of court; 15*d*.
John Coulyng and Ralph Porth, 1 acre Cornish, in socage; no suit of court; 15*d*.

Elwans, Bodruthyn, Pentir [*Efflins, Bedruthan and Pentire, in St Eval*]:
Elizabeth Ralegh, in Elwens, Bodruthyn and Pentir, by knight's service, 2 acres, without suit of court; 1 red rose.

Trewarvena [*Trevenna, in St Mawgan in Pyder*]:
Henry Dayow, by his wife's right, 3 ferlings, by knight's service;

common suit of court; 7s.
Samson Reis, 3 ferlings, by knight's service; common suit of court; 6s.

Total [of free tenants], 27s. 6d.

Conventionary tenants

Trevedrus [*Trevedras, in St Mawgan in Pyder*]:
Robert Trevedrus, the whole vill; 20s., and for a day's work at harvest, 1d. [?]

Trewarvena [*Trevenna, in St Mawgan in Pyder*]:
George (*Jeorgius*) Donston, 1 holding; 9s., and for a day's work, 2d.

Lanvyen [*Lanvean, in St Mawgan in Pyder*]:
Robert Fenten, 2 holdings; 18s. and 2d.
John Jack [David . . . , *added later*], 2 holdings; 18s. and 2d.
Ralph Came [Nicholas T..., *added later*], 1 holding; 9s. and 2d.
John Snell [James B..., *added later*], 1 . . . with 1 acre; 2s. 4d.

Penpons [*Penpont, in St Mawgan in Pyder*]:
John Wodcok [James . . . , *added later*], 1 holding; 5s.

Newham [*lost, in St Mawgan in Pyder*]:
The same John [James [?] . . . , *added later*], 1 close; 2s.

Wyndesor [*Windsor, in St Mawgan in Pyder*]:
John Thom', 1 holding; 16s. and 2d.

Tregonvan [*Tregonning, in St Mawgan in Pyder*]:
John Hick [Th..., *added later*], 1 holding; 20s. and 2d.

Tregewstak [*Tregustick, in St Columb Minor*]:
Ralph Wan [?] [*illegible name added later*], 1 holding; 16s. 8d. and 2d.
James Richard [*illegible name added later*], 1 holding; 16s. 8d. and 2d.
John Tregethiow, 1 holding; 8s. 4d. and 2d.
James Ric' Mayow, 1 holding; 8s. 4d. and 2d.

Trevelgy [*Trevelgue, in St Columb Minor*]:
John Hokkyn, 1 holding; 22s. and 2d.
John Bloyhow, 2 holdings; 22s. and 2d.

Penfoos [*Penvose, in St Mawgan in Pyder*]:
John Budy, 1 holding; 5s. and 2d.

Trevorek Downe [*name rewritten; downs named from 'Trevorrick' (lost), near Penvose, in St Mawgan in Pyder*]:
The same John, in Trevorek Dow...; 3s. 4d.

Kenhewys [*Carnewas, in St Eval*]:
John Samuell [*illegible name added later*], 1 holding; 19s. and 2d.

Pras [?] Carnan [*meadow named from Carnanton, in St Mawgan in Pyder*]:
Reginald Crabbe; 3s. 4d.

H...llenparke ['*Halyn Parke' (lost), in St Mawgan in Pyder*]:
Thomas Tomyow, clerk; 7d., plus a best beast as heriot.

Lanhern down:
In hand; used to pay 8s.

Mill of Lanhern:
In hand; used to pay 53s. 4d.

Demesne land:
In hand; used to pay £6 13s. 4d.

[Trevy]..[v]el[gy] [*name rewritten; Trevelgue, in St Columb Minor*]:
In hand; used to pay 30s.

Total [*of conventionary tenants*], £[23] 11s. 5d.,
plus [15?] days' work.
Total of free and conventionary tenants, £24 18s. 11d.

* * *

Treloy
[*Treloy, in St Columb Minor*]

Extent made [*blank*] January, 14 Henry VII [1499].

Free tenants

Polgren [*Polgreen, in Newlyn East*]:
John Willmur, by right of his wife, 3 acres, by knight's service; common suit of court; 5s.
[*added over*] 'Cau... ... hiis 2d.' [*or 3d.*]

Gargois, Chipitt, Bovelek, Talgragyn, Reis, Banallek, Kelestek Rewall, Breanek [*Gargas and 'Chypitt' (lost, cf. Pittsdowns), in Cuby; Boswellick and Tolgroggan, in St Allen; Rees, Bennallack and Callestock-ruall, otherwise Little Callestick, in Perranzabuloe; and Bryanick, at St Agnes churchtown*]:
William Trevaignon, 2 acres Cornish [*at Gargas*], by knight's

service; common suit of court; 12d.;
the same William, in Bossevelek, 1 [?] acre Cornish, by knight's service; common suit of court; 6d.;
the same William, in Rays, ½ acre Cornish, by knight's service; common suit of court; 1d.;
the same William, in Kelestek [and] Breanek,[6] 1 [?] acre, by knight's service; common suit of court; 2s.

Trencruk [*Trencreek, in St Columb Minor*]:
John Petit Predannek, 1 [?] acre Cornish, in socage; common suit of court; 12d.
John Tentyn, 1 acre Cornish, in socage; common suit of court; 2s. 8d.

Wiket [*Wicket, in Newlyn East*]:
John Copleston, ½ acre Cornish, in socage; common suit of court; 10d.

Trelegh [*Traleath, in Newlyn East*]:
The same John, ½ acre Cornish, in socage; common suit of court; 10d.

Trelest [*Trelaske, in Cubert*]:
Thomas Pynent, by right of his wife . . . , 1 [?] acre Cornish, in socage; common suit of court; 20d.

Pentirven [*Pentirevean, otherwise East Pentire, in Crantock*]:
Alice Tremayn, 1 acre Cornish, in socage; common suit of court; 2s.

Trefewa [*Trevowah, in Crantock*]:
John Treworga, 1 acre Cornish, in socage; common suit of court; 2s. 6½d.
John Godolhen, by right of his wife, 1 ferling, in socage; 4d.

Helwyn [*Halwyn, in Crantock*]:
John Treaga, 1 parcel; common suit of court; 6d.

Tresevyan [*Tresean, in Cubert*]:
Joan Treveele, ½ acre Cornish, in socage; common suit of court; 12d.

Hendre Pawle [*Hendra Paul, in St Columb Minor*]:
Robert Gibbe, ½ acre Cornish, by knight's service; common suit of court; 3s.

---

[6] *Kelestek* added later.

John Trethias, ½ acre Cornish, by knight's service; common suit of court; 3s.

Trevargh [*Trevarth, in Gwennap*]:
The heir(s) of Henry Bodrugan, [*blank*] acres [*blank*]; 2 [?] suits of court; 5s.

Talcarn Morrek [*Tolcarne Merock, in St Mawgan in Pyder*]:[7]
Paul Benny, 1 acre Cornish, in socage; common suit of court; 43s. [?]
[*interlined*: now in the lord's hand . . .]

Hendre Mostell [*'Hendra Mussell' (lost), in St Columb Minor*]:
Peter Syntaubyn, by right of his wife, 1 acre Cornish, by knight's service; 2 suits of court; 13¾d.
[John Bray, Richard Carv...h and John ...ys [= Boys], *added later*]

Trenynnek [*Treninick, in St Columb Minor*]:
Robert [*sic; read* John?] le Veer, earl of Oxford, 6 acres Cornish, by knight's service; common suit of court; 1 *lb*. [pepper]

Caskeis [*(Higher) Keskeys, in St Columb Minor*]:
John Resogan, ½ acre Cornish, in socage; 2 suits of court; 13d.

Treworder Wast [*downland in Kenwyn parish, named from Treworder there*]:[8]
John Nevell, [*blank*]; 6s. 6d.

M...gam [*'Mingham' (lost), in St Columb Major*]:
Walter Gau'ygan, ½ acre Cornish, in socage; common suit of court; 18s.

     Total [*of free tenants*], 59s. 10¼d. and 1 *lb*. pepper

Conventionary tenants

Treloy Newton [*Treloy and 'Newton' (lost), in St Columb Minor*]:
Reginald Chycois [John Newham, *added later*], ½ vill of Treloy; 36s. 8d.
John Treloy [William Lusky, *added later*], ½ same vill; 36s. 8d.

Pentir [*(West) Pentire, in Crantock*]:
John Treyaga [William Engew [?], *added later*], ½ acre Cornish; 6s.

---

[7] *in convenc'*, added above; in 1460 this place appears as both a free and a conventionary tenement, as here (pp. 29–30); but in 1480 as a conventionary tenement only (p. 69). Its presence here seems to be an error.
[8] Name rewritten.

Bodrogow [*Bedrugga, in St Columb Minor*]:
Thomas Noill [John Bodrogow, *added later*], ½ acre Cornish; 8s.

Kestell [*Kestle, in St Columb Minor*]:
Thomas Waty [Richard Tom Rawlyn, *added later*], one-third of the vill; 17s.

Treveglos [*Treviglas, in St Columb Minor*]:
Andrew Baker [Robert Cady, *added later*], ½ acre and 1 ferling; 24s.
Robert Milhenek [Odo . . . , *added later*], 1 holding; 2s. 4d.

Trethowall [*Trethowell, in Kea*]:
John Trethowall, whole vill; 26s. 8d.

Mengam ['*Mingham' (lost), in St Columb Major*]:[9]
David Moile, whole vill; 18s.

Penpoll [*Penpoll, in Crantock*]:
John Penpoll [Thomas Hendre, *added later*], whole vill; 30s.

Stret Nuham ['*Strete Newham', otherwise 'Newhamstret' (lost), in Truro (in Kenwyn)*]:
John Skeberiow, 1 holding; 12d.

Melynvran [*Mellanvrane, in St Columb Minor*]:
John Scovern [Richard Cawga [?], for term of years, *added later*], the mill, 13s. 4d.

Trerebeow [*Trebby, in St Columb Minor*]:
Now waste; used to pay 10s.[10]

Tripkunyn [*Trekenning, in St Columb Major*]:[11]
Delivered to the heir(s) of Tripkunyn, in exchange for land and holding(s) in Lanhaddron.

Trebedannen [*Trebudannon, in St Columb Major*]:
Delivered to the same, in exchange for land in Seynt Goran.

Penrynburgh [*Penryn town, in St Gluvias*]:
With Tripkynyn, in exchange for land in Seynt Goran.

---

[9] *inter lib' tenentes*, added.
[10] 'All the tenants hold' (*omnes tenentes tenent*), interlined.
[11] The exchange mentioned in this entry and the next (no deed survives for the exchange in Penryn, in the following entry) was effected with Ralph Tripkunyn in May 1459 (AR1/48 and 268–69). Tripkunyn's land had been in Rescassa, in Lanhadron manor and Goran parish; he received also a close in St Columb town. See also pp. 53 and 118.

Talcarn Morekke [*Tolcarne Merock, in St Mawgan in Pyder*]:[12]
Remfrey Olyuer, 1 acre Cornish, conventionarily (*in convenc'*); 28s., [and] 1 capon for 1 day's work at harvest.

Total [of conventionary tenants], £11 9s. 8d.[13]

Total of free and conventionary tenants, £14 19s. 6¼d.

* * *

Bodwenek
[*Bodwannick, in Lanivet*]

Free tenants

Resevelyn [*Rosevallon, in Bodmin parish*]:
John Kympe by right of his wife, John Rescarrek, and Richard Boscawen, the whole vill; 2 suits of court; 20d.

Boskeir [*Boskear, in Bodmin parish*]:
John Ber,[14] [½ acre Cornish, by knight's service, *added later*]; common suit of court; 12d.

Treffry [*Treffry, in Lanhydrock*]:
John Phelip, 3 ferlings Cornish, by knight's service; 2 suits of court; 4s. 6d.
John Treffry, ½ acre Cornish, by knight's service; 2 suits of court; 3s.
Thomas Jenkyn, by right of his wife, 1 ferling Cornish, by knight's service; 2 suits of court; 18d.

Boskedek [*Bokiddick, in Lanivet*]:
William Rescasa, 1 ferling Cornish, by knight's service; common suit of court; 5d.
Thomas Lacy, 3 ferlings Cornish, by knight's service; 2 suits of court; 20d.

Frogham in Seyntlaurens [*'Frogham' (lost), in Lanivet, close to St Lawrence in Bodmin parish*]:[15]
William Hoigge, 1 holding [½ acre, by knight's service, *added later*]; 2 suits of court; 6d.

---

[12] See also among the free tenements (p. 112 and n.).
[13] This includes the 10s. for Trebby, but not the 28s. for Tolcarne Merock.
[14] 'now Mr Bevyll', inserted.
[15] The words *Frogham in* added later; compare the 1480 rental (p. 97).

Moor (*mora*) of Tremaile, Tre... More, and Boscaire More [*names added later; moors named from Tremayle, in Lanivet, and Boskear, in Bodmin parish*]:
John Herry [now John Brian and John Rich..., *added later*], 1 holding; 2 suits of court; 7s. 6d. during term of 100 years; after 100 years, rent 10s. and relief 5s.
Thomas Lanhergy [within Tremayle Downe and Tremayle, 2 acres, by knight's service, *added later*]; 2 suits of court; 12d.

Total of free tenants, 22s. 9d.

And 8d. from Flamanck, for a mill-pool (*pro gurgit' molendini*), total 23s. 5d. [*entry added later.*][16]

Conventionary tenants

Bodwenek [*Bodwannick, in Lanivet*]:
John Rogger, 1 holding; common suit of court; 32s. plus 4 capons.
John Brode, 1 holding; common suit of court; 12s. 6d. plus 3 capons.
William Broude, 1 holding; common suit of court; 12s. 6d. plus 3 capons.
John Broude, 1 holding; common suit of court; 32s. 4d. plus 7 capons.

Attley [*Atley, in Lanivet*]:
Nicholas Braben, 1 holding; common suit of court; 21s. plus 6 capons.

Tremaile [*Tremayle, in Lanivet*]:
Richard Oppy, 1 holding; common suit of court; 17s. 2d. [?]
John Richard, 1 holding; common suit of court; 15s. 2d. plus 4 capons.

Lanyet [*Lanet, in Lanivet*]:
Sibilla Law, 1 holding, for her life; common suit of court; 18s. 8d.
Nicholas Stevyn, 1 holding; common suit of court; 13s. 4d. plus 2 capons.

Lannenwell [*Laninval, in Lanivet*]:
Martin Bailey, 1 holding; common suit of court; 10s. 6d. plus 2 capons.
John Lobbe, 1 holding; common suit of court; 12s. plus 3 capons.
Thomas Martyn, 1 holding; common suit of court; 19s. 6d. plus 3 capons.

---

[16] In the rental of c.1586 this is described as 'the mill pool of Gere' (AR2/1343), presumably for a mill of Tregear, in Bodmin parish.

Boskedek [*Bokiddick, in Lanivet*]:
John Luky ['Ped' [?] . . . , *added later*], 1 holding; common suit of court; 8s. plus 2 capons.

Wodley le Ouera [*Higher Woodley, in Lanivet*]:
John Stevyn, 1 holding; common suit of court; 13s. 4d. plus 2 capons.
John William, 1 holding; common suit of court; 14s. plus 2 capons.

Wadley le Nethir [*Lower Woodley, in Lanivet*]:
John Tailour, 1 holding; common suit of court; 9s. plus 2 capons.
John Ede, 1 holding; common suit of court; 10s. plus 2 capons.
John Dyngell, 1 holding; common suit of court; 14s. plus 2 capons.
John Richowe, 1 holding; common suit of court; 14s. plus 2 capons.

Corn-mill:
Thomas Bryand; common suit of court; 24s. plus 2 capons.

Tucking mill (*Molend fullon'*):
Andrew Touker; common suit of court; 13s. plus 2 capons.

Atford [*Forda, in Lanivet*]:
John Tredwyn, 1 holding; common suit of court; 16s. plus 2 capons.

Newtown [*Newton, in Lanivet*]:
John Michell [now Philip Brabin [?], *added later*], 1 holding; common suit of court; 9s. plus 2 capons.

Seyntlaurens [*St Lawrence, in Bodmin parish*]:
Richard Calwey, 1 holding; used to pay 15s., pays 14s.

Roshill [*unidentified*]:
Richard Watta, a blowing mill (*molend' sufflatic'*); 20d.

Total [*of conventionary tenants*], £19 6s. 2d.,[17]
plus 9s. 10d. for capons

Total *of free and conventionary tenants*, £20 7s. 11d.

[For a water-course at Lanenwill, 3d.;[18] total £20 8s. 2d.; *added later*.]

* * *

---

[17] A revised total of £18 14s. 8d. for conventionary tenants was added later, and seems more accurate, but was not used in the grand totals given.
[18] See comment in the 1480 rental, above (p. 98n.).

Nansladdron
[*Nansladron alias Lanhadron, in St Ewe*]

Free tenants

Pille [*Pill, in Lanlivery*]:
John Curteis, 1 acre Cornish, by knight's service; 2 suits of court; 1 *lb*. cummin, value 4*d*.

Will [Parke, *added later*] [*lost, in Lanlivery*]:
John Rescumer, by right of his wife, 1 acre Cornish, by knight's service; 2 suits of court; 6*d*.

Pengelly [*Pengelly, in St Ewe*]:
Peter Eggecomb, 2 acres Cornish, by knight's service; common suit of court; 15*d*.

Tregirthek [*Tregerrick, in Goran*]:
The same Peter, 4 acres Cornish, by knight's service; 2 suits of court; 1 pair of gilt spurs or 3*d*., [and] 12*d*.

Nansgronek ['*Nansfrinick alias Nanruan' (lost), in Goran*]:
The same Peter, 1 ferling Cornish, by knight's service; 2 suits of court; 6*d*.

Crukcon' Olas [*(Lower) Cotna, in Goran*]:
The same Peter, 1 ferling, by knight's service; and for a mill leat (*bed' molend'*) there, 6*d*.

Hontyngdon [*Hunting Down; also 'Bloughan' (lost) and Castle, otherwise Little Lantyan; all in Lanlivery*]:
The same Peter, Hontyngdon, Blasslond [?] and Castell, ½ knight's fee, by knight's service; 1*d*. [?]

Carloos [*Carloose, in Creed*]:
Thomas Carloos, ½ acre Cornish, by knight's service; 2 suits of court; 2*s*.

Seyntcrida [*Creed churchtown*]:
Halnathet' Malm'e, by right of his wife, 1 acre Cornish, by knight's service; 2 suits of court; 12½*d*. and ...
Nicholas Arundell Treris, 1 acre Cornish, by knight's service, and [*blank*] whenever relief [arises].

Bossulyan [*Bossillian, in Creed*]:
John Trevelyan and Thomas Tregarthyn, ½ acre Cornish, in socage; 2 suits of court; 12½*d*.

Trewarvena [*Trewarmenna, in Creed*]:
John Tretherff, 2 acres Cornish, in socage; 2 suits of court; 17½d.

Rescasa [*Rescassa, in Goran*]:[19]
William Rescasa, [*blank*] acres Cornish, [*blank*]; common suit of court; 18d.

Bonhurdon [*Benhurden, in Goran*]:
Thomas Trevelwith, ½ acre Cornish, by knight's service; 2 suits of court; 3d.; nothing, because in . . . [the lord's hand?]

Total of free tenants, 11s. 1½d.

Conventionary tenants

Rescorlan [*Rescorla, in St Ewe*]:
William Euryn, 1½ holdings; common suit of court; 15s. 8d., plus 2d. for a day's work, and 2 capons.
John Nicoll, 1½ holdings as above; 16s. 4d., plus 2d. and 2 capons.
Richard Penstrasow, 1 holding; 18s., plus 2d.

Bossu [*Bosue, in St Ewe*]:
John Hokkyn, 1 holding; 22s., plus 2d.
Vivian Hick, 1 holding; 24s. 6d., plus 4d.
John Hawys, 2 closes called Parke Engrouse; 13s. 4d.

Laworan [*at Goran churchtown*]:
John Goly, 1 holding; used to pay 17s.; pays 15s., plus 2d. and 2 capons.
Thomas Tom [now Symon, *added later*], 1 holding; 10s., plus 2d.
Walter Hegon [now John Taylour [?], *added later*], ½ holding; 10s., plus 2d. and 1 capon.
John Will, ½ holding; 10s. plus 2d.;
the same John, 1 holding, formerly William Th' Davy; 8s. 8d., plus 2d.
Robert Henry [now [*blank*], *added later*], 1 holding; 8s., plus 2d.
Thomas Tregarthyn, 1 workshop (*shopa*); 8d.
Robert William, 1 holding; 10s. 4d., plus 2d. and 1 capon.

Crukcon' [*Cotna, in Goran*]:
The same Robert, 1 holding; 16s., plus 2d.

---

[19] Note that this has now been fully absorbed into Lanhadron manor, unlike its separate appearance in 1463 (above, p. 53).

Penhale [*Penhale, in Goran*]:
Thomas Hunte [Richard Penhale, *added later*], 1 holding; 10s., plus 2d.
John Tomkin, 1 holding; 10s., plus 2d.

Menagwyns [*Menagwins, in Goran*]:
The same Thomas and John, whole vill; 5s. 4d.

Laworan [*at Goran churchtown*]:
The same Thomas and John, 1 holding; 4s. 3d.

Bonhurdon [*Benhurden, in Goran*]:
Walter Tomherry, whole vill; used to pay 26s. 8d.; pays 22s., plus 2d.

Corn mill:
Robert Hoskyn, the whole mill; used to pay 56s. 8d.; pays 40s., plus 2d. and 4 capons.

Penburgligh [*Pengrugla, in St Ewe*]:
John Stevyn, 1 parcel; used to pay 3s. [4d., *deleted*]; pays 20d.

Halendeves [*lost, presumably in St Ewe*]:
Nil, because in hand.

Lanewy [*Lanuah, in St Ewe*]:
Nil here, because in lord's park; used to pay 17s.

Rescasa [*Rescassa, in Goran*]:
William Rescasa, ½ holding, formerly Richard Hore; 4s.
John Kerow, ½ holding; 4s., plus 2d.;
the same John, 1 holding; used to pay 20s.; pays 18s. 8d.
James Benet, 1 holding; 8s.;
the same James, another holding; 6s.

Sticker [*Sticker, in St Merryn*]:
Thomas Houper; used to pay 43s. 4d.

Trelowith Wartha [*(Higher) Treloweth, in St Mewan*]:
The same Thomas, the whole vill; 17s. 4d. [now 26s. 8d., *added later*].

Lanhaddron Park [*in St Ewe*]:
[*blank*]

Gretemedow:
John Hawys; 10s.

Litellmedow:
Now in hand; used to pay 6s.

    Total [*of conventionary tenants*], £19 0s. 3d.,
    including days' work, plus 12 capons.
  Total *of free and conventionary tenants*, £19 11s. 4½d.[20]

* * *

Truruvyen
[*Truro Vean, in St Clement*]

Free tenants

Robert Coulyng, 1 close called Gwele Connyan;[21] 2 suits of court; 2s. 6d.

John Spernan, 1 close there, [*blank*], and 2 suits of court; 4s. 6d.

John Walsch and Richard Carvegh, 1 close, formerly Richard Treffry; common suit of court; 2s.

William Laghar, 3 tofts with 3 gardens, for him and his heirs; 2 suits of court; 2s.
The same William, 1 close in Gwele Conyan; 8d.

William Trevenour, 1 close in Gwele Connyan; 6d.

Peter Bevill, 1 close in Gwele Conyan, by knight's service; 3d.

Stephen Polwhile, 1 holding, 1 suit of court at Michaelmas; 20s.

John Alen, 1 toft with garden; 12d.

    Total [*of free tenants*], 33s. 5d.

Conventionary tenants

Treruburgh [*Truro borough*]:
Oto Norton and Nicholas Symon, 1 holding with garden annexed.
The same Oto and Nicholas, another holding by the sea shore.
Gwele Crokprynnyer: the same Oto, 1 parcel containing 16 acres.[22]

---

[20] A note at the end reads, 'Nota md. to inquer whether ye grete medow and ye lytell medow be allowed in ye accompte, ye or no; and yff not ye ryffys [= 'reeves'] doyth lost it. Ideo inquer' melius;' [*all deleted*] 'oneratur, ideo exoneratur.'

[21] The site of *Gwele Con(n)yan* is indicated by the house called Conium, now Tremorvah, in Truro (St Clement); compare p. 60n.

Truruvyen: the same Oto, 1 close called Truruvyen.
Gwele Nansmeur: the same Oto, 2 acres in Gwele Nansmeur.[23]

[Joint sub-total], £4 3s. 11d.

Gweleyet: the same Oto, 1 close in Gweleyet.[24]
Coskeir: the same Oto, 1 close in Coskeir.[25]

[Joint sub-total], 9s.

Seynt Clemens stret [*St Clement Street, in Truro*]:
Thomas Triggean, 1 close, for term of [*blank*] years; 2 suits of court; 3s. 4d.
John Triggian, 1 close, [*blank*] years, as above; 6s. 4d.
John Engooff, 1 close, at will; common suit of court; 2s.

Truruburgh [*Truro borough*]:
Walter Cordalion and Pascoe (*Pascasius*) his son, 1 holding with garden, for their lives; 14d.

Chiwarren: [David Logan, *added later*].[26]

Tresympill: [*blank*].

Carnek: [*blank*].

Tregontelion: [*blank*].

Total [*of conventionary tenants*], 105s. 9d.

Total of free and conventionary tenants, £6 19s. 2d.

* * *

---

[22] The site of *Gwele Crokprynnyer* is indicated by the house called Comprigney, in Truro (Kenwyn).
[23] Presumably an open-field close to Nancemeor, in St Clement.
[24] Unidentified open-field, in either Kenwyn or St Clement parish.
[25] *Coskeere*, 1659 rental; apparently different from *Camp Close(s)* (in St Clement), found in both the 1659 and 1717 surveys.
[26] These four tenements (the first and third unidentified; the second Tresemple, in St Clement; and the last *Tregatillion*, lost near Tregurra, in St Clement) are otherwise unknown as tenements of Truro Vean manor, except in the rental of c.1586 (AR2/1343), which, as here, has no detail apart from the place-names themselves. Note that there is no mention of Arundell's quarry at *Truru-vyhan*, which is mentioned four years later, in 1503 (Henderson, 'Ecclesiastical Antiquities', p. 457).

Kenell
[*Kennall, in Stithians*]

Free tenants

Treskewys [*Treskewes, in Stithians*]:
William Jerueis, 1 plot, by knight's service; 16*d*.

Penmena [*sic; Penmenor, in Stithians*]:[27]
Richard Brent and Thomas Baker, 2 acres Cornish, in socage; 1 suit of court, at Michaelmas; 4*s*.

Resegh [*Roseath, in Stithians*]:
John Resegh, ½ acre Cornish, by knight's service; common suit of court; 3*s*.

Enys [*Ennis, in Stithians*]:
Martin Enys, 3 parts of 1 acre Cornish, by knight's service; common suit of court; 14¾*d*.;
the same Martin, 1 ferling, by knight's service; common suit of court; 14¾*d*.

Tregonan [*Tregonning, in Stithians*]:
John Butside, ½ acre Cornish, in socage; common suit of court; 2*s*. 4*d*.
John Duront, ½ acre Cornish, by knight's service; 16*d*.[28]

Hendre [*Hendra, in Stithians*]:
The same John, ½ acre Cornish, by knight's service; 3*s*.

Total [*of free tenants*], 17*s*. 5½*d*.

Conventionary tenants

Kenell [*Kennall, in Stithians*]:
Roger Jakluky, 2 plots as 1 holding (*sub una tenura*), for term of 42 years; all services as others [do], and 6*s*. 8*d*. as heriot; at 4 dates, 26*s*. 8*d*.
John Alen, 1 holding; common suit of court; 13*s*. 4*d*.
John Adam, 1 holding, as above; 13*s*. 4*d*.

Treberveth [*Trebarveth, in Stithians*]:
Richard Jaktom, 2 holdings; 16*s*. 6*d*.

---

[27] *Tre* appears after this name, probably for *Tregonan*: compare p. 77.
[28] '2 suits of court', added later, applying to this entry and the next.

Tremenhir [*Tremenheere, in Stithians*]:
John Hick, 1 holding; 10s.

Trembroth [*Trembroath, in Stithians*]:
Pentecost John, 1 holding; 8s. 6d.
Ralph Treher, 1 holding; 8s. 6d.

Mill of Kenell:
Henry Hogan, the mill, for term of 30 years; 13s. 4d.

Thomas Polmargh, 1 parcel of land, with 2 blowing-mills (*molend' sufflatic'*); 5s.
John Kellygrewe, John Cavell and others, for a water course there, 16d. [*Last two entries added later.*]

Total [*of conventionary tenants*], 110s. 2d.[29]

Total [*of free and conventionary tenants*], £6 7s. 7½d.

* * *

Tregarn
[*Tregarne, in St Keverne*]

Free tenants

Trelanvyen [*Trelanvean, in St Keverne*]:
John Reskum', ½ acre Cornish, by knight's service, at 4 dates, *viz.* St Andrew, mid-Lent, St James and Michaelmas; 2 suits of court and relief; 7s.

Congvynyan [*Polgwidnan, in St Keverne*]:
David John Laurens, 1 ferling Cornish, in socage; no suit of court; ½d.

Tregarn [*Tregarne, in St Keverne*]:
Thomas Rescruk, 3 ferlings Cornish; common suit of court; 12d.

Monglegh [*Mongleath, in Budock*]:
Thomas Keligrew de Arwennak, [*blank*]; common suit of court; 2s.

Nansdreisek [*Nancetrisack, in Sithney*]:
John Arundell Talvern, [*blank*]; common suit of court; 6d.

Penwheras [*Penwerris, in Budock*]:
The same John, the whole vill; 1 pair of gloves or 1d.

---

[29] The total does not include the last two entries.

Gelly [*Gilly, in Mawgan in Meneage*]:
John Petit, [*blank*]; 2 suits of court; 1*d*.

Baghow [*Bahow, in St Keverne*]:
Thomas [John, *deleted*] Baghow, 1 acre [?]; no suit of court; 7*s*.

Total [*of free tenants*], 17*s*. 8½*d*.[30]

Penwheras contains ¼ knight's fee 'by the record of Mr Kelligrewe' [*sentence added*].

Conventionary tenants

Tregarn [*Tregarne, in St Keverne*]:
Thomas Golleth, 1 holding, as before; common suit of court; 20*s*.
Thomas Nans, ½ holding; common suit of court; 6*s*. 1*d*.
John William, ½ holding, as above; 6*s*. 1*d*.
Richard Tomluky, 1 holding, as above; 13*s*. 8*d*.

Helwyn [*Halwyn, in St Keverne*]:
John William, 1 holding, as above; 8*s*.
Richard Hoskyn, 1 holding, as above, for term of his and his wife's lives; recognisance 3*s*. 4*d*.; [rent] 16*s*.

Tregevys [*Tregevas, in St Martin in Meneage*]:
Thomas Jamys, 1 holding; 14*s*. 2*d*.
William John, 1 holding; 7*s*. 1*d*.
Richard Jamys, 1 holding; 10*s*. 8*d*. ['1*d*.', *added*]

Hendrewike [*Landrivick, in Manaccan*]:
John Gooff, the whole vill; 15*s*.

Condorow [*Condurrow, in St Anthony in Meneage*]:
George Peryn, 1 holding; 10*s*. 4*d*.
Simon Henr', 1 holding; 10*s*. 4*d*.
John Perow, 1 holding; 10*s*. 4*d*.
John Henr', 1 holding; 10*s*. 4*d*.

Penpoll [*Penpoll, in St Anthony in Meneage*]:
Thomas Herry clerk, whole vill; 9*s*.

Bodenvyan [*Boden Vean, in St Anthony in Meneage*]:
John Will Perow; 20*s*.

---

[30] There seems to be no basis for a revised total of 19*s*. 1½*d*., which has been added later.

The mill [*Tregarne Mill, in St Keverne*]:
John Phelippe, the mill; 22s.

Total [of conventionary tenants], £10 9s. 2d.

Total of free and conventionary tenants, £11 6s. 9½d.

* * *

Carmynow
[*Carminow, in Mawgan in Meneage*]

Free tenants

Redalen, Huthnans, Karioghall, Trener, Roddowr, Keligow [*Redallan, Huthnance, Crawle, Trenear, Ruthdower and Treliggo, all in Breage*]:
The heir(s) of Larcedeken, [*blank*] knight's fee; by homage, fealty and scutage, for all service.

Treueglos, Treuembr', Tregynryth [*Treveglos, Tremeader, Tregerthen* [?]; *also 'Carlibby' (lost), all in Zennor*]:
John earl of Oxford, ½ acre Cornish in Treveglos, 3 acres in Trevemed', 1 acre in Tregynryth, and 1 ferling in Carlibbe, by knight's service; by homage and fealty [*only*].

Tregedill [*Tregiddle, in Cury*]:
John Petit Predannek, 1 acre Cornish, in socage, by homage and fealty; common suit of court; at Sts Philip and James, 12d.

Gurlyn, Trevillian [*Gurlyn and Trelean, both in St Erth*]:
The heir(s) of Ralph Soor, 2 parts of the vill of Gurlyn and ½ the vill of Trevilian, by knight's service; given in free marriage with one *Margar'* daughter of Carmynow, and now in the lord's hand in Pengwenna.[31]

Growse [*Angrouse, in Mullion*]:
William Gurlyn, 3 acres Cornish, by homage and fealty; common suit of court, at 4 dates; 5s.

Rosmodr' [*Rosemorder, in Manaccan*]:
John Reskym', ½ acre Cornish, by homage and fealty; 20d.

---

[31] Presumably the manor of Pengwedna, in Breage, is meant; but Gurlyn and Trelean actually appear as free tenements of Prospidnick manor in 1468–69 and 1509 (below, pp. 146 and 149), and not in Pengwedna manor.

Polgren [*Polgrean, in Cury*]:
Philippa (*Phelippa*) Carmynow, 1 acre Cornish, by homage and fealty; common suit; 19s.

Helston burgh [*Helston town*]:
William Jak Davy, by right of his wife, 1½ plots and 1 close; 6s.

Total of free tenants, 32s. 8d.

Conventionary tenants

Lannargh [*Lamarth, in Mawgan in Meneage*]:
William Lannargh, 1 acre Cornish, for term of lives of James Lannargh, Lucy his wife, and John, William and Robert their sons; 2 [*altered from* common] suits; at 4 dates, 11s.

Bronywik Wartha, Bronywik Wolas [*Higher and Lower Burnuick, in Mawgan in Meneage*]:
John Godolhan, ½ acre and ½ ferling in Bornywik Wartha and 1 ferling in Bornywik Wolas, term [*blank*]; used to pay 23s. 6d.; 20s.

Chynythen, Hendre, Killiengreth ['*Chynythen' (lost) and Hendra, both in Cury, and Killianker, in Mawgan in Meneage*]:
John Snoboll, in Chynythyn 1 acre ½ ferling, in Hendr' ½ acre; 17s.
Thomas Mester, in Hendr' 3 ferlings, in Kelliengreth 1 acre, at will; 17s.

Clyse Olynsy ['*Clies Olingey' (lost), part of Clies, in Mawgan in Meneage*]:
Ralph Cleise, 3 ferlings, term [*blank*]; 16s.

Chiwarloo [*Chyvarloe, in Gunwalloe*]; contains 4 acres Cornish:
John Gregour, 1 holding, for term of his life; 10s.
John Engooff, 3 holdings, at will; 20s. 8d.
John Bacheler, 1 holding; 6s. 8d.
John London, 1 holding; 13s. 4d.
Richard Calamee, 1 holding; 12s.
William Symon, 1 holding; 6s. 8d.

Nanspyen [*Nampean, in Gunwalloe*]:
John Herry alias Verlich [?], ½ acre Cornish; 14s.

Gom, Hee ['*Goome' (lost) and Anhay, both in Gunwalloe*]:
Thomas Tom, the whole vill; 50s.

Hendr' Dodda [*Burgess, in Gunwalloe; also 'Chynythen', in Cury*]:[32]
Roger Burges, ½ acre Cornish, and ½ ferling in Chynethyn; 16s.

Chynals [*Chinalls, in Gunwalloe*]:
Simon John, 3 ferlings; 13s. 4d.

Beaurripper [*Berepper, in Gunwalloe*]:
John Jenkyn, 1 ferling; 10s.

Morrebloo, Polscovornow [sic], Clise meene [*'Morebloe' (lost), in Gunwalloe; 'Polscovornogow' and 'Clies Men' (unidentified)*]:
containing in Polcornygow 2 acres, in Clisemene 1 acre and in Morrebloo 4 acres [*sic, no tenant or rent given*].

The mill:
Ralph Hick, the lower mill with mill-land annexed; 20s.

Burnow [*Burnow, in Cury*]:
William Robert, whole vill, for term of his life and of Joan his wife; 27s.

Demesne of Carmynow:
Ralph Cleise, 2 closes, Parke Payn and Parke Cardelys; 15s.
John Snoboll, 1 close by Dorwenek; 8s.

Carmynow Bally [= *bailiff's*]:
Ralph Cleise and John Snoboll, for term of 14 years; £4.

Le Ouer Mill:
decayed and ruinous.

Total [of conventionary tenants], £20 2s. 8d.

Total of free and conventionary tenants, £21 15s. 4d.

* * *

Wynnyanton
[*Winnington, in Gunwalloe*]

Free tenants

Tregowres, Hengeyther, Cornhogh [*Tregowris, Nangither and Carno, all in St Keverne*]:
John Rescumer, 2 acres Cornish, in socage; common suit of court; at St Andrew, mid-Lent, St James and Michaelmas, 10s. 2d.

---

[32] For *Hendr' Dodda* identified as Burgess see above, p. 15 (1459 extent).

Treris [*Trerise, in Ruan Major*]:
John earl of Oxford, 1 acre Cornish; by homage and fealty, for all service.

Trenansbyen [*Trenance Vean, in Mullion*]:
The same, ½ acre Cornish, in socage; 2s. 5½d.

Treseis [*Trezise, in St Martin in Meneage*]:
The same, ½ acre Cornish, in socage; common suit of court; 2s.

Boschym, Pentir [*Bochym and Pentire, both in Cury*]:
Joan Wyndeslate, 1 acre Cornish, by knight's service; common suit of court; 4s. 11d.

Trevynwon [*Trenoon, in Ruan Major*]:
James Erisy, ½ acre Cornish, in socage; common suit of court; 6s. 8d.

Hendree [*Hendra, in Ruan Major*]:
The same James, 3 ferlings Cornish, in socage; common suit of court; [*blank*];
the same James, 1 ferling Cornish, as above; 4s. 11d.

Tresprison [*Tresprison, in Mullion*]:
Richard Trispreson [*sic*], ½ acre Cornish, in socage; common suit of court; 2s. 6d.

Eresy [*Erisey, in Grade*]:
The heir(s) of Henry Bodrugan, ½ acre Cornish; common suit of court; 20d.

Tregadreth Meur, Tregadreth Vyan, Treris, Nansploth [*Tregaddra, in Mawgan in Meneage, and Trease and Nanplough, both in Cury*]:
John Chamond, 2 acres 1 ferling Cornish; common suit of court; 20d.

Total [*of free tenants*], 36s. 11½d.

Syntsewena [*Sowanna, in Gunwalloe*]:
½ acre Cornish which used to pay 4s. 11d. is in hand because it descended by hereditary right to Matthew Syntsewena, lord's bondman (*nativus*); now it is granted as conventionary land (*traditur convens'*).[33]

---

[33] See above, p. 18n.

MANOR OF WINNINGTON

Conventionary tenants

Tolle [*Toll, in Gunwalloe*]:
James Tolle, 3 ferlings; common suit of court; payable as before, 20s.

Gonynsycok [*'Goninsey Cock' (lost), close to Chepye, in Gunwalloe*]:
John Nicoll, 1 acre Cornish; 10s.

Gonynsypye [*Chepye, in Gunwalloe*]:
The same John, 3 ferlings; 10s.

Trenowith [*Trenoweth, in Gunwalloe*]:
John Bosustow, 1 acre Cornish; 17s.

Roos [*'Rosehendra' (lost), in Cury*]:
Roger Burges, 1 ferling; 2s.

Nynsy [*Hingey, in Gunwalloe*]:
Ralph Roos, 1 acre Cornish; 16s.

Wynnyanton [*Winnington, in Gunwalloe*]:
John William, 1 acre Cornish; 12s.
John Nicoll, 1½ acres Cornish; 20s.

Chicastell [*'Choy Castle' (lost), adjacent to Gunwalloe church*]:[34]
Ralph William chaplain (*capell'*), 1 toft; for all service, 4d.

The quarry (*Le Quarr'*):
Robert Jacke, le Quarry; 2s. [*entry added later*]

Total [*of conventionary tenants*], 109s. 4d.[35]

There are there various casual profits, *viz.* of ward, marriage, scutage, aid, escheat, heriot, wreck of sea and strays for the Hundred of Kerriar.

Total *of free and conventionary tenants*, £7 6s. 3½d.

* * *

---

[34] The tenement of *Chicastle* (possibly the same tenement as *Curte* in 1480: see p. 82n.) was described in a lease of 1585 as 'standing nere the churche of Gonewallo', and in another of 1692 as adjoining the church (AR4/993-94); in the surveys of 1659 and 1717 it was merged with the tenement of Winnington, also adjoining the church.

[35] This total includes 2s. for the quarry, but not the tenement of Sowanna, granted conventionarily but currently in hand.

Conerton
[Connerton, in Gwithian]

Free tenants

Trencromme, Nansawallen [*Trencrom and 'Nansavallan' (lost), both in Lelant*]:
Edward Hastyng knight, 1 acre Cornish, in socage; common suit of court; at the 4 dates usual in Hundred of Penwith, 4s.

The water of Lanant [*stream at Lelant*]:
The same Edward, water of Lanant; at Easter, 6d.
Offering (*offre*) and aid: the same Edward owes [?] offering and aid (*tenet offr' et auxilio*); at Michaelmas, 3d.[36]

Boswithgy, Boscuden [*Bosworgey and Boscudden, both in St Erth*]:
The same Edward, 1 acre Cornish, with the tithing of Conerton (*cum decenna de Conerton*); [*blank*].[37]

Talscoys [*Taskus, in Gwinear*]:
John Kyllygrewe, by right of his wife, ½ acre, in socage; common suit of court; 15d.

Bosuerhes [*unidentified*]:
The heir(s) of Carsulek,[38] 25 acres English, in socage; common suit of court; nil.

Trenowith [*Trenoweth, in Gwinear*]:[39]
The same heirs, 2 parts of 1 [*blank*] Cornish, [*blank*]; common suit of court; and offering at Michaelmas (*offretorium ad festum Sancti Michaelis*), 3d.

Amalibri, Nanscludry, Chyenglasen [*Amalebra, Nancledra and Chylason, all in Towednack*]:
Robert Broughton knight, 2 acres Cornish, in socage; common suit of court; 8s.

Polkynhorne [*Polkinghorne, in Gwinear*]:
The same Robert, ½ acre Cornish; 12d.

Trenawyn Wartha [*Trenowin, in Gwinear*]:
The same Robert, 1 ferling [*blank*]; common suit; 1 *lb.* cummin or 4d.

---

[36] For this phrase see above, p. 40 n. 42.
[37] For the explanation of this remark see above, p. 40 n. 43.
[38] *Her' Carsulek* is written over a deleted word or words.
[39] This seems to be a duplicate entry for Trenoweth, below (p. 132).

MANOR OF CONNERTON 131

Eggloshaile [*Egloshayle, at Phillack churchtown*]:
John Arundell Talvern, ½ acre Cornish, in socage; common suit of court; 6s. 9d.

Trethengy [*Trethingy, in Phillack*]:
The same John, 1 acre Cornish, in socage; 1d.;
the same John, for offering and aid (*pro offr' et auxilio*), 3d.

Conerwartha [*Connorwartha, near Gwithian churchtown*]:
John Trevesys,[40] by right of his wife, ½ acre Cornish; common suit of court; 12d.

Ponsreles [*'Ponsfrellas' (lost), in Gwithian*]:
The same John, as above, ½ acre Cornish; common suit; 1d.

Graften [*'Grafton' (lost), in Gwithian*]:
The same John, as above, 1 ferling, in socage; 2s.

Treuasek, Ventenlegh [?] [*Trevassack and Ventonleague, both in Phillack*]:
Edmund Arundell knight, 2 acres Cornish, by knight's service; 3s.

Arde [*Ayr, in St Ives parish*]:
Joan Carnarthur, 3 parts of 1 acre, in socage; common suit of court; 2s.

Hendre [*Hendra, in St Ives parish*]:
Elizabeth Ralegh, 1 acre Cornish, by knight's service; 1 suit of court; 1 pair of spurs or 6d.

Trenawyn [*Trenowin, in Gwinear*]:
John Mohun, 1 acre Cornish, in socage; 2 suits of court; 12d.

Hellenwon [*Hellynoon, in Lelant*]:
The same John, 1 croft; 2 suits of court; 2s.

Carewyn [*Carwyn, in Phillack*]:
John Godolhen, 1 acre Cornish, in socage; common suit of court; 2s.

Boskeures Wolas [*Boskerris Woollas, in Lelant*]:
The heir(s) of John [*sic*],[41] ½ acre Cornish, by knight's service; common suit of court; 6s. 8d.

Trenywyn [*probably Treven, in St Erth*]:[42]
John Mohun, 2 acres Cornish; 2 suits of court; 5s.

---

[40] '*viz.* her' Laurens Sherston', added above.
[41] Written later, over an erasure; presumably of John Trevogherth (p. 87).
[42] The first *n* in the name is rewritten, possibly over a *g*.

Carneny, Carbons, Chiengwele, Eggloshaile, Trewelysek Heile [*Carninney, Carbis and Chyangweal, in Lelant; Egloshayle, in Phillack; and Trelissick, in St Erth*]:
Thomas marquess of Dorset, 1 acre Cornish in Carneny [and] Carbons, 1 ferling in Chiengwele, ½ acre in Egglosheyle, ½ acre Cornish in Trewhelisik Heile, all in socage; common suit of court; 7s. 7d.; and for offering and aid, 3d.

Trethegember [*Tregembo, in St Hilary*]:
Alice Fortescue, 1 acre Cornish, in socage; common suit of court; 12d.; and for offering and aid, 3d.

Gornogow, Westua [*'Carnogowe' (lost) and Westway, in Lelant*]:
John Mohun, 1 acre Cornish, by knight's service; common suit of court; 1 pair of gloves or 1d.

Arde [*Ayr, in St Ives parish*]:
Elizabeth Ralegh, 3 parts of 1 acre, by knight's service; common suit of court; 16d.

Trevascois [*Trevaskis, in Gwinear*]:
The same Elizabeth, 3 parts of 1 acre, by knight's service; common suit of court; 12d.

Trewronnan [*Trevarnon, in Gwithian*]:
William Clemow, 2 acres Cornish, in socage; no suit of court; 6d.

Trenowith iuxta Trevascois [*Trenoweth, in Gwinear*]:
[*blank*] Carsulek, 2 acres Cornish, in socage; common suit of court; 2s.; and for offering [and] aid, 2d.

Legha, Trewon [*Leah and Trewoone, both in Phillack*]:
James Tomlyn, 1 ferling, in socage; common suit of court; 15d.

Egglosheyle [*Egloshayle, at Phillack churchtown*]:
John Bois, 1 ferling, in socage; 2 suits of court; 13¼d.;
the same, for offering and aid, 1½d.
Richard Bois, 1 ferling, in socage; 13¼d.;
the same, for offering and aid, 1½d.

Legha, Trewon [*Leah and Trewoone, both in Phillack*]:
The same Richard, 1 ferling, in socage; 15d.

Nansderow [*Nanterrow, in Gwithian*]:
John Tregenna, by right of his wife, and James Tomlyn, as above, 2 acres Cornish, by knight's service; common suit of court; 10s.; and

for offering, 4d.

Pennas [sic; Pennance, in Gwithian]:
Henry Pennans, ½ acre Cornish, in socage; common suit of court; ½ lb. pepper or 8d.
Remainder of the whole vill in hand, by escheat.
The same Henry, for aid, 2d.

Treffrynk, Ard' [Trink, in Lelant, and Ayr, in St Ives parish]:
[blank] Carnarthur, in Treffrynk, 1 acre, and 3 parts of 1 acre in Ard', in socage; common suit of court; 4s. 8d.
The same, for offering and aid, 3d.

Treffrynk [Trink, in Lelant]:
Stephen Calmady, ½ acre Cornish, in socage; common suit of court; 2s. 6d.

Ard' [Ayr, in St Ives parish]:
John Nanscothen, one-sixth acre Cornish, in socage; common suit of court; 12d.

Helles Vyen [Hellesvean, in St Ives parish]:
The same John, 1 ferling, in socage; common suit of court; 16d.

Carenuer, Wotfold [Crenver and Oatfield, both in Crowan]:
John Arundell Treris, Carenuer and Wotfolde, in socage; for all service, 1 grain of wheat.

Treuleghan [Treloyan, in St Ives parish]:
John Martyn, ½ acre Cornish; common suit of court; 3s.

Boskeures Wartha [Boskerris Wartha, in Lelant]:
John Tremayn esquire, ½ acre Cornish, by knight's service; common suit of court; 2s.; and for offering [and] aid (offr' auxilii), 3d.

Trelighon [Treloyan, in St Ives parish]:
John Martyn Trelighan, 1 ferling, in socage; common suit of court; 4s.
John Trelighan, 1 ferling, in socage; common suit of court; 3s.

Tregena [Tregenna, in St Ives parish]:
William Hick Elen, 1 ferling; common suit of court; 2s.
Oto Tregena, ½ acre [blank], by knight's service; common suit of court; 20d.; and for offering and aid, 3d.
John Plymen, by right of his wife, and Nicholas Rusch, 1 ferling; common suit of court; 2s.; and for offering and aid, 3d.

Coyswyn [*Lanyon, formerly 'Coswinwolward', in Gwinear*]:
John Lanyen, 2 acres Cornish, in socage; common suit of court; 7s. 8d.; and for offering and aid, 3d.

A sanding-way (*via zabulo* [sic]) [*at Pulsack, in Phillack*]:
The heir(s) of Nicholas Polulsek, for a way [from] Polulsek to the sand (*que tendit Polulsek vers' zabul'*); 6d.

Trevalscos [*Trevaskis, in Gwinear*]:
Alan John, 1 ferling [*blank*]; 12d.;
the same Alan, 1 ferling [*blank*]; 12d.

William Mohun, for the multure of tenants outside Haile [?] (*pro multur' tenens' extra Haile*);[43] 1 *lb.* cummin or 4d.

Total [*of free tenants*], 116s. 1½d.

Welcomb' iuxta Hertlond [*Welcombe (parish), Devon*]:
The heir(s) of Robert Corune, the manor of Welcomb', by service etc., because he showed a charter to John Corke, to be distrained to show the charter (*distr' ad monstrand' cart'*); 1 clove gillyflower.

Conventionary tenants

Demesne [*at Connerton, at Gwithian churchtown*]:
The tenants hold the whole demesne and pay at 4 dates, [plus] heriot, farleu and common suit of court.[44]
John Rawe, 1 holding; 24s. 6d.
Robert Wodwer held (*tenuit*) 1 holding; 19s. 6d.
John Richard held (*tenuit*) 1 holding; 16s. 8½d.
Thomas Jack, 1 holding; 11s.
William Penros held (*tenuit*) 1 holding; 25s.
Stephen Kelliou, 1 holding; 20s.
John Clerk, 1 holding; 11s.
Joan Lowda, 1 holding; 8s. 4d.
Peter Nansise, 1 holding; 11s. 1d.
John Rawe, 1 holding; 19s. 8d.

Penfentenyow [*Penfentin, in Gwithian*]:
John Bossosowe, 1 holding; 33s. 4d.

---

[43] *tenens'* is presumably for *tenentium*; the sense of *extra Haile* is obscure, possibly 'away from [the estuary of the river] Hayle', or 'except [for a mill at] Hayle'. The town of Hayle is a nineteenth-century creation.

[44] The tenancies are expressed in the present tense, except for three.

MANOR OF CONNERTON

Nanscrasscyas [*sic; Negosias, alias Nantasier, in Gwithian*]:
Nicholas Gregour, 1 holding; 23s.

Talseghan [*Tolzethan, in Gwithian*]:
Henry Jenyn, 2 holdings; 24s.

Halglasen [*'Haleglasan' (lost), near to Tolzethan, in Gwithian*]:[45]
Michael Jenkyn; 2s. 8d.

Pennans Meur [*Pennance (Veor), in Gwithian*]:
Nicholas Jenyn, 1 holding; 20s.

Halenvelyn, Gargasen [*'Halenvelan' and 'Gargason' (both lost), in Gwithian*]:
William Jamys, 1 holding; 20s.

Pennans Vyen [*Pennance Vean, in Gwithian*]:
Henry Pennans, 1 holding; 13s. 4d.

Engew [*Angew, in Gwithian*]:
Nicholas Tomperkyn, 1 holding; 20s. 6d.
John Sandry, 1 holding; 7s. 6d.

Vppetoun [*Upton, in Gwithian*]:
Walter Symon, 1 holding; 18s.
John Clerk, 1 holding; 16s.
Hugh Thomas, 1 holding; 8s. [*illegible marginale, ... 7s.*]
Thomas Jamys, 1 holding; 25s.

Est'lo [*'Easter Low' (lost in the sand), in Gwithian*]:
John Cok, 1 holding; 22s.

Penpoll iuxta Lanant [*Penpoll, in Phillack*]:
John Frawen, 1 holding; 24s.
Roger Bloyhowe, 1 holding; 24s.

Engarrake [*Angarrack, in Phillack; entry added later*]:
Richard Pers'; 18s.

Trevascoys [*Trevaskis, in Gwinear*]:
John Jack, 1 holding; 10s.
William Edward, 1 holding; 10s.

Dryme [*Drym, in Crowan*]:
Roger Frances, 1 holding; 20s.

---

[45] In 1659 and 1717 the adjacent tenements of Tolzethan and Angew, together with *Haleglasan*, formed a single, merged, tenement.

John Pons, 1 holding; 20s.

Treffrynk [*Trink, in Lelant*]:
Peter Trevanyon, 1 holding; 15s.

Nans [*Nance, in Lelant*]:
William Nans, 1 holding; 13s.

Vynwyn [*Venwyn, in Lelant*]:
David Vynwyn, 1 holding; 18s. 8d.

Gorfos [*Vorvas, in Lelant*]:
John William, 1 holding; 10s.

Boskerrys Wolas [*Boskerris Woollas, in Lelant*]:
Thomas Roly, 1 holding; 13s. 4d.
Thomas Symon, 1 holding; 13s. 4d.

Treloighan [*Treloyan, in St Ives parish*]:
Michael Nicolas, 1 holding; 11s.

Fowhyer [*Vow, in St Ives parish*]:
Oliver Cadwodley and *Marina* his wife, 1 holding; 20s.; he used to pay 28[s.]

Polleow [*Poleo, in Crowan*]:
Nicholas Polkynhorn, 1 holding; 6s.

Enwethen [*Withen, in Lelant*]:
Richard Renowdyn, 1 parcel of land; 10s.

Porrupter [*'Barrepta' (lost), near Carbis, in Lelant*]:
John Tremeur, 1 cottage (*cotag'*); for all service and heriot, 4d.
Warinus Trevethow, 1 cottage; 4d.
Richard Nicolas, 1 cottage; 4d.
David Vynwyn, 1 cottage; 4d.
Henry Tom Gregor, 1 cottage; 4d.
Thomas Henry Trevethek, 1 cottage; 4d.
Roger Benet, 1 cottage; 4d.
Stephen Calmady, 1 cottage; 4d.
John Davy Hoskyn, 1 cottage; 4d.
Michael Nicolas, 1 cottage; 4d.

Total [*of conventionary tenants*], £33 19s. 9½d.
Total of free and conventionary tenants, £39 15s. 11d.

* * *

Medischoll

[*Mitchell, in St Enoder*]

Free tenants

John Godolhen, by right of his wife, 2 plots, formerly of William Scatera, and 1 plot, formerly of William [*error for* Walter?] Wynkele; common suit of court; 3s. 11½d.;
the same John, 1 plot, formerly of Thomas Treiagu by gift of William Berken' (*quam Thomas Treiagu ex dono Willelmi Berken'*); common suit of court; 3s. 6d.;
the same John, 1 plot with a *lawda* [*sic*] called Gon Enbayly, which (*quas*) the said Thomas had by gift of Joce Faober ['the smith']; common suit of court; 2s. 6d.;
the same John, 1 plot which he had by gift of John Sket; 12d.;
the same John, 1 plot which he had by gift of the same John; common suit of court; 7d.;
the same John, 1 plot, formerly of the said Thomas Treiagu which he had by gift of Thomas Burges; common suit of court; 9d.;
the same John, as above, 2 plots formerly of John Trenowith; 15d.;
the same John, as above, 2 plots which the said John Trenowith esquire [*sic, no verb*]; common suit of court; 18d.;
the same John, as above, the *landa* of Gonmargh [*Goamarth (field), in St Enoder*]; common suit of court; 6s., payable at Invention of the Cross 2s., Nativity of St John the Baptist 2s., and St Francis 2s.

Oto Gibbes, 1 house (*domus*) called Chienpoll; 2 suits of court; ½d.;
the same Oto, 3 plots and ¼ of the *landa* called Gonbayly; common suit of court; 8s. 8d.;
the same Oto, 1 plot, formerly of Maidow; common suit of court; 9d.[46]

John Tretherff, 1 plot which he had by gift of Agnes Skytt, and 1 acre English which he had by gift of Stephen H...uos, and 1 acre which he purchased (*perquisivit*) from William Gillot; common suit of court; 15d.;
the same John, 1 acre in the *landa* called Kergruggyer; without suit of court; 5d.;
the same John, 1 parcel formerly of Simon Fall', in Gonmargh [*Goamarth (field), in St Enoder*]; common suit of court; 18d.;
the same John, 1 plot formerly his father's, 1 plot opposite, 3 acres

---

[46] '9/5/ob.', interlined.

in the *landa* beside Fosbras, and ½ plot, which (*quas*) Gonnet' formerly held; 8 acres in the *landa* beside Kergruggier; and 1 acre English between the roads leading to St Michael's Mount and Truru (*inter vias que tendit* [sic] *versus montem Sci Michaelis et Truru*); suit as above; 2s. 7d.;

the same John, 1 plot formerly of Simon Fall', 4 acres English in the land (*terra*) called Sekerlegh, and ½ acre English formerly of Henry Longes; common suit of court; 2s. 2d.

Thomas Hellond, by right of his wife, 4 plots; common suit of court; 2s. 9½d.;

the same Thomas, as above, 2 acres English beside the land (*terra*) of Simon Fall; common suit of court; 6d.;

the same Thomas, as above, 1 plot formerly of Robert Ronsyn; common suit of court; 8d.;

the same Thomas, as above, the acre of St Francis (*acr' Sancti Frauncissi*); 4d; and to St Francis (*et Sancti Frauncissi* [sic]), 6d.[47]

William Carnsuyow, by right of his wife, 1 plot with its portion (*cum porcione sua*) in Gonenbaily, which John Mark formerly held; no suit of court; pays by hand of John Tretherff, 8s. 2d.

Henry Trevysa, 1 plot and 2 acres English in Gonmargh [*Goamarth (field), in St Enoder*]; 2 suits of court; 9d.

Robert Tann', 3 plots with their portion in Gonenbaily, viz. ¼ part there; common suit of court; pays, apart from (*ultra*) 21d. which the lord has released to him and given in exchange for 1 messuage and 1 acre in Medischoll which the said John had (*que dominus ei relaxavit et dedit in excambium pro uno mes' et una acra in Medischoll que predictus Johannes habuit*); used to pay 3s. 3d.; pays 18d.

John Tretherff, 1 plot formerly of Stephen Heuos; common suit of court; 6d.

Reginald Cary, 1 plot formerly of William Bond; common suit of court; 4d.

Nantelyowe [*Nantillio, in St Enoder*]:
Richard Nantelyow, ½ acre Cornish; common suit of court; 4s.

[*Total of free tenants, 58s. 5½d.?*][48]

---

[47] '4/9/ob.', interlined.
[48] The grand total and the conventionary rents imply a sum of 58s. 5½d. for the free rents, but those given above seem to total 57s. 11½d. instead.

Conventionary tenants

William Trehar, ½ the vill of Na...eliow [*Nantillio, in St Enoder*]; common suit of court; 8s.

Martin Rawlyn, 1 holding and 1 close called Parke nowith, reserving the lord's fair held there (*salv' nund' domini ibidem tent'*), and Gonhughell [*unidentified*], for term of 40 years; 18s. 4d.

Total of free and conventionary tenants, £4 4s. 9½d.

* * *

Enyscaven
[*Enniscaven, in St Dennis*]

Free tenants

Enyscaven [*Enniscaven, in St Dennis*]:
John Roche, ½ acre Cornish, in socage; common suit of court; 4s. 6d.
John Gau'gan, one-eighth acre Cornish, in socage; common suit of court; 13½d.

Mena [*Menawollas, in St Dennis*]:
The heir(s) of Archedeken',[49] ½ acre Cornish, in socage; common suit of court; 5¾d. and 1 pair of white gloves; and for tin fine, 1½d.

Trelowargh [*Trelavour, in St Dennis*]:
Peter Bevill, 1 ferling; 2 suits of court; 5¾d.

Menawartha [*Mennawartha, in St Dennis*]:
John Dauy Mena, 1½ ferlings; common suit of court; 9d.

Trelowargh [*Trelavour, in St Dennis*]:
Laurence Penkevell, John Pascow, William Pascow and Odo Michell; 2 suits of court; 3s.

Total [of free tenants], 10s. 5½d.[50]

Conventionary tenants

Nenys [*Ennis, in St Dennis*]:
William Michell Stevyn, 1 holding; common suit of court; 3s. 4d.

---

[49] Written over an erasure; the phrase appears again (presumably redundantly) between the names of Peter Bevill and John Dauy Mena.
[50] The amount written appears as 10s. 6½d.; but both the rents and the total for the manor show that 5½d. was intended.

Trelowargh [*Trelavour, in St Dennis*]:
William Richard, 3 holdings, for term of 60 years; 17s. 9d. [6d., *deleted*].
John Thomas, 1 holding, for term of 60 years; 11s.

Enyscaven [*Enniscaven, in St Dennis*]:
Thomas Michell, 1 holding, for term [*blank*]; 10s.
John Tomkyn, 1 holding, for term of 60 years; 10s.

Total [*of conventionary tenants*], 51s. 10d.[51]

Total of free and conventionary tenants, 62s. 3½d.

Enysmere [*Ennis (Veor), in St Dennis*]:
Michael Stephyn, in fee tail, and pays 2s. for all services, as seen by an indenture by seal of John Arundell knight, dated 12 November 7 Edward IV [1467]; Walter Gau'gan now holds, etc.

* * *

Penles Treviscan
[*Perlees, in St Breock, and Trevisker, in Padstow*]

Free tenants

Resker [*Roskear, in St Breock*]:
John Ber', 1 ferling, [*blank*]; [*blank*]

Wade [*Wadebridge, in St Breock*]:
The heir(s) of Richard Criff, in Wade; because in hand, [*blank*]

Trevansen [*Trevanson, in St Breock*]:
John Carew, 1½ ferlings; 17½d.

Bodelek [*Bodellick, in St Breock*]:
Nicholas Braban, 4 ferlings [*sic*]; 18d. [*added later*]

Tredenek [*Tredinnick, in St Issey*]:
Nicholas Trewyns, 7 selions, conventionarily (*in convens'*); 2s.

Trenoyow [*Treniow, in Padstow parish*]:
John Noell, 1 ferling; 2s.

Treneyren [*Trenearne, in Padstow parish*]:
John Trenayren, 3 ferlings; 22d.

Total [*of free tenants*], 8s. 9½d.

---

[51] This sum is based upon the original rent for William Richard (17s. 6d.).

Conventionary tenants

Penles [*Perlees, in St Breock*]:
Thomas Braben, ½ the vill; common suit of court; 40s.
John Slee, other ½ of the vill; 40s.

Trevansen [*Trevanson, in St Breock*]:
Richard Lovetop, 3 ferlings; 13s. 4d.

Nascaw [*Nanscow, in St Breock*]:
Richard Loury, ½ acre Cornish; 16s. 8d.

Treviscan [*Trevisker, in Padstow parish*]:
[*blank*], 1 acre Cornish; 26s. 8d.

Rskelian [*sic*] goff' [*Roscullion, in Little Petherick*]:[52]
William Harry, 1 acre Cornish [for term of 60 years, *added later*]; 26s. 8d.
John Ede, 1 acre Cornish; 26s. 8d.

Crukmeur [*Crugmeer, in Padstow parish*]:
Thomas Sherpe, 2 parts of a ferling; 3s. 4d.

Tresalen [*Tresallyn, in St Merryn, presumably*]:
John Tresalen, ½ acre Cornish; 10s.[53]

Wadebrigge [*Wadebridge, in St Breock*]:
John Leche, 1 cottage; 6s.

Total [*of conventionary tenants*], £10 9s. 4d.

Total *of free and conventionary tenants*, £10 18s. 1d.

Payment to the lord of Poweton for lands and tenements following, as seen by copy of an extent of the lord:[54]

Pelles, Trevanson, Reskere, Bodelek, Tregonowe [*Perlees, Trevanson, Roskear, Bodellick, and Tregunna* [?], *all in St Breock*]:[55]

---

[52] Name added later.
[53] 'Richard Borlas and Joan his wife, John Bischop [*blank*] and his wife have that land to themselves and the said John's heirs of body for ever, by gift of John Arundell knight,' added later.
[54] The great bishop's manor of Pawton, in St Breock. Some of the tenements listed in what follows are not otherwise known as tenements of Perlees manor. For a good extent of Pawton manor half a century later, in 1548, see Stoate, *Cornwall Manorial Rentals*, pp. 97–114.
[55] Tregunna is not elsewhere mentioned as a tenement of Perlees manor.

Jocelin de Penles, 2 acres Cornish arable, to mark and bound [?] (*ut patet* [?] *et metet*), worth ½d.;

the same Jocelin, 5 ferlings in Trevanson; ½ acre in Reskere, ½ acre in Bodelek, ½ acre in Tregonowe; pays 9s. 6d., 4 sheep (*oves*) and 3 feet of 1 sheep,[56] and for aid 2s., and does suit; 2 arable cliffs, to mark and bound [?] (*duas cleff' arabil' ut patebit et metet*), worth ½d.

Trevysken, Tredenek, Trevemed', Treneyren [*Trevisker, in Padstow parish; Tredinnick, in St Issey; Trevemedar, in St Eval; and Trenearne, in Padstow parish*]:

Roger de Trevysken, 3 acres Cornish there, 1 acre in Tredenek, ½ acre in Trevemed', 3 ferlings in Treneyren; 10s. 6d., 5 sheep and 1 foot, and for aid 6d. and 1 [?] arable cliff, to mark and bound [?] (*clyffe arabil' ut patebit et metet ut supra*), worth ½d.[57]

---

[56] For this method of reckoning rent in sheep (berbiage), again in Pawton manor, compare Stoate, *Cornwall Manorial Rentals*, pp. 97–114; also on Duchy manors: Hatcher, *Duchy of Cornwall*, pp. 68–69; *Caption of Seisin*, ed. Hull, p. 183.

[57] Two attached schedules give (1) a list of free and conventionary tenants of Penles manor (tenants' names only, no place-names), slightly different from the above; (2) a list of tenancies of *Nanscawe, Penles, Trevansen* and *Trevithcan* (the last similar to the list given for Roger de Trevysken, above).

RENTALS OF THE FOUR CHANTRY-ENDOWMENT MANORS, 15th–16th CENTURIES

(AR2/1338, parts)

Contents

Manor of Pengwedna, 1468–69 144
Manor of Prospidnick, 1468–69... 146
Manor of Pengwedna, 1509 147
Manor of Prospidnick, 1509 149
Manor of Bodbrane, 1515 150
Manor of Reperry, 1515 152
Manor of Reperry, mid-16th century ... 154

144

CHANTRY-ENDOWMENT MANORS, 15th–16th CENTURIES

Pengwenna
[*Pengwedna, in Breage*]

Extent made there by John Perkyn and Henry Roswyn, 8 Edward IV [1468–69].[1]

Free tenants

Pryske [*Priske, in Mullion*]:
Hugh Pryske, [*blank*] acres;[2] no suit of court; 32s. 3d.[3]

Bosfrawell [*Bosprowal, in Gwinear*]:
John Bosfrawell, [*blank*] acre; 2 suits of court; 1d.[4]

Caterbederan [*Cathebedron, in Gwinear*]:
Richard Caterbederan, [*blank*]; common suit of court; 6d.[5]

[Redolen (*Redallen, in Breage*):
Heir of Carmynowe, [*blank*] acres Cornish, in socage; [*blank*] suits of court; 6d.][6]

Kerthen [*Kerthen, in Crowan*]:
Robert Coulyng, [*blank*]; suit of court; 6s. 1d.[7]

Total of free tenants, 38s. 11d.[8]

---

[1] On rot. 4d.; another copy of this rental, with the same date, appears on rot. 18r., giving sometimes more information, sometimes less; significant variants from it appear in the notes. The second maker of the extent (who appears as 'Henry [*blank*]' on rot. 18r.) is probably the tenant Henry Boswyn, at Ruthdower; the first is the tenant at Pengwedna.
[2] 'William Priske, now John [*blank*]', rot. 18r.; 1 acre Cornish in c.1586 (AR2/1343).
[3] 'in addition to rent and suit of court which he pays to the lordship of Predannecke, on behalf of the lord (*in exoneracione domini*)', rot. 18r.
[4] 'Heir of Bosfrawell, 1 acre Cornish, in socage', and paying 1½d., rot. 18r.; paying 7d. in 1509 (below, p. 147), but 1d. again in later rentals (after 1516, rots 9r. and 15r.); 1½d. again in 1571 (below, p. 205).
[5] In rot. 18r. two tenants, John Resogan and the heir of Sentabyn, each hold 1 acre Cornish here, paying 6d. each, with common suit of court.
[6] This entry is lacking on rot. 4d., and supplied from rot. 18r.; rent not included in the total.
[7] '[*blank*] acres Cornish, by knight's service', rot. 18r. Written below this entry on rot. 4d. are the words 'Et hoc . . . Et . . . de Whalysbor...'.
[8] The total is left blank on rot. 18r. (actually 39s. 11½d. there).

Conventionary tenants

Pengwenna [*Pengwedna, in Breage*]:
John Perkyn; 10s.
John Bagh; 6s. 8d.
Richard Kalevan; 3s. 4d.
John Kelyan; 17s.

Caryorall [*Crawle, in Breage*]:
John Bosveell; 20s.

Tylygowe [*Treliggo, in Breage*]:
James Goeff; 8s.

Treneyr [*Trenear, in Breage*]:
Peter Jankyndauy; 13s. 4d.

Ruthwas [*sic; Ruthdower, in Breage*]:[9]
Henry Boswyn; 14s.
William Wenna; 5s.

'Persecutus C..., 3s.'[10]

Total of conventionary tenants, £4 17s. 4d.

Total receipt, without toll of tin, £6 19s. 3d.[11]

* * *

---

[9] Probably an error for *Ruthwar*, a spelling of Ruthdower at this period (e.g. in 1525–31, AR2/269–71); the scribe appears to have written in error a form of the name of Ruthvoes, in St Columb Major.

[10] The meaning of this phrase is unclear; the 3s. is not included in the total of conventionary tenants, but is needed to make the overall total stated.

[11] Toll of tin is not normally mentioned in the rentals; if it appears in manorial accounts it usually comes under 'perquisites of court' (as in the account for the neighbouring manor of Prospidnick in 1433–34, AR2/887, m. 2) or under other revenues, not under rents.

Pryspynnek
[Prospidnick, in Sithney]

Extent made by James Perowe [*probably* 1468–69].[12]

Free tenants[13]

Gurlyn [*Gurlyn, in St Erth*]:
William Gurlyn, [*blank*] acres, by knight's service; 2 suits of court; 20s.

Treflyan [*Trelean, in St Erth*]:
William Trewynard, [*blank*] acres, by knight's service; common suit of court; 12d.

Relegh [*Releath, in Crowan*]:
Richard Wydeslade, [*blank*] acres, in socage [?]; common suit of court; 2s.

Trewheferek [*Treworvack, in Constantine*]:
John Arundell Trerys, [*blank*] acres, by knight's service; common suit of court; 2s.

Pennarth [*Penare, in St Keverne*]:
Heir(s) of Sergeaux, [*blank*] acres Cornish, by knight's service; common suit of court; 2s.

Total [*of free tenants, blank*; 29s.]

Conventionary tenants

Pryspynnek Sore [*Prospidnick, in Sithney*]:
James Perowe, 1 holding; 19s.
Richard Jankyn, 1 holding; 18s.
Richard [?] J...an holds there; 15s. 4d.
John Ferly holds there, 1 holding; 6s. 10d. [7s. 2d. deleted].

Chyenha.. [*Chynhale, in Sithney*]:
John Tomaset holds there; 10s. 2d.

Penpras [*Penpraze, in Sithney*]:
Janyn Lastreynes holds there; 14s.

---

[12] On rot. 4r.; probably of the same date as the dated rental of Pengwedna on the dorse, in the same hand (above, p. 144).
[13] The free tenants are actually listed after the conventionary ones, but are given first here for consistency's sake.

Nanskyrwes [*Nanskerres' (lost), in Sithney, near Trevarno*]:[14]
John Dauy holds there; 10s. 8d.

Trevarnowe [*Trevarno, in Sithney*]:
Peter Jakperowe holds there; 18s. 2d.

Nansdreysek [*Nancetrisack, in Sithney*]:
Richard [?] Nansdreysek holds there; 8s.

Treweferek [*Treworvack, in Constantine*]:
Richard Michell holds there; 6s.

Total [*of conventionary tenants*], [*blank*; £6 6s. 2d.?]

* * *

Pengwenna
[*Pengwedna, in Breage*]

Rental made 1 December 1 Henry VIII [1509].[15]

Free tenants

Preske [*Priske, in Mullion*]:
William Preske, [*blank*]; 32s. 3d., and shall pay all rents on behalf of the lord (*exonerabit dominum de omnibus redditibus*), [*blank*].[16]

Penhale [*Penhale, in Breage*]:[17]
Heir(s) of Sergeaux, [*blank*]

Caterbedran [*Cathebedron, in Gwinear*]:
John Resogan; suit of court; 19d.

Bosfrawell [*Bosprowal, in Gwinear*]:
Heir(s) of Bosfrawell; 7d.[18]

Kyrthen [*Kerthen, in Crowan*]:
Heir(s) of Cowelyn; 5s.

---

[14] The location is shown by an entry in a court roll of 1521–22, where Thomas Nantrysak was accused of encroaching land at Trevarno hill and Nanskerres, bringing it into his own land at Nancetrisack (*accrochiavit certam terram apud collem de Trevarnowe et Nanskyrwys ad terram suam de Nantrysak*): AR2/253.
[15] On rot. 8r.
[16] See above, in 1468–69 (p. 144 n. 3).
[17] Presumably Penhale-an-Drea (near Pengwedna), rather than Penhale Jakes (near Rinsey).
[18] See above, in 1468–69 (p. 144 n. 4).

Redalen [*Redallen, in Breage*]:
Heir(s) of Nanfan; [*blank*].

Total of free tenants, [*blank*].

Conventionary tenants

Pengwenna [*Pengwedna, in Breage*]:
John Thomas; 18s. 6d.[19]
John Prior; 18s. 6d.

Carhyhoghall [*Crawle, in Breage*]:
John Pascowe; 20s.

Rethwar [*Ruthdower, in Breage*]:
John Perin [?]; 19s.

Trenere [*Trenear, in Breage*]:
William Thomas; 13s. 4d.

Telegaw [*Treliggo, in Breage*]:
Thomas Hughnans; 8s.

Total [*of conventionary tenants, blank;* £4 17s. 4d.?]
Rents paid:
to the heir of Godolhan [*Godolphin, in Breage*], 1d. for the leat (*bed'*) of a mill;
to the heir of Spernan [*Spernon, in Breage*], 8d. for the leat (*bed'*) of a mill;
to the heir of Pomery, for high rent of the manor of Pengwenna, 10½d.[20]

[*Total, of free and conventionary tenants?*], £6 7s. 10½d.

* * *

---

[19] In the rental on rot. 15r., which is datable to after 1516, this tenancy appears as follows: John Thomas, Mabel his wife, and Thomas John, William John, Ralph John and Alice John their children, by copy made for them successively (*per copiam eis factam successive*), dated Sunday before St Luke, 19 Henry VII [15 October 1503], for term of 99 years; 18s. 6d.

[20] A fuller list of payments made by the manor in 1433-34, including some not mentioned here and evidently lapsed, gives payments of 11½d. to the lord of *Tregony* (i.e. to Tregony Pomeroy) for *Pengwenna*; 10d. to the lord of *Spernen* for the water-course of *Reddour* (i.e. Ruthdower) mill; and 1d. to the lord of *Godolghan* for its mill-leat (*bedum*) (account roll, AR2/887, m. 2).

Manor of Perispynneck
[Prospidnick, in Sithney]

Rental made there 1 December 1 Henry VIII [1509].[21]

[Free tenants]

Pennarth [*Penare, in St Keverne*]:
Heir of the earl of Oxford; 3s. 1d.

Releigh [*Releath, in Crowan*]:
Heir of Vinslate;[22] 3s. 8d.

Trevillian in St Erth [*Trelean, in St Erth*]:[23]
Heir of William Trewynnerd,[24] by knight's service; 4s. 6d.

Gurlyn [*Gurlyn, in St Erth*]:
Heir of Gurlyn, 1 knight's fee; 20s. 6d.

Nansdryseck [*Nancetrisack, in Sithney*]:
Heir of Antron, the mill leat (*beda molend'*); 4d.

Total of free tenants, [*blank*; 32s. 1d.?]

Customary tenants

Pryspyneck [*Prospidnick, in Sithney*]:
Stephen Richard; 19s.
Pears Richard;[25] 18s.
John William; 7s.
John Hick; 15s. 4d.

Penprase [*Penpraze, in Sithney*]:
Genyn Penprase; 24s.[26]

Nanskerwis ['*Nanskerres*' (lost), *in Sithney*]:
Henry Nanskerwis; 10s. 8d.

Trevenow [*sic; Trevarno, in Sithney*]:
Richard Trevernow; 18s. 2d.

---

[21] On rot. 19r.–d.; another copy of this rental, also dated 1509, appears at rot. 10r., and significant variants from that copy are given in the notes; the name of the manor appears there as *Pryspennek*.
[22] *Wynslate*, rot. 10r. (i.e. Winslade).
[23] *Trelyan*, rot. 10r.
[24] William Trewennard [not his heir], rot. 10r.
[25] *Perys* Richard, rot. 10r.
[26] A further entry here, 'Treweffrak tenet ibidem, 12s.', rot. 10r.

Nansdryseck [*Nancetrisack, in Sithney*]:
Thomas Nansdryseck; 8s.

Helston Borowgh [*Helston town*]:[27]
[*blank*], 1 tenement; 6s. 8d.
[*blank*], 1 tenement and 1 close; 8s. 8d.

Blowing howse [*at Nancetrisack, in Sithney*]:[28]
[*blank*], 1 blowing-mill (*molend' sufflatic'*); 3s. 4d.

    Total of customary tenants, [*blank*; £6 18s. 10d.?]
    Total rent of the manor, [*blank*; £8 10s. 11d.?]

* * *

[*Bodbrane, in Duloe*]
Rental made 20 September 7 Henry [VIII] [1515].[29]

Free tenants[30]

The Fooss [*Voss, in Duloe*]:
John Champlett; common suit of court; 2s. 2d.

Lamelyn [*Lamellion, in Liskeard*]:
John Copelston; 2 suits of court; 13d.

Gonmeleck [*Gormellick, in Liskeard*]:
John Lawharen; 2 suits of court; 2s. 2d.
John Pyper; 2 suits of court; 13d.
Heir(s) of Robert Daw; 2 suits of court; 13d.
Heir of Robert John; 2 suits of court; 14d.

Algallys Wallys iuxta Leskerd [*'Argalls Walls alias Grove Park' (lost), in Liskeard parish*]:[31]
John Kymppe; 3s. 6d.

[27] These last three entries, and the totals, are omitted on rot. 10r.
[28] The blowing-house is specified as being at Nancetrisak, at the same rent, in an undated rental on rot. 11d.
[29] On rot. 13r.; a fair copy of this rental, undated and now less legible, appears at rot. 6r.; it contains no significant variants.
[30] The free tenants actually appear after the conventionaries; but are here given first for consistency's sake.
[31] The name appears here, corruptly, as *Algall ys Wallys le iuxta Leskerd*; better as *Algareswall'* in 1461-62 (rot. 5, estreat roll). The identification is provided by a later rental, of 1739 (AR2/1356); the tenement must have been near the site of the present Grove Park Terrace, near the railway station.

['Great Place' (lost), in Liskeard town]:[32]
Reginald ('Renold') Bere; 2s. 6d.
Heir of Bowcom; 1 *lb.* pepper.

Total of free tenants, 14s. 9d.,
plus 1 *lb.* pepper.

[*Conventionary tenants*]

Bodbrane [*Bodbrane, in Duloe*]:
Meliora Pytt; 25s., plus 13d. for days' work (*pro vorke syluer*).
John Pytt; 24s., plus 13d.[33]

Nether Stockes [*Lower Stock, now Stock's Cottage, in Duloe*]:
William Hockyn; 20s., plus 13d.
John Renold; 12s. 6d., plus 4d.

Bonoke [*Benoak, in Duloe*]:
Thomas Jagow; 14s., plus 9d.[34]
Richard Carne; 14s. 6d., plus 9d.
John Barett; 14s. 6d., plus 9d.[35]
Robert Strett; 7s., plus 6d.

The Ouer Stokes [*Higher Stock, in Duloe*]:
William Hockyn; 13s. 4d., plus 9d.

Lyttyl Penbegyll [*Penbugle, in Duloe*]:
Meliora Pytt; 6s. 8d., plus 6d.

Myllond [*'Millparke' (lost), in Duloe*]:
The same, for days' work (*pro vorke syluer*), 8d.[36]

Total of conventionary tenants, £7 11s. 6d.;[37]
plus, for days' work (*opera*), 8s. 3d.

Total [*of free and conventionary tenants, blank;* £8 14s. 6d.]

* * *

---

[32] The later name of this tenement is given by the same rental of 1739; the tenement included an impressive courtyard building, at the bottom of the present Baytree Hill.
[33] John Pytt was reeve of the manor in 1520–21 (account roll, AR2/950).
[34] Thomas Jagowe was dead by 9 May 1533 (court roll, AR2/327).
[35] John Baret was reeve of the manor in 1524–25 (court roll, AR2/322).
[36] *Sic*, no rent stated; the modern form *Millparke* (in Duloe) appears in the 1659 and 1717 surveys. The two last entries are lacking on rot. 6r.
[37] The total seems to imply a rent of 9s. 4d. for *Millparke*.

Repery
[Reperry, in Lanivet]

[Rental; no date, but presumably 1515.][38]

Free tenants

Resgerans [*Roserrans, in St Columb Major*]:
John Moyle; 12*d*.

Pennans [*Pennance, in St Stephen in Brannel*]:
John Rosogan; 10*s*. 11*d*.

Trelyu' [*Treliver, in St Wenn*]:
John Trelyu'; 1*s*. 1*d*.

Tregomer [*Tregamere, in St Columb Major*]:
David Treg...rrek; 4*d*.

[*Treliver, in St Wenn*]:
Heir of Anger, John Dunsy; 20*d*.

Bodman Whytles [*Whitley, in Bodmin parish*]:
John Sadler; 3*s*. 9*d*.

Synt Nyclys Parke [*St Nicholas, in Bodmin parish*]:
John Tryplett; 7*d*.

Bodman [*tenements in Bodmin town and parish*]:[39]

[*'Quarry Parke', now Copshorn, in Bodmin parish*]:[40]
John Kympton, 1 close called Quarre Parke; 5½*d*. [?]

[*'Borehill Close' (lost), in Bodmin parish*]:
Martin Newalle, 1 close called Bore Hyll Parke; 5½*d*. [?]

[*Fore Street, in Bodmin town*]:
Benedict Burnarde, 1 house; 1*d*.
Joan Herr'; 21*d*.
John Grynsy; 16*d*.

---

[38] Also on rot. 6r.; presumably of the same date as Bodbrane, above.

[39] This heading serves for the remainder of the free tenements; Fore Street and Bodiniel are identified from the 1571 rental, AR2/1341 (below, p. 200).

[40] The identification is provided by the surveys of 1659 (*Quary Parke alias Cobshorne*) and 1717.

[*Bodiniel, in Bodmin parish*]:
John Samoll; 2½d.
John Phelypp; 2½d.
Heir of Glyn of Morwall [*Morval (parish)*], 1 close; 4d.

Boskere [*Boskear, in Bodmin parish*]:
John Bere; 6d.

[*added later*]
Canalegy [*Cannalidgey, in St Issey*]:
Heir of Falmouth, now Nanscawen, 1 acre Cornish; common suit of court; 3s.

[*Total of free tenants, 27s. 8d.*]

[*Conventionary tenants*]

...pery [*Reperry, in Lanivet*]:
John Edwarde; 20s.[41]
John Hoskyn; 24s.
Petrock (*Petrocus*) Jenkyn; 10s.[42]
Thomas Jenkyn; 10s.

[*Tredenham, in Lanivet*]:[43]
Peter Marchant; 15s.

Trenans [*Trenance (Wolas), in Withiel*]:
John Herry; 20s.

Canalyse [*Cannalidgey, in St Issey*]:
John Thomas; 14s.
John Seaby; 7s.
Benedict Trehare; 8s.[44]

[*Total of conventionary tenants, £6 8s.*]

[*Total of free and conventionary tenants, £7 15s. 8d.*]

* * *

---

[41] John Edward was reeve of the manor in 1521–22 (court roll, AR2/748).
[42] Petrock Jenkin was reeve of the manor at various dates between 1518–19 and 1533–34 (account roll, AR2/948; court rolls, AR2/281, 285 and 287).
[43] This tenement is not named, and is grouped with the preceding ones; but the 1571 rental (below, p. 201) provides the identification.
[44] A tenement in *Borelane*, in Bodmin town, might be expected here, as in 1571 (below, p. 201); but Trehare's entry is not separated from the other two, and the rent of the *Borelane* tenement in 1571 (20d.) does not agree with any of those given here.

Respere
[Reperry, in Lanivet]

[Rental of free tenants only, no date; c.1550–65?][45]

[*Free tenants*]

Resgarens vel Reserans [*Roserrans, in St Columb Major*]:
Heir of Moyle, now John Moyle; 12*d*.

Pennans [*Pennance, in St Stephen in Brannel*]:
Heir of Resogan, now John Bevyll esquire, 1 acre, by knight's service; 9*s*. 10*d*. [?][46]

Trelyu' [*Treliver, in St Wenn*]:
Heir of Trelyu', now James Trelyu', 1 acre, by knight's service; 12*d*.

Tregem' [*Tregamere, in St Columb Major*]:
Heir(s) of Tregareke and Boscawan; 4*d*.

Trelyu' [*Treliver, in St Wenn*]:
Heir(s) of Anger, now John Dengy, 1 acre, by knight's service; 6*d*.

Canalysy [*Cannalidgey, in St Issey*]:
Heir(s) of Falmouth, now William Kendall, 1 acre, by knight's service; 3*s*.

Bodman Whytles [*Whitley, in Bodmin parish*]:[47]
Heir of Sadler, now John Harry; 3*s*. 9*d*.

[*St Nicholas, in Bodmin parish*]:
Heir of Trepylet, now Nicholas Oppy; 7*d*.

[*Bodmin town*]:
Heir of Kempton, now John Pasco [?]; 5½*d*.
Heir of Newall, now [*blank; no rent given; 5½d.?*].

[*Fore Street, in Bodmin town*]:
Heir of Harry, now Robert Sturgion; 20*d*.

---

[45] On rot. 1r. The list of tenants shows that this rental is later in date than that on rot. 6r., above (1515?); the names are mostly the same as those given in 1571 (below, pp. 199–201), but one or two appear to be earlier.

[46] Compare the earlier rental (above), and that of 1571 (below).

[47] *Bodman* here serves as a heading for the remainder of the free tenants; the identifications are supplied from the 1571 rental (AR2/1341).

Heir of Grynsy, now Oto (*Ot'*) Treluddar; 16*d*.

[*Bodiniel, in Bodmin parish*]:
Heir of Samell, now [*blank*] Hewet; 2½*d*.
Heir of Phelyp, now William Capper; 2½*d*.
Heir of Glyn, now Peter Northaye; 4*d*.[48]

[*Boskear, in Bodmin parish*]:
Heir of Checker, now William Bauden; 7*d*.

[*Fore Street, in Bodmin town*]:
Heir of Burnard, now [*blank*] Barret; 1*d*.

[*Total of free tenants, 26s. 4d.?*]

---

[48] '[*blank*] Norrys', deleted; Peter Northaye appears here again in 1571.

TWO MANORS OF THE EARL OF OXFORD, 1549
(AR2/1333)

Contents

Manor of Roseworthy 157
Manor of Bejowan 161

TWO MANORS OF THE EARL OF OXFORD, 1549

Roseworye
[Roseworthy, in Gwinear]

Rental renewed at a court held there, Thursday after the Annunciation, 3 Edward VI [28 March 1549].

Free tenants

Roose Vydneye Vyan [*Little Rosevidney, in Ludgvan*]:
Marquess of Dorsett, 1 acre Cornish, by knight's service, in Roose Vydneye Vyan; 8*d*., plus 12*d*. for suit of court.

Nansdiron [*Nanterrow, in Gwithian*]:
Sir John Arundell of Lanhern knight, 1 acre Cornish, by knight's service, in Nansdiron; 1 pair of gilt spurs or 2*s*. 6*d*., plus 12*d*. for suit of court.

Caterbedron [*Cathebedron, in Gwinear; also Nancemellin, in Gwithian* (?), *and Bosprowal, in Gwinear*]:
The same, 2 [?] acres 1 ferling ('farthing') Cornish in Nansmelyng,[1] Bosse Frawell and Caterbedron; 6*d*.

Trevabon [and?] Park & Gere [*Trevabyn and Gears* [?], *both in St Hilary*]:[2]
Sir John Arundell Treryse knight, ½ acre Cornish, by knight's service, in Trevabon [and?] Park & Gere; 15*d*.

Trewrasowe [*Treassowe, in Ludgvan*]:
Thomas Arundell Tallfern esq., ½ acre Cornish, by knight's service, in Trewrasowe; 2*s*., plus 12*d*. for suit of court.

---

[1] The name appears rather as *Nanfinelyng*, by copying error.

[2] The rental of c.1586 describes these as in 'Legvan alias Legevan parish', but that must be an error, at least in the case of Trevabyn; unlocated in the 1659 rental, and absent in 1717. In 1659 the manor paid a high rent of 15*d*. to the lord of *Trithwall* (Truthwall, in Ludgvan) for *Trevabin Parke and Geare*. It is unclear how to divide the names: are they *Trevabyn Park* (not otherwise known) and *Gear*, or (more likely) *Trevabyn* and *Park an Gear* (not otherwise known)? Gears is adjacent to Trevabyn; compare *Trevavon* and *Gayr*, together in an undated deed (*Catalogue of Ancient Deeds*, IV, A.9967).

Stret, Penpons and Resongros [*Start, Pedon Pons (near St Erth Bridge) and Rose-an-Grouse, all in St Erth*]:
John Reskemer esq., 1 acre Cornish in Stret,[3] Penpons and Resongros; 2s.

Bossevargham, Trewrasoo and Chiwen [*Boswarthan, in Madron* [?], *and Treassowe and 'Chywoone' (lost), both in Ludgvan*]:[4]
Joan Plumyn lately wife of John Velle, 1 acre Cornish, by knight's service, in Bossevarghame, Trewrasoo and Chiwen; 6s. 8d.

Trevrasoo [*Treassowe, in Ludgvan*]:
The same Joan, 1 ferling ('farthing') Cornish, by knight's service, in Trevrasoo (parish of Lugean); 16d., plus 12d. for suit.
Richard Jenkeyn, ½ acre Cornish, in socage, at Trewrasoo; 20d., plus 12d. for suit of court.

Trewanton [*Trengwainton, in Madron*]:
William Cowlyn, heir of John Teffreye [sic], 5½ acres Cornish, by knight's service, in Trenquenton; 1d.

Caterbedron [*Cathebedron, in Gwinear*]:
John Rosogon esq., ¼ acre Cornish, by knight's service, in Caterbedron; 6d., plus 12d. for suit of court.

Panhall Warthaye [*Penhale, in Gwinear*]:
Margery Treverth widow, 1 acre Cornish, by knight's service, in Penhalewartha; 6s., plus 12d. for suit of court.

Cosewynsowsen [*Coswinsawsin, in Gwinear*]:
Thomas Spernam [sic], 1 acre Cornish, by knight's service, in Cosewynsowsen; 8s.

Ponse Ferreis [*Ponsferrance, in Gwinear*]:
Robert Boes, heir of William Chicoes, 1 ferling ('farthing') Cornish, by knight's service, in Pense Ferreis; 2s., plus 12d. for suit of court.

Tallgolow [*Tolgullow, in Gwennap*]:
William Trewynnard esq., [blank], by knight's service, with 2 suits of court, in Tallgolowe (parish of Gwynnoppe); 3d., plus 6d. for

---

[3] Perhaps an error for *Stert*: the place is called *Sturt* in 1333 (*Catalogue of Ancient Deeds*, IV, A.10342), but note *Streat alias Steart* in the surveys of 1659 and 1717. The name is Old English *steort*, 'tail of land'.

[4] *Busworran, Trerasow* and *Chywoone*, in *Ludgan* parish (1717); but no name conforming to *Bossevargham* or *Busworran* is known there.

suit of court.

> *Total of free tenants*, 43s. 11d.,
> including 8s. 6d. in fines for suit of court.

Tenants by copy, indenture and at will

Penhalle [*Penhale, in Gwinear*]:
Sir William Godolphan knight, senior, and Sir William Godolphan knight, junior, 1 enclosure ('encloser') at Penhale Wolas; 46s. 8d., plus suit of court and heriot.
John Hoosekyn, Mary his wife and John their son, 1 tenement in Panhale; 16s., plus suit of court and heriot.
Richard Humfraye, by right of Beatrice his wife, and John Morveth her son, 1 tenement in Penhale; 18s. 6d., plus suit of court and heriot.

Roseworye [*Roseworthy, in Gwinear*]:
David John and John son of John Ingowe, 1 tenement in Rosworye; 34s., plus suit of court and heriot.
John Rawe Cosewyn, 1 tenement with various pieces of land, estimated 50 acres; 26s. 10d., plus suit of court and heriot.
John Trehan, 1 tenement; 23s. 9d., plus suit of court and heriot.
Alan John, Thomas John his son and Nicola wife of Alan, 1 tenement; 17s. 9d., plus suit of court and heriot.

Cosewynsowson [*Coswinsawsin, in Gwinear*]:
Joan Baron widow and Joan her daughter, 1 tenement in Cosewynsowson; 23s. 4d.
James John, 1 tenement with various pieces of land, pasture and meadow, estimated 24 acres; 16s., plus suit of court and heriot.

Carnhell [*Carnhell, in Gwinear*]:
John Snoden, Joan his wife and [*blank*], 1 tenement with various pieces of land, pasture and meadow, estimated 38 acres; 26s., plus suit of court and heriot.

Revyar [*Riviere, in Phillack*]:
Geoffrey Browne and James his son, 1 tenement with various pieces of pasture, land and marsh, estimated 40 acres, in Revyar (parish of Phelik); 56s., plus suit of court and heriot.

Pengelly [*Pengelly, in Crowan*]:
Pascoe Joyce, Ralph Thomas and Mary Thomas, 1 tenement, with various pieces of land, pasture and meadow, estimated 33 acres,

with 22½d. paid to the manor of Bennerton [*Binnerton, in Crowan*]; 9s., plus suit of court and heriot.

Carnhell [*Carnhell, in Gwinear*]:
Richard Crane, and William Crane and Thomas Crane his sons, 1 tenement with various pieces of land, pasture and meadow, estimated 29 acres; 26s., plus suit of court and heriot.

Rosewory Myll [*Roseworthy Mill, in Gwinear*]:
Elizabeth Vyan widow and Matilda her daughter, wife of Richard Crane above, 1 tenement with a water mill called Rosewory Myll, next to Roseworye, and 1 house called a blowing house; 53s. 4d., plus suit of court and heriot.

Roseworye Stampen Mell:
James William, 1 mill called a stamping mill in Roseworye; 6s.

Roseworye More [*'Hallgoose Moore' (lost), in Gwinear*]:
Martin Baowchampe, deputy of the bailiff, 1 moor called Hallgose More, in Roseworye; 4s.

Total of tenants by copy, indenture and at will, £20 3s. 2d.

Total of all tenants, £22 7s. 1d.

Rents resolute:
To the manor of Bynnerton [*Binnerton, in Crowan*] for 1 tenement held by Pascoe Joyce [*i.e. at Pengelly*], 22½d.

Remains clear: £22 5s. 6d. [*sic*], including 8s. 6d. in fines for suit of court.
Remains in rents and farm: £21 16s. 9d. [*sic*]

[*Nanseglos, near Madron churchtown*]:
Memorandum of 2s. yearly rent paid from certain lands 'sumtyme Nanseglos', now in the king's hands because of the attainder of Nanseglos; thus to be inquired whether Nanseglos was attainted for treason or felony.

Memorandum of 15d. rent from lands lately held by Hugh Osberne: it is unknown where they are; to be inquired.

* * *

Boosywen
[Bejowan, in St Columb Minor]

Rental dated Wednesday 3rd April, 3 Edward VI [1549].

Free tenements

Kestell [*Kestle, in St Columb Minor*]:
Sir John Arundell of Lanherne knight, one-third acre Cornish in Kestell, by knight's service; 4s.

Tallkarnye [*Tolcarne Merock, in St Mawgan in Pyder*]:
The same, one-third acre Cornish in Tallkarne (parish of Saynt Mogane), in socage; 9s., plus 12d. for suit of court.

Treloye [*Treloy, in St Columb Minor*]:
The same, 1 acre Cornish in Treloye, in socage; 12d.

Gavrygan [*Gaverigan, in St Columb Major*]:
John Gavrigan, 1 acre Cornish in Gavrigan, in socage; 4s., plus 12d. for suit of court.

Rutfoose [*Ruthvoes, in St Columb Major*]:
Laurence Hendrye, 3 acres Cornish in Rutfoose, in socage; 1d., plus 12d. for suit of court.

Treverran, Treverryn, Treverren [*Trevarren, in St Columb Major*]:
Henry Rowse, 1 acre Cornish in Trerren [*sic*], in socage; 4s.
John Trewolla, by right of Alice his wife, 1 acre Cornish in Treverren, in socage; 12s., plus 12d. for suit of court.
John of Byslond [*sic*], ½ acre Cornish in Treverren, in socage, now occupied by John Copyethorn; 3s. 7d., plus 12d. for suit of court.
John Hopkyn, heir of John Hopkyn, lately of Robert Vdan, [*blank*] in Treverren, [*blank*]; 2s. 4d., plus 12d. for suit of court.
Richard Mylhenek, 1 ferling ('ferthinge') in Treverren, [*tenure blank*]; 16d.

Hendra [*Hendra, formerly 'Hendra Mullier', in Colan*]:
The same Richard, 1 acre Cornish in Hyndramytler (parish of Saynt Colane), [*tenure blank*], now held by John Pynnowe; 20d.

Treverren [*Trevarren, in St Columb Major*]:
Samson Trewloghan, [*blank*] in Treverren, [*tenure blank*]; 4d.

Kyllyworge [*Killaworgey, in St Columb Major*]:
Richard Opye, ½ acre in Kyllyworge, in socage, 'late John

Serloses', with 4s. 3d. paid to the lord of Hastinges; 7s.

Henry Rowse, 1½ acres Cornish in Kyllyworge, in socage; 4s.

Carveior [*'Cavears' (lost), in Colan*]:
The tenants of 1 acre Cornish, in Carveior (parish of Saynt Colane), lately belonging to a chantry called 'Jesus Chawntrye' in the parish of Saynt Colane, in socage; 18d., plus 12d. for suit of court.

Bossoughan [*Bosoughan, in Colan*]:
Richard Craynsewe esq., heir of Nywlyn, [blank] in Bossoughan, now in the tenure of Thomas Marvell, in socage; 6d., plus suit of court [sic].

Tolkaryn [*Polgreen, in Newlyn East, rather than Tolcarne, in St Columb Minor (?)*]:[5]
Alexander Wollacumme esq., heir of 'Mychell Stowe',[6] 1 acre Cornish in Tolkaryn, in socage; 5s., plus 13d. for suit of court.

Towyn [*Towan, in St Columb Minor*]:
Francis Bluett esq. and Ralph ('Rauffe') Vyvyan,[7] by right of their wives the heirs of Richard Colan, 1 acre Cornish in Towyn, in socage; 8d., plus 13d. for suit of court.

Porteveer [*Porth Veor, in St Columb Minor*]:
The same Francis and Ralph, by right of their wives, certain parcels of land, estimated 9 acres, in Porthveer, in socage; 8s.

---

[5] Identified as Tolcarne in St Columb Minor, with the same tenant, acreage and rent, in the rental of c.1586 (AR2/1343); but in the 1659 rental it is called '(*Polgreen* alias) *Tolcarne Wollacombe*, in *Nulen* parish' (the words '*Polgreen* alias' added later), and in the 1717 survey this tenement appears as *Polgreen* (in Newlyn parish), held by Roger Woollacombe, esq., at the same rent. Compare the relief paid to the manor upon the death of Thomas Wolecumb, for his tenement at 'Polgreen', in 1510–11 (account roll of Bejowan, AR2/847). There is no Tolcarne in Newlyn East, nor any Polgreen in St Columb Minor; perhaps the adjacency of Polgreen and Tolcarne Merock (both in St Mawgan in Pyder) assisted the confusion (see below, *Tollkarn Morak*).

[6] i.e. of Michaelstow (family); compare the heir of Mark Mighelstowe, holding Polgreen (in Newlyn East) as a free tenement of Treloy manor, in the 1460 rental (above, p. 27).

[7] *Sic*, but presumably an error for Ralph Dewen; compare 'Richard' Dywan at Trebelzue (below, p. 164 and n.); and Ralph Dewen at Towan in the 1575 survey (below, p. 208).

MANOR OF BEJOWAN

Towyn [*Towan, in St Columb Minor*]:
John Cowlyn, ½ acre Cornish in Towyn, now in the tenure of Robert Trevevik [*sic*], in socage; 6*d*.
Robert Trygenfelde otherwise Trygonnold, ½ acre Cornish in Towyn, lately of Michael Trygestaye, in socage; 8*d*., plus 12*d*. for suit of court.

Portveer [*Porth Veor, in St Columb Minor*]:
Sir John Arundell of Lanhern knight, various parcels of land in Portveer, in socage; 16*d*., plus suit of court.

Hyndrover [*Hendra Veor, in St Columb Minor*]:
Florence Arundell Tallverne widow, [*blank*] in Hyndrover; 16*d*., plus suit of court.

Traveglos, Treveglus [*Treviglas, in St Columb Minor*]:
Sir John Arundell of Lanherne knight, various lands in Trevegles, in socage; 16*d*., plus 3*d*. for 1 sheep, and suit of court.
Richard Chapell, heir of Homer, [*blank*] in Treveglus, in socage, now in the tenure of Richard Chapell [*sic*]; 16*d*., plus 3*d*. for 1 sheep and 13*d*. for suit of court.
John Pollgrene, parcels of land amounting to one-third acre Cornish, in socage, in Treveglus; 16*d*., plus 3*d*. for 1 sheep and 13*d*. for suit of court.

Tollkarn Morak [*Tolcarne Merock, in St Mawgan in Pyder*]:
John Norton, messuages and tenements in Tollkarn Morak next Pollgrene (parish of Saynt Maugane), granted by John Veer esq. to Henry Norton and his heirs of body, by deed dated 10 October 15 Edward IV [1475]; 23*s*., at 3 dates (Easter, St John the Baptist and Christmas), suit of court twice yearly, re-entry clause, and heriot.

Trebervethe, Treberveth [*Trebarva, in St Columb Minor*]:
Henry Dottysson, by right of Christine his wife, lately the wife of Erysye, daughter and heir of Sir Humphrey Arundell knight, various lands and tenements, *viz.* [*blank*], in socage, in Treverveth; 2*s*. 6*d*., plus 13*d*. for suit of court.
The same Henry Dottyson, ½ acre called Gobeacre in Treverveth Treylowlane; 9*d*.
John Kylygryce [*sic*], 1 acre Cornish in Treverveth, in socage, now in the tenure of Richard Robert; 2*s*., plus 13*d*. for suit of court.
The same, ¼ acre called Gobyacre, in Trevertheth Treylowlane; 4½*d*.

John Holles and William Ryskemer, by right of their wives, ¼ acre called Gobyacre, in Treverveth; 4½d.

Treveglus [*Treviglas, in St Columb Minor*]:
Richard Cok, heir of John Hoskyn, 1 acre Cornish in Treveglus, in socage; 9d., plus suit of court.

Trevelsywe [*Trebelzue, in St Columb Minor*]:
Francis Blewett esq. and Richard Dywan,[8] by right of their wives the heirs of Richard Colan, various lands, *viz.* [*blank*], in Trevelsywe, in socage; 10s., plus suit of court. ['Sed ... ad maner' ... Carnanton' [?], *added*.]

Trethrysak [*Treisaac, in St Columb Minor*]:
Martin Trewynnard, by right of his wife, lately wife of Chenallce, 1 acre Cornish, in socage, in Trethrysak, now in the tenure of John Treygoose; 1d., plus suit of court.

Boessywen [*Bejowan, in St Columb Minor*]:
John Cheverton otherwise Boessywen, lands and tenements in the village of Boessywen (parish of Saynt Columb the Lower), granted by John Veer esq., son and heir of Robert Vere knight, to John Trewarton, otherwise to William and Mabel his wife, and their heirs of body, by deed dated All Saints, [*blank*] Edward IV; 10s., at 2 dates, with 2 suits of court, 6s. 8d. relief, and re-entry clause.

[*Total of free tenants*, £6 4s. 10d., plus 14s. 6d. fines for suit of court?]

Tenants by copy of court roll and at will

Kestell [*Kestle, in St Columb Minor*]:
John Henry Carthu, Margery his wife, and John their son, 1 tenement in Kestell, by copy of court roll for term of their lives; 13s. 6d., plus suit of court and heriot.
John Coseworthe, 1 tenement in Kestell, lately of John Rycharde, by copy of court roll for term of his life; 13s. 6d., plus suit of court and heriot.

---

[8] Presumably an error for Ralph Dywan: compare Towan, above (p. 162 and n.). In the rental of c.1586 both Towan and Trebelzue are said to have been held by Francis Bluett and Ralph Dewen (or Dewyn), by right of their wives (AR2/1343).

Trevalsywe [*Trebelzue, in St Columb Minor*]:
John Roberd, and Richard John and Henry John his sons, 1 tenement in Trevelsywe, by copy of court roll for term of their lives; 22s. 2d., plus suit of court and heriot.
Robert Carthewe and John his son, 1 tenement in Trevelsywe, by copy of court roll for term of their lives; 22s. 2d., plus suit of court and heriot.
Thomas Davyd, by right of Elizabeth his wife, 1 tenement in Trevelsywe, by copy of court roll for term of her life; 22s. 3d., plus suit of court and heriot.

Porver [*Porth Veor, in St Columb Minor*]:
James Roberd and Joan his wife, 1 tenement in Purver, by copy of court roll for term of their lives, with 15s. 7d. paid to the manor of Ryall [*Rialton, in St Columb Minor*] for the village of Purver; 28s. 4d., plus suit of court and heriot.
Joan Olde, lately wife of Richard Olde, and Peter his son, 1 tenement in Purver, by copy of court roll for term of their lives; 14s. 2d., plus suit of court and heriot.
Robert Rychard, Henry Rychard, and Alice daughter of Robert, 1 tenement in Purver, by copy of court roll for term of their lives; 7s. 1d., plus suit of court and heriot.
Joan Opye widow, 1 tenement in Purver which she holds by [*blank*]; 7s. 1d., plus suit of court and heriot.

Tresawsyn [*Tresawsen, in Perranzabuloe*]:
William Trengoo and Katherine his sister, 1 tenement in Tresawsyn, at the lord's will, with 6s. 1d. paid to the manor of Lamborn [*Lambourne, in Perranzabuloe*]; 15s., plus suit of court and heriot.

Bossywon, Bossyowen [*Kestle Mill and Bejowan Meadows, both in St Columb Minor*]:
Thomas Thraher, and John and Richard his sons, 1 water mill at Kestell called Bussywon Myll, with water-courses belonging, by copy of court roll for term of their lives; 20s., plus suit of court and heriot.
Richard Cogar, 1 enclosed meadow, parcel of Bussywen Medowes, at will; 8s.
John Bussywen, 1 meadow called Bussywen Medow, at will; 8s.

Tolkarn [*Tolcarne and Bedrugga, in St Columb Minor?*]:[9]
Reginald ('Raynolde') Mayhewe, 2 tenements in Tolkarn [and] Bodrogowe, by copy of court roll for term of his life, with 5s. 9d. paid to the manor of Carnenton; 26s. 8d.

Total of tenants by copy of court roll and at will, £11 7s. 11d.

Total of all tenants, £19 8s. 2d.

[*Deductions*]
Rents resolute: £4 14s. 0½d.
Fines for suit of court: 19s. 6d.[10]

Remains clear in rents and farm: £14 19s. 6½d.

Memorandum of a rent of 4s. which ought to be paid to the lord for 1 acre Cornish called Mymghan [*sic; 'Mingham' (lost), in St Columb Major*], now in the hands of [*blank*] Gavrigan, sometime of Sir John Arundell of Lanhern; to be inquired whether John Arundell or Gavrigan should pay.

---

[9] This holding must include the conventionary tenement of the manor at Bedrugga, not otherwise represented here. But the rent for Bedrugga in both 1575 (below, p. 211) and c.1586 (AR2/1343) was only 6s. 8d., so presumably Mayhewe's two tenements were one at Tolcarne and one at Bedrugga; hence the heading. Tolcarne and Bedrugga are not close to one another within the parish. For Bedrugga as a tenement of Bejowan at an earlier date, compare a high rent for *Bodrog(g)owe* paid to the lord of Carnanton by the manor of Bejowan in 1511-12 (account rolls, AR2/847-848). Note that a conventionary tenement of Treloy manor was also located at Bedrugga (above, pp. 30, 69 and 113).

[10] These are the fines to be paid to other manors, not the fines received for suit of court (which total instead 14s. 6d.); hence their inclusion here. But the sums do not agree anyway.

THREE MANORS OF THE EARL OF OXFORD, 1563
(PRO, SP12/31 no. 30, parts)

Contents

Manor of Roseworthy 168
Manor of Domellick 170
Manor of Tregorrick 171

SURVEY OF THE EARL OF OXFORD'S LANDS, 1563 (parts)

The true estate of all manors, lands and tenements of the Right Honourable Edward earl of Oxford[1] within the county of Cornwall demised by lease or by copy of court roll.

[Manor of Roseworthy, in Gwinear]

The manor of Roseworry lies in the west part of the shire within 6 miles of the mount called St Michaell, not above 16 miles from the uttermost part of this land in a place where the north sea and south sea are not distant above 8 miles; towns of any note for market or other repair or traffic are Helleston, 6 miles, Penzans, 8 miles, and St Jees [St Ives], 4 miles.

Tenant by indenture[2]

[Roseworthy Mill, in Gwinear]:
Richard Crane the younger, William Crane and Catherine wife of Richard, by indenture of 12 April 6 Edw. VI [1552], 1 corn mill called Roseworry Mill and another mill called Roseworry blowing mill, for their lives; 8 acres; rent 53s. 4d.; heriot; fine £13 6s. 8d. Livery and seisin not delivered.[3]

Tenants by copy of the manor court

Roseworry *[Roseworthy, in Gwinear]*:
David Angowgh alias John, by copy for term of his life only, 1 capital messuage; 51 acres; rent 34s.; fine 20s. [*Copy of*] 26 Hen. VIII [1534–5].

---

[1] Survey made before the sale of this estate to Sir John Arundell of Lanherne.
[2] As indicated by the preamble to this set of surveys, free tenants are omitted. For these see above, pp. 157–9.
[3] In the document acreages, rents and fines are set out in columns to the right of the main text, all of this being in a single hand. A second hand has added more detail, including, in places, dates of copies, in the left-hand margins; within each entry printed here, the second hand is indicated by the beginning of a new sentence after acreage, rent and fine.

Nicola John, widow, for term of her life only, 1 tenement; 36 acres; rent 17s.; fine 17s. 9d. [*Copy of*] 26 Hen. VIII [1534–5].
David Angowgh, 1 tenement late of John Rawe, deceased; 39 acres; rent 26s. 10d. Tenement is in the lord's hands and David offers a fine of £40.
John James alias Pentevion, 1 fulling mill only, occupied a long season without copy; rent 6s. James offers a fine of 6s.
David Angowgh, by copy for term of his life only, another tenement; 33 acres; rent 23s. 9d.; fine 26s. 8d. [*Copy of*] 26 Hen. VIII [1534–5].

Penhale [*Penhale, in Gwinear*]:
John Hoskie, by copy, 1 tenement for term of life only; 15 acres; rent 16s.; fine 33s. 4d. [*Copy of*] 26 Hen. VIII [1534–5]. Hoskye would renew this copy.
John Drewe, 1 tenement late of [*blank*] Roydon, occupied a long time by assignment of Roydon; 25½ acres; rent 18s. 6d.; fine 20s. Drewe offers a fine of £6 13s. 8d. Roydon has left his copy with Drue and has dwelt 7 years from the tenement.
Francis Goodolphin esq., piece of ground; 40 acres; rent 46s. 8d.; fine 20s. Mr Goodolphyn offers a fine of £30, but it is supposed that more will be given.

Revyar [*Riviere, in Phillack*]:
James Jeffrey, son of Jeffrey Browne, has relinquished the possession of a tenement into the hands of Richard Crane gent., who has the copy; 190 acres; rent 56s.; fine 26s. 8d. This tenement is greatly impaired by the abundance of sand which has choked a great quantity of it. Will notwithstanding yield fine.

Pengilly [*Pengelly, in Crowan*]:
Marion Thomas, by copy for term of her life only, 1 tenement; 28½ acres; rent 9s.; fine 20s. [*Copy of*] 37 Hen. VIII [1545–6].

Coswynsowsyne [*Coswinsawsin, in Gwinear*]:
Thomasine John, daughter of James John, 1 tenement; 17½ acres; rent 16s.; fine 14s. [*Copy of*] 3 & 4 Philip & Mary [1556–7].
Thomas Philipps, 2 tenements held in stitchmeal without division; my lord's part, with 8 acres of wood enclosed, 25½ acres; rent 23s. 4d. Tenement held in stitchmeal with Spernam. Philipps offers a fine of 20 marks.

Carnehell [*Carnhell, in Gwinear*]:
Richard Crane esq., by copy for term of his life only, 1 tenement; 36 acres; rent 26s.; fine 60s. [*Copy of*] 3 Edw. VI [1549–50].
John Snawden, 1 tenement, garden and ½ the town of Carnehell; 44 acres; rent 26s.; fine £8 beyond 60s. paid to John Lucas.

[*Down*]:
The commons called Roseworry Downe, where the tenants of the town of Rosworry claim common without stint, contain 80 acres of heath.

[*Penhale Moor, in Gwinear*]:
The moor called Penhale Moore, where the inhabitants of the tenements in Carnehell (now Richard Crane and John Snowden) and the tenants of the tenements in Penhale (now John Drewe and John Hoskye) claim common without stint, contains 40 acres of very good pasture ground. The tenants of the manor of Conorton [*Connerton, in Gwithian*], being Sir John Arrundell's, claim common there.[4] Mr St Albane claims ½ this common as belonging to his manor of Catabetherne [*Cathebedron, in Gwinear*].

[*Polmenor Downs, in Gwinear*]:
The common called Penmeaneth, in which the tenants of the town of Tresausine [*Coswinsawsin*] and the tenants of tenements of John Drewe and John Hoskye in Penhale claim common without stint, contains 16 acres.

[*Wood*]:
The wood called Roseworry Wood contains 100 acres and is of very small growth not fit to be cut for many years; herbage enjoyed by Richard Crane during the minority of my lord ever since the last cutting, supposed to be about 10 years. The lord is paid nothing for it, for Crane claims it as his fee for keeping the wood.

* * *

Demylyock
[*Manor of Domellick, in St Dennis*]

The manor of Demyliocke lies in the parish of St Dennys 2 miles

---

[4] This and the next sentence are crammed into the left-hand margin, and could relate either to Roseworthy Down or to Penhale Moor; the latter is more likely.

MANOR OF DOMELLICK 171

directly eastwards from Tresethny [*Tresithney, in St Columb Major*], about 4 miles from the north sea and from the south sea 6 miles, within 8 miles of Bodman the chiefest market town of Cornwall.[5]

Tenants by copy of the manor court[6]

Enys Vyen [*Ennis (Vean), in St Dennis*]:
William Pascho, for term of his life only, 1 tenement and 4 closes; 36 acres; rent 8s. besides 8d. high rent; fine 6s. 8d.

Penrose Vien [*Penrose Vean, in St Dennis*]:
[*Blank*], 1 tenement late of Richard Luke deceased; 38 acres; rent 15s. Richard Pasco offers a fine of £35.

[*Goss Moor, in St Dennis*]:
A certain moor called Gosmore containing 100 acres, where the tenants have common without stint together with tenants of diverse other lords who common there also, by what title they know not.
Memorandum: Edward Pascho, Eweth Anne Busshe and Powell Styple have several works of tin in the common which toll the 13th dish to the lord, paid to Richard Crane the younger, bailiff there.

* * *

[*Manor of Tregorrick, in St Austell*]

The manor of Tregorreck lies in the parish of St Austell within 1 mile of Tregennoe [*Tregenna, in St Ewe*] towards the north-east and within 1 mile of the south sea.[7]

[*Tenants by copy of the manor court*][8]

Tregorreck [*Tregorrick, in St Austell*]:
John Avrean, by copy for term of his life, the remainder to his wife

---

[5] A survey of the manor of Tresithney is included in this document, but not transcribed here because a fuller survey, only twelve years later, is available: below, pp. 229–34.

[6] As indicated by the preamble to this set of surveys, free tenants are omitted. For these see below, p. 236.

[7] A survey of the manor of Tregenna is included in this document, but is not transcribed here because a fuller survey, only twelve years later, is available: below, pp. 220–28.

[8] As indicated in the preamble to this set of surveys, free tenants are omitted. For these see below, p. 237.

and daughter, ½ of certain lands and tenements; 55 acres; rent 40s. besides 3d. high rent; fine £12 10s. [*Copy of*] 1 Edw. VI [1547–8].

[*St Austell town*]:
John Tirrell, ½ of 2 parcels of land under the town of St Austell; ½ acre; rent 3s. 9¼d. Joan Hannoforde offers a fine of 13s. 4d. William Daddo, 1 tenement late of John Vivean, deceased, whereof my lord's part is a moiety; 2 acres; rent 10s. Daddo offers a fine of 40s.

Tresalster [*Rosewastis, in St Columb Major*]:
Richard Carter and Joan his wife, for term of their lives, by copy, 1 tenement; ½ of 15 acres; rent 7s. 9d. besides 5s. high rent; fine 20s. [*Copy of*] 31 Hen. VIII [1539–40].

Trevaldg [*Trevemedar, in St Eval*]:
Moiety of certain lands called Mynneyleas in the tenure of [*blank*]; rent 23½d. besides 6½d. high rent.

Part of a wasterly moor there, not yet divided, contains, in the whole, 7½ acres.[9]

Memorandum: Martin Powell alias Poyle died holding this manor by knight's service; heirs are 3 daughters under age.

---

[9] The proportion of the moor owned by the earl of Oxford was specified by the surveyor, but is now faded and illegible.

SURVEY OF DINHAM'S LANDS, 1566
(Devon Record Office, Z17/3/19, parts)

Contents

Manor of Downinney	174
Manor of Cardinham	177
Carnabeggas	188
Fee of Cardinham	190
Manor of Bodardle	193

SURVEY OF DINHAM'S LANDS, 1566 (parts)

Doneckney
[*Downinney, in Warbstow*]

Inquisition taken 11 August 8 Eliz. [1566] by Henry Compton esq., one of the lords of the manor.

Free tenants

[*Treskellow, in Treneglos*]:
John Fulford kt, in Treskellowe, 1 tenure and ½ acre Cornish, by knight's service and common suit; relief 3s. 8¾d.; rent nil except suit.

[*Treneglos (parish)*]:
Edward Morthe, in Treneglod [sic], 1 fee with 1 water mill, by knight's service and common suit; relief 16s. 8d.; yearly rent at the 4 terms 13s. 4d.

[*Trewonnard, in Treneglos*]:
Anthony Burie gent., in Trewonarde, 1 tenure with ½ acre Cornish, by knight's service with common suit; relief 3s. 8d.; rent nil except suit.

Sum of free tenants yearly, 13s. 4d.

Customary tenants

[*Treglith, in Treneglos*]:
Thomas Harrye, by copy dated under the seal of John Rudgeway and others, 22 October 4 Edw. VI [1550], 1 tenement in Treglighs which is measured and divided between him and Thomas Pope, house in which he lives, garden and orchard, ½ rood, close called Above Towneparke, 4 acres beyond 1 acre of his own bought from Morthe, close called Longeaker, 2½ acres beyond 1 acre of his own, 2 closes lying together called Inner Sowth and Homere South, 5 acres, park called Haye Syde, 2 acres, close beyond the water called a ponifold, 3 acres, close called Treglissedowne newly enclosed, 10 acres; yearly rent 13s. 6d.

Thomas Poope, by copy dated as above, the other tenement in Treglihes equally divided between him and Thomas Harrye, house in which he lives, garden, close called the Parke Above the Towne,

2 acres, close called Longe Akers of which part is meadow, 3 acres, close called Wylland, 3 acres, close called the Wyll Parke, 2½ acres, close called the Parke by the House, 2 acres, close called a down newly enclosed, 10 acres, close called North Parke, 1 acre; rent 13s. 6d.

[*Nether and Higher Scarsick, in Treneglos*]:
John Congdon, by copy dated 3 September 10 Hen. VIII [1518] under the seal of John Fourd, for a fine of 6s. 8d., 1 tenement in Nethescasocke, house in which he lives, other necessary buildings, garden, orchard, close called Coldon, 10 acres, close called Middell Parke, 8 acres, close called Myll Parke, 8 acres, close called Myllham, 1 acre, close called Queyna Parke, 8 acres, close called Bakes Parke, 2 acres, close called Wyll Parke, 1 acre, close called Bove Parke, 2 acres; yearly rent 16s.
John Rowse, Katherine his wife and John their son, by copy dated under the seal of Norleigh, 20 October 37 Hen. VIII [1545], 1 tenure in Overskascok, house in which he lives, barn, other buildings necessary for husbandry, orchard and garden, close called the Parke under Hay, 3 acres, close called the Bant, 1 acre, close called the Litell Neweparke, 1 acre, close called the Est Towne, 6 acres, close called Coldon next to the moor, 40 acres, close called Moore Close, 4 acres, 3 closes lying together called Breches, 4 acres, grove of meadow, 1½ acres; rent 14s.

[*Tregenna, in Treneglos*]:
Michael Staddon, by copy dated at the audit of the lords held at Exeter, 23 October 5 Edw. VI [1552] under the seal of Norleigh, 1 tenement in Tregennowe, house in which he lives and other buildings necessary for husbandry, close called Litell Parke under Towne, 5 acres, close above the town, 5½ acres, close lying at Helland, 4½ acres, 7 acres of arable at Downe; rent 4s.
John Here, by copy dated under the seal of Norleigh, 24 Hen. VIII [1532–3], for a fine of 26s. 8d., 1 tenement in Tregennowe, house in which he lives, close called the Parke under the Towne, 10 acres, close called Hellands, 4½ acres, close above the town, 10 acres, part of the land above the wall, 4 acres, arable land upon lez Downe, 7 acres; yearly rent 8s.

[*Trewonnard, in Treneglos*]:
Henry Bray, by copy dated 4 June 4 Edw. VI [1550] by Rudgeway and others, 2 tenements in Trewonard, house in which he lives,

garden and orchard, close under town, 7 acres, close called Wyllparke, 10 acres, 4 parks lying together, 4 acres, close above the town, 14 acres, arable land upon lez Downe, 15 acres; rent 26s.

[*Higher Scarsick, in Treneglos*]:
Joan Harrye, by copy dated 24 July 33 Hen. VIII [1541] by Norleigh, 1 tenement in Over Skasseck, house in which she lives, garden, 2 closes called Sowth Parkes lying together, 10 acres, close called the Moore, 6 acres, close called Coldon Parke, 40 acres, close called the Parke above the Towne, 2 acres, close called Bates Parke, 1 acre, 2 closes called Whete Parkes, 2 acres, 1½ acres of meadow, moor in severalty, 1½ acres; rent 14s.

Sum of customary tenants yearly, 109s.

Sum total of yearly value of the manor, £6 2s. 4d.

Customs and remembrances

Two parts of this manor belong to John Arundell and Mr Compton esqs and the other two parts to Thomas Heale gent. It is false.[1]

To this manor belongs a court baron to which all tenants, free and customary, are bound to sue.

Tenants dying seized of customary lands pay for every tenement their best beast in the name of a heriot and likewise upon every alienation or surrender.[2]

The tenants yearly choose amongst themselves a reeve and tithing-man who gathers rents and perquisites of courts and pays them yearly at the audit at Exeter as other reeves in the county of Devon do.[3]

No widow after the death of her husband shall enjoy any lands or tenements in which her husband dies seized unless named upon her husband's copy.

Tenants dying seized of customary lands pay for every tenement their best beast for a heriot and a farleu upon every alienation.

Waste

There belongs to the manor common waste ground called Myllesdowne [*probably at Wilsey Down, in Treneglos*] containing

---

[1] Sentence added later: relates to Heale.
[2] This information is repeated, more accurately, in the last custom, below.
[3] Much of this ex-Dinham estate lay in the county of Devon.

200 acres, beginning at a ditch called Townewell and thence by a way which leads towards Boscastle to Litle Downe Corner and thence ascending to a certain cross called Half Drounked Crosse [*now Hallworthy, in Davidstow*], and thence by the way to Tregenna Combeshed and thence to the ditch called Hoole Crepe.

Also note a small coppice there of 3 acres or thereabouts [*added later*].

* * *

Cardinham

Inquisition taken 12 August 8 Eliz. [1566] by Henry Compton esq., one of the lords of the manor.

Free tenants

[*Deviock, in Cardinham*]:
William Courteney gent., 1 acre Cornish in Devyok, by knight's service with 2 suits of court; yearly rent at Michaelmas 10s.

[*Kenketh, in Cardinham*]:
Nicholas Carmynowe, 1 acre Cornish in Kenkeyth, by knight's service with 2 suits of court, as above; rent 4s.

[*Pinsla, in Cardinham*]:
William Tredenecke gent., in right of his wife, the daughter and heir of Nicholas Bosworbeth [*sic*], 1 acre Cornish in Pynchloe, by knight's service and 2 suits; rent 2s. 5d.

[*Newland Preeze, in Cardinham*]:
Roger Coppinge and others, 2 acres [Cornish][4] in Newland Paies [*sic*], by knight's service, as above, and suit; rent 2s.

[*Lahays, in Cardinham*]:
The tenants at the Hay, lands and tenements there (formerly the priory of Tywardreth); yearly rent 6d.[5]

[*Old Cardinham*]:
Thomas Pound, in Old Cardinham, ½ acre by knight's service, with 2 suits; rent 6d.

---

[4] Supplied from a seventeenth-century survey, AR2/1346.
[5] For the priory's ownership of Lahays, see Picken, 'Trezance, Lahays'.

[*Probably Trewithen, in Stithians*]:
The heirs of St Wrath [*Sewrah, in Stithians*], in Trevoythan; rent 15s.

[*Heligan, in Warleggan*]:
Robert Hill, the mill leat in Helligan; yearly rent 6d.

Diverse men and the inhabitants of Trevorder in Warlegan [*Trevorder, in Warleggan*] pay for the watercourse at Michaelmas merely 6d.

Sum of free tenants yearly, 41s. 7d.

Customary tenants

[*Higher Colvannick, in Cardinham*]:
Robert Davy, by copy dated under the seal of John Stclere and others dated 11 September 30 Hen. VIII [1538], 1 tenement in Over Calvanak, house sufficient for the tenement, close called the Great Close with a moor adjacent, 7 acres, 2 closes of meadow called Lower Meadowe and Over Meadowe, 2 acres; yearly rent 7s. 9d.

[*Lower Trezance, now Teason, in Cardinham*]:
Robert Davy, by copy dated 22 August 35 Hen. VIII [1543] under the seal of John Stcler and others, 1 tenement called lez Nether Tresans, house in which he lives, orchard, garden, close called the Close Above Towne, 2½ acres, close called the Hollywill Parke,[6] 2½ acres, close called the Middel Parke, 3 acres, close called lez Bye, 3 acres, close called the Clieff Parke, 1½ acres, close undergarden and a small meadow lying together, 2 acres, close called the Downe Close, 2 acres; rent 8s.

[*Gnatham, in Cardinham*]:
Joan Semon widow, during her widowhood, by copy dated under the seal of John Seyntcler and others 2 September 32 Hen. VIII [1540], 1 tenure in Gnatteham which Agnes Jule formerly held, house in which she lives, garden, 1 rood, close called Above Towne, 1 acre, close called Newe Parke, ¼ acre, close called High Park, 1 acre, close called Grene Parke, ¼ acre, close called Velny Park, ¼ acre, close called Under Towne, 1½ acres; rent 6s. 6d.

---

[6] *ibid.*, p. 205 for this holy well.

[*Lower Colvannick, in Cardinham*]:
John Groose, by copy dated in the name of Cardinal Thomas, legate *a latere*, Archbishop of York,[7] 6 October 21 Hen. VIII [1529], 2 tenements in Ney' Calvanack which Stephen Grosse formerly held, messuage in which he lives, garden, close called the Haysyde, 4 acres, close called the Church Parke, 1 acre, close called the Geare, 2 acres, close called the Parke Above Towne, 1½ acres, close called the Mett Parke, 1½ acres, close called the Longe Parke, 1 acre, close called the Middell Parke, 2 acres, close called the High Parke, 2 acres, close under town,[8] 2½ acres; rent 16*s*.

[*Old Cardinham*]:
Thomas Abraham, by copy made by John Fourd, 20 April 13 Hen. VIII [1522], 1 tenement in Old Cardinham, house in which he lives, close called Above Toune, 3 acres, close called the Weste Close, 3 acres, close called Cross Parke, 2½ acres, close called Littell Close, 1 acre, close called a rough ground, 1 acre, a small meadow, ¾ acre; rent 6*s*. 2*d*.

[*'Clapper Moor' (lost), in Cardinham*]:
The same Thomas Abraham, by copy dated 24 August 28 Hen. VIII [1536], 2 acres at Clapermoore between the land of Henry once marquess of Exeter on the west side and land once Robert Hill's on the east side; rent 3*s*. 4*d*.

[*Outer Bury, now Higher Bury, in Cardinham*]:
Stephen Lawarne, by copy dated 19 Hen. VIII [1527–8] under the seal of John Fourd, 1 tenement in Utterbury, house in which he lives, orchard, garden, close called Longeaker, 5 acres, close called the Blacklond, 2½ acres, close called Thistell Park, 4 acres, close called Barneparke, 2 acres, close called the Hill Parke, 2 acres, close under town, 3 acres, close called Bremell Parke, 2 acres, close called the Bury Parke, 4 acres, two closes called the Castell Parkes, 4 acres, close called Erishe Castell, 2 acres, close called Neweground, 3 acres, close called Rye Park, 5 acres, two closes above town lying together, 2½ acres; rent 14*s*. 5½*d*.

---

[7] This is Thomas Wolsey who became Archbishop of York in 1514 and papal legate *a latere* in 1518: Mackie, *Early Tudors*, pp. 289–90. There seems to be no clue as to why this copy should have been granted by him.

[8] Possibly 'under down': the first letter is smudged.

[*Treslea, in Cardinham*]:
Thomas Holm, by copy dated under the seal of John Stcler, 11 September 30 Hen. VIII [1538], 1 tenement in Sley, house in which he lives, close called Highclose, 3½ acres, close called Middelparke, 2½ acres, close called Above Towne, 2 acres, close under town, 1 acre, meadow, ½ acre, close of rough ground, 6 acres; rent 11s. 1¾d.

Elizabeth Rich, by copy dated 26 Hen. VIII [1534–5] under the seal of John Fourd, reversion of 1 tenure in Tresseley, house in which she lives, close called Longe Parke, 2½ acres, close called Highparke, 2 acres, close called Middell Parke, 2 acres, close above town, 1½ acres, close behind town, 2 acres, close under town, 2½ acres, close called the Lee Ley, 1½ acres, rough ground, 6 acres; rent 11s. 2d.

['*Tanna mill*' *(lost), in Cardinham*]:[9]
Robert Davy, by copy dated under the seal of John Fourd, 24 August 28 Hen. VIII [1536], 1 piece of land at Tannyngemylhill on the east side of Lamerthforth [*ford named from Lemar, in Cardinham*] and the west side of Luttecoot [*Lidcutt, in Cardinham*], 12 acres; rent 3s. 4d.

[*Treswithick, in Cardinham*]:
Elizabeth Garrowe widow, without copy, 2 tenements in Treswythyak, house in which she lives, other buildings necessary for the tenement, orchard, 1 rood, close called the Great Above Towne, 4 acres, close called Tayle Parke, 4 acres, close called Middell Parke, 4 acres, close called the Rough Parke, 4½ acres, close called the Newe Parke, 2 acres, close called the Bakehouse Park, 1½ acres, close called the Litle Abovetowne, 1½ acres, close called the Hayleparke, 2½ acres, close called the Roodeparke, 1½ acres, close called the Halseparke, ¾ acre, close called Jukelparke, 2½ acres,

---

[9] A 'newly constructed' mill called 'Tanmylle' is recorded in a manorial account roll of 1482–3 for Cardinham, though by 1489–90 it was 'totally decayed': AR2/450 mm. 1, 7 ('newly constructed' need not be taken at its face value, because the term was often carried over from one account to another for many years). Medieval tanning mills, which ground bark, are also recorded at Truro, near Tavistock and at Okehampton: *Caption of Seisin*, ed. Hull, p. 73; Finberg, *Tavistock Abbey*, pp. 153–4, 196; P.R.O. S.C.6 1118/6.

close called the Lanehed, ¼ acre, a small meadow, ¼ acre; yearly rent 15s. 5½d.

[Old Cardinham]:
William Goodinge, by copy made by Stclere and others, 30 September 32 Hen. VIII [1540], 1 tenure in Old Cardinham which Thomasine Wyll formerly held, house in which he lives, garden, close called ... [*word stained*] Parke, 4 acres, close called Calvan Parke, 3 acres, close called the Best Parke, 3 acres, close called the Backe Parke, 3 perches, close called the Castle, 2 acres; yearly rent 10s.

[Treslea, in Cardinham]:
Thomas Rowe, by copy made by John Stcler and others at the audit at Exeter, 23 October 33 Hen. VIII [1541], reversion of 1 tenure which Joan Nycholyn widow formerly held in Treslee, house in which he lives, garden, close called Abovetowne, 2 acres, close called Wyllparke, 2 acres, close called Thistleparke, 2 acres, close called Middell Parke, 2 acres, close called Crosse Parke, 1 acre, close called Browne Parke, 2½ acres, close called Parke over the Water, 1 acre, close called the Medowe, 1 acre; rent 10s. 1½d.

[Callabarrett Wood, in Cardinham]:
John Stanwey, by copy dated under the seal of Norleigh and others, 5 May 36 Hen. VIII [1544], ½ close of land and wood pasture (*pastur' bosc'*) called Kellybarrett, provided always that he will not use for grazing any part of the wood within 6 years of that part being felled by the lords; rent 3s. 4d.
Joan Garrowe, by copy made at the Exeter audit, 23 October 36 Hen. VIII [1544] by Seintcler, ½ that land and wood pasture called Kellybarrett, proviso as above [*entry for Stanwey*]; yearly rent 3s. 4d.

[Penpoll and Inner Bury, now Little Bury, in Cardinham]:
Nicholas Wyll, by copy made by John Rydgway esq., farmer during the minority of Henry Compton esq., 2 tenures, one called Penpoll, the other called the Ynner Bury, house in which he lives, garden, orchard, 1 rood, close called Undertowne, 2½ acres, close called the Great Mede Parke, 2 acres, close called Crosse Parke, 2 acres, close called Abovetowne, 3½ acres, close called the Vellwey, 3 roods, close called the Litell Parke above Lane, 1½ acres, close called Wyllparke, 3½ acres, 2 closes lying together called Middell

Parkes, 4 acres, close called Lome Parke, 1 acre, close called Under Buryhouse, 1 acre, close called Above ye Bury House, 2½ acres, close called the Rough Close, 4 acres, close called the Downe Parke, 2 acres, meadow called the Parkes Foote, 3 roods, meadow called Litell Medowe, 3 roods; yearly rent 15s. 1d.

[*Welltown, in Cardinham*]:
John Stanwaye, by copy made by Richard Paliner[10] and others, the lords' surveyors, dated Tuesday before the feast of the Apostles Simon and Jude 14 Hen. VIII [21 October 1522] for a fine of 10 marks, 1 tenure in Wylton, house in which he lives, barn and other buildings, garden, 2 orchards, 1 rood, close called Above Towne, close called High Parke, 4½ acres, close called Bynlane, 4 acres, close called Struell Barne, 1 acre, close called Litlebovetowne, 1 acre, close called Longeparke, ½ acre, close called Benethbakes, 3 roods, close called the Maydeswill, 2 acres, close called Benethtowne, 2 acres; rent 13s. 9d.

['*Peach*' (*lost*), *in Cardinham*]:
David Hockin, by copy dated at Gretediche,[11] 23 Hen. VIII [1531–2], 1 tenement at Peache, 1 cottage house, close called Pechesmoore, 2 acres, close called Woodparke, ¼ acre, close called Colwyll Parke, 1 acre, close called the Crossemoore, ¼ acre; rent 7s.

[*Lower Cardeast, in Cardinham*]:
The same David, by copy dated by John Seintcler and others, 30 September 36 Hen. VIII [1544], 1 tenure in Ney' Cadest, house in which he lives, garden, orchard, ½ acre, close called Benethe ye Towne, 1½ acres, close called Longlinge, 1¼ acres, close called Horseparke, ¼ acre, close called Newe Parke, 3 acres, close called the Park afore the Doore, 4½ acres, close called Higha Parke, 4 acres, close above town, 3 acres; rent 7s. 2½d.

[*Treslea, in Cardinham*]:
John Curtys, by copy dated 10 October 34 Hen. VIII [1542] by John Stcler and others, reversion of 1 tenement in Tresly, house in

---

[10] Possibly 'Palmer'.
[11] The leet courts of the Dinhams in this part of Cornwall were held at the Great Ditch (now demolished) on the parish boundary, near to Council Barrow on the present A30. See below, pp. 186, 190 and 193, and Picken, 'Trezance, Lahays', p. 204.

which he lives, close above town, 2 acres, close called Styleparke, 2½ acres, close called the High Parke, 4 acres, close called the Ronde Parke, 1½ acres, close called Hilparke, 1 acre, close called Hilbrightonparke, 1½ acres, rough ground called Conory, 2 acres; yearly rent 9s. 1d.

[*Colvannick, in Cardinham*]:
William Byllinge and William his son, by copy dated at the lord's audit at Exeter, 22 October 6 Edw. VI [1552], under the seal of John Ridgeway, John Butler, Robert Webbe and Thomas Gervys, the lord's surveyors, for a fine of £10, 1 tenure in Calvanack, house in which he lives, barn, other necessary houses, garden, close called the Close at Cause Ende, 2½ acres, close called Undertowne, 2 acres, close called Brodeparke, 2 acres, close called Longeparke, 1 acre, close called Medeparke, 1 acre, close called the Close next to Grosse, 1 acre, close called Above Towne, 1 rood, meadow, ½ acre, 3 acres in Colpheneck ye Higher [*Higher Colvannick, in Cardinham*]; rent 14s. 9d.

[*Lemar, in Cardinham*]:
Robert Edy, by copy made under the seal of John Seynclere and other surveyors dated 11 September 30 Hen. VIII [1538], for a fine of 6s. 8d., a certain parcel of land and appurtenances in Lamarth on which Robert built 1 dwelling house; barn, garden, orchard, 1 rood, close called Abovetowne, 6 acres, close called Westparke, 7 acres, close called Estparke, 2 acres, close called Undertowne, 1 acre 1 rood; rent 6s. 4d.

[*Milltown, in Cardinham*]:
Joan Hoblyn widow, without copy, 1 cottage in Mylton Combe, dwelling in which she lives, close above the house, 2 acres, 1 small moor; rent 3s. 11d.

[*Lidcutt, in Cardinham*]:
William Bathe, by copy made under the seal of John Seincler and other surveyors of the lords dated 22 August 35 Hen. VIII [1543], for a fine of £4, 1 tenure called Lutcote, house in which he lives, garden, close called the Higher Parke, 10 acres, close called the North Parke, 8 acres, close called Above Towne, 5 acres, close called Quary Parke, 4 acres, close called Flockford Parke, 1 acre, close called Litle North Parke, 1½ acres, close called Wyll Parke, 3 acres,

close called Heith Parke, 12 acres of heath, 2 meadows lying together, ½ rood; yearly rent 10s. 9d.

[*Higher Colvannick, in Cardinham*]:
William Garland, by copy made under the seal of John Stcler and other surveyors dated 11 September 30 Hen. VIII [1538], for a fine of 70s., 1 tenure in Over Calvaneck, house in which he lives, barn, garden, close called Crosse Parke, 2 acres, close called High Parke, 2 acres, close called Longeparke, 1 acre, close called the Parke above the House, 1 acre, close called Downe Parke, 3 roods, meadow, ½ acre; rent 7s. 7d.

[*Benorth, in Cardinham*]:
Peter Edward, by copy made under the seal of Robert Norleigh by demise of John Ridgeway dated 16 January 6 Edw. VI [1553], 1 tenure in Benorth, house in which he lives, garden, orchard, ½ acre, close called Abovetowne, 7 acres, close called Grenepitt, 2 acres, close called Brodeparke, 3 acres, close called Wyllparke, 3 acres, 2 small closes lying together called Geyreparke and Middelparke, 3 acres, parcel of land called the Clieffe planted with hazel withies and other underwood, 5½ acres, meadow, 1 acre; rent 8s.

Robert Davy, by copy made under the seal of John Glyn sen., merely by demise of the surveyor, dated 3 August 17 Hen. VIII [1525], 1 tenure, no dwelling house, 6 closes, in all 12 acres; rent 7s. 5½d.

[*Carblake, in Cardinham*]:
Margaret Grosse widow, during her widowhood, according to the custom of the manor, by a copy made by John Stcler and other surveyors dated 11 September 30 Hen. VIII [1538], 1 tenure in Carbleth, house in which she lives, barn and other necessary buildings, garden, close called the Church Parke, 2 acres, close called Bynyeatt, 2 acres, close called the Mede Parke, 1 acre, close called the Tayle Parke, 3 roods, close called Lomeparke, 1 acre, meadow, 3 roods; rent 14s. 5½d.

[*Trezance, in Cardinham*]:
Alice Wyll widow, during her widowhood, by copy made under the seal of John Fourd steward dated 5 August 24 Hen. VII [1532], for a fine of 60s., 1 tenure in Over Tresant, house in which she lives, barn and other buildings, garden, orchard, ½ acre, close called

Pempell Hall, 1 acre, close called Style Parke, 1 acre 1 rood, close called Blendwyll, 1 acre, close called the Helstedes, 1 acre 1 rood, close called the Longelond, 1½ acres, close called Above Towne, 1½ acres, close called the Narrowelane, 2 acres, close called Crosse Park, 3 roods, close called Abovelane, 2 acres, 1 meadow called [*blank*], 1 acre; rent 9s. 3d;

the same Alice, during her widowhood, by copy made by Ridgeway and other surveyors dated at the lord's audit held at Exeter 23 October 2 Edw. VII [1548], 1 tenure in Over Tresant, orchard, close called ... [*stained*], 3 acres, close called the Hillstiche, ½ acre, close called Longeparke, 1 acre 1 rood, close called the Litle Hilstiche, ½ acre, close called Rondparke, 1 acre 1 rood, close called Bowelane, 3 acres, close called Crosseparke, 3 acres, close called Neweparke, 1 acre, close called Litlelongeparke, 3 roods, meadow, 3 roods; rent 11s. 8½d.

[Benorth and Higher Cardeast, both in Cardinham]:
Eleanor Mold widow, by copy made under the seal of John Fourd, 5 August 24 Hen. VIII [1513], 2 tenements in Benorth and another in Over Cadest. Belonging to the tenements in Benorth, house in which she lives, garden, close called Grenepitclose, 4 acres, close called Higer Grenepitt, 5 acres, close called Abovelane, 3 acres, close under lane, 1 acre, meadow, ¾ acre, close under town, 3 acres; rent 7s. 6d. Belonging to the tenement in Over Cadest, sheephouse, close above towne, 8 acres, close called Bakehouse Parke, 2 acres, close called Undertowne, 3 acres, close called Fursyhill, 1½ acres, close called Aishparke, 6 acres; yearly rent 7s. 1½d.

[Lower Colvannick, in Cardinham]:
John Roger, without copy, 1 tenement lying in Lower Calvanack, house in which he lives, close called the Highparke, 2 acres, close called the Brodeparke, 2 acres, 2 closes called Middellparkes lying together, 3 acres, meadow called Bakehousemead, 1 acre, close called Underlane, 1½ acres, orchard; rent 7s. 8d.

[Sixpenny Land, in Cardinham]:[12]
William Tredeneck, without copy, close next to the land of the rector called Sixepennyland, 1½ acres; yearly rent 6d.

---

[12] Close to Cardinham churchtown, to the east of it where the glebe was located. The location of the glebe is clear from bounds given in *Calendar of Cornish Glebe Terriers*, ed. Potts, p. 14. The tithe map and apportionment show that the glebe also contained land called Sixpenny Land.

Thomas Abraham, close next to the same land, 1¼ acres, formerly William Wyll's and after St Congon; [rent] 20*d*.

[*Unlocated cottage*]:
Emma Jule, 1 cottage once Joan Hodge's; rent 6*d*.

The reeve of the manor of Cardinham and the tenants and residents of Cardinham pay yearly for having pasture and common in Fowy Moore [*Bodmin Moor*], as appears by an ancient extent made in 18 Hen. VIII [1526–7], 13*s*. 4*d*.

<p style="text-align:center">Sum of customary tenants yearly, £15 14s. 9d.
Total yearly value of the manor, £17 16<i>s</i>. 4<i>d</i>.</p>

[*Allowances and payments*]

Paid yearly to the heirs of Mr Bewmand for a yearly rent for Standon Ball [*part of Stannon Downs, in St Breward*] in Fowymoore [*Bodmin Moor*], 6*d*.

Paid yearly to the heirs of lez Pyrne [*Respryn, in St Winnow*][13] now Mr Carmynowe for an allowance made to him of old, as is testified by the homage, for a remittance made by the lords, 6*s*. 8*d*.

Paid to the feodary of the duke of Cornwall for homage and suit of court yearly, 14*s*. 4*d*.

<p style="text-align:center">Sum of allowances and payments, 20s. 6d.
Remains clear, [<i>blank</i>].</p>

Customs

There belongs to this manor the patronage of the benefice of Cardinham, incumbent Robert Bucher, worth yearly £24.

The earl of Bathe, Lord Zouche, John Arundell and Henry Compton esqs are lords of the manor.

There belongs to this manor a court baron. Lords may choose their steward and keep court every 3 weeks. Two law courts are yearly kept at Grett Dyche[14] because the court of the fee of Cardinham is kept there, and the free tenants ought to appear.

Each lord may keep a court of survey at his pleasure and may grant his own part by copy of court roll for term of 2 lives and the wife's widowed estate.

---

[13] Compare John Carmynowe, at Respryn, below, p. 191, and Nicholas Carmynowe, esq., of Respryn, in 1569 (Douch, *Muster Roll*, p. 25).

[14] See above, p. 182 n. 11.

Every customary tenant pays after death, surrender or forfeiture his best beast as relief or heriot to all the 4 lords and so does every widow after death, surrender or forfeiture.

Belonging to this manor is toll tin in Fowey Moore [*Bodmin Moor*], Polmellecke Moore, Kermoore, Skorden Moore, Claper Moore ['*Clapper Moor*' *(lost), in Cardinham*] and elsewhere.

Belonging to this manor is a great waste of moor and heath where the customary tenants have a common of pasture; free tenants have the drift of the common and the reeve pays yearly to the 4 lords, for the profit, 13s. 4d.

Woods

One wood called Lutcote Grove [*Lidcutt Wood, in Cardinham*] of 40 years growth, containing 15 acres.

One other wood called Kyllyberret Wood [*Callabarrett Wood, in Cardinham*] of 40 years growth, containing 50 acres.

One other wood called Horestocke [*Hurtstocks Wood, in Cardinham*] begins at Petheckes Combe and so eastwards by the water of Thurelake; of 34 years growth, containing 80 acres.

One other wood called Glyan Wood [*named from Glynn, in Cardinham*] begins from Thurelake on the south and east sides unto a certain wood there (8 acres) which is limited for the reparations of the tenants in Cardinham and Boderdell, containing 12 acres.

One other wood called Lanhuskley Wood [*Laneskin Wood, in Cardinham*] begins from Ekenswell on the north and east side unto Gotton Lake [*Golden Lake, in Cardinham*] on the south side; age 43 years, containing 18 acres.

Another wood called Lan Cade Woodde [*named from 'Lancada Well' (lost), in Cardinham*] beginning at Newe Bridge [*Newbridge, in Cardinham*] on the south and west sides unto Lomcale Wyll ['*Lancada Well*' *(lost), in Cardinham*] on the north and east side; age 50 years, containing 30 acres.

Another wood called Boodygywood beginning at the way which leads from Newebride [*sic*] to Lyskerd on the west side and [land?] now called Gnattham [*Gnatham, in Cardinham*] on the south; age 43 years, containing 23 acres.

Another wood called Boodygywood [between the way?] which leads from Newe Bridge unto Lyskerd on the west and Dress Lake on the east side; age 53 years, containing 20 acres.

* * *

Carbugus
[Carnabeggas, in St Erth]

Extent made 13 May 8 Eliz. [1566].

All tenants owe suit of court every 3 weeks where it pleases the steward to hold it within the hundreds of Penwith and Keryer.

Free tenants[15]

[Trenedros, in St Erth]:
William Godolhan kt, ½ acre Cornish in Trewooddres, by knight's service with common suit, lately Sir Robert Brooke's; rent 2s. 6d.

[Rinsey, in Breage, Trengothal, in St Levan, Bosehan, in St Buryan, and Chyanhor, in St Levan]:
The same William, 1 acre in Rynsy, 2 acres in Tregothell, 1 ferling in Bosseghan, 1 ferling in Chyenhorth, by knight's service with suit of court as above, previously John Godolhan's; rent 12s. 10d.

[Chenhalls, in St Erth]:
Heirs of Chienhals next Carbugus, formerly Edward Hastinges, ⅓ ferling, by knight's service; yearly rent at Easter and Michaelmas 4d.

[Trenerth, in Gwinear, presumably]:
John Killigrewe esq., formerly John Pedit, 2 acres Cornish in Trenerth by knight's service and suit as above; rent 3s. 4d.

[Chenhalls, in St Erth]:
Heirs of John Reskymer, in Chyenhals next Carbugus, ⅔ ferling, by service [and] suit; rent 8s.

[St Erth churchtown, in St Erth]:
Reginald Mohun esq., in St Erth, 1 ferling, in socage without suit of court; rent 3d.

[Treskillard, in Illogan, presumably, and Tregoose and St Erth churchtown, both in St Erth]:
Richard Lanyen, in right of his wife, ½ acre in Trustulard, in socage, and 1 ferling in Tregoys [and] 1 ferling in St Erth and owes suit; rent 17d.

---

[15] Only free tenants are listed here and in Cardinham Fee: compare p. 190, below, and see the Introduction.

[*Collorian, in Ludgvan, Porthmeor and Bosporthennis, both in Zennor, and Cucurrian, in Ludgvan*]:
John Kylligrewe esq., 2 acres in Kylirian, ½ acre in Porthmer, 1 ferling in Bosportenes, ½ acre in Karkeryan, by knight's service with common suit; rent 3s. 4½d.

[*Bodraverran, in St Erth*]:
John Arundell of Talvren esq. [*Tolverne, in Philleigh*], 1 ferling in Bodreveren, by knight's service with common suit; rent 12d.

[*Tregellast and Cargease, both in Ludgvan, and Bosporthennis, in Zennor*]:
John Killigrewe esq., ½ acre Cornish in Tregellest and Cargose and 1 ferling in Bosportines, by knight's service with common suit; rent 4½d.

[*Trenowin, in Ludgvan*]:
John Vivian gent., ½ acre in Trenekyn alias Trenevyn in the parish of Ludvan, by knight's service; rent 2s.
Heirs of Otto Colyn now John Trefry and others, 1 ferling in Trenevyn, by knight's service; rent 12d.
Heirs of Colroger and Tregennowe, 1 ferling, by knight's service and suit of court; rent 12d.

[*Bosigran, in Zennor*]:
John Cosewyn, 1 acre in Bosygarn, by knight's service and suit of court; rent nil.

[*Porthmeor, in Zennor*]:
John Arundell of Talvren esq. [*Tolverne, in Philleigh*], ½ acre in Porthmer in the parish of Senor, by knight's service; rent 12d.

[*Foage, in Zennor*]:
Heirs of Caunterbury, in Boys in the same parish, 1 acre, by knight's service with common suit; rent 4s.

[*Unidentified*]:
Heirs of [*blank*], in Tresven, for the mill leat there, 4d.

[*Treviades, in Constantine*]:
Richard Trevises alias Trefusas, 1 acre Cornish there, by knight's service with common suit; rent 13s. 4d.

[*Probably Tregellast, in Ludgvan*]:
William Mylleton esq., in Tregellaston, ½ acre Cornish with common suit; rent 18d.

[*Treworgie, in Manaccan*]:
John Kylligrewe, 2 acres in Treworgy, by knight's service with common suit; rent 20*d*.

[*Trevaddra, in Manaccan*]:
John Treggedellen, lately Richard Vivian and before that John Tregonwall, 1 ferling in Trevardreth next to Stythians, by knight's service with common suit; rent 3*s*.

Sum of free tenants yearly, 54*s*. 11*d*.

* * *

Cardinham Fee

Extent of the fee made and renewed 13 August 8 Eliz. [1566].

Free tenants[16]

[*Landulph (parish)*]:
Heirs of the marquess of Exeter, 1 knight's fee in Landilpe, common suit at the Gretediche;[17] relief 5 marks; yearly rent 14*d*.

[*Cartuther and Tencreek, both in Menheniot*]:
Robert Beckett, Peter Coryton and George Kyrkeham esq., 2 knight's fees in Cartuther and Trencrek, common suit at Gretediche; fine for suit of court, 6*s*.

[*Lanreath*]:
Christopher Chiddeleigh esq., manor of Lanreythowe, by service of 3½ knight's fees, common suit as above; fine for suit of court, 2*s*. 6*d*.

[*Helligan, in St Mabyn*]:
Robert Hyll, in right of his wife (heir of Flamacke), manor of Hellygan, by service of 2 fees, common suit as above; fine for suit of court, 12*d*.

[*Colquite, in St Mabyn*]:
Thomas Howard kt, Lord Howard, in right of his wife (heir of Mareney), manor of Colquytt, by service of 3½ [*or* 4½] knight's fees, suit as above; fine for suit of court, 2*s*.

---

[16] As at Carnabeggas, only free tenants are given; see p. xxix.
[17] See above, p. 182 n. 11.

[*Trelay, in Pelynt, apparently*]:
Heirs of Larchedecon, 1 knight's fee in Treley in the parish of Pelynt; should pay yearly 3s. [*reading uncertain*], now nil.

[*Eglosrose, in Philleigh*]:
John Arundell of Guernecke [*Gwarnick, in St Allen*], manor of Eglos Rose, by service of 2 knight's fees, suit as above; fine for suit, 12d.

[*Lawhittack, at Colan Barton, in Colan*]:
Francis Blewett and Ralph Dulyn, in right of their wives, 1 knight's fee in St Colan, suit as above; fine for suit, 12d.

[*Trebartha, in North Hill*]:
Thomas Spore, 1 knight's fee in Trebarth, suit as above; fine for suit, 20d.

[*Unidentified; possibly Foage, in Zennor*]:
Heirs of Gervis, ¼₄ knight's fee in Levos, suit as above; fine for suit, 2s. 6d.

[*Streigh, in Lanlivery*]:
Nicholas Kendall, 1 knight's fee in Streythe, by knight's service, suit as above; fine for suit, 12d.

[*Pencarrow, in Egloshayle*]:
Lady Hungerford and Nicholas Oppey, ½ knight's fee in Pencarrowe, suit as above; fine for suit, 6d.

[*Amble, in St Kew*]:
Reginald Mone esq., ½ knight's fee and ⅑ knight's fee in Amell Richard next to St Kewe, suit as above; fine for suit, 12d.

[*Arrallas, in St Enoder*]:
Heirs of Trethyreff, 1 knight's fee in Argawles; 2s. 4d. [*payment added later*].

[*Lower Helland, in Helland, presumably*]:
John Rescarrecke and Peter Corryton esq., ¼ and ¹⁄₁₀ knight's fee in Hellond le Nethera, suit as above; fine for suit, 6d.

[*Respryn, in St Winnow*]:
John Carmynowe, in Reprynna, ¹⁄₁₀ knight's fee, suit as above; fine for suit, 6d.

[*Trenowin, in Ludgvan*]:
Richard le Rouse, ¹⁄₁₀ knight's fee in Trenewyn, suit; fine for suit, 6d.

Note: should pay 2s. as appears by a rental of 18 Hen. VII [1502–3] [*sentence added later*].
Richard Vivian, ⅙ knight's fee in Trenewyn.

[*Polscoe, in St Winnow*]:
Heirs of Litelton, 1/12 knight's fee in Polscoith next to Lostythyell; rent 6d.

[*Trethew, in Menheniot*]:
Heirs of Lord Broke, 1 knight's fee in Trethewe next Liscard, suit; fine for suit, 12d.

[*Polsue, in St Erme*]:
The earl of Oxford, 1 fee in Polsewe, suit; fine for suit, 2s.

[*East Anstey (parish), Devon*]:
John Prouce of Chagford and the heirs of Bere in Hunstham [*Huntsham, Devon*] and Thomas Hexte, in right of their wives, by knight's service in Ansty Crewes, suit as above; fine for suit, 12d.

[*Unidentified; possibly Tregongon, in Veryan*]:
Robert Tregongon, in Tregongon, by knight's service and suit as above; fine for suit, 6d.

[*St Ingunger, in Lanivet*]:
Nicholas Opy, by knight's service, in Styngorgar in Lan Nyvett, suit as above; fine for suit, 6d.

[*Penquite, in Lanlivery*]:
Heirs of Goodman, by knight's service, in Penquite next to Boderdell, suit as above; fine for suit, 6d.

[*Cotleigh (parish), Devon*]:
Robert Yeo, by knight's service, in Cotleigh next Honyton [*Honiton*] in Devon, suit as above; fine for suit, 12d.

Sum of free tenants yearly, 29s. 9d.

[*Higher and Great Beer, in Marhamchurch*]:
Heirs of Beachym, now George Speeke kt, in Overa Beere and Nethar Beere next to Maramchurch, by knight's service; fine for suit of court, 12d. [*all added later*].

[*Little Modbury, in Modbury, Devon*]:
Heirs [*blank*], in Littell Modburie in Devon [*blank*]; 12d. [*all added later*].

* * *

Boderdell
[*Bodardle, in Lanlivery*]

Inquisition taken there 14 August 8 Eliz. [1566] by Henry Compton esq., one of the lords of the manor.

Free tenants

[*Penquite, in Lanlivery*]:
Stephen Goodman, 1 ferling in Penquyt, by knight's service with 2 suits of court at the Great Ditch[18] and relief; rent 14*d*. Relief 3*s*. 1*d*. in 8 Hen. VIII [1516–17] [*relief added later*].

[*Roseney, in Lanlivery*]:
Lawrence Tregonya, 1 ferling in Tresney, by knight's service with suit; rent 3*s*. 6*d*.

[*Tregantle, in Lanlivery*]:
Nicholas Kendall gent., 1 ferling in Tregantell, previously the coheirs of Robert Davy, by knight's service with 2 suits of court; rent 18*d*.

Sum of free tenants yearly, 6*s*. 2*d*.

Customary tenants

[*Westow, in Lanlivery*]:
John Thoma alias Skott, by copy dated under the seal of John Sentclere, 14 October 31 Hen. VIII [1539], 1 tenure in Wystowe, then John Hockin's, house in which he lives, close called Long Aker, 3 acres, close called Wyll Parke, 1½ acres, close called Over Wyll Parke, 1¼ acres, close called the Gomme, 1½ acres, close called the Parke Above the ..wne[19], 1½ acres, close called Above the Shewte, ¼ acre, close called the Crosse Stiche, 1 acre, close called Torre Wyll, 5 acres, 4 parcels of land called Hemphayes, ¼ acre, close called lez Backsyde, ¾ acre; yearly rent 6*s*. 8*d*.

[*Roselath, in Lanlivery*]:
John Sweet, by copy dated under the seal of John Moyne, 1 September 10 Hen. VIII [1518], 1 tenement in Roslath, to which belongs, as appears by the extent made 18 Hen. VII [1502–3], ⅓ of Rosloth, 18 acres; rent 4*s*. 8*d*.

---

[18] See above, p. 182 n. 11.
[19] Initial letters are badly formed and uncertain.

[*Penquite and Demesnes, both in Lanlivery, and Trescoll, in Luxulian*]:
Walter Kendall, by copy made by John Stcler, 25 October 35 Hen. VIII [1543], reversion[20] of lands with appurtenances in Penquytt, Liteldymen and Rosegawle which John Godman now holds; belonging to the tenement in Penquyte are 7 closes, 36 acres; 2 closes called Litle Demyn, 7 acres; yearly rent 36s. 8d.

[*Trevilmick, in Lanlivery, and land presumably near Lesquite, in Lanivet*]:
Nicholas Kendall gent., 1 tenure in Trevilmock, 6 closes, 54 acres, and a parcel of land called the Quyte, 3 acres; rent 14s. 1d. of which 7d. for lez Quyte.

[*Chark, in Lanlivery*]:
Joan Trelevyn widow, by copy dated 1 September 10 Hen. VIII [1518] under the seal of John Moyne clerk, surveyor, 1 tenure in Charke, house in which she lives, barn and other necessary buildings, garden, close called Above Towne, 4 acres, close called Brodeparke, 1 acre, close called Hodge Parke, 5 acres, close called Bargins Parke, 2 acres, close called the Bakes Parke, 3 roods, close called Blownes Hill, 1 acre 1 rood, close called Horsnagrasse, 2 acres, close called Barneparke, 3 roods, common pasture in Redmore, close called Yonglond, 3 acres, 2 small closes lying together, 1 rood; yearly rent 9s. 5d.

[*Roseney Mill and Roseney, in Lanlivery*]:
Lawrence Tregonyen, by copy dated 1 September 10 Hen. VIII [1518] demised by John Moyne clerk, surveyor, 1 tenure in Roseney Mill, Over Roseney and Lower Roseney; [*in Over Roseney*], close called the Newe Parke, 1 acre 1 rood, close called Old Parke, 1 acre 1 rood, close called Brodefeld, 4 acres, close called the Rede, 2 acres; in Roseney the Lower, close called Stegges Parke, 2 acres, close called Horseparke, 3 acres, close called Keybyn, 3½ acres, close called Above Towne, 2 acres, parcel of land called the Downe; rent 8s. 6d. for the tenement, 6s. 8d. for the mill.

[*Pennant, in Lanlivery*]:
John Curteys sen., by copy dated under the seal of John Fourd, 25 Hen. VIII [1533–4], 1 tenure in Pennaunt which John Swete

---

[20] 'reversion' qualified by an obscure word, *perpertic*' ('perpetual'), or the like.

forfeited into the lords' hands, 6 closes called Heyley Closes, 15 acres, and 39 acres of arable land, 3 roods of meadow; rent 12s.

[*Tregantle, in Lanlivery*]:
Nicholas Kendall jun., son of the late Lawrence Kendall, 1 tenement in Tregantell and ½ of a parcel of land called lez Devytt; the former containing 5 closes, 12 acres, and 6 acres of arable land, the latter 4 acres of pasture; rent 10s. 8d.

[*Crift, in Lanlivery, presumably*]:
Richard Bryne, by copy dated under the seal of John Moyne, 1 September 10 Hen. VIII [1518], 1 tenure at lez Croft, 4 closes, 10 acres, and 12 acres of arable; rent 8s. 4d.;
the same Richard, without copy, half 1 pasture called lez Devyt, 4 acres; rent 4d.

[*Boslymon, in Lanlivery*]:
Thomas Bartlet, without copy, 1 tenure at Boseloman, 2 closes, 18 acres, common for his animals; rent 5s. 10d.
Nicholas Carlian, by copy dated under the seal of John Moyne, 13 April 7 Hen. VIII [1516], 1 tenure with 4 closes, 18 acres, in Boseloman; rent 8s.

[*Creney, in Lanlivery*]:
Thomas Littelton gent., without copy, 1 tenure in Creweney, 4 closes, 27 acres; rent 6s. 8d.

[*Roseney, in Lanlivery*]:
Thomas Trenanz, without copy, 1 tenement in Rosewey, 7 closes, 27 acres; rent 10s.

[*Chark, in Lanlivery, and Trescoll, in Luxulian*]:
John Hewett, in right of Joan his wife, by copy dated under the seal of John Fourd, 26 Hen. VIII [1534–5], reversion of 1 tenure in Chark, Rosegowly and Buntesmede formerly John Tylbott's [*sic*], 5 closes, 5½ acres, moor called Buntesmede, 10½ acres, and 28 acres of arable land; rent 9s. 5d.

[*Breney, in Lanlivery*]:
Henry Pethick, without copy, 1 tenure in Breyny, with 1 close, ½ acre, and 18 acres of arable land, once Thomas Brode's, rent 5s. 1d.; 1 tenement with 1 close, ½ acre, and 18 acres of arable land in Breyny, rent 5s. 1d., once John Richardes's; another tenure there

with 18 acres of land, once Thomas Brode's and John Richardes's, rent 5s.; total yearly rent 15s. 2d.
Philip Josep, without copy, 1 tenure, 5 closes, 18 acres, land called Fursedown, 18 acres; yearly rent 20s. 4d.

[*Bodwen, in Lanlivery, presumably*]:
John Helman, without copy, 1 tenement, close and garden, ½ acre, and 18 acres of arable land, in Ney' Bodlben [*sic*]; rent 7s.
John Heliar, without copy, 2 tenures, 2 closes, ½ acre, and 54 acres of arable land, in Bodwen; rent 17s.

[*Land presumably near Lesquite, in Lanivet; at Demesnes and at Bodardle, both in Lanlivery; and 'Howpers Mill' (lost)*]:
The same John, a parcel of land called Lez Quyte; rent 7d.;
the same, 1 tenement, 6 closes, 54 acres of arable land, in Demmen; rent 32s. 8d. (usually let by indenture and not by copy [*added later*]);
the same, 1 pasture called Boderdell Close, 3 acres; rent 8s.;
the same, in Boderdell, once Elizabeth Sweate's, 1 close, 6 acres; rent 10s. 8d.;
the same, 1 corn mill called Howpers Mill, 2 closes, 3 acres of land and ¼ acre of wood; formerly should pay 8s. and, because the mill is totally decayed, now only 3s. 4d.;
the same, 3 closes called Hayly Closes, 10 acres, in Boderedell; rent 20s.

[*Red Moor, in Lanlivery*]:
The tenants and residents within the manor hold common pasture in Redmoore; yearly rent 20s.[21]

Tenants pay yearly in lieu of days' work, 12d.

[*Hell Grass Common, in Lanlivery*]:
Tenants in Roseney, Breyny and Wystowe hold 1 moor called Haylegras and pay 7d.

    Sum of customary tenants yearly, £15 13s. 11½d.

    Sum total yearly value of the manor, £16 1½d.

---

[21] An addition, slightly later, names the tenants and tenements enjoying common; not transcribed here, because partly cramped and illegible.

Paid to the reeve yearly for his stipend, for collecting and raising the rents of the manor, as was the ancient usage, 5s. 4d.

Sum of allowances and repayments, 5s. 4d.
Remains clear [blank].

Customs

The tenants present that John Arundell, Henry Compton and Nicholas Kendall, esqs and John Helyar are lords of this manor.
The 4 lords may choose a steward to keep their courts every 3 weeks.
There belongs to this manor a court baron.
The lords time out of memory of man have had stray goods.
Every lord may keep a court of survey of his part and set and let for his own part by copy of court roll for term of 3 lives.
Every customary tenant dying seized of customary land pays best beast for a heriot and, upon surrender or forfeiture, a farleu.
The wife of every customary tenant dying seized of customary lands ought to have her widow's estate by the custom of this manor.
There belong to this manor toll tin in Redmoore, Hallegrasse, Saddellbacke and Tregaron Moore [*Red Moor, Hell Grass Common, and 'Sadleback' (lost), all in Lanlivery; and possibly moor below Tregarden, in Luxulian*], made at the 16th dish; tenants yearly choose one to gather toll, called the toller; his allowance, 4s. 8d. for sacks.
Every customary tenant shall be reeve and tithingman; reeve's allowance, 5s. 4d.
There is a wood of oaks and hazel of 40 years growth, containing 3½ acres.
There belongs to this manor 1 acre of land at Roche whereby the lords are patrons of the church of Roche; [*blank*] is now incumbent; benefice worth yearly £20.

EXTENT, 1571
(AR2/1341, parts)

Contents

Manor of Reperry 199
Manor of Bodbrane 202
Manor of Prospidnick 204
Manor of Pengwedna 205

EXTENT OF 1571 (parts)

Repery
[*Reperry, in Lanivet*]

Free tenants

Resgarens, in St Colombe Over [*Roserrans, in St Columb Major*]: Heir of John Moyle, now Richard Moyle of St Austell, 1 acre [Cornish];[1] yearly rent, without [with *deleted*] suit of court, and other service, 12*d*.

Pennans, within the parish of St Stephens in Brannel [*Pennance, in St Stephen in Brannel*]:
Heir of John Rosogan, now Peter Bevill gent., the son of John Bevyll esq., 1 acre [Cornish] in socage;[2] yearly rent, and suit of court, as above, 10*s*. 11*d*. Tenant says that he pays only 9*s*. 10*d*.

Treliver [*Treliver, in St Wenn*]:
Heir of John Treliver, now Thomas Kerne [James Trelyuer *deleted*], son of Pascoe (*Pascasii*) Kerne, 1 acre [Cornish] in fee Gloucester, by knight's service;[3] yearly rent with suit of court, as above, 12*d*. [2*s*. 1*d*. *deleted*]. Tenant says that it is only 12*d*. rent. Relief, 11*s*. 1¼*d*. and ½ of ¼*d*. as appears in 20 Eliz., 1578, for the death of Pascoe Kerne.[4]

Tregomer, in St Columbe Over, on the northern side of the vill [*Tregamere, in St Columb Major*]:
Heir of David Tregarreck and Richard Boscawen, now Nicholas

---

[1] In this, and in some of the following entries, 'Cornish' has been supplied from a seventeenth-century survey, AR2/1346.
[2] 'socage' replaces 'knight's service', deleted. The few other changes by the scribe to the nature of tenure are not noted below; the final version is given here for this and the following three manors.
[3] This is the larger 'acre' of Cornish land held of the duke of Gloucester's former fees, not the smaller Cornish acre of fee Mortain.
[4] In this and the following manors, a later hand has added details of reliefs in the margin for some of the free tenants, and other alterations, particularly to names of tenants, have been made in several hands; see above in the Introduction.

Boscawen and Francis Penkevell esq., [*service blank*]; rent, as above, 4*d*.

Trelyver, in St Wen [*Treliver, in St Wenn*]:
Heir of Anger, now John Dengy, 1 acre [Cornish], by knight's service with common suit; yearly rent, as above, 6*d*. [9*d*. *deleted*].

Bodmin Whitles [*Whitley, in Bodmin parish*]:
Heir of John Sadler, now William Woolcock son of Thomas Woolcock [John Hary *deleted*], [*blank*] acre(s); yearly rent without [with *deleted*] suit of court and other service, as above, 3*s*. 9*d*.

Synt Nichus Parkes [*St Nicholas, in Bodmin parish*]:
Heir of John Triprolett, now Thomas [Nicholas *deleted*] Oppy, [*blank*] acre(s); yearly rent, without [with *deleted*] suit of court, and other service, as above, 7*d*. [8*d*. *deleted*].

Bodman [*Bodmin parish*]:
Heir of John Kempton, now John Pasco, 1 close called Quarr Parke [*now Copshorn*]; yearly rent, as above, 5½*d*.
Heir of Martin Newall, now [*blank*], 1 close called Bye Hill Parke; yearly rent with service, as above, 5½*d*.

Bodmyn Forstrete [*Fore Street, in Bodmin town*]:
Heir of Benedict Burnard, now [*blank*], 1 house; yearly rent with service, as above, 1*d*.
Heir of Joan (*Janna*) Harr', now Robert Sturgyon, 1 barn; yearly rent, as above, 20*d*. [21*d*. *deleted*]. Query if he holds by indenture in fee or by terms of years.
The heir of John Grinsye, now Otto Teluddar [*sic*]; yearly rent, 16*d*.

Bodynnyell, in Bodmyn parish [*Bodiniel, in Bodmin parish*]:
Heir of John Samell, now Thomas Oppye; rent, as above, 2½*d*.
Heir of John Phillippe, now William Cappar; rent, as above, 2½*d*.
Heir of Glynn of Morwall [*Morval (parish)*], now Peter Northaye, 1 close, by service; yearly rent, as above, 4*d*.

Boskere, in the parish of Bodmyn, on the northern side of St Laurence [*Boskear, north of St Lawrence, both in Bodmin parish*]:
Heir of Cheke [Beare *deleted*], now Richard Coundye, formerly of Bodmyn; rent, as above, 7*d*.

Canalegy [*Cannalidgey, in St Issey*]:
Heir of Nicholas Nascaven [Falmouthe *deleted*], now William

Kendall, 1 acre Cornish by knight's service in the fee of Gloucester; rent, with common suit of court, as above, 3s. 9d. Relief, 11s. 1¼d. and ½ of ¼d. William purchased it from Nicholas who did fealty on 16 October 3 Eliz., 1561, and Thomas Beere gent. used to buy an outer garment, *viz.* a tunic, for which he will pay the lord 4d.[5]

Conventionaries

Respery [*Reperry, in Lanivet*]:
John Jankyn, 1 tenement; rent at the 4 yearly terms, and other service, 20s. and 1 day in autumn;
the same, 1 corn mill and 1 stamping mill with 1 blowing house [*last 4 words deleted*] in diverse parcels next to the water; yearly rent with service, as above, 6s. 8d. and 20d. [*20d. deleted*];
the same, 1 blowing house called Sente Bennettes Howse and ½ acre annexed to it; rent, as above, 20d.
John Edward, 1 tenement; rent, as above, 26s. 8d.

Canalysy [*Cannalidgey, in St Issey*]:
Thomas Joce, 1 tenement; rent, as above, 21s.

Trenance Wolas [*Trenance (Wolas), in Withiel*]:
Nicholas Jobe, 1 tenement; rent, as above, 20s.

Tredenan [*Tredenham, in Lanivet*]:
Peter Marchaunt, 1 tenement; rent, as above, 15s.

Canalysy [*Cannalidgey, in St Issey*]:
Henry Bennett, 1 tenement; yearly rent 10s.

Borelane in Bodmyn [*presumably a lane off Bore Street, in Bodmin town*]:
John Blight, schoolmaster, at the lord's will, 1 small meadow on the west side of a garden belonging to the land of the heirs of John Blight, merchant; rent 20d.

Sum, [*blank*].

* * *

---

[5] The last sentence has been crammed into an empty space in the manuscript; the reading is nevertheless clear, though the sense is obscure.

Bodbrane
[*Bodbrane, in Duloe*]

Free tenants

Lamelyn alias Lametton [*Lamellion, in Liskeard parish*]:
John Coplestone,[6] now John Harryes, by knight's service, 1 acre Cornish; yearly rent, with 2 suits of court, and other service, 3*d*. Relief, 12*s*. 6*d*. in 22 Eliz., 1580, for the death of John Harrys.

Gormelleck [*Gormellick, in Liskeard parish*]:
Heir of John Lawharen, now Robert Moye [John Harrye *deleted*], ⅛ acre Cornish, service [*omitted*]; rent, as above, 2*s*. 2*d*. And 5*s*. relief when it arises.
Heir of John Piper, now [John Broune *deleted*] Christopher Come in right of his wife the daughter of the said Browne, ⅕ acre Cornish, in socage, by service of 2 suits of court; yearly rent, as above, 13*d*. Relief, 2*s*. 6*d*. in 5 & 6 Philip & Mary, 1558.
Heir of Robert John, now John Harryes, ⅕ acre [Cornish] which Harris purchased from John Marke jun., with 2 suits of court; yearly rent, as above, 13*d*. Relief, 2*s*. in 22 Eliz., 1580.
Heir of Robert Dawes, now John Harryes, Richard Laundry and Alice Mone, ⅕ acre [Cornish] in socage; yearly rent, as above, 13*d*. and relief for the death of any of them. Harrys pays 2½*d*., Laundry 2½*d*. and Moune 8*d*. For Harrys ¹⁄₂₀ of the relief, 7½*d*. Alice Mone, 7½*d*. Landery, for ¹⁄₁₀, 15*d*.

Algall Wallis in Lyskerd ['*Argalls Walls alias Grove Park*' (*lost*), *in Liskeard parish*]:
Heir of John Kempe, now Robert Kempe, ½ acre, by service of 2 suits of court; yearly rent, as above, 3*s*. 6*d*. Relief 6*s*. 3*d*.

['*Great Place*' (*lost*), *in Liskeard town*]:
Heir of Reginald Bere, now Richard Roscarrock esq., ½ acre by service of court; yearly rent, as above, 2*s*. 6*d*. Relief 6*s*. 3*d*.
Heir of Thomas Lamellyn [Bowcome *deleted*], now Jonathan (*Jenothas*) Trelawny, 1 acre by service of court; yearly rent, as above, 1 *lb*. of pepper.

---

[6] The sense would suggest that the scribe should have written 'Heir of' before 'John'.

Penbugell and the Fosse [*Penbugle and Voss, both in Duloe*]:
Heir of John Champlet, now William Gryllys, ½ acre [Cornish],[7] with common suit, in socage; yearly rent, 2s. 2d. For the death of William Grilles, a relief of 6s. 3d. as appears by the court roll of 20 Eliz., 1578, and the account.

Sum, 13s. 11d. and 1 *lb*. of pepper.

Conventionaries

Bodbrane [*Bodbrane, in Duloe*]:
Elizabeth Clementes, 1 tenement; rent at the 4 yearly terms, with suit of court and other service, 30s., and for work silver, 13d.

Meade ['*Meade*' *(lost), in Duloe*]:
John Carne, 1 tenement; yearly rent, as above, 7s., and for work silver, 6d.

Benok [*Benoak, in Duloe*]:
The same, 1 tenement; yearly rent, as above, 19s. 3d., and for work silver, 9d.
Alice Jagowe, 1 tenement; yearly rent, as above, 20s., and for work silver, 9d.
Walter Barret, 1 tenement; rent, as above, 20s., and for work silver, 9d.

Stokes [*Stock's, in Duloe*]:
Robert Abraham, 1 tenement; rent, as above, 17s., and for work silver, 8d.

Stokouer [*Higher Stock, in Duloe*]:
Henry Hockin, 1 tenement; yearly rent, as above, 16s., and for work silver, 9d.

Stokenether [*Lower Stock, now Stock's Cottage, in Duloe*]:
The same, 1 tenement; rent, as above, 24s., and for work silver, 13d.
Cecilia Hockin, widow, 1 tenement; rent, as above, 25s. 1d. [*all deleted*].

Penbugell and Millonde [*Penbugle and 'Millparke' (lost), both in Duloe*]:
John Comgann, 1 tenement; yearly rent 13s. 4d., and for work money, 6d.

---

[7] Supplied from a seventeenth-century survey, AR2/1346.

Bodbrane [*Bodbrane, in Duloe*]:
John Horsdon, 1 tenement; yearly rent 42s., and for work silver, 13d.; 1 capon.

        Sum of customary rents, £10 9s. 5d.
 Sum of free and customary rents, £11 3s. 4d. and 1 lb. of pepper.
    Sum of sale of days' work, 7s. 11d. and 2 capons.[8]
             Sum, [*blank*].

       * * *

Prospinnek
[*Prospidnick, in Sithney*]

Free tenants

Pennarth, in the parish of St Keveren [*Penare, in St Keverne*]:
Heir of the earl of Oxford, now John Kylligrew esq., [*blank*] land[9] by knight's service, with common suit; yearly rent 23d.

Relegh [*Releath, in Crowan*]:
Heir of William Windeslade, now William Moham esq., [*blank*] acre[10] by [*blank*]; rent, as above, 3s. 1d.

Trevillian, within the parish of St Erth [*Trelean, in St Erth*]:
Heir of William Trewinard, now John Nance esq., [*blank*] acre Cornish,[11] by knight's service; yearly rent, as above, 4s. 6d.

Gurling [*Gurlyn, in St Erth*]:
Heir of William Gurlin, *viz.* James Nanspian, 1 knight's fee, by knight's service with suit of court; rent, as above, 20s.

Nansdrysek [*Nancetrisack, in Sithney*]:
Heir of Richard Antron, now George Paynter, 1 mill-weir; rent 4d.

Conventionaries

Nansdrysek [*Nancetrisack, in Sithney*]:
John Thomas, 1 tenement; rent at the 4 yearly terms, with other service, 11s. 5d.

---

[8] Probably an error for '1 capon', because one only is mentioned above.
[9] 1 acre Cornish in a seventeenth-century survey, AR2/1346.
[10] 1 acre Cornish in the same survey.
[11] 1 acre Cornish in the same survey.

Treverno [*Trevarno, in Sithney*]:
Alexander Trevernowe holds there; rent, as above, 20s.

Nanskerris ['*Nanskerres' (lost), in Sithney*]:
William John holds there; rent, as above, 10s. 8d.

Penpras and Chyenhale [*Penpraze and Chynhale, both in Sithney*]:
John Penpras, 2 tenements; yearly rent, as above, 30s.

Prospenek [*Prospidnick, in Sithney*]:
John Tamlyn, 1 tenement; yearly rent, as above, 22s. 4d.
Eleanor (*Elim'*) Pears, 1 tenement; as above, 20s.
Thomas Sandery, 1 tenement; yearly rent, as above, 17s. 8d.
William Davy, 1 tenement; yearly rent, as above, 13s. 4d.

Trewheverack [*Treworvack, in Constantine*]:
John Jaunken, 1 tenement; yearly rent, as above, 12s.

Helstonburgh [*Helston town*]:
John Penhenneck, 1 tenement; yearly rent 6s. 8d.;
the same, 1 tenement and 1 close; yearly rent 8s. 8d.

Blowing mill:[12]
John Penrose, 1 blowing mill, for term of years; yearly rent 3s. 4d.

Sum, [*blank*].

* * *

Pengwenna
[*Pengwedna, in Breage*]

Free tenants

Browfrowell [*Bosprowal, in Gwinear*]:
Heir of Browfrowell, now John Smythe gent.,[13] 1 acre Cornish in socage; rent, with 2 suits of court and other service, 1½d. Relief, 12s. 6d. as appears from an account of 22 Eliz., 1580.

Catabedran [*Cathebedron, in Gwinear*]:
Heir of John Pettit, now John Seyntaubin esq., 1 acre [Cornish];[14] rent, with common suit, 6d.

---

[12] The name *Chenhall* (Chynhale, in Sithney) has been added here, then deleted. An earlier rental places the mill at Nancetrisack, in Sithney: above, p. 150.
[13] Replaces an obscurely written personal name.

John Stawbyn, 1 acre [Cornish]; yearly rent with common suit, as above, 6d.

Preske [*Priske, in Mullion*]:
Heir of William Preske, now William Prysk, 1 acre Cornish; yearly rent 35s.

Redolen [*Redallen, in Breage*]:
Heir of John Carmyno, now John Carmynaw esq., 1 acre [Cornish], by knight's service; yearly rent 6d.

Kyrthen, in Crowen [*Kerthen, in Crowan*]:
Heir of William Cowlyn, now Francis Godolghan, [*blank*] acre(s), by knight's service; yearly rent with suit, as above, 6s. 1d.

Penhall [*Penhale-an-Drea, in Breage*]:
Earl of Oxford and John Kyllygrew, [*blank*] acre(s) Cornish;[15] rent, as above, [*blank*].

Sum, 42s. 8½d.

Conventionaries

Pengwenna [*Pengwedna, in Breage*]:
Henry Johan, ½ the vill; rent, at the 4 yearly terms, with other service, 18s. 6d.
Mabel Prior, the other ½ of the vill; rent, as above, 20s.

Carrioghall [*Crawle, in Breage*]:
William Ripper, 1 tenement; rent, as above, 23s. 4d.

Trevere [*Trenear, in Breage*]:
William Jenyn, 1 tenement; rent, as above, 16s.

Telligowe [*Treliggo, in Breage*]:
John Huchnance, the whole vill; yearly rent, as above, 8s.

Reddower [*Ruthdower, in Breage*]:
[*Blank*], the whole vill and mill; rent, as above, 26s. 8d. [19s. *deleted*].

Sum, £5 12s. 6d.

---

[14] In this, and in some of the following entries, 'Cornish' has been supplied from a seventeenth-century survey, AR2/1346.
[15] 2 acres Cornish in AR2/1346; compare p. 147n.

THREE MANORS OF THE EARL OF OXFORD, 1575
(AR2/464, 477 and 482)

Contents

Manor of Bejowan 208
Manor of Tregenna 220
Manor of Tresithney 229

SURVEY OF BEJOWAN, 1575
(AR2/464)

Manor of Bossueyn
in the parishes of St Columb Major and Minor, Colan
and Mowgan
[Bejowan, in St Columb Minor]

Survey made by Edward Hubberte esq.[1] and Edward Worstley gent., in August 17 Eliz. [1575] by a commission from William Lord Burleye, from examination of ancient rentals and by view and perambulation.

Free tenants within the parish of St Columb Minor

[Kestle, in St Columb Minor]:
John Arondell kt, by knight's service, ⅓ acre Cornish in Kestell; yearly rent, beyond suit of court, ward, marriage and other service, 4s.[2]

[Treloy, in St Columb Minor]:
The same, in socage, 1 acre Cornish in the vill of Treloye; yearly rent, beyond suit of court and other service, 12d.

[Treviglas, in St Columb Minor]:
The same, by charter, diverse parcels of land in Trevegles; yearly rent, beyond [*this word deleted*] suit of court and with 3d. for a sheep, and other service, 19d.

[Tolcarne, in St Columb Minor]:
Alexander Wollacome esq., in socage, 1 acre Cornish in the vill of Talkerne; yearly rent, beyond 12d. for suit of court and other service, 5s.

[Towan, in St Columb Minor]:
Francis Blewet esq. and Ralph Dewen gent., in right of their wives who were the heirs of [*blank*] Collan, in socage, 1 acre Cornish in

---

[1] Described as 'of Birchanger' (Essex) in 1576 (AR1/859) and as receiver general of the earl of Oxford in 1575 (AR1/856 and below, p. 220).
[2] For almost all of the free tenants in this survey, the stated nature of the tenure (by knight's service, socage, etc.) is followed by 'so it is said'.

the vill of Tewen; yearly rent, beyond 12*d*. for suit of court and other service, 8*d*.

[*Porth Veor, in St Columb Minor*]:
The said Francis and Ralph, in socage, certain parcels of land, 9 acres, in Porth Vere; yearly rent, beyond 12*d*. for suit of court and other service, 8*s*.

[*Towan, in St Columb Minor*]:
John Cowlyn, in socage, ½ acre Cornish in the vill of Towen; yearly rent, beyond suit of court and other service, 6*d*.
Robert Tregenfelde alias Tregonall, in socage, ½ acre Cornish in the said vill; yearly rent 8*d*., denied.

[*Hendra Veor, in St Columb Minor (near Treloy)*]:
John Arondell of Talverne esq. [*Tolverne, in Philleigh*], in socage, [*blank*] in the vill of Hendrevere; yearly rent, beyond suit of court and other service, 16*d*.

[*Treviglas, in St Columb Minor*]:
Richard Chappell, in socage, [*blank*] in the vill of Trevegles; yearly rent, beyond 12*d*. for suit of court, with 3*d*. yearly for a sheep, and other service, 19*d*.;
the same, in socage, ⅓ acre Cornish once John Polgrene's, in the said vill; yearly rent, with 3*d*. for a sheep, and other service, 19*d*.

[*Trebarva, in St Columb Minor*]:
James Erysye gent., in socage, diverse lands in the vill of Trebarvithe; yearly rent, beyond 12*d*. for suit of court and other service, 2*s*. 6*d*.
John Coswarthe gent., in socage, 1 acre Cornish in the said vill; yearly rent, beyond 12*d*. yearly for suit of court and other service, 12*d*.
John Hollys gent. and the heirs of William Ryskymer, in socage, ¼ acre Cornish called Gobye Acre in the said vill; yearly rent, beyond suit of court and other service, 4½*d*.
John Nance, 1 acre [Cornish] in Treb..vethe;[3] yearly rent, with common suit as above, ... [*faded*].

[*Treisaac, in St Columb Minor*]:
Pascoe ('Pasca') Tresylyan, in socage, 1 acre Cornish lying in the

---

[3] One, inserted, letter is obscure.

vill of Tredrysacke; yearly rent, beyond 12d. for suit of court and other service, ... [*faded*].

[*Bejowan, in St Columb Minor*]:
The heirs of John Cheverton, in socage, 1 tenement and certain land in the vill of Bossuyen; yearly rent, beyond suit of court and other service, 40s.

Francis Blewet and Ralph Dewyn gent., in right of their wives, certain lands and tenements in socage in the said vill; yearly rent 10s.

Free tenants within the parish of Mowgan

[*Tolcarne Merock, in St Mawgan in Pyder*]:
John Arondell kt, in socage, ⅓ acre Cornish in the vill of Talkerne; yearly rent, beyond 12d. for suit of court and other service, 9s.

John Norton, in socage, certain land in the vill of Talkerne; yearly rent, beyond suit of court and other service, 12s.

Free tenants within the parish of St Columb Maior

[*Gaverigan, in St Columb Major*]:
John Gavrigan gent., by charter in socage, 1 acre Cornish in the vill of Gavrigan; yearly rent, beyond 12d. for suit of court and other service, 4s. Relief 12s. 6d.

[*Ruthvoes, in St Columb Major*]:
John Trypconye gent., by charter in socage, 3 acres Cornish in the vill of Ruthvous; yearly rent, beyond 6d. for suit of court and other service, 1d. Relief ... s. [*faded*] 6d.

[*Trevarren, in St Columb Major*]:
Henry Rowse, by charter in socage, 1 acre Cornish in the vill of Trevarran; yearly rent, beyond suit of court and other service, 4s. Relief 12s. 6d.

John Trewollaye gent., in socage by charter, 1 acre Cornish in the vill of Trevarran; yearly rent, beyond 12d. for suit of court and other service, 8s. Rent of 4s. yearly denied.

John John of Blysland [*Blisland (parish)*], in socage, ½ acre Cornish in the said vill; yearly rent, beyond 12d. for suit of court and other service, 3s. 7d.

[*Blank*], ⅓ acre Cornish as one of the heirs of Hoskye; yearly rent 9¼d. Relief 4s. 2d.

John James, in socage, in right of his wife who was one of Hoskye's

heirs, ⅓ acre Cornish in the said vill; yearly rent, beyond 12*d*. for suit of court and other service, 9¼*d*. and ½ of ¼*d*. Relief 4*s*. 2*d*.
John Cooke of Trurow, ⅓ acre Cornish in socage which he purchased from William West, one of Hosky's heirs; yearly rent, beyond common suit of court, 9¼*d*. and ½ of ¼*d*. Relief 4*s*. 2*d*. as appears from the account of 21 Eliz., 1579.
Richard Mylheneke, by charter in socage, 1 ferling in the said vill; yearly rent, beyond suit of court and other service, 16*d*.

[Killaworgey, in St Columb Major]:
Richard Oppye, in socage by charter, ½ acre Cornish in the vill of Kyllyworga; yearly rent, beyond suit of court and other service, 7*s*.
Henry Rowse, in socage, 1 acre Cornish in the said vill; yearly rent, beyond suit of court and other service, 4*s*. Relief, when it occurs, 12*s*. 6*d*.

Free tenants within the parish of Colan

[Hendra, formerly 'Hendra Mullier', in Colan]:
Richard Mylheneke, in socage by charter, 1 acre Cornish in the vill of Hendra; yearly rent, beyond suit of court and other service, 20*d*.

[Bosoughan, in Colan]:
Richard Carnesewe esq., by charter, [*blank*][4] in the vill of Bossoghan; yearly rent, beyond 12*d*. for suit of court and other service, 6*d*.

Sum of rents of free tenants yearly, £7 7s. 3½d.

Customary tenants

Bodrowgow [*Bedrugga, in St Columb Minor*]:
Robert James, by copy dated 2 October 3 & 4 Philip & Mary [1556], 1 tenure in Bodrowgoe for his life and the life of Barbara James daughter of the late Thomas James; yearly rent 6*s*. 8*d*. at the usual terms for this manor; all burdens, services and customs, heriot, suit of court at Michaelmas only.

[Trebelzue, in St Columb Minor]:
Elizabeth Davy, widow, by copy dated 29 October 26 Hen. VIII [1534], 1 tenure in Trevelsue during her widowhood; yearly rent,

---

[4] 1 acre Cornish in a seventeenth-century survey, AR2/1346.

at the usual terms within the hundred of Pider, 22s. 3d.; suit of court, heriot, other services.

John Carthue, by copy dated 26 October 28 Hen. VIII [1536], 1 tenure in Trevelsue for life; yearly rent 22s. 2d. at the usual terms for this manor; suit of court, heriot and other services. Reversion by indenture to Edward Arondell esq., William Lyon and Thomas Worthyvall, yeoman, for their lives, by Edward de Veer earl of Oxford, 19 May 14 Eliz. [1572].[5]

John Rawlen [*deleted and* dead *added*], by copy dated as above, 1 tenure in Trevelsue for life; yearly rent 22s. 3d.; suit of court and other services.

[*Porth Veor, in St Columb Minor*]:
Richard Olde, by copy dated 19 May 14 Eliz. [1572], 3 tenures in Porte Veer within the parish of St Columb Inferior, *viz.* 1 once in the tenure of Thomas Tirrell for a yearly rent of 14s. 2d., another once in the tenure of Philip Oppye for a yearly rent of 7s. 1d., and the third once in the tenure of Robert Richard for a yearly rent of 7s. 1d. as appears in the terrier;[6] for his life and the lives of Joan his wife and John Olde son of John Olde the brother of Richard; yearly rent, beyond suit of court and 3 heriots, 1 for each tenement, 28s. 4d.

Henry James, by copy dated 2 October 3 & 4 Philip & Mary [1556], 1 tenure in Porth Veer for life; yearly rent, beyond suit of court, heriot and other services, 28s. 4d.

[*Bejowan, in St Columb Minor*]:
William Carvolghe, by copy dated 2 October 3 & 4 Philip & Mary [1556], 2[7] meadows in Bossuyen for his life and the lives of John his son and Alice his daughter; yearly rent, beyond suit of court and 3d. for heriot, 16s.

[*Kestle Mill, in St Columb Minor*]:
Nicholas Trahare alias Carne, George Wolcocke and Roger Trahare alias Carne son of Nicholas, by copy dated 19 May 14 Eliz. [1572],

---

[5] Details of the reversion are crammed into the margin and are not all readable; the gist is given here. See also p. 213.
[6] i.e. the list of fields later in the survey.
[7] The reading of '2' is slightly uncertain; 3 meadows are specified later in the survey.

1 water mill for corn in Kestle with multure and the watercourse belonging, for their lives; yearly rent at the 2 usual terms, beyond suit of court, heriot and other services, 20s.

Sum of rents of customary tenants yearly, £8 6s. 10d.

[*Tenants by indenture*]

Demesne in Talkerne [*Tolcarne Merock, in St Mawgan in Pyder*]:
John Maye, Donnet his wife and Jane their daughter, by indenture dated 28 November 2 & 3 Philip & Mary [1553], by John de Veer, earl of Oxford, messuage or tenement with all lands, meadows, feedings, pastures, commons, barns, stables, orchards and gardens once in the tenure of Reginald Myghe, for their lives; yearly rent 20s. in equal portions at the Annunciation, Nativity of St John, Michaelmas and Christmas; indenture void if rent is in arrears; best beast as heriot.

Kestell [*Kestle, in St Columb Minor*]:
Thomas Atkynson, by indenture dated 28 January 17 Eliz. [1575], 1 tenement lying in Kestell once in the tenure of Thomas Coswarthe and 1 tenure in Kestell once in the tenure of John Cossewyer and formerly in the tenure of Thomas Coswarthe, for 41 years; yearly rent at the Annunciation and Michaelmas, 27s.; best beast or chattel as heriot; distraint if rent is in arrears.

Trevlesewe [*Trebelzue, in St Columb Minor*]:
Edward Arondell esq., by indenture dated 19 May 14 Eliz. [1572], lands and a tenement within the vill and fields of Trevelsue alias Treveliewe in the parish of St Columb Minor; reserved the rents, suit and services of all free tenements in Trevlesue alias Treveliewe, and all the broken ground for the tin works there; for the lives of Edward, William Lyon and Thomas Worthyvall; yearly rent 66s. 8d.; re-entry if rent is in arrears. But cancel this because it is earlier under the heading of customary tenants.[8]

Sum of the farm of demesne land yearly, beyond 66s. 8d.[9] already charged among the rents of the customary tenants, 47s.

Sum total of the whole manor yearly, ... [torn away].

---

[8] See above, p. 212, entry for John Carthue.
[9] Refers to the fact that Edward Arundell's rent of 66s. 8d. (see the last entry above) should not be included in this sum total.

Deductions

To the queen's manor of Carnanton [*in St Mawgan in Pydar*] for acquittance of rent from certain free land of Francis Blewet and Ralph Dewyn in the parish of St Columb Minor [*probably Towan*], yearly 10s.

To the queen, to the same manor for rent from customary land in the tenure of Robert James [*Bedrugga*], yearly 5s. 5d.

To the queen's manor of Carnanton [*in St Mawgan in Pyder*], for rent from customary land in the tenure of Elizabeth Davy, John Carthue and John Rawlen [*Trebelzue*], yearly 66s. 8d.

To the queen's manor of Royalton [*Rialton, in St Columb Minor*], for customary land in the tenure of Richard Olde (7s. 9½d.) and Henry[10] James (7s. 9½d.) [*Porth Veor*], yearly 15s. 7d.

To the earl of Huntingdon for rent from certain free land of Richard Oppye in the vill of Kyllyworga and parish of St Columb Maior [*Killaworgey, in St Columb Major*], yearly 4s. 3d.

To John Arundell's manor of Lanherne for quit rent from free land of John Gavrigan [*Gaverigan*], yearly 2s.

Remains clear yearly beyond deductions, £12 ...[11]

Value of the said lands if they were improved

[*Customary tenants*]

Bodrogowe [*Bedrugga, in St Columb Minor*]:
Robert James, by copy, 1 tenement and a barn roofed with straw; in a common field called Bodrogowe Fielde on the west side 39 parcels of arable land, 9 acres 1 rood 24 perches, at 5s. the acre, value 62s. 6d., the parcels intermingled in the fields [*sic*] with the lands of the queen's majesty and the free lands of Sir John Arondell, kt; 7 parcels of pasture, 1½ acres 1 rood, in a several close of pasture called the Well Parke at 10s. the acre, value 17s. 6d., likewise intermingled; 6 pieces of pasture, 1½ acres, in a several close of pasture called Newe Close at 4s. the acre, value 6s., likewise intermingled; 7 small pieces of arable land, 1½ acres 10 perches, in a field called the Higher Feild adjoining New Parke at 4s. the acre, value 6s.; a several meadow called Bodrogowe Meadow, ½ acre, value 5s.; ¼ of a several close of pasture called the Down, 6 acres, at 4s.

---

[10] 'Henry' deleted, 'Robert' added and then deleted.
[11] The rest of this line is torn away.

the acre, value 24s., likewise intermingled without any division or bounders; total yearly value, £6 12d. Meadow, ½ acre; pasture, 9 acres 1 rood; arable, 11 acres; yearly rent 6s 8d.[12]

[*Trebelzue, in St Columb Minor*]:[13]
John Carthue, by copy of court roll for his life, 1 tenement roofed with straw and a curtilage belonging, ½ acre; certain pieces of arable land in 38 parcels divided, 22½ acres 1 rood, in a common field there called Easte Felde at 2s. 8d. the acre, value 60s. 8d.; 7 pieces of arable land, 2½ acres 1 rood, in a common field there called the West Felde on the west side of the way leading towards Tregoryan [*Tregurrian, in St Mawgan in Pyder*] at 2s. the acre, value 5s. 6d.; rough and furzy pasture, 12 acres, in a pasture called the common heathy down being without any division at 20d. the acre, value 20s.; certain pieces of pasture, 12 acres, in diverse parcels divided in a close called Chappell Parke, at 3s. the acre, value 36s.; 7 pieces of pasture, 3½ acres, in a field called the Olde Close at 3s. the acre, value 10s. 6d.; little parcel of pasture, 1 rood, value 10d.; a several close of pasture near the well, ½ acre 1 rood, value 2s. 6d.; a several close of pasture called the Haye, 20 perches, value 6d.; in the town place there called Trevlesew, 1 rood 22 perches, value nil; total yearly value £6 16s. 6d. Pasture, 28½ acres; meadow, nil; arable, 25½ acres; yearly rent 22s. 6d.

Elizabeth Davye, by copy of court roll for her life, 1 tenement roofed with straw and a curtilage belonging, ½ acre; certain pieces of arable land in 38 parcels divided, 22½ acres 1 rood, lying in a common field called the East Felde at 2s. 8d. the acre, value 60s. 8d.; 7 pieces of arable land, 2½ acres 1 rood, in a common field there called the West Feld, on the west side of the field[14] leading towards Tregoryan [*Tregurrian, in St Mawgan in Pyder*] at 2s. the acre, value 5s. 6d.; rough and furzy pasture, 12 acres, in a pasture called the common heathy down being without any division at 20d. the acre, value 20s.; certain pieces of pasture, 12 acres, in diverse parcels

---

[12] In this section of the document the central part of each entry ends with a statement of the yearly value. Acreages and the rent are entered in the margins. For some entries there are other marginal memoranda; these are printed here after the rent.
[13] Most place-names in this section have been supplied from earlier in the survey.
[14] The text reads 'field', but 'way' is intended: see the previous entry.

divided in a close there called Chappell Parke at 3s. the acre, value 36s.; 7 pieces of pasture, 3½ acres, in a field called the Olde Close at 3s. the acre, value 10s. 6d.; little parcel of pasture, 1 rood, value 10d.; a several close of pasture near the well, ½ acre 1 rood, value 2s. 6d.; a several close of pasture called the Haye, 20 perches, value 6d.; in the town place there called Trevlesewe, 1 rood 22 perches, value nil; total yearly value £6 16s. 6d. Pasture, 28½ acres; meadow, nil; arable, 25½ acres; yearly rent 22s. 3d.

[*Meadows named from Bejowan*]:
William Carvolghe, by copy, 3 several meadows called Bossuyen Meadowes, *viz.* 1 containing 3 acres, another lying in strakes[15] containing 2 acres, the third containing ½ acre, adjoining the lands of Sir John Arondell kt called Myll Parke, at 10s. the acre; total yearly value 55s. Meadow, 5½ acres; yearly rent 16s.

[*Porth Veor, in St Columb Minor*]:
Richard Olde, by copy, 1 tenement called Porte Veere roofed with straw, a barn and a curtilage, ½ acre of pasture, value 5s.; little close of pasture in 2 parts divided, 1 acre, near the tenement, value 13s. 4d.; a several close of pasture called the Moore Close, 1 acre, value 5s.; 2 several closes of pasture, 3 acres at 6s. 8d. the acre, value 20s., at the west end of the close called the Well Felde; a little several close of pasture called Lambe Close, ½ acre, value 3s. 4d.; in a field there enclosed called Well Felde 3 acres of arable land at 5s. the acre, value 15s.; a several close called Oxe Close, 3 acres of pasture at 6s. 8d. the acre, value 20s.; a several close of pasture called Newe Close, 1½ acres, value 10s.; arable lands in a field called the Higher Felde, 9 acres in diverse parcels at 5s. the acre, value 45s.; arable lands in a field called Corcollam in sundry small parcels, 1 acre, value 6s. 8d.; arable lands in a field called the Midle Feilde in diverse parcels, 9 acres at 5s. the acre, value 45s.; arable lands and some pasture in a field called Lower Feilde in diverse parcels, 13 acres at 5s. the acre, value 65s.; total yearly value £12 13s. 4d. Pasture, 10½ acres; arable, 35 acres; meadow, nil; yearly rent 28s. 4d.

Henry James, by copy, 1 tenement called Port Veer, a barn roofed with straw and a curtilage and 2 little pightles of pasture adjoining

---

[15] O.E.D., s.v. strake, gives 'strip' as one meaning of this word, and cites its use for a strip of meadow in a legal document of 1503.

the tenement, 1 rood, value 20s.; arable land in a close called Wellfelde in sundry parcels divided, 3 acres at 5s. the acre, value 15s. 0d.; a several close of pasture called Midle Parke, 1½ acres at 6s. 8d. the acre, value 10s.; a several close of pasture called the Highwaye Close, 3 acres at 8s. the acre, value 24s.; arable lands in a field called the Higher Felde, 9 acres in diverse parcels at 5s. the acre, value 45s.; arable lands in a field there called Corcollam in sundry small pieces, 1 acre, value 6s. 8d.; arable lands in Midlefeld, 9 acres in diverse parcels at 5s. the acre, value 45s.; arable land and some pasture in Laver Felde in diverse parcels, 13 acres at 5s. the acre, value 65s.; total yearly value £11 10s. 8d. Pasture, 4 acres 3 roods; meadow, nil; arable, 35 acres; yearly rent 28s. 4d.

[*Kestle Mill, in St Columb Minor*]:
Nicholas Carne, by copy, 1 water mill called Bossuyen Mill roofed with straw and 1 acre of pasture; value 100s. Pasture, 1 acre; yearly rent 20s. Note that the mill was well worth 100s. yearly when the tenants of the manor used to grind their corn there and not elsewhere and when the stream fishing was not hindered by Quyntrell.

Sum of the value of the customary lands, £51 13s.

[*Tenants by indenture*]

Talkerne [*Tolcarne Merock, in St Mawgan in Pyder*]:
John Maye, by indenture for term of 3 lives, 1 tenement in Talkerne, barn and stable roofed with straw and an orchard belonging, 1 rood of pasture, value 13s. 4d.; 2 parcels of pasture in a field called the Higher Field of Talkerne, 5½ acres at 6s. 8d. the acre, value 36s. 8d., intermingled with the free lands of Sir John Arondell kt and one John Norton; arable lands in a field enclosed called Penhendrey in 6 parcels divided, 3 acres at 8s. the acre, value 24s., all likewise intermingled; piece of pasture, 2 acres, in a field called the Crosse Feilde of Talkerne at 8s. the acre, value 16s., likewise intermingled; arable lands in 6 parcels divided in a field enclosed called Penclyes, 2½ acres at 8s. the acre, value 20s., likewise intermingled; 3 pieces of arable land, 3 acres, in a field called Tonkreke on the north side of the field called Crosse Feilde at 8s. the acre, value 24s., likewise intermingled; a several close called the Newe Close, 1 acre 1 rood of pasture at 8s. the acre, value 10s.; a several close of arable land called Pengelly, 1 acre, value 8s., likewise intermingled; piece of pasture, 1 acre 1 rood 10 perches, in a field called Lite Penclyes at 8s. the acre, value 10s., likewise intermingled; close of arable land

called the Litle Close above the garden, ½ acre, value 5s.; piece of pasture, 1½ acres, in a close of pasture called Lampeyan at 8s. the acre, value 12s., likewise intermingled; piece of pasture, 1 acre, in a field enclosed called the Newe Parke, value 10s., likewise intermingled; 4 pieces of arable land, 3 acres, in a field enclosed called Landemeyre at 8s. the acre, value 24s., likewise intermingled; 7 pieces of pasture, 3 acres, in a close of pasture enclosed called the Gellye at 4s. the acre, value 12s., likewise intermingled; piece of meadow, 2 acres, in a several meadow called Talkerne Meadowe at 13s. 4d. the acre, value 26s. 8d., likewise intermingled; piece of meadow, 3 roods, lying in 5 parcels, value 10s., in a meadow called the Higher Meadow of Talkerne, likewise intermingled; total yearly value £13 20d. Meadow, 2½ acres; pasture, 15½ acres 1 rood 10 perches; arable, 13 acres; yearly rent 20s.

Trevlesewe [*Trebelzue, in St Columb Minor*]:
Edward Arondell esq., by indenture among other lands, 1 tenement late the customary tenement of John Rawlen deceased, roofed with straw and a small curtilage belonging, ½ acre; pieces of arable land in 38 parcels divided, 22½ acres 1 rood, in a common field called Est Felde at 2s. 8d. the acre, value 60s. 8d.; 7 pieces of arable land, 2½ acres 1 rood, in a common field called the West Felde upon the west side of the way leading towards Tregoryan [*Tregurrian, in St Mawgan in Pyder*] at 2s. the acre, value 5s. 6d.; rough and furzy pasture, 12 acres, in a pasture called the common heathy down, without any division at 20d. the acre, value 20s.; certain pieces of pasture, 12 acres, in diverse parcels divided, in a close called Chappell Parke at 3s. the acre, value 36s.; 7 pieces of pasture, 3½ acres, in a field called the Olde Close at 3s. the acre, value 10s. 6d.; little parcel of pasture, 1 rood, value 9d.; a several close of pasture near the well, ½ acre 1 rood, value 2s. 6d.; a several close of pasture called the Haye, 20 perches, value 6d.; in the town place called Trevlesewe, 1 rood 22 perches of ground, value nil ...[16] Yearly rent 22s. 3d.

Kestell [*Kestle, in St Columb Minor*]:
Thomas Atkynson, by an indenture along with other property, 2 tenements called Kestell roofed with straw and 2 gardens belonging, value 13s. 4d.; in a several close called Kestle Close in

---

[16] Total value and summary of land use torn away.

diverse parcels 80 acres of pasture at 3s. 4d. the acre, value £13 6s. 8d.; in a certain moory or meadow ground 2½ acres at 4s. the acre, value 10s.; total yearly value £14 10s. Pasture, 80 acres; meadow, 2½ acres; yearly rent 27s. Small elms about the 2 tenements, 12. Note: Sir John Arondell has also a tenement here called Kestell and ⅓ of the land besides my lord's ⅔.

Total value of the farm lands yearly worth to be let, £34 8s. 2d. Sum total value of demesne lands and customary lands yearly, £86 14d.

[*Total customary and demesne land of the whole manor*]: pasture, 206½ acres 1 rood 20 perches; meadow, 10½ acres 1 rood; arable, 170½ acres; the mill's pasture, 1 acre.

Sum, [blank].

* * *

SURVEY OF TREGENNA, 1575 (AR2/477)

Manor of Trigennowe Wolas and Trigennowe Warthow
[*Tregenna, in St Ewe*]

Survey by Edward Hubbarte esq., receiver general of Edward de Veer earl of Oxford, and Edward Worstley gent., in August 17 Eliz. [1575] by a commission from William Cecil Lord Burleye, from examination of ancient rentals and by view and perambulation.

Free tenants

[*Trelean Vean, in St Ewe*]:
John Wadham and Anthony Tanner esq., by charter, ½ tenure and land called ... [*torn*],[1] 6 acres; yearly rent, with 12*d*. yearly for suit of court called suit fine and other service, 2*s*.[2]
Nicholas Kempthorne gent., by charter, ½ the said tenure and land called Trelyan Vyan, 6 acres; yearly rent, with 12*d*. for suit of court called suit fine and other service, 2*s*.

[*Trelean Veor, in St Ewe*]:
Nicholas Resega gent., as above [*i.e. by charter*], 1 tenure and land in Trelyan Vere, 6 acres; yearly rent, beyond suit of court and other [service], 4*d*.
[*Forename lost*] ... Trevethicke, by charter, 1 tenure and land adjoining, [*blank*] acres; yearly rent nil, except suit of court.

Sum of rents of free tenants yearly, 4s. 4d.

Customary tenants

[*Trelaske, in Cubert*]:
William Carvolghe, by copy dated 6 March 37 Hen. VIII [1546], 1 tenement in Trelaste for his life and the lives of John and Helen his children; yearly rent, beyond suit of court, heriot and other service, 13*s*. 4*d*.

---

[1] Place-name lost through a tear, but supplied in the heading here from a seventeenth-century survey (AR2/1346) and by the sense of the next entry.
[2] The words 'by charter' followed by 'so it is said' in this and some of the following entries.

[*Trelean Veor, in St Ewe*]:
John Mellhuys jun., by copy dated 8 October 3 & 4 Philip & Mary [1556], reversion of lands and tenements lying in Trelyoen Veer formerly of the late John Rescase, for his life and the lives of Margaret Melhuys and Alice Melhuys his sisters; yearly rent, beyond suit of court, heriot and other service, 36*s*. Memorandum: this copy is thought to be scarce good in law because it was taken in reversion for 3 lives and 1 life in possession besides; therefore query it.

[*Withiel churchtown*]:
John Dennys, by copy dated 20 May 14 Eliz. [1572], 1 tenement and land adjoining in Withyell, for his life and the lives of Henry and Margaret Dennys his children; yearly rent, beyond suit of court, heriot and other service, 10*s*. Note: Nicholas Kendall demands in the right of the queen 22*d*. of quit rent as to her manor of Withyell; therefore query it.

[*St Austell town*]:[3]
Christopher Woolcocke, Jane his wife and George their son, by copy dated 22 May 14 Eliz. [1572], a house and garden called Priesthouse in Sancte ... [Austell],[4] formerly in the tenure of the late John Bossitho, for their lives; yearly rent, beyond suit of court, heriot and other service, 2*s*. 6*d*.

Reskevys [*Reskivers, in Veryan*]:
Martin Newton, by copy not shown, pasture and arable ground in the town of Reskeves, for life; yearly rent, beyond suit of court, heriot and other service, 10*s*.

Sum of rents of customary tenants yearly, 71*s*. 10*d*.

[*Tenants by indenture*]

Demesne in Tregennow Wartho [*Tregenna Wartha, in St Ewe*]:
John Randall alias Trigennowe sen., by indenture made by Lady Alice Courtenay widow, once wife of the late Walter Courtenay, to one Nicholas Hoper, dated 13 November 3 Hen. VIII [1511], all messuages, lands and tenements, for 80 years; yearly rent

---

[3] Place-name almost totally obliterated, but supplied from later in the survey.
[4] Likewise.

26s. 8d. at Christmas, Easter, Nativity of St John the Baptist and Michaelmas; suit to the common court of the manor of Trygennow Wartho and best beast as heriot; re-entry if rent is in arrears. *Le mullett*, 4d., paid to the queen to her manor of Trebas [*Tybesta, in Creed*].[5]

Demesne in Trigennowe Wolas and Avalsamore [*Tregenna Wolas and Levalsa (Meor), both in St Ewe*]:
John Randall jun. alias John Tregennowe, by indenture made by Edward de Veer earl of Oxford, dated 10 November 14 Eliz. [1572], all messuages, gardens, orchards, lands, meadows, feedings, pastures, underwoods, heaths, moors, commons, wastes, marshes and moors (the earl to have access to break the land for tin), for his life and the lives of Martha and Margaret his daughters; yearly rent at the Annunciation and Michaelmas, 28s.; suit of court to the manor of Tregennowe Wartha and best beast as heriot or farleu on death or withdrawal; re-entry if rent is in arrears.

Land in the vill of Trelyan Vere [*Trelean Veor, in St Ewe*]:
John Melhues, by indenture made by Edward de Veer earl of Oxford, dated 10 December 16 Eliz. [1573], 1 tenement with all messuages, lands, meadows and pastures once in the tenure of John Coswarthe deceased, for his life and the lives of Mary his wife and Mary his daughter; yearly rent 17s. 10d. at Christmas, the Annunciation, Nativity of St John the Baptist and Michaelmas; suit of court to the manor of Tregennowe Wartha; indenture to be null and void if the tenant makes waste in any of the lord's wood ... [*rest torn away*].

[*Either Sourne, otherwise Tresournes, in Probus, or less likely Soarns, in Probus*]:
[*Details torn away.*][6]

Land called Pollprye [*Poll Fry, in Menheniot*]:
John Trehake gent., as assignee of James Brandon gent., by indenture made by the late John de Veer earl of Oxford dated 1 October 3 & 4 Philip & Mary [1556], ⅓ of certain land, meadow and

---

[5] *Mullett, mollet* or *motlet* does not appear in O.E.D. nor in Neilson, *Customary Rents*. It is frequent in Cornwall: e.g. *Caption of Seisin*, ed. Hull, pp. viii, xxv, 9, 10, 62, 72, 80, 97. It appears to have had some connection with tin.

[6] Identification of place supplied from later in this survey.

pasture called Pollprye (wood and underwood reserved), for 21 years; yearly rent 20s. at the Annunciation and Michaelmas; heriot; re-entry if rent is in arrears.

[*Treguth, in Cubert*]:
William Carvolghe, at will, ½ of certain land in Trygewe.

[*Totals torn away.*]

Deductions

To [*blank*] Pomerye's manor of Tregney Pomerye [*Tregony, in Cuby*] for rent from customary land in the tenure of John Melhuys jun. [*Trelean*], yearly 8d.
To the queen for quit rent from customary land now in the tenure of John Denys [*Withiel*], 22d.
To John Arondell's manor of Tareloye [*Treloy, in St Columb Minor*], yearly for quit rent from customary land in the tenure of William Carvolghe [*Trelaske*], 16½d.
To the queen's manor of Trebasta [*Tybesta, in Creed*], yearly for rent called *le mullett*[7] from demesne land lying in Levasowe [*Levalsa (Meor), in St Ewe*] now in the tenure of John Randall jun. alias Trigennowe, 2½d.
To the bailiff of the stannary yearly for tin fine, 2½d.
To Peter Edgcombe's manor of Pestresvo [*Penstrassoe, in St Ewe*] for the aforesaid demesne land in Levasowe [*Levalsa*], yearly 13d.
To Edward Trevanyon's manor of Treverlyne [*Treverbyn, in St Austell*] for rent from demesne land in Trigennowe Wolas in the tenure of the said John Randall alias Tregennowe, yearly 13d.
To the queen's manor of Trebasta [*Tybesta, in Creed*] for *le mullett*, 4d.
To [*blank*] Pomerye's manor of Pomerye Tregney [*Tregony*] for quit rent yearly from demesne land in the tenure of John Melhuys [*Trelean*], 23d.
To Peter Edgecombe's manor of Trelowthas [*Trelowthas, in Probus*] for quit rent and suit from demesne land within the parish of Probus called Sworne [*either Sourne, otherwise Tresournes, in Probus, or less likely Soarns, in Probus*] now in the tenure of Francis Tregian esq., 4s. However, query it.

---

[7] See above, p. 222 n. 5.

To the lord of Helliclasse [*Ellenglaze, in Cubert*] for yearly rent from land in the parish of St Cubert now in the tenure of William Carvolghe [*Treguth*], at the lord's will, 12*d*.

Sum of deductions yearly, 13*s*. 8½*d*.

Value of customary and demesne lands if they were improved

Customary tenants

[*Trelaske, in Cubert*]:
William Carvolghe, by copy, 1 tenement roofed with slate in Trelaste, barn and stable roofed with slate, curtilage and garden, value 13*s*. 4*d*.; in a close of pasture called Parkangewe, 5 acres at 5*s*. the acre, value 25*s*.; a several close of pasture adjoining the 'harber',[8] ½ acre, value 3*s*.; parcel of arable land called the Small Park, ½ acre 1 rood, value 4*s*. 6*d*.; in a close of pasture called Chymney Parke, 3 pieces, 7 acres at 4*s*. the acre, value 28*s*.; in a little piece of moory ground, 1 acre of pasture, value 4*s*.; in a close of pasture called the Newe Parke in 2 parts divided, 7 acres at 4*s*. the acre, value 28*s*.; in a close called Water Myll Parke, 3 acres of arable land at 4*s*. the acre, value 12*s*.; in a close of arable called the Furzye Parke in 2 parts divided, 7 acres at 4*s*. the acre, value 28*s*.; in the down pasture, 30 acres of pasture at 24*d*. the acre, value 60*s*.; total yearly value £10 5*s*. 10*d*. Pasture, 56½ acres; arable, 10½ acres 1 rood; meadow, nil; yearly rent 13*s*. 4*d*. Memorandum: Peter Edgcombe esq. has within this farm another moiety of land *viz*. a tenement and as much land in quantity as my lord's part and intermingled with my lord's land.[9]

[*Trelean Veor, in St Ewe*]:[10]
John Melluys jun., by copy, 1 tenement, barn and stable roofed with straw and 2 little gardens adjoining, 1 rood, value 10*s*.; close of pasture called Litle Penrigle, 1 acre, value 5*s*.; close of pasture called

---

[8] i.e. vegetable garden, Cornish *erber: Padel, *Cornish Place-name Elements*, p. 95.

[9] In this section of the document the central part of each entry ends with a statement of the yearly value. Acreages and the rent are entered in the margins. For some entries there are other marginal memoranda; these are printed here after the rent.

[10] Place-names in this section have been supplied from earlier in the survey.

Pendue, 3½ acres at 5s. the acre, value 17s. 6d.; close of pasture called the Litle East More, 1½ acres at 5s. the acre, value 7s. 7d. [sic]; a several close of pasture called the Pale Parke, 6 acres at 4s. the acre, value 24s.; in a close of pasture called East Felde 1½ acres at 4s. the acre, value 6s.; a several close of pasture called the Newe Parke, 3 acres 1 rood at 4s. the acre, value 13s.; close of pasture called the Lambe Parke, 2½ acres at 4s. the acre, value 10s.; close of pasture called Lysborne besides ½ acre there of Nicholas Trevithike's, 3 acres at 4s. the acre, value 12s.; in a little close of pasture called the Litle East Feilde, 1 acre, value 4s.; a several close of pasture called Bewes Close, 3 acres at 4s. the acre, value 12s.; moiety of close of pasture called Lanehyre, 3 acres at 4s. the acre, value 12s.; a several meadow called the Litle Medowe with a little garden adjoining on the east side of a tenement called Tubbs, 1 acre, value 6s. 8d.; a several meadow called the Higher Medowe, 3½ acres 1 rood at 6s. 8d. the acre, value 25s., which meadow lies on the west side of the said tenement; a several meadow called the Lower Medowe, ½ acre 1 rood, value 6s.; a several meadow called the Moore, 2 acres at 10s. the acre, value 20s.; ¼ of close of pasture called the Weste Close, 6 acres at 4s. the acre, value 24s.; ¼ of close of arable called Tubbs Close, 2 acres 30 perches at 10s. the acre, value 22s.; ¼ of close of arable called the Waye Close, 7½ acres at 5s. the acre, value 37s. 6d.; ¼ of close of arable called the Beef Close, 7½ acres at 5s. the acre, value 37s. 6d.; ¼ of 2 closes of pasture called the Downes, 4 acres 20 perches at 5s. the acre, value 20s. 6d.; total yearly value £11 12s. 2d. Pasture, 35½ acres 1 rood; meadow, 7½ acres; arable, 20½ acres 20 perches; yearly rent 36s.

[*Withiel churchtown*]:
John Denys, by copy, 1 tenement, little house adjoining roofed with straw, curtilage, orchard and meadow called the Garden Meadow, 1 rood, value 20d.; moiety of close of pasture called Cocks Feilde, 6 acres with a moory piece adjoining at 5s. the acre, value 30s.; moiety of close of arable called the Geyre, 5 acres at 5s. the acre, value 25s.; total yearly value 56s. 8d. Meadow, 1 rood; pasture, 6 acres; arable, 5 acres; yearly rent 10s. Elms, 12. Oaks growing in the Geyre, 12 worth for sale 20s.

[*St Austell town*]:
Christopher Woolcocke, by copy, 1 tenement roofed with straw called Pryests House in St Austwell and an orchard, 20 perches;

close of arable land on the backside of the tenement, 1 rood; total yearly value 20s. Arable, 1 rood; yearly rent 2s. 6d. Elms, 14; ashes, 4; apple trees, 24.

[*Reskivers, in Veryan*]:
Martin Newton, by copy, little piece of waste ground adjoining the tenement of Nicholas Bowyer gent. on the east side, on which sometime was built a tenement, 10 perches; a several close of pasture, ½ acre, value 3s. 4d., lying to [*sic*] the highway leading to Kellybogyan [*'Callibudgia' (lost), in Veryan, near Tregony*]; in a close of arable called the Higher Feilde, 5½ acres at 4s. the acre, value 22s.; close of pasture called the Lower Feilde, 6 acres ... [*rest torn*].[11]

[Sum of value of customary lands] yearly, £30 ...[12]

Tenants by indenture

Demesne in Trigenowe Wartho [*Tregenna Wartha, in St Ewe*]:
John Randall sen. alias Tregennowe, by indenture, 1 tenement roofed with slate commonly called Trigennowe Wartho, stable and barn roofed with straw, orchard, curtilage and garden lying on the backside of the tenement, the whole 1 acre, value 20s.; a several close of pasture called Parke an Monker near the wood, 7½ acres at 5s. the acre, value 37s. 6d.; a several close of pasture called Parke Wartho, 9 acres at 5s. the acre, value 45s.; a several close of pasture called Parke Anventon, 3 acres at 5s. the acre, value 15s.; a several close of pasture called Parke an Marragge with a garden adjoining, 1 acre, value 6s.; moiety of meadow called the Under Towne Medowe, 1 acre, value 10s.; moiety of meadow called the Lower Meadowe, 2 acres at 10s. the acre, value 20s.; moiety of close of pasture called the Torren, 2 acres 1 rood at 5s. the acre, value 11s. 3d.; moiety of close of pasture called the Parkeengowe, 5 acres at 5s. the acre, value 25s.; moiety of close of arable called the Newe Parke, 2 acres at 5s. the acre, value 10s.; moiety of close of arable called Penjohn Warne, 1 acre, value 5s.; moiety of close of pasture called ..wbathowe [*letters lost*], 2½ acres at 5s. the acre, value 12s. 6d.; all in Tregennowe Woolas and Tregennowe Wartho; also the moiety of a several common or waste ground called Trigennowe

---

[11] Much of this page is missing, but it is certain, from comparison with the earlier part of the survey, that no further whole entry has been lost.
[12] Shillings and pence lost.

Downe, 125 acres at 6d. the acre, value 62s. 6d.; claims to hold by force of his indenture the herbage and weeding of 25 acres of coppice wood called the Higher Woode of Trigennowe Wartho now let to Roger Beanes gent., so it is said, and a little coppice or grove called Parkamonker Grove, 2 acres, at 4d. the acre, value together 9s; total yearly value £14 8s. 9d. Pasture, 30 acres 1 rood; meadow, 3 acres; arable, 3 acres; waste and common, 125 acres; herbage of wood, 27 acres; yearly rent 26s. 8d.[13] Item a wood called Lambecerry Godno, 1 rood, value 15s. Item a parcel of wood called the Acre, 3 acres at [60s.] the acre, value £9. Item 1 little copse called Parkamonker, 2 acres, value 40s.

[*Tregenna Wolas and Levalsa Meor, both in St Ewe*]:[14]
[John Randall],[15] ... herbage of ... [*word lost*] of ground lately felled called the Wood Park, 2 acres at 4d. the acre, value 8d.; ¼ of close of pasture called Pentarnns, 1½ acres at 4s. the acre, value 6s.; ¼ of close of pasture called the Chappell Parke, 1 rood, value 16d.; moiety of a several close of arable called the Wood Close, 1 acre, value 5s., all in Levasowe; a several garden plot, pasture, ½ acre 1 rood, value 4s., called Parcus Minns; ¼ of close of pasture called Wellclose, 1 acre, value 5s.; moiety of meadow called the Undertowne Medowe, 1 acre, value 10s.; moiety of meadow called the Lower Medowe, 2 acres at 10s. the acre, value 20s.; moiety of close of pasture called the Torren, 2 acres 1 rood at 5s. the acre, value 11s. 4d.; moiety of close of pasture called the Parkengewe, 5 acres at 5s. the acre, value 25s.; moiety of close of arable called the Newe Parke, 2 acres at 5s. the acre, value 10s.; moiety of close of arable called Penjohnvarne, 1 acre, value 5s.; moiety of close of pasture called Stowbathowe, 2½ acres at 5s. the acre, value 12s. 6d.; a several close of pasture called Nawhibber, 2 acres at 2s. 8d. the acre, value 5s. 4d.; a several close of pasture called Litle Nawhibber, 1 acre, value 2s. 8d.; all in Trigennowe Wolas and Trigennowe Wartho; moiety of a several common or waste ground called Trigennowe Downe, 125 acres at 6d. the acre, value 62s. 6d.; ⅛ of

---

[13] A torn and faint memorandum about the coppice wood has not been transcribed.
[14] This heading, and most others below, supplied from information earlier in the survey.
[15] Name supplied from earlier in the survey; much of the first part of this entry is lost.

a waste ground or common called Levasowe Downe, 5 acres at 8*d*. the acre, value 3*s*. 4*d*.; claims to hold by force of his indenture the herbage and weeding of 25 acres of coppice wood called the Lower Wood of Trigennowe Wolas now let to Roger Beanes gent. by indenture among other things, so it is said; herbage of a little grove of wood called ..eterye Godno,[16] 1 rood ... [*several words lost*], value 8*s*. 8*d*.; herbage and weeding of 3 acres of wood called the Acre at 12*d*. the acre, value 3*s*.; total yearly value ... [*lost*]. Pasture, 26 acres; meadow, 6 acres; arable, 4 acres 1 rood; waste and common, 130 acres; herbage of wood, 30 acres 1 rood; ... [*rent lost*].

[*Trelean Veor, in St Ewe*]:
John Melhues, by indenture, 1 tenement roofed with straw, 3 little gardens, 1 rood of pasture; close of pasture called the Greate Moore Close, value yearly 70*s*. ... [*rest mostly lost*].[17]

[*Either Sourne, otherwise Tresournes, in Probus, or less likely Soarns, in Probus*]:
[Francis][18] Tregian esq., by indenture, moiety of pasture and arable lands called Sworne, lying together in 2 several closes, 40 acres at 4*s*. the acre, value £8. Pasture, 30 acres; arable, 10 acres; yearly rent 9*s*.

Lands called Pollprye [*Poll Fry, in Menheniot*]:
John Trehake, as assignee of James Brandon, by indenture, ⅓ of meadow and pasture called Pollprye, 20 acres at 5*s*. the acre one with another, value 100*s*. Pasture and meadow, 20 acres; yearly rent 20*s*.

[*Treguth, in Cubert*]:
William Carvolghe, at will, 1/12 of 24 acres of arable land lying in Trigewe at 5*s*. the acre, value 10*s*.; 1/12 of 12 acres of pasture called the Common of Tregeste, value 3*s*. 4*d*.; 1/12 of 12 acres of meadow or moory ground, value 6*s*. 8*d*.; total yearly value 20*s*. Pasture, 1 acre; meadow, 1 acre; arable, 2 acres; yearly rent 4*s*.

Total value of farm lands and lands let at will, £54 17*s*. 1*d*.[19]

* * *

---

[16] See 'Lambecerry Godno' in the previous entry.
[17] Field names which can be read are 'Parke Ansen' and 'Brome Close'.
[18] Forename supplied from earlier in the survey.
[19] The summary of land use, as in the other surveys, is torn away.

SURVEY OF TRESITHNEY, 1575 (AR2/482)

Manor of Tresithney
in the parishes of St Columb Maior, St Colan,
St Peran in Sabulo and Gwenepe
[*Tresithney, in St Columb Major*]

Survey by Edward Hubbart esq. and Edward Worsteley gent., in August 17 Eliz. [1575] by a commission from William Cecill kt, Lord Burley, from examination of ancient rentals and by view and perambulation.

Free tenants within the parish of St Columb Maior

[*Nankelly, in St Columb Major*]:
John Crabbe, by charter,[1] 1 ferling in the vill of Nankillye; yearly rent 20*d*. Relief 3*s*. 1½*d*. for 1 ferling, as appears by the account of 19 Eliz. [1576–7].[2]
John Rowse, by charter, 1 ferling in socage there; yearly rent 20*d*. Relief 3*s*. 1½*d*. for 1 ferling, as appears by the court roll and account of 27 Eliz., 1585, then received from Remfrey Rowse and Richard Rowse sons of Jenkin Rowse.

[*Trebudannon, in St Columb Major*]:
Pascoe ('Pasca') Kerne of Tresylian [*Tresillian, in Newlyn East*], by knight's service of the fee of Gloucester, 1 ferling in the vill of Trebydadnan; yearly rent 12*d*. Relief 2*s*. 9¼*d*. and ½ of ¼*d*., as appears by the account of 20 Eliz. [1577–8] then received from John Kerne son and heir of Pascoe upon his death.
Richard Watt, by charter as above, certain land there; yearly rent 12*d*.

[*Tregaswith, in St Columb Major*]:
Heirs of John Beacham, by charter in socage, 1 ferling in the vill

---

[1] The words 'by charter' followed by 'so it is said but by what service is not known' in this and the following entry.
[2] Details of reliefs in this section have been added, probably slightly later, in the left-hand margin.
[3] Cf. John Kerne alias Tresylyan of Tresylyan (Newlyn East), AR14/6.

of Tregaswith; yearly rent 12d. Relief 3s. 1½d., as appears by the court roll and account of 25 Eliz. then received for the death of Richard Carter, 1583.

John John of Blysland [*Blisland*], by charter as above, certain land there; yearly rent 12d.

[*Padstow town*]:
Joan ... [*faded*] widow, in fee farm, 1 tenement and garden in the vill of Padstowe; yearly rent 4s. 11d.

Sum of rents of free tenants yearly, 13s. 3d.

Customary tenants

[*Tregaswith, in St Columb Major*]:
John Horrell, by copy dated 20 May 14 Eliz. [1572], 1 tenement in Tregaswithe, for his life and the lives of Richard 'alias Rithow' Adam; yearly rent, beyond suit of court and other service, 9s.

Bosoughan [*Bosoughan, in Colan*]:
John Vivian, by copy dated 1 March 37 Hen. VIII [1546], 1 tenement in Bosoughan, for his life and the life of Mary his sister; yearly rent, beyond suit of court and other service, 7s. 6d.

Tresawsyn [*Tresawsen, in Perranzabuloe*]:
Nicholas Kempthorne, in the right of Katherine his wife once wife of the late William Crane, by copy dated 20 May 14 Eliz. [1572], 1 tenement in Tresawsin, for the lives of Katherine, Humphrey Crane and John Kempthorne son of Nicholas; yearly rent, beyond suit of court and other service, 15s.

Cosvarne [*Cusgarne, in Gwennap*]:
Jane Saundrye widow of the late Richard Saundrye, by a certain copy not shown, 1 tenement roofed with straw; yearly rent, beyond suit of court and other service, 13s. 8d.

Sum of rents of customary tenants yearly, 45s. 2d.

[*Tenants by indenture*]

[*Tresithney, in St Columb Major*]:
Thomas Atkynson, by indenture made by Edward de Veer earl of Oxford dated 28 January 17 Eliz. [1575], site of the manor of Tresithney with all houses, buildings, barns, stables, orchards, gardens, meadows, feedings, pastures and other hereditaments, for 41 years; yearly rent, at the Annunciation and Michaelmas, 53s. 4d.

and 19s. paid to the earl of Huntingdon; entry and distraint if rent is in arrears.

Kalyon [*Chellean, in Gwennap*]:
John Thomas, by indenture so it is said, not shown, 1 tenement roofed with straw and land adjoining; yearly rent 9s. 7d.[4]

Sum of the farm of demesne land yearly, £4 23d.

Sum total of all the manor yearly, £6 19s. 4d.

Deductions

To William Bevell's manor of Resoghan [*Rosesuggan, in St Columb Major*] for quit rent from customary land in the tenure of John Horrell [*Tregaswith*], 2s.
To the queen's manor of Royalton [*Rialton, in St Columb Minor*] for rent from customary land in the tenure of John Vivyan [*Bosoughan*], 2s. 6d.
To the heirs of the late Edward Arondell kt to their manor of Kalestack [*Callestick, in Perranzabuloe*] for rent from customary land in the tenure of Nicholas Kempthorne [*Tresawsen*], 6s.
To James Eryssye's manor of Pensignans [*Pensignance, in Gwennap*] for rent from customary land now in the tenure of Jane Saundrye widow [*Cusgarne*], 20d.
To the earl of Huntingdon's manor of Farlethe [*Cotford Farley, in Colan and St Wenn*] for rent from the site of the manor, 19s.
To James Erysye's manor of Pensgnans [*sic*] for rent from customary land in the tenure of John Thomas [*Chellean*], 7d.

[*Sum of deductions*], 31s. 9d.
Remains clear yearly beyond the deductions, £5 7s. 7d.

Value of customary and demesne lands if they were improved

Customary tenants

[*Tresawsen, in Perranzabuloe*]:[5]
Nicholas Kempthorne, by copy in the right of his wife, 1 tenement and barn roofed with straw, little garden plot on the backside of the tenement, little garden plot, 20 perches of pasture, on the back-

---

[4] A good deal of this entry is blank because the tenant failed to produce his lease.
[5] Place-names in this and the following section have been supplied from earlier in the survey.

side of the barn; a several close of arable ground called the Garden Close, ½ acre, value 2s.; a several close of arable called the Rounde Close, 2½ acres at 3s. the acre, value 7s. 6d.; a several close of arable called the Longe Close, 4½ acres at 3s. the acre, value 13s. 6d.; a several close of arable called the Newe Close Above the Towne, 2½ acres at 3s. the acre, value 7s. 6d.; a several close of arable called the Litle Close above the Towne, 1½ acres 1 rood at 3s. the acre, value 5s. 3d.; moiety of several close of pasture called the Standerde, 10 acres at 3s. the acre, value 30s.; in the common arable fields [sic] there called the Greate Feilde on the west side of the town, 6 acres of arable being 6 parcels, at 3s. the acre, value 18s.; a several close of pasture called the Parke Anythen, 1 acre, value 3s. newly taken out of the common of Tresawsyn; moiety of common called Tresawsyn Moore without any division, 8 acres, value 10s.; total yearly value £4 16s. 9d. Pasture, 11 acres 23 perches; arable, 17½ acres 1 rood; common, 8 acres; yearly rent 15s. Elms about the tenement, 7. Note: Richard Tremayne and one [blank] Opye hold in coparceny the other moiety of the village called Tresawsyn.[6]

[*Bosoughan, in Colan*]:
John Vivian, by copy, void piece of ground where sometime a tenement was built, now utterly decayed and wasted; moiety of a several close of pasture called the Haye, 20 perches, value 12d.; lands in a close of pasture there called the Higher Felde, 12 acres lying in diverse parcels at 3s. 4d. the acre, value 40s.; arable lands in a close or field called the Churche Waye Close, 4 acres at 4s. the acre, value 16s.; arable lands in a close or field called the Nere Parke in diverse parcels, 3 acres at 3s. the acre, value 9s.; total yearly value 66s. Pasture, 12 acres 20 perches; arable, 7 acres; yearly rent 7s. 6d.

[*Tregaswith, in St Columb Major*]:
John Horrell, by copy, 1 tenement roofed with straw; in a close of arable land called the Park under the Towne, 2½ acres at 8s. the acre, value 20s.; a several close or field of pasture or meadow called Dore, 2½ acres at 10s. the acre, value 25s.; a several close of arable land called the Rese, 2½ acres at 5s. the acre, value 12s. 6d.; a several

---

[6] In this section of the document the central part of each entry ends with a statement of the yearly value. Acreages and the rent are entered in the margins. For some entries there are other marginal memoranda; these are printed here after the rent.

close of arable land called the Overfeilde containing, with 1 acre of arable land above the highway and part of Overfeilde, 4 acres at 6s. the acre, value 24s.; in a close of pasture called Gorgulfa, 2½ acres at 8s. the acre, value 20s.; close of pasture called the Utter Feilde, 4 acres at 2s. the acre, value 8s.; total yearly value, 109s. 6d. Pasture, 6½ acres; meadow, 2½ acres; arable, 9 acres; yearly rent 9s. Note: within this village called Tregaswith my lord's part amounts to a full third as is said.

[*Cusgarne, in Gwennap*]:
Jane Saundrye widow, by copy not shown upon this survey, 1 tenement roofed with straw, backside and orchard, 1 rood 20 perches of pasture, value 2s.; a several close of pasture called the Churche Close, 3 acres 1 rood at 5s. the acre, value 16s. 3d.; a several close of arable called the Stone Parke, 3½ acres at 4s. the acre, value 14s.; a several close of arable called the Close above the Towne, 3½ acres at 6s. the acre, value 21s.; a several close of pasture at the lane end, 1 acre, value 6s.; in the commons called Cosvarne Downes unlimited common of pasture, value 40s.; total yearly value £4 19s. 3d. Pasture, 8 acres; arable, 3½ acres; yearly rent 13s. 8d.

Sum value of customary lands yearly, £18 11s. 6d.

[*Tenants by indenture*]

[*Tresithney, in St Columb Major*]:
Thomas Atkynson, by indenture, the site of the manor of Tresithney, barn roofed with slate, stable, kitchen and other outhouses roofed with straw, curtilage, orchard with a little pightle adjoining, the whole containing 1 acre, value 33s. 4d.; meadow called Litle Meadowe, 1½ acres at 10s. the acre, value 15s.; plot of meadow adjoining, 1 rood, value 2s. 6d.; little parcel of pasture leading into the Beif Close, 1 rood, value 2s.; little piece of pasture, 1 rood, lying at the end of Beif Close, value 2s.; a several close of moory or meadow ground now in 2 parts divided, 6 acres at 6s. the acre, value 36s.; a several close of pasture called the Beif Close, 16 acres at 8s. the acre, value £6 8s.; a several close of arable called the Corne Parke Close above the Beif Close, 16 acres at 5s. the acre, value £4; a several close of pasture called the Furzye Close alias Downe Close, 8 acres at 3s. 4d. the acre, value 26s. 8d.; a several close of pasture called the Newe Downe Close alias Longe Close, 7 acres at 3s. the acre, value 21s.; a several close of pasture lying on the north side

of Beef Close called the Asshe Close, 13 acres at 6s. the acre, value 78s.; a several close called the Litle Close, of pasture, 3 acres 1 rood at 4s. the acre, value 13s.; close of pasture called the Mowe Haye, 2½ acres at 5s. the acre, value 12s. 6d.; close of arable called the Bett Close, 1½ acres 1 rood at 6s. the acre, value 10s. 6d.; piece of pasture lately enclosed from the way leading to the mansion house, 3 roods at 4s. the acre, value 3s.; little pightle of pasture adjoining the orchard on the east side, 1 rood, value 20d.; total yearly value £23 5s. 2d. Pasture, 50½ acres 1 rood; meadow, 7½ acres 1 rood; arable, 17½ acres 1 rood; yearly rent 53s. 4d.

[*Chellean, in Gwennap*]:
John Thomas, by indenture not shown at this survey, 1 tenement roofed with straw and a little outhouse adjoining, backside and orchard containing 1 rood of pasture; waste piece of ground called the Towne Place lying before the door against the watercourse on the south side, 1 rood, value 12d.; close of arable called the Meadow, ½ acre 1 rood at 5s. the acre, value 3s. 9d.; a several close of arable called the Towne Close, 2½ acres 1 rood at 6s. the acre, value 16s. 6d.; a several close of arable called the Higher Close, 5 acres at 4s. the acre, value 20s.; a several close of pasture called the Moore, ½ acre, value 3s.; close of pasture taken out of the common, 1 acre, value 3s. 4d., on the east side of the south highway; a several down, 3 acres of pasture, value 13s. 4d.; ⅓ of a close called the Parke Enene taken likewise from the common, 1 acre, value 3s. 4d.; ¼ of the common south downs, value 13s. 4d.; total yearly value 77s. 7d. Pasture, 6 acres; arable, 8½ acres; yearly rent 9s. 7d.

Sum value of farm lands, £27 2s. 9d.

Sum total value of demesne lands and customary lands, £45 13s. 3d.

[*Total customary and demesne land of the whole manor*]: pasture, 94½ acres; meadow, 10 acres 1 rood; arable, 63½ acres; common, 8 acres.

RENTAL, *c.*1586
(AR2/1343, parts)

Contents

Manor of Domellick 236
Manor of Tregorrick 237

RENTAL, c.1586 (parts)
Two of the earl of Oxford's former manors

Demilyocke
in the parish of Sanctus Dionisius
[*Domellick, in St Dennis*]

Free tenants

[*Domellick*]:
[*Blank*], 1 ferling Cornish, in socage; common suit of court; rent 5s.

[*Ennis Vean, in St Dennis*]:[1]
[*Blank*], 3 ferlings Cornish, [*tenure blank*]; common suit of court; rent 6d.

Nenys Veer [*Ennis (Veor), in St Dennis*]:
[*Blank*], 1 ferling Cornish, in socage; [*blank*] suit of court; rent 2s. 6d.
[*Blank*], 1 ferling Cornish, in socage; common suit of court; rent 2s. 6d.

Kersela [*Carsella, in St Dennis*]:
John Arundell of Gwarneck esq. [*Gwarnick, in St Allen*], 1 ferling Cornish, in socage; common suit of court; rent 4s.
[*Blank*] Boscawen, 1 ferling Cornish, in socage; common suit; rent 4s.

Penrose Veer [*Penrose Veor, in St Dennis*]:
[*Blank*] Pascow, 1 ferling Cornish, in socage; [*blank*] suit of court; rent 4d.

Total of free tenants, [*blank*; 18s. 10d.]

Customary tenants

Penrose Vyan [*Penrose Vean, in St Dennis*]:
[*Blank*] Pascow, 1 tenement; common suit of court; rent 15s.

---

[1] In 1717 the first two free tenements of this manor were Domellick, paying 5s., and Ennis Vean, paying 6d.

Ennys Vean [*Ennis (Vean), in St Dennis*]:
[*Blank*], 1 tenement; suit of court; rent 8s.

Total of customary tenants, [blank; 23s.]

Rents paid

To [*blank*] manor of Trevevas [*unidentified; possibly Trethevas, in Landewednack*],[2] for land in [*blank*], 23d.

* * *

Tregorreck
[*Tregorrick, in St Austell*]

[*Free*] *tenants*

[*Tregorrick, in St Austell*]:
[*Blank*] Danvers and [*blank*] St Albon, lands in the vill of Tregorreck, [*tenure blank*]; [*blank*] suit of court; rent 9¾d.
[*Blank*] Clowberye, [*blank*] land Cornish, [*tenure blank*]; rent 2s. 10d., plus 6d. fine for suit of court.
[*Blank*] Menhire, [*blank*] acre(s) Cornish, [*tenure blank*]; [*blank*] suit of court; rent 7½d.
[*Blank*], [*blank*] Cornish, [*tenure blank*]; [*blank*] suit of court; rent 2½d.
[*Blank*] Doungye, [*blank*] Cornish, [*tenure blank*]; [*blank*] suit of court; rent 3¾d.
[*Blank*] Vivian, [*blank*] Cornish, [*tenure blank*]; common suit of court; rent 1¼d.

[*Total of free tenants, 4s. 10¾d.*]

[*Customary tenants*][3]

[*Name lost*]:
[*Name lost*] Carter, 1 [*lost*]; [suit] of court; rent 17s. 9d.

---

[2] In 1506 Domellick appears to have been held of the manor of Trethevas, in Landewednack (Black Book of Merthen, RIC).

[3] The names of the customary tenants and tenements are mostly lost, but are evidently the same as in the earlier survey of 1563 (above, pp. 171–2), and in that of 1659. In order, they are probably: Rosewastis (in St Columb Major); uncertain (perhaps in St Austell town?); Tregorrick; and two holdings in St Austell town. With the surname of the third tenant, compare that of John Avrean, at Tregorrick, in the survey of 1563 (above).

[*Name lost*]:
[*Name lost*] Ca..., ½ [*lost*], [and] half a close called Over [*lost*]; rent 10s.

[*Name lost*]:
[*Name lost*] ...rean, ½ [*lost*]; suit of court; rent 40s. [*lost*].

[St] Austell [*St Austell town*]:
[*Blank*], ½ tenement; rent 4[s.].
[*Blank*], 1 piece of land; rent 2d.

Trevemether in the parish of Vvall [*Trevemedar, in St Eval*]:
[*Blank*], certain land; rent 23d.

              [*Total of customary tenants, 73s. 10d. (?)*]

Rents paid
To the queen's manor of Carnanton, for customary land in Tresalstre [*Rosewastis, in St Columb Major*], 5s.
To [*blank*] Pomerye gent.'s manor of Tregney Pomerie [*Tregony, in Cuby*], for customary land in Tregorreck, 3s.
To the queen's manor of Treverbyne Courtneye [*Treverbyn, in St Austell*], for demesne land in St Austell, 9¾d.

INDEXES

INDEX OF PLACES

This index lists, in the great majority of cases, the modern forms of place-names, the forms appearing in italics in the edited text. Early forms, whether of 'lost' places (i.e. those whose location is unknown, though they may appear in later documentation) or of 'unidentifiable' ones (i.e. those unknown from other documentation), are given here in *italics*; where such names occur more than once, the latest recorded form is used, with cross-references from earlier variants where needed. Names of manors and other administrative units surveyed in this volume are in **bold**. Places within Cornwall have in brackets the parish in which they were anciently located (as in the identifications within the text); places elsewhere have their county similarly. All place-names, including field-names, are included from surveys down to 1563, but the numerous fields and closes in those of 1566–75 are not indexed.

aboueteheberne (field, Mawgan in Pyder), 99
aboueteheforge (field, Mawgan in Pyder), 99
Amalebra (Towednack), 40, 86, 130
Amble (St Kew), Middle, 1 & n., 24, 73, 106; *Amell Richard*, 191
Angarrack (Phillack), 46, 91, 135
Angew (Gwithian), 47, 91, 135 & n.
Angrouse (Mullion), 13, 16n., 83, 125
Anhay (Gunwalloe), 15, 84, 126
An Poule (field, St Enoder), 95
Anstey, East, parish (Devon), 192
Antony, West, manor, lxxiv
Argalls Walls (alias *Grove Park*, Liskeard), 150 & n., 202
Arrallas (St Enoder), xxxii, 191
Arundell's Wood (Constantine), see Merthen Wood
Ashburton (Devon), lxxvii, xcv
Atley (Lanivet), 56, 97, 115
Ayr (St Ives), 41–2 & n., 44, 87, 89, 131–3

Bahow (St Keverne), 22, 79, 124
Barrepta (*Porthrepter*, Lelant), 48, 93 & n., 136
Battishorne (Devon), xvi–xvii
Baytree Hill (Liskeard), 151n.
Bear's Downs (St Ervan), cviii n.
Bedrugga (St Columb Minor), lxxxi, lxxxiii, 30, 69, 113, 166 & n., 211, 214–15

Bedruthan (St Eval), 32–3, 65, 108
Beer (Marhamchurch), Great & Higher, 192
Bejowan (St Columb Minor), manor, xxxii–xxxv, xlvi–xlvii, xlix, lxvi, lxxv, lxxxi, lxxxv, xciv, 161–6, 208–19; meadows, 165, 212, 216; mill, see Kestle Mill; tenement, 164, 210, 212
Benhurden (Goran), 8, 52, 118–19
Bennallack (Perranzabuloe), 110
Benoak (Duloe), 151, 203
Benorth (Cardinham), lxxii, cix, 184–5
Berepper (Gunwalloe), 15, 84, 127
Bin Down (Morval), xcii, xcv
Binnerton (Crowan), manor, 160
Birchanger (Essex), 208n.
Blackmore, stannary, cxiii
Blakes Keiro (St Minver), 2, 24, 73, 106
Blarrick (Antony), lxxx
Blisland, lord of, 2; parish, 161, 210, 230
Bloughan (Lanlivery), 9, 51n., 117
Blowing House (Cardinham), xxxvi
Bochym (Cury), 17, 81, 128
Bodardle (Lanlivery), manor, xxviii–xxix, xxxi, xlviii–xlix, li, lxix–lxx, lxxv, lxxxi, 187, 193–7; mills, 194, 196
Bodbrane (Duloe), manor, xxi–xxii, xlv–xlvi, 150–1, 202–4; tenement, 151, 203–4
Bodellick (St Breock), 140–2
Boden Vean (St Anthony in Meneage), cxvi n., cxxvi, 23, 80, 124

241

Bodiniel (Bodmin), 152n., 153, 155, 200
Bodmin, town, xcvi, cxii, 152 & n., 154 & n., 171; parish, 200; streets, 152, 153n., 154–5, 200–1
Bodmin Moor, 186–7
Bodraverran (St Erth), 189
Bodwannick (Lanivet), manor, xviii–xix, xli, xlv, cx–cxii, cxvi–cxvii, cxxii–cxxiii, cxlv–cxlvi, 55–8, 96–9, 114–16; mills, cxii, cxvii, 57–8, 98, 116; tenement, cxvii, 56, 97, 115
Bodwen (Lanlivery), 196
Bokiddick (Lanivet), 56–7, 97–8, 99n., 114, 116
Bollowal (St Just in Penwith), lxxxiii–lxxxiv
Boodygywood (Cardinham), wood, 187
Borehill Close (Bodmin), 152; see also Bye Hill Parke
Borelane (Bodmin), 153n., 201
Boscastle (Forrabury), borough, xcvii; way to, 177
Boscudden (St Erth), 40, 49, 85, 130
Bosehan (St Buryan), 188
Bosigran (Zennor), 189
Boskear (Bodmin), 55, 96, 114–15, 153, 155, 200
Boskerris (Lelant), 40n., 48; B. Wartha, 45, 89, 133; B. Woollas, 42, 87, 92, 131, 136
Boslymon (Lanlivery), 195
Bosoughan (Colan), lxxxi, 162, 211, 230–2
Bosporthennis (Zennor), 189
Bosprowal (Gwinear), 144 & n., 147, 157, 205
Bossillian (Creed), 8, 50, 117
Bosue (St Ewe), 11, 51, 118
Bosuerghes (unidentified), 40 & n., 85, 130
Boswarthan (Madron) [?], 158 & n.
Boswellick (St Allen), manor, lxxxii, 28, 68, 110–11
Boyton, manor, xcvi
Bosworgey (St Erth), 40, 49, 85, 130
Breney (Lanlivery), 195–6
Brown Willy (St Breward), xcii
Bryanick (St Agnes), 28, 68, 110–11
Bugford (Devon), manor, xcii
Buntesmede (Lanlivery & Luxulian), 195
Burgess (Gunwalloe), 15 & n., 84, 127 & n.; see also Hendradodda; Rosehendra

Burnow (Cury), 16, 127
Burnuick (Mawgan in Meneage), Higher & Lower, 14, 83, 126
Bury (Cardinham), Higher, 179; Little, 181
Bye Hill Parke (Bodmin), 200; see also Borehill Close

Callabarrett Wood (Cardinham), 181, 187
Callestick (Perranzabuloe), manor, 231; Little C. (alias *Callestock-ruall*), lxii, 28, 68, 110–11
Callibudgia (Veryan), 226
Camp Close(s) (St Clement), 121n.
Cannalidgey (St Issey), 153–4, 200–1
Capson Howse (Gunwalloe), c n.
Caradon Prior (Linkinhorne), manor, lxxiv
Carbis (Lelant), 42, 88, 132, 136
Carblake (Cardinham), 184
Cardeast (Cardinham), Higher, lxxii, cix, 185; Lower, 182
Cardinham, manor, xxviii, xxxi, xxxv–xxxvi, xlviii–xlix, li, lxix, lxi, lxxv, lxxxi, xciv, cix, cxii n., 177–87; barony, xiv, xxix; benefice, 186; churchtown, 185n.; fee, xxix, xxxii, xlviii, 186, 190–2; Old C., see Old Cardinham
Cargease (Ludgvan), 189
Cargoll (Newlyn East), manor, lxxi
Carlibby (Zennor), 13, 83, 125
Carloose (Creed), 8 & n., 50, 117
Carlumb (St Minver), 24, 73, 106
Carminow (Mawgan in Meneage), manor, xvi–xvii, xxiv, xlv, xcix, cv, cxxi–cxxiii, cxlv–cxlvi, 13–16, 19n., 82–5, 125–7; demesne, lix, 16, 85, 100, 127; mills, 16 & n., 84, 127; C. Bally, 127
Carnabeggas (St Erth), fee, xxix, xxxii, xlviii, 188–90
Carnanton (Mawgan in Pyder), manor, lxxxii, 34n., 164, 166 & n., 214, 238; C. meadow, 34 & n., 66, 110
Carnek (St Clement?), 121 & n.
Carnewas (St Eval), 2, 9n., 34, 65, 110
Carnhell (Gwinear), 159–60, 170
Carninney (Lelant), 42, 88, 132
Carno (St Keverne), 17, 81, 127
Carnogowe (Lelant), 42, 87, 132
Carsella (St Dennis), 236

INDEX OF PLACES

Cartuther (Menheniot), 190
Carvedras (Kenwyn), xxiv, xxxix, 77
Carwyn (Phillack), 42, 87, 131
Castle (alias Little Lantyan, Lanlivery), xc, 9, 51n., 117
Cathebedron (Gwinear), 144, 147, 157-8, 205-6; manor, 170
Cavears (Colan), 162
Chagford (Devon), 192
Chapel (St Columb Minor), cii, 27, 55, 75, 107
Chark (Lanlivery), 194-5
Chellean (Gwennap), 231, 234
Chenhalls (St Erth), 188
Chepye (Gunwalloe), 18 & n., 82 & n., 129
Chideock (Dorset), xxv
Chienpoll (St Enoder), 62, 93, 137
Chinalls (Gunwalloe), 15, 84, 127
Chiwarren (Truro Vean manor), 121 & n.
Choy Castle (Gunwalloe), 82n., 129 & n.
Chyangweal (Lelant), 42, 88, 132
Chyanhor (St Levan), 188
Chylason (Towednack), 40, 86, 130
Chynhale (Sithney) 146, 205 & n.
Chynythen (Cury), 14-15, 84, 126-7
Chypitt (Cuby), 110
Chyvarloe (Gunwalloe), 14-15, 84, 126
Chywoone (Ludgvan), 158 & n.
Clapper Moor (Cardinham), 179, 187
Clies (Mawgan in Meneage), *C. Men*, 16, 127; *C. Olingey*, 14, 84, 126
Climsland Prior (Stoke Climsland), manor, xcv
Colan Barton (Colan), 191
Collorian (Ludgvan), 189
Colquite (St Mabyn), manor, 190
Colvannick (Cardinham), lxxiii, 183; Higher, 178, 183-4; Lower, 179, 185
Comprigney (Kenwyn), 121n.
Condurrow (St Anthony in Meneage), 23, 80, 124
Conium (*Gwealcunnion*; = Tremorvah, St Clement), 60n., 120 & n.; *see also Runbovetown*
Connerton (Gwithian), manor, xiii-xv, xvii, xxiv, xxxii, xxxix, xlv, li n., lvii, lix-lx, lxii-lxiii, lxvi, cx-cxiii, cxvi-cxvii, cxxii-cxxiii, cxlv-cxlvii, 39-49, 85-93, 130-6, 170; demesne, lix, 46, 90-1, 134

Connorwartha (Gwithian), 41, 86, 131
Copshorn (formerly *Quarry Parke*, Bodmin), 152 & n., 200
Coskeere (St Clement?), 121 & n.
Coswarth (Colan), *see* Cotford
Coswinsawsin (Gwinear), 158-9, 169-70
Coswinwolward, see Lanyon
Cotford (Colan & St Wenn), manor, 87; C. Farley, 231
Cotleigh (Devon), parish, 192
Cotna (Goran), 10, 51, 118; Lower, 9, 50, 117
Council Barrow (Cardinham), 182n.
Court (Gunwalloe), 82 & n., 129n.
Cowclose (field, Mawgan in Pyder), 99
Crafthole (Sheviock), borough, xcvii
Crawle (Breage), 13, 82, 125, 145, 148, 206
Creed, churchtown, 9, 50, 117
Creney (Lanlivery), 195
Crenver (Crowan), 9n., 44, 89, 133
Crift (Lanlivery), 195
Crigmurrick (St Merryn), cxvi, 26, 55, 75, 107
Crugmeer (Padstow), xxvi, 141
Cruk Bras (= *Gonhughell*? St Enoder), 95 & n.
Cucurrian (Ludgvan), 189
Cusgarne (Gwennap), 230-1, 233

Degembris (Newlyn East), manor, xxxix, xcviii
Demesnes (Lanlivery), (Little), 194, 196
Deviock (Cardinham), 177
Domellick (St Dennis), manor, xxxii-xxxiv, xlvii, xlix-l, xciv, 170-2, 236-7; tenement, 236
Dorwenek (field, Mawgan in Meneage), 127
Dounrew (Lanherne & Trembleath manor), 4
Downinney (Warbstow), manor, xxviii-xxix, xxxi, xlviii, lxix, lxxxi, xcv, 174-7
Dress Lake (Cardinham manor), 187
Drym (Crowan), 47, 92, 135-6
Dyffryn Clwyd (Denbighshire), lordship, cxxxv

East ..., *see under second element*
Easter Low (Gwithian), 47 & n., 92, 135

Eastway (Morwenstow), manor, xci–xcii & n., xcvi
Eathorne (Mabe), manor, xxxii, xxxv
Efflins (St Eval), 33, 65, 108
Egloshayle (Phillack), 41–3, 86, 88, 131–2
Eglosrose (Philleigh), manor, 191
Ekenswell (Cardinham), 187
Ellenglaze (Cubert), manor, 224
Engollan (St Eval), lxxxi, ciii, 1, 3, 5, 26 & n., 32, 54, 65, 75, 107–8
Ennis (St Dennis), 59, 96, 139; *E. Veor*, 59n., 140, 236; E. Vean, 171, 236–7
Ennis (Stithians), 20, 78, 122
Enniscaven (St Dennis), manor, xx, xxxii, xli, xlv, lvi, cxxii–cxxiii, cxlv, 58–9, 95–6, 139–40; tenement, 58–9, 95–6, 139–40
Enysmaugan (Mawgan in Pyder), 4, 34
Erisey (Grade), 17, 81, 128
Exeter (Devon), cxxvii n., 176, 181, 183, 185; bishops of, xiii, xiv n., xxv, 4n.

Foage (Zennor), 189, 191 [?]
Forda (Lanivet), 58, 98, 116
Fore Street (Bodmin), 152 & n., 154–5, 200
Fosbras (St Enoder), 62, 94, 138
Frogham (Lanivet), 56n., 97, 114 & n.
Fursedown (Lanlivery?), 196

Gargas (Cuby), 28, 68, 110
Gargason (Gwithian), 46 & n., 91n., 135
Garrah (Mullion), lxxxiii
Gaverigan (St Columb Major), 1 & n., 32, 65, 108, 161, 210, 214
Gears (*Parke and Geare*, St Hilary), 157 & n.
Gilly (Mawgan in Meneage), 22, 79, 124
Gluvian Marth (St Columb Major), 1
Glynn Wood (Cardinham), 187
Gnatham (Cardinham), 178, 187
Goamarth (field, St Enoder), 61–2, 93–4, 137–8
Gobye Acre (field, St Columb Minor), 163–4, 209
Godolphin (Breage), 148 & n.
Goenenbayly (St Enoder), moorland, 61–3, 93–4, 137–8
Golden Lake (Cardinham), 187
Gonenbaily, see Goenenbayly
Gonhughell (St Enoder), 95n., 139

Goninsey (Gunwalloe), *G. Cock*, 18 & n., 129; *G. Pye*, 18n., 82 & n., 129
Goome (Gunwalloe), 15, 126
Goosehill (Advent), cviii
Goran, churchtown, 10–11, 51–53, 113 (?), 118–19
Gormellick (Liskeard), 150, 202
Goss Moor (St Dennis), xciv, 171
Grafton (Gwithian), 41, 86, 131
Great ..., *see under second element for names other than the following*
the Great Close (St Columb town), 38–9, 72
Great Ditch (Cardinham), xxix, 182 & n., 186, 190, 193
great meadow (of Lanherne), 99
Great Place (Liskeard town), 151 & n., 202
Grete medow (of Lanhadron), 119, 120n.
Grove Park, *see Argalls Walls*
Grynwyth (St Dennis?), 59n.
Gunenbayly, see Goenenbayly
Gunvenna (St Minver), 3 & n.
Gurlyn (St Erth), 13, 83, 125, 146, 149, 204; manor, xxix
Gwarnick (St Allen), 191, 236
Gwealcunnion, see Conium
Gwele Crockprynner (= Comprigney, Kenwyn), 120–1 & n.
Gwele nansmeur (field, St Clement), 121 & n.
Gweleyet (field, Kenwyn or St Clement), 121 & n.

Haleglasan (Gwithian), 135 & n.
Halendevas (St Ewe), 52 & n., 119
Halenvelan (Gwithian), 46, 91, 135
Hallas (Gwithian), moor, 46
Hallgoose Moore (Gwinear), 160
Hallworthy (Davidstow), 177
Halwyn (Crantock), 29, 67, 111
Halwyn (St Eval), 26 & n., 32 & n., 54, 65, 75, 107
Halwyn (St Keverne), 22, 80, 124
Halyn Parke (Mawgan in Pyder), 34 & n., 66, 110
Harlyn (St Merryn), 1, 24 & n., 73–4, 105–6
Harrold (Bedfordshire), cxxxv

INDEX OF PLACES

Hartland (Devon), xxxii
Haryngton (unidentified), lord of, 88
Haygrove (Cardinham), xxxvi
Hayle (Lelant), estuary, 40n., 134n.
Heligan (Warleggan), 178
Helland, parish, 42n.; Lower, 191
Helland (Treneglos), 175
Hellesvean (St Ives), 44, 133
Hell Grass Common (Lanlivery), 196–7
Helligan (St Mabyn), manor, 190
Hellynoon (Lelant), 41–2, 87, 131
Helston, town, lxxvii, xcvi & n., 14, 83, 126, 150, 168, 205
Helstone in Trigg, manor (Lanteglos by Camelford), lxxxvi, lxxxix, cvi, cviii
Hendra (formerly *Hendra Mullier*, Colan), 161, 211
Hendra (Cury), 14, 84, 126
Hendra (St Ives), 41, 42n., 87, 131
Hendra (Ruan Major), 17, 81, 128
Hendra (Stithians), 20, 78, 122
Hendradodda, see Burgess; *Rosehendra*
Hendra Mussell (St Columb Minor), 29 & n., 68, 112
Hendra Paul (St Columb Minor), 29, 67–8, 111, 113
Hendra Veor (St Columb Minor), 163, 209
Higher ..., *see under second element*
Hingey (alias *Nensey*, Gunwalloe), 19 & n., 82, 129
Holwood (Quethiock), lxxiv
Honiton (Devon), 192
Hoole Crepe (Treneglos?), 177
Hornacott (North Tamerton), manor, lxx
Howpers Mill (Lanlivery?), 196
Hunting Down (Lanlivery), 9, 51n., 117
Huntsham (Devon), parish, 192
Hurtstocks Wood (Cardinham), 187
Huthnance (Breage), 13, 82, 125

Ideford (Devon), xvi–xvii
Inkpen (Berkshire), 29
Inner ..., *see under second element*

Kaergrugyer, Kergruggyer (St Enoder), moorland, 62, 93–4, 137, 138
Keiro Veor (St Minver), 2 & n., 24, 73, 106
Kennall (Stithians), manor, xvi–xvii, xxiv, xlv, lvi, cxxii–cxxiii, cxlv–cxlvi, 19–21, 77–8, 122–3; mills, 21, 78, 123; tenement, 20, 78, 122
Kenketh (Cardinham), 177
Kenton (Devon), manor, xxviii, lxxiv
Kergruggyer, see *Kaergrugyer*
Kermoore (Cardinham?), 187
Kerrier, hundred, 19 & n., 129, 188
Kerthen (Crowan), 144, 147, 206
Keskeys, (St Columb Minor), Higher, 29, 68, 112
Kestle (St Columb Minor), lxxv, lxxxi, 30, 69, 113, 161, 164, 208, 213, 218–19; K. Mill (= Bejowan mill), 165, 212–13, 217
Killaworgey (St Columb Major), 161–2, 211, 214
Killianker (Mawgan in Meneage), 14, 84, 126
Knyght is Chamber (St Columb town), 105

Lahays (Cardinham), 177 & n.
Lamarth (Mawgan in Meneage), 14, 16n., 83, 126
Lambourne (Perranzabuloe), xx, xxii, 165
Lamellion (Liskeard), 150, 202
Lancada Well (Cardinham), 187
Landrayne (North Hill), manor, xcii
Landrivick (Manaccan), 23, 80, 124
Landulph, manor, lxxv, xcvi, 190
Laneskin Wood (Cardinham), 187
Lanet (Lanivet), 57, 98, 115
Langoran, see *Lanworan* (Goran)
Langurra (Crantock), 25, 74, 105
Lanhadron or **Nansladron** (St Ewe), manor, xx, xxii, xxxii, xl, xliii–xlv, cxxii–cxxiii, 8–11, 49–53, 53n.,113n., 117–20; demesne, 53; meadows, 119–20 & n.; mill, 11 & n., 52, 119; Park, 52, 119; *see also* **Rescassa**
Lanherne (Mawgan in Pyder), manor, x–xvii, xxii, xxiv, xxxix–xli, xlv, xlix, cxix, cxxii–cxxiii, cxlv, 1–7, 22n., 26n., 32–5, 65–6, 108–10, 214; barton lands, 99; church, see St Mawgan; demesne, lix, 35, 66, 99 & n., 110; Down, 35, 66, 110; mills, 6 & n., 35, 66, 110; Park, 99 & n.; rabbit farm, 65, 99; *see also* **St Columb town**; **Trembleath**
Laninval (Lanivet), 57, 98, 115; water, 99 & n., 116

Lanreath, manor, 190
Lantyan, Little (Lanlivery), *see* Castle
Lanuah (St Ewe), 10, 51, 119
Lanvean (Mawgan in Pyder), 6–7, 33, 66, 109
Lanworan (Goran), xx, xliv n., 11, 51, 52–3, 118–19; *see also* Goran
Lanyon (formerly *Coswinwolward*, Gwinear), 45 & n., 90, 134
Launceston, 46
Lawhittack (Colan), 191
Laworan, *see Lanworan*
Leah (Phillack), 43, 88, 132
Leigh Durrant (Pillaton), manor, lxxvi, lxxix, xcvi
Lelant, stream at, 40 & n., 49, 85, 93, 130
Lemail (Egloshayle), xcii n., 24 & n., 73 & n., 105
Lemar (Cardinham), 183
Lesquite (Lanivet), 194, 196
Levalsa (St Ewe), L. Meor, 222–3, 227
Levos, *see* Foage [?]
Lidcutt (Cardinham), 180, 183; L. Wood, 187
Liskeard, town, 192; way to, 187
Little ..., *see under second element except for*
  Litellmedow (of Lanhadron), 120 & n.
Loddiswell (Devon), xvi–xvii
Lostwithiel, town, xxviii, 192
Lower ..., *see under second element*
Lucyes, manor, *see* Rosuick
Ludgvan, manor, xxviii

Manuels (St Columb Minor), 27, 29n., 55, 75, 107
Mawgan Porth (Mawgan in Pyder), 32, 65, 108
Meade (Duloe), 203
Medland (temple), lxxii
Medlyn (Wendron), lxxiii n.
*Melingoth (Mawgan in Pyder), 6 & n.
Mellanvrane (St Columb Minor), civ, 31, 69, 113
Menagwins (Goran), 10–11 & n., 52, 119
Menawollas (St Dennis), 59 & n., 95, 139
Mennawartha (St Dennis), cxxxvi, 59, 96, 139
Merthen (Constantine), manor, xvi, 19n.; M. Wood, xvi
Middle ..., *see under second element*

Millingworth (St Ervan), mill, cii–civ, 27, 55, 75, 107
Millook (Poundstock), xcv
Millparke (Duloe), 151 & n., 203
Milltown (Cardinham), 183
Mingham (St Columb Major), 31, 69, 112, 113n., 166
Mitchell (St Enoder), borough, xiv–xv, xvii, xlii, xlv, li, lvii n., xcvi, xcviii & n., cxxii–cxxiii, xlv–xlvi, 61–3, 93–5, 137–9
Modbury (Devon), Little, 192
Mongleath (Budock), 22, 79, 123
Morchard Arundell (Devon), xiii, xv, xvii
Morebloe (Gunwalloe), 16, 127
Morval, parish, 153, 200
Myllesdowne (Treneglos), 176–7
Mynneyleas (St Eval), 172

Nampean (Gunwalloe), 15, 84, 126
Nance (Lelant), c n., 47, 92, 136
Nancegollan (Crowan), 89
Nancemellin (Gwithian), 157 [?] & n.
Nancemeor (St Clement), 121 & n.
Nancetrisack (Sithney), cix, 22 & n., 79, 123, 147, 149–50, 204; blowing mill, 150 & n., 205 & n.
Nancledra (Towednack), 40, 86, 130
Nangither (St Keverne), 17, 81, 127
Nankelly (St Columb Major), 229
Nanplough (Cury), 18, 81, 128
Nanruan (Goran), *see Nansfrinick*
Nansavallan (Lelant), 39 & n., 85, 130
Nanscow (St Breock), 141, 142n.
Nanseglos (Madron), 160
Nansfrinick alias Nanruan (Goran), 9, 50 & n., 117
Nanskerres (Sithney), cix, 147, 149, 205
Nansladron, *see* **Lanhadron**
Nantasier, *see* Negosias
Nanterrow (Gwithian), lxvi, 43, 88–9, 132, 157; moor, 49, 93
Nantillio (St Enoder), 63, 94–5, 138–9
Nantornan (St Columb Minor), 32, 65, 108
Negosias (alias *Nantasier*, Gwithian), 46, 91, 135
Nensey, *see* Hingey
Nether ..., *see under second element*
Newbridge (Cardinham), 187
Newham (Kenwyn), manor, xxiv
Newham (Mawgan in Pyder), 33n., 109

INDEX OF PLACES

Newhamstret, see Strete Newham
Newland Preeze (Cardinham), manor, xxxv–xxxvi, xlix–li, lxi, 177
Newton (Lanivet), 58, 98, 116
Newton (St Columb Minor), 30, 112

Oatfield (Crowan), 9n., 44, 89, 133
Okehampton (Devon), 180n.
Old Cardinham (Cardinham), xxxvi, 177, 179, 181
Oldeparke (field, Mawgan in Pyder), 99
Outer ..., *see under second element*

Padstow, town, 74n., 230
Parke and Geare, see Gears
Parke Cardelys (field, Mawgan in Meneage), 127
Parke Engrouse (fields, St Ewe), 118
Parke Engrowse (field, St Columb Major), 102
Parke Envelyn (field, St Columb Major), 105
Parke Enys, Le (field, St Ervan), cxlii
Parkenfenten (field, St Columb Major), 36, 102–3
Parke Nowith (field, St Enoder), 139
Parke Payn (field, Mawgan in Meneage), 127
Parke Trembleyth (field, St Ervan), 27; *see also* Trembleath
Park Tresithney (field, St Columb Major), 102
Pawton (St Breock), manor, xxv, 4 & n., 141–2 & nn.
Peach (Cardinham), 182
Pedon Pons (St Erth), 158
Penare (St Keverne), 146, 149, 204
Penberthy (St Hilary), manor, xx, xxii
Penbugle (Duloe), 151, 203
Pencarrow (Egloshayle), 191
Pendrift (Blisland), lxxx, lxxxiv
Penfentin (Gwithian), cx n., 134
Pengelly (Crowan), 159–60, 169
Pengelly (St Ewe), 8 & n., 11, 49 & n., 117
Pengrugla (St Ewe), 52, 119
Pengwedna (Breage), manor, xx, xxii, xlv–xlvi, cxxv, 125 & n., 144–5, 146n., 147–8, 205–6; mill, 206; tenement, 145, 148, 206

Penhale (Breage), Penhale-an-Drea, 147 & n., 206; Penhale Jakes, 147n.
Penhale (St Enoder), manor, xxxii, xxxv, lxxxii
Penhale (Goran), 10–11, 52, 119
Penhale (Gwinear), 158–9, 169–70; Moor, 170 & n.
Penmenor (Stithians), 19–20, 77–8, 122
Pennance (St Stephen in Brannel), 152, 154, 199
Pennance (Gwithian), P. Vean, 47, 91, 135; P. (Veor), 43, 46 & n., 48–9, 89, 91 & n., 133, 135
Pennant (Lanlivery), 194
Penpoll (St Anthony in Meneage), 23 & n., 80, 124
Penpoll (Cardinham), 181
Penpoll (Crantock), 31, 69, 113
Penpoll (Phillack), xci, cxii, 47, 92, 135
Penpont (Mawgan in Pyder), 33 & n., 66, 109
Penpraze (Sithney), 146, 149, 205
Penquite (Lanlivery), 192–4
Penrose (St Dennis), P. Vean, 171, 236 & n.; P. Veor, 236
Penrose (St Ervan), lxxxii, cii, 4, 25, 54, 75, 107
Penryn (St Gluvias), town, 30–1, 113 & n.
Pensignance (Gwennap), manor, 29n., 231
Penstrassoe (St Ewe), manor, 223
Pentewan (Mevagissey), 52
Pentire (Cury), 17, 81, 128
Pentire (Crantock), East, *see* Pentirevean; West, 30, 112
Pentire (St Eval), 33, 65, 108
Pentirevean (alias East Pentire, Crantock), 28, 67, 69, 111
Penvose (Mawgan in Pyder), 1, 3, 32, 34, 65, 108–9
Penwerris (Budock), xx, xxii, 22, 79, 123, 124
Penwith, hundred, xiv & n., xvii, xlviii, 40n., 188
Penzance, town, xcvi, 168
Perlees (St Breock), manor (with Trevisker), xxv–xxvii, xliv–xlv, 74n., 106n., 140–2; tenement, 141
Petheckes Combe (Cardinham), 187
Philleigh (parish), glebe, xvi, xliii, 85

Pill (Lanlivery), 8, 49, 117
Pinsla (Cardinham), 177
Pittsdowns (Cuby), 110
Plymouth (Devon), xcvi
Plympton (Devon), priory, xviii n.
Poleo (Crowan), 48 & n., 92, 136
Polgrean (Cury), 14, 83, 126
Polgreen (Mawgan in Pyder), 32, 65, 108, 162n.
Polgreen (Newlyn East), 27–8, 67, 110, 162 & nn.
Polgwidnan (St Keverne), 21, 79, 123
Polkinghorne (Gwinear), 40, 86, 130
Poll Fry (Menheniot), 222–3, 228
Polmellecke Moore (Cardinham), 187
Polmenor Downs (Gwinear), 170
Polscoe (St Winnow), 192
Polscovornogow (Carminow), 16, 127
Polsue (St Erme), manor, xxxii, xxxv, 192
Ponsferrance (Gwinear), 158
Ponsfrellas (Gwithian), 41 & n., 86, 131
Porth, *see* Mawgan Porth
Porthrepter (Lelant), *see* Barrepta
Porth Veor (St Columb Minor), lxx, lxxxi, lxxxiv–lxxxvi, 162–3, 165, 209, 212, 214, 216
Porthmeor (Zennor), 189
Praas Gulcer (Gwithian or Phillack), 90
Predannack (Mullion), P. Wartha, manor, cxxxv, 16n., 144n.; P. Wollas, manor, xxxii, xxxv, lxxxiii
Priesthouse (St Austell), 221, 225
Priske (Mullion), 144, 147, 206
Prospidnick (Sithney), manor, xviii–xix, xxii, xlv–xlvi, xcvi n., 22n., 125n., 146–7, 149–50, 204–5; tenement, 146, 149, 205
Pryests House, *see* Priesthouse
Pulsack (Phillack), 45, 90, 134

Quarry Parke, *see* Copshorn

Red Moor (Lanlivery), 196–7
Redallan (Breage), 13, 82, 125, 144, 148, 206
Rees (Perranzabuloe), lxii, 28, 68, 110–11
Releath (Crowan), 146, 149, 204
Reperry (Lanivet), manor, xx, xxii, xlv–xlvi, xcvi, 152–5, 199–201; mills, 201; tenement, 153, 201

Rescassa (Goran), 53 & n.; tenement, 53, 113n., 118 & n., 119; *see also* **Lanhadron**
Rescorla (St Ewe), 8–10, 50–1, 118
Reskivers (Veryan), 221, 226
Respryn (St Winnow), 186 & n., 191
Restormel (Lanlivery), xxxi; castle, xiv, xxviii
Retallick (Roche), 25 & n., 74, 105
Rialton (St Columb Minor), manor, 165, 214, 231
Rinsey (Breage), 147n., 188
Riviere (Phillack), cxxv, 159, 169
Roche (parish), benefice, 197
Roscullion (Little Petherick), xxvi, 141 & n.
Rose-an-Grouse (St Erth), 158
Roseath (Stithians), 20, 78, 122
Rosehendra (Cury), 15n., 19, 82, 129; *see also* Burgess; *Hendradodda*
Roselath (Lanlivery), 193
Rosemorder (Manaccan), 13, 16, 83, 125
Roseney (Lanlivery), 193–6; Over & Lower R., 194; R. Mill, 194
Rosenithon (St Keverne), manor, xxxii, xxxv
Roserrans (St Columb Major), 152, 154, 199
Rosesuggan (St Columb Major), manor, 231
Rosevallon (Bodmin), 55, 96, 114
Rosevidney (Ludgvan), Little, 157
Rosewastis (St Columb Major), 172, 237n., 238
Roseworthy (Gwinear), manor, xxxii, xxxiv, xciv, 157–60, 168–70; mills, 160, 168; tenement, 159, 168; wood, 170; Down, 170 & n.
Roshill (Lanivet?), 116
Roskear (St Breock), 140–2
Rosuick or *Lucyes* (St Keverne), manor, xvi, 16 & n.
Ruan Major (parish), advowson, xvi
Ruan Minor (parish), advowson, xvi
Runbovetown (St Clement), 60 & n., 76; *see also* Conium
Ruthdower (Breage), 13, 82–3, 125, 144n., 145 & n., 148 & n., 206
Ruthvoes (St Columb Major), 1, 32, 65, 108, 145n., 161, 210

INDEX OF PLACES 249

Sadleback, tin-moor (Lanlivery), 197
St Andrew's (Tywardreath), priory, lxxix
St Austell, town, lxxv, 52n., 172, 221 & nn., 225, 237n., 238
St Bennets (Lanivet), blowing mill, 201
St Clement street (Truro), 121
St Columb (St Columb Major), town, xiii, xv, xxii, xxxii, xxxviii–xxxix, xli, xliv–xlv, li, lvii n., xcvi–cxviii, cxxii–cxxiii, cxliii–cxlvi, 2, 35–9, 70–3, 102–5, 113; *see also* **Lanherne**; bakehouse, 38, 73; chantry, xix, xxi–xxiv, xxxviii, xli, xlv–xlvi, xlviii–xlix, cross, 36; demesne, 4; Great Close, 38–9, 70, 72; mills, 39, 52n., 73, 105; smithy, 37; well, 36, 102
St Erth, churchtown, 188
St Francis, acre of (St Enoder), 63, 94, 138
St Ingunger (Lanivet), 192
St Ives, town, xcvi, cxiii, 168
St Lawrence (Bodmin), 56–7, 58 & n., 97n., 98, 114, 116, 200
St Mawgan in Pyder, church, xxii, xxiv, rector of, 66
St Michael's Mount, 168; way to (St Enoder), 62, 94, 138
St Minver (parish), 24, 73–4, 106; lands in, xiii, xv, xl, lxv; vicar of, 75
St Nicholas (Bodmin), 152, 154, 200
St Stephen's (Launceston), priory, lxxix
St Tudy (parish), advowson & lands, xxi n., xxii, xxxviii
Saltash, town, xcvi
Scarsick (Treneglos), Higher, 175–6; Nether, 175
Sekerlegh, Sikerlych (St Enoder), 62, 94, 138
Sewrah (Stithians), 178
Sidbury (Devon), xcv
Sixpenny Land (Cardinham), 185 & n.
Skewes, Great (St Wenn), 25, 74, 106
Skorden Moore (Cardinham), 187
Soarns (Probus), 222–3, 228
Sourne alias Tresournes (Probus), 222–3, 228
Sowanna (Gunwalloe), lix, 18 & n., 128, 129n.
Spernon (Breage), 148 & n.
Stannon Downs (St Breward), 186
Start (St Erth), 158 & n.
Stephen Gelly (Lanivet), 99 & n.
Sticker (St Mewan), xxxix, 119

Streigh (Lanlivery), 191
Strete Newham (alias *Newhamstret*, Kenwyn), 31, 69, 113
Sticker (St Merryn), 119
Stock (Duloe), Stock's, 203; Higher S., 151, 203; Lower S., alias Stock's Cottage, 151, 203
Stratton, town, xcvi; hundred, cix
Stuffle (St Neot), lxxii

Tamerton, manor, 19n.
Tanna Mill (Cardinham), 180 & n.
Taskus (Gwinear), 40, 85, 130
Tavistock (Devon), 180n.
Teason (alias Lower Trezance, Cardinham), lxviii–lxix, cix, 178
Tencreek (Menheniot), 190
Tewington (St Austell), manor, 11 & n.
Thurelake, stream (Cardinham?), 187
Tintagel (parish), glebe, lxxvi; manor, c n.
Tinten (St Tudy), lxxx
Tolcarne (St Columb Minor), 162 & n., 166 & n., 208
Tolcarne Merock (Mawgan in Pyder), lxxxi, lxxxiv, 29–30 & n., 69, 112 & n., 114, 161, 162n., 163, 210, 213, 217
Tolgarrick (St Stephen in Brannel), manor, lxxxii
Tolgroggan (St Allen), 110
Tolgullow (Gwennap), 158
Toll (Gunwalloe), 18, 82, 129
Tolverne (Philleigh), xviii–xxiii, 9n., 22n., 79n.; *see also* Index of Persons, Arundell of Tolverne
Tolzethan (Gwithian), 46, 91, 135 & n.
Ton Engrouse (field, St Ervan), 26, 54–5
Towan (St Columb Minor), 25, 74, 106, 162 & n., 163, 164n., 208–9, 214
Towan (St Merryn), lxxxi, 24, 73, 105
Townewell (Treneglos?), 177
Traleath (Newlyn East), 28, 67, 111
Trease (Cury), 18, 81, 128
Treassowe (Ludgvan), 157–8 & n.
Trebartha (North Hill), 191
Trebarva (St Columb Minor), 163, 209
Trebarveth (Stithians), 21, 78, 122
Trebby (St Columb Minor), ciii, cvi, 31, 69, 113
Trebelzue (St Columb Minor), lxxvii, lxxxi–lxxxii, lxxxiv, xc–xci, cxxv, 162n.,

164 & n., 165, 211, 213 & n., 214–16, 218
Trebudannon (St Columb Major), 31, 53, 113, 229
Trecaine (Creed), lxxxvi, lxxxix
Tredenham (Lanivet), 153 & n., 201
Tredinnick (St Issey), lxxxi, 140, 142
Tredrizzick (St Minver), lxv, 6, 25, 54, 75, 106
Treffry (Lanhydrock), 56, 97, 114
Tregaddra (Mawgan in Meneage), 18, 81, 128
Tregamere (St Columb Major), 152, 154, 199
Tregantle (Lanlivery), 193, 195
Tregarden (Luxulian), moor named from, 197
Tregarne (St Keverne), manor, xx, xxii, cxvi n., cxxii–cxxiii, cxlv–cxlvi, 21–3, 79–80, 123–5; mill, 23, 80, 125; tenement, 22, 79, 123–4
Tregaron Moore, see Tregarden
Tregarthen (Ludgvan), 8n.
Tregaswith (St Columb Major), 229–33
Tregatillion (St Clement), 121 & n.
Tregawne (Withiel), xxvii & n.
Tregear (Bodmin), 99, 115n.
Tregellast (Ludgvan), 189
Tregembo (St Hilary), 42, 88, 132
Tregenna (St Ewe), manor, xxxii–xxxiv, xlvii, xlix, lxix, lxxv, 171 & n., 220–8; T. Wartha, 221–2, 226–7; T. Wolas, 222–3, 226–8; demesne, 221–2
Tregenna (St Ives), 45, 89–90, 133
Tregenna (Treneglos), 175, *T. Combeshed*, 177
Tregenryth, see Tregerthen
Tregerrick (Goran), 9, 50, 117
Tregerthen (= *Tregenryth*? Zennor), 13, 83, 125
Tregevas (St Martin in Meneage), 23, 80, 124
Tregiddle (Cury), 13, 83, 125
Treglith (Treneglos), xciii n., 174–5
Treglyn (St Minver), lxv, 2 & n.
Treglynes (St Minver), 2 & n.
Tregona (St Eval), lxxxvii–lxxxix, xci, cii–ciii, 5 & n., 26, 54, 75, 107
Tregonan (Stithians), 122n.
Tregongon (Veryan), 192 (?)

Tregonning (Mawgan in Pyder), 3–4 & n., 34, 66, 109
Tregonning (Stithians), 19–20, 77–8, 122
Tregony (Cuby), manor, 148n., 223, 238; town, xcvi
Tregoose (St Erth), 188
Tregorrick (St Austell), manor, xxxii, xxxiv, xlvii, l, 171–2, 237–8; tenement, 171, 237
Tregowris (St Keverne), 17, 81, 127
Tregunna (St Breock), 141–2 & n.
Tregurra (St Clement), 121n.
Tregurrian (Mawgan in Pyder), lxxxi–lxxxii, xci, xcv; way to, 215, 218
Tregustick (St Columb Minor), 5 & n., 34, 109
Tregustick (Withiel), 5n.
Treguth (Cubert), 223–4, 228
Tregwinyo (alias Trevengenow, St Ervan), cviii, cxlii, 27, 54n., 55, 75, 107
Treisaac (St Columb Minor), 164, 209–10
Trekenning (St Columb Major), cii n., 30, 53, 113 & n.
Trelanvean (St Keverne), 21, 79, 123
Trelaske (Cubert), 28, 67, 111, 220, 223–4
Trelavour (St Dennis), 59, 96, 139–40
Trelawder (St Minver), 6 & n.
Trelay (Pelynt), 191
Trelean (St Erth), 13, 83, 125, 146, 149, 204
Trelean (St Ewe), T. Vean, 220; T. Veor, 220–5, 228
Treligga (St Teath), xcv
Treliggo (Breage), 13, 82–3, 125, 145, 148, 206
Trelissick (St Erth), 42, 88, 132
Treliver (St Wenn), 152, 154, 199–200
Treloweth (St Mewan), xxxix, 119; T. Wood, xvi
Trelowthas (Probus), manor, 223
Treloy (St Columb Minor), manor, x–xi, xiii, xv–xvii, xxii, xxxii, xlv, xlix, lxii–lxiv, lxvi, ci–cviii, cx–cxi, cxiii, cxv–cxvii, cxxii–cxxiii, 27–31, 67–9, 110–14, 161, 162n., 166n., 208, 223; mill, *see* Mellanvrane; tenement, cvii–cviii, cxvi, 30, 68, 112
Treloyan (St Ives), 45, 48, 89–90, 92, 133, 136
Tremayle (Lanivet), 57, 97–8, 115; T. Down, 97, 115

INDEX OF PLACES

Trembleath (St Ervan), manor, x, xiii, xv–xvii, xxvi, xxxix–xli, xlv, lxv, lxxxvii, xcii n., xcviii & n., ci–cv, cviii, cx–cxi, cxiii, cxv–cxvii, cxix, cxxii–cxxiii, cxlv–cxlvi, 1–7, 24–7 & n., 32n., 54–5, 73–6, 105–7; demesne, lix, 107; mill, *see* Millingworth; tenement, cxvi, 26, 54 & n., 75; *see also* **Lanherne**
Trembroath (Stithians), 19–21, 77–8, 123
Tremeader (Zennor), 13, 83, 125
Tremenheere (Stithians), 21, 78, 123
Tremorvah (St Clement), *see* Conium
Trenance (Mawgan in Pyder), 32, 65, 108
Trenance (Mullion), T. Vean, 17, 81, 128
Trenance (Withiel), *T. Wolas*, 153, 201
Trenayles (St Ervan), cxlii, ciii, cvi, cviii, 27, 54n., 55 & n., 75, 107
Trencreek (St Columb Minor), lxxxii, 28, 67–8, 111
Trencrom (Lelant), 39–40, 85, 130
Trenear (Breage), 13, 82, 125, 145, 148, 206
Trenearne (Padstow), xxvi, 140, 142
Trenedros (St Erth), 188
Treneglos, parish, 174
Trenerth (Gwinear), 188
Trengothal (St Levan), 188
Trengwainton (Madron) 158
Trenhillocks (St Columb Major), (with St Columb town) 70–3, 102–5; *see also* **Lanherne**
Treninick (St Columb Minor), xxxii, 29, 68, 112
Treniow (Padstow), xxvi, cii n., 74 & n. [?], 106 & n., 140
Trenoon (Ruan Major), 17 & n., 81, 128
Trenoweth (Gunwalloe), 18n., 19, 82, 129
Trenoweth (Gwinear), 43, 86, 130 & n., 132
Trenowin (Gwinear), 41, 86–7, 130–1
Trenowin (Ludgvan), 189, 191–2
Trerice (Newlyn East), 9n.
Trerise (Ruan Major), 17, 81, 128
Tresallyn (St Merryn), 141
Tresawsen (Perranzabuloe), lxxv, lxxxiv, xciii n., 165, 230–2
Trescoll (Luxulian), 194–5
Tresean (Cubert), 29, 67, 111
Tresemple (St Clement), 121 & n.
Tresillian (Newlyn East), cxxiv, cxxviii, 229

Tresithney (St Columb Major), manor, xxxii, xxxiv, lxix & n., lxxv, lxxxi, 171 & n., 229–34; tenement, lxx, 230, 233
Treskellow (Treneglos), 174
Treskewes (Stithians), 19–20, 77–8, 122
Treskillard (Illogan), 188
Treslea (Cardinham), 180–3
Tresournes (Probus), *see* Sourne
Tresprison (Mullion), 17, 81, 128
Tresven (unidentified, member of Carnabeggas), 189
Treswithick (Cardinham), 180
Trethauke (St Minver), 1 & n., 24, 73–4, 106
Trethevas (Landewednack), manor, xvi, 237 & n.
Trethew (Menheniot), 192
Trethewell (St Eval), xxi, 5n.
Trethias (St Merryn), cii and n., 24, 73, 75, 105–6
Trethingy (Phillack), 41, 86, 131
Trethowell (Kea), lxiii–lxiv, cv–cviii, cxv, 31 & n., 69, 113
Trevabyn (St Hilary), 157 & n.
Trevaddra (Manaccan), 190
Trevanger (St Minver), 1 & n., 2, 24, 73, 106
Trevanson (St Breock), xci, 140–2 & n.
Trevarno (Sithney), 147 & n., 149, 205
Trevarnon (Gwithian), 43, 88, 90, 132
Trevarren (St Columb Major), 161, 210
Trevarrian (Mawgan in Pyder), lxxxi, lxxxii n., xci
Trevarth (Gwennap), 29 & n., 112
Trevarthian (St Hilary), xvi
Trevaskis (Gwinear), 42n., 43, 45, 47, 87, 90, 92, 132, 134–5
Trevassack (Phillack), 41, 86–7, 131
Trevedras (Mawgan in Pyder), 3 & n., 33, 109
Treveglos (Zennor), 13, 83, 125
Trevelgue (St Columb Minor), cxliii, 3 & n., 5 & n., 34, 65, 109–10
Trevella (Crantock), 25, 74, 106
Trevellion (Luxulyan), xc
Trevemedar (St Eval), 142, 172, 238
Treven (St Erth), 42 & n., 87, 131 & n.
Treveneage (St Hilary), manor, xx, xxii
Trevengenow (St Ervan), *see* Tregwinyo
Trevenna (Mawgan in Pyder), 33, 66, 108–9

Treveor (St Merryn), 24, 73, 105
Treverbyn (St Austell), manor, 223, 238
Trevia (Lanteglos by Camelford), lxxx, lxxxix
Treviades (Constantine), 189
Treviglas (St Columb Minor), 31, 69, 113, 163–4, 208–9
Trevilmick (Lanlivery), 194
Trevio (St Merryn), 24 & n., 73, 105
Trevisker (Padstow), manor (with Perlees), xxvi, 140–2; tenement, 141–2
Trevollard (Lanreath), lxxx
Trevorder (Warleggan), 178
Trevorek Downe (Mawgan in Pyder), 109
Trevowah (Crantock), 25, 28–9, 67, 74, 105, 111
Trewarmenna (Creed), 9, 11n., 50, 118
Trewartha (Veryan), lxx
Trewellard (St Just in Penwith), manor, lxxxii
Trewen (Lanteglos by Camelford), lxxxvi
Trewinnick (St Ervan), 26–7 & n., 54
Trewinnion (St Enoder), xxxix
Trewinnow (Creed), lxxxviii
Trewithen (Stithians), 178
Trewonnard (Treneglos), 174–6
Trewoone (Phillack), 43, 88, 132
Treworder (Kenwyn), 112
Treworgie (Manaccan), 190
Treworlyn (Gunwalloe), 14–15 & n.
Treworvack (Constantine), 146–7, 149 n., 205
Treyarnon (St Merryn), 24, 73, 105
Trezance (Cardinham), xxix, 184–5; Lower T., *see* Teason
Trezise (St Martin in Meneage), 17, 81, 128
Trinity (Lanlivery), xxxi
Trink (Lelant), 44, 47, 89, 92, 133, 136; manor, xxii, xxxviii
Truro, borough, xxxix, 120–1, 180n., 211; Dominican friary, 77 & n.; streets, 31, 69, 113, 121; way to (St Enoder), 62, 94, 138
Truro Vean (St Clement), manor, xxiv, xli, xlv, cxxii–cxxiii, cxlv–cxlvi, 60, 76–7, 120–1; quarry, c n., 121n.
Truthall (Sithney), xxi
Truthwall (Ludgvan), manor, 157n.

Tubbs (St Ewe), 225
Tybesta (Creed), manor, lxxxvi, lxxxviii–lxxxix, cvi, 11 & n., 49n., 53n., 222–3
Tywardreath, priory, xxviii, 177 & n.; manor, xxix
Tywarnhaile, stannary, cxiii

Uphay (Devon), lxxiv
Upton (Gwithian), 47, 91, 135
Uton Arundell (Devon), xiii, xv, xvii

Ventonleague (Phillack), 41, 86–7, 131
Venwyn (Lelant), 47, 92, 136
Virly (St Minver), 2n.
Vorvas (Lelant), 48, 92, 136
Voss (Duloe), 150, 203
Vow (St Ives), cxi, 48–9, 92, 136

Wadebridge (St Breock), 140–1
Weens (St Minver or St Kew), 6 & n.
Welcombe (Devon), manor, lx, lxii–lxiii, 45, 90, 134
Welltown (Cardinham), 182
West Close, Le (field, St Ervan), cxlii
Westow (Lanlivery), 193, 196
Westway (Lelant), 42, 87, 132
Whitley (Bodmin), 152, 154, 200
Whitstone (parish), advowson, xvi; glebe, xliii, 85
Wicket (Newlyn East), 28, 67, 111
Wille (Lanlivery), 8 & n., 49 & n., 117
Wilsey Down (Treneglos), *see* Myllesdowne
Windsor (Mawgan in Pyder), 34, 66, 109
Winnington (Gunwalloe), manor, xvi–xvii, xxiv, xlv, lix, cxxii–cxxiii, cxlv, 15n., 17–19, 81–2, 127–9; tenement, 19, 82, 129; quarry, c n., 129
Withen (Lelant), 48 & n., 92, 136
Withiel, churchtown, lxxv, 221, 223, 225; manor, 221
Woodley (Lanivet), Higher, 57, 98, 116; Lower, 57–8, 98, 116

York, archbishop of, 179 & n.

Zennor, churchtown, lxxxix–xc, xcii

INDEX OF SURNAMES

This is primarily an index of names, rather than persons. That is to say, it does not presume to decide whether two people mentioned in separate places within the text are to be identified as one or not; and it does not usually list persons mentioned in the text but not named (such as the reeve of a manor or the vicar of a parish). The decision on whether two individuals with the same name (or even with different names) can be equated is left to the reader's own judgement and additional knowledge. However, in the case of major land-holding families (particularly the Arundells but also some others), individuals are distinguished where possible.

In order to suggest the sphere of activity of a person appearing in the index, the parish where he or she held land is sometimes given, and/or the date when they are mentioned. It should be emphasised that the parish is that where a person held land, not necessarily their parish of residence. Similarly it is possible in some cases that people were dead at the date when they were mentioned in the surveys.

For discussion of the surnames and their significance, see the Introduction, pp. cxxiv–cxxxvii. Two-part surnames (see pp. cxxxi–cxxxvii) have been indexed under both the second and the third parts, with either cross-references or duplicated entries; when sometimes written as a single word (e.g. Jakgillowe), a two-part surname is given a separate index entry, but with cross-references to the component parts where appropriate.

The head-forms are chosen from among those appearing in the text (i.e. spellings have not been modernised), with variant spellings given in brackets after the head-form. In cases of uncertainty whether two surnames are variants of one another or not, both are indexed, with cross-references. Names present in the text but later deleted appear as ordinary entries. When a name does not survive in full (e.g. when only a christian name survives in the text, or when too little of a surname survives for it to be guessed), that person is not indexed.

Entries are filed in modern alphabetical order, word by word. Thus *u*, *v*, *w* and *i*, *j*, *y* are treated as separate letters in alphabetical order, with *see* or *see also* cross-references. French indexing conventions are followed in putting 'de' after names in which it occurs ('Rosworugan, John de', rather than 'de Rosworugan, John'), and in putting 'le' before the names that have it ('le Brit'), but disregarding it in alphabetical ordering.

Abbas, Richard, 52
Abraham, Robert, 203; Thomas, 179, 186
Adam, John, chaplain (St Columb town), 103; John (Stithians), 122; Richard (St Columb Major), 230
Ady, John, 31
Alan (Alen), John (St Clement), 120, (Stithians), 122; Peter John A., 48
Aly Carnarthur, John, *see* Carnarthur
Androwe (Andreu, Andrev), John (St Columb Minor), 3n., (Goran), 10 & n.;

William Tom A., 27; Thomas A. Taylour, *see* Tailor; John A. Treghar, *see* Trehar
Anger, heir(s) of, 152, 154, 200
Angowgh, David John alias A., cxxx, 159, 168–9; *see also* Goff, Ingowe
Anne Busshe, *see* Busshe
Antron, heir of, 149; heir of Richard, 204
Archedeken (Larcedeken, Larchedecon, Lercedekne), family, xxxiv; heir(s) of (St Columb Major), 108, (St Dennis),

139 & n., (Pelynt), 191; John, 1; Warin,
& daughter Philippa (married Hugh
Courtenay), xxxiv; heir(s) of Warin
(Breage), 13, 32, 82, 125

Arundell (Arondell, Arrundell, Arundel,
Darundel)

(1) Arundell of Lanherne
(previously of Trembleath, previously of
Treloy)
family, ix–xii, xvi, xxii, cxvii–xcviii & n.
Ralph son of Remfrey I [d.1275–6], xiv,
xxvii [?], lxii, xcviii, & wife Eve, xiii,
lxv, 3n.
Remfrey II [d.1278–81], lxiii, & wife
Alice, xiii–xv
John I [fl.1290–1306], xiv–xv, xviii
John, son of John [1323], xiv–xv, 1n.;
Joan, widow of John, xxxix–xl, [1328],
6n.; John, & wife Elizabeth Carminow
[c.1334], xv; John, [1339], 5n.; John de
[1346], 1n.; Sir John [1347], 3n.; Sir
John [1358], 44n.; John [1374], lxiv
John [d.1433–5], xvii–xxiv, xxxviii, xl,
48n.
John, of Bideford [d. by 1424], xx–xxi
Remfrey [fl.1420s–30s], xxii
John [b.1421, d.1471–3], xx–xxi, xxiii,
xxvii, xliv, 52n., 53n., 59n., 140
Thomas [d.1485], xi, xxvii, xxix–xxx,
xliii–xliv
Sir John [d.1545], xi, xxiv, xxx, 102n.,
141n.
Sir John [d.1557], xi, 157, 161, 163, 166
Edward, esq. [d.1587], 212–13 & n., 218
Sir John [d.1590], xxxii–xxxiii, lxvi, 168n.,
170, 176, 186, 197, 208, 210, 214,
216–17, 219, 223
Sir John [d.1701], xii
Richard Bellings A., xii, li
Mary Bellings A., xii

(2) Arundell of Trerice
family, xi
Ralph/Randulph [1343], xi & n., 2 & n.,
9n., [1358], 44n.; Joan his wife, 2n., 9n.
Nicholas [1378, 1400], xi, 2n., 9n., 44n.,
89n.; his heir(s), 44 & n., 89 & n.
Ralph, & wife Joan [1404], xix
John [1468–9], 146

heirs of John [1480], 89 & n.
John [1499], 133
Nicholas [1499], 117
Sir John [1549], 157

(3) Arundell of Tolverne
family, xxi
Thomas, xx
Sir John [1460–99], 22 & n., 79 & n., 86,
123, 131
Thomas, esq. [1549], 157
Florence, widow [1549], 163
John [1566–75], 189, 209

(4) Arundell of Gwarnick
John [1566], 191
John [c.1586], 236

(5) Arundell of Wardour
family, xi–xii, xv, xlii
Henry, 7th Lord [1739], xii
[Henry], 8th Lord [1771], 61n.
Thomas [d.1551], xi

(6) Arundell (other)
Christine (Erysye, later Dottysson),
daughter of Sir Humphrey A. [1549],
163
(Sir) Edmund A. [1499], 102, 106, 131
heirs of Sir Edward A. [1575], 231
Humphrey, xi
heirs of Laurence A. [1459–99], 24, 73,
105
heir(s) of Sir John A. [1459], 25, 74
(Sir) Remfrey A. [1459–60], 25, 36, his
heirs, 70, 74, 86
Robert [12th century], x
Roger [12th century], x n.

Arwennack, Thomas Keligrew de, *see*
Killigrewe
Atkynson, Thomas, 213, 218, 230, 233
Atley, *see* Ley
Auny, heir of John, 20; Nicholas, 11
Avrean (...rean), John, 171, 237n., 238,
his wife & daughter, 171–2

Bacheler, John, 126
Baddecok (Badcok), William, cxlii, 75
Badyn, Stephen, 5
Bagh, John, 145

INDEX OF SURNAMES

Bahow (Baghowe), John, 124; Richard, 22, 79; Thomas, 124
Bailey (Bailly), Henry, 75; Martin, 115
Baker (Bakeur), Andrew, 113; Janyn, 51; John, & wife, 77; Thomas, 122
Baowchampe, *see* Beacham
Barbour, John, 104
Baron, Joan, widow, & daughter Joan, 159
Barret(t), ..., 155; John, 151 & n.; Walter, 203
Barry, John Martyn, & wife, 33
Bartlet, Thomas, 195
Basset, John, 59; Ralph, 38; Thomas, 4
Bathe, William, 183; earl of, 186
Bathurst, family, xlii
Bauden (Bawdyn), Nicholas, 103; William, 155
Bayly, *see* Bailey
Beacham (Baowchampe, Beachym), heirs of (Marhamchurch), 192; heirs of John (St Columb Major), 229; Martin, 160
Beanes, Roger, gent., 227–8
Beauripper, Richard, cxxvii, cxliv, 84
Beckett (Beket), Edmund, 55; Robert, 190
Beer (Beere, Bere, Ber', Beare), ... (Bodmin), 200; of Huntsham, heirs of, 192; John, 96, 114, 140, 153; Reginald, 151; heir of Reginald, 202; Thomas, gent., 201
Beket, *see* Beckett
Bellings Arundell, *see under* Arundell of Lanherne
Bennett (Benet), Henry, 201; James, 119; Roger, 136
Benny (Bynny), John, cxvi, 27, 30, 68; Laurence, 30; Paul, 29, 37–8, 112
Berban, William, 61, 93
Bere, *see* Beer
Berk(e)le, Bartholomew de, 3 & n.
Berken', William, 137
Berkle, *see* Berk(e)le
Berowe, *see* Perow
Betty, Richard (Lanivet), 57, 98, (St Dennis), 59; Thomas, 58, 98
Bevell (Bevill, Bevyll), Mr (Bodmin), 114n.; John, esq., 154, 199; Peter (St Clement), 120, (St Columb town), 102, (St Dennis), 139, (St Stephen in Brannel), 199; William, 231
Bewmand, heirs of Mr, 186

Billo(u)n (Byllun), John, (de Trethywol) [1343], 3, 5 & n.; [c.1400], xxi–xxii
Bischop, John, & wife & heirs, 141n.
Blake, Thomas, 25
Blewet(t) (Bluett), Francis, (& wife) (St Columb Minor), 162, 164 & n., 208–10, 214, (Colan), 191
Blight, heirs of John, merchant, 201; John, schoolmaster, 201
Blisland, *see* John, of Blyslond
Bloyhow(e) (Bloyowe), ..., 65 [?]; John, 65, 109; Roger, 135
Bluett, *see* Blewett
Boddrugan, *see* Bodrugan
Boden, Henry, 22; Thomas, 79
Bodrogow, John, 113
Bodrugan (Boddrugan), (Sir) Henry, 29n.; Henry, (esq.), 17, 29, 49–50, 81, heir(s) of Henry, 112, 128; Sir William [1435], xxiv; heirs of William [1385], 9
Body, John (de Penrynburgh), 30–1; *see also* Budy
Boes, *see* Boys
Boessywen, *see* Bussywen
Bois, *see* Boys
Bolenowe, Walter, 89, 91, & wife Joan, 89
Bonda, William, 63, 94, 138
Bonythorn, Richard, 81
Borlas, Richard, & wife Joan, 141n.
Boscaffyn, *see* Boscawen
Boscawen (Boscawan, Boscaffyn), (St Dennis), 236; heir of (Bodmin), 55; heir(s) of (St Columb Major), 154; Hugh, 24, 73; John, 102; Nicholas (St Columb Major), 199–200; Richard (Bodmin), 114; heir of Richard (St Columb Major), 199; B. Roos, Richard (St Merryn, etc.), 105; *see also* Falmouth
Bosfrawell (Browfrowell), heir(s) of, 144n., 147, 205; John, 144
Bossitho, John, 221
Bossosowe, John (Gwithian), cxxvii, 134
Bossu, Simon, 11
Bosustow (Bossustowe), John (Gunwalloe), 82, 129
Bosveell, John, 145
Bosveysek, Thomas, his daughter Joan (Rosougan), 29
Bosworbeth, daughter of Nicholas, 177
Boswyn, Henry, 144n., 145
Bothet, *see* Botthet

Botreaux, Richard B. de Coisvogherth, cxxxv, 87; William lord of B., 39–40, 49, heirs of William, 85
Botthet (Bothet), Matthew, 10; heirs of Richard, 8
Boughton, see Broughton
Bowcom(e), heir of (Liskeard), 151, 202
Bowyer, Nicholas, gent., 226
Boys (Bois, Boes), John (St Columb Minor), 29, 112, (Phillack), 88, 132; heir of Olimpi(as) or Olimpus, 43, 88; Richard, 132; Robert, 158; Stephen, & wife Joan, 90; see also Tregenna
Braben (Braban, Brabin), Nicholas (St Breock), 140; Nicholas (Lanivet), 115; Philip, 116; Thomas, 141
Braggour, William, 10
Brande, William, 56
Brandon, James, gent., 222, 228
Bray, Henry, 175; John B. (Treworlas), 29, 112
Brent, Richard, 122
Brenton, Richard, 57; William, 58
Brian, John, 115; see also Bryand
Briand, see Bryand
le Brit, heir of William, 17
Brode, John (Lanivet) 57, 115; John, sen. (Lanivet), 97; Thomas (Lanivet), 56; Thomas (Lanlivery), 195–6; see also Broude
Broid(i)er (Broyder), John, xliv n., 82, 84
Brooke (Broke), heirs of Lord, 192; Sir Robert, 188
Broude, family, cxvii; John (Lanivet), 115; Thomasia, 97; William, 97, 115; see also Brode
Broughton (Boughton), John, 86; (Sir) Robert, 130
Browfrowell, see Bosfrawell
Browne (Broune), Geoffrey/Jeffrey, & son James (Phillack), cxxv, 159, 169; John, & daughter (Liskeard), 202
Bryand (Briand), family, cxvii; Reginald, 57 & n., 98; Thomas, 116
Bryne, Richard, 195
Bucher, Robert, 186
Buckingham, duke of, xi, xxx
Budda, Mark, 5; Thomas, 5
Budy, John (St Eval), 34, (Mawgan in Pyder), 108–9; Thomas, 71, 103; see also Body

Burgess (Burges, Burgeys), John, 84; Roger, 127, 129; Thomas, 61, 93, 137
Burie, Anthony, gent., 174
Burley(e), William (Cecil), Lord, 208, 220, 229
Burnard(e), Benedict, 152, his heir, 155, 200
Burwyk (Burwik), Thomas, & wife Isabel, 88, his heir(s), 43
Busshe, Eweth Anne, 171
Bussywen (Boessywen), John, 165; John Cheverton alias B., 164; see also Cheverton
Butler, John, 183
Butside, John, 122
Byan, cxxxi; John, 37; see also Vyan
Byllinge, William, & son William, 183
Byllun, see Billon
Bynny, see Benny

Cadwodley, Oliver, & wife *Marina*, 136
Cady, Robert, 113
Caiser, see Keiser
Calamee, Richard, 126
Calmady, John, cxli; Stephen, cxli, 89, 133, 136
Calwey, Richard, 116
Came, Ralph, 66, 109
Campo Arnulphi (Champernowne), Henry de, xxviii; William de, 9n.
Cappar (Capper), William, 155, 200
Caran, Henry, 46; see also Carne
Carbura, John, lxxxvi, 24, 26, 54; John, jun., 26; Ralph, 54; William, ciii, 24, 26
Cardinan, Isolda de, xxvii–xxviii
Carew, Sir Edmund, xxx; John, 140
Carlyon (Carlian, Cordalion, Curlean), Nicholas, 195; Walter, 77, & son Pascoe, 121
Carloos, Thomas, 117; compare Corlo(y)s
Carminow (Carmynow(e), Carminov, Carmynaw, Carmyno), heir of (Breage), 144; Mr (St Winnow), 186 & n.; Elizabeth (married John Arundell), xv–xvi; Joan (d.1396), xvi; John, heir of John (Breage), 206; John (St Winnow), 186n., 191; Margery daughter of C., 13, 83, 125; Nicholas (Cardinham), 177; Nicholas (St Dennis), 58; Nicholas (St Winnow), 186n.; Philippa, 126; Richard, 4; Roger de, 19n.; heir of Thomas, 50

INDEX OF SURNAMES

Carn, see Carne
Carnarthur, ..., 133; Joan, 131; John Aly C., 44, 89; Walter, 89
Carne (Carn, Carun'), John (St Columb town), 38, (Duloe), 203; Nicholas (Trahare alias) C., 212, 217; Richard, 151; Roger Trahare alias C., 212; Vivian, 71, 103; see also Caran; Kerne; Trehar
Carnesewe (Craynsewe, Carnsuyow), Richard, esq., 162, 211; William, & wife, 138
Carnky, Richard, 46, 90
Carpentar', Ralph, lxxxvii, 26
Carsul(l)ek, ..., 132; heir(s) of, 85–6, 130 & n.
Carter (Kerter), ... (St Columb Major?), 237; Luke, 38, 73; Richard, 230, & wife Joan, 172; Sampson, 107
Carthewe (Carthu, Carthue), John (St Columb Minor), 165, 212, 213n., 214–15; John Henry C., cxxxv, & wife Margery & son John (St Columb Minor), 164; Robert, 165
Carun', see Carne
Carvegh, Richard (St Clement), 60, 76, 120, (St Columb Minor), 29, 112
Carvolghe, William (St Columb Minor), 216, & daughter Alice & son John, 212; William (Cubert), 223–4, 228, & daughter Helen & son John, 220
Cary, heir(s) of Reginald, 63, 94; Reginald, cxliv n., 138
Caterbederan, Richard, 144
Caunterbury, heirs of (Zennor), 189
Cavell, John, 123
Cawga [?], Richard, 113
Caylewy, John, 5n.; Roger, 5n.
Cecil, see Burleye
Ceny, Reginald, 3
Chamond, John, 128; Thomas, 81
Champlet(t), John, 150; his heir, 203
Chap(p)ell, Richard, 163, 209
Cheke (Checker), heir of (Bodmin), 155, 200
Chenallce, see Chienhals
Cheverton (Trewarton), heirs of John C., 210; John T., 164; John C. alias Boessywen, cxxviii, 164, (165); William [T.?], & wife Mabel, 164; see also Bussywen

Chiddeleigh, Christopher, esq., 190
Chideock, John, xxv; Katherine (married William Stafford and John Arundell), xxv, xxvii, xliv; Margaret (married Sir William Stourton), xxv
Chienhals (Chenallce, Chynals), heirs of, 188; late wife of, 164; heir(s) of (Henry), 21, 79
Chycois (Chicoes), Reginald, 112; heir of William, 158
Chynale, John, cxli–cxlii, 80
Chynals see Chienhals
Cissor, cxxx; Nicholas, 11; Walter, 20; see also Tailor, Trehar
Cleise, see Clies
Clementes, Elizabeth, 203
Clemow(e) (Clemov, Clymov), John, 35, 70, 102, 104; William, 88, 132
Clerk(e), John, cxliii, 91, 134–5; Thomas, 65, 99
Cleys (Cleise), Henry, 84; John, 15; Ralph, cxxvii, 126–7; Richard, 15; John C. Mottry, cxxxvii n., 14
Clowberye (St Austell), 237
Clymov, see Clemow
Coisvogherth (Coysvogherth, Coysvghford), Reginald, 54, 75; Richard Botreaux de, 87
Cogar, Richard, 165
Cok(e) (Cooke), John, 92, 135; John, of Truro, 211; Richard (St Columb Minor), 107, 164; see also Couk'
Cokyn, Michael, 103
Colan (Collan), heirs of (Richard), 162, 164, 208
Colbroke, Alice daughter of Walter (married John de Vere), xxxiv
Colroger, heirs of, 189
Colshull, Joan (married Remfrey Arundell), xxii
Colyn, John (de Lananta, de Lenanta, de Hellond), 87, his heir, 42 & n.; Odo/Ot(t)o (de Hellond), 33, 42n., his heir(s), 87, 189; Thomas C. de Hellond, xix
Come, Christopher, & wife, 202
Comgann, John, 203
Compton, (Henry), 174, 176–7, 181, 186, 193, 197
Condorowe, Geoffrey de, 23
Congdon, John, 175

Conyn, heir(s) of Henry, 62, 93
Cooke, *see* Cok(e); Couk'
Copleston(e), John (Liskeard), 150, his heir [?], 202 & n.; John (Newlyn East), 111, & wife, 28; Ralph, 67
Coppinge, Roger, 177, & family, xxxv–xxxvi
Copyethorn, John, 161
Cordalion, *see* Carlyon
Cork(e), John (steward of Arundell), 46, 90, 134
Corl(o)ys, heir of John, 43; John, 88; *compare* Carloos
Cornhogh, John, cxlii
Cornwall (Cornewall, Cornewayll, Cornuwayll, Cornuall), John (de Roche), 59 & n., 95; Nicholas, 52; Richard earl of, xxviii; duke of [1566], 186
Cor(r)yton, Peter, (esq.), 190–1
Corun(e), heir(s) of Robert, 45, 90, 134
Coryton, *see* Cor(r)yton
Coseworthe, Cossewyer, *see* Coswarthe
Cosewyn, John (Zennor), 189; John Rawe C. (Gwinear), 159
Coswarthe (Coseworthe, Cossewyer) John (St Columb Minor), 164, 209, 213, (St Ewe), 222; Thomas, 213
Cotha, heir of Pascoe, 14
Couk' [?], Thomas, 10; *see also* Cooke
Coulyng, *see* Cowlyn
Coundye, Richard, 200
Courtenay (Courtney), Henry, marquess of Exeter [1538], lxxix; Hugh, knight [d.1425], xxxiv; Joan (married Robert Vere), xxxiv; Walter, & widow Alice, 221; William, gent., 177
Courtes, Courteys, *see* Curtys
Couswarn, John, 108; Richard, 104
Cousyn, Nicholas, 51
Cowlyn (Cowelyn(g), Coulyng), John (St Columb Minor), 163, 209, (Mawgan in Pyder, St Merryn), 33, 106, 108, & wife Katherine, 24 & n., 74; Robert (St Merryn), cxvi & n., 26, 55, 75, 107, (St Clement), 60, 76, 120, his heir(s), 147, (Crowan), 144; William, (Madron), 158; heir of William (Crowan), 206
Coysvghford, Coysvogherth, *see* Coisvogherth

Crabbe (Crabba), Joan, 77; John, 229; heir(s) of Michael, 37, 71; Reginald, 66, 103, 110
Crak, Maud, 4
Crane, Humphrey, 230; Richard, 160, 169–70, & wife Matilda (Vyan) & son Thomas, 160; Richard jun., 171, & wife Catherine, 168; William (Gwinear), 160, 168, (Perranzabuloe), his widow Katherine (Kempthorne), 230–1
Cras, heir of Robert, 41; Thomas, 87
Craynsewe, *see* Carnsew
Creheer [?], Roberta wife of, 4
Criff, heir(s) of Richard, 140
Crosse, John, 104
Crugow(e), Thomas, cxliv, 72–3, 102
Crukdur, Thomas, 10
Cryer Melender, David, 23; *see also* Melender
Curlean, *see* Carlyon
Curnow, Peter, 47n.
Curtys (Courte(y)s, Curteis, Curteys), John (Cardinham), 182, (Lanlivery), 117; John sen. (Lanlivery), 194; Robert, 49; Thomas, 8
Cuthbert (Cutbert), Henry, 76; Robert, 60

Daddo, William, 172
Dago(u)n, William, 59, 96
Dalbene, *see* Dawene
Danvers, 237
Darre, Oliver, cxliv, 98 & n.
Darundel, *see* Arundell
Daune(y), *see* Dawene
Davy(e) (Dauy, Davyd), Elizabeth, widow, 165, 211, 214–15; John, 147; John D. Mena, *see* Mena; John D. Hoskyn, *see* Hoskyn; John Toma D., 52; Ralph John D. (Cubert), cxxxiii; Robert (Cardinham), lxviii–lxix, cix, 178, 180, 184; coheirs of Robert (Lanlivery), 193; Thomas, 165; William (Sithney), 205; William Jak D. (Helston), 83, & wife, 126; William Toma D. (Goran), 51, 118; *see also* Jankyndauy
Daw, *see* Dawes
Dawene (Daune, Dauney), (Sir) John, 1–2 & nn.; John, 47; Martin, 46
Dawes (Daw), heir(s) of Robert, 150, 202

INDEX OF SURNAMES

Dayow, Henry, & wife, 108–9
Dengy (Dunsy, Dunge, Doungye), 237; John, 152, 154, 200; Robert, lxxxvii; Thomas, cxlii, 76
Den(n)ys, John, 223, 225, & children Henry & Margaret, 221; Robert, 69
Denshill (Denesel), Humphrey, 99; John, 3
Denys, see Den(n)ys
Dewen (Dewyn, Dywan, Vyvyan), Ralph, gent., 214, & wife, 162 & n., 164 & n., 208–10; see also Dulyn
Dinham, family, xxvii–xxx; lands of, xxx–xxxii, xlviii–xlix; John [d.1501], xxvii, xxx; Katherine (married Thomas Arundell), xxvii, xxix–xxx; Oliver [1268], xxviii
Dodda, heir of, & wife, 50 & n.; Stephen, 8–9
Doll(e), John, 37, 71
Doly, Hilary, 4
Donowe, Richard, 27
Donston, see Dunstan
Dorset, marquess of, 157, & wife Cecily, 88; Thomas, marquess of, 132
Dottysson, Henry, & wife Christine (née Arundell, formerly Erysye), 163
Doungye, see Dengy
Dounrew, Elias, 4; John de, 4
Drewe (Drue), John, 169–70
Dulyn, Ralph, & wife (Colan), 191; see also Dewen
Dunge, see Dengy
Dunstan (Donston), George, 66, 109; Thomas, lxxxvii, 75, 107
Dunsy, see Dengy
Durant (Duront), John (Stithians), 78, 122, (St Columb town), 104; Thomas, 20
Dure, Robert, 54; see also Endure
Dyngell, John, 116
Dywan, see Dewen

Ede, John (Lanivet), 116, (Little Petherick), 141; Robert, 183; see also Udy
Edg(e)combe (Eggecomb), Peter [1499], 117, [1575], 223–4
Edward(e), John, 153 & n., 201; Peter, 184; Randolph Hicke E., 51; William, 135

Edy, see Ede
Eggecomb, see Edg(e)combe
Elen, William Hick, 133
Endure, Robert, ciii, 26; see also Dure
Eneys, see Enys
Engew [?], William, 112
Engollan, see Hengolon
Engooff, see Goff
Enhere, John, cxxxi, 89; see also Hire
Envelyn, Andrew, 20
Enys (Eneys), heir of Henry de, 20; Martin, 122; heir(s) of Ralph, 78; Remfrey, 71; Thomas, 37
Erisey (Erysy(e), Eryssye, Erisy, Heresy), heirs of, 102; Christine (Dottysson) lately wife of, 163; James (St Columb Major, Gwennap), 209, 231, (Ruan Major), 128; John, 37, 71; Thomas, 81; heir of William, 17
Erlond, John, 34; Laurence, cxliv n., 69
Erysy(e), see Erisey
Esterloo, Richard, 47
Euryn, William, 118
Exeter, bishop of, 16; (Henry) marquess of, 179, his heirs, 190
Ey(e)r, heir of, 41–2; Richard, 87

Faber (Faober), cxxx; Joce, 61, 137; John, 33; see also Goff, Smyth(e)
Facy, Thomas, 38; William, 37
Fall(e) (Fal), Simon, 62, 93–4, 137–8
Falmouth, heir(s) of, 153–4, 200; see also Boscawen
Faven, William, 66; see also Fevian
Felghour, John, 35
Fel(i)pp, Felpp, see Phillippe
Fenten (Fynten), John, 33, 66; Robert, 109
Ferly, John, 146
Fevian, Odo, 105
Fisher, William, 106
Fitzwarin, Elizabeth, xxx
Fitzwater (Fitz Waulter), heir of, 41; William, 87
(le) Flamank (Flamacke, Flamak, Flamanck), heir of (St Mabyn), 190; James, 32; Mark (le), 1 & n.; Richard (Mawgan in Pyder), 108, (Bodmin) 96, 99, 115
Foggeur, Thomas, 48
Folfrank, Ralph, 4–5
Fortescue, Alice, 132

Fourd, John, 175, 179–80, 184–5, 194–5
Fowy (Foy [?]), John, 107; heir(s) of John, 62–3, 94, Joan daughter of John, 94, her heir, 62
Frances (Fraunceys), Roger, 92, 135
Frawen, John, cxii–cxiii, 135
Fulford, Sir John, 174
Fursedon, George, 25n.
Fynda, Ralph, 94; William, 94, his heir, 63
Fynten, *see* Fenten
Fyttock, John, 48

Garland, William, 184
Garrowe, Elizabeth, 180; Joan, 181
Gatty, Isolda, 51
Gaverigan (Gauergan, Gau'gan, Gau'ygan, Gavrigan), (St Columb Major), 166; John (St Columb Major), 161, 210, 214, (St Dennis), 139; Richard, 58; Walter (St Columb Major), 112, (St Dennis), 140; William, 95
Geffre(y) (Giffra, Jeffr(e)y), James, cxxv, (159), 169; John, 80; Richard (Gwithian), 46, 91; Thomas (Goran), 53, (Phillack), 92; Wilmot, lxxxvii
Gelda, Martin Hicke, cxxxvii n., 90; *see also* Hick
German (Germayne), William, 98; John, 98
Gervis (Jerueis, Gerue(y)s, Gerveys, Gervys), heirs of (Zennor?), 191; John (St Ervan?), 4, (Gunwalloe), 82; Peter, 16; Thomas, 183; William, 122
Gibbe, Robert, 111
Gibbes, Oto, 137
Giffra, *see* Geffrey
Gillot, William, 62, 94, 137
Gloucester, Robert earl of, lv; Robert his son, xiii, lxiii
Gluvyon, heir of Richard, 28
Glyn(n), of Morval, heir of, 153, 155, 200; John, sen., 184; Margaret, 90; *see also* Tregenna
Godman, *see* Goodman
Godolphin (Godol(g)han, Goodolphin, Gotholhan, Godolphan, Godolhen, Goodolphyn), heir of (Breage), 148 & n.; Francis 169, 206; John, 87, 126, 131, 188, & wife, 111, 137; Thomas, 42, 87;
William [1566], 188; Sir William jun. [1549], 159; Sir William sen. [1549], 159
Godrevy, heir(s) of Reginald, 13, 83
Godzhis, Richard, 11
Goff (Goef, Gooff, Engooff), cxxx; James, 145; John, 121, 124, 126; heir of John, 44; Oto/Odo (St Columb Minor), 69, (St Columb town), 104; Richard, 36, 70; Thomas, 33; *see also* Engew, Ingowe, John (Angowgh), Faber, Smyth(e)
Golleth (Golla), Thomas, 79, 124
Goly, John, 51, 118
Gondry, John, 92 & n.
Gonfold, Maud, 3
Gonnet', *see* Gunneta
Goodinge, William, 181
Goodman (Godman), heirs of, 192; John, 194; Stephen, 193
Goodolphin, *see* Godolphin
Gooff, *see* Goff
Gorfos, Joan, 48
Gotholhan, *see* Godolphin
Gouernour, (St Columb Minor), 27
Gourlyn, *see* Gurlyn
Gregor(y) (Gregour, Grigor), Henry Tom(me), 93, 136; John (St Dennis), 59, 96, (Gunwalloe), 84, 126; Michael, 38, 71; Nicholas, 135; Stephen, 48, 92
Grinsye (Grynsy), heir of, 155; John, 152; heir of John, 200
Groby, Thomas, 30
Grosse (Gros, Groose), John, 179; Margaret, widow, 184; Martin, 63; Stephen, 179
Gryllys (Grilles), William, 203
Gunere (*for* Gundre?), John, 92 & n.
Gunneta (Gonnet'), 62, 94, 138
Gurlyn (Gurlin, Gourlyn), William (St Hilary), 42, 88; William (St Erth), 146, his heir, 149, 204; William (Mullion), 83, 125
Gwarnick, Arundell of, *see* Arundell
Gweader, John, cxxx, 33; *see also* Textor, Webbe
Gwyndreth, John, cxlv n.
Gynnon, William, lxxxvi

Hagge, *see* Hogge
Hamely, heir of John, 45, 90

INDEX OF SURNAMES

Hankyn (or Haukyn), Thomas, 57
Hanly, daughter of John, 28
Hannoforde, Joan, 172
Hardi, John, 6
Harr', see Harry
Harris (Harry(e)s), John, 202; see also Harry
Harry(e) (Harr', Hary, Herry), heir of (Bodmin), 154; Joan (Treneglos) [1566], 176; heir of Joan (Bodmin) [1571], 200; John (Bodmin), 154, 200, (St Columb Major), 72, 103, (Gunwalloe; alias Verlich?), cxlv n., 84, 126, (Lanivet), 98, 115, (Liskeard), 202, (Withiel), 153; John (H.) Norton (St Ervan), cxxxii, cxlii, 76, see also Norton; John Tomme H. (Lanivet), 99, see also Thomas; Oto Tom H. (Truro), cxxxiii; Richard (St Columb town), 71, 102–3, (Gwithian), 92; Thomas, 174; Thomas, clerk, 124; Thomas H. Seynt Erven, cxxxiv; William, 141; see also Harris; Jakharry; Tomherry
Harry(e)s, see Harris
Hary, see Harry
Hastinges (Hastyng), lord, 102; (Sir) Edward, 130, 188
Hauke, John, 96
Haukyn, see Hankyn
Hawell, Richard, 103
Hawys, John, 118–19
Hayly, see Heyly
Heale, Thomas, gent., 176 & n.
Hee, Ralph, 84
Hegon, Walter, 118; see also Hogan; Hogge
Heliar (Helyar), John, 196–7
Hell Porthia (Helle de Porthia), John, 41, his heir, 44, 87
Hellond, Thomas, cxlv n., & wife, 138; see also Colyn
Helman, John, 196
Helwyn, Nicholas, 22; William, 54
Helyar, see Heliar
Hendre (Hendr', Hendrye), Richard atte, 6; Henry (de), 17, 81; Thomas, 113; Laurence, 161
Hendrevyk, Robert, 23
Hendrye, see Hendre
Hengolon, John de, 3
Henry (Henr'), Joan, 5; John, 124; Simon, 124; Robert, 118; John H. Carthu, see Carthu; Thomas H. Trevethek, see Trevethek; see also Harry; Herry
Here, John, 175
Heresy, see Erisey
Herr', Joan, 152
Herry, see Harry; Henry; Tomherry
Hervy (Heruy), John, 47; William Jak H., 91
Heuos, Stephen, 62–3, 94, 137–8
Hewet(t), see Huwet
Hexte, Thomas, & wife, 192
Heyly (Hayly), John (St Ervan), 24, 26, (St Eval), lxxxvii, 107; Thomas, cxlv n.
Hichopkyn, Humphrey, 46; see also Hopkyn
Hick(e) (Hicka, Hikke, Hykke), Andrew, cxliv n.; James, 46, 48; John (St Columb Minor), 69, (Cury), 14, 84, (Gwinear), 45, 90, (Lanivet), 97, (Mawgan in Pyder), 109, (Sithney), 149, (Stithians), cxlv n., 123; John (H.) Mathy, see Mathy; Martin H. Gelda, see Gelda; Matthew, 18; Nicholas, 51; Ralph, 127; Randolph H. Edward, 51, see also Edward; Richard Jake H., 52; Thomas (Gwithian), 47, (St Dennis), cxliv n., 96; Vivian, 118; William H. Elen, 133
Higon, see Hogan
Hikke, see Hick
Hill (Hyll), Robert (Cardinham & Warleggan), 178–9; Robert, & wife (St Mabyn), 190
Hire, cxxxi; heir of John, 45; see also Enhere
Hoblyn, Joan, widow, 183
Hockin (Hockyn, Hokkyn), Cecilia, widow, 203; David, 182; Henry, 203; John (St Columb Minor), 109, (St Ewe), 118, (Lanlivery), 193; William, 151
Hodge, Joan, 186; see also Hogge
Hoer (Hore), Richard, 53, 119
Hogan (Hogen, Higon), Henry, 123; John, 61, 93; Richard, 61, 93; see also Hegon
Hogge (Hagge, Hoigge), John, 11; Thomas, 97; William, 56, 114; see also Hodge

Hokkyn, *see* Hockyn
Hollys (Holles), John, 209, & wife, 164
Holm, Thomas, 180
Homer, heir of, 163
Hoosekyn, *see* Hoskyn
Hoper, *see* Ho(u)per
Hopkyn, Henry, 80; James, 15; John (Crantock), 69, (Gwithian), 47, 91, (St Anthony in Meneage), 23; John, & John Hopkyn his heir (St Columb Major), 161; wife of John (St Dennis), 59; heir of John (Roche), 25; Richard (Gwithian, Lelant), 91–2; Walter, 78; William (Stithians), 21; heir(s) of William, (Roche), 74, 105
Horrell, John, 230–2
Horsdon, John, 204
Hosky(e) (Hoskie), heirs of (St Columb Major), 210–11; John (Gwinear), 169–70; *see also* Hoskyn
Hoskyn (Hoosekyn), John, wife Mary & son John (Gwinear), 159; John (Lanivet), 57, 153; heir of John (St Columb Minor), 164; John Davy H. (Lelant), 136; Richard (Gwithian), 91, (St Keverne), 124; Robert, 119; *see also* Hosky(e)
Ho(u)per, Nicholas, 221; Thomas, 119
Howard, Thomas Lord, & wife, 190
Hubbart(e) (Hubberte), Edward, esq., 208 & n., 220, 229
Huchnance, *see* Hughnans
Huchoun, Nicholas, 4
Huet, *see* Huwet
Hughnans (Huchnance), John, 206; Thomas, 148
Humfraye, Richard, & wife Beatrice (formerly Morveth), 159
Hungerford, Lady, 191
Hunte, Thomas, 119
Huntingdon, earl of, 214, 231; Henry earl of, xxxv
Hurde, ... (Lanivet), 98; John (Lanivet), 57
Husband, family (Kea), 31n.
Huwet (Hewet(t), Huet), 155; Henry, 31; John [1343], 3 & n.; John [1460], 31, 34; John, & wife Joan [1566], 195
Hykke, *see* Hick
Hyll, *see* Hill

Ilcomb, heir of Margery, 49
Ingowe, cxxx; John, & son John, 159; David John I., 159; *see also* Engooff; Goff; John (Angowgh)
Ionnian, John, 7
Ive, Francis, 47; William, 14
Iveron, John, 51
Iwyn (Yewan), James, 75; John, cxlii, 76

J...an, Richard [?] (Sithney), 146
Jack(e) (Jak, Jakke), John (Gwinear), 135, (Mawgan in Pyder), 66, 109; Robert, 129; Thomas, 134; *see also compound names beginning* Jak-
Jagow(e), Alice, 203; John (St Ewe), 51, (Gwithian), 47, 91; Michael, 103; Thomas, 151 & n.; Walter John J., cv–cvi, cxv, 69
Jak, *see* Jack
Jak Davy (Jak Dauy), William, 83, & wife, 126; *see also* Davy
Jake Felipp, *see* Phelip
Jake Hicke, *see* Hick
Jakenhell, Richard, 46; Simon, 46
Jaket, John, 52
Jakgillowe, Nicholas, 48
Jakharry (Jakherry), John, cxxxii, cxlii, 76; *see also* Harry
Jak Hervy, *see* Hervy
Jakke, *see* Jack
Jakluky, Roger, 122; *see also* Luky
Jak Pascowe, Pentecost, 78; *see also* John *and* Pascow
Jakperowe, Peter, 147; *see also* Perowe
Jakraulyn, Jankyn, 47; *see also* Rawlyn
Jakrobyn (Jakke Robyn), *Eurinus*, 27; John (Cury, Mawgan in Meneage), 14; *see also* Robyn
Jaktom (Jaktomma, Jaktomme), John, 66; Richard (St Ervan), 25, 76, (Stithians), 122; *see also* Thomas
Jak Wone, John (St Keverne), 80
James (Jamys), Barbara, 211; Henry, 212, 214 & n., 216–17; John, & wife (St Columb Major) [1575], 210–11, (Cury), cxliv n., 84, (Gunwalloe), 84; John J. alias Pentevion (Gwinear), 169; heir(s) of John (St Columb town) [1480], 71; Laurence, 84; Margaret, 46; Richard, 124; Robert, 211, 214 & n.; Thomas (St Columb Minor), 211,

INDEX OF SURNAMES

(Gwithian), 135, (St Martin in Meneage), 124; Walter, 91; William, 135
Jankyn, *see* Jenkyn
Jankyndauy, Peter, 145; *see also* Davy
Jannowe, Francis, 28
Janyn, *see* Jenyn
Jaunken, *see* Jenkyn
Jedwart, Thomas, 11
Jeffrey, *see* Geffrey
Jenkyn (Jenkin, Jankyn, Jaunken, Jenkeyn), John (Constantine), 205, (Gunwalloe), 127, (Lanivet), 201; John J. alias Pascowe (St Columb Major), 72, *see also* Pascow; Michael (Gwithian), 91, 135; Petrock, 153 & n.; Richard (Ludgvan), 158, (Mawgan in Meneage), cv, 83-4, (Sithney), 146; Richard J. Wilkyn, 26, Richard J. Wylkyn de Seynt Irven, *see* Synt Erven; Thomas (Lanivet), 153, & wife (Lanhydrock), 114
Jenyn (Janyn), Henry, 135; Joan, 79; John (St Columb Minor), 34, (St Ewe), 51, (Lelant), 92; Nicholas (St Ervan), cxlii, 76, (Gwithian), 91, 135; Ralph (St Columb town), 39, 104; Richard, 72; Robert, chaplain, 76; Thomas, 34; William, 206
Jerueis, *see* Gervis
Jobe (Jobbe), Thomas, cxlv n., 69; Nicholas, 201; *see also* Joopp
Joce (Joyce), Pascoe, 159-60; Thomas, 201
John (Johan), Adam, cxlv n., 78; Alan (Gwinear), cxxv, 134, 159; Alice J. daughter of John Thomas (Breage), cxxv, 148n.; David J. (alias Angowgh), 159, 168-9, *see also* Engooff, Goff, Ingowe; Henry (Breage), 206; Henry J. son of John Roberd (St Columb Minor), cxxv, 165; James, 159, & daughter Thomasine, cxxv, 169; John J. of Blysland, 210, 230; Nicola wife of Alan, 159, widow, 169; Pentecost, 123, *see also* Jack; Ralph J. son of John Thomas, cxxiv-cxxv, 148n.; Richard J. son of John Roberd, cxxv, 165; heir of Robert J., 150, 202; Simon, 127; Thomas J. son of John Thomas (Breage), cxxv, 148n.; Thomas (St Columb Minor), 68, (Gwinear), cxxv, 159; Thomas J. Matthy, cxliv n.; Thomasine, cxxv, 169; William J. son of John Thomas (Breage), cxxv, 148n.; William (St Martin in Meneage), 124, (Sithney), 205
John Alan, Peter (Lelant?), 48
Jo(o)pp, John, 34; Nicholas, 58 & n.; *see also* Jobe
Josep, Philip, 196
Joyce, *see* Joce
Jule, Agnes, 178; Emma, 186

Kalevan, Richard, 145
Kayll, heir of Robert, 49
Keiser (Caiser), John, cviii, 107; Reginald, 102, 105; Richard, cviii, 107
Kelean (Kel(l)yan), Thomas, 90; Stephen, 91; John (Breage), 145, (Gwithian), 47
Kelligrewe, *see* Killigrewe
Kelliou, Stephen, 134
Kellyan, *see* Kelean
Kellygrewe, *see* Killigrewe
Kelyan, *see* Kelean
Kempe (Kymp(p)e), John, & wife (Bodmin), 114; John (Liskeard), 150, his heir, 202; Robert, 202
Kempthorne, Nicholas (gent.), 220, & wife Katherine (formerly Crane), 230-1; John, 230
Kempton (Kympton), heir of (Lanivet), 154; John (Bodmin), 152, his heir, 200
Kendall (Kendell), Lawrence, 195; Nicholas (gent.), 191, 193-4, 197, 221; Nicholas jun., 195; Richard, 79; Walter [1566], 194; Walter [1659], 8n.; William, 154, 200-1
Kentrevek, Simon, 13, 15, 19, 84
Kern(e), John, cxxviii, 229; Pascoe, 199, Pascoe K. of Tresylian, cxxiv, cxxviii, (209), 229; Thomas, 199; Walter, 77; *see also* Carne
Kerow, John, 119
Kerter, *see* Carter
Killigrewe (Keligrew(e), Kellygrewe, Kyllygrew(e), Kylligrewe), heir(s) of (Budock), 79; Mr, 124; John (Stithians) [1499], 123; John, esq. [1566], 188-90, [1571], 204, 206; John, & wife (Gwinear) [1499], 130; Simon (Budock), 22; Thomas jun. (St Columb

Minor), 67; Thomas K. de Arwennak (Budock), cxxxv, 123; *see also* Kylygryce
Knapp, heir of Thomas, 33
Knyght (Knygh'), cxxx; Mark, cxliii–cxliv, 37, 73
Kylligrewe, Kyllygrewe, *see* Killigrewe
Kyllywyn, Walter, 88
Kylygryce, John (St Columb Minor), 163
Kymp(p)e, *see* Kempe
Kympton, *see* Kempton
Kyrkeham, George, esq., 190

Lacy, heirs of Alice, 97; Thomas, 56, 114
Laghar (Laugher *or* Langher), Thomas, 77 & n.; William, 77, 120
Lamargh (Lannargh), Ralph, 83; James, wife Lucy, & sons John, Robert & William, 126
Lambron, Sir William, & daughter Annora (married John Arundell), xvii, xx, xl
Lamellyn, heir of Thomas, 202
Landery, *see* Laundry
Langher [?], *see* Laghar
Lanhadron, Joan (married Sir William Lambron), xvii, xx, xl; John, & wife Amity, xx, xl
Lanhergy, Thomas, 55–6, 97, 115
Lanherne (Lanhern, La Herne), Alice (married Remfrey Arundell), xiii–xv, lxiii; John, xiii, lxii–lxiii; *see also* Arundell
Lanlaron, Serlo de, 8n.
Lannargh, *see* Lamarth
Lanuighan, Marina de, 6; Peter de, 7; Robert de, 7
Lanyon (Lanye(e)n, Lanyeyn), John [1463], 45 & n., [1480, 1499], 90, 134; Richard, & wife, 188; Tobias, 45n.
Larcedeken, Larchedecon, *see* Archedeken
Lastreynes, Janyn, 146
Laughe, *see* Law
Laugher, *see* Laghar
Laurence (Laurens), David John L., 123; James, 46, 91; John, lxxxvii, 104, 107; William, lxxxvii, 107
Laundry (Landery), Richard, 202
Laury, John (St Columb town), 72, (St Ervan), 26, (St Eval), 34, 65–6, (St Ives), 48; *see also* Loury

Law (Laughe), Henry, 57–8, & widow Joan, 57n.; *Sibilla*, 115
Lawarne (Lawharen), John, 150, his heir, 202; Stephen, 179
Laye, *see* Ley
Leche, John, 141
Lenanta, John Colyn de, *see* Colyn
Lercedekne, *see* Archedeken
Leta, Roger, 5
Ley (Laye), John, 56, 97
Lit(t)elton, heirs of, 192; Thomas, gent., 195
Lobbe, John, 115
Logan, David, 121
London (*or* Loudon), John, 82, 84, 126
Longes, Henry, 62, 94, 138
Loryng, Nigel de, 86, 88, his heir, 40, 42
Loude (Louda, Lowda), Joan, 134; Michael, 91; William, 46
Loudon, *see* London
Loury, Richard, 141; *see also* Laury
Lovetop, Richard, 141
Lowda, *see* Loude
Lucas, John, 170
Luke, Richard (St Dennis), 171
Luky, ... (Lanivet), 98 [?]; John (Lanivet), cxlv n., 116; Richard (Lanivet), 98; *see also* Jakluky, Tom(a)luky
Luscott, Joan (married John Arundell & William Lambron), xvi, xx
Lusky, William, 112
Lymbery, Thomas, xxvi–xxvii
Lyon, William, 212–13

Maenheyr, *see* Menhire
Maidow (Maydov), 62, 93, 137
Malm'e, *Halnathet'*, & wife, 117
Mangyer (Mangeyr), Andrew, 10 & n., 11
Manyer, Alan, 89, his heir, 43; William, 85–6, his heir, 40, 43
Marcha(u)nt, Peter, 153, 201
Mareney, heir of, 190
Mark(e), John (St Enoder), 62, 138; John jun. (Liskeard), 202; Stephen, 32, 34
Marrek, Martin, cxxx, 55
Martyn, John (Goran), 10, (St Ives), 133; John M. Barry, & wife (Mawgan in Pyder), 33; John M. Trelighan (St Ives), 133; Nicholas, 57; Thomas, 115
Marvell, Thomas, 162

INDEX OF SURNAMES

Massely, Thomas, 17
Mata, Walter, 22
Mat(t)hy, John (Hicke) M., 27, 30; Thomas John M., cxliv
Maydov, see Maidow
Maye, John, 217, & wife Donnet & daughter Jane, 213
Mayhewe (Mayow(e), Mayov), James Ric' M., 109; Reginald, 166; Richard, 34; Thomas, 10
Mechell, see Michell
Melender (Melynder), cxxix, David Cryer M., cxxxvi, 23; Ralph, 21; Thomas, 84; see also Miller
Mel(l)huys (Melhues, Melluys), Alice & Margaret, 221; John (jun.), 221-4, 228, his wife Mary & daughter Mary, 222
Melyonek, see Mylhenek
Mena, John, 59, 96, John Dauy M., cxxxvi, 139
Meneythgwyns, Alice, 10
Menhire (Menhyr, Maenhyr), 237; heirs of Ralph, 8; heir of Walter, 50
Menughter, William, 22
Mercer (M'ce', Merceur), Philip, 48; Ralph, 46, 91, 93
Mester, John, 10; Thomas, 126
Michell (Michall, Mechell), John (Gwithian), 49, (Lanivet), 116, (St Columb town), 35-6, 38, 70, 102-3; Odo (St Dennis), 139; Richard (Constantine), 147, (St Eval), 26, chaplain (St Columb town), 103; Thomas, cxliv n., 96, 140; William (St Columb town), 36, 39, 72; William M. Stevyn, (St Dennis), 139, see also Stephen
Mighelstowe (Myghelstowe, Mychell Stowe), heir(s) of, 67, 162 & n.; heir of Mark, 27, 162n.
Milhenek, see Mylhenek
Miller, William, cxxx, 51; see also Melender
Moham, William, esq. (Crowan), 204
Mohun (Mohoun, Mo(u)ne, Movne), Alice, 202; John, 131-2; Reginald, esq., 188, 191; Thomas, 24, 73, 106; William 87, 134; see also Mowna
Moile, see Moyle
Mold, Eleanor, widow, lxxii, cix, 185
Mone, see Mohun
Morley, Thomas Lord, & daughter Elizabeth (married John Arundell), xxv
Mortain, Robert count of, lv
Morthe, Edward, 174
Morval, Glyn of, see Glyn(n)
Morveth, John, & mother Beatrice (Humfraye), 159
Mottry, John Cleys, cxxxvii n., 14; see also Clies
Mouna, see Mowna
Moune, see Mohun
Mowna (Mouna, Movna), John, 104; Stephen, 38, 72; see also Mohun
Moye, Robert, 202
Moyle (Moile, Moyll), heir of, 154; David, 113; John, 152, 154, his heir, 199; Oto/Odo, 35, 69-70; Richard (St Columb town) [1499], 104; Richard M. of St Austell (St Columb Major) [1571], 199
Moyne, John, clerk, 193-95
Myghe, Reginald, 213
Mylhenek(e) (Milhenek, Melyonek), Richard, 161, 211; Robert, (chaplain), 69, 113
Mylleton, William, esq., 189

Nance (Nans), John, 204, 209; Thomas, 124; William, cxxvii, 47, 92, 136
Nanfan (Nanffan), heir(s) of (Breage), 148, (Crantock), 67; James (Crantock), 29, (Cury), 14, 83; John, xxi n., xxii, 32; Richard, 108
Nans, see Nance
Nanscawen (Nascaven), ..., heir of Falmouth [1515], 153; Nicholas, [heir of] Falmouthe, 200; see also Falmouth
Nanscothen, John, 133; Robert, 87
Nanscuuel, see Nanskevell
Nansdelyowe, Nansdillyowe, Nansdyllyowe, see Nantelyow
Nansdreysek (Nansdryseck, Nantrysak), Richard (?), 147 & n.; Thomas, cix, 147n., 150
Nanseglos, 160
Nansise, Peter, 134
Nanskerwis, Henry, 149
Nanskevell (Nanscuuel, Nanscuvell, Nanscuuel), John de (St Columb town), 2, John (St Columb town), 37, 71, 102, (Mawgan in Pyder), 66; Odo de, 2

Nanspian (Nanspyan), 90; James, 204; Richard (de) (Gunwalloe), 15, 84
Nanswhiden (Nanswhidan), Thomas, 32; John, 108
Nantelyow (Nansdyllyowe, Nansdelyowe, Nansdillyowe), heirs of Richard (de), 63, 94; Richard, 95, 138
Nantrysak, see Nansdreysek
Nascaven, see Nanscawen
Nawen, Joan, 52
Nensy, John, 18
Nenys, Thomas, 102
Nevell, John, 112
Newall(e), heir of, 154; Martin, 152, his heir, 200
Newham, John, 112
Newlyn, see Nywlyn
Newton, Martin, 221, 226
Nicholl, see Nicol(l)
Niclys, see Nicolas
Nicol, see Nicol(l)
Nicolas (Niclys), Michael, 92, 136; Richard, 136
Nicol(l) (Nicholl), James, 92; John (St Ewe), 118, (Goran), 10–11, (Gunwalloe), 18, 82, 129; Richard, 47; Thomas, 105
Noell (Noiel, Noill, Nole), John (St Columb Minor), 55, (Padstow), 140, (Stithians), 21 & n., 78; Thomas, 113; Walter, 38, 39
Norleigh, (Robert), 175–6, 181, 184
Norrys, ..., 155n.
Northaye, Peter, 155 & n., 200
Norton (Nortoun), Henry, & heirs, 163; John (St Clement), 76–7, (Mawgan in Pyder), 163, 210, 217; John (Harry) N. (St Ervan), cxxxii, cxlii, 76, see also Harry; Oto, cxxxii–cxxxiii, 120–1
Nycholyn, Joan, widow, 181
Nywlyn, heir of, 162

Oby, Robert, 82; Thomas, 19; see also Opye
Oen, heir of John, 45
Olde, John brother of Richard, & son John [1572], 212; Richard, his widow Joan, lxxxv, & son Peter [1549], 165; Richard [1572, 1575], 214, 216, & wife Joan, 212

Olyuer, John, 59; Remfrey, 114; Richard, 31; heir(s) of Robert, 36, 70
Opye (Opy, Opp(e)y, Oppye), (Perranzabuloe), 232; Joan, widow, lxxxv, 165; John, 98; Nicholas, 154, 191–2, 200; Oura, 57, 98 [?]; Philip, 212; Richard (St Columb Major), 161, 211, 214, (Lanivet), cxliv–cxlv nn., 98, 115; Thomas, 200; see also Oby
Osberne, Hugh, 160
Oxford, earls of, xxxiv–xxxv; heir of earl of, [1509], 149, 204; (Edward) (de Veer), earl of [1566–75], xxxii–xxxiii, 192, 206, 208n., 212, 220, 222, 230, his manors [1563], xlvii–xlviii, lxxviii, 167–72; John, earl of [1499], 125, 128; John de Veer, earl of [1553, 1556], 213, 222, his manors [1549], xlvi–xlvii, 156–66; Robert [for John] le Veer, earl of [1460, 1499], 29, 112; see also Veer

Pafford, John, 3
Paler, John, 4
Paliner (or Palmer), Richard, 182 & n.
Parson, John, 21, 23
Pascow(e) (Pascawe, Pasc(h)o, Pascov), (St Dennis), 236; Edward, 171; John (Bodmin), 154, 200, (Breage), 148, John (St Columb town), 104, John Jenkyn alias P. (St Columb Major), 72, John (St Dennis), 139, (St Eval), lxxxvii, 75, (Gunwalloe), 19, (Stithians), 21, 78; John Jak P. (St Just in Roseland), cxxxiii; Nicholas, & wife, 59, 95; Pentecost Jak P., 78, see also John; Richard, 171; Thomas (St Keverne), 22; William [1499], 139, [1563], 171
Pasket, 11
Paul(e) (Paull), Richard (St Columb town), 37, 71, 102, 104, (St Minver), 6; Oliver, 38
Paynter, George, 204
Payoun, William, 13, 15–16
Pears (Pers', Perys), Eleanor, 205; John (St Columb Minor), 30, (Lanhydrock), 56, his heirs, 97; Richard (Phillack), 135
Pedit, Pedyt, see Petit
Peen, John, 104

INDEX OF SURNAMES

Pencors, Peter, 4; William (Bodmin), 55, (St Merryn), 24, 73, his heir, 105
Penfos, John de, 1
Pengwyn, John, cxxxi, 104
Penhale, Richard, 119
Penhalov, Roger, 11
Penhelege, Alexander, 1 & n.
Penhenneck, John, 205
Penkevell, Francis, esq., 200; Laurence, 139
Penles, Joce de, & wife Margaret [1350], xxvi; Jocelin de, 142; Philip de [c.1300], xxvii
Penmeneth, John, cxliv n.
Pennans, Henry, cxxvii, 133, 135; heir of Joan, 43; Richard, 91
Penpoll, John, 113; Thomas, 47
Penpras(e), John, 205; 'Genyn', 149
Penros, John (St Ervan), 25, (Phillack), 41, 86, (Sithney), 205; John Raulyn de, 55; Thomas, 30; William, 134
Penrynburgh, John Body de, see Body
Pensignance, Thomas lord of, 29n.
Penstrasow, Richard, 118
Pentevion, John James alias P., 169
Pentyr, Francis, 30
Penwern, Thomas, 88
Perdannek, see Petit Predannek
Perin (Peryn), George, 124; John (St Anthony in Meneage), 80, (Breage), 148, (St Columb town), 104; Michael, 72
Perkyn, John, 63, 144–5; see also Tomperkyn
Pernel, Joan, 6; Thomas, 6
Perow(e) (Berowe), James, 146; John (St Anthony in Meneage), 80, 124, (Gwithian), 47; John, weaver (St Columb Minor), 31; John Will (Tomma) P. (St Anthony in Meneage), cxxvi, cxxxiv, cxlv n., 124; John P. Sergeaunt (Gwithian), cxxxvi, 47; Thomas, 34, [d.1447], cxxvi; William Toma B. (alias William Tomperowe), cxxvi, 23, 80
Pers', see Perys
Peryn, see Perin
Perys, see Pears
Pethick, Henry, 195
Petit (Petyt, Pedyt, Pedit, Pettit), John (Gwinear), 85, 188, his heir, 205; John (Mawgan in Meneage), 22, 79, 124, (Mullion), 16 & n.; John P. Predannek, cxxxv, (St Columb Minor), 28, 111, (Cury), 13, 83, 125; heir of Michael, 40, 85
Petycru, Ralph, 2
Petyt, see Petit
Peverell, family, xxxv
Phelip(p)(e), Phelyp(p), see Phillippe
Philipps, Thomas, 169
Phillippe (Phelyp(p), Phelip(p), Phelippe, Felipp, Felpp), John (Bodmin), 153, his heir, 155, 200; John (St Columb Major, Mawgan in Pyder), 32, 38–9, 108, (St Keverne), cxlii, 80, 125, (Lanhydrock), 56, 97, 114; John Jake F. (Phillack), 47; Robert, 51, Thomas, 169
Pig', John, 6
Pincerna, Richard, and granddaughter Margery (married John de Lanhern), xiii
Piper, John, 150, heir of John, 202
Piterel, William, 6
Plumyn (Plymen, Plymmayn), Joan, widow (of John Velle), 158; John, & wife, 133; Peter, 89
Pluven, Luke, 35, 70
Plymen, Plymmayn, see Plumyn
Polgren(e) (Pollgrene, Polgrun), John, 163, 209; Roger, 32; Thomas, 108
Polgwest, John, 22
Polkynhorn (Polkenhorn), John, 48 & n., Margaret his wife, 48n.; Nicholas, 48n., 92, 136
Polmargh, Thomas, 123
Polpeer, Marion, 90
Polpenruth, Walter, 15
Pol(s)ulsek, heir(s) of Nicholas, 45, 90, 134; John, 90
Polwhile, Stephen, 120
Pomery(e) (Pomeroy), lord of Tregony, 148n., 223, 238; heir of, 148
Pons, John, 136
Ponsnewyth, John, 11
Po(o)pe (Popa), Gervase, lxxxvi; Thomas, 174
Porth, John, 32; Ralph, 33, his heirs, 65; Ralph, 108
Porthbyan, Geoffrey, 15
Porthia, see Hell Porthia
Pound, Thomas, 177

Powell alias Poyle, Martin, 172
Predannek, see Petit
Prelot, Simon, 91
Preske, see Priske
Pridias, Geoffrey, xix n.
Prio(u)r, John (Breage), 148, (Crowan), 92, (Gwinear), 47; Mabel, 206
Priske (Prysk(e), Preske), Hugh, 144 & nn.; John, 144n.; William, 144n.; William [1509], 147, his heir, 206; William [1571], 206
Prouce, John, of Chagford (Devon), 192
Prouest, heir of Nicholas, 50
Prynke, John, cv
Purlad, Simon, 46
le Py, family, 18n.
Pynent, Thomas, & wife, 111
Pynnowe, John, 161
Pyper, see Piper
lez Pyrne, see Respryn
Pytt, John, 151 & n.; Meliora, 151

Quarter', William, 6
Queynte, George, 33
Quyell, see Quynell
Quyke, John, 51
Quynell (Quyell), John, 25, 74; heir(s) of Richard, 105
Quyntrell, 217

Raffull, Isabel, 82; Thomas, 16
Ralegh, Elizabeth, 108, 131-2
Randall, John R. jun. (alias Tregennowe, Trigennowe), 222-3, 227, his daughters Margaret & Martha, 222; John R. sen. (alias Tregennowe, Trigennowe), 221, 226; see also Tregennow(e)
Randowe, Edward, 51
Raskerrak, see Roscarrock
Raulyn, see Rawlyn
Rawe, Henry, 48; Hervey, 90; John (Gwinear), 169, (Gwithian), 46, 91, 134; Stephen, 46
Rawlyn (Raulyn, Raulen), John (St Columb Minor), 212, 214, 218; John R. de Penros (St Merryn), 55; Martin, 95, 139; Odo, 57; Richard Tom R., 113; *Thomasia*, 98; see also Jakraulyn
Raynward, see Reynward
Reche, see Rich
Reis, Sampson, 109

Renawdon (Renaudyn, Renavdyn, Renawdyn, Renoudon, Renowdyn), Benedict, 15; John (St Martin in Meneage), 21, 23; heir of John (St Columb Major), 38; Richard (Lelant), 48, 136, (Mawgan in Meneage), 23, 80
Renold, *Fridisweda*, lxxxvii; John, 151
Renward, see Reynward
Rescarrek, see Roscarrock
Rescas(s)a (Rescase), John (St Ewe), 221; Thomas (Goran), 53, (Lanivet), 56, 97; William (Goran), 118-19, (Lanivet), 114
Rescorlan, see Roscorlan
Rescruk, Thomas, 123
Rescum(er), see Reskymer
Resega, Nicholas, gent., 220; see also Ressegh
Resgerens, Odo, & wife Alice, 41, 86
Reskarrek, see Roscarrock
Reskemer, see Reskymer
Reskere, Walter, 88
Reskymer (Rescumer, Reskum', Reskym', Reskemer, Resky(m)mour), John (Lanlivery), 117, (Manaccan, St Keverne), 79, 81, 123, 125, 127; John, esq. (St Erth) 158, his heirs, 188; Ralph, 13, 17, 21, 83; William, & wife, 164, his heirs, 209
Resogan, see Rosogan
Ressegh, Joan, 78; John, 20, 122; see also Resega
Re(s)talek, Ralph, 103, 105
Restarrock, see Roscarrock
Reswalstus, John de, 2
Retalek, see Re(s)talek
Reynward (Raynward, Renward), Reginald, 88, his heir, 43
Ric', Ricard, see Richard
Rich(e) (Reche), Elizabeth, 180; Richard, 89, his heir, 45
Rich... , John (Bodmin), 115
Richard(e) (Ric', Rychard(e), Ricard, Richardes), Henry (St Ervan), 76, & wife Nicola & son William, 107; Henry (St Columb Minor), 165; James, 109; James R. Mayow, 109, see also Mayow; John (St Columb Minor), 164, (Gwithian), 134, (Lanivet), 115, (Lanlivery), 195-6, (Mawgan in Pyder), 99; John William R. (Penryn), cxxxiii;

INDEX OF SURNAMES

'Pears'/'Perys', 149 & n.; Robert, lxxxv, 212, & daughter Alice, 165; *Salmon'*, 34; Stephen, 149; Thomas, lxxxvii, 75; William, cxlv n., 96, 140
Riche, *see* Rich
Richowe (Richov), John, 116; William, 58
Ridgeway (Rudgeway, Rydgway), John, (esq.), 174–5, 181, 183–5
Ripper, William, 206
Robert (Roberd), James, lxxxv, & wife Joan, 165; John [1480], 75; John [1549], & sons Henry John & Richard John, cxxv, 165; Martin, 78; Michael, 91; Nicholas, 79; Richard, 163; William, & wife Joan, 127
Robyn, John (Gunwalloe), 15, 19, (Lanivet), 56; John Jakke R. (Mawgan in Meneage), 14, *see also* Jakrobyn; Martin, 75
Roche (alias Tremodret), family, 6n.; Eve daughter of Richard (married Ralph Arundell), xiii–xiv, lxv; John (St Dennis), 139; John (Mawgan in Pyder), 3; Nicholas, 95
Rog(g)er, John (Cardinham), 185, (Lanivet), 115; Thomas, 98
Rois, *see* Roos
Roly, Thomas, 136
Ronsyn (Roncyn), Robert, 62, 94, 138
Roos (Rois, Rose), Ralph (Gunwalloe), cxliv–cxlv nn., 82, 129; Boskawen R., *see* Boscawen; *see also* Rowse
Roscarrock (Raskerrak, Rescarrek, Rescarrecke, Reskarrek, Rescarrock, Restarrek, Restarrock), John [1499], 105 & n., 114, [1566], 191; Richard, esq., 202; Thomas, 24, 55, 73
Roscorlan (Rescorlan), Henry, 10; Ralph, 8–9
Rose, *see* Roos
Rosmoddres (Rosmoddros), William, 49, 88
Roso(u)gan (Rossogan, Resogan, Rosworugan, Tresogan), ... (Lanivet), 98; John de [1343], 2; John [1465], xxvii, [1480, 1499], 68, 71, 102, 112; John (Gwinear), 144n., 147, 158, (St Stephen in Brannel), 152, his heir, 154, 199; Richard, 37, & wife Joan, 29; Thomas (Lanivet), 57
Roswyn, Henry, 144; *see* Boswyn

le Rouse, *see* Rowse
Rowe, Thomas, 181
Rowse (le Rouse), Henry, 161–2, 210–11; John (St Columb Major), 229; John, wife Katherine & son John, (Treneglos), 175; Remfrey & Richard, sons of Jenkin (St Columb Major), 229; Richard (Ludgvan), 191; *see also* Roos
Roydon, (Gwinear), 169
Roys, *see* Roos
Rudgeway, *see* Ridgeway
Ruffos, heirs of, 74n.; Thomas, 74 & n.
Rusch (Ruys), Nicholas, 133; Robert, & wife, 89
Russell, John, 36–8, 102–3, his heir(s), 38, 71
Ruys, *see* Rusch
Rychard(e), *see* Richard
Rydgway, *see* Ridgeway
Ryskymer, *see* Reskymer

Sad(e)ler, John (St Anthony in Meneage), 80, (Bodmin), 152, his heir, 154, 200
St, *see also* Sanctus, Sent, Seynt, Synt
St Austell, *see* Soor
St Congon, 186
St Ervan, *see* Synt Ervyn
St Wrath, *see* Sewragh
Sage, Roger, lxxxvi
Salman, Oto, 92
Salt, John, 33
Sam(u)ell (Samoll), John (Bodmin), 153, his heir, 155, 200, (St Eval), 110
Sancto Albino, de, *see* Seyntaubyn
Sancto Austel, Soor de, *see* Soor
Sanctus Albinus, *see* Seyntaubyn
Scawen, Tryphena, xlii n.
Saundrye (Sand(e)ry), Jane widow of Richard, 230–1, 233; John, 135; Thomas, 205
Scatera, William, 61, 93, 137
Scovarn (Scovern), cxxxi; John, xxvi, (St Columb Minor), 113, (St Eval), lxxxvii, 26, (Mawgan in Pyder), 33, 35; John jun. (St Ervan), 27
Seaby, John, 153
Sein(t)cler, *see* Seyntcler
Semon, Joan, widow, 178; cf. Symon
Seneschal, family, xxxv
Sentabyn, *see* Seyntaubyn

Sentclere, *see* Seyntcler
Serdewyne, *see* Sherdewyne
Sergeaunt, John Perowe S., cxxxvi, 47; *see also* Perow
Sergeaux, family, xxxv; heir(s) of, 68, 146–7; heir(s) of Sir Richard, 13, 17, 81, 83; Alice sister of Richard (married Richard de Vere), xxxv
Serlose, John, 161–2
Sewragh (St Wrath), heirs of, 178; John, 78
Seynclere, *see* Seyntcler
Seyntaubyn (St Albane, Stawbyn, Seyntaubin, St Albon, Sanctus Albinus, de Sancto Albino, Sentabyn, Syntaubyn), (St Austell), 237, (Gwinear), 170; heir of, 94, 144n.; heir(s) of John (St Enoder), 62; John (Gwinear), 205–6; Peter, & wife, 29, 112; Thomas, 68
Seyntcler (Stcler(e), Sein(t)cler, Sentclere, Seynclere), John, 178, 180–4, 193–4
Seynt Irven, *see* Synt Ervyn
Seynt Sewana, *see* Syntsewana
Seynterven, *see* Synt Ervyn
Seys, John, cxxxi, 10
Sherard, Richard, 104
S(h)erdewyne (Shirdewyn), cxxxi; Richard, 38, 72; John, 36, 38–9, 70, 103; Remfrey, 104
Sheriston, *see* Sher(y)ston
Sherpe, Peter, cv; Thomas, 141
Sher(y)ston (Sheriston), heir(s) of Laurence (St Enoder), 94, (Gwithian), 86, 131n.
Shirdewyn, *see* Sherdewyne
Skauerel, John, 30
Skeberiow (Skeberyowe), John, 113; Richard, 69
Sket, *see* Skyt(t)
Skott, John Thoma alias S., *see* Thomas
Skynner, heir(s) of Alice, 63, 94
Skyt(t), *see* Sket
Skyt(t) (Sket), Agnes, 94, 137; John, 61, 93, 137
Slaffe, Thomas, 11
Slee, John, 141
Smyth(e), cxxx; John, 55; John, gent., 205; *see also* Faber, Goff
Snell(e) (Snele), John, 109; Thomas, 33, 66

Snoboll, John, 126–7
Snou, Richard, lxxxvi
Snowden (Snawden, Snoden), John, 170, & wife Joan, 159
Soor (Soer, le Soor), family, xviii; John (Philleigh), 9n., (St Anthony in Meneage), 23; John S. de Sancto Austel (St Columb Major), 2; Peter, 23; Ralph, xviii, heir(s) of Ralph, 13, 83, 125; Rose (Pridias) wife of John, xix n.
Southwode, Thomas, 100
Speeke, (Sir) George, 192
Spernall, John, 54
Spernan (Spernam), heir of (Breage), 148; heir(s) of (David) (St Clement), 60, 77; John, 120; Thomas, 158, (169)
Spore, Thomas, 191
Staddon, Michael, 175
Stafford, William, and son Humphrey, earl of Devon, xxv
Stanlowe, John, & wife, 77–8
Stanwaye (Stanwey), John, 181–2
Stephen (Stevyn, Stephyn, Stephin), John (Crantock), 69, (St Ervan), 76, (St Ewe), 119, (Gwithian), 91, (Lanivet), 116; Michael (St Columb town), 71, (St Dennis), 140; Nicholas, 115; Thomas, 103; Werin John S. (Constantine), cxxxiii; William Jack S. (St Hilary), cxxxiii; William Michell S. (St Dennis), 139, *see also* Michell
Stonart, John, 8
Stork('), William, 8, 10
Stouka (*or* Stonka), Benedict, 5; John, 5
Stourton, Sir William, xxv
Stoute, Henry, 77
Strangman, John, 39
Strett, Robert, 151
Sturgyon (Sturgion), Robert, 154, 200
Styple, Powell, 171
Summonur, William, 5
Sutter, Robert, 72
Sweet (Sweate, Swete), Elizabeth, 196; John, 193–5
Sweyn, Richard, 15
Syluester, Humphrey, 49
Symon, (Goran), 118; Ivo, ciii, 54, 75; John (St Columb Minor), 31, (Lanivet), 56; Michael Tom(me) S., 38, 71, 103; Nicholas (John) S., cxxxii–cxxxiii, 120; Oto John S., cxxxii; Thomas, 136;

INDEX OF SURNAMES

Walter, 135; William, 126; see also Semon
Syntaubyn, see Seyntaubyn
Synt Ervyn (Seynterven, Seynt Erven, Seynt Irven, Synt Irvan, Seynyrvan), John, cxxxiv; Richard, 76, 107, Richard Jankyn Wylkyn de S., cxxxiv, (26), 54, see also Wilkyn; Thomas Harry S., cxxxiv
Syntsewena (Seynt Sewana), Matthew (de), 18, 128

Tabard, James, 19
Tailour (Taylour), cxxx; John (Goran), 118, (Lanivet), 116; Thomas Androwe T., cxxx n., cxxxvi, 54; see also Cissor, Trehar
Talcoys, John, 88
Tallfern, Tallverne, Talvern, see Arundell (of) Tolverne
Tamlyn, John, 205
Tanner (Tann'), Anthony, esq., 220; Robert, 138
Taylour, see Tailor
Teffrye, see Treffry
Teluddar, see T(r)eluddar
Tentyn, see Tynten
Textor, Odo, cxxx, 6; see also Gweader, Webbe
Thomas (Thoma, Thom', Th', Tomas, Tom(a), Tomm(e), Tomma), Edward, 78; Hugh, 135; John, & wife Mabel (Breage) & children, cxxv, 148 & n.; John (St Columb Major), 31, (St Dennis), 140, (Gwennap), 231, 234, (Gwinear), 92, (Gwithian), 47, 91, (St Issey), 153, (Manaccan), 80, (Mawgan in Pyder), 109, (Sithney), 204; John T., scribe, 49; John T. alias Skott (Lanlivery), 193; Mark (St Columb town), 36, 70, 103; Mary (Marion), 159, 169; Ralph, 159–60; Thomas (Goran), 118, (Gunwalloe), cxlv n., 126; William (Breage), 148, (Stithians), 20; see also compound names beginning Tombelow
Thraher, see Trehar
Tirrell (Tyrell), John, 172; John, & wife Emma, 52 & n.; Thomas, 212
Tolle, James, cxxvii, cxlv n., 129; Peter, cxliv–cxlv nn., 82
Tolverne, Arundell of, see Arundell
Tom(a), Tomas, Tomma, Tomme, see Thomas
Toma Berowe, see Perow
Toma Dauy, see Davy
Tom(a)luky, Richard, 80, 124; see also Luky
Tom Androwe, see Androwe
Tomaset, John, 146
Tomenty, Richard, 102
Tomeov, see Tomyow
Tom Gregor(y), see Gregor
Tomherry, Walter (Goran), 119; see also Harry
Tomkin (Tomkyn), John (St Dennis), 140, (Goran), 119
Tomluky, see Tom(a)luky
Tomlyn, James, 88, 132; Warin, 93
Tomme Gregory, see Gregor
Tomme Harry, see Harry, Tomherry
Tomme Symon, see Symon
Tomperkyn, Nicholas, 135; see also Perkyn
Tomperowe, see Perow
Tom Rawlyn, see Rawlyn
Tom Symon, see Symon
Tomyow(e) (Tomeov, Tomyow), Richard (Bodmin), 58, (St Columb town), 38, 72; Thomas (St Columb town), 102, clerk (Mawgan in Pyder), 110
Ton, Thomas, 7
Totam, heir of John, 45
Touke(u)r, cxxx; Andrew, cxii, 116; John, cxii, 58, 98
Towan, see Dewen
Trahare, see Trehar
Treaga, see Treyagu
Trebervet(h), Ralph, 77; Richard, 78
Treburgheur, John, 42; see also Trevogherth
Tredeneck(e), William, 185, & wife, 177
Tredreysec, Geoffrey de, 6
Tredwyn, John, 116
Trefew(h)a, Gregory, 105; heir of Maud, 28; Robert, 25, 74
Treffry (Trefry(e), Teffrye), John (Lanhydrock), 97, 114, (Ludgvan), 189, (Madron), 158; Richard, 60, 76, 120; Thomas, 56
Trefrynk (Trefyng), heir of William, cxli, 44; William, 89 & n.

Trefry(e), *see* Treffry
Trefusas, *see* Trevises
Treg...rrek, John, 102; *see also* Tregarreck
Tregadreth, heir of Thomas de, 18
Tregarn (Tregaryn), James, 86; William, 21
Tregarreck (Tregareke, Treg...rrek), David, 37, 71, 152, his heir, 154, 199
Tregarthyn, John (St Ervan), cxlii, 75; Thomas (Creed, Goran), 117–18
Tregaryn, *see* Tregarn
Tregassowe, John, 98; Oliver, 59, his heirs, 96
Tregena, *see* Tregen(n)a
Tregenfelde (Trygenfelde, Trygonnold, Tregonall), Robert, 163, 209; *see also* Tregonwall
Tregenfren (Tregenwran), Silvester de, 8 & n.; John his son, 8n.
Tregengy, William, 53
Tregen(n)a (Tregene), heir of Alan, 45; Joan Boys & Margaret Glyn, daughters of Alan, 90; John, & wife (Gwithian), 132; Oto, 133; Peter, 89
Tregennow(e) (Trigennowe), heirs of (Ludgvan), 189; John Randall alias T., sen. (St Ewe), 221, 226; John Randall alias T., jun. (St Ewe), 222–3, 227
Tregenwran, *see* Tregenfren
Tregethiow, John, 109
Treggedellen, John, 190
Treghar, *see* Trehar
Tregheustek, William de, 5
Treghures, Joan, 5
Tregian, (Francis), esq., 223, 228
Tregois, *see* Tregoys
Tregonall, *see* Tregenfelde
Tregonben, John, 4n.
Tregongon, Robert, 192
Tregonwall, John, 190; *see also* Tregenfelde
Tregonya (Tregonyen), Lawrence, 193–4
Trego(y)s (Tregois), John, 103; Thomas, cxliii–cxliv, 99; William, 86, his heir, 41; *see also* Treygoose
Trehake, John (gent.), 222, 228
Trehan, John, 159
Trehar(e) (Treher, Trahare, Thraher, Treghar), cxxx; Andrew, 36; Benedict, 153 & n.; John Androwe T., lxxxvii,

cxxx n., cxxxvi, 26; Nicholas T. alias Carne, 212, 217; Ralph, 123; Reginald, 105; Roger T. alias Carne, 212; Thomas, 72; Thomas, & sons John & Richard, 165; William (St Enoder), 139, (Gunwalloe), 13, 15; *see also* Cissor, Tailor
Treiagu, *see* Treyagu
Trelawader, Roger de, 6
Trelawny, Jonathan, 202
Trele(e)k, Walter, 15, 84
Trelevyn, Joan, widow, 194
Trelighan, *see* Treloyghen
Treliver (Trelyu', Trelyuer), James, 154, 199; John, 152, his heir, 199
Treloddrowe, *see* Treluddrow
Treloy, John, 112; Thomas, cxlv n.
Treloyghen (Trelighan), John, 89, 133; John Martyn T., 133
T(r)eluddar, Ot(t)o, 155, 200
Treluddrow (Treloddrowe), John, 105; Nicholas, 39, 72
Treluri, Simon, & wife Alice, 4
Trelyu(er), *see* Treliver
Tremayle, Thomas, cxlii, 76
Tremayn(e) (Tremeen), family, cxvii; Alice (St Columb town), 103, (Crantock), 111; John (St Columb town), 38, 72, (Crantock), 67, (Lelant), 133; Nicholas, 45, 89; Richard, 232; Thomas, 89
Trembras, heir of Philip, 42, 87
Tremeen, *see* Tremayn
Tremenhyr(e), John, cxliv; Peter, 21
Tremodret, family, *see* Roche
Tremur(e) (Tremeur), John, 136; William de, & wife Joan, 6n., heirs of William (de), 29, 68
Trenanz, Thomas, 195
Trenayren, John, 140
Trencrik (Trencruk, Trencryk), heir of Henry, 28; heir(s) of Ralph, 67; William (de), 20, his heir(s), 78
Trengoo, William, & sister Katherine, 165
Trenowith (Trenewit, Trenowyth, Trenowth), John, cxlv n., 61, 93, 137; Maud, 37; Stephen de, 4
Trepkunyn, *see* Trypconye
Trepylet, *see* Tryplett
Treres (Trerys), Michael (de), & daughter Joan (married Ralph Arundell), xi,

INDEX OF SURNAMES

2n., 9n.; Odo son of Michael, 9n.; *see also* Arundell (of) Trerice

Tresafnowe, Richard, 39; *see also* Treysathnov

Tresalen, John, 141

Tresawell, John, 107; Walter, cxliv, 75

Tresithny (Tresythny), Joan (married Walter Colbroke), xxxiv; John, 94; Nicholas, 37, 71, his heirs, 102; Thomas, 37, 71

Treso(u)gan, *see* Roso(u)gan

Tresprison (Tresprysoun, Trispreson), heir of Henry, 17; Richard, cxxvii, 81, 128

Tresylyan (Tresylian), Pascoe, 209, Pascoe Kerne (of T.), 199, 229; *see also* Kerne

Trethaek, John, 19–20

Tretheas, *see* Trethias

Tretherf(f) (Trethyreff), heirs of (St Enoder), 191; John (Creed, St Enoder), 93, 118, 137–8, (St Wenn), 106; Reginald (Creed, St Enoder), 9, 94, his heir, 50, 62; Thomas, 25n.

Trethias (Tretheas), John (St Columb Minor), 29, 67, 112, (St Merryn), 106

Trethowall (Trewothowall), Francis de, (cv), 31; John (de) [1460], (cv), 31, [1499], cxv, 113

Trethyreff, *see* Tretherff

Trethywol, John Byllun de T. (St Eval), (3), 5 & n.

Treuarthan, Michael, 62, 94

Treueglos, John de, 1

Treuelg(h)y, Joce de, 5; Roger de, 3 & n.; Vincent de, 3 & n.

Treuelgyn, William, 62, 94

Treuelwyth, *see* Trevelwith

Treuysa, *see* Trevisa

Trevaigno(u)n, *see* Trevanyon

Trevalscoys, Alan, 90

Trevanion (Trevanyon, Trevaigno(u)n, Trevaynon, Trewanyan), family, lxxxii; Edward, 223; John, esq., 68; Peter, 136; Richard, 92; Roger, 47; Thomas, 28, 68; William, 110–11

Trevarthian, family, xvi

Trevedrus, Robert, 109

Treve(e)le, Joan, 111; John, 29, his heirs, 67

Trevelwith (Treuelwyth), John, 25, 74, 106; Thomas [1385], 8, [1499], 118

Trevelyan (Trevilian, Trevylyan), John, esq. (Creed), 50, 117, (St Minver), 106

Trevenour, William, 60, 76, 120

Trevernow(e), Alexander, 205; Richard, 149

Treverth, Margery, widow, 158

Trevesys, John, 131; *see also* Trevises

Trevethicke (Trevethek), ... (St Ewe), 220; Thomas Henry T., cxxxv, 136; *see also* Trevithike

Trevethow, *Warinus*, 136

Trevevik, Robert, 163

Trevga, John, 37, 71

Trevilian, *see* Trevelyan

Trevisa (Treuysa, Trevysa), Henry, 94, 138; John, 62

Trevises (alias Trefusas), Richard, 189

Trevisithik (Trevysithek), Henry, 48, 93

Trevithike, Nicholas, 225; *see also* Trevethicke

Trevnwyth, Oto, 49; Thomas, & wife Isabel, 88

Trevogherth, John, 87, his heir(s), 131n.; *see also* Treburgheur

Trevylyan, *see* Trevelyan

Trevysa, *see* Trevisa

Trevysithek, *see* Trevisithik

Trevysken, Roger de, 142

Trewanyan, *see* Trevanyon

Trewarton, John, 164; William, & wife Mabel, 164; *see also* Cheverton

Trewarvena, Isabel, cxlii, 66

Treweffrak, 149n.

Trewenna, Andrew, lxxxvi; John de, lxxxvi

Trewinard (Trewyn(n)ard, Trewynnerd, Trewennard), Martin, & wife, 164; William, esq. (St Erth, Gwennap), 146, 149n., 158–9, his heir, 149, 204

Trewloghan, Samson, 161

Trewolla(ye), John, gent., 210, & wife Alice, 161

Trewolvas, Odo, 105

Trewonwall (Trewounwall), Laurence, 60, his heir(s), 76

Treworga (Trewurga), heir(s) of, 67; John, 111

Treworlas, John Bray T., 29, (112)

Trewothowall, *see* Trethowell

Trewounwall, *see* Trewonwall
Trewurga, *see* Treworga
Trewynard, *see* Trewinard
Trewynean, John, 76
Trewynhelek (Trewenhelek), heir(s) of, 36, 70
Trewyns, Nicholas, 140
Treyagu (Treiagu, Tre(y)aga), John, 111–12; Thomas, 61, 93, 137
Treygoose, John, 164; *see also* Trego(y)s
Treys, Thomas, 99
Treysathnov, Richard, 72; *see also* Tresafnowe
Triggean, John, 121; Thomas, 121
Trigennowe, *see* Tregennow(e)
Tripkunyn, Tripkynyn, *see* Trypconye
Triprolett, *see* Tryplett
Trispreson, *see* Tresprison
Tros(s)e (Trous), John, 72; Juliana, 34; William, 66
Truro, *see* Cooke, John
Trygenfelde, *see* Tregenfelde
Trygestaye, Michael, 163
Trygonnold, *see* Tregenfelde
Trypconye (Tripkunyn, Tripkynyn, Trepkunyn, Trypkunyn), heir(s) of, 113; Elizabeth, 106; James, 102; John, gent., 210; Ralph, 35–6, 53n., 70, 113n.
Tryplett (Trepylet, Triprolett), heir of, 154; John, 152, his heir, 200
Tyek, John, 30, 34, 67; Richard, 103
Tylbott [*for* Tybbott?], John, 195
Tynten (Tynten), John (de) [1343], 1, his heir, 32; John [1499], 108, 111
Tyrell, *see* Tirrell

Udan, *see* Vdan
Udy (Ude, Vda, Vdy), Joan, 51; John, 57, 98; heir(s) of Michael, 36, 70; Robert, clerk, 37; Warin, lxxxvi; *see also* Ede
Umfraville, John, & son John, xiv–xv
Urban, Robert, 39

Vdan, Robert, 161
Vdy, *see* Udy
Veel, heir of John Wilkyn V., 45
Veer (Vere), family, xxxii–xxxv; their manors, xlvi–xlix, li, lxvi, lxxviii; John, esq., 163–4; Sir Robert, 164; *see also* Oxford, earls of
Velle, John, & widow Joan (Plumyn), 158

Vere, *see* Veer
Veyse, William, 77
Vicar (Viker, Vycar), Sir John, 10; Richard, 10; William, ciii, 24, 26
Vincent, Luke, 11
Vinslate, *see* Windeslade
Virly, John, 2 & n.
Vivian (Viuyan, Vyuyan, Vivean, Vyvyan), (St Austell) [c.1586], 237; John (St Austell), 172, (Ludgvan), 189, (Colan), 231–2, & Mary his sister, 230; Odo, 36, 70; Ralph, *see* Dewen; Richard (Ludgvan), 192, (Manaccan), 190, (St Columb town), 39
Volanty, Ralph, 31
Vyan, cxxxi; Elizabeth, widow, & daughter Matilda (Crane), 160; John Wolcok V., cxxxvi, *see* Wo(o)lcocke; William, 54; *see also* Byan
Vycar, *see* Vicar
Vynwyn, David, 136; William, 47–8, 92–3
Vyuyan, *see* Vivian

Wadham, John, 220
Walesbrew, *see* Whalesborough
Walsch, John, 120
Walter (Waultere), Henry, 6; John (Bodmin), 57, (St Minver), 6; William Fitz W., *see* Fitzwater; *see also* Watt
Wan..., Ralph (St Columb Minor), 109
Watkyn, Richard, 10
Watt(a), John, 72; Richard (St Columb Major), 229, (Lanivet), 116; William, 104; *see also* Walter
Waty, Thomas, 113
Waultere, Fitz, *see* Fitzwater
Webbe, Robert, cxxx, 183; *see also* Gweader, Textor
Welle, Thomas (St Ewe), 11; *see also* Will(e)
Wenna, William, 145
Wennon', John, 6
West, William, 211
Whalesborough (Walesbrew, Whalisbrewe, Whalesburgh), John, 2 & n.; Thomas, 24, 73
Wilcock, Richard (St Dennis), 59, (Stithians), 20
Wilkyn (Wylkyn), Richard Jankyn W., 26, Richard Jankyn W. de Seynt Irven, *see* Synt Erven; John W. Veel, *see* Veel

INDEX OF SURNAMES

Will(e) (Wyll, Wylle), Alice, widow, 184–5; John (Goran), 118; Nicholas, 181; Thomas (Mawgan in Meneage), 14; heirs of Thomas (St Clement), 60, 76; Thomasine (Cardinham), 181; William, 186; John W. Perow, *see* Perow; *see also* Willy

William (Willyam), Elizabeth, lxxxvii; James, 160; John (Gunwalloe), 129, (St Keverne), 80, 124, (Lanivet), 57, 98, 116, (Lelant), 136, (Sithney), 149; John Thomas W. (Ludgvan), cxxxiii; Ralph, chaplain, 129; Robert, 118; Tebat Jac W. (St Columb Major), cxxxiii; Thomas, 34; *see also* Willy

Willmur, John, & wife, 110

Willy (Wylly), Henry, 89, heir of Henry, 45; *see also* Will, William

Willyam, *see* William

Windeslade, *see* Winslade

Windesore, heirs of, 67; Thomas, 29

Windeslade (Wyndeslate, Wydeslade, Vinslate, Wynslate), Joan, 128; Richard (Cury), 10, 81, (Crowan), 146, his heir, 149 & n.; heir of William, 204

Wise (Wyse), Oliver, (Cubert), 67, (St Ewe), 52

Wodcok, John, 109

Wodwer, Robert, 134

Wolcocke, Wolcok, *see* Wo(o)lcocke

Wolecumb, Wollacome, Wollacumme, *see* Woollacombe

Wolsey, Thomas, archbishop of York, 179 & n.

Wone, John Jak W., cxxxv, 80

Woolcock(e) (Wolcocke, Wolcok), Christopher, 225, & wife Jane & son George, 221; George, 212; John, 53; John W. (Vyan), cxxxvi, his heir(s), 38, 71; Mabena, cxliv n.; Martin, ciii, cxlii, 54, 75–6; William son of John, 200

Woollacombe (Wolecumb, Wollacome, Wollacumme), Alexander, esq., 162, 208; Roger, esq., 162n.; Thomas, 162n.

Worst(e)ley, Edward, gent., 208, 220, 229

Worthyvall, Thomas, 212–13

Wraan, Richard, 11

Wydeslade, *see* Windeslade

Wyghen, William, 3

Wylkyn, *see* Wilkyn

Wyll(e), *see* Will

Wylly, *see* Willy

Wyn, Thomas, 10

Wyndeslate, *see* Windeslade

Wyndesore, *see* Windesore

Wynkele, Walter, 61, 93, William (*for* Walter?), 137

Wynslate, *see* Winslade

Wyse, *see* Wise

Yeo, Robert, 192

Yewan, *see* Iwyn

Zouche, family, xxx; Lord, 186

INDEX OF SUBJECTS

An asterisk after a word indicates that it occurs very frequently in the documents printed and has not been indexed in them, but only in the Introduction.

almshouse, xxiv
Arundell family, ix–xii
  heraldry, x, xcvii–xcviii & n.
  name, ix–x
assessments, lviii, cxviii

Black Death, lxxxix, ciii, cxii
buildings, xcviii–xciv & n., cv–cvi, cxlii n.
  almshouse, xxiv
  bakehouses, cxliii–cxliv, 38, 73
  barns, xcix, 175, 182–4, 194, 214, 216–17, 224, 232–3
  capstan house, c n.
  church house, xcvii
  corn-drying barn, xcii & n.
  cottages, cxix, cxlii, 33, 51, 66, 136, 141, 182–3, 186
  dry house, xcix
  farmhouse, cvii
  houses, 2, 16, 31, 62, 82, 93, 137, 152, 174–6, 178–85, 193–4
  inn, xcvii
  kitchen, 233
  manor houses, 168, 230–1, 233–4
  outhouse, 233–4
  pigs' house, xcix
  plots for building, 35, 39, 70
  sexton's house, xcvii
  sheephouse, lxii, xcix, cix, 185
  shop, xcvii
  smithy, 37, 71
  stables, 217, 224, 233
  workshops, xcvii, 52, 118
  see also mills; tinning; textile industry
by-laws, xcii & n.

chevage, 6–7
church matters
  advowson, xvi, xxii, xliii n.
  benefice, 186, 197
  chantries, xix, xxi, xxii–xxiv, xlv, 162
  chapels, xcii, xcviii & n., cxliv, 73

church matters, continued
  chaplain, 69, 76, 103, 129
  church, 197
  crosses, 36, 38, 52, 177
  friary, 77 & n.
  glebe, xvi, xliii & n., lxxxix–xc, 85, 185n.
  guild, xcii & n.
  holy well, 178n.
  priory, 177 & n.
  rector, 66, 85
Codner's Survey (1618, AR2/1346), xxxi, l, lv n., lviii, lxxvi n., cvi n., cviii n., 177n., 199n., 203n., 204nn., 206nn., 211n., 220n.
conventionary tenements, see under tenants and tenements
copyhold, see under tenants and tenements
Cornish acre, see under land, measurement

demesne lands, lix, & n., lxix n., cxxii, cxxiii n., cxliii & n., cxliv n., 4, 16, 35, 46, 53, 54n., 55, 66, 85, 90, 98–100, 107, 110, 127, 134, 213, 221–3, 226, 230–1, 233–4, 238
Dinham's Lands, xxx–xxxii, xlviii, lxxv, 173–97
dower, xxxix–xxx, 3n., 50
Duchy (earlier Earldom) **of Cornwall**
  lands or manors of, lxxiv–lxxvi, lxxix–lxxx, lxxxiv–lxxxvi, lxxxviii–lxxxix, xcii, xcv–xcvi, xcix n., civ, cvi, cviii, cxxviii n., 11 nn., 40n., 53n., 142n., [223]
  tenants of, cxi, cxvii n., cxviii
  tenures on, liii n., lv, lviii–lix, cxix
dues owed by tenants
  berbiage, 142 & n.
  entry fine, lvii
  farleu, lviii, 134, 176, 197, 222
  heriot*, lviii
  motlet, 222 & n., 223

INDEX OF SUBJECTS 277

dues owed by tenants, *continued*
   offering and aid, 19, 40 & n., 41–45, 85 & n., 86–90, 129–34
   recognisance, 124
   relief*, lv
   scutage, 9, 13, 19, 125, 129
   work money, work silver, lvii, 151, 203–4
   see also rents in kind; tinning

enclosure, lxix & n., lxxix, lxxxiii & n., xciii & n., xcv & n., 174–5, 232, 234
enclosures
   closes, lxviii–lxxvii, lxxxii, lxxxviii–lxxxix, xc, 27, 36–9, 54, 60, 70–7, 99, 102–5, 109, 113n., 118, 120–1, 126, 139, 150, 152, 159, 171, 174–6, 178–86, 193–6, 200, 214–18, 224–8, 232–4, 238
   closes enclosed from common, xciii n., xcv n., 174–5, 232, 234
   crofts, 41, 87, 131
   encroachments, cix, 147n.
   hedges, lxx, lxxii–lxxv, lxxvii, lxxxi–lxxxii, cxlii, 16
   park, the lord's, cxliii n., 52, 119
   parks (closes), lxxvii, 83, 176
   tofts, 120, 129

farming, types of
   arable, lxxi, lxxx–lxxxi, ciii
   pastoral, lxxi–lxxiii, lxxix–lxxxi, ciii
   fuel, xcii
ferling, *see under* land, measurement
fine for suit of court, *see under* manorial courts
fishing, lxxxi, c & n., cxiii, 217
free tenure
   homage*, lv
   knight's fees*, xxix, lv
   knight's service*, liv
   fees Gloucester, l, lv, 199 & n., 201, 229
   fees Mortain, lv, 199n.
   socage*, liv
   see also dues owed by tenants; tenants and tenements

heriot, *see under* dues owed
holdings
   engrossing, ciii, cvii–cviii
   inheritance, lvi, cxiii–cxx

holdings, *continued*
   size, cv–cvi
   see also tenants and tenements
homage, *see under* free tenure
housebote, xcix n., 20, 187

knight's fee, knight's service, *see under* free tenure

labour services, lvii, 10, 25, 30, 68, 75, 106–107n., 109, 114, 118, 120, 151, 196, 201; *see also* dues owed by tenants
land, measurement of
   acres, Cornish*, l, liv–lv
   acres, English, 7, 31, 33, 40, 62, 66, 85, 94, 138
   ferlings*, liv
land-use
   arable, lxxi, xci, xciv, 142, 160, 175–6, 195–6, 214–19, 221, 224–8, 232–4
   cliff, 142
   common land, lxxii, lxxviii–lxxxii, xci–xciii, xcv, civ, cvii–cviii, 47n., 170–7, 187, 194–6, 214–15, 218, 226–8, 232–4
   downs (*landa*, moorland), lxix, lxxii, xciii–xcvi, 35, 61–2, 66, 93–4, 110, 137–8, 175, 179n., 215, 218, 224, 234
   furze or gorse, lxxvi, lxxxiii, xcv n., 215, 218
   gardens, lxviii, 5, 36, 66, 69–70, 77, 100, 102, 120–1, 170, 174–6, 178–85, 194, 196, 201, 218, 221, 224 & n., 226–8, 231
   heath, xciv, 170, 184, 187, 218
   marsh, *see* moor
   meadow, 33n., 34 & n., 65–6, 91, 99, 110, 119–120 & n., 159, 160, 165, 175–6, 178–9, 181–5, 195, 212 & n., 214–19, 222, 224–8, 232–4
   moor (*mora*, marsh), lxxii, xciv, cxiii, 20, 31, 39, 46, 48–9 & n., 93, 114–15, 159–160, 170–2 & n., 175–6, 183, 187, 195–6, 219, 224–5, 228, 233
   moorland, *see* downs
   orchards, lxviii, lxxvi, 174–6, 178–85, 217, 225–6, 233–4
   outfields, xciv–xcvi

land-use, *continued*
  pasture, lxix, lxxi–lxxii, lxxxiii, cviii, 159–60, 170, 195–6, 214–19, 221, 223–8, 231–4
  rushes, 104
  warrens, cxliii & n., 65, 99
  waste, lxxii, lxxxii, xci, xciv, cviii, 3, 11, 51–2, 66, 112–13, 172, 176, 187, 222, 226–8, 234
  see also woodland

manorial courts
  courts baron, 176, 186, 197
  courts leet, 182 & n., 186, 190, 193
  courts of survey, 186, 197
  court profits, cxxi
  suit of court* and fine for suit of court*, liii–liv, lvii
  summoner, cxxxvi
markets and fairs, xv n., xcvi, xcviii & n., cxii, 39, 139, 168, 171
mills, cii–ciii & n., civ, cxvii, cxxix, cxlii, 4, 6 & n., 11, 16 & n., 21 & n., 23, 27, 31, 35, 39, 52 & n., 55, 69, 73, 75, 78, 80, 84, 98–9, 105, 107, 110, 115n., 116, 119, 123, 125, 127, 160, 165, 168, 174, 194, 196, 217
  repair of, 23, 27, 80
  suit of, xciv, 1, 3n., 10, 14, 18, 20, 22, 29, 30, 68, 79, 82, 83, 134
  tanning, 180n.
  mill-land, 127
  mill-leat, 1 & n., 11n., 50, 117, 148 & n., 149, 189
  mill-pool, 115 & n.
  mill-stones, 27, 52n.
  mill-weir, 99, 204
  multure, *see* suit of mill
  see also tinning; textile industry

occupations
  chaplain, 69, 76, 103, 129
  clerk, 37, 110, 124, 194
  merchant, 201
  miller, civ, cxxix
  rector, 66, 85
  schoolmaster, 201
  scribe, 49
  servant, cxviii–cxix, cxxxvi

occupations, *continued*
  smith, cxxx, 33, 61
  tailor, cxxx
  tucker, cxxx
  weaver, cxxx
  see also tinning: tinners
officials (manorial, estate, etc.)
  bailiff, lxxii, cxliii & n., cxliv n., 66, 85, 91, 160, 171
  bailiff of stannary, 223
  reeve, lviii, cxxvi, cxliv & n., cxlv & n., cxlvi, 10, 20, 21n., 25, 30, 151n., 153n., 176, 187, 197
  receiver general, cxliii & n., 208n., 220
  surveyor, 182–5, 194
  steward, xxvii, xxxiii, 186, 188
  tithingman, 10, 30, 40n., 176, 197

peat (turves), lxxvi, 20
Prayerbook Rebellion, xi

quarries, c & n., 121n., 129 & n.

rabbits, cxliii, 65, 99
relief, *see under* dues owed
rents
  buoyant, cxi–cxii
  high, chief or resolute*, xliii, lxi & n., lxii–lxvii
  reduction, cii–cv, cxiii
rents in kind
  capons, lviii, 11, 56–8, 97–8, 114–16, 118–20, 204 & n.
  cummin, liii, lv, 8–9, 11, 32, 41, 86, 108, 117, 130, 134, 151
  gillyflower, clove, lx, lxiii, 46, 90, 134
  gloves, lxii & n., 9, 11, 22, 59 & n., 79, 87, 95–6, 123, 132, 139
  pepper, 29, 43, 44, 46, 68, 89, 112, 133, 151, 202–4, 231
  red rose, 108
  sheep, 142 & n., 163, 208–9; *see also* dues owed (berbiage)
  spurs, lv, lxvi, 9, 11, 24, 41, 50, 73, 87, 105, 117, 157
  wheat grain, 44, 89, 133
  see also dues owed
roofing materials
  slate, xcix, 224, 226, 233
  thatch, xcix, cv, 16, 214–18, 225–6, 228, 231–4

INDEX OF SUBJECTS

rural settlement
  desertion, cvii–cx
  hamlets, lxxvii–xciii, cvii–cviii, 99
  town-place, xci, 215–6, 218
  see also holdings; strip-field systems

sand
  covering tenements, 47 & n., 92, 135, 169
  sanding, lxxxi
  sanding-way, 5n., 45, 90, 134
school, xxiii
socage, see under free tenure
strays, 19 & n., 129, 197
strip-field systems, lxxvii–xciii, xcv–xcvi, 140, 169, 214–19, 232
  divisions (bounders), 215
  enclosure, lxxix lxxxiii & n.
  selions, xc, 31, 69, 140
  shareholding, lxxxiv–xciii, xcvi
  stitches, lxxxii–lxxxiii, xc, xcv n.
  stitchmeal, lxxviii, lxxxi n., lxxxii, 169
  strakes, 216 & n.
suit of court, see under manorial courts
surnames
  definition, cxxiv
  descriptive, cxxxi, cxxxvi
  fluidity, cxv–cxvi, cxxv–cxxviii
  occupational, cxxix–cxxxi, cxxxvi
  patronymic, cxxv–cxxvii, cxxxi–cxxxiv, cxxxvi
  three-part, cxxxiv–cxxxv
  toponymic, cxxvii–cxxviii, cxxxv–cxxxvi
  two-part, cxxxi–cxxxvii

tenants and tenements
  bondmen, lix & n., 5, 7, 18, 34, 128
  conventionary*, lvi–lix & n., lxiv, ci–cxx, cxli–cxlii
  copyhold*, lvii–lviii
  cot-land, 4, 5
  cottars, cottagers, lix, cxviii–cxix, 4, 7
  free*, liii–lvi, lix–lxvii, ci, cxli
  plot-holder, 102
  smallholding, 4
  term of years, lvii n., 3, 27, 31, 35–9, 47n., 70–1, 76–7, 103–5, 107, 113, 115, 121–3, 127, 139–41, 148n.
  see also free tenure; holdings

textile industry, cxi–ii & n.
  fulling or tucking mills, xcii & n., xcvii, cxii, cxxx, 58, 98, 116, 169
  wool, lxxii
  see also occupations
tinning, xvi, xxxv, lxxvi, lxxxi, c, cxii & n., cxiii, cxvii
  black tin, 52n.
  blowing houses or mills, c n., cxii, 116, 123, 150 & n., 160, 168, 201, 205 & n.
  mullett, 222 & n., 223
  stannaries, cx, cxiii, cxvii, 223
  stannary bailiff, 223
  stamping mills, c n., 160, 201
  tin-bounds, li
  tin-fine, 59 & n., 95, 139
  tinners, cxi–cxiii
  tin-works, xciv, 171, 213, 222
  toll of tin, xciv & n., cxiii, cxxi, cxxviii n., 145, 171, 187, 197
  toller of tin, 197
towns, xiv–xv & n., lvii n., xciii & n., xcvi–xcviii, cxii–cxiii, cxxii, cxxx–cxxxi, cxxxiv, 168, 171
trees, lxxiv–lxxvi, cxlii n.
  apple, 226
  ash, lxxv, 226
  elm, lxxv, 219, 225, 226, 232
  hazel, 184, 197
  oak, 197, 225
  see also woodland
tunic, 201

widow's estate, 176, 186, 197
woodland, xvi, xxxv, lxxiv–lxxvi, xcix & n., 99, 169–70, 181, 187, 196–7, 222–3, 226–8
  age, 187, 197
  coppice, xcix n., 177, 227 & n., 228
  herbage, 170, 227–8
  reserved for house repairs, 187
  underwood, 184, 223
  weeding, 227
  wood-pasture, xcix n., 181
  see also housebote, trees
wreck, rights of, 19, 129

THE DEVON AND CORNWALL RECORD SOCIETY

(Founded 1904)

Officers (1998–9)

President:
Sir Richard Carew Pole, Bt., DL

Hon. Secretary:
J. D. Brunton, LLB, BA, c/o Devon and Exeter Institution,
7 Cathedral Close, Exeter EX1 1EZ

Hon. Treasurer:
J. Baldwin, c/o Devon and Exeter Institution,
7 Cathedral Close, Exeter EX1 1EZ

Hon. Editors:
Professor N. I. Orme, MA, DPhil, DLitt, FSA, FRHistS
Mrs Margery M. Rowe, BA, DAA

The Devon and Cornwall Record Society (founded 1904) promotes the study of history in the South West of England through publishing and transcribing original records. In return for the annual subscription members receive the volumes as published (normally annually) and the use of the Society's library, housed in the Westcountry Studies Library, Exeter. The library includes transcripts of parish registers relating to Devon and Cornwall as well as useful genealogical works.

Applications to join the Society or to purchase volumes should be sent to the Assistant Secretary, Devon and Cornwall Record Society, c/o Devon and Exeter Institution, 7 Cathedral Close, Exeter EX1 1EZ. New series volumes 7, 10, 13, 16, and 18, however, should normally be obtained from the Treasurer of the Canterbury and York Society, St Anthony's Hall, York, YO1 2PW.

PUBLISHED VOLUMES, NEW SERIES
(Volumes starred are no longer available)

*1. *Devon Monastic Lands: Calendar of Particulars for Grants, 1536–1558*, edited by Joyce Youings (1955).

2. *Exeter in the Seventeenth Century: Tax and Rate Assessments, 1602–1699*, edited by W. G. Hoskins (1957, reprinted in 1973).

*3. *The Diocese of Exeter in 1821: Bishop Carey's Replies to Queries before Visitation*, edited by Michael Cook, Volume I, Cornwall (1958).

4. *The Diocese of Exeter in 1821: Bishop Carey's Replies to Queries before Visitation*, edited by Michael Cook, Volume II, Devon (1960).
*5. *Cartulary of St. Michael's Mount, Cornwall*, edited by P. L. Hull (1962).
6. *The Exeter Assembly: The Minutes of the Assemblies of the United Brethren of Devon and Cornwall, 1691–1717, as Transcribed by the Reverend Isaac Gilling*, edited by Allan Brockett (1963).
7. *The Register of Edmund Lacy, Bishop of Exeter, 1420–1455: Registrum Commune*, Volume I, edited by G. R. Dunstan (1963).
*8. *The Cartulary of Canonsleigh Abbey*, calendared and edited by Vera C. M. London (1965).
*9. *Benjamin Donn's Map of Devon, 1765*, with an introduction by W. L. D. Ravenhill (1965).
10. *The Register of Edmund Lacy, Bishop of Exeter, 1420–1455: Registrum Commune*, Volume II, edited by G. R. Dunstan (1966).
*11. *Devon Inventories of the Sixteenth and Seventeenth Centuries*, edited by Margaret Cash (1966).
12. *Plymouth Building Accounts of the Sixteenth and Seventeenth Centuries*, edited by Edwin Welch (1967).
13. *The Register of Edmund Lacy, Bishop of Exeter, 1420–1455: Registrum Commune*, Volume III, edited by G. R. Dunstan (1968).
14. *The Devonshire Lay Subsidy of 1332*, edited by Audrey M. Erskine (1969).
15. *Churchwardens' Accounts of Ashburton, 1479–1580*, edited by Alison Hanham (1970).
16. *The Register of Edmund Lacy, Bishop of Exeter, 1420–1455: Registrum Commune*, Volume IV, edited by G.R. Dunstan (1971).
17. *The Caption of Seisin of the Duchy of Cornwall (1337)*, edited by P. L. Hull (1971).
18. *The Register of Edmund Lacy, Bishop of Exeter, 1420–1455: Registrum Commune*, Volume V, edited by G. R. Dunstan (1972).
19. *Cornish Glebe Terriers, 1673–1735, a calendar*, edited by Richard Potts (1974).
20. *John Lydford's Book*, edited by Dorothy M. Owen (1975).
21. *A Calendar of Early Chancery Proceedings Relating to West Country Shipping, 1388–1493*, edited by Dorothy A. Gardiner (1976).
22. *Tudor Exeter: Tax Assessments 1489–1595, including the Military Survey, 1522*, edited by Margery M. Rowe (1977).
23. *The Devon Cloth Industry in the Eighteenth Century: Sun Fire Office Inventories, 1726–1770*, edited by Stanley D. Chapman (1978).
24. *The Accounts of the Fabric of Exeter Cathedral, 1279–1353. Part I: 1279–1326*, edited by Audrey M. Erskine (1981).
25. *The Parliamentary Survey of the Duchy of Cornwall, Part I: (Austell Prior–Saltash)*, edited by Norman J. G. Pounds (1982).

THE DEVON AND CORNWALL RECORD SOCIETY

26. *The Accounts of the Fabric of Exeter Cathedral, 1279–1363, Part II: 1328–53*, edited by Audrey M. Erskine (1983).
27. *The Parliamentary Survey of the Duchy of Cornwall, Part II: (Isles of Scilly–West Antony and Manors in Devon)*, edited by Norman J. G. Pounds (1984).
28. *Crown Pleas of the Devon Eyre of 1238*, edited by Henry Summerson (1985).
29. *Georgian Tiverton: the Political Memoranda of Beavis Wood, 1768–98*, edited by John Bourne (1986).
30. *The Cartulary of Launceston Priory*, edited by P. L. Hull (1987).
31. *Shipbuilding on the Exe: the Memoranda Book of Daniel Bishop Davy (1799–1874)*, edited by Clive N. Ponsford (1988).
32. *The Receivers' Accounts of the City of Exeter, 1304–53*, edited by Margery M. Rowe and John M. Draisey (1989).
33. *Early-Stuart Mariners and Shipping: the Maritime Surveys of Devon and Cornwall 1619–1635*, edited by Todd Gray (1990).
34. *Joel Gascoyne's Map of Cornwall, 1699*, with an introduction by W. L. D. Ravenhill and Oliver Padel (1991).
35. *Nicholas Roscarrock's Lives of the Saints: Cornwall and Devon*, edited by Nicholas Orme (1992).
36. *The Local Customs Accounts of the Port of Exeter, 1266–1321*, edited by Maryanne Kowaleski (1993).
37. *Charters of the Redvers Family and the Earldom of Devon, 1090–1217*, edited by Robert Bearman (1994).
38. *Devon Household Accounts, 1627–1659, Part I*, edited by Todd Gray (1995).
39. *Devon Household Accounts, 1627–1659, Part II*, edited by Todd Gray (1996).
40. *The Uffculme Wills and Inventories, 16th to 18th Centuries*, edited by Peter Wyatt, with an introduction by Robin Stanes (1997).

FORTHCOMING VOLUMES

42. *Liberalism in West Cornwall: The 1868 Election Papers of A. Pendarves Vivian, M.P.*, edited by Edwin Jaggard (forthcoming, for 1999).
43. John Hooker's *Synopsis Chorographicall of the County of Devon* (for 2000).
44. Maryanne Kowaleski, *Havener's Accounts of the Duchy of Cornwall* (for 2001).
45. Richard Carew, *The Survey of Cornwall* (for 2002).

THE DEVON AND CORNWALL RECORD SOCIETY

EXTRA SERIES

I. *Exeter Freemen, 1266–1967*, edited by Margery M. Rowe and Andrew M. Jackson (1973).
II. *Guide to the Parish and Non-Parochial Registers of Devon and Cornwall, 1538–1837*, compiled by Hugh Peskett (1979): a new edition, including Somerset, is in preparation.